# TAKEN FOR A RIDE

## DETROIT'S BIG THREE AND THE POLITICS OF POLLUTION

*Jack Doyle*

**FOUR WALLS EIGHT WINDOWS**
**NEW YORK / LONDON**

© 2000 by The Tides Center/*Corporate Sources*

Published in the United States by

Four Walls Eight Windows
39 West 14th Street, room 503
New York, NY 10011

http://www.4w8w.com

U.K. offices: Four Walls Eight Windows/Turnaround
Unit 3 Olympia Trading Estate
Coburg Road, Wood Green
London, N22 6TZ

First printing April 2000.

Library of Congress Cataloguing-in-Publication Data:

Doyle, Jack, 1947-

    Taken for a ride : Detroit's big three and the politics of
pollution / Jack Doyle.
        p.   cm.
    Includes bibliographical references and index.
    ISBN 1-56858-147-5
    1. Automobiles—Motors—Exhaust gas—Environmental aspects—United
States. 2. Automobile industry and trade—Environmental aspects—United
States. 3. Air—Pollution—United States. 4. Air—Pollution—Government policy—
United States. 5. Global warming—Government policy—United States. I. Title
    TD886.5 .D68 2000
    363.739'21'0973—dc21

                                                            99-088236
                                                               CIP

Printed in Canada
10 9 8 7 6 5 4 3 2 1
Interior design by Terry Bain

# TAKEN FOR A RIDE

# Contents

# Acknowledgments

I am indebted to a number of individuals and organizations for guidance, encouragement, and assistance in undertaking and completing this project, now stretching over nearly three years. Among those who have supplied information, reviewed parts of the manuscript, agreed to be interviewed, or otherwise provided assistance or support as this project followed a not-always-predictable course, are the following: Jeff Alson, Dick Ayres, Phil Barnett, Bill Becker, Dan Becker, Bruce Bertelsen, Paul Billings, Leon Billings, John Blizard, Stan Briggs, Andy Brooks, Joe Browder, Luther and Marsha Carter, Martha Casey, Joe Caves, Joan Claybrook, Michael Colbert, Steve Connolly, Bill Curtiss, Clarence Ditlow, Louise Dunlap, Rachel Finson, Chuck Freed, Wade Greene, Sonia Hamel, Hal Harvey, Janet Hathaway, Dave Hawkins, Denis Hayes, Betsy Hemming, Roland Hwang, Gene Karpinski, Dick Kircshten, Drew Kodjak, Jim Krier, Jonathan Lash, Sam Leonard, Cynthia Lenhart, Don and Jean Lenhart, Louis Lombardo, Amory Lovins, Beth Lowry, Sheila Lynch, Jim MacKenzie, Jason Mark, Cecile Martin, Bob Massie, Gladys Meade, Paul Miller, Denny Minano, John Mooney, Danny Moses, Judy Mullins, Frank O'Donnell, Charlotte Pera, Carl Pope, Joe Povey, John Quarles, Paul Rogers, Bob Rose, Marc Ross, Arlie Schardt, Jeff Schwartz, Deborah Silverman, John Wallace, Mike Walsh, and John V. White.

Special thanks to those who gave their expertise or lent their names in the formation of *Corporate Sources,* the nonprofit project of the Tides Center that enabled the research for this book. Among those individuals are Joan Bavaria, Jim Browne, Mike Clark, Kris Finn, John Guffey, Denis Hayes, Mardi Mellon, Keith Mestrich, Harriet Parcells, Jane Rissler, Hope Shand, Andy Smith, Ted Smith, Joel Thomas, and Allen White. At the Tides Center, thanks are owed to Sheela Jhaveri, Dahnesh

Medora, Miyoko Oshima, Carl Pascual, Drummond Pike, Justin Probert, David Salniker, Harry Taylor, and Yeshica Weerasekera.

Thanks to book agents Ronald Goldfarb and Robbie Hare at Goldfarb & Silverberg in Washington for placing the book with its current publisher. At Four Walls Eight Windows in New York, very special thanks to my editor, JillEllyn Riley, and publisher John Oakes. For funding support of book and author, and to *Corporate Sources* while I worked on the project, I am indebted to Joan Bavaria, Mike Fremont, the Alida R. Messinger Charitible Trust, Ted Stanley, and anonymous donors. My immediate family, especially my parents, John and Eleanor Doyle, believed in and stood by this project in its most troubled times. Brothers and sisters Tim, Tom, Ellen, Teresa, and their significant others, all rendered useful views and opinions during this sojourn. My daughter, Dana Jaros, gave her support and made sure I didn't go off the deep end. In Pennsylvania, felines Blue and Tober and border collies Teddy and Mirk helped me through as well. And loyal basketballers at the Lebanon, Pennsylvania, YMCA and in Washington kept me aerobically challenged and usefully exhausted when I needed it most.

## AUTHOR CAVEATS

A few caveats and warnings follow. First, this work is not meant to be the definitive political history of the auto-industrial struggle over smog and global warming. As anyone who has worked these issues or ventured into their history knows well, there is an enormous trove of material available, all of it subject to, and filled with, nuance, detail, personal impression, and interpretation. What follows in these pages, in one sense, is likely to be the proverbial tip of the iceberg. As I discovered in my searches, there are files and files of material in government offices and other places—dump trucks full, and each one worth a book in itself. What I have tried to do here is tell just a part of this story in a new way—one that lays out the politics, business, and technologies of the "clean car" fight over fifty years. It is also a story that travels roughly from the discovery of LA smog in the 1950s to today's concerns over SUVs and global warming—from about 1953 to 2003. Still, I have not covered every twist and turn in this fifty years. I admit up-front that I have not gone out of my way to provide in great and exacting detail the automakers' perspective, as I believe they are fully capable of doing that. The reader is directed to any of the automaker web sites or the Alliance of Automobile Manufacturers in Washington for auto industry materials and perspective. I have, however, tried to give at least the basics of industry's positions and views in the major controversies and policy fights featured in the book. I have also been selective in the fights chosen. While I have spent a good twenty years in the active environmental community, the views and interpretations that follow are my own and do not automatically line up with any particular consumer or environmental perspective. In fact, some environmental and consumer activists will undoubtedly have differing views and positions on the stories included here. However, on initiating this project I did conclude that some of the richest parts of this contemporary business/environmental history—the activist and political process parts in particular—appeared in danger of ebbing away with time, though they hold much relevance to current events. For that reason, and to insure that the younger generation has a "package of time" on the clean-car fight longer than a few years, I wrote this book.

As to my sources, I have interviewed catalyst industry lobbyists and scientists, former congressional staff and members, former and current EPA officials, consumer and environmental leaders, and a few auto industry officials. In using secondary sources, I have tried to rely as much as possible on business and auto industry sources, citing respected industry analysts or journalists who have either been auto industry beat reporters, have had special access to and approval of an auto company on one or more investigation, and auto company executives writing first-person accounts of their own experiences, such as Lee Iacocca and Robert Lutz. I have tried to document every fact and conversation as to date, origin, and source. As a writer, I prefer, as much as possible, to stay out of the reader's way and let events speak for themselves. And in this case I think the history tells a powerful tale all by itself, though I have made a few observations here and there. In many ways, I have mostly assembled, trying to pull events together in a new way for readers, describing the pattern over time. The book is meant to be provocative, to stimulate other work to follow, and to prod policymakers, engineers, activists, reporters, and others. It is aimed, too, at educators and business schools, and the next generation. For the debates to come will certainly be as important as those covered here. Yet there are lessons in these stories from Washington and Detroit that can illuminate the road ahead and help in charting tomorrow's course.

—Jack Doyle
Washington, December 1999

# Abbreviations

| | |
|---|---|
| AMA | Automobile Manufacturers Association, trade association representing automakers from 1932 to 1972 |
| AAMA | American Automobile Manufacturers Association, trade association representing the Big Three from 1992 to 1998 |
| AAM | Alliance of Auto Manufacturers formed in 1998, includes BMW, DaimlerChrysler, Ford, General Motors, Mazda, Nissan, Toyota, Volkswagen, and Volvo |
| ACEEE | American Council for an Energy Efficient Economy |
| AIAM | Association of International Auto Manufactures |
| ALA | American Lung Association |
| ALAPCO | Association of Local Air Pollution Control Officials |
| AMC | American Motors Corporation |
| API | American Petroleum Institute |
| CAA | Clean Air Act of 1970; may also be used to refer generically to subsequent amendments of that act in 1977 and 1990 |
| CAFE | Corporate Average Fuel Economy; refers to fuel economy standards, or "CAFE standards" for automakers, established under the Energy Policy and Conservation Act |
| CAP | Chrysler Clean Air Package |
| CARB | California Air Resources Board |
| CAS | Center for Auto Safety |
| CAWG | Clean Air Working Group; coalition of Fortune 500 companies and industrial trade groups in the auto, oil, steel, chemical, and coal industries, among others |
| CDC | Centers for Disease Control and Prevention |

| | |
|---|---|
| CO | carbon monoxide |
| $CO_2$ | carbon dioxide |
| CEQ | Council on Environmental Quality |
| DOE | US Department of Energy |
| DOT | US Department of Transportation |
| EGR | exhaust gas recirculation, often used in the context of a pollution control system, as in EGR system |
| EPA | US Environmental Protection Agency |
| EPCA | Energy Policy and Conservation Act of 1975 |
| EV | electric vehicle |
| FTP | Federal Test Procedure |
| GAO | US General Accounting Office |
| GCC | Global Climate Coalition |
| GCIP | Global Climate Information Project |
| GM | General Motors Corporation |
| HC | hydrocarbons |
| ICE | internal combustion engine |
| I & M | inspection and maintenance |
| LEV | low emission vehicle or low emission vehicle regulation |
| MECA | Manufacturers of Emission Controls Association |
| MVMA | Motor Vehicle Manufacturers Association; trade association representing US and some foreign automakers between 1972 and 1992 |
| MY | model year (as distinct from calendar year, refers to car models introduced in the fall preceding calendar year) |
| NAS | National Academy of Sciences |
| NAAQS | National Ambient Air Quality Standards |
| NESCAUM | Northeast States for Coordinated Air Use Management |
| NHTSA | National Highway Traffic Safety Administration |
| NOx | nitrogen oxides |
| NRDC | Natural Resources Defense Council |
| NUMMI | New United Motor Manufacturing, Inc., a GM–Toyota joint venture |
| OMS | Office of Mobile Sources (EPA) |
| OTC | Ozone Transport Commission |
| PIRG | Public Interest Research Group; nonprofit organizations operating at the state and national level, as in Vermont PIRG or US PIRG, or PIRGs, plural |
| PNGV | Partnership for a New Generation of Vehicles |
| R & D | research and development |
| RFG | reformulated gasoline |
| STAPPA | State and Territorial Air Pollution Program Administrators |

SUV    sport utility vehicle, classified as light truck in most cases, although some have grown in recent years to above 8,500 lbs, putting them in the commercial truck category

TIER 1    auto emissions standards required by the amendments to the Clean Air Act of 1990, effective in mid-1990s

TIER 2    auto emissions standards required under EPA authorized by the amendments to the 1990 Clean Air Act that will apply in the 2004-2009 time frame

UAW    United Auto Workers of America

UCS    Union of Concerned Scientists

ULEV    ultra-low emission vehicle

USABC    US Advanced Battery Consortium

VOCs    volatile organic compounds

ZEV    zero-emission vehicle or zero-emission vehicle regulation

# Introduction

They called it the "Arsenal of Democracy," and it was truly one of the twentieth century's most astounding feats of industrial accomplishment. The year was 1941 and the place, Detroit, Michigan. The American automobile industry was just climbing out of an economic depression and hoping for better days ahead. Then came World War II. The Japanese attack on Pearl Harbor on December 7, 1941, brought the Americans fully into the war. The automakers—some of whom had already begun doing contract work for the government—were shortly enlisted to become the Allies' full-time military manufacturers. Most civilian auto production was halted as the entire industry was converted to wartime production. The scale of the undertaking that followed was breathtaking, unlike anything the world had ever seen before and rarely since.

From a standing start in late 1941, the automakers converted—in a matter of months, not years—more than 1,000 automobile plants across thirty-one states. Not only did the automakers undertake the manufacture of unfamiliar and sometimes entirely new products, they also had to produce these items in unprecedented volume, far exceeding anything in their civilian experience.[1] Yet they delivered a dazzling industrial performance, turning out an incredible array of vehicles, weapons, and other war materials.

In one year, General Motors developed, tooled, and completely built from scratch 1000 Avenger and 1000 Wildcat aircraft for the US Navy's carrier forces. GM's Oldsmobile division produced 48 million rounds of artillery ammunition and 350,000 precision parts for aircraft engines. "The most intricate assignment," explains one report of GM's output, "was the aerial torpedo, requiring 5,000 parts and 20,000 separate operations." GM also produced the amphibious "duck"—a watertight steel hull enclosing a GM six-wheel, 2.5 ton truck that was adaptable to land or water. GM's Duck "was designed, tested, built, and off the line in ninety days."[2] Chrysler built Sherman tanks and a new factory to make them featuring an assembly line one-third of a mile long. Ford used its massive Willow Run plant in Yipsilanti, Michigan—called "a city with a roof on it"—to build the B-24 bomber known as the Liberator. At Willow Run, Ford turned out one B-24 every 63 minutes, a pace that allowed the price of the planes to be cut nearly in half. Studebaker built big 6x6-wheel-drive military trucks and aircraft engines. Pontiac produced antiaircraft guns. Ford and Willys Overland cranked out more than 660,000 open-air Willys jeeps between 1939 and 1944.[3] Barely a year after Pontiac received a Navy contract to build antishipping missiles, the company began delivering the completed product to carrier squadrons around the world. "The industry was geared for swift action," says the Motor Vehicle Manufacturers Association, "converting from tank hulls to aircraft wing sections . . . in an amazingly short time by many companies."[4]

In the end, the auto industry had converted well over 85 percent of its capacity to military production, turning out more than 2.8 million tanks and trucks, 27,000 fully assembled aircraft, and more than 5.9 million weapons. Detroit had turned out one-fifth of the total US industrial output during the 1942-45 period. "Never before had an industry produced more goods in such a short time," says the MVMA. "When Detroit was referred to . . . as the Arsenal of Democracy," says Harley Shaiken, "it meant just that. It was a productive capability that went beyond what anyone could imagine a decade before."[5] The automakers' war effort, says Shaiken, "redefined what was possible."[6]

Nor was World War II the end of the auto industry's contribution to national technical leadership. In the 1950s, President Harry Truman appointed Chrysler CEO Kaufman T. Keller to organize the Pentagon's guided missile program. In 1952 a few dozen Chrysler engineers were assigned to work on the Redstone missile in Huntsville, Alabama.[7] The auto industry had become America's technical beacon; government went there for advice and leaders. Out in the country, Americans were singing along with Dinah Shore. "See the USA in your Chevrolet" became more than an advertising jingle; it was a national anthem of American optimism at a time when anything seemed possible. And Detroit's products were providing the good life and access to it.

By the 1960s, some of the best minds in the auto industry were turned to the space program and NASA. GM, in fact, designed and manufactured the mobility system for the lunar roving vehicle that astronauts David Scott and James Irwin would use to explore the moon's surface in 1971. Yet down on earth, things in Detroit were changing. When it came to a problem called smog and cleaning up tailpipe exhaust, the auto industry seemed to lose its "can do" spirit. Derring-do was being replaced by cost accounting. Auto engineers appeared to be taking a backseat to managers and accountants. Suddenly, the industrial machine that won the war and "redefined what was possible" could not manage to solve what were believed to be fairly straightforward technical problems. Soon, a new dimension of industrial stubbornness began emanating from Detroit. And out on Dinah Shore's suburban American tapestry, the music had changed, too. Forty-five years later, there was considerably less singing.

## ATLANTA 1999

Visitors to Stone Mountain, Georgia, could see the smog shrouding the city of Atlanta from afar. It was summer, 1999. In downtown Atlanta, those who went to the observation deck on the top of the seventy-two story Westin Peachtree Hotel were appalled at the view on smoggy days.[8] "I moved to Atlanta from Miami thirteen years ago," says Sharon Bagatell, a forty-year-old teacher who lives in the city's Ormewood Park area, "and my asthma has gotten significantly worse. My doctor says it's because of the dirty air here. . . ." Bagatell soon left Atlanta for cleaner skies.[9]

Gary Palmer, like Bagatell, had moved to Atlanta. An avid jogger from Boston, he came to Atlanta in 1986 with the idea that his new southern home would allow him to jog year-round. It didn't work out that way. By the late 1990s, Palmer had to quit his daily run because the air was so bad. Expressing his disgust with Atlanta's pollution, he said, "I'm no tree hugger, but this is ridiculous."[10]

Indeed, Atlanta is ridiculous. For some, it has already become the Los Angeles of the East. Like other metropolitan areas, Atlanta has used highway building to grow, lacing together a sprawling urban region with little rugged terrain to contain it. "Concrete and commerce" is the label used by some transportation critics who believe the region has spun out of control. Atlanta's highways serve business, feed the real estate market, help service a busy regional air hub, and bring thousands of commuters into the city every day. Since 1990, more than 415,000 out-of-state residents have poured into the Atlanta region—a thirteen-county area of more than 3.2 million people. Traffic is a nightmare throughout the region. Irate drivers stuck in lengthy jams have already taken to shooting out red lights. Atlanta is rated No. 1 nationally in "daily per capita VMT," as transportation experts call it—meaning vehicle miles traveled per person per day. Atlanta's rate of daily per capita VMT is 34.1, eclipsing other auto-intense capitals such as Dallas (30.1), Los Angeles (21.5), and Washington, DC (22.6). Growth and traffic, of course, mean more pollution, smog, and high ozone—the stuff that burns the throat, smarts the eyes, and more.

Ozone shielding the earth in the upper atmosphere is a good thing, helping to screen damaging ultraviolet rays of the sun. At ground level, in the streets of Atlanta and other cities, ozone is a biologically invasive compound—actually a poisoned version of oxygen. "Ozone is capable of destroying organic matter, including human lung and airway tissue," explains the American Lung Association (ALA). "It essentially burns through cell walls, and it is capable of doing this at . . . levels frequently encountered in many US cities."[11]

Research Atlanta, a nonprofit organization associated with Georgia State University, has found that asthma-related visits to the pediatric emergency clinic at Grady Memorial Hospital go up by a third during Atlanta's high ozone days. In the four metropolitan Atlanta counties that have ozone levels exceeding the national standard —DeKalb, Douglas, Rockdale, and Fulton—over 10 percent of the population suffers from either asthma or chronic bronchitis and emphysema. If ozone levels continue at the current rate, Research Atlanta estimates, about 1,000 additional persons each year will develop chronic bronchitis and emphysema.[12] In the summer of 1999, Atlanta had a record sixty-nine bad air days—thirty-seven of which were back-to-back from mid-July to mid-August. "Every day they are getting worse," explained Dr. Gerald Staton, a lung specialist at Atlanta's Crawford Long Hospital in August 1999. He was referring to the strain on asthmatics and others during consecutive days of bad air. "At my level, this is a very real thing. Real people are calling me and they're sick, and it is because of the air."[13]

Ten-year-old Ryan Laneaux, an asthmatic who lives in Atlanta, has to slow down when playing if he feels his chest tightening up. He can't go at full speed, especially on bad air days—days when the ozone is high. "The air is heavy and you can't breathe," he says, "even though you can breathe, you know?"[14] More than 5 million children in America have asthma; last year 200 children under the age of fifteen died of asthma. Asthma of all kinds, including adult onset, seems to be growing. The Centers for Disease Control and Prevention (CDC) estimates there were 17.3 million US asthmatics in 1998, compared with 6.8 million in 1980.[15]

Ozone concentrations become a problem for asthmatics and others when they reach the 80-to-120 parts per billion (PPB) range. "Parts per billion" might not sound like a lot. Yet the average person takes 20,000 breaths a day, repeatedly ferrying into the lungs whatever the air contains. Children, of course, take more breaths than adults, and the elderly have to labor with diminishing lung capacity. And those who exercise breathe more often and more deeply, as do laborers who work outside. Perfectly healthy adults can be affected as well. In fact, one research team—which included members from Harvard's Medical School and its School of Public Health—found that day hikers who climbed Mount Washington in New Hampshire on high ozone days had lost lung function by the time they came down the mountain. That didn't happen to hikers making the same trek on low ozone days.[16]

"Repeated exposure to ozone pollution for several months," says EPA, "may cause permanent structural damage to the lungs." Anyone who spends time outdoors in the summer is at risk, according to EPA. "Even when inhaled at very low levels, ozone can trigger a variety of health problems, including aggravated asthma, reduced lung capacity, and increased susceptibility to respiratory illnesses like pneumonia and bronchitis."

Jan Lucas, a forty-nine-year-old university relations official at Towson State University near Baltimore, Maryland, had never been hospitalized for her asthma when she lived in Columbus, Ohio. Yet, during the summer of 1999, after moving to the Baltimore area, she was rushed to the Greater Baltimore Medical Center unable to breathe. She has had a number of other visits as well. "I only found out after I moved here that the air pollution in this area is about as bad as it gets east of the Mississippi."[17] Baltimore is in the belt of cities running up the East Coast from Richmond, Virginia, to Boston and beyond—a region with many counties falling short of the National Ambient Air Quality Standard (NAAQS) for ozone, some in "serious nonattainment." At least 100 million Americans live in areas that do not meet EPA's new eight-hour air quality standard for ozone.

Back in Atlanta, meanwhile, the bad air days are not only threatening the region's public health, but also the region's economy. Major businesses have already refused to come to the area because of the bad air. In 1996, EPA threatened to cut off federal highway funds for Atlanta's metropolitan counties unless a tough ozone cleanup plan was forthcoming. In March 1999, Atlanta created the overarching Georgia Regional Transportation Authority, empowered to veto highways, order new mass transit, and even turn away big traffic-generating projects like malls and subdivisions. Atlanta is now trying to use a population density formula to justify big projects. Still, the prognosis for the immediate future is not good. "With continued urban sprawl and the probability of more cars and hot, dry summers," says Ron Methier, head of Georgia's Air Quality Branch, "there is a likelihood we will continue to have ozone exceedances by the year 2003."[18] Longer term, it doesn't look good either. In the region's twenty-five-year plan, also aimed in part at reducing ozone, Atlanta officials are forecasting regional growth of a million more people by 2025, most of whom will continue to drive. Atlantans will then spend an average of ninety minutes a day in their cars, up from eighty minutes in 1999.[19] But it's not just Atlanta.

During the summers of 1998 and 1999, ozone-limit violations occurred regularly along the East Coast—in Delaware, Maryland, New Jersey, Pennsylvania, New York, North Carolina, Washington, DC, West Virginia, and Virginia. They also occurred in cities like Milwaukee, Cincinnati, Dayton, Toledo, St. Louis, Kansas City, Dallas, Austin, Houston, and, of course, Los Angeles and southern California. But even places like Wichita, Kansas, and Salt Lake City, Utah, now worry about becoming ozone nonattainment areas.[20] Nor have rural retreats and popular vacation destinations been spared, as ozone moves with the wind and is produced in part by traveling vehicles. In the great Smoky Mountain National Park, for example, ozone levels exceeded those recorded in every southern city except Atlanta. Lancaster County, Pennsylvania, known for its Amish farmland and bucolic rural setting, had twice as many bad air days in the summer of 1999 as Philadelphia. Kennebunkport, Maine, also had ozone levels as high or worse than Boston, as did Maine's beautiful Mount Desert Island at Acadia National Park. The eastern shore of Maryland, in Chesapeake Bay Country, had air pollution equal that of Washington, DC.[21]

## THE ICE

The reason ozone is such a problem today in so many places, and seems to follow us wherever we go, is due in large part to the automobile — and more specifically, the internal combustion engine, or the ICE, as it is called.

The ICE, of course, is the thing that makes the world move and Detroit hum. It is a major part of the global economy, giver of jobs, and maker of money—the central ingredient of motive power found under the hood of every car, truck, and SUV on the planet. It is also a chamber of fire, producing millions upon millions of repeated tiny explosions, combusting fossil fuels to produce the power that drives the car. But every time this engine's spark plugs fire, moving pistons within their cylinders after each repeated explosion—millions upon millions of times every second somewhere on the planet—waste gases waft off into the air and atmosphere. These little bits of chemistry and tiny particles are primarily carbon monoxide (CO), nitrogen oxides (NOx), hydrocarbons (HC), or volatile organic compounds (VOCs), particulate matter (PM), and carbon dioxide ($CO_2$)—the last compound a leading actor in global warming.

The ICE's mischief in making ground-level ozone, for example, comes from its NOx and volatile hydrocarbons, which travel up into the summer sky where they are "cooked" by the sun to make the ozone that burns the throat, smarts the eyes, and more. But it's not just ozone. The ICE is also a major player in global warming.

At last count, there were 600 million motor vehicles moving around the planet with internal combustion engines; a number that is slated to double to more than a billion in a mere twenty years. Every minute of every day, globally, more than 100 new ICE-powered vehicles are produced—or roughly, 6,900 an hour, 1.2 million a week, 60 million a year. Each and every car, truck, and SUV that rolls off the assembly line is ready to be fired up with petroleum products to begin an expected ten-year career of fossil-fuel combustion, contributing to both urban smog and global warming.

The worst of the global warming forecasts are indeed bleak: sea levels rising between a half foot and three feet by 2100; global mean temperature up 1.8 to 6.3 degrees Fahrenheit; places like the Florida Keys wiped out; more very hot summers, more smog, and more severe weather. As much as a quarter of the global warming problem is because of the ICE and the refining of its fuel. We have learned that what we burn in the ICE and other industrial processes does not go away—especially the greenhouse part. It stays around for a good long time. $CO_2$ released in 1910 is still up there. Every twenty-gallon tank of gasoline that is burned yields about 380 pounds of $CO_2$, which goes wafting into the blue beyond for a century of heat-trapping havoc. When the ice sheets thin, as they have over Greenland recently, the $CO_2$ coming from the tailpipes of cars and trucks is part of the reason. And because fuel economy in many vehicles today is not what it could be, more carbon is being burned per mile of travel. Yet the cars and trucks keep coming, and more are on the way.

Globally, the big automotive markets still wait. China, India, and Latin America are places where car and truck growth will continue years into the future. Yet air pollution in many cities abroad is already savage, as any traveler to Mexico City or Bangkok will report. Driving downtown in some European and South American cities is now being banned or restricted because of urban pollution. "All too often these days," reports the Associated Press' Angela Doland from Paris in September

1999, "the Eiffel Tower is shrouded in smog, emergency rooms are crowded with people suffering from bronchial distress, and visitors to Paris go away with memories of clogged streets and hazy skies."[22]

## BIG THREE BOOM

Meanwhile, back in the states, Detroit is smiling. The Big Three automakers—General Motors, Ford, and now, DaimlerChrysler, the three companies that today account for about 35 percent of all vehicles sold globally and nearly 70 percent in the US—are enjoying record sales. Annual profits in the last few years running in the $4-billion-to-$6-billion range have not been uncommon. In fact, the last seven years of the 1990s have been the best period of sustained auto growth in Detroit's history. US sales in 1999 set an all-time record, with more than 17 million vehicles sold. Light truck sales—encompassing minivans, pickup trucks, and sport utility vehicles (SUVs)—have been booming, and now comprise nearly one half of all US vehicles sold. Profits on a big SUV can be $15,000 and up. Because of their prosperity, the automakers now have lots of cash. Ford has more than $20 billion in cash, for example. Much of the Big Three's money is going into new or expanded truck and SUV capacity. But what about cleaning up the ICE?

The Big Three say they have made tremendous progress in pollution control. By the year 2007, they say, the ICE will burn at "near-zero pollution." They have also promised to improve fuel economy. Yet some of today's vehicles are abominations when it comes to environmental performance—some, for example, getting less than fifteen miles to the gallon, with no improvement for the last fifteen years. Some SUVs pollute at three times the level of passenger cars. And even in the new and improved cars and trucks that are meeting "grams-per-mile" emission standards, the grams per mile add up when there are millions of vehicles all in one place, making repeated and more frequent trips. Generally, in fact, the growth in vehicle sales plus the rising use of those vehicles are threatening, overtaking, and in some cities, preventing cleanup gains. VMT is doubling about every ten or fifteen years. So as Detroit tries to make that old ICE burn just a little bit cleaner, with a tweak here or a new controller chip there, VMT eats up the gain, and more. Incremental ICE cleaning just doesn't cut it anymore. "Zero emissions" technology is needed. Clean cars period, not just cleaner cars.

## HOLDING BACK

Today we are told the auto industry is on the verge of the clean car. New hybrid vehicles are here now. And the fuel cell, the automakers say, is just around the corner. Still, as former Senator Ed Muskie, the father of the Clean Air Act, used to say, each year's production of vehicles at the current pollution standard really means ten years of pollution into the future at those levels. Each vehicle rolling off the assembly line had an average ten years of life. Therefore, 1975 vehicles would pollute at 1975 levels well into the 1980s. So today, if we don't have clean vehicles until after the year 2010, that means between now and then there will be something like *600 million more vehicles*—roughly, 60 million per year for ten years, globally—polluting urban air and adding atmospheric carbon at today's standards. And the bad news doesn't end in 2010, of course, since the last batch of vehicles produced under the old standards in 2010 will remain on the road through 2020. Millions and millions of them.

This lag time in cleaning up vehicle pollution is the product of a highly evolved political art form—an art form invented and perfected by Detroit's Big Three automakers. And that, in essence, is the tale of *Taken for a Ride*—a story about determined industrial delay and technological negligence on a seventy-year scale. It tells a story that didn't have to be—how America's most prominent and gifted corporations, full of talent and resources, held back their capabilities, their leadership, and their technologies. For fifty years in the past—and now looking forward for another twenty years—General Motors, Ford, and Chrysler have not done, and will likely not do, what was and is within their power to do in cleaning up and/or replacing the internal combustion engine. During this time, America and Americans have been duped, deceived, and misled by Detroit about the possibilities for producing cleaner cars, trucks, minivans, and SUVs.

Time and time again in the 1950s, 1960s, 1970s, 1980s and through the 1990s, the automakers said, "we don't have the technology," "it's impossible," "we don't have the money," "we don't have the engineers," "we're at a competitive disadvantage," "jobs will be lost," "it will take ten years," "we can't change our models that quickly," "it will be too disruptive," "it will make cars unsafe," etc. Yet this is an industry that once never shrank from technological challenge, an industry filled with capability and dynamic leaders, CEOs of action and "can do" engineers ready to tackle any problem. But as the regulatory wars began in 1950s Los Angeles and 1970s Washington, a continuing struggle began over the internal combustion engine that now continues into the twenty-first century. What follows, then, is both a political chronicle and a business history; a story about the continuing contest between big business and big government and why public policy is often needed to push business innovations that protect public health, safety, and the environment.

Sadly, though, this is also an examination of missed opportunities—business opportunities *and* environmental opportunities—as Detroit repeatedly lost market share to the competition, failing to see a new generation of products in fuel-efficient, nonpolluting motor vehicles. It is also a story of misapplied capital and poor investments. Huge profits were squandered in the mid-1980s on empire-building and fanciful technological diversions, with the Big Three missing a chance to become global leaders in fuel economy and pollution control. Detroit also missed—and never really envisioned—the environmental potential of the so-called quality revolution in building cars and trucks. Energy and environmental values were never seen as product starting points; as core business values to shape and guide vehicle design, engineering, and marketing—or for strategic business planning.

Today, there are signs these values are finally taking hold, as there is the promise of a green car race unfolding among the world's major automakers. Yet still, this "better engine" of business purpose and product development may be slow to replace existing technologies and the industry's business-as-usual attitude. For even as new hybrid vehicles now reach the streets, the Big Three are rapidly becoming the "Big Six" as a frenzy of auto industry mergers and joint ventures reshapes the global marketplace. As the competition dwindles, will the green car race proceed? Or will lowest-common-denominator "world car" strategies follow? New entanglements of business and government like the Big Three–White House "supercar" venture—lending official sanction to certain kinds of automotive technology—may make public challenge more difficult.

Yet the bottom line, fifty years after the discovery of smog is this: pollution by car, truck, and sport utility vehicle is still a major public health and environmental problem in the United States and throughout many parts of the world. Fuel economy is going backward. Oil consumption and vulnerable nation-state dependencies are rising. Meanwhile, as the auto and oil industries spend millions to put off and weaken international agreements to help reduce greenhouse gases, the global fleet of cars and trucks is slated to double in twenty years, making global warming and other environmental problems worse, not better. While there is some hope that cleaner technologies will take hold, a lot will depend on which corporate philosophies and marketing approaches emerge as preeminent. New leadership in Detroit can help too, as can the innovations and initiative recently shown by some Japanese automakers.

Still, there is little reason for complacency. The auto-industrial complex of tomorrow will need to be pushed often and pushed hard. It is therefore hoped that the younger generation, and those that follow, will heed and act upon the concerns raised here. There is no time to waste. For the smog and greenhouse dangers of 2010 and 2020 will be thanks, in part, to what isn't accomplished in the first years of this century.

# I

## Polishing the Oval

The love affair with the automobile might not be over yet, but the honeymoon is.
                                                                —*William Clay Ford, Jr.*

William Clay Ford, Jr., the forty-year-old great-grandson of Henry Ford—inventor of the Model-T and founder of the Ford Motor Company—was scheduled to give a talk to the Detroit chapter of the Society for Automotive Engineers at the Greenbriar Hotel in White Sulfur Springs, West Virginia. The Greenbriar is one of those secluded places in the country where corporate executives often go to meet in private. It was October 1997. At the time, young Bill Ford was rumored to be in the running to become chairman of Ford Motor. The Ford family still held 40 percent of the voting stock in the company, but a family member had not run the firm since 1980. So when Bill Ford came to give his talk, he had his listeners' attention. Ford's audience that day included scientists, engineers, and auto executives. His topic was provocative, too: the automobile and the environment.

"Cars and trucks have begun to be seen by some as a social liability, primarily because of their impact on the environment," Ford said. "I want to talk about what we have to do to address those concerns, and rekindle the love affair with the automobile.[1]

"I believe the environmental issues the world faces are real and daunting. And I believe that for the public—which includes our customers, our employees, our stockholders, and voters—environmental preservation is going to be one of the most important issues for the twenty-first century." Indeed, as Ford spoke, the world of nations was preparing to meet in Kyoto to discuss an international treaty on global warming and ways to reduce greenhouse gases—many of which result from burning fossil fuels in cars, trucks, and various industrial processes.

Back in Detroit, however, Bill Ford was not directly engaged in the day-to-day management of the Ford Motor Co. and did not have, in the eyes of some observers, enough of an executive profile to run the company. True, he had worked in the company for fifteen years, almost immediately after completing his formal education—

Hotchkiss boarding school in Connecticut, a degree from Princeton University, and an MBA from the Sloan School of Management at the Massachusetts Institute of Technology. In fact, Bill Ford had been on a management track since 1979—commercial trucks, advanced vehicle planning, vehicle design, and corporate strategy— rising to become a vice president in the 1980s. But in 1994 he stepped down from active management to succeed his father, William Clay Ford, Sr., as chairman of the board's finance committee. At about the same time, he became vice chairman of the Detroit Lions football team, also owned by the Ford family, and later took over the team, also becoming active in National Football League financial affairs. He also pursued some outside interests: starting a home insulation company at one point, then buying up a fly-fishing rod company in Telluride, Colorado, to pursue his passion in fly-fishing with a childhood friend as business partner.[2]

For some in the company, Bill Ford's departure from day-to-day management surely meant he was out of the running to succeed then-chairman Alex Trotman, who had successfully led the company in the 1990s, but who might not stay on beyond 1999. Yet Bill Ford's remarks at the Greenbriar—hinting at a new era ahead—had the sound of something more than just another speech.

"I truly believe there is a competitive imperative to be responsive to environmental concerns," he continued, "and woe be it to the company that ignores them. I think companies that are not environmentally responsive will have difficulty selling their products, attracting investors, and recruiting bright young employees."[3]

Bill Ford, it turns out, also had some environmental stripes of his own. In recent years, he served on the board of directors of the Nature Conservancy, the Greening of Detroit group, and Conservation International in Washington, DC. And meanwhile, in his various roles on Ford's board—which he joined in 1988—he was also "encouraging environmental action." All of this greenness, especially outside of the company, did not escape the notice of some of the more traditional members of Ford's management. They warned young Bill not to hang out with environmentalists. But he refused to heed that advice. "We need to know these people," he said, "and we need to talk with them."[4]

At the Greenbriar, Ford laid out the environmental challenges facing the auto industry and why the Ford Motor could not ignore them. "There are 625 million cars and trucks in service around the world today. In the next thirty years, that number is expected to reach one billion as new markets open and living standards rise. As the number of vehicles increases, so will concerns over emissions, energy usage, and over-crowded roads.

"That concern is manifesting itself in many ways. In some major cities in the United States, loose-knit groups of pedestrians and bicyclists have taken to blocking traffic and protesting cars as the predominant method of transportation. In the UK, Deputy Prime Minister John Prescott has said in this new transportation strategy 'some stark and difficult choices may have to be made'—possibly including the elimination of the two-car family. Actually, restrictions on automobile use have already been witnessed all over the world—including driving bans in Milan and Sao Paulo."[5]

The auto industry, of course, had not been sitting still through all of this, and Bill Ford acknowledged the positive changes that had occurred. He praised the industry's engineers and scientists who had found ways to double fuel efficiency in Ford cars since the 1970s; reduce emissions more than 96 percent nationally; and recycle more than 75 percent of the content of most automotive vehicles. "I know my great-grand-father would have been proud of our progress," he said. "Henry Ford was one of this century's environmental pioneers. He strongly believed in preserving the natural environment as well as recycling."[6] Ford then turned to the future and the new undertakings of the Ford Motor Company—especially the new technologies that lay ahead.

"I believe that a significant part of the automotive fleet in the future will be vehicles that run on alternative fuels. But we don't know today which technology or which fuel will be the winner ten years from now. The general strategy in the industry has been to pursue all technologies that show promise, continuously improve them, and let future developments and the marketplace decide."[7]

Ford Motor was then working on a range of new vehicles, some of which were on the road: "flexible fuel vehicles," cars that ran on both ethanol and gasoline; cars that could run on natural gas; and the "P-2000" car, a prototype, lightweight vehicle using an advanced propulsion system that would get three times the mileage of today's cars with very low emissions. Then there was the joint research effort with the federal government, called "The Partnership for a New Generation of Vehicles." Begun in 1993 with a prod from Bill Clinton and Al Gore, the PNGV, as it was called, is a ten-year, moon-shot type endeavor designed to yield "pre-competitive technologies" and a prototype vehicle by the year 2004 that would have a fuel efficiency of about 80 MPG, or three times today's family car, without sacrificing affordability, utility, or safety. "The program has the best minds of Ford, Chrysler, and GM, auto suppliers, government laboratories and universities working together," Ford explained. "The issues are so enormous that the only hope of victory is if government and industry work together to meet the goal of a cleaner future."[8]

Ford cautioned, however, that "public policy should not prescribe the technological solution." A better approach, he offered, "would be government purchase of new technologies, like alternative fuel vehicles, that would help create demand and reduce the cost of early low-volume production." As for government regulation, he added, the regulatory process should not keep turning into "an adversarial confrontation."

But perhaps William Clay Ford, Jr.'s most interesting remarks came when he departed from his prepared text to talk about global warming.

## GLOBAL WARMING

Global warming, Ford told his listeners, "is real enough that we all ought to be concerned." The auto industry, he suggested, should not be slow in reacting to this problem, as it had been in the past on issues such as auto safety, urban smog, and automotive fuel economy. "If we're seen as dragging our feet and once again saying no," he said, "I don't think it's going to be good for our companies. I think we need to act as if it's real. I think we need to plan as if it's real. I think there's a risk that we'd be marginalized in the court of public opinion if they make up their mind and we don't do anything about it."[9]

The US auto industry, however, was not planning as if global warming were real. In fact, for the most part, Detroit's Big Three were hoping it would go away. For nearly a decade, and even through the last several years as more scientific consensus formed around the likelihood of global warming, the Big Three and their colleagues in the chemical, coal, and oil industries took the view that global warming was only theory, that there was no scientific proof, and that any actions taken to regulate industrial emissions or alter new products to meet that challenge would be premature. In the months prior to Bill Ford's speech at the Greenbriar, the auto industry laid out $13 million for an advertising campaign to wage public relations war against the Clinton administration and the possibility of an international treaty to regulate greenhouse gases. This treaty, soon to be considered in Kyoto, Japan, promised to have more teeth than the 1992 version signed in Rio de Janeiro that called on nations to make voluntary greenhouse gas reductions. The new treaty was proposing mandatory reductions with a proportionally greater share coming from advanced nations, which the Clinton administration supported but not with reductions as steep as some environmentalists and Europeans wanted.

About a week before Bill Ford's speech at the Greenbriar, the Big Three executives—Alex Trotman of Ford, Jack Smith of GM, and Robert Eaton of Chrysler, plus Stephen Yokich of the United Auto Workers (UAW)—met privately with President Clinton and several cabinet members at the White House to make their views known. "We believe the treaty would be bad for the United States in terms of jobs and the economic vitality of the country," said Ford's Alex Trotman to the media after the meeting. The automakers said the proposed treaty would increase gas prices by 50 cents a gallon and boost electricity prices by 20 percent, raising the cost of making cars.[10]

## A NEW COURSE?

So, was William Clay Ford, Jr. saying something different at the Greenbriar? True, he also took his shots at the proposed Kyoto treaty, saying that by excluding some nations, the treaty wasn't fair and would prove ineffective. "We believe in a global economy," he said. "Environmental degradation is a global problem. We can't have regional solutions." Still, the young Ford sounded more positive about the environment and the economy. "I'm chairman of the finance committee and the environmental committee of Ford's board of directors," he said, "and I don't see the two as being in conflict. In fact, I see tremendous business opportunity for the company that can take the lead in technological breakthroughs that protect and preserve the environment.[11]

"I think we're going to find that not only are economic growth and environmental protection compatible, they're complementary. We welcome an opportunity to produce vehicles more compatible with our environmental goals. That's what we want, and, most importantly, what our customers will demand. It is America's responsibility, as the world's leading economy, to lead the way."

David Versical, managing editor of *Automotive News*, who covered the Greenbriar gathering, called Ford's speech "remarkable." Another listener thought the young Ford's positions "naive." Still another was disappointed Ford didn't push his audience to do more.[12] Yet, Bill Ford appears to be an executive with a sure understanding of what kind of company Ford Motor should be.

"The Ford Motor Co. should stand for something more than cars and trucks. There is a Ford way of doing things that we cannot lose. . . . We need to be continuously polishing that Ford oval." At times, Bill Ford even appears to have a social agenda in mind. As the company expands into Asia and Latin America, he says, he would like to find a way to emulate his great-grandfather's involvement in helping to build hospitals, schools, and highways abroad.[13] At home, he has fought to help revitalize Detroit, pushing a deal to bring a new stadium and the Detroit Lions back to the city from the Silver Dome in Pontiac. He says the Lions should have never gone to the suburbs in the first place. When the NFL tried to cancel the annual Thanksgiving Day game that has been a hallmark of Detroit for many years and give it to a better team, Ford chided NFL team owners at his first meeting: "This game doesn't belong to you or to us. It belongs to the fans who've been watching it since 1934—which predates most of the franchises trying to take it away."[14]

Those who have dealt with Bill Ford are impressed. "He's a brilliant man," says Detroit mayor Dennis Archer. "He has maturity and intellect beyond his young age. . . . If he looks you in the eye and tells you something, you can take it to the bank. . . ."[15]

At the Greenbriar, Ford left his listeners with these words.

The love affair with the automobile might not be over yet, but the honeymoon is. Environmental stewardship is a heartfelt concern of our customers and of policymakers around the world. It should be a top priority for the auto industry in the twenty-first century. The challenge is clear: we must lead the green revolution.

I'm confident that our engineering community is up to this challenge. By meeting it, we'll show the world that the auto industry leads the world in technological progress. We will also ensure that future generations enjoy the personal freedom and prosperity that our industry produces.

And our clean vehicles will allow our children and grandchildren to continue the love affair with the automobile.[16]

William Clay Ford, Jr.'s remarks—though careful and in the tradition of an up-and-coming executive, and certainly not revolutionary—were still bucking up against a "culture of resistance" on environmental matters; an attitude and way of doing business deeply embedded not only at Ford, but at General Motors, Chrysler, and throughout the US auto establishment. Environmentalism, where it existed at all among the Big Three, had come about only grudgingly, as a force imposed upon them from the outside. Environmentalism was largely seen by the automakers as a threat; as something to be opposed and resisted—and when that failed, maneuvered around or endlessly litigated. This is the way it had always been, for nearly five decades.

Indeed, Bill Ford had a considerable legacy to overcome if he was truly the environmental Renaissance man he projected himself to be. Could he move the Ford Motor Company, and, through that movement, push the entire US auto industry into a new era? Could Ford become a global leader?

Less than a year after Bill Ford made his remarks at the Greenbriar, it was announced in Dearborn that he would become the company's next chairman, effective in 1999. He would share power with Jac Nasser, fifty-one, who would serve as president and chief executive officer. On May 13, 1999, Bill Ford was formally installed as the new chairman of the Ford Motor Company. His opening remarks at the company's annual shareholders' meeting, regarded as a bit of contemporary business history, were broadcast live on the large NBC-Panasonic TV screen at Times Square. Ford used the time to restate his administration's goals of corporate and environmental responsibility, noting that company polling of consumers worldwide had found that "universally people are demanding corporate responsibility, especially young people."[17]

Once in his new position, Bill Ford continued to speak out on environmental issues. In July 1999, Darren Gersh of the *Nightly Business Report* asked him why environmental issues were becoming so important to his company. "First of all, it's the right thing to do," said Ford. "Secondly, each succeeding generation is going to demand it from us. As you know, as children are taught in preschool and kindergarten about the environment, their expectation about environmental friendliness is only going to grow as they get older. So, for us to capture the consumer in the next century, we have to get on the right side of this issue. Finally, we see it as a competitive advantage. The field is wide open. Nobody has carved out a reputation for themselves as an environmentally friendly industrial company and certainly not an automaker. We would like to change that equation."[18]

Gersh later asked Ford about the future. "Your family has an incredible legacy. When people look back on your term at Ford, what would you hope your legacy would be and how will you contribute to that family history?"

"Henry Ford really, in many ways, defined the twentieth century," said Bill Ford. "[P]rior to the assembly line and the Model-T, most people never traveled in their entire lifetime more than twenty miles from home. Ford Motor Company changed that. What I would like for people to look back upon is to say that in the twenty-first century, Ford Motor Company undid the excesses of the prior industrial revolution; that we made personal mobility possible with no social trade-offs."

# 2

# *Bad Air*

The Ford engineering staff, although mindful that automobile engines produce gases, feels that these waste vapors are dissipated in the atmosphere quickly and do not present an air pollution problem. . . .

—*Ford Motor Co., 1953*
*letter to Kenneth Hahn*[1]

Los Angeles had been called "the valley of the smokes" by Indians as early as the 1500s, owed in part to the campfire smoke that hung across the valley even then. But the reports of a "pall of haze" over the city of the 1940s was something new; something that residents during the time of World War II mistook for Japanese gas attacks. The color was different: a yellowish brown.

By 1943, Los Angeles began to experience days when "the low-lying smoke and fume bank [i.e., smog, haze] engulfed the city and environs and sent cursing citizens, coughing, and crying, running for the sanctuary of air-conditioned buildings." But it was the "daylight dimout" of September 8, 1943, that really got people's attention. "Everywhere the smog went that day, it left a group of irate citizens...," reported the *Los Angeles Times*. "Public complaints reverberated in the press.... Elective officials were petitioned."[2]

A month later, Los Angeles County formed a Smoke and Fumes Commission and in 1945 the city of Los Angeles began limiting smoke emissions from certain industrial sources. In 1947 the state passed the California Air Pollution Control Act, empowering counties to establish air pollution control districts and regulate emissions. Los Angeles County, meanwhile, banned burning in open dumps in 1948 and two years later restricted the burning of smoky fuel between April 15 and November 15. Still, the hazy variety of air pollution persisted.

## A POLLUTED FOOTBALL GAME

Automobiles, for the most part, had escaped California's early regulatory initiatives. However, an air pollution incident at a November 1949 football game between the University of California and Washington State at a stadium in Berkeley, California, later led state legislators to suspect automobiles as major culprits.

On the day of the game, thousands of fans drove into Berkeley with resulting traffic congestion. Later that day, during the game, the pollution became so bad that "many thousands of persons attending . . . experienced intense eye irritation." In the California General Assembly, meanwhile, the Committee on Air and Water Pollution investigated the incident, noting that the only unusual occurrence that day "was the concentration of automobiles at the football game in Berkeley, accentuated by the idling of motors, starting and stopping, which occurs in such a traffic jam." It could only be concluded, the committee said, "that the cause of this particular eye irritation was in some way directly related to automobile exhaust." In fact, the committee suggested that the pollution in Berkeley that afternoon was really quite similar—"very striking" in their words—to what was occurring in Los Angeles on a daily basis. The stadium area that day, they suggested, was actually a microcosm of what was happening over a much larger area in Los Angeles, where "the crowding of existing freeways leading to the downtown area results in daily traffic jams as the flood of cars enters the city in the morning, with resulting accentuation of the exhaust problem by idling, stopping, and starting." Although there was little hard science to verify their hunch, they believed that vehicle exhaust, a form of combustion, was certainly contributing to the LA pollution problem.[3]

About that same time a professor of biochemistry at the California Institute of Technology, Dr. Arie J. Haagen-Smit, began propounding his ideas about "smog." Haagen-Smit suggested that the "smog" in the Los Angeles Basin was actually produced in a photochemical reaction of other pollutants—primarily those coming from oil refineries and automobiles. This was new information to Los Angeles authorities, whose air pollution engineers thought auto exhausts were only a minor part of the problem.

Haagen-Smit, for his part, was drawn into the smog issue almost by accident. He had been researching the biochemistry of flavor compounds, analyzing fruits and vegetables, and factors related to taste. At the time, he also happened to be a member of the scientific committee of the Los Angeles Chamber of Commerce. The chamber had received complaints about unusual crop damage, and Haagen-Smit got the job of looking into these complaints. He soon began filtering and testing thousands of cubic feet of Pasadena air, studying its effects and activity. When the Los Angeles County Air Pollution Control District (LAPCD) learned of his research talents, they hired him in March 1949 as an advisor. In Los Angeles, meanwhile, smog was becoming more apparent. On October 14, 1950, for example, "a nauseous blanket of smog cut visibility to less than two city blocks and caused Gov. Goodwin J. Knight to . . . see what action he can take . . . to help alleviate the sickening siege," explained the caption on an Associated Press wire photo showing the haze.

## THE HAAGEN-SMIT HYPOTHESIS

In November 1950, Haagen-Smit went public with his laboratory experiments. He explained that through a photochemical process, sunlight transformed pollutants like hydrocarbons and oxides of nitrogen found in the LA air into what was called *smog*.[4] Haagen-Smit had tested mixtures of these gases in a test chamber using ultraviolet light to simulate sunlight. The resulting chemical reaction caused the formation of the eye-irritating haze, or smog, known technically as ozone (o-3). It was a new kind of pollution that could also damage crops and crack rubber tires. The hydrocarbons in the smog, Haagen-Smit reported, came from many sources, but automobiles, oil refineries, and refuse burning then appeared to be the most significant. Haagen-Smit cautioned that his findings constituted a research "hypothesis." However, it did "fit the known facts very well." Personally, he regarded the findings significant enough to begin a program to control the sources of hydrocarbons. Although the LAPCD was convinced, and ordered an investigation into controlling automobile pollution, the public was not. Some felt the "little guy and his automobile" would be singled out.

The oil industry—a prominent industry in Southern California—took issue with Haagen-Smit and hired the Stanford Research Institute (SRI) to review his findings. SRI went about attacking the fundamentals of Haagen-Smit's research, arguing that smog was still a mystery. The SRI attack caused Haagen-Smit to spend nearly two years defending his work and responding to charges. In the fall of 1953, however, there was a severe, five-day siege of smog that focused public attention on the lack of progress in cleaning up the air in Los Angeles County. Public opinion then swung against the local authorities for weak enforcement and blame shifted to the oil refineries. The oil companies, meanwhile, were pointing at the automobile.

Automobiles came to southern California with the great rush of settlement that occurred in the state during the early 1900s. In 1906, there were about 6,500 cars in the entire state. By 1918, there were 365,000. Ten years later, by 1929, there were 1.9 million, with more than one million of those in southern California. In Los Angeles, automobile registration grew five times as fast as the population during the 1920s. Unlike the railroads, which had played a key role in bringing the first wave of immigrants to southern California in the 1880s, the automobile played a more lasting role. "For this was a case, not of the locomotive bringing the man," observes historian Ashleigh Brilliant, "but of every man bringing his own locomotive."[5]

Indeed, in a very real sense, the automobile made industrial fire portable; each vehicle carrying its very own furnace—the Otto Cycle, internal combustion engine. By the 1950s when Haagen-Smit advanced his theory about smog, the internal combustion engine was at the center of the storm. By then, there were more than 2 million motor vehicles in LA County alone.

## Not Our Smog

In the auto industry, meanwhile, there had been some interest in the auto exhaust problem, and in fact, a body of knowledge was emerging on the techniques of exhaust gas measurement and how the internal combustion engine contributed to air pollution.* Acknowledging this in a March 1953 letter to Los Angeles Supervisor Kenneth Hahn, GM's technical director, John Campbell, assured Hahn there was no need to worry:

> GM has been cognizant of the exhaust gas problem for many years and the research laboratories of GM have been responsible for the discovery of much of the basic information on exhaust gas that is available today on this subject.
>
> Carbon monoxide has generally been considered the principal component of exhaust gas that is injurious to health. Through improvements in carburetion, ignition, and engine design, we have reduced the average carbon monoxide content of exhaust gases by a very significant amount over the past twenty years.[6]

Mr. Campbell added that GM and others were "continually seeking practical solutions" to the problem. As fast as such solutions were found—"even partial ones"— they would be put into commercial use, "because of the continual competitive incentive toward making engineering improvements in the automotive industry."

By 1953, the Automobile Manufacturers Association (AMA) had formed a committee charged with investigating the auto pollution problem. In early 1954, ten leading automotive engineers were dispatched to Los Angeles from Detroit to see firsthand the "peculiar new form of air pollution" known as smog. The auto engineers sent to study the problem assured reporters at the time that the industry was "vitally interested" and had for "many years" been conducting research on the problem. After a week of observations and study, the visiting delegation of engineers said the problem required further investigation to determine the exact contribution of all sources. The auto industry, the team said, needed to study the effects of proposed controls, develop better instruments for measurement, and study health effects. "A tremendous amount of work needed to be done," said the group. Still, the auto industry would "do whatever we possibly can to assist in the situation of automobile exhaust fumes' part in air pollution. We are dead serious. We mean business. We didn't come out here to fool around."[7]

However, for the next six years, the automakers did fool around; they stalled in acknowledging the automobile's role in the LA pollution mess. "Whatever its motivation," public policy historians James Krier and Edmund Ursin observe, summarizing the period in their book, *Pollution and Policy*, "the industry was remarkably

---

* For example, a 1922 paper published in the *Franklin Institute Journal* covered the "Sampling and Analysis of Automobile Exhaust Gas." In 1936, another paper appearing in the *SAE Journal* (Society of Automotive Engineers) explained, in part, "Complete exhaust gas analyses for $CO_2$, $CO$, hydrogen, methane, and oxygen have been related to directly measured air-fuel ratios for three engines over a range of operating conditions and with varied air-measuring equipment." A paper delivered at the 1952 National Air Pollution symposium in Pasadena reported on "Hydrocarbon Constituents of Automobile Exhaust Gases."

slow in conceding what had become obvious to everyone else—the importance of automotive emissions."[8]

First, the industry insisted on definitive proof. General Motors had already written in March 1953, for example, that while Los Angeles studies indicated that exhaust gases "may be a contributing factor to the smog," other cities did not appear to have the same problem. Thus, for GM, "some other factors," peculiar to Los Angeles, "may be contributing to this problem." Ford officials, also writing in March 1953, had taken the view that automobile exhaust was not a problem. They also contended that the need for a pollution control device "to more effectively reduce exhaust vapors had not been established."[9]

Next, after the automakers conceded in 1954 that the automobile was the largest single source of hydrocarbons in Los Angeles, and that auto exhausts were capable of forming ozone, industry officials wanted further work to substantiate the exact cause-and-effect relationship between auto pollutants and smog. In 1955, the automakers held that the evidence did not prove auto pollutants produced smog and its harmful effects, such as eye irritation and plant damage, etc. In 1957, when definitive proof was found that the automobile was the primary cause of photochemical air pollution, industry reverted to an earlier held position that the problem was peculiar to Los Angeles. It continued to espouse this view for three more years.[10]

In a late February 1960 statement before Congress, the AMA's Karl M. Richards conceded that Los Angeles' smog may well come from automobiles, but the aggravating quality was not due to anything in the automotive gases per se, but was caused by the unique nature of the Los Angeles Basin's topography and meteorology. Photochemical smog, he explained, was only caused when the unique combination of all the LA factors came into play: persistent temperature inversion, encircling mountains, very light wind movement, and intense sunlight. Further, photochemical smog, he said, "is not likely to occur anywhere else on earth with the frequency and intensity found in this area."[11] Richards added that the auto industry would not consider controls on its vehicles in other parts of the country until it was demonstrated that hydrocarbons presented a problem elsewhere.

## Not Just Los Angeles

Commercial airline pilots in the 1950s and 1960s reported seeing the skies over broad regions of the US becoming less and less clear—and not just over urban areas. Captain W. Lain Guthrie of Eastern Airlines, for example, explained that pilots could see the sources of pollution emanating from distrust sections of the earth's surface below. Guthrie, in fact, would accuse the US Weather Bureau of issuing false reports on air quality, misleading the public into thinking that air visibility and pollution problems were natural haze, when in fact they were smog and industrial pollution.[12]

## "They Have a Responsibility"

In February 1953, Kenneth Hahn, a Los Angeles County supervisor, wrote a letter to Henry Ford II to ask what Ford's company knew about automobile pollution and what the company's research plans were. Mr. Ford replied, through his staff, that there was really no problem, and therefore, no need for research. "The Ford engineering staff, although mindful that automobile engines produce gases, feels that these waste vapors are dissipated in the atmosphere quickly and do not present an air pollution problem," replied Ford's public affairs manager, Dan J. Chabak. "Therefore, our research department has not conducted any experimental work aimed at totally eliminating these gases." Hahn was later assured by Detroit that an industrywide study of the exhaust problem had begun. Mr. Hahn, however, kept writing, pushing for action.

In 1955 he was told in one reply, "We will soon be in a position to make recommendations which should point the way to reduction of hydrocarbons in automotive exhaust gases." Nearly two years passed. Hahn again inquired about exhaust controls. Will they be ready for 1957 models? "We have . . . established the 1958 model year as the goal for the production of deceleration devices." Still, there was little progress. Finally, in October 1960, the president of General Motors, replying to Hahn, wrote, "I am gratified to report that positive crankcase ventilation is available on all 1961 General Motors passenger cars being delivered to California. We believe that this relatively inexpensive device will perform a major job of reducing air pollution." Positive crankcase ventilation—based on a technique known to industry since the 1930s—took care of gases in the engine proper, but only about 25 percent of hydrocarbon exhaust. Hahn wrote back to express his disappointment.

In January 1964, when Hahn testified before two US Senate committees, he handed out a little booklet of the collected correspondence he had made with the automakers, explaining to the senators:

> . . . I have tried to tell [the auto executives]. . . that they have a responsibility on air pollution and they have not met it. . . .
>
> . . . [T]hey know about the problem. . . . They have been here; there are devices manufactured that have been proven. . . . [A]nd it is strange why they have not put it on all their cars. . . .
>
> . . . Now they have had ten years of warning, all documented with answers back from their own officials saying they are studying the problem and researching it. They can research this to death; in the meantime we haven't licked the problem. . . .

It would not be until 1966—thirteen years after Mr. Hahn began his inquiries of the automakers—that exhaust controls would be required on new California cars. And even then, it would only be by force of law. Meanwhile, Ken Hahn's 1953-1967 correspondence with the automakers leaves behind a record as good as any of the industry's attitudes toward pollution control at the time.

The smog problem, the nation was discovering, was not unique to Los Angeles. Los Angeles, in fact, was the urban equivalent of the miner's canary; the harbinger of what lay ahead for other cities. While smog may have emerged in its most intense form in some cities like Los Angeles, the air pollution problem was worsening nationwide. "Los Angles-type smog" was being reported in New York, Philadelphia, and other cities by the late 1950s and spreading to rural areas in some places. California's vast San Fernando Valley, once a smog-free agricultural region, had begun to be plagued by smog almost as badly as Los Angeles. Sacramento, one of state's most pristine cities in the early 1950s, with some of the cleanest air found anywhere, began succumbing to smog in the fall of 1958, recording some twenty air pollution episodes.[13] California's growth—and the explosion of automobile ownership and use in particular—was spreading the pollution. In 1945 there were about 3 million motor vehicles in California; by 1950, 5 million; and by 1956, more than 7 million.

In Washington, DC, meanwhile, the federal government was starting to pay more attention to air pollution. By 1955, both California and the federal government had adopted laws providing for the study of the air pollution, its causes, effects, and possible control strategies. The federal law, however, left matters principally to the states, while California's law deferred to local authorities. In 1957, Representative Paul Schenck (R-OH), introduced a strongly worded bill in Congress to prohibit the use of any motor vehicle in interstate commerce that discharged unburned hydrocarbons in levels found dangerous by the US surgeon general. Schenck's bill—one of the first ever proposed to directly involve the federal government in the matter of automobile pollution—did succeed in generating congressional hearings in 1958, but was opposed by the Eisenhower administration and died in committee. Schenck persisted with subsequent bills, but his prohibition provision was watered down to a US surgeon general's study of the effects of motor vehicle exhaust on the public health. Still, this was a key recognition of the potential public health problem. Eisenhower signed this bill in mid-1960, and the law that became known as the Schenck Act.[14]

As the Kennedy administration came to power in Washington, nearly 400 US communities were collecting pollution data and there was a growing recognition of the problem nationwide.[15] "It is estimated that all 232 communities with populations over 500,000 have air pollution problems and about 40 percent of the communities of 2,500 to 50,000 population," reported US Department of Health, Education and Welfare (HEW) undersecretary Ivan A. Nestingen to a gathering of engineers in Washington in 1961. Nestingen estimated that some 90 percent of the American population then lived in localities with air pollution problems.[16] It wasn't just Los Angeles anymore, as the auto industry had maintained.

"Los Angeles no longer has, if it ever had, a monopoly on photochemical smog," stated the US Department of Agriculture in its 1963 *Yearbook of Agriculture*. "The characteristic symptoms [of pollution damage] in plants have been found in almost every metropolitan area in the country. . . . [T]he entire coastal area roughly from Washington, DC, to Boston has come to rival southern California." To this, the US

Public Health Service added, "The data show that although Los Angles experiences photochemical smog incidents more frequently, smog incidents in other cities are severe and not infrequent."

## SLOW TO EMPOWER

Although the Kennedy administration had asked for an expanded federal role in pollution control, Congress was not willing to go much beyond technical grants to the states and further federal study. Only fifteen states had any control programs at the time. By February 1963, Kennedy recommended legislation to Congress that offered more grants for states and localities, but there had also been some discussion about the need for a stronger federal power to help abate pollution problems. At the recommendation of Wilbur Cohen of HEW, Kennedy's bill also included a federal abatement power. At the time, in fact, the American Medical Association was favoring a more active federal role, including the power to abate pollution, and Cohen advised Kennedy not to adopt a position that would be to the right of the nation's doctors. A bill would eventually pass in Congress—the Clean Air Act of 1963—that allowed for federal investigative and abatement authority, signed by then-President Lyndon Johnson in December 1963. Yet these early federal provisions were more "bark than bite," say public policy historians James Krier and Edmund Ursin, and were essentially "hedged in by a set of complex and time-consuming [agency] procedures."[17] Although abatement provisions were on the books, for all practical purposes they would not be used.

California, on the other hand, had become a little more aggressive with automobile pollution by this time, passing the 1960 Motor Vehicle Pollution Control Act—the first state act directed at motor vehicle emissions. The act created a Motor Vehicle Pollution Control board to certify pollution control technology for motor vehicles, which would later become important in spurring the automakers forward. Certified technology, for example, would be required as a condition to register new vehicles. Getting the new technology, however, would prove to be the problem.

Back in Washington, the Johnson administration was now being pushed by some in Congress to enact tougher measures. Johnson told Congress in a February 1965 address that his administration would initiate discussions with the auto industry to help solve the exhaust problem. But no discussions ensued. Was Johnson stalling? Editorials in a few major newspapers at the time "hinted at a 'love affair' between Johnson and the automobile industry."[18] The auto industry, now eyeing an emerging national concern, was still insisting that if new air pollution control programs were needed, they were best left to the states. Big Three executives, though, were still barely inching away from their steadfast position that smog was only a problem in California.

General Motors vice president Harry F. Barr, speaking on behalf of the four major automakers in June 1965, said the industry did not rule out the possibility that an auto pollution problem might exist outside California. However, he added, "the situation probably needs more definition."[19] Officials from HEW were more certain about the problem and told Congress as much that same month. "The evidence of photochemical smog reaction products outside of California is clear. . . . Significantly high concentrations of carbon monoxide and nitrogen oxides are now occurring in all metropolitan areas where pollutants are monitored. . . . Current evidence indicates the widespread occurrence of photochemically produced pollutants and their deleterious effects. . . ."[20] As some states in addition to California started to develop legislation of their own—New York, for example, proposed standards tougher than California's—the auto industry changed its tune about state control. Still not admitting to a national smog problem, however, the industry began to say that it might equip new vehicles with exhaust controls should Congress decide that was necessary. Congress and the Johnson administration began working together and essentially agreed on the need for auto emissions standards, but such standards would not be written into law. HEW would also be given wide discretion in setting and establishing deadlines. Congress had considered a 1966, and then a 1967 deadline in proposed bills, but these were removed. In October 1965, the Motor Vehicle Air Pollution Control Act became law. Before regulations were promulgated under the '65 act, Congress passed the Air Quality Act of 1967, adding language that preempted state regulation of emissions—except for California. The first federal regulations for auto emissions developed under the 1967 act—those pertaining to crankcase emissions—essentially had little practical effect. Exhaust standards were set for model year 1968, for hydrocarbons (HC) and carbon monoxide (CO). These, however, were later extended to the 1970 model year. Standards for nitrogen oxides (NOx) were not expected until 1973.

Pollution from automobiles worsened in the 1960s, particularly NOx emissions. In 1964, automobiles accounted for an estimated 430 tons per day of NOx; by 1968 it was up to 645 tons per day. By 1968, Los Angeles County was recording a third to a half of its calendar year had pollutants at the "adverse level"—132 days in excess of the California nitrogen dioxide standard, then set at 0.25 PPM for one hour, and 188 days in excess of the state's 0.15 PPM oxidant (ozone) standard.[21]

## TURNED THE CORNER?

Meanwhile, auto industry executives were predicting progress with pollution control devices on automobiles. "We have turned the corner so far as motor vehicle emissions are concerned," claimed GM's vice president Harry F. Barr in February 1967. Barr explained that the 1968 model cars would contain pollution control devices that would reduce emissions by 60 percent. Chrysler's president Virgil E. Boyd was also optimistic. He explained that in ten years—by 1977—the older cars would be off the road, and the newer cars would take their place, resulting in cleaner air. "As a result," he said, "along with a 30-percent increase in car population [i.e., from 94 million to 120 million by 1977], you have a 7-percent decrease in each car's harmful exhaust. The result is a net decrease in auto-caused pollution by nearly half—in ten year's time."[22]

Yet those enforcing California's early pollution laws were finding poor performance on the 1966-67 model cars equipped with new pollution control devices. Louis J. Fuller, director of the Los Angeles Air Pollution Control District, testified before Congress in March 1967 that many cars carrying the devices were beginning to emit pollution exceeding legally permissible levels after only 5,000 miles of driving, even though the devices were supposed to keep pollution below those levels for 50,000 miles. Fuller criticized the testing practice of "averaging"—whereby automobiles with pollution control devices would be randomly averaged at the factory. Fuller called the practice "a clear evasion" of the law and asked for tighter quality controls on car production to insure the emission systems would perform as they were supposed to.[23]

And despite the optimism expressed by some in Detroit about the future of auto pollution control, others were not happy about the record to date. In January 1968, Richard S. Morse of the Sloan School of Management at MIT addressed the Society of Automotive Engineers, singling out the auto industry for its historic resistance and lack of initiative in addressing automotive pollution.

> ... [T]he 'smog' photosynthesis reaction was postulated as early as 1951, and unfortunately history suggests that without California and federal action, the auto industry would voluntarily not have made the limited progress presently achieved in reducing harmful emissions. And I think it should be pointed out that we have yet to see the public announcement from the auto industry of pollution control concepts more effective than those required to meet the current standards. The ideas which give us hope have come from elsewhere.[24]

In March 1969, on Capitol Hill, the Senate Commerce Committee released a March 1969 report that concluded in part, "Present emission standards will not stabilize, much less reduce, vehicular air pollution. . . . Under existing controls, automobile air pollution in the United States will more than double in the next thirty years because of the projected increase in both number of vehicles and miles driven by each vehicle."

In August 1969, Dr. Fred Bowditch, GM's director of emission control, reported in Los Angeles that progress was being made in controlling auto emissions. Crankcase controls, he explained, in place in California since 1961, had brought hydrocarbon emissions down to 454 grams, or about one pound per day. With exhaust controls, instituted in the state in 1966, hydrocarbon emissions came down even further, to 208 grams per day. And finally, with evaporative emission controls, which would be installed in the early 1970s, hydrocarbon emissions would come down to an estimated 108 grams per car per day—an overall reduction of 80 percent since 1960s models. "I think there can no longer be any doubt that the worst part of the automotive problem is behind us," he said, suggesting that auto-produced smog in southern California would never again be as high as it was at that time.[25]

Yet, just as Bowditch was making his pronouncements about the auto industry's purported progress in cleaning up LA smog, a new drama was unfolding back in Washington, DC. The US Justice Department was charging that the auto industry had been engaged in a technological conspiracy for the previous sixteen years, purposely holding back the use of pollution control technology on automobiles.

# 3

## Smog Conspiracy

... [T]he automobile manufacturers, through AMA, conspired not to compete in [the] research, development, manufacture, and installation of [pollution] control devices, and collectively did all in their power to delay such research, development, manufacturing, and installation.

*—US Department of Justice*
*confidential memo, 1968*

It was August 1969. Richard Nixon was president of the United States, American troops were being withdrawn from Viet Nam, and baseball's New York Mets were on their way to a National League pennant. In upstate New York, 400,000 young people gathered for a music festival called Woodstock. A month earlier, Neil Armstrong had become the first man to walk on the moon.

In Washington, Lloyd Cutler, then a well-known and respected fifty-one-year-old attorney at Wilmer, Cutler, and Pickering, was tending to a little business on behalf of one of his clients, the Automobile Manufacturers Association (AMA). Cutler had been in and out of meetings at the US Justice Department (DOJ) for weeks. He was defending his client against a charge of industrial conspiracy. Nine months earlier, the AMA—along with American Motors, Chrysler, Ford, and General Motors—had been named by the Justice Department in an antitrust lawsuit accusing them of conspiring for sixteen years to prevent and delay the manufacture and use of pollution control devices for automobiles.[1]

"Beginning at least as early as 1953, and continuing thereafter. . . ," alleged the DOJ complaint, "the defendants and coconspirators have been engaged in a combination and conspiracy in unreasonable restraint of interstate trade and commerce in motor vehicle air pollution control equipment. . . ." The complaint charged that the automakers, in violation of the Sherman Act, had:

- engaged in a conspiracy to eliminate competition among themselves in the research, development, manufacture, and installation of pollution control equipment;
- engaged in a conspiracy to eliminate competition among themselves in purchasing patents on new pollution control equipment developed by outside parties;

- agreed to install air pollution technology only when all parties to the agreement settled on a common date for doing so;
- agreed among themselves in 1961 to delay national installation of crankcase emission control devices until 1963, despite the fact that this could have been done in 1962;
- agreed among themselves in late 1962 and 1963 to delay installation of improved crankcase devices in California; and,
- conspired among themselves to tell California regulatory officials that exhaust emissions control devices could not be installed before 1967.

## WHERE'S THE TECHNOLOGY?

The DOJ's "smog conspiracy case," as it became known, had its origins in the Lyndon Johnson administration of 1965. However, it was a local official in Los Angeles who first planted the seeds of a possible conspiracy case. Los Angeles had been choking on smog since the early 1950s, with city and county officials there pushing the auto industry for action, without much success. The frustration soon boiled over.

"What has the industry accomplished in the last ten years?" asked Los Angeles County Pollution Control Board executive S. Smith Griswold in a June 1964 speech at the annual meeting of the Air Pollution Control Association. Griswold was then alluding to a 1953 joint agreement the automakers had made with one another, supposedly to pool their research on air pollution and come up with a solution. The automakers said they would make progress jointly and even set up cross-licensing agreements to insure that progress by one would be progress by all. "How has this worked out?" asked Griswold. "Apparently, it has served to guarantee that no manufacturer would break ranks and bring into this field of air pollution control the same kind of competitive stimulus that spokesmen for the industry frequently pay homage to. . . ."[2]

Griswold, without really knowing it, had hit upon a possible antitrust issue that was driven home to him later by a maverick attorney named Ralph Nader. Nader was just beginning what would become a long, distinguished career as the nation's leading consumer advocate and pioneer of "public interest" law. In addition to alerting Griswold of the possible collusion, Nader also briefed Justice Department officials on what he thought was the basis for a major antitrust suit. In Los Angeles, Griswold helped draft a resolution for the LA County Board of Supervisors citing the industry's lack of progress on pollution control technology. The resolution, adopted in January 1965, specifically requested the US attorney general to initiate an investigation and take legal action to prevent the automakers from engaging in "further collusive obstruction." By this time, the Justice Department had already subpoenaed records from the industry, and a formal investigation was underway.

During 1967-68, an eighteen-month grand jury investigation was convened in Los Angeles. Justice Department attorneys handling the case had initially sought a criminal indictment, but higher-ups hedged and delayed action.* Finally, a civil suit was filed against the automakers just as the Johnson administration left office in January 1969, handing the case to the Nixon administration's new attorney general John Mitchell.

## CUTLER TO THE RESCUE

Lloyd Cutler, meanwhile, had been plying his craft at Justice. A well-known heavy hitter on matters of corporate law and skilled at backroom negotiating, Cutler had lobbied on Capitol Hill for the AMA a few years earlier in the 1965 auto safety debate. He was credited with persuading Congress on two key parts of the legislation: not to include criminal penalties in the bill and replacing specific auto safety design standards with performance standards. Cutler also crafted language for the Senate report requiring that cost be considered in determining what safety features would be added to cars. Cutler's firm—though not Cutler himself—had also been retained for several years as legal counsel for General Motors. Cutler, however, had represented the AMA in other Justice Department matters. One attorney at the agency described him as, "hands down, the best lobbyist in Washington."[3] The automakers, no doubt, were pleased to have Lloyd Cutler on their side. During negotiations in the antitrust case over several months, there soon came rumor of a deal in late summer 1969.

Sure enough, on September 11th, the Justice Department announced that the case would be settled by consent decree. In the legal trade, consent decrees are viewed as a way to save face, save cost, and not drag all the parties through a public display of charge and countercharge. For the automakers, that was good news. There would also be no findings or admissions of illegal activity in the decree. Still, the fact that there had to be a federal settlement at all—and that the attorney general was involved, however remotely—revealed the seriousness of the allegations. The settlement, in fact, specifically prohibited the four automakers and the AMA from obstructing the development and installation of automobile pollution control devices.**

---

* As the case evolved inside Justice, there was debate over whether the grand jury should seek a criminal or civil indictment. The civil route won out. Four federal judges who might receive the case were strongly opposed to criminal sanctions in antitrust cases. In addition, it had been long-standing Justice Department policy to reserve the criminal route for price-fixing and other traditional cases in which there is no question of blatantly illegal conduct. However, the pollution case was not traditional. Some, like Nader, argued "product fixing"; that restraint of technology was restraint of trade, preventing competition. This, however, was a very novel approach at the time, especially in the closed and ponderous world of conservative antitrust adjudication.

** In the government's settlement, there were a couple of key restrictions that were to apply for at least a decade. First, the automakers were restricted from entering any agreement "to

Attorney General Mitchell said the decree would "spur aggressive and competitive research and development efforts." He also said it would be "a substantial benefit to the health and welfare of all metropolitan area residents." The president's science advisor at the time, Lee A. DuBridge, said the resolution of the case "represents an important step forward in the fight against pollution."[4] Others, however, were furious. They saw it as a clear victory for the auto industry, a way to avoid a public airing of the case, essentially escaping more than fifteen years of illegal activity. Ralph Nader wrote to DOJ's antitrust chief Richard W. McLaren, asserting that criminal wrongdoing was uncovered by the grand jury, that the consent decree was weak by comparison, containing insufficient enforcement procedures, and that key provisions of the decree would expire after ten years. Nader and others asked Justice to rescind the decree and bring the matter to trial.[5]

A key issue became the evidence compiled by the grand jury investigation. That evidence would be sealed forever by the consent decree. However, if the case were brought to trial and the defendants found guilty of conspiracy, under the antitrust laws, any injured parties could then bring their own suits to recover three times the damages suffered. Triple damages are designed to serve as a deterrent to future violations, and in this case, future conspiracies against the public good. Earlier on Capitol Hill, as rumors swirled about a settlement, a group of nineteen congressmen, led by Representatives George Brown (D-CA) and Bob Eckhart (D-TX), sent a letter to Attorney General Mitchell expressing their concern that a full trial was needed to show the public that corporate lawbreaking was no different than any other violation of law.[6] The Justice Department, nevertheless, proceeded with its agreement.

In Los Angeles, meanwhile, Supervisor Kenneth Hahn told the press that Los Angeles County would demand the unsealing of "a roomful of federal grand jury evidence" gathered by the grand jury. According to Hahn, foreman of the grand jury Martin Walshbren was quite angry over the Justice Department's consent agreement. In fact, when asked by a *Los Angeles Times* reporter if there was more to the case than the consent decree suggested, Mr. Walshbren said, "Yes."

LA TIMES: "How much more?"
WALSHBREN: "A great deal more."

---

exchange restricted information" with one another, including trade secrets, and unpublished policy and technical information relating to pollution control devices. Second, the auto companies were prohibited from filing any jointly authored statements relating to emission standards or regulations with any governmental regulatory agency. These restrictions were to be in force for ten years, with the proviso that the federal government could apply for an extension, which the government did. However, in the 1980s the Reagan administration dropped the matter, and Congress passed legislation more favorable to allowing joint industry research programs.

LA TIMES: "If the federal judge refuses to release [the grand jury testimony], what are you going to do?"

WALSHBREN: "There isn't much I can do unless I wish to risk going to jail."

LA's Kenneth Hahn, however, was not happy. "The presidents of General Motors, Ford, and Chrysler should be brought to trial right here in Los Angeles. . . . The big manufacturers all conspired. If one wouldn't put the devices on, the others wouldn't either. . . . This case is the most important legal battle in the history of the air pollution fight. If we lose it, we will go back twenty years."[7] The California attorney general, Thomas Lynch, also planned to file a separate antitrust action against the auto companies, but said he too was being hampered by the seal on the grand jury records. He was unable to question key grand jury witnesses. Still, there was one last chance for those opposing the settlement and wanting the proceedings made public: the consent decree had to be approved by a federal judge.

A brief but intense campaign to prevent the approval of the decree ensued. Thousands of individuals, scores of congressmen, and numerous municipalities petitioned Federal District Court Judge Jesse W. Curtis not to approve the decree. Other related developments at the time were:

- The Los Angeles County Board of Supervisors asked the federal courts to allow them to intervene in the original suit and to sue the manufacturers for $100 million in damages. At the time, other municipalities were also being asked to join Los Angeles in the intervention. With other parties joining the case, it was thought that the court might be reluctant to agree to the settlement before holding an open trial.
- Members of the Judiciary Committees in both Houses of Congress were asked to sign a letter urging the Justice Department to review its policy on the use of consent decrees in antitrust cases.
- Rep. George Brown (D-CA) started a statewide petition drive requesting the Justice Department to withdraw the settlement, and he also introduced a resolution in the House, part of which requested the full transcript of the 1966-67 grand jury investigation, including subpoenaed documents.[8]

On October 28, 1969, the two sides came before the judge at the US District Court in the Central District of California. Lloyd Cutler rose for his clients.". . . [This] is the first case I am aware of that has ever been brought against an industry for cooperating in the exchange of technology in order to solve a public health problem. . . ." A few hours later, Judge Curtis approved the decree; the auto industry had its deal.* Yet, the public only had a fleeting glimpse of what this case was

---

* In addition to the federal case, there were twenty-eight states and another ten cities and counties that brought private actions against the automakers after the federal case was settled. These actions, modeled on the Justice Department's antitrust case, sought damages for

all about, and more importantly, what the auto industry had done to deserve this level of federal action.


## PHIL BURTON'S DISCLOSURE

In May 1971, nearly two years after the government's conspiracy case against the automakers was settled, Representative Phil Burton (D-CA) obtained a copy of the original Justice Department memorandum on the case. According to Burton, the memo—which had been kept under wraps since it was written in 1968—contained "previously undisclosed evidence" not available when the case was settled. Citing Justice Louis Brandeis' maxim that "sunlight is the best of all disinfectants," Burton submitted the DOJ memo to the *Congressional Record*.[9] It revealed, among other things, that a criminal proceeding was recommended rather than the civil case that DOJ finally did bring.

"The disclosures are especially painful in light of the settlement of the government's civil case . . . ," said Burton, submitting the DOJ memo to the public record on the floor of the House. In Burton's view, the settlement "deprived the public of an open trial on all the issues"; a trial that he believed "would educate the unreformed and deter the potential violator, especially in the auto industry, which has for too long been dealt with by gentlemanly trust-busters. . . ." He also charged that

---

automotive air pollution. Later consolidated into one case in California, the suits sought a variety of remedies, asking, for example, that auto companies be ordered to take steps to eliminate smog, make contributions toward the establishment of mass transit systems, and provide free emissions testing of automobiles. In June 1973, the US Court of Appeals in San Francisco ruled that the plaintiffs could not sue for damages in the case but they could seek equitable protection under the antitrust law. However, in October 1973, Federal Judge Manuel Real dismissed thirty-four of the thirty-eight cases saying that the antitrust laws did not give him the power to force the automakers to find a solution to the pollution problem. The automakers argued that antitrust laws were reserved for the regulation of business conduct and the adjudication of business damage. The cases brought, they argued, were not about business damage in the strictest sense of antitrust tradition, as in price-fixing. Judge Real agreed. "Certainly, in the battle against smog, the hour is late," he said, adding that in the conduct of their business, the automakers had caused "substantial discomfort and sometimes actual illness" for "uncountable millions of Americans." However, this was "not the result of any conspiracy or combination in restraint of trade." The antitrust laws, he explained, "are not intended—nor do they purport to be—a panacea to cure all the ills that befall our citizenry by the accident that some damage or injury may have been caused by a business enterprise." The suits had asked the judge to depart from traditional antitrust law to "find a solution to this most perplexing social problem." Some later speculated that the states might have fared better had they pursued a public nuisance argument rather than mimicking the federal government's antitrust case.

the settlement "increased the legal burdens for later litigants, failed to provide for any restitution of damage done, failed to contain adequate reporting requirements, and failed to prohibit the destruction of past documents—all in tradition of ex parte negotiations which form the cornerstone of the consent decree program."[10] Burton urged Attorney General John Mitchell to reopen the case, conduct both a Justice Department investigation and convene a new grand jury to consider a conspiracy indictment—none of which occurred.[11]

Yet, the disclosure of the DOJ memo clearly brought new evidence to the public record, showing how the auto industry and its trade association dealt with the growing auto pollution problem during the 1953-1967 period; how they held back and delayed pollution control technologies even while assuring public officials they were going all out to develop those technologies.

## "COOPERATION" BEGINS

In 1953, the automakers began to meet among themselves on the air pollution issue, mostly through their trade association, the AMA. The AMA convened two key committees that would play a central role in how industry responded to the air pollution issue: the Vehicle Combustion Products Committee (VCP) and the Engineering and Advisory Committee (EAC). By 1954, the VCP was empowered to deal with the auto pollution matter through a noncompetitive industrywide "team" approach, covering not only research and development matters, but also the installation and marketing of pollution control devices.[12] This initiative became known as "the industry cooperative program" among auto industry participants and was publicly acknowledged by auto industry officials on certain occasions. In 1954, for example, Charles A. Chayne, then General Motors VP and chairman of AMA's Engineering and Advisory Committee, noted in a speech:

> ... [L]et me pause to add my personal salute to the civic spirit that launched the cooperative program, 'Operation Teamwork' which went into effect last August [1953]. It is the kind of teamwork which we have adopted in the automotive industry on a number of historic occasions when it was obviously more beneficial to the American people generally for us to set aside for a time our concern about the immediate advantages of competitive action, and apply the combined talents and facilities of the whole industry to the solution of some problem that affected the public interest adversely.[13]

Publicly, the automakers' cooperative venture appeared to be a laudable undertaking, as the companies began working together to reduce automobile air pollution. But unbeknownst to the public, "the agreement" would work its will on any company that stepped out ahead of the others, retarding progress, not pushing it forward.

By 1955, the AMA had taken the cooperative research agreement one step further: it devised procedures for uniformly handling each automaker's and their outside suppliers' potential technological innovations for pollution control devices. AMA adopted a formal cross-licensing agreement that provided for the royalty-free exchange of patents on such devices among the participants. This agreement also included a formula for sharing the costs of acquiring such patents from third parties. The intent was clear: if something important was invented, all parties would be licensed to use it together; no one party would be advantaged. In fact, concern over this point surfaced "many times" in the industry's discussions during 1954 and in AMA's Patent Committee. According to the minutes of one April 1955 Patent Committee meeting, for example, "Mr. Heinen has repeatedly expressed the feeling of his committee (the VCP) that no one company should be in a position to capitalize upon or obtain competitive advantage over the other companies in the industry as a result of its solution to this problem." So much for competition.*

## FORD'S MISSTEP

In 1957, however, Ford Motor released some publicity about a new piece of pollution control equipment called the vanadium pentoxide device—a very early version of the catalytic converter. Ford received nationwide attention on the device. This sudden notoriety for Ford on a matter that fell under the cooperative agreement—which held that all parties were to move forward together or not at all—was not well received by the other companies. During DOJ's grand jury investigation, Robert T. Van Derveer, formerly head of the Fuels and Exhaust Emissions Department at American Motors, was questioned on the publicity that Ford received and on the other automakers' reactions.

Q: So, Ford issued a publicity statement on the vanadium pentoxide device, and it achieved nationwide recognition.
A: Yes.
Q: And it was a device? A prototype device had been developed?
A: Yes.
Q: Tested on cars.
A: Yes. Not very extensively, but yes.
Q: And then there was some unhappiness in the industry over Ford's publicity?
A: Correct.
Q: Now, who was the source of the unhappiness?

---

* However, as the DOJ memo explains, "Quite evidently the cross-licensing agreement was not needed for the protection or use of any patent. As a matter of fact, no significant patents were then known to exist affecting the development of pollution control devices and no lists of patents were then nor have they ever been annexed to the cross-licensing agreement or any extension thereof. It is submitted that the cross-licensing agreement was merely a vehicle to accomplish the non-competitive and delaying activities of the signatories. . . ."

A: Well, Heinen [Charles Heinen of Chrysler] was probably the most vocal on the thing.

Q: All right. What did Heinen say?

A: . . . Well, he said lots of things, actually. But, more or less of a breach of a promise: the fact that this put Ford in a lot better light. And just the fact that the company was getting nationwide attention for something; the other people were working equally hard on other things and they weren't getting any publicity. That sort of thing.

Q: Was there a little feeling that Ford was reaping too much advantage out of its publicity, and therefore, Ford should not have issued the publicity statement?

A: Well, that was certainly part of it. . . .

Q: . . . So, there was an attempt to dampen the publicity that was issued a little while before.

A: It wasn't actually a retraction, I guess.

Q: Not a retraction, but an attempt to dampen down the publicity.

A: As I remember, yes.

Q: What was the impetus of Ford to dampen down the publicity: Was it because Heinen was disturbed about this?

A: I am sure it was Heinen and General Motors being disturbed, too. I am sure General Motors had an opinion on it. I never heard it expressed particularly. . . . [14]

## CONTROLLING PUBLICITY

After the Ford incident, the AMA committees held discussions aimed at firming up the cooperative agreement, paying particular attention to publicity procedures. One set of minutes from a January 10th, 1958 meeting of the Engineering Advisory Committee (EAC) indicated that members wanted to insure there was "no misconception" about what was intended regarding the exchange of information between companies and publicity on smog research and any resulting developments. Provision was made, for example, that "plans for speeches and text" regarding any announcements about research or new devices be submitted "ahead of time," which the committee approved, with GM's Charles Chayne adding that company public relations directors be apprised of this procedure, asking them to join in the effort to carry the policy out properly. The EAC also voted that day to reaffirm "the idea of a single announcement and a uniform adoption date for any device which the industry may decide to use for smog control."[15]

Nor would these 1958 sessions be the end of the publicity discussion. In 1962, the matter would come up again. Within American Motors, for example, one internal document of November 1962 explained, "In the area of press releases there has been a tacit understanding, if not a written policy, that all individual company press releases will be reviewed by the AMA Public Relations Committee and the VCP. Ford has been the only flagrant violator of this policy, since on two occasions they have issued releases that caught the rest of the industry by surprise (announcement of vanadium pentoxide exhaust catalyst in 1957, and blowby control system in 1962)."[16]

American Motors added, however, that the AMA public relations policy on pollution control devices had been "initiated by GM," which was seen by some as "a 'veiled threat' to Chrysler because of that company's success (and related publicity) in making their cars meet the California standard for exhaust emissions without an exhaust treating device." Chrysler at the time was testing an improved, better tuned engine approach—essentially, a better tuned engine with improved carburetion. General Motors, however, had "overwhelming dominance in smog research," according to American Motors' memo. And with its support of the AMA unified public relations policy, GM was in effect "saying to Chrysler, 'Slow down on this approach and don't break the industry front or we will completely submerge you, publicity-wise.'"[17]

The AMA committees continued to debate the AMA policy on publicity of auto company pollution control devices, especially as some of the companies wanted to have more such publicity by 1962. Yet, even at this date, in December 1962, a critical demarcation was suggested between how "activities" in the pollution control field would be handled versus "solutions."

> The [EAC] is in complete agreement with both the Public Relations Committee and the [VCP] Committee with regard to the need for more and better publicity about industry activities in the air pollution field.
>
> The [EAC] does, however, share the concern of the [VCP] Committee regarding the dangers of ill-conceived unilateral publicity. The EAC recommends, therefore, that the proposal for increased publicity by the individual companies, as well as by the [AMA], be approved with the proviso that such releases concern only "activities" and that releases concerning specific "solutions" be issued by AMA.
>
> It is essential that all releases be coordinated through AMA and that procedures be established to handle such coordination expeditiously.[18]

Finally, during DOJ's 1964 grand jury investigation, William L. Scherer, manager of the AMA's Patent Department, reiterated under questioning that as part of the cooperative agreement, no one company would advertise or publicize the merits of its equipment versus the equipment of another company; that all the companies had agreed to a date when they would jointly announce the development of any pollution control device; and that, up until the time of the grand jury proceedings, the agreement was essentially still in effect and that no device had been adopted unilaterally by any one company.[19]

## THE BLUSTER ON "BLOWBY"

In the late 1950s and early 1960s, three parts of the automobile were seen as the primary targets for addressing pollution: the crankcase, the carburetor/fuel tank, and the exhaust system. At the time, experts estimated that 25 percent of the pollutants came from the crankcase, 15 percent to 25 percent from evaporation losses at the carburetor and fuel tank; and 50 percent to 60 percent from the exhaust system.

The first part of the automobile to receive attention was the crankcase, the engine compartment directly below the combustion chamber in which firing pistons located in sleevelike cylinders above turn a crankshaft to provide driving power. GM had patented the Positive Crankcase Ventilation Valve (also known as the PCV valve) in 1959 and is generally credited with "discovering" that the PCV valve was effective in the elimination of crankcase gases.[20] These gases were known in the industry as "blowby" since they escaped around the pistons during combustion and went into the crankcase. The gases, however, did not go into the exhaust system, but rather, were vented directly into the atmosphere. "Positive crankcase ventilation" took the blowby gases back into the engine's intake manifold where they were consumed, at least partially, in the combustion process.

The PCV valve itself, however, wasn't really a new technological breakthrough. It had been known since the 1940s—and the principle of vacuuming off the gases from the crankcase back to the carburetor or intake manifold for recombustion— long before that. Howe Hopkins, an industry old-timer, former federal emissions official, and long-standing member of the American Society of Automotive Engineers (SAE), offered this account in 1969. ". . . From 1921-1923, Ludlow Clayton of the Sun Oil Company wrote numerous papers for the SAE Journal on drawing crankcase gases out by creating a small vacuum. Back in about 1936, I went down to the Studebaker plant to meet W.S. James, the company engineer who demonstrated for me a simple tube attachment from the crankcase to the intake manifold to recirculate and recombust the crankcase gases. They were offering a conversion kit for this which was essentially only a length of copper tubing. . . ."[21]

The PCV valve, in fact, was used extensively in the early 1940s on army vehicles for the purpose of keeping the crankcase of those vehicles free of dust, mud, and sand. Yet, even though by the late 1950s there was certainly a sufficient understanding of crankcase blowby,* some in the industry portrayed crankcase ventilation as a new

---

* For example, in the proceedings of the 2nd National Air Pollution Symposium dated May 1952, there is this discussion of crankcase blowby emissions: ". . . The rates of blowby relative to exhaust are quite low, however, the higher concentration of noxious products make blowby a factor to be considered in regard to air pollution. The effect of deteriorating engine condition is to increase blowby and, consequently, to increase the total amount of noxious products. This change may be greater than tenfold at low speeds typical of city driving.

"Of the products identified as definitely or probably present in blowby, aldehydes and acids have characteristic irritating effects on the nose, eyes, or both. Combinations of these with other exhaust and blowby products or with other air pollutants may accentuate these effects. Organic hydroperoxides identified as probably present have been blamed in past theories as being serious contributors to air pollution." J.O. Payne & H.W. Sigworth, "The Composition and Nature of Blowby and Exhaust Gases. . . ," Proceedings of 2nd National Air Pollution Symposium, Pasadena, CA, May 1952, pp. 62-70.

development. Almost magically, 1959 had become the year industry discovered what to do with crankcase pollutants. "In 1959, through a truly extraordinary stroke of good fortune," reported one account from the AMA "—the crankcase was discovered to be a more important source of emissions than had been suggested by prior government and other studies."[22]

Auto industry officials, then eyeing possible statewide regulation in California with strong pressure from local officials in Los Angeles, soon began to see that installing the relatively simple PCV device on California cars might be a way to forestall even tougher state action. W.S. Berry of American Motors, writing in November 13, 1959, urged his colleagues to go ahead with the PCV action in California for the following reasons:

1. The opportunity for the industry to do something in California which will make a major reduction in emissions at a relatively low cost. . . . [T]he AMA staff used a cost to the customer figure of around $10.
2. On December 4th there will be a hearing in Berkeley which will be held [by] the California State Department of Health to finalize recommendations on tailpipe emissions. An announcement before that date would possibly slow down any regulatory action on this matter. Likewise, this announcement may deter Governor Brown from holding a special session of the Legislature dealing with the air pollution problem.[23]

When GM president John F. Gordon wrote to LAs' Kenneth Hahn in October 1960 to report that the company's 1961 models in California would carry the PCV device, he did so as if breaking new ground. "I am gratified to be able to report that positive crankcase ventilation is available on all 1961 General Motors passenger cars being delivered to California," he wrote. "We believe that this relatively uncomplicated, inexpensive device will perform a major job of reducing air pollution.

"As you know," he continued, "the automobile industry is collectively working on the problem. The voluntary offering of these devices by the entire automobile industry to the new car buyers of California, I believe, is concrete evidence of the sincerity of our efforts."[24] Yet others believed the threat of statewide California regulation was the real motivating force.

Nationally, the automakers were also being pushed to take voluntary action with the device, but only with the threat of federal legislation. Senator Maurine Neuberger (D-OR), for one, wrote a letter to fourteen automakers in May 1961 urging them to move voluntarily to install the device on all models, suggesting that in the alternative, "responsible legislation to prohibit . . . interstate commerce of vehicles without the protective device" would be introduced.[25] Others in Congress, such as Representative John E. Fogarty (D-RI), were also wondering why the automakers were moving so slowly on a relatively simple device.

I cannot escape the conclusion that the automobile industry has been dragging its feet in the matter of factory installation of blowby devices. These, as you probably know, are relatively inexpensive devices for controlling emissions from automobile crankcases. While they will not solve the larger problem of exhaust emissions. . . , they do eliminate from one-fourth to one-third of the motorcar's total contribution to our air pollution problem.

Such devices were factory installed on new cars sold this year in the one State of California and are available—at a higher price, of course, as optional dealer-installed equipment on new American cars in other localities. In view of the mounting evidence that air pollution is not only is costly but may be highly hazardous to human health—and since this new device eliminates a part of it at low cost—it would have seemed both good business and good public relations for the auto industry to install such a device at the factory for all new cars sold in this country. . . .[26]

The AMA, meanwhile, had set about asking all of the automakers to come up with reasons why the PCV valve could not be made standard equipment on all cars.[27] "[T]hey are specifically looking for problems that will justify a negative decision," explained GM engineer G.R. Fitzgerald. The AMA found, however, that engineers at Ford, International Harvester, Studebaker-Packard, and American Motors thought the device could be installed on all 1962 models. In fact, a technical paper by International Harvester's James Chandler indicated the device could have been installed on 1961 models.[28]

Although Studebaker-Packard and American Motors agreed to the release of the PCV device for all 1962 model cars, "none of the companies did so." The reason, according to DOJ, was "the industry agreement."[29] At an early December 1961 meeting of the AMA board of directors, it was agreed that the PCV device would be installed as standard equipment on all 1963 model cars—two years later than requested. In fact, one GM engineer, Robert J. Templin, assistant chief engineer at the Cadillac division, wrote in September 1961, "To sum it up, there is nothing to prevent our going to positive crankcase ventilation as standard equipment for 1963, if policy dictates it. Our lives will be less troubled, however, if we don't do it."[30] Templin was arguing for even further delay.

Abraham Ribicoff, then secretary of Health Education and Welfare, like Senator Neuberger, had also threatened to push for federal legislation requiring the crankcase controls unless the industry installed them. Coupled with the latest round of possible legislation, industry saw the writing on the wall and did in fact install the PCV valve on all 1963 models nationally. But that wasn't the end of the matter. In 1964, Ford began removing the devices from its automobiles without notifying the government. When Ford was caught having removed the devices, the company claimed that it had been having maintenance problems with the devices, though no other automaker had reported similar problems.[31]

## THE CLOSED CRANKCASE DEVICE

Air pollution control officials in California and New York, discovering that additional crankcase pollutants could be eliminated with something called the closed crankcase device, had actions pending to require those devices be installed in 1963 and 1964 model cars. But once again, the AMA requested its members to produce reasons why this could not be done.[32] In fact, GM's Charles A. Chayne, vice president in charge of engineering, delegated AMA's EAC to prepare a specific list of technical problems that might prevent GM's car divisions from supplying reliable crankcase ventilation systems for 1964 models.[33] Meanwhile, the companies held to the cooperative agreement, not taking any individual steps to add the devices early. Memos from both Chrysler and American Motors officials show them holding firm to the agreement. In fact, in one March 1963 interoffice memo, by H.F. Barr, GM's member on the EAC, noted in part:

> I have recently had a call from Mr. Paul Ackerman of Chrysler which indicates they are pulling back their 1964 start of production releases and will release later, effective January 1, 1964, if required at that time by the California law. We are, of course, all hopeful that this [i.e., closed crankcase device requirement] will be further extended to start of production of 1965 models before time for this action arrives.
>
> It is therefore quite important that no General Motors Division make any changes in their 1963 releases for start of 1964 model year production. Since changes would jeopardize the industry position that is being taken with the Air Pollution Board of California.[34]

However, the industry's attempt to delay the installation to the 1965 model year failed, as California required the devices by January 1, 1964. Moreover, during the DOJ grand jury investigation, it was revealed that the devices could have been installed years before that. One government expert witness, Wallace Linville, testified:

> Q: Is there any reason why [installing the device] couldn't have been done by the industry prior to 1964?
> A: No. It is similar to a system that you find and have found for years on particularly dump trucks where they are operating in very dirty areas, and again on the army equipment that we mentioned in the second World War, where they're running in convoy. . . , operating in very dusty terrain, and as a result of this they have had the system closed by means of this tube to the air cleaner for a good number of years, so I see no reason why this should have offered a substantial or major problem at all.[35]

In addition to Linville, Errol J. Gray, an industry consultant for TRW and others, when asked the same question replied, "Hell, they could have done it prior to 1938, if necessary."[36]

By 1964, some California officials, having battled Detroit for more than a decade seeking pollution controls, concluded that the automakers were really not making any progress at all. LA County's pollution control executive, S. Smith Griswold, noted in one speech, ". . . I term it a great delaying action, because that is what I believe the auto industry has been engaged in for a decade. Everything the industry has disclosed it is able to do today to control auto exhaust was possible technically ten years ago. No new principle has been developed, no technological advance was needed, no scientific breakthrough was required. Crankcase emissions have been controlled by a method in use for half a century. Hydrocarbons and carbon monoxide are being controlled by relatively simply adjustments of the most basic engine components. . . ."[37] Griswold's remarks were those that later helped to precipitate DOJ's investigation of the automakers. But California at this time was about to push the automakers into new territory: requiring them to begin treating automobile exhaust.

## CATALYTIC REACTION

As early as December 1959, California had signaled its intent to the auto industry that exhaust-treating devices might be required. The automakers, however, were not excited by such a prospect. "They [the Big Three] are not . . . interested in making or selling devices. . . ," wrote Dr. Donald Diggs, a technical manager at Du Pont, in an April 21, 1959 report. "[B]ut [they] are working solely to protect themselves against poor public relations and the time when exhaust control devices may be required by law."[38]

In May 1959, Ford's James Chandler took the position that the smog problem "is not bad enough to warrant the enormous cost and administrative problems of installing three million afterburners." Chandler, in fact, believed that one of the functions of the AMA working group was to "contain" the smog problem.[39] "We gathered that the automobile industry will continue to do whatever it can within the scope of California legislation and of political pressure to postpone installation of exhaust control devices. . . ," wrote J.D. Ullman, another Du Pont technical expert in April 1960.[40] An official of the Maremont Automotive Products Co., also doing business with Detroit, confided to a Du Pont colleague in May 1960 that the automakers "were keeping up a good front, but were not pushing as rapidly as they could toward a solution of the smog abatement problem."[41]

What the automakers feared most, however, was that some outside interest might begin to meddle in the core of their business in a way that could affect control over what was produced. This fear surfaced as a new group of businesses began working on catalytic devices to be installed in exhaust systems to treat and reduce auto pollution.

Catalysts are substances used to facilitate a chemical reaction without themselves being consumed in the reaction. By the time catalysts were being considered for pollution control in the auto industry, they had been used for years in various industrial processes. In the petroleum industry, a platinum-palladium catalyst was used in the "cracking" of petroleum molecules for making gasoline. The use of catalysts to clean the fumes from petroleum engines was reported by the French in 1898. Catalysts were also used in the coal mining industry to deal with the carbon monoxide problem in enclosed spaces. In the 1920s, researchers at Johns Hopkins and the US Bureau of Mines produced a substance called "hopcalite" to control CO. Separately, in fact, Johns Hopkins researchers had applied the substance to automobiles about the same time and published a research report about the attempt.

Detroit, however, was never keen on catalytic devices, especially those made by others, and would do all in its power to delay the day such devices would be required. True, in 1957 the vanadium pentoxide device that Ford Motor had tested and bragged about to the press was an early, crude version of what would become the catalytic converter. However, Ford's converter was big and cumbersome; so crude, in fact, that some speculated the company's device was purposely put forward to show that such exhaust treatments wouldn't work—but from which Ford could still glean some public relations benefit.

Still, if Ford's intent was to kill the catalyst with the vanadium pentoxide device, it actually had the reverse effect. For what surprised many chemists who learned of this device was that the catalyst approach worked at all in an automobile. They were surprised that after some thousands of miles of being run in Ford test cars, there was still activity in the catalyst medium, which suggested the catalyst approach generally might be worth further research.[42] Shortly thereafter, as California had made clear that exhaust devices of some sort were going to be required on what amounted to about 10 percent of the nation's cars, a fairly sizeable market, several nonautomobile companies began investigating the catalytic converter in earnest. Among them, each later teaming up with muffler manufacturers, were American Machine & Foundry Co./Chromalloy; Universal Oil Products/Arvin Industries; W.R. Grace/Norris-Thermador Corp.; American Cyanamid/Walker Manufacturing; and Engelhard Industries.

## AMA Seeks Delay

Meanwhile, in California, the operative trigger for setting in motion the state's requirement for installing exhaust controls was state certification of any two new devices. One year following such certification, automobiles then sold in California would have to be equipped with one or the other device. By the end of 1963 and early 1964, it was clear that two devices being produced by nonauto manufacturers would be certified, thereby triggering the law, and requiring their installation on all 1966 models. At the AMA, meanwhile, a March 1964 memorandum from William Sherman, secretary of the EAC to Harry Williams, AMA director, explained the predicament for the automakers, and how they might adopt a one-year delay strategy.

While we certainly have the objective of holding the line until 1967 models, we know that the stated purpose of the California MVPCB is to approve two catalytic devices in the next few months and trigger the law so it will apply to 1966 models.

It seems to me that we would be exercising very poor judgement if we suggested or implied that we wanted them to hold off the triggering of the law, or to let ourselves get into any controversial position about it.

If they do act in the near future to approve the catalytic devices, our companies would probably have to take the position, anyhow, that there is not enough engineering time to fit the catalytic converters under the frames and chassis of cars in time to meet the schedule of 1966 model production and there would be strong likelihood of various delays until 1967 introductions.

It would be very much to our advantage to avoid this topic—shrug it off or ignore it—for a month or two. In the interim, a lot of things might change. . . , including even the withdrawal of the catalytic devices now on tests when the submitters analyze the future possibilities for themselves.

Thus, the problem will have some tendency 'to go away' if we don't aggravate discussion of it at this time.[43]

But again, in one of the industry's carefully timed maneuvers to project voluntary action in advance of possible government requirements, the AMA issued a press release on March 10th, 1964, one day before the California Motor Vehicle Pollution Control Board was to meet and possibly certify exhaust control devices targeted for 1966 model year cars. The AMA press statement said that its member companies "have set a target date of the fall of 1966 in their programs to make 1967 model automobiles and passenger-like cars for sale in California comply with the state's motor vehicle emissions standards."[44] Yet, as revealed in one confidential Ford Motor Co. memo of June 1964, while the automakers were posturing with the public line "we-can-only-do-1967-models," they were engineering for the 1966 model year. "It should be recognized," explained the Ford memo, "that our external program as presented to California is to meet Job 1, 1967, but that our internal program is to meet Job 1, 1966. It is recommended that the 1967 goal remain our public posture."[45]

California, however, did not blink in the face of auto industry's gambit. Three days after AMA's statement, the MVPCB notified the automakers that the state was testing four exhaust control devices on an accelerated basis. MVPCB's chairman, J.B. Askew indicated the board was hopeful industry "would work with us to achieve exhaust controls for 1966 models." In June, the board approved four exhaust devices manufactured by nonautomotive manufacturers. In July, it requested the industry plans for meeting the 1966 model-year (MY) requirement. On August 12, 1964, the automakers formally presented their intentions to comply with the 1966 model year deadline.

As it turned out, however, none of the automakers used the approved catalytic devices developed by the outside manufacturers. J.B. Askew of the California MVPCB, in fact, would later reveal that the board was not satisfied with any of the catalytic devices produced by these manufacturers, but approved them anyway to force the industry to install their own systems in 1966 and 1967—systems which, according to Askew, did a better job than the four outside-manufactured devices at that time.[46] What emerged in place of the catalytic devices was a "combustion control" approach Chrysler was pushing called the "Clean Air Package."

## THE CLEAN AIR PACKAGE

Chrysler's Clean Air Package, however, was not exactly rocket science. The "system" for controlling exhaust emissions had two essential elements: more complete combustion and retarding the spark. Adjusting the fuel/air ratio reduced the amount of gasoline burned, thereby reducing the amount of unburned gases that went out the exhaust pipe. Adjusting the timing of the spark at the combustion chamber had the net effect of making the engine run at higher temperatures, thereby burning up some of the exhaust gases outside the combustion chamber. This was not, however, new technology.

"The technological breakthrough that is the Clean Air Package," concluded the Nader Task Force investigating the industry, "consists generally of . . . [a] different rubber hood seal, different cylinder gaskets, reduced production tolerances, and a different manifold heat valve. The carburetor and distributor employ very simple control valves."[47] "I knew about the effect of retarding timing on combustion efficiency in 1925," said longtime auto expert Howe Hopkins. "But of course, others knew about it before that. The Model-T Ford had a manual device so that the owner could advance or retard the spark. . . ."[48]

It soon became apparent that the adjustments in engine timing and spark used as a pollution-control strategy in the Clean Air Package were highly dependent upon regular maintenance and adjustments to local driving conditions to consistently stem pollution. Chrysler's "package" deteriorated with use and would not cut pollution in 50 to 80 percent of operating vehicles. Engine adjustments made for cars in Los Angeles weren't necessarily appropriate for stop-and-go driving in major cities of the Northeast. But for the auto industry, the CAP, as it was called, was a masterpiece of strategy; it was a low-cost, Band-Aid application when something more like a tourniquet was needed.

Chrysler's Charlie Heinen, the engineer and auto emissions strategist who had led the first team of engineers to Los Angeles in 1953 to investigate the "new problem" of smog, was instrumental in convincing California authorities to accept the Clean Air Package, which was later certified in time to use for the 1966 model year. Heinen and Chrysler, however, appeared to be playing both sides of the street with the CAP, on the one hand providing Los Angeles authorities with CAP-equipped vehicles to show that these cars could control emissions, yet on the other hand, still

## RIPPING OUT THE TRACKS

Another charged conspiracy—this one from the 1930s involving a concerted attack by General Motors and others to dismantle and replace mass transit systems with buses, trucks, and automobiles—also involved a federal investigation. Excerpts from four different writers tell that tale.

*Starting in the 1930s, National City Lines, a company backed by General Motors, Standard Oil, Phillips Petroleum, Firestone Tire and Rubber, Mack Truck, and other auto interests, systematically bought up and closed down more than 100 electric trolley lines in forty-five cities across the country. In 1949, a federal grand jury convicted GM and the other companies of conspiring to replace electric transportation systems with buses and to monopolize the sale of buses. (These corporations were fined a trifling $5,000 each for their actions.) But the long-term damage had already been done. In 1947, when the destruction of mass transit was just beginning, 40 percent of US workers relied on public transportation to get to their jobs. In 1963, only 14 percent did. By that time, electric trolley lines were virtually extinct in the United States. The trend has continued: today less than 5 percent of the working population commutes by way of public transportation.*

*In 1974, antitrust lawyer Bradford Snell testified before Congress on the corporate conspiracy to wreck mass transit. The Big Three automakers—GM, Ford, Chrysler—"used their vast economic power to restructure America into a land of big cars and diesel trucks," Snell contended. These companies "reshaped American ground transportation to serve corporate wants instead of social need." (excerpted from Steve Nadis and James J. MacKenzie,* Car Trouble, *1993)*

*. . . The transcript and other evidence from the GM case are in two battered packing cartons in a federal warehouse near Chicago. That material makes this point beyond a reasonable doubt: There was for many years a criminal conspiracy behind our national transportation policy. . . . As spelled out in the court record, the conspirators did their work in many cities. They schemed from the mid-1930s through the 1940s. Electrified rail mass transit systems which carried millions of riders were bought and junked. Tracks were literally torn out of the ground, sometimes overnight. Overhead power lines were dismantled, and valuable off-street rights of way were sold.*

*After reading the testimony and court filings, I interviewed dozens of transit officials all over the country to find out if the old electrified system could have served us today. . . . Not more than three of these officials were even aware of the GM conspiracy case, and none knew the details. They were, however, aware that a series of "mistakes" had been made in transportation planning back in the 1930s and 1940s. . . .*

*. . . Transit officials who remember the rails, power lines, and generating stations that were once in place say these facilities, if left intact, could have formed the nucleus for a modern American transit system. . . . (excerpted from Jonathan Kwitny,* Harper's, *February 1981)*

*Before a Senate hearing in 1974, San Francisco mayor Joseph Alioto lamented the loss of his city's electric mass transit system. "We had . . . something we called the Key system. . . . It had 180 electric streetcars, and it had 50 rather sleek and fumeless electric passenger trains." [I]n 1946, NCL came in and "two days after they acquired the system, they announced that they were going to convert the system to buses, and . . . did in fact purchase 200 [GM] buses."*

*In 1954, eight years after the [NCL] acquisition and at a time when San Francisco was contemplating building a Bay Area Rapid Transit System (BART), NCL and its associate companies announced their intention of abandoning the remaining electric rail system that ran across the bridge. . . . "It is very difficult to escape the inference, in light of the total context, that they did this for the very purpose of slowing up and perhaps making impossible the development of our BART system. . . . Nevertheless, regardless of motive, the fact is clear. They pulled up the track. Now for BART we have to spend $200 million to create that same corridor in the form of a tube on the bed of the bay." (excerpted from Russell Mokhiber,* Corporate Crime and Violence, *1988)*

*Mayor Tom Bradley of Los Angeles told the subcommittee Feb. 27 [1974] that Southern California thirty-five years ago was served by the Pacific Electric System, the world's largest interurban electric operation.*

*In prepared testimony . . . Bradley said the destruction of the system was begun by GM, SoCal, and Firestone in 1940 through NCL affiliates. By 1944, Bradley said, the system of 3,000 trains operating over 1,164 miles of track in 56 incorporated municipalities was "totally destroyed."*

*The public was left "with little alternative but to use what GM and the oil companies produced," Bradley said. Los Angeles, more than any other city, suffered the consequences, listed by Bradley as: "poor mobility, poor air quality, lack of adequate fuels, a high rate of fatal accidents, and inefficient land use." (excerpted from Morton Mintz,* Washington Post, *May 1974)*

trying to abide by the "industry agreement" not to go out on its own ahead of the other automakers.*

In any case, GM, Ford, and American Motors eventually adopted the Chrysler CAP, or approaches similar to it, for their cars as well.** As for the emerging cat-

---

*According to the DOJ's grand jury documents, "the rest of the industry felt that this [Chrysler's CAP] was a breach . . . of the [AMA] agreement." And that the "final straw" came after Chrysler received word from LA County government that they would buy only Chrysler products in appreciation for Chrysler's work on lowering emissions. Still, according to DOJ, "Chrysler showed it came back into line" with the AMA agreement in 1964 when it agreed to a resolution by the automakers that called for delay of controls until the 1967 model year. And Chrysler did delay the CAP on its own models for at least one year, admitting it could have installed the CAP on its 1965 cars if required.

** Yet with the CAP and CAP-like systems, another major auto pollution problem was

alytic converter industry, once it was learned that Chrysler's Clean Air Package would be certified by California in 1964, most of the companies engaged in making catalytic devices either stopped or shelved their programs. CAP-like systems would also be used nationwide to satisfy federal standards and would continue to be the primary "technology" used to control auto pollution through the early 1970s.

## BATTLE WON!

Within a few years after the automakers began meeting the California and new federal requirements, a few of their leaders began crowing about how the industry was solving the problem. In April 1969, Chrysler's Charles M. Heinen, essentially speaking for the entire industry,[49] gave a talk entitled, "We've Done the Job—What Next?" In that speech, Heinen stated, "The main battle against automotive air pollution has been won," pointing to reductions in hydrocarbon and carbon monoxide emissions. "The technical job to reduce what's left is going to be rough, and it looks like it will be very expensive—in the billions of dollars. . . . " He questioned whether any "next steps" to bring about further reduction in auto emissions "is really necessary and is worth it from a societal, scientific, medical and economic standpoint."[50] A year earlier, the National Air Pollution Control Administration (NAPCA) had projected that unless more stringent national controls were instituted after 1970, vehicular pollution levels would continue to rise, especially by the late 1970s.[51]

Heinen, however, also challenged the need to regulate nitrogen oxides, for which NAPCA was then proposing some modest standards for 1973 models. He concluded that "a . . . review of the medical position would seem to say that the situation is not critical now or, indeed, even serious in the opinion of nearly everyone except those in California." The probable cost to control NOx, said Heinen, would involve "a national expenditure of ten billion dollars plus."[52] Mr. Heinen also disputed the federal government's prediction that pollution levels would rise as the number of cars and the mileage per vehicle increased. The reduction in pollution per vehicle, he claimed, would offset any such increase.

The passing of time, however, would prove Charlie Heinen and his colleagues wrong by a wide margin. The job wasn't done. Automobile pollution would continue to be major public health problem in the years ahead. As for the battle being won, the real battle—over a new Clean Air Act and its enforcement during the next forty years—was just beginning.

---

made worse. Since the CAP caused the engine to produce higher temperatures by combusting excess gases in the engine compartment, other pollutants began to form, and most notably, nitrogen oxides (NOx), a chief component of photochemical oxidants, or smog. NOx was then not regulated, so for industry, it did not figure into the pollution control fix at the time. Yet for some critics, the fact that industry knew about the NOx problem at this juncture and knew as well that it would be a problem, but proceeded essentially to engineer around it, was another indication of the industry's disregard for public health.

# 4

## *Eternal Combustion*

...Inherently, the internal combustion engine can never be a clean machine....
—*Frank Stead, former chief, California Division of Environmental Sanitation, 1969*

The late 1960s were a tumultuous time in the United States. Robert Kennedy and Martin Luther King Jr. were assassinated, the Viet Nam war was raging, and authority was being challenged by a younger generation. The seeds of the modern environmental movement had already been planted with Rachel Carson's 1962 publication of *Silent Spring*, a landmark book exposing the ecological dangers of pesticide chemistry. Up on Capitol Hill in 1965, a young lawyer named Ralph Nader was raking General Motors over the coals for its unsafe Corvair. Detroit was into its "muscle car" era, as Pontiac GTOs, Ford Mustangs, and Dodge Chargers roamed the nation's streets and highways.

Despite the passage of updated federal air quality laws in 1965 and 1967, air pollution was becoming a growing national problem. In November 1966, an air pollution episode in New York city led to eighty deaths and a declaration of emergency by Governor Nelson Rockefeller (R). California had already passed its own pollution control act. Of the estimated 146 million tons of pollutants discharged into the US atmosphere in 1966, nearly 60 percent—86 million tons—came from motor vehicles. The average car, travelling 10,000 miles annually without pollution controls, spewed 1,700 pounds of carbon monoxide, 520 pounds of hydrocarbons, and 90 pounds of nitrogen oxides. Automobiles were also the major source of lead pollutants. Depending on the particular city or county, 60 to 80 percent of atmospheric pollution was attributed to motor vehicles—in some places, like Orange County, California, the motor vehicle's share was over 95 percent.

### LATE '60S ENGINE DEBATE

On Capitol Hill, a unusual series of Senate hearings began in early 1967 probing automobile pollution. These hearings were focused on alternatives to the internal combustion engine—the core technology of the auto industry. At the time, there were also bills pending that proposed to bring the federal government into alternative engine research and federal purchase of alternative vehicles for government fleets. Senator Warren Magnuson's (D-WA) Commerce Committee and Senator Edmund Muskie's Public Works Subcommittee on Air & Water Pollution held joint hearings and took testimony from a variety of witnesses.

Ford's witness said his company had been researching alternative engines since 1956. GM's witness said company engineers had been working on the problem since the late 1940s. And Chrysler's witness sung the praises of the company's gas turbine engine. In practically every case, when pressed on what the real chances were for an alternative to the ICE, industry witnesses would point to their research and talk about the future. In March 1967, Senator Howard Baker (R-TN) questioned Ford Motor's vice president for scientific research, Michael Ference, Jr. The topic that day was the prospects for the electric car.

> BAKER: . . . Which will we get to first: the practical electric car, or the practical clean, gasoline engine?
>
> FERENCE: I think the latter.
>
> BAKER: Would you care to speculate on the times for either one of them?
>
> FERENCE: Since it is in the research area, that would be a tough one for me. I feel strongly from the kind of effort that is going on in this area, and the kinds of problems to be overcome, that we will solve the air pollution problem from our internal-combustion engine before we have large-scale practical electric cars. This would be my thinking.
>
> BAKER: Are we talking in terms of ten years?
>
> FERENCE: Ten years. That is the order of magnitude.
>
> BAKER: Thank you.[1]

At this hearing and others, the report of the automakers was consistently the same: while some of the alternatives to the internal combustion engine showed promise, they all had drawbacks. The ICE was deeply embedded in industry programs. Ford Motor and Mobil Oil formed the Inter-Industry Emissions Control (IIEC) program in 1967, the purpose of which, according to Mobil, was to conduct research upon "the basic premise . . . that the conventional gas-powered ICE will be the automotive power plant for some years to come." Still, one of the Senate hearings in 1968 focused on an intriguing alternative at the time called the Rankine Cycle engine, a new kind of steam engine.

## KILLING THE STEAM CAR

The Rankine Cycle engine was not a "Stanley steamer" engine, but rather, a modern engine that ran quietly and smoothly with good acceleration and very low emissions.

The hearings came about as a result of government reports and the efforts of nonindustry inventors who found that the Rankine engine showed promise as a propulsion system for modern automobiles. An October 1967 US Department of Commerce study entitled *The Automobile and Air Pollution* concluded, in part, that "vehicles such as the piston-type steam engine of advanced design, potentially offer a satisfactory alternative to the present automobile and should have very low pollution and noise. . . ."[2]

Two nonindustry inventors—the Williams brothers of Ambler, Pennsylvania—had also testified before Congress about their steam car and had impressed some senators with rides in the new machine around Capitol Hill. At the hearings, Lawrence R. Hafstad of General Motors, then vice president of the company's research laboratories, stated that GM had worked for forty years trying to perfect a modern steam engine. However, the company found the steam engine too costly, too heavy, too inefficient, and too dangerous. But a Ralph Nader investigative team, reporting in a 1970 study, *Vanishing Air*, spoke with another GM engineer who charged that Hafstad's testimony—which took about four weeks to prepare—was about as much time as GM had spent on steam-powered automobiles. GM, he charged, merely "dabbled around with the steam engine," and the work GM did undertake on the steam car didn't really start until after Hafstad testified. "They already had the conclusion [that the steam engine was not a feasible alternative] and we were told to prove it. . . ," explained the GM engineer.

GM did build a steam car to show off with some of its other alternative vehicles. In May 1969, at the unveiling of the company's new Research Vehicle Emissions and Safety Laboratory in Warren, Michigan, GM brought out a cavalcade of twenty-six new vehicles in its "Progress of Power" show. Hybrid gas-electric vehicles and others powered by gas turbines, liquified petroleum gas, and various external combustion engines were all on display. Two steam cars were also featured. One, a 1969 Pontiac Grand Prix, was described by GM as "the world's first steam car with complete power accessories, including air conditioning." But as the assembled onlookers and journalists started to read the fine print of the GM handouts, they soon learned that most of the cars had "problem areas"—which GM highlighted. The steam-powered Pontiac, for example, had a much heavier engine than the one it replaced with half the horsepower. The Williams brothers' engine, however, weighed much less than the conventional ICE.

Ralph Nader's team called the GM steam car a "Rube Goldberg" machine. ". . . the GM contraption made wheezing, clanging noises like an untuned calliope. Furthermore, even though all experts agree that the steam engine is less polluting than the internal combustion engine, this machine sputtered out huge quantities of smoke and soot. The engine weighed 500 pounds more than the conventional type because GM claimed that its concern for public safety had impelled it to design the engine to meet the American Society of Mechanical Engineers Boiler Code—a code prepared for factory boilers. GM got its message across: a great deal more time was needed back . . . at the drawing boards. . . ."

A Senate Commerce Committee staff report, summarizing Senate hearings, noted "The Rankine cycle (steam) propulsion engine is a satisfactory alternative to the present internal combustion (gasoline) engine in terms of performance and a far superior engine in terms of emissions." Other analysts would also mention the Rankine engine in their studies.* Even Ford Motor acknowledged in 1968 that a Rankine-style engine could fit under the hood of its cars.

In 1969, William Lear, of Lear jet fame and then president of Lear Enterprise of Reno, Nevada, entered the steam car fray. Goaded by the automakers who said steam engines could never be competitive, Lear charged into the controversy, promising to build a steam-powered racecar for the famed Indianapolis 500. Lear assembled a top-notch crew of engineers—a team that had nearly won the Indy two years earlier with a turbine car. But in the end, neither Lear's dream of steam-powered race car nor a mass-produced steam powered automobile ever materialized.** However, in California, a major political fight was brewing over alternatives to the ICE, in which Lear became involved.

## CALIFORNIA CRUSADER

In 1969, Nicholas C. Petris, a state senator in California representing Oakland, became something of a crusader against the internal combustion engine when he began investigating the possibility of banning the engine and putting in its place low-polluting alternatives, like the steam engine. "Our lungs are turning gray with inhaled grime," he would say, "we are living in an envelope of poison."[3] Petris believed the

---

* "From the standpoint of automotive users," wrote Robert Ayres and Richard McKenna in their 1972 book *Alternatives to the Internal Combustion Engine*, ". . . at least three technological alternatives—the gas turbine, Rankine-cycle (steam) engine, or hybrid—could be adapted to automotive purposes with no significant sacrifices in terms of performance. . . ."

** In January 1972, Lear testified before the Senate Public Works Subcommittee on Air and Water Pollution, touting a vapor turbine steam bus his company had produced, which he believed represented progress toward production of a cleaner car. "I believe we can now promise combustion emissions which will meet or exceed the 1976 requirements. In the laboratory and on our chassis dynamometer we have met the standards and this work further reinforces our confidence that a car can be built to meet the standards. . . . A clean car must be equal in every way in performance, comfort, convenience, acceleration, and miles per gallon to present automobiles. We have adopted this specification for the Lear vapor turbine car. . . . Such an automobile power plant is now in the final engineering stages and we will soon start road tests. . . ." But Lear had spent more than $12 million by then, and he acknowledged to the subcommittee, "we can no longer go it alone." Lear developed what he believed was "an excellent engineering prototype that could solve the automobile air pollution problem," but he did not have the money to develop it further. "We cannot build additional . . . prototypes without the financial assistance of the government or the automotive industry."

automobile industry could produce a smog-free engine if it pushed hard enough. He pointed to the work being done on steam, gas turbines, battery-powered cars, and other alternatives. At one of Petris' hearings, William Lear testified, taking issue with pollution control devices on the ICE, which he characterized as "a patch on a patch and cannot be relied upon to work with even 90 percent efficiency for more than six months." Lear was asked if he believed a 1975 phaseout of the internal combustion engine was practical. "Yes," he said, "if this committee and others like it across the country have the guts to take the pressure such an act would generate."[4]

Petris, for one, was up to the challenge. He introduced SB 778 in early 1969 that would prohibit the sale of all diesel- and gasoline-powered internal combustion engines in California by January 1, 1975. Auto industry lobbyists thought Petris' bill comical. They all laughed. However, the laughing stopped in July 1969 when the California Senate approved Petris' bill by a vote of 26-5 and sent it to the California Assembly. "People are demanding that we move rapidly to reverse this trend of polluting our air and water and the whole environment," said Petris upon passage of his bill.[5]

Industry lobbyists thought Petris' measure was crazy, "idiotic," and out of the question.[6] "I thought it was nutty bill," said Kent H. Redwine, lobbyist for the Motor Car Dealers Association, a group then representing some 2,500 new car dealers. Redwine, however, admitted that "I should have opposed [the bill] in committee, but I never thought it had a chance."[7] The automakers also failed to show up for consideration of a related bill in the Senate Finance Committee, which at the time had approved a $1 million expenditure to study alternative engines. Some of the senators supporting Petris' bill did so in part because of the industry's cavalier attitude. Others believed that Petris' bill actually prevented a more stringent regulatory measure from coming up, one that would have tightened down on auto emissions well beyond those then in effect. Still, other senators were genuinely concerned by the industry's lack of progress.

"If the human race can send a man to the moon," said one, "surely it can clear up smog." Another senator added of the vote on the Petris bill, "this is a kind of favor to the automobiles industry. Now the industry has ample time in which to clear up the mess it is making in California."[8] Petris himself acknowledged his bill was meant to get the industry's attention; to make its executives "sit up and take notice" of the urgent need to do something about smog.[9] Auto lobbyists said Petris was really backing William Lear's steam car project, a charge Petris denied. "I don't care if it's electric, turbine, steam, jet—or rubber band." He had also introduced a companion bill proposing to allocate up to $1 million in state funds to private concerns for research into cleaner engines.[10]

By the time Petris' bill came to the assembly, the auto industry was paying a lot more attention. California auto dealers were present in force, and nationally, the AMA issued a statement by Ford Motor's D.A. Jensen, also chairman of the AMA's Emissions Standards Committee, describing the bill as a major departure from the regulatory course the state had already set with its emissions standards.* But most of all—with California alone accounting for 10 percent of the national new car market and a thriving, 2.5-million-vehicles-per-year California used car market—industry was making economic appeals.

"We believe that enactment of this legislation would economically destroy California," said Jim Gorman, executive vice president of the Motor Dealers Association of Southern California. "Our members, in all-out united effort, are undertaking to contact their assemblymen urging them to vote against this legislation." Gorman said it was "sheer futility" to think that an alternative engine could be developed by 1975.[11]

"The automotive industry has advanced too far to change things, and a change now would be foolish," said Dodge dealer Paul Judd of Earl Ike Dodge in Englewood, California. "All they're trying to do is get rid of a little smog, and this would be a very foolish move."[12] If worse came to worse, said lobbyist Kent Redwine, there was always Governor Ronald Reagan. "I just can't see the governor signing it," he said.[13] Indeed, one source reportedly "close to Reagan," stated in early August, "if the assembly approves the bill, the governor will surely veto it."[14]

Meanwhile, in the assembly, the Transportation Committee, considering Petris' bill, conducted a seven-hour hearing on August 10, taking testimony from a variety of witnesses. Frank Stead, former chief of California's Division of Environmental Sanitation, urged the committee to support the Petris bill and ban the piston engine. According to Stead, the smog-control devices then being used did not substantially reduce emissions. In fact, he called the devices "fraudulent." Stead argued that with the little time bought with existing regulations, the state ought to be getting ready for the 1980s "by preparing to ban the [internal combustion] engine altogether."[15]

"A program of control by fractional reduction buys time," he said, alluding to the current program of emission controls, "it does not solve the problem. Inherently, the internal combustion engine can never be a clean machine."

Petris, meanwhile, had taken a poll of the committee and determined he was one vote short needed to pass the ban.[16] He then substituted a strict regulatory bill with standards twice as tough of those on the books for 1974 models. Industry opposed that measure as well. Ford's Jensen said the bill should not be adopted because the standards "seem to go far beyond any air quality levels which have ever been proposed by scientists." Asked whether it would be possible for the automakers to meet the stricter standards in Petris' substitute, Jensen replied, "We don't know we can't do it, but on the other hand, we don't know that we can."[17]

In arguing for his revised bill, Petris pointed to "an unwillingness by the auto-

---

* Jensen's statement emphasized that the regulatory approach established up to that point had been one of setting performance standards rather than determining which technologies might be acceptable or unacceptable, and allowing manufacturers to figure out how best to meet those standards. Yet, the AMA was clearly concerned about Petris' bill, with Jensen pointing out that California often set the pace for national and even global emissions standards.

mobile industry to take one step beyond what the law says they have to do." The automakers did everything in their power to evade and delay existing California provisions. "They will have to knuckle under to a harsher law than we now have," he said, referring to his substitute, "and I urge passage."[18] But it was not to be. The committee, by voice vote, rejected both the ban and the substitute. Petris later vowed to submit his bill again in the next session of the legislature, noting, "at no stage in the hearings did the auto industry refute any of the medical testimony" relating to the health effects of smog.[19]

In the wake of the final vote killing Petris' bill, one San Jose auto dealer commented, "The damage has been done. The car is now looked upon like some kind of dangerous drug that [has to be] taken off the market. It now has the same reputation as DDT, and the car's image as a proud symbol of modern-day America is no longer true." Another auto lobbyist predicted that because the Petris bill was passed "by an idiotic Senate and did make some headway" it would thereby "encourage every nut in the country in any legislature to introduce similar bills to show what a big hero he is and how he is protecting the health of the people."[20]

Petris, on the other hand, defended his actions. "People are no longer willing to wait while additional studies, additional lead time, and the like are requested by the auto industry," he said. "We are faced with a crisis in California, and we must act on that basis."[21] Petris reintroduced his bill in the next session of the legislature, but the measure ultimately died a quiet death.

## FARBSTEIN'S BILL

Meanwhile, in the US Congress, Representative Leonard Farbstein (D-NY) took a somewhat different approach in a September 1969 bill that also singled out the internal combustion engine. Farbstein's bill sought to prohibit the manufacture or sale of any new motor vehicle powered by an internal combustion engine that could not meet very strict antipollution controls. His amendment proposed that by January 1978— then eight years away—auto exhaust emissions would be limited to .5 grams/mile of hydrocarbons, 11 grams/mile of carbon monoxide, and .75 grams/mile of oxides of nitrogen. Only vehicles meeting those standards could be sold in the US after January 1, 1978 under Farbstein's proposal. The congressman explained that the automakers, then earning millions of dollars on the sale of automobiles, should assume responsibility for cleaning them up—specifically by making engines that would not produce smog. Representative James Harvey (R-MI), however, reminding his colleagues that "one out of every seven workers' jobs" was traceable to the auto industry, said he would be very careful before writing standards that might alter the status quo.[22]

But Representative George Brown (D-CA), then in the thick of fighting the Nixon Justice Department over the proposed "smog conspiracy" antitrust settlement with the automakers, thought the Farbstein amendment too moderate. Brown suggested the ban on automobiles with internal combustion engines be imposed in three years, not eight. He said that the auto industry had failed to take any action toward stopping pollution.

"They have actually conspired over the last 10 years . . . to avoid doing anything about controlling this problem," he said, pointing to the government's pending antitrust suit against the automakers. But Brown also explained that for less than $5 billion a year—the cost of a regular annual model change—the industry could produce a completely redesigned automobile that would not pollute the atmosphere. Representative Ed Koch (D-NY), later to become New York's mayor, also supported Farbstein's bill, asserting the automakers would never do anything for public safety unless the law compelled them to act. Still, Farbstein's bill was defeated in a standing vote of members, 99 to 22.[23]

Farbstein would later join sixteen other House colleagues issuing a report in March 1970 that concluded that the internal combustion engine "cannot lower emission levels sufficiently to give us the clean air we require." The report also said that since the auto industry had such a "huge financial stake" in the present engine it had little interest in developing an alternative.[24]

"The only way that we will be able to eliminate automobile air pollution in this country," said Farbstein, "is by setting pollution standards not based on what the inherently dirty internal combustion engine can achieve, but on the basis of the cleanest propulsion systems," which Farbstein believed were steam cars and gas turbine engines.[25]

Two years later, in December 1969, when Dr. Paul F. Chenea of GM testified before the House Commerce Committee, he listed the problems with each alternative, one by one. The gas turbine engine, he said, had poor fuel economy and inadequate response in traffic. The steam engine had problems relating to size, cost, fuel consumption, lubrication, weight, and cold-weather freezing. Electric cars were still experimental and might prove hazardous to public safety on urban expressways. Range, speed, and cold-weather usefulness were also problems with the electric vehicle, as was finding a battery that met all the requirements for a general purpose passenger car.[26]

"In my judgement," said Dr. Chenea, "the internal combustion engine is the best overall power plant for the short term. . . . There are fewer problems remaining to be solved in improving the piston engine. Therefore, we believe we can achieve a production version of a lower emission piston engine sooner than for any other engine. The improved piston engine thus represents the fastest route to lower vehicle emissions for the short term."[27] Still, the idea of alternatives to the ICE had enough political currency that even the president of the United States got into the act.

## NIXON'S MOVE

Richard Nixon saw environmental issues as a potential threat to his presidency, and by 1969 his administration was moving to protect its flanks. Two senators on Capitol Hill were of particular concern to Nixon—Senator Henry "Scoop" Jackson (D-WA) and Senator Edmund Muskie (D-ME). Both were potential presidential contenders for 1972 and they each occupied key positions on environmental lawmaking committees: Jackson on the Energy and Natural Resources Committee and Muskie on the Public Works Committee, chairing the Environmental Pollution Subcommittee. Muskie was already the author of the 1963 and 1967 Clean Air acts and was moving a water pollution bill that Nixon would later sign into law. Jackson, too, was writing major environmental legislation and would author the National Environmental Policy Act of 1969 (NEPA) that Nixon would sign on January 1, 1970.* But it was Ed Muskie who would become the thorn in the side of the Nixon White House on automobile air pollution.

In late November 1969, a White House conference on environmental issues and auto pollution was held. Among the attendees were Ed Cole, president of General Motors; Lee Iacocca, vice president of Ford; Virgil Boyd, president of Chrysler; Roy D. Chapin, chairman of American Motors; and Frank Ikard, president of the American Petroleum Institute. Also present for the administration were Lee Du Bridge, Nixon's science advisor; Elliott Richardson, secretary of state (and later HEW); and Robert Finch, secretary of HEW. At the meeting, the auto executives learned that Nixon was considering using federal money to speed research on alternatives to the internal combustion engine. They also learned the administration's future goals on auto emission controls for 1975 were going to be three to five times more stringent than existing levels. By 1980, there would be tougher standards, which the internal combustion engine might not be able to meet. Yet on Capitol Hill the prospects for industry were even less inviting, as Senator Gaylord Nelson (D-WI) had introduced a bill to phase out the internal combustion engine and Ed Muskie also had a bill pending to rewrite the 1967 Clean Air Act.

The auto executives, though not keen on any tougher controls, threw their lot in with Nixon, at least rhetorically. GM president Ed Cole, an engineer, said he thought the Nixon program could be achieved, "providing we obtain enough time." Said Cole, "We have the technical ability to do the job and handle it properly, but the question is of the manufacturing feasibility." However, Cole was not speaking of alternative engines, but rather of new emissions-control hardware** the company was

---

* NEPA, as it was called, was a watershed piece of legislation, not only creating the President's Council on Environmental Quality, but more importantly, the "environmental impact statement (EIS)," a thorough environmental review of all major federal projects before they could proceed. NEPA and the EIS were the opening salvo in a new kind of "environmental due process" for government-funded public works projects.

** Among the devices GM was considering at the time were: a thermal reactor, tanklike devices slung on each side of the engine, which burned excess gases at high temperature; an exhaust gas recirculation system; and the exhaust-treating catalytic converter that would need lead-free gasoline to work properly.

then testing on internal combustion engines. Still, the administration went ahead with its plans for research on alternative engines, calling for a "virtually pollution free automobile within five years."

In late January 1970, Nixon mentioned the program in his State of the Union address and elaborated on why the program was needed in his environmental message to Congress in February:

> . . . Based on present trends, it is quite possible that by 1980 the increase in sheer number of cars in densely populated areas will begin outrunning the technological limits of our capacity to reduce pollution from the internal combustion engine. I hope this will not happen. I hope the automobile industry's presently determined effort to make the internal combustion engine sufficiently pollution-free succeeds. But if it does not, then unless motor vehicles with an alternative, low-pollution power source are available, vehicle-caused pollution will once again begin an inexorable increase.
>
> Therefore, prudence dictates that we move now to ensure that such a vehicle will be available if needed.
>
> I am inaugurating a program to marshal both government and private research with the goal of producing an unconventionally powered virtually pollution free automobile within five years.[28]

"Whatever the President's actual intentions were," wrote Henry D. Jacoby and John D. Steinbruner in *Clearing the Air*, "it looked very much like a deft political finesse on a major developing issue." Although the Nixon program—dubbed the Advanced Automotive Power Systems program (AAPS)—was actually funded and research begun,* within a few years it faded into bureaucratic oblivion.

---

* The Nixon program actually grew out of a 1969 inquiry launched as the Ad Hoc Panel on Unconventional Propulsion under the Office of Science and Technology. Its mission was to assess the possibilities of achieving low emissions with the ICE as compared with other technologies. The panel officially reported in 1970, concluding that modifications of conventional engines was not a promising route to low emissions. The panel's recommendation—to begin an alternative technology to achieve emissions control—was essentially incorporated into the president's initiative. Initially, HEW began to move on Nixon's order. In March 1970, HEW Secretary Robert Finch, issuing priorities for 1971, urged agency heads to "shift research and development efforts to realize an unconventionally powered vehicle within five years. . . ." The AAPS soon moved to EPA, and there the program actually laid out a plan to develop steam and gas turbine engines—from prototypes to production—by 1980. The program later drifted back to focus on how the conventional internal combustion engine could be modified to help meet federal air pollution compliance deadlines and eventually lost direction. It also suffered from inadequate funding. Authorized at $55 million over three years, Congress, not keen on funding an administration venture, never appropriated more than $11 million in any year. Interestingly (especially in the context of the Clinton administration's Partnership for a New Generation of Vehicles, for example), the president's own Office of Management and Budget cut the program's budget requests, arguing that it was industry's business to conduct

But it was Nixon's proposed federal legislation that would put in play major changes for the Clean Air Act. The administration, in fact, called for cutting auto emissions by as much as 93 percent by 1980, regardless of cost or the effect on car performance. The Nixon guidelines for 1980 were "the end of the line for internal combustion engine control technology," said Chrysler's emission control engineer Charles Heinen in March 1970. "If more than that is required," he said, "it's going to mean electric cars." But Henry Ford II allowed that his company might consider alternative engines if it became necessary. "We have a strong vested interest in the survival of the internal combustion engine, but we have a far stronger vested interest in the survival of our company."[29] Mr. Ford, in fact, announced to the world in an April 6, 1970 *Look* magazine article that his company would produce virtually emission-free internal combustion engines by 1975.

## EARTH DAY & THE ACTIVISTS

A few weeks later, on college campuses across the nation, the automobile was impugned as the symbol of the nation's environmental deterioration, as students mounted teach-ins and other demonstrations on the first Earth Day. The nationwide event was the brainchild of Senator Gaylord Nelson, who had read about the anti-war teach-ins and concluded the same technique could be used to help direct the rising public concern over the environment. Although maligned by right-wing organizations as a celebration of Lenin's birthday, Nelson explained that April 22 was actually the birthday of St. Francis of Assisi, one of the first environmentalists. Nelson later raised enough money from speaking fees and other sources to hire three students from Harvard to organize the event, one of whom was Denis Hayes, who became national coordinator.* Earth Day 1970 proved an enormous success with more than 20 million people becoming involved, according to *Time* magazine.

---

automotive research. "The result," concluded Jacoby and Steinbruner in *Clearing the Air*, "is a nominal effort that can be cited as evidence of federal concern in response to pro-environmentalist political pressure, but which offers no serious possibility of developing a marketable alternative technology."

* In addition to Gaylord Nelson and Denis Hayes, a number of other people figured prominently in the event and its aftermath. To name a few: Representative Paul McCloskey (R-CA), who would cosponsor the event with Nelson; Linda Billings, a former Nelson aide who became one of the organizers and later a lobbyist for the Sierra Club; Barbara Reid, who ran the Clean Air Coalition from Environmental Action, and later a key lobbyist on the 1970 Clean Air Act; Linda Katz; Bob Waldrup; Kent Conrad, director of volunteers; and others. Among the Earth Day/Environmental Teach-In national advisory committee, in addition to McCloskey and Nelson were Sydney Howe, president of the Conservation Foundation; Professors Paul Erlich of Stanford University and Harold C. Jordahl of the University of Wisconsin; investment broker Daniel Lufkin; Charles Creasey of Federal City College; Glenn L. Paulson of Rockefeller University; and Doug Scott of the University of Michigan.

Major rallies were held in Washington, New York, and San Francisco, and assorted actions took place at more than 10,000 schools, and 1,500 colleges and universities. At the University of Minnesota there was a ceremonial burial of an internal combustion engine. On other college campuses, entire cars were buried. In New York city, GM's new office building was picketed by a local action group, Environment! Using the slogan "GM Takes Your Breath Away," the group accused GM of producing one-third of the nation's air pollution. But the street theater was only part of the activism that came in the wake of Earth Day. A new brand of environmental lobbying was also born, one that included the United Auto Workers among its first participants.

Not long after Earth Day, in fact, Denis Hayes helped to arrange a strategy meeting for moving environmental issues forward on the public policy agenda. "The Clean Air Act of 1970 was not an immaculate conception, fashioned by enlightened legislators without serious public pressure," recalls Hayes. "Early in 1970, Earth Day organizers learned that Muskie would push clean air legislation, and we strongly encouraged our local activists to focus on the issue." Hayes and others in the environmental vanguard, gathered the best of the local Earth Day activists together with other environmental leaders to plan priorities and strategy. They met at the UAW Conference Center in Black Lake, Michigan, and chose to focus on clean air and the Highway Trust Fund. The first Coalition for Clean Air was formed, led by Environmental Action with the participation of the Sierra Club, Friends of the Earth, and other groups willing to lobby. This coalition also worked with Ralph Nader's "clean air task force," led by John Esposito.[30] Out in the country, meanwhile, local hearings were organized to gin up grassroots support for clean air, some with help from the Oil, Chemical, and Atomic Workers Union and its legislative director, Tony Mazzochi.

"Two things made the coalition significant," recalls Denis Hayes of the early lobbying and public education efforts to support the Clean Air Act. First was the full participation of the United Auto Workers. In fact, Walter Reuther joined Hayes at the first national Clean Air Coalition press conference, as did Bill Dodds, the UAW's chief lobbyist who worked on Capitol Hill. "This really muted the jobs issue," recalls Hayes of UAW's involvement. Second, was the grassroots nature of the environmental and citizen lobbying effort to push the Clean Air Act. "It drew strength from its authenticity," says Hayes. "These were *real people*—not professional green lobbyists. I'd argue that the 1970 Clean Air Act campaign was the first successful lobbying effort of the modern environmental movement."[31]

## GAYLORD NELSON & THE ICE

In the US Congress, meanwhile, the House passed its version of the Clean Air Act of 1970 on June 11th with an overwhelming vote of 374-to-1. The House bill incorporated many elements of Nixon's proposal.[32] In July, just as the Senate began its debate on the Clean Air Act, a mass of stagnant air became lodged over the east-

## "The Great Dirty Cloud"

"Through the polluted haze that for days has hung over the East Coast from New York to Atlanta," wrote the *New York Times*, "nothing is clear but a timely warning. Urban areas are getting perilously close to the point where they have to chose between the internal combustion engine and breathable air. . . .

". . . [W]hat has up to now been regarded as personally hysterical and economically unthinkable may yet become a reality," offered the *Times*. "Until the gasoline engine can be made pollution-free or a clean substitute for it developed—eventualities at least ten years in the future—the automobile may actually have to be banned from the centers of major American cities. . . . In the present New York crisis a prohibition on all nonessential traffic may yet have to be invoked in certain areas. . . . "

Interestingly, a few days later, half a world away in Tokyo, it would be learned that city officials there had done just that, producing dramatic results. "Tokyo closed 122 of the busiest streets to cars today [a Sunday], and for a short while part of the world's most populous city was free of the exhaust fumes that have plagued it recently," reported a *Washington Post* correspondent on August 3, 1970. ". . . It was part of Tokyo Gov. Ryokichi Miniobe's campaign to show the 11.5 million residents what life could be like without the noise and stench of the internal combustion engine. . . .The improvement in the air was dramatic. Meters recording carbon monoxide levels nosedived, and for a few minutes in the West Tokyo area of Shinhuku the needle rested on zero. . . ."

Back in the United States, meanwhile, there were questions about the slated clean-car timetable. Calling the East Coast pollution cloud a "dangerous cesspool of air that now hangs over this city," the *Washington Post* said the incident "raises the immediate question of whether the public can wait the ten years the automobile industry has said it needs to produce clean cars." The *Post*, in fact, wondered, "Has an independent group thoroughly looked into this timetable to see if ten years really is needed? Or is it a comfortable pace the industry has set for itself?" On Capitol Hill, apparently, there were a few people listening to such appeals, among them Senator Edmund Muskie. President Nixon, offering his pollution control package to Congress, essentially bought into the industry's ten-year proposal. Muskie, however, would cut that in half, making the deadline for achieving auto emissions standards 1975, not 1980.

ern seaboard of the United States, putting a lid on the entire region and trapping all manner of industrial and automotive pollutants. Gaylord Nelson used the pollution episode to dramatize the need for tougher regulation, and in particular his proposed amendment to the Clean Air Act to ban the sale of the internal combustion engine by 1975.

". . . [F]or several days last week, a massive pollution cloud lingered over the seventeen states along the eastern seaboard. . . . It was but an ominous messenger of the future; a messenger warning of pollution more frequent and more intense. . . ." Nelson charged that no one—not the president, Congress, or industry had taken responsibility for the air pollution problem, even though for more than twenty-five years there had been scientific findings and health warnings about its growing threat to public health. "The staff report of Senator Magnuson's Commerce Committee projects that the air pollution from automobiles will double in the next 30 years," said Nelson. ". . . Imagine the air over New York City or Los Angeles twice as polluted as it has been in the past few days. . . ."[33]

Nelson then outlined how he would strengthen federal pollution standards and actions, including those on the automobile. ". . . [T]he automobile pollution problem must be met head on with the requirement that the internal combustion engine be replaced by January 1, 1975. While we have delayed confronting this problem, the auto industry has skillfully filibustered and sweet-talked the Nation out of forcing it to do anything meaningful." Nelson explained that it was "necessary to pass legislation" to replace the ICE "because the auto industry will not do so voluntarily." In his remarks, Nelson also addressed the matter of cost:

> . . . [I]t will cost the automotive industry $3-to-$5 billion to convert to an alternative engine. Spending that much money is obviously a real concern of the manufacturers.
>
> It is valid to point out, however, that the taxpayers are paying for air pollution damages estimated at $30 billion annually. The automobile is responsible for more than half that $30 billion.
>
> . . . [T]he cost to the automotive industry for converting to a substitute for the internal combustion engine is only one-third the annual economic damages caused by the present internal combustion engine.
>
> What the auto industry has spent, however, has been inadequate and directed solely to rigging a jerry-constructed internal combustion engine that will have attained some slight degree of social acceptability and be a little cleaner. . . .
>
> . . . According to its own estimates, the auto industry is investing $11 billion to $15 billion to strengthen its bond to the internal combustion engine, expenses that ultimately the consumer pays for in the final product. . . .[34]

Nelson's bill soon got the attention of Detroit. A few days after it was introduced, GM lobbyist Bill Chapman began trying to set up a meeting between Senator Nelson and GM president Edward Cole. On August 14, 1970, Cole talked with Nelson about the progress GM had made toward cleaning up the internal combustion engine.[35]

## CATALYTIC CONVERSION

One of the items Cole discussed with Nelson and others on Capitol Hill was industry's renewed interest in the exhaust-treating device called the catalytic converter— the device that had almost come on the scene in California in the early 1960s. New progress had been made.

Although many of the nonautomotive companies that had been involved with catalytic devices in the early 1960s had abandoned their programs after the Chrysler Clean Air Package was approved to meet California's standards, Engelhard Industries had kept its research going. Engelhard was working with devices to control fumes on gasoline and diesel-powered forklifts used in enclosed factories and warehouses. Engelhard's Carl D. Keith had invented a new kind of converter, called the monolithic converter, which the company had tested with promising results. Engelhard had also learned about leaded gasoline, which poisoned the catalyst, and tested the device with unleaded fuel and found the catalysts lasted much longer. Ford Motor Co., later noticing an Engelhard patent on one catalyst system, soon began working with Engelhard. At one point, Henry Ford II was to go to Congress in 1968-69 and say the automakers could clean up the air with catalysts, but would need fair regulation and unleaded fuel to do so. For whatever reasons, Henry Ford never made the visit. GM's Ed Cole did, however, visiting Senators Muskie and Howard Baker, and Representative Paul Rogers (D-FL) in November 1969. Still, the automakers had made no public commitments to use the catalytic converter, calling all such technologies experimental.

The automakers, meanwhile, had begun on their own to meet with the oil industry about the lead issue. In January 1970, for example, Ford sought the reaction of Sun Oil executives to plans for new cars that could operate on regular-grade, unleaded gasoline. "From our standpoint," wrote Ford, ". . . the sooner lead-free fuel is available, the better."[36] GM also met with Sun officials and other oil companies individually, noting that a bill had been introduced in California calling for the complete elimination of lead by January 1974. GM's Cole raised the lead issue publicly in a mid-January 1970 speech to the Society of Automobile Engineers. Cole said he expected auto emissions standards to be required for 1975 and 1980, but industry would not be able to meet them unless lead was removed from gasoline. By mid-February, in his environmental message to Congress, Richard Nixon urged the oil industry to voluntarily remove lead from gasoline beginning in 1971 or face the prospect of legislation.

Meanwhile, the business interest in catalytic converters had picked up considerably. In addition to Engelhard, Allied Chemical, W.R. Grace, Matthey Bishop, Universal Oil Products had each restarted earlier programs or begun new ones. Corning Glass Works, of Corning, New York, a company that would play a pivotal role in producing the substrate ceramic material that held the catalyst in the core of the converter unit, also became a key player in the development of the catalytic converter.

In April 1970, a delegation of businessmen from Corning visiting General Motors officials in Detroit on routine business had a chance encounter with GM's Ed Cole that changed their business. At one point in the meeting, one of Corning's men pulled a small piece of ceramic honeycombed material from his briefcase and handed it to Cole. "Here's something that might be useful for your work on the gas turbine," he said, referring to a GM engine then in research. Cole looked at the material and responded immediately saying it was just what they were looking for—but not for turbines. Rather, Cole saw the material as a potential medium to carry a pollution-control catalyst GM was testing in catalytic converters for use on its cars. The Corning team "lost no time getting across Grand Boulevard to the St. Regis Hotel," recalls one of the participants, where they telephoned the home office to prepare for a briefing of GM engineers. "We're going into the substrate business," said the caller.[37]

Back in Washington, as the clean air debate raged on during the summer of 1970, a cross-country "Clean Air Race" had been organized by HEW, with college students driving cars that had been equipped with emissions control systems. In forty-three of fifty catalyst-equipped cars that crossed a Capitol Hill finish line, the cars produced emission levels meeting the 1980 standards that Richard Nixon had proposed in his bill. The race received wide publicity, helped to show Congress that emissions could be reduced, and boosted the prospects for catalytic converters.

Still, in Congress, the legislative fight was just beginning.

## THE MUSKIE BILL

On August 20, 1970, Senator Edmund Muskie held a press conference to announce that his Air and Water Pollution Subcommittee had approved a new clean air bill that he expected would soon be approved by the Senate Public Works Committee and the full Senate. Muskie had introduced a modest bill the previous year that would have extended the 1967 Clean Air Act and given HEW power to set auto emission standards. Yet this new bill was different and much tougher. Although it didn't call for banning the internal combustion engine as Gaylord Nelson's bill did, it did call for an aggressive timetable and tough standards. Introduced shortly after the East Coast pollution episode, Muskie's bill blended Nixon's call for a 90 percent reduction of pollutants and Nelson's 1975 deadline.

At the news conference—which was also attended by Senator J. Caleb Boggs (R-DE) who supported the bill—Muskie called the new bill "a tough piece of legislation." It had the power to halt sales of new cars on January 1, 1975 if the automakers did not, by that time, reduced exhaust pollutants by 90 percent of 1970 levels. He explained it was necessary to have a 1975 deadline rather than 1980 because of the length of time it took to move older, higher-polluting cars off the road through attrition. If new cars did not become minimal polluters until 1980, he explained, it would actually take until 1990—then twenty years away—before old-car attrition combined with the 1980 new-car deadline to achieve the desired public health standards.[38] Calling the automobile "a pollution monster" that consumed most of his subcommittee's time, Muskie challenged American ingenuity to rise to the task of solving the auto pollution problem.

In the House of Representatives, however, some members doubted that Muskie's 1975 deadline would be acceptable. The House bill, passed earlier that summer, had no deadline. "Some of us feel that it can't be done by setting any specific target date because the auto industry is perplexed and has told us it doesn't know when it can achieve such standards," said Representative Ancher Nelsen (R-MN). "It's like trying to set a date next week, or next month to pull out of Viet Nam. It can't be done that way."[39]

Ed Muskie believed it could. His bill allowed five and half years to get to its goal. In fact, an unnamed source at General Motors the next day suggested the industry was not impossibly far from meeting the demands by 1975 for an automobile that would be almost pollution free.* Muskie, a determined legislator, believed it was important to push the industry.

### BIG ED FROM MAINE

Unlike others in the US Senate, Ed Muskie was not a man of great wealth. In 1946 he began his law practice in Waterville, Maine, in a modest office above a dress shop. Not long thereafter, he was recruited by a moribund Democratic party to run for the state legislature, where he later became minority leader. By 1954, recruited again by his Democrat colleagues, Muskie waged a tireless campaign and surprised party leaders by becoming Maine's governor, reviving the Democratic party in a state where Republicans were practically set in stone. "A key factor" in the change was Ed Muskie himself, observed the authors of the *Almanac of American Politics*. "His plain and sincere manner, coupled with his clearly honest idealism, convinced many Yankee Republicans that Democrats were not all big city hacks, and that Muskie and his followers were decent men who could be trusted with government." Standing at six-foot-six, with a patient rural manner about him, Ed Muskie evoked a certain Lincolnesque quality. He was part professor, part everyman; capable of intimidating expert witnesses from his committee chairman's seat, or wooing others to his cause through his insight and earnestness. In 1960, Muskie was elected the US Senate. Ed Muskie, however, befitting his Maine heritage, liked his independence— and he paid a price for it. When he arrived in the Senate, he refused to pledge allegiance to then-Senate Majority Leader Lyndon Johnson, who ran a very tight ship. Muskie's committee assignments suffered as a result. But by 1963, he managed to convince his colleagues on the Senate Public Works committee to create the Air and Water Pollution Subcommittee, where as chairman, he began an illustrious career crafting air and water pollution control laws, "before environmental causes became fashionable."[40]

"None of us knew very much about air pollution," said Muskie, reflecting on the issue years later. "We educated ourselves in the subcommittee hearings."[41] Indeed

---

* The GM source mentioned two approaches that were being undertaken in research at that time "to take autos out the pollution business." One involved the catalytic muffler and the other a new kind of exhaust manifold that would be hot enough to burn off unused fuels and gases.

they did. Muskie began holding hearings all over the US. In California, he listened Governor Edmund Brown tell him of the state's problem in keeping up with automotive pollution, and that progress there had been modest. Brown urged a more aggressive federal role. "The automobile industry," Brown told Muskie, "is in interstate commerce and the Federal Government clearly has jurisdiction." Hearing this plea in other locations as well, Muskie concluded automotive emissions were indeed a national problem, and in an October 1964 report entitled *Steps Toward Clean Air*, Muskie's subcommittee recommended, among other things, national standards for vehicular emissions.[42] Though the 1965 and 1967 Clean Air Acts were somewhat cautious in their reach and impact, and Muskie would later be criticized by some activists for not being aggressive enough with polluters, he had been moving the government role gradually forward. There was more to come.

In 1968, Ed Muskie became the Democrat's vice presidential candidate running with Hubert Humphrey. During that campaign, Muskie's "quiet Yankee style, his willingness to let opponents speak their piece, impressed votes all over the country in a year of political turbulence."[43] No wonder Richard Nixon worried about him. Environmental issues, in fact, would be at the core of the political maneuvering between Muskie and Nixon. In fact, by April 1970 Nixon would sign the Water Quality Improvement Act that Muskie authored.[44] By the time Muskie came to speak at the April 1970 Earth Day rally on the Washington mall, ten thousand college students, activists and others "applauded him more vigorously than they did such youth-culture heros as Rennie Davis, Phil Ochs, and I.F. Stone."[45] But it was Muskie's proposed 1970 clean air bill that drove the automakers wild.

## "WE'LL HAVE TO LIQUIDATE"

When some of the automakers' lobbyists first saw a draft the Muskie clean air bill in late August 1970, they read the riot act to Leon Billings, Muskie's chief environmental aide. "It was a little tense," said Billings at the time. American Motors' representative declared on the spot that the bill would require his company to liquidate. GM's William Chapman and James M. Morris complained about the lack of hearings on the bill, and that they had not had a chance to comment on its specific provisions. Four days later, on August 25, Ed Cole, Lee Iacocca, John Riccardo, Gerald Meyers, and Thomas Mann all met with Muskie, informing him of the burden the requirements placed on their companies. The auto executives also lobbied other senators and sought the assistance of Nixon administration officials. In still other meetings on Capitol Hill, Lloyd Cutler and GM assistant general counsel Fraser Hilder went to Leon Billings with an alternative industry proposal. Billings saw the proposal as an attempt to undo everything Muskie's subcommittee had done on the bill. That meeting, according to Billings, was "acrimonious."[46]

In Dearborn, Michigan, at Ford Motor headquarters, Lee Iacocca let loose with his broadside on the Muskie proposal, a twenty-page statement with charts and graphs released to the press.

> The Senate Subcommittee on Air and Water Pollution chaired by Senator Muskie of Maine has just adopted an amendment to the Clean Air Act. Some of the changes in this bill could prevent continued production of automobiles after January 1, 1975. Even if they do not stop production, they could lead to huge increases in the price of cars. They could have a tremendous impact on all of American industry and could do irreparable damage to the American economy. And yet, in return for all of this, they would lead to only small improvements in the quality of air.[47]

Muskie began to hear more from the auto executives as the bill moved through full committee and closer to the Senate floor. "General Motors does not at this time know how to get production vehicles down to the emissions levels that your bill would require for 1975 models," complained Ed Cole to the senator in a September 17, 1970 letter. "Accomplishment of these goals, as far as we know, simply is not technologically possible within the time frame required."[48] Cole's letter was distributed to the entire House and Senate, key people in the administration and the press. GM ran at least one national newspaper advertisement with the headline, "Does GM Care About Cleaner Air? You Bet We Do." The ad, which described GM's activities to reduce air pollution, was misleading in its abbreviated definitions of certain pollutants, found in the ad's "glossary." Carbon monoxide, for example, was defined as "a colorless, tasteless gas resulting from the combustion of carbon with insufficient air."

The same day Ed Cole's letter was circulating on Capitol Hill, the Muskie bill was reported by the Senate Public Works Committee with one amendment—a provision, however, that would later prove important to industry. It gave the automakers the right to petition HEW (later EPA) for a one-year extension of the 1975 deadline if the necessary technological breakthrough was not made by January 1, 1973. But industry wanted more. Additional alternative language was prepared in late September 1970 that included six changes: the right to appeal earlier than 1973 for extension of the deadline; federal pre-emption of state standards; provision for a defect warranty on pollution equipment rather than a performance warranty; assurance that tests used to check compliance under the warranty provision were comparable to the original factory tests; deletion of any section permitting citizen suits against HEW for failing to enforce the law; and permission for the manufacturers to disregard the standards on cars made for export.

The automakers, however, could not find a willing sponsor to propose these amendments before the full Senate. In fact, given the public mood, there was little lobbying by the automakers against Muskie's bill when it came to the Senate floor. "We did nothing about the bill in the full Senate," said GM lobbyist James M. Morris at the time. "I wouldn't think of asking anybody to vote against that bill."[49] Muskie's

# Does GM Care About Cleaner Air?

*General Motors ran this 1970 ad in major US newspapers, restating the company's public pledge "to solve the problem of vehicle emissions in shortest possible time." (1978 GM Corp. Used with permission of GM Media Archives.)*

bill passed, 73-0. But GM would not have received the votes in any case, even with an all-out effort. For GM and the auto industry had not endeared themselves to many senators and senate staff who had dealt with their lobbyists and executives on other matters.

"The industry's statements before this committee as to what they are capable of, and their performance in California in claiming that the state standards could not be met," explained Leon Billings in November 1970, "have made us skeptical of what they say." The industry, and GM in particular, had also wounded itself badly during the mid-1960s auto safety debate, leaving a distinctly bad impression on many senators. In 1965, when GM appeared before Senator Abraham Ribicoff's (D-NY) Government Operations Subcommittee, then very concerned about the rising frequency of serious injuries in auto collisions, the company's witnesses told the senators that GM was satisfied with its progress in safety but was unable to provide the committee with data on how much it was spending on safety research. A year later when the Senate Commerce Committee began hearings on the Traffic Safety Bill, GM and the other automakers argued for self-regulation rather than federal standards. Ralph Nader, meanwhile, was suing GM for having him followed and investigated by private detectives. All of this hurt the industry's image, and, more seriously, devalued its word on Capitol Hill as the Clean Air Act was being considered.[50]

Still, even after Muskie's bill passed in the Senate, the automakers continued to rail against the standards, believing there was opportunity to influence the House-Senate conferees as they made their final deliberations. Ed Cole, in a November 1970 speech to the American Petroleum Institute, said the standards being considered by Congress "simply aren't attainable." He proposed in their place a HC standard of 1.0 GPM vs. the 0.3 to 0.5 GPM being considered in conference; a CO standard of 11 GPM vs. 4.7 GPM being considered; and a NOx standard of 3.0 vs. 0.4 GPM.[51] GM, in other words, wanted HC and CO standards that would allow two-to-three times more pollution, and a NOx standard that would allow seven times more pollution than the standards being put forward by Congress.

As the Clean Air Act of 1970 came to its final debate in the House-Senate conference, most environmental organizations were pushing for Muskie's bill. However, many environmentalists were then being especially careful with their political activities, given a pending challenge by the IRS to the tax exempt status of environmental organizations engaged in environmental litigation. Still, some organizations created solely for lobbying, such as Environmental Action, and its legislative director, Barbara Reid, did push for the bill. Carl Pope, then with Zero Population Growth who also worked with Environmental Action, lobbied as well, as did Ted Pankowski of the Izaak Walton League. Arthur Mackwell, a lobbyist for Engelhard Industries, also worked with environmentalists fighting for tough auto emission standards and deadlines. But during the final sessions of the House-Senate conference in December all eyes were on Muskie. "It's up to Muskie to hold the line," said John Esposito, then working at Ralph Nader's Center for the Study of Responsive Law in Washington.

The auto industry, meanwhile, had turned to the Nixon administration to help supply pressure on the conferees. After a pause for the 1970 congressional elections, the House-Senate conference reconvened to negotiate the remaining differences—with the Senate version having the tough 1975 deadline. Nixon administration officials began to weigh in on the fight in late November. Edward David, Nixon's science advisor, attacked the deadlines as unwise. HEW Secretary Elliott Richardson pressed Congress to relax the proposed deadlines. William Ruckelshaus, then nominated to head EPA, asked for authority to extend the deadlines. The administration essentially pushed for the House version of the bill.

Despite the administration's pressure, however, the conferees went with the Senate version of the bill and held to the tougher standards and the deadlines with two exceptions: it allowed for a single one-year extension of the deadlines by the EPA administrator after certain findings were made, and it required the National Academy of Sciences to conduct a study of technical feasibility for meeting the standards and deadlines.

The final bill from the conference committee was agreed to by the full House and Senate on December 18, 1970. Title II, known as the National Emissions Standards Act, included emissions standards for hydrocarbons and carbon monoxide for new cars in 1975 and a standard for oxides of nitrogen for 1976. These standards were to achieve a 90 percent reduction below 1970 levels of CO and HC and 90 percent below the 1971 level of NOx (these standards were later specified as .41 grams/mile HC, 3.4 grams/mile CO and 0.4 grams/mile NOx). EPA was designated to carry out certification tests to confirm compliance; to conduct research; to establish fuel regulations; to require and enforce warranties from auto manufacturers; and to certify and subsidize inspection and testing programs. For violations of the emissions standards—i.e., marketing vehicles not certified—the law would impose a fine of $10,000 per vehicle. Theoretically, there was also the power to shut down auto manufacturing operations producing vehicles that were not certified to meet the standards. EPA's administrator was given power to subpoena and obtain documents from the auto companies, and there were also allowances for "citizen suits" under certain circumstances.

Over at the White House, however, Richard Nixon had threatened a veto, since he was especially perturbed at Muskie's 1975 deadline for meeting auto emissions standards. In the end, however, Nixon signed the bill into law, but Ed Muskie was not invited to the ceremony. Still, it was clearly Muskie's victory.

"Muskie has pushed to final passage a bill that is by far the toughest anti-pollution measure ever approved by Congress," wrote *National Journal's* Richard Corrigan, summarizing the action. "The [Nixon] Administration found itself publicly siding with corporate polluters—even though the legislation was based, to a substantial degree, on a White House proposal."

## "TECHNOLOGY FORCING"

The Clean Air Act of 1970 was a first-of-its-kind piece of federal legislation. It would become known as a "technology forcing" statute driven by public health goals. "A sharp turn to a very new philosophy" is how authors James Krier and Edmund Ursin described it in their excellent history of the early air pollution fight, *Pollution and Policy*. "The old way was to pay heed to economic and technological feasibility. . . . The new way was simply to protect public health, and feasibility was 'not to be used to mitigate against' this goal. If technology were inadequate or uneconomic, it would have to catch up."[52] No one put this better or more eloquently than the sponsor of the legislation, Senator Muskie, in opening Senate debate on the bill in September 1970.

> The first responsibility of Congress is not the making of technological or economic judgments—or even to be limited by what is or appears to be technologically feasible. Our responsibility is to establish what the public interest requires to protect the health of persons. This may mean that people and industries will be asked to do what seems to be impossible at the present time. But if health is to be protected, these challenges must be met. I am convinced they can be met.[53]

Ed Muskie and several of his Senate colleagues knew they were pushing the industry hard, forcing them to innovate. "Everyone understood that the goal could not be reached with state-of-the-art technology," Leon Billings would later explain. "But the debate was not over the 90 percent cut. It was over what could be done if the automobile industry could not meet the standard. Muskie's theory was that a bureaucrat would always extend the deadline, so he wanted Congress to make the decision."[54] And that became a key feature of the 1970 Act: mandated deadlines and statutory standards written into the law itself.

"Three fundamental principles shaped the 1970 law," wrote Senator Muskie describing some of the Senate chemistry that led to the act's three-part structure. "I was convinced that strict federal air pollution regulation would require a legally defensible premise. Protection of public health seemed the strongest and most appropriate such premise. Sen. Howard Baker [R-TN] believed that the American technological genius should be brought to bear on the air pollution problem, and that industry should be required to apply the best available technology. Sen. Thomas Eagleton [D-MO] asserted that the American people deserved to know when they could expect their health to be protected, and that deadlines were the only means of providing minimal assurance."[55]

## NEXT MOVES

Within a few months of passage of the Clean Air Act, the auto industry, still reeling from what had occurred in Congress, began to evaluate its options. First, there were deadlines it had to meet under the act. But these were tempered somewhat by the possibility of a one-time extension if the automakers could show EPA why they needed more time. Second, there was the problem of the automobile's public image as a polluter and the industry as uncaring and insensitive toward the pollution problem. By early 1971, industry began to move on both of these fronts simultaneously—attacking the new law for its "impossible" provisions and producing ads and

## LEON G. BILLINGS

A key player in the national clean air debates of the 1970s was not a US senator, or even a congressman. Rather, the man who would become as important as any elected official in writing the Clean Air Act, amending it, and even holding sway over its implementation was Leon G. Billings, chief of staff for Ed Muskie's Environmental Pollution Subcommittee. Born in Helena, Montana, and raised in the time when big mining companies like Anaconda Copper ran the state, Leon Billings was schooled in the prairie populism of agrarian fairness and liberal politics. His parents edited what Billings has called "the only liberal newspaper in the state of Montana," the *People's Voice.*

In his early twenties, Billings went off to work as a reporter and farm organizer in the rural politics of California. By 1963, he was lured east to work for the American Public Power Association (APPA) in Washington, where he became a lobbyist fighting for municipally run electric utilities. In his work with APPA, Billings became acquainted with the Senate Public Works Committee and one of its rising young senators, Democrat Edmund Muskie of Maine. Muskie at the time was the prime mover behind a federally supported hydroelectric power project in Maine known as the Dickey-Lincoln School project, which APPA backed. Muskie became chairman of the new Public Works Subcommittee on air and water pollution in 1963, and in 1966 Leon Billings was hired to help Muskie run that subcommittee. And so began a career in environmental public policy on Capitol Hill. During Muskie's tenure in the Senate through 1980, Leon Billings helped write not only clean air legislation, but also a major new water pollution control act, legislation aimed at prying open the highway trust fund, and various other laws dealing with noise, energy, and solid waste.

During the tumultuous fights over auto emissions standards, Leon Billings was often at the center of the storm, parsing out briefings and interpretations to demanding senators trying to make sense of a difficult issue. Billings garnered the respect of the Republicans and Democrats he worked with, but also built a reputation as something of a character, being direct and sometimes confrontational with lobbyists and other staffers. Auto industry lobbyists would leave his office shaking their heads as he criticized their proposals—often in blunt and very earthy language. On the other side of the fight, there were disagreements with Ralph Nader and his associates, some of whom had criticized Muskie sharply for his pre-1970 role in what they believed were weak initiatives. House staffers who had come to Billings to discuss the pending 1977 House-Senate conference on the Clean Air Act amendments remember him taking charge of the operation in no uncertain terms. Still, while some may have bridled at his style, few doubted his dedication to cleaning up the nation's air and water—and to making Big Business responsible for its technology.

After Ed Muskie left the Senate in 1980 to serve as secretary of state, Leon Billings went with him as his executive assistant. In the mid-1980s, after a stint as director of the Democratic Senatorial Campaign Committee, Billings made an unsuccessful bid for Congress as the Democratic candidate for the Eighth Congressional District in Maryland. However, in 1991, Billings became a member of the Maryland House of Delegates, a seat he still holds today, fighting for environmental and other causes. In private practice, too, Billings has also continued to work on energy and environmental issues, forming a consulting partnership with two other Muskie colleagues, Bob Rose and Charlene Sturbitts. And in 1995, with Ed Muskie and former Senator Robert Stafford (R-VT) as founding cochairs, Billings formed The Clean Air Trust, a nonprofit organization in Washington to watchdog the Clean Air Act.

But clearly, for Billings, it has been Ed Muskie's environmental vision and their work together in the US Senate that has left the most enduring mark. Muskie's Air and Water Pollution Subcommittee and the laws it spawned, says Billings, were among the prime movers of modern environmentalism, pushing that movement beyond traditional conservation issues and into the more volatile arena of public health policy. "Ed Muskie made it national policy to protect human health by protecting the air, the water, and the land," said Billings in a 1996 tribute to Muskie at his death. "That policy and that philosophy have now spread across the planet."

Still, Leon Billings, as Muskie's right-hand man and legislative architect, also made such new protections possible. In fact, *Environmental Reporter* called Billings "probably the most influential man in America" drafting environmental legislation during the late 1960s and early 1970s. And as this book goes to press, Leon Billings is once again strategizing with colleagues over the fights to come with Congress and the Clean Air Act, this time taking that law beyond 2003.

television spots to show the public that the auto companies were already acting on the problem.

In February 1971, Ed Cole and John Riccardo asserted to *Look* magazine business editor Al Rothenberg that the act's requirements for meeting 1975 standards were not based on any scientific evidence. Cole cited a 1967 study that was "specific to the automobile without regard to other pollution sources." Cole said the authors indicated their findings were preliminary and "not intended as final or adequate for establishing legal standards." Riccardo charged that the US Senate had no basis for its unanimous 73-0 vote passing the act. "When the bill came up for a vote in the Senate, which senator had the information he should have had before the vote?" asked Riccardo. He answered his own question. "None, because none exists." Still, Riccardo was not specifically critical of the Senate passing the bill. "I would have voted for it if I had been a senator and knew as much as they did."[56] In a separate speech in Tennessee, Ed Cole said the act contained a number of provisions "which are unrealistic and technologically impossible." Yet he added that since it was the law, GM would do everything possible to comply.[57]

In 1971 television ads, meanwhile, both GM and Ford projected their companies as caring and concerned about air pollution, with GM claiming it had been working "to solve these problems" since the 1950s. In one of its ads, GM explained its work on the catalytic converter. "GM made you a promise to get the car out of the pollution problem," said the GM announcer, "and General Motors is doing it." Ford explained in a January 1971 TV spot, "Now, if you think Ford Motor Company just woke up and discovered virtue because people are talking more about safety and pollution, check the record." Ford cited its installation of seat belts in 1956 and an antipollution system in 1961.

But a few months later, in a private meeting at the White House with President Richard Nixon and his aide John Ehrlichman on the morning of April 27, 1971, Henry Ford II and Lee Iacocca sang a somewhat more distressing tune on safety and the environment.

## A Meeting with Richard Nixon

At the outset of that meeting, Nixon assured his two guests that personally, when it came to environmental or consumer matters, he was "extremely pro-business." But he also let his guests know that environmental concerns were in the forefront of national issues—what he called "the environment kick" as being all the rage. "[I]t's in your ads," he told them. There was also the "safety kick," said Nixon, "'cause Nader's running around squealing about this and that." But Nixon did acknowledge the pollution problem. "You can fly over various places and you can see the stuff in the air. [T]he general principle I believe in," he said, still breaking the ground with his guests, but giving them a feel for his views, "is that . . . we'll do the best we can to . . . eliminate the toxins." But, he added, "we can't have a completely safe society or safe highways or safe cars and pollution-free, and so forth, or . . . (we'll go back to living) like a bunch of damned animals. . . ."

Nixon wanted to set his visitors at ease, letting them know they could speak candidly. He assured them that he was "for the system" as it was—unlike the "environmentalists" and "the consumerism people. They're a group of people that aren't really one damn bit interested in safety or clean air. What they're interested in is destroying the system. They are enemies of the system. So what I'm trying to say is this: that you can speak to me in terms that I am for the system."

Henry Ford explained that the purpose of their visit was to talk about safety issues, not auto emissions. "I don't think we want to talk to you today about emissions," said Ford. "It's very political." Then Ford proceeded to do just that, adding, "we lost seventy-three-to-nothing," referring to the Senate vote on Muskie's bill, apparently etched deep in Ford's brain (even Michigan's Republican senator Robert P. Griffin, who complained about the Muskie bill, did not vote against it). "Mr Ruckelshaus has just come in," Ford said of Bill Ruckelshaus' appointment to become head of EPA. "Lee's [Iacocca] already been in to see him." Ruckelshaus was scheduled to convene an EPA hearing to consider extending the auto emission deadlines. Ford also mentioned EPA's test procedures for automobiles. ". . . [I]f he [Ruckelshaus] can help us a little bit," said Ford—apparently referring to the upcoming hearings and possibly the test procedures, too—"we can probably meet the '75 schedule. We hope we can, we're not sure we can." But Ford added, "'76 is gonna be impossible" because the requirements were tougher. Then Ford turned back to what they really came to talk about, safety.

Still, in parts of the discussion, environment and safety were lumped together in terms of the cost these requirements were imposing on the industry and how this might imperil America's economy and auto industry. Ford stressed to Nixon the importance of the automobile to the economy, reminding him that the auto industry contributed about one-sixth of the gross national product. Then he jumped on the regulations. "It's the safety requirements, the emissions requirements, the bumper requirements . . . All of these things are going to cost money," Ford said. "If these prices get so high that people stop buying cars . . ."

NIXON: "um-hum"

FORD: ". . . they're gonna buy more foreign cars; you're going to have balance of payments problem. . . ."

NIXON: "Right I'm convinced. . . ."

FORD: "granted, the foreign [automakers] have got to do the same thing, but they're doing it at a wage rate that's half [ours]."

Lee Iacocca joined the conversation at that point, talking about the emissions issue, and how Nixon and his White House team had originally talked about a 1980 goal, but that Muskie had set the tougher 1975 goal. Iacocca acknowledged that he thought Ruckelshaus was on the spot, given the way the law was written. Ruckelshaus could grant an extension to the automakers, but he had to determine first whether the automakers were making a good faith effort to meet the standards. Iacocca wasn't convinced that the "good faith" requirement was such a good idea and seemed a little concerned after his earlier meeting with Ruckelshaus because the new EPA administrator seemed to know clearly what he had to do. "[H]ow [do] they determine good faith" was Iacocca's concern. Perhaps the National Academy of Sciences could help, he had said to Ruckelshaus. But Ruckelshaus said it was his call. Iacocca recounted this meeting to Nixon, suggesting that Ruckelshaus was going to end up with "fifty different standards for fifty different manufacturers" and that the law may wind up penalizing "the guy who does the best job." Iacocca concluded by saying that he only mentioned it because the Ruckelshaus-EPA hearings were coming up in about a week. "I think they will work with us on the technical level," Iacocca said, concluding his remarks about EPA and emissions.

When Iacocca turned to safety, his focus was on some earlier discussions he had with DOT officials. Iacocca clearly felt the DOT safety proposals went too far. But in recounting that meeting for Nixon, Iacocca appeared to be playing safety off emission regulations. He recalled having said "we don't wanna short clean air"—which translated into "we can't do both."

Iacocca made his most impassioned plea to Nixon about rising costs, citing inflation, pollution control costs, and safety regulations as key factors. "We're not only frustrated, we've reached the despair point. We don't know what to do anymore. Except we're booking numbers. . . . And I would predict to you that our Pinto will be closer to three thousand dollars in '75 than it is to two thousand now." If the Japanese weren't deterred at 3,000-dollar Pintos, then "the ball game's over." America's viable auto industry would be made into "a sick industry."

The Pinto was then doing fairly well. "The reason we've underpriced General Motors by a hundred and fifty," he explained, was that Ford decided to make all of its transmissions, axles, and engines entirely overseas. "So we have the benefit of low-cost components. Now we're bringing 'em in at nineteen-nineteen." Still, the Germans were beating them with their little VW bug. "Volkswagen is sold out. You can't get one. You've got to wait in line for one."

But the Japanese were making inroads as well, Iacocca reported, "underpricing us a hundred, too."

"With what?" Nixon asked. "With their Toyotas?"

Yes, replied Iacocca, "Toyotas, Datsuns." Then he went into his Japanese-threat rant, noting that most US radios were now from Japan, implying that cars might be next. "Well, it can't happen here, I keep saying to myself," said Iacocca. "We're up to 15 percent foreign cars when we've given them our best shot at nineteen-nineteen [per] Pinto, using German componentry to do that. . . . On the West Coast . . . year to date, about twenty-seven percent of all cars are foreign. In Vancouver, it's up to fifty; Toyota outsold all Ford products in Vancouver."

"[W]e're in a downhill slide," said Iacocca later in the conversation, "the likes of which we have never seen in our business. And the Japs are in the wings ready to eat us up alive. So I'm in a position to be saying [to the regulators, DOT in this case], 'Would you guys cool it a little bit? You're gonna break us.'" Regulation, coupled with inflation, explained Iacocca, were "the load that's breaking our back. . . . [W]e are now projecting price increases between 50 and 53 percent. I can almost predict this fall's price increase for you. And the fall of '72, because of emissions and safety and inflation . . ."

Iacocca and Ford were after regulatory relief on safety, and Nixon made no commitments, but he did acknowledge there might be ways for senior economic advisors—then Pete Peterson and Paul McCracken—to be aware of "how decisions we make may make our [auto] industry noncompetitive with the Japs." Nixon also acknowledged that the addition of "these damn gadgets" might be a problem for the industry. John Ehrlichman added that the Department of Commerce might be used on behalf of the industry point of view on "the environment thing" as "sort of counterweight."

The meeting ended with some casual conversation on the issues, with Nixon appearing to ask about the industry's trade group, and at one point why "the whole industry don't stick together on this . . . Dodge, GM, Ford . . . Chrysler . . ." (transcript has omissions at this point, and "this" is not clearly identified). "[W]hile one [company] may be able to do it," says Nixon, "the problems of all [the companies] are really involved here. . . ." Nixon and Erhlichman appear to huddle briefly to discuss follow-ups intended for selected advisors and cabinet officers mentioned in the meeting. "I will not judge it until I hear the other side," says Nixon. Ford and Iacocca thank the president for the meeting.[58]

## THE FIGHT BEGINS

The AMA, meanwhile, had already begun the formal process of challenging EPA's first actions under the new Clean Air Act. In January 1971, EPA published notice of its proposed ambient air quality standards for hydrocarbons, carbon monoxide, nitrogen dioxide, and oxidants. The standards, while not directly affecting automobile engines, would nonetheless guide state and local governments in their pollution control activities and transportation planning to protect public health, potentially affecting car use and car sales. The AMA filed ninety-two pages of comments. "On the basis of available evidence," charged the AMA in part, "the proposed ambient air quality standards for hydrocarbons, carbon monoxide, nitrogen dioxide and oxidants are disproportionate to any demonstrated health or safety need...."[59] This is a drumbeat that would continue for the next thirty years under various guises.

Individually, the automakers would also begin to mount their own company campaigns attacking the new law. By October 1972, for example, General Motors had released a report entitled *Study on the Environment*, which concluded that the pressure on Congress to pass the Clean Air Act of 1970 was the result of twenty years of faulty print and broadcast reporting on air pollution. GM fully expected this "public misperception" would change, however. First, the public would discover that air pollution had reached its peak and realize that automotive pollution, in particular, "is not significant in many localities." This change would come about, in part, "because of the effect of automotive industry public information programs...." There would also be "penalties in reduced driveability and increased fuel consumption" with the installation and use of emissions control systems—penalties, according to GM, the public "will not willingly accept." Further, with the exception of those localities where automotive air pollution "is considered a serious problem, there probably will be an adverse reaction to the cost of such control systems."[60]

Both AMA's regulatory comments and GM's study were typical of the posture and tactics the auto industry would employ for the next thirty years, picking away at rules and regulations at every turn, mounting public disinformation campaigns, filing petitions and appeals, and going to the courts and Congress to overturn or change the law in any way it could.

# 5

## Attack & Delay

... "Ninety-three was the first model year we ever built a model certified to seventy-five standards."

—*Sam Leonard, General Motors.*[1]

It was April 1972, and William "Bill" Ruckelshaus, the newly appointed administrator of the US Environmental Protection Agency (EPA), was on the hot seat. The thirty-nine-year-old Ruckelshaus, an Indiana attorney who had served briefly in the Nixon Justice Department, was now presiding over what would become one of EPA's first major decisions: whether to grant the auto industry a one-year extension of deadlines under the Clean Air Act.

The battle over this issue—and it was a battle, undertaken amidst a feisty new environmental politics in the full glare of the electronic media—began during three weeks of public hearings in Washington at an undistinguished Department of Commerce auditorium. To an unsuspecting tourist who may have wandered into these proceedings it may have seemed like ordinary business—"just a bunch of bureaucrats talking." But for those wrapped up in this little corner of national governance—lobbyists, scientists, government officials, congressional staff, and press—it was the political equivalent of High Noon. On one side, eager to make its mark, was the EPA, the new federal agency. On the other, some of the world's largest and most determined industrial powers, and namely, the Big Three automakers: General Motors, Ford, and Chrysler.

Each day at the hearings, the witnesses were asked to stand and be sworn in. The stakes were high. EPA's credibility, the wisdom of Congress, and to some degree, the future of environmental lawmaking were on the line for the government. At issue for the automakers was their economic power, wielding hundreds of thousands of jobs and risking millions in capital investment. In the middle was Bill Ruckelshaus, soon to be thrust into the national spotlight as one of the "good guys" in the otherwise bleak Watergate fiasco. But for the next year or so, it would be automobiles and air pollution that would consume his attention.

### INDIANA REPUBLICAN

Bill Ruckelshaus was an Indiana Republican who had made a run for the US Senate in 1968, but was soundly beaten by incumbent Democrat Birch Bayh. Educated at Princeton and Harvard, Ruckelshaus had worked as an assistant attorney general for Indiana and had prosecuted a few industrial polluters there. Beyond that, he had no special training in environmental science. After Nixon was elected, Ruckelshaus made his way to the Justice Department in Washington, where he worked as assistant attorney general. When the search was opened to find an administrator for EPA, his name was put forward by friendly White House staff. In the nomination process, Ruckelshaus received key support from Attorney General John Mitchell, who had been impressed by his work at Justice. Once at EPA, Ruckelshaus was required by the 1970 Clean Air Act to take on the auto emissions deadline decision. But as he did, he was walking into a widening chasm between the automakers and the federal government that had been developing practically since the day the Clean Air Act of 1970 was signed into law.

## POLITICAL MANEUVERING

Each of the automakers had petitioned EPA for the one-year extension by February 1972. But the maneuvering by industry and the Nixon administration to delay the auto standards had been going on for months leading up to EPA's hearings. In January 1972, President Nixon's "western White House" in San Clemente, California, was used to host a two-day, invitation-only gathering on the Clean Air Act. The closed-door session was attended by fifty-five representatives from industry, government, and the scientific community, and concluded, among other things, that "amendments should be sought to the Clean Air Act."[2] The White House Science Office, issuing its own report, concluded the act's auto emission standards were too stringent and would add $755 to the retail price of the average car. The National Academy of Sciences (NAS), reporting on the auto emissions standards as required by Congress, found that most of the automakers could comply with the standards, but the cost would be high. NAS recommended extending the act's deadline to allow the automakers time to improve their cars' performance.

On Capitol Hill, meanwhile, Senator Thomas Eagleton, conducting hearings in March 1972, became frustrated listening to industry witnesses and scientists explain why the act wouldn't work. "I am concerned that too large a portion of the scientific community lines up with industry and tells us that while dirty air is technologically feasible, clean air may not be either technologically feasible or cost effective, and that we must have dirty air and the health problems it brings as a price of our technological progress." Eagleton also took aim at the industry-administration gathering in San Clemente and what he saw as an orchestration of Clean Air Act criticism. "Since that meeting," he said, "we have been virtually inundated with industry and administration pronouncements against the clean air effort."[3]

GM's vice president for environmental affairs, Ernest S. Starkman, told Eagleton, "We sincerely believe that more time is required. . . . The very stringent levels prescribed . . . do not appear to be warranted, either to protect health, prevent plant damage, or to provide aesthetic quality of the air in even the most severely stressed communities of this nation."* Others who testified, however, took a somewhat different view. John G. Harlan, Jr. of Engelhard Industries, one of the major catalyst makers, stated, "It is my firm belief that current efforts to meet the 1975 standards will be successful provided development programs which are now in high gear throughout the industry are not permitted to slacken. . . . It should be realized that the millions of automobiles produced in 1975 will be on the roads of this nation for an average of at least ten years. A postponement of the 1975 standards means a postponement for ten years for all the cars produced in 1975.[4]

Soon, the action shifted to the scheduled main event: the showdown between EPA and Detroit's big automakers.

## THE RUCKELSHAUS HEARINGS

In making his decision on whether or not to grant the one-year extension requested by the automakers, Bill Ruckelshaus would listen to a parade of witnesses on all sides of the question and weigh the facts. EPA was, afterall, an independent federal agency—and a new one at that. But before Ruckelshaus made the final call, he also had to make three special findings, specified in the 1970 Clean Air Act: that an extension was essential to the public interest; that the companies asking for the extension were making a "good faith effort" to meet the law; and finally, that the technology to do the job was not available.

John Quarles, then deputy EPA administrator and one of Ruckelshaus' right-hand men at the auto standards hearings, remembers the setting. "On Monday, April 10, public hearings opened in the auditorium at the Department of Commerce. . . . It was not much different from a typical high school auditorium, with a raised stage . . . and a sloping floor with rows of several hundred theater seats. Most of the seats were filled and the stage was bathed in the glare of floodlights. Two long tables were placed at angles to each other facing out toward the audience, one for the six-man

---

* GM, in fact, would release a report of its own in October 1972 entitled *Study on the Environment*, which concluded that the pressure on Congress to pass the Clean Air Act of 1970 was the result of twenty years of faulty print and broadcast reporting on air pollution. GM fully expected this "public misperception" would change, however. First, the public would discover that air pollution had reached its peak and realize that automotive pollution, in particular, "is not significant in many localities." This change would come about, in part, "because of the effect of automotive industry public information programs. . . ." There would also be "penalties in reduced driveability and increased fuel consumption" with the use of emissions control systems—penalties, according to GM, the public "will not willingly accept." Further, with the exception of those localities where automotive air pollution "is considered a serious problem, there probably will be an adverse reaction to the cost of such control systems." Indeed, if GM's "public information programs" had anything to do with it, there most certainly would be such a reaction.

EPA panel, the other for the witnesses. . . . At ten o'clock, Bill Ruckelshaus began to read his introductory statement, looking up into the television cameras. . . . The hearing schedule was jammed with a variety of witnesses—forty-four in all—selected to cover every side of the problem. . . ."[5]

Going ahead with the 1975 deadline would essentially mean equipping cars with catalytic converters, since the automakers hadn't made much progress on alternative engines or other devices. The EPA hearings, in fact, became a mini-debate between the automakers and the catalyst makers over the state of the technology. "The auto companies said that catalysts were plagued by problems," says Quarles, recounting the testimony. "The catalyst companies replied that the problems had been solved." The automakers also said the catalysts might burn up or cause safety problems. In fact, at one point during the hearings, Chrysler's Charles Heinen "presented a melted down hunk of metal as evidence" of the catalyst's alleged safety threat. There was also criticism about the automaker's murky test data submitted to EPA, some of which failed to identify which model of catalyst had been used or why failures had occurred. Argument also ensued about the auto companies' lack of promptness in testing improved models as soon as the catalyst makers had developed them. But as the hearings unfolded, some catalyst makers believed they had the edge.[6] "We think we can do it, and I think the guys up there [Ruckelshaus and the EPA panel] are beginning to get the feeling it can be done too," said Joe Povey, representing catalyst maker Matthey Bishop, Inc.[7]

"[I]t became apparent," says John Quarles, relaying the views of the EPA officials after the first few days of hearings and technical briefings, "that the auto companies were much closer to achieving the 1975 standards than we had supposed. At that point we realized that we might deny the [auto companies'] applications. . . ."[8]

Three weeks later, a turning point came, which John Quarles attributes to the testimony of a young attorney for the Natural Resources Defense Council (NRDC), David Hawkins. "[H]is clear analysis established the perspective that controlled the final decision," says Quarles. "If EPA were to grant a suspension on the record that had been established, [Hawkins] argued, it would demolish the ability of the agency at any later time to insist that industry push itself harder to satisfy the pollution control requirements."

Hawkins was one of a new breed of environmentalists; a former high school teacher who had become an activist and litigator in an era when environmental activism would increasingly turn on knowledge of the law and how to wield it for the public's advantage. Another activist at that time—who with Hawkins played a determined role in holding up the public interest side of the ledger during the long auto emissions debate—was Clarence Ditlow. Ditlow, a Lehigh University engineer and Harvard lawyer, had come to Washington to work with Ralph Nader. He first worked on the auto pollution issue with Nader's US Public Interest Research Group (PIRG), but would later head up the Nader-founded Center for Auto Safety (CAS). During the EPA hearings, Ditlow and Hawkins became important unofficial adjuncts to the investigation, attending the sessions every day and feeding questions to EPA staff for the parade of witnesses that gave testimony.

## RUCKELSHAUS DECIDES

As the hearings neared their conclusion, Ruckelshaus appeared to be leaning towards a denial of the automaker's request to extend the deadline. He seemed to be swayed in part by the progress that was being made on the catalytic converter and other devices. Ruckelshaus would later tell Senator Muskie, "The evidence now available in my judgement clearly establishes that catalysts are both safe and highly effective in reducing emissions."[9] Privately, however, in the midst of weighing the pros and cons, Ruckelshaus went off to enlist the support of the White House to support him if he turned down the automakers' request. He then held a Saturday morning meeting with his key staff—Quarles, George Allen, and Robert Fri. The decision was made: a denial would be issued. John Quarles recounts the politically charged May 12 press conference announcing the decision and its aftermath.

> The large conference room was packed. . . . Ruckelshaus approached the podium jammed with microphones. . . . He reviewed the statutory and technical background . . . [and] all the analyses made by the agency. . . . He read on . . . : "My judgement . . . is that these manufacturers have not established that present control technology is not available to meet the Act's requirement for 1975 cars." Across the room, the tension broke. Someone in the back began applauding. With surprised expressions, the newsmen exchanged glances. Ruckelshaus kept reading: "I want to stress that the issue is a close one. . . ."
>
> The decision had an instantaneous effect on the employees of EPA. A sense of jubilation rippled through the ranks. Employees took the decision as confirmation of the agency's strength and integrity. I rode back from the press conference to EPA with three members of the staff. . . . One of the secretaries put it simply, "I feel proud of our agency. I think we stood up to the auto companies and did what was right."
>
> The decision demonstrated the [EPA's] capacity to make an independent appraisal of the facts. . . . The enormous stakes made this a test of the agency's stature . . . and gave it a far-reaching effect. The significance of EPA's strict handling of the auto industry was not lost on the rest of American business. On this account alone the auto decision was a significant event in the history of the environmental movement.
>
> . . . The announcement was fully covered on the evening newscasts. It was also widely reported on the front pages of the papers the following morning and was applauded in editorials around the country. Everywhere the decision was hailed as a victory for the environment and a triumph for the public welfare over the special interests of industry.[10]

Three weeks after Ruckelshaus made his decision, however, the auto companies appealed. In December 1972, the appellate court sent the issue back to Ruckelshaus, directing him to consider an NAS report that had questioned whether catalyst technology could be perfected and implemented in the available time frame. Ten days later, Ruckelshaus reaffirmed his earlier decision, saying his conclusion was consistent with the NAS findings. The automakers went back to court again, this time asking for a court-ordered extension. The court refused to order an extension, but in February 1973 did order Ruckelshaus to conduct another round of hearings on the technology and assume the burden of proof in denying the automakers' request.

### "BUSINESS CATASTROPHE"

On the first day of the new hearings, on March 12, 1973, GM's Ernie S. Starkman painted a grim economic picture if the extension was not granted.

> [I]f GM is forced to introduce catalytic converter systems across the board on 1975 models, the prospect of unreasonable risk of business catastrophe and massive difficulties with these vehicles in the hands of the public may be faced.
>
> It is conceivable that complete stoppage of the entire production could occur, with the obvious tremendous loss to the company, shareholders, employees, suppliers, and communities. Short of that ultimate risk, there is a distinct possibility of varying degrees of interruption, with sizeable dislocations.[11]

A week later, in sharp contrast to GM's dire warnings, was the testimony of Hideo Sugiura, director of the Honda Motor Company, who declared that his company had developed cars with a cleaner engine capable of meeting the federal standards. Honda was ready to export 250,000 such cars for sale in the United States in 1975. The cars used a piston engine known as the stratified-charge engine and would meet the emissions standards without a catalytic converter. A report from the National Academy of Sciences' Committee on Motor Vehicle Emissions had called the Honda engine the "most promising" of the new emission control technologies.[12]

Nevertheless, on April 11, 1973, Ruckelshaus granted Detroit the one-year delay, noting at a crowded news conference that the postponement was issued to avoid the "potential societal disruptions" the automakers said would result if the pollution control equipment was required on all 1975 model cars. Instead, Ruckelshaus set interim standards for 1975—both for California and the rest of the nation. Those standards, compared to uncontrolled (pre-1968) and 1970 Clean Air Act levels, were as follows:

|  | Hydrocarbons | Carbon Monoxide |
| --- | --- | --- |
| Uncontrolled (pre-1968) | 8.7 GPM | 87.0 GPM |
| 1970 Act | .41 | 3.4 |
| National interim | 1.50 | 15.0 |
| California interim | .90 | 9.0 |

The Big Three at the time, although savoring victory on EPA's giving ground on its first major auto industry ruling, were still unhappy with the outcome, especially

## "Someone Is Lying"

On September 22, 1972 at the Chrysler building in Highland Park, Michigan, a meeting was being held in the office of Rinehart Bright, Chrysler VP for Product Development and Purchasing. There were five or six people present but the principals were Bright and Robert S. Leventhal, executive vice president of Engelhard Industries, a New Jersey manufacturer of catalysts. The subject of the meeting was a contract for catalysts Engelhard was expecting to receive from Chrysler. However, that morning, by way of the *Wall Street Journal*, Leventhal had learned that Universal Oil Products (UOP), a competitor, had received the contract. Leventhal was stunned, as his company had been working with Chrysler testing the catalysts. While there were still some bugs in the technology, Engelhard's catalyst was believed to be superior to UOP's, which had less testing. Jumping on a plane with colleague Carl Keith, Leventhal wanted to know first-hand from Chrysler what had gone wrong.

At the meeting in Bright's office, Leventhal asked if Engelhard had been eliminated from the business. Bright said yes, pointing to factors such as Engelhard's inflexibility and high price. But "above all," said Leventhal, later recounting and reciting Bright's reasons for giving UOP the contract, was that "Engelhard was just too aggressive in its testimony at the EPA hearings." At the Chrysler meeting, however, Leventhal kept his cool and remained courteous, reiterating Engelhard's willingness to negotiate over price and other matters. As the meeting ended, Bright held out the possibility that Engelhard might still have a chance for "50 percent of the business." Leventhal followed up a few days later with a courteous letter acknowledging that possibility, inviting Chrysler officials to inspect Engelhard's operation. But Engelhard would obtain no business from Chrysler, neither then nor in the future. The automaker was playing hardball.

Chrysler's decision to penalize Engelhard—normally a private contract matter that would never surface publicly—became a matter of some public controversy during EPA's March 1973 hearings. Normally, if Chrysler wanted to use its business leverage to punish Engelhard, that was its prerogative. In the nuance of the Clean Air Act, however, there was a legal requirement that brought the incident forward. Before EPA's Ruckelshaus could grant an extension to any automaker, he was obligated to make a finding that "a good faith effort" had been made by the automaker to meet the 1975 standards. The charge that Chrysler had dumped Engelhard for political reasons came up only through the technical-legal context: was Chrysler doing all that it could to obtain the best available technology to meet the standards. It became such a serious matter, in fact, that two additional days of hearings were held and six volumes of documents were subpoenaed. At the hearings, both Bright and Leventhal testified. Bright denied he had made the statement attributed to him. Leventhal stood by his memorandum. However, still in the running for future Chrysler business, Leventhal downplayed the incident, saying that Bright was just "blowing off steam." Leventhal would later tell Carl Keith and reiterate to EPA officials what he thought Chrysler was doing: "Before giving us the business, they [Chrysler] wanted to give us the business—and we took it." Still, the EPA hearings were deadly serious, and those who testified did so under oath. A set of leaked, handwritten notes on the meeting surfaced that did not jibe with Chrysler's official written account. One EPA official commented at the time, "It is clear that someone is lying in the Chrysler–Engelhard dispute." Even Ruckelshaus stated, "If we should decide that somebody perjured themselves . . . then we would of course refer that to the Justice Department."

In the end, Ruckelshaus could not find bad faith on Chrysler's part, given conflicting testimony. But he left no doubt what he thought about the whole affair, in effect condemning Chrysler without exactly saying so:

"The record does not support a determination as to whether or not Chrysler's decision against purchasing catalysts from Engelhard was materially influenced by antagonism aroused by the testimony of Engelhard. . . . I am particularly disturbed by this question because of a possible conflict in the testimony under oath by representatives of Engelhard and Chrysler. . . .

" . . . If I were forced to choose between one or the other of these versions, the one put forward by Mr. Leventhal . . . would seem more probable. One salient fact inclining me to that view is that the handwritten notes from which the official Chrysler minutes of the meeting were prepared indicate that Mr. Bright of Chrysler made a statement similar to the one which both Engelhard representatives present at the meeting testified he made.

"On such a record, the gravest questions as to Chrysler's compliance with the statutory requirements arise. But a determination that they have not been met cannot be lightly made. . . .

" . . . I conclude with serious reservations that the statutory requirements concerning good faith have been met. In reaching this conclusion, I am placing decisive reliance upon the consideration that the sanction that arises from a negative finding . . . could force that manufacturer to close down in 1975. Such a result would not only create extreme hardship for large numbers of innocent employees . . . but would also severely impact numerous suppliers . . . and ultimately the public at large. Thus, despite the very serious questions I have concerning the record as it relates to Chrysler . . . I do not believe that Congress intended me to make a finding of bad faith in the absence of a very high degree of certainty that acts of a particular manufacturer require such a finding. . . ."

the California standards.[13] GM issued a statement saying the company was "disappointed and dismayed" by the EPA action. Yet, within two months of the decision granting the delay, GM announced it would install catalysts across the board on all models, despite its earlier warnings of "business catastrophe" and shutdown scenarios. But the automakers weren't finished with the Clean Air Act.

## BROADER ATTACK

Having managed to get a one-year extension from EPA, there was still the matter of the standards themselves, which industry wanted to weaken, if not dismantle. Chrysler, which had already attacked the act with newspaper ads, also issued a booklet entitled, *Let's Have Clean Air—But Let's Not Throw Money Away*. The booklet was distributed by the thousands in early 1973. "Even if automotive engineers could meet the 1975-76 federal motor vehicle standards," said the company, "Chrysler ... would oppose them because they are wasteful, unnecessary and unrealistic. . . ." In addition to deferring the 1975 standard—which in Chrysler's view "would avoid investing millions in the next few months for control systems the country does not need"— Chrysler also proposed that Congress review the original Clean Air Act, "revoke the 1975-76 standards, and transfer to EPA [from Congress] authority for setting any new ... standards. . . ."[14] Industry typically preferred agency discretion over congressional specificity.

Lee Iacocca had already given Ford Motor's views on the standards and the act in a February 15, 1973 speech in New York.

> Despite the claims and counterclaims that pop up in the news from time to time, the simple fact is that nobody we've heard of yet in this highly competitive, one-upsmanship auto world has managed to produce that breakthrough device that could consistently achieve the '75 standards on a variety of production vehicles of different size, weight and power. . . .
>
>   As for the 1976 standards on nitrogen oxides—no way ... the goal isn't even really in sight.
>
>   ... Our inability to meet completely the arbitrary standards within the arbitrary time frame set by Congress is, fortunately, not even a small threat to the health and welfare of any of us. A lot of new information and data have become available since 1970 concerning atmospheric pollution. These new facts not only clarify the relationship between pollution and health, but also bring into question the feasibility and good sense of what has been a headlong, cost-be-damned approach to the problem. In short, they suggest that we may be out of our minds if we don't reexamine the criteria established by the 1970 Clean Air Amendments.[15]

Iacocca proposed that the 1975 standards be scrapped (except in California), and that less stringent standards be put in place until 1977 or later, pending further study. Such an approach would not require a "crash program" involving the installation of expensive catalytic converters.

## Muskie's Review

By April 1973, Senator Muskie convened a series of hearings to review the Ruckelshaus decision and also to learn what progress the automakers had made since the passage of the Clean Air Act.* Muskie opened the hearing by recounting some recent

* As he began his oversight in a new Congress, Muskie had to confront a new political dynamic as well. The Senate Public Works Committee had just gone through a major overhaul thanks to the 1972 elections. Suddenly, there was a new crop of senators on the key committee

history, especially earlier auto industry commitments to address the problem. He noted, for example, that in June 1964, industry officials generally supported emissions controls and establishing performance standards. They also recognized that some government surveillance would be necessary to monitor progress. In the mid-1960s, in fact, industry pledged that once the specifics of the problem were identified and well understood, it would "work unstintingly" on the problem "in the public interest."

The data were now in, said Muskie, some of it twenty years old: automotive air pollution was well-established fact. He also reminded his listeners that nearly a year prior to the 1970 Act, in late 1969 at a White House conference, industry had agreed that it could achieve clean-car goals, albeit by 1980. With the Clean Air Act, Muskie explained, Congress decided to accelerate the deadline, moving it up to 1975 to help clean up the air in the nation's cities. Then Muskie turned to the business at hand.

> Now, in 1973, we are told those [1975] deadlines cannot be met. In most cases the auto industry argues that they cannot produce and guarantee cars which comply with auto emission standards set forth in the law. And, they argue that even if they could, those standards are not necessary.
>
> I want to know why not. I want to know what the industry has done in the past three years. I want a public explanation from the industry for the course they have chosen, a course that has not been altered since 1969.[**]
>
> I want to know what the industry is going to do in the coming year to overcome past failures.
>
> I want to know what commitment the auto industry is willing to make to the American people. And I intend to challenge the assumptions on which the industry's failures have been based. . . .[16]

Senator Muskie was not alone in raising questions about the industry's progress and intentions. The *Wall Street Journal* editorial page added its voice, suggesting that the automakers' move to roll back the clean air standards after just receiving a one-year extension from EPA was not a good tack.

---

that would oversee the Clean Air Act. The Senate Public Works Committee now had a cast of nine new senators, outnumbering the five who remained from 1970. The new members included Lloyd Bensten (D-TX), Joe Biden (D-DE), Quentin Burdick (D-ND), Dick Clark, (D-IA), James McClure (R-ID), James Buckley (R-NY), Pete Domenici (R-NM), Robert Stafford (R-VT), and William L. Scott (D-VA). Only Muskie, Chairman Jennings Randolph (D-WV), Joseph Montoya (D-NM), Mike Gravel (D-AK), and Howard Baker (R-TN) remained from 1970.

** Arguably, industry had been on notice long before 1969. In fact, in one February 1967 exchange between Muskie and Thomas C. Mann, then president of the AMA, Mann said he considered the federal standards then in effect for 1968 models (weaker than the '70 standards, to be sure) to be reasonable and practical. But he also added that "a series of stated goals, projecting what will be required of the industry as far ahead as 1975 or 1980" would help the industry to focus its R & D on specific problems.

... Having been given a year's grace, the manufacturers above all else must demonstrate good faith. They can not do so by swarming over Capitol Hill, taking full-page advertisements, and having vice presidents fan out over the countryside making speeches denouncing the standards. We would suggest they leave that issue to Mr. Ruckelshaus's EPA technicians, perhaps the National Academy of Sciences, and Congress.

Detroit would strike a more positive posture by squarely confronting the questions raised by Sen. Muskie: What is the industry willing to commit itself to do? When will it commit itself to do it? And what guarantees is it willing to give the public?

The automakers, afterall, are in no position to make credible presentations on the nation's health requirements. They should not even try. It is only when the public sense the manufacturers have accepted public policy, as good citizens, and have pulled out all the stops in an attempt to meet it, that they will have public support should they stumble. . . .[17]

Instead, some of the automakers, such as Chrysler, had blasted the Clean Air Act with full-page newspaper ads, like one placed in the *New York Times*. "The fact is," said Chrysler in its ad, "with the reductions already achieved, there is no scientific evidence showing a threat to health from automotive emissions in the normal, average air you breathe. Not even in crowded cities." Muskie, for one, was furious with the ad's suggestion that the federal health standards were somehow arbitrarily concocted:

... May I say that neither this subcommittee, nor the full committee, nor the Congress is interested in any way in picking a health standard out of the air and laying it down as an impossible challenge for the American automobile industry. We are not scientists. We are not doctors. We are not the Public Health Service.

We believed in 1970, and we believe today, that we have a right to rely upon the professional advice of the nation's doctors and the Public Health Service to lay down the standard that we have a right to require. . . . That is what we have done. That is what we will continue to do.

... [W]e are aware of the dispute; of the fact that there will never be full agreement, especially from the automobile industry, the industry to be regulated, as to what the facts are. But we also agree from the evidence ... that we have never overstated the health effects or the public health and welfare effects of pollutants.

We found it to be true that as our information is enlarged, as it becomes more refined, our estimates of damage have been underestimated rather than overestimated in the past. That doesn't lead us to conclude that overestimation may not at some time be the result of any basis we lay down. But that has not been our experience.

I am really using this ... because I think it is critical to the challenge the industry has laid down to the Congress. Industry has made no secret of its intention to try to change this law. In response to that I say to them and to the American people, we are not interested in laying down an arbitrary standard nor will we. But we will rely, as we think we have a right to rely, upon the advice of that scientific community which is paid to serve the Government of the United States, the people of the United States, and the Congress of the United States on this subject.

*This Chrysler ad, which challenged the need for the auto emissions standards under the 1970 Clean Air Act, brought an angry reaction from Senator Ed Muskie."*

We will not be panicked by such advertisements as that to which I have referred
.... We recognize the importance of this issue. ... It is our intention to fully exam-
ine it as this year goes on. ...[18]

Muskie and his committee mainly questioned Ruckelshaus on his decision to grant
the one-year extension and to review some of the technological choices the automakers had while they considered how to meet the standards. Of some interest to Muskie
and other members at the time was why the American automakers seemed to have
cast their lot with the catalytic converter while three foreign automakers—Honda,
Mazda, and Mercedes Benz—had already met the 1975 standards using alternative
engine designs—Honda using the stratified charge engine, Mazda using a Wankel
rotary engine, and Mercedes using a diesel (all internal combustion engines).
Muskie remarked that he did not think the American auto industry had made a
"good faith effort" to explore the feasibility of a diesel or stratified charge engine,
particularly since the industry had known of those alternatives since 1964.[19]

## BIG THREE RESPOND

A few weeks later, in early May, the automakers had their turn in Congress, each
reporting that EPA's current one-year extension wasn't enough, and that they needed
more time. The main contribution of the extension, said Lee Iacocca, was to "keep
us in business for another year."

"It most certainly did not give us an additional year in which we could concentrate our full resources on efforts to meet the statutory standards," he said. "On the
contrary, the EPA Administrator established a new set of stringent deadlines for
1975 that will challenge our abilities and strain our resources to the fullest, up to and
beyond the beginning of 1975 model production." Iacocca called for an additional
one year of delay in meeting the standards generally and for a less stringent NOx
standard, which he asked to be reevaluated. "We simply don't know how to meet it
either," he said, referring to the NOx standard, adding that NOx controls would
also exact "a stiff penalty in fuel consumption." NOx controls would also "work against
efforts to control the other two pollutants (HC and CO)." Ford Motor, he explained,
had spent all of its time modifying the internal combustion engine to meet the 1975
HC and CO standards—"we had absolutely no choice" given "the little time allowed
us by the law." Muskie countered that the automakers knew as early as 1969 that
stringent auto emissions standards would be put into effect.[20]

A week later, Ed Cole, appearing before Muskie on May 30, 1973, also attacked
the 1976 statutory limits for HC and CO, calling them "more stringent than intended."
He asked Congress to commission a reexamination of the regulations. He also charged
that EPA's deadline extension had not given GM the relief it sought. GM too, had
focused on the catalytic converter, he said, because it was "the best choice of available alternatives at this time from the standpoint of emissions control, durability,
low maintenance, fuel economy, driveability, and cost to the consumer." He added

that none of the potential alternative engines satisfied all of these requirements and, at the same time, had realistic prospects to meet all the 1975 and 1976 standards. GM had a few experimental models at the time that could meet the prescribed 1975 emission control levels—some for the specified durability periods. "However," said Cole, "we could not assure that each of the 4.5-to-5-million cars we mass-produce each year would do that for the required 50,000 miles or five years." Cole also wanted a review of the NOx standards, saying "we do not yet know adequate technology for meeting all the requirements of this standard" for mass-produced vehicles.[21]

By this time, Muskie's subcommittee and Congress as a whole were receiving mail on the auto emissions issue. But the messages coming in, according to Richard A. Hellman, then minority counsel to the subcommittee, was dominated by "form letters from Dodge dealers and other industry-generated mail."[22]

## Ford's Road Show

Ford Motor Co. had also begun a public relations campaign in the spring of 1973 aimed at bringing grassroots pressure on Congress to change the Clean Air Act. The campaign—which eventually traveled to at least thirty-seven cities—included press briefings, luncheons, and speeches by Ford executives who were critical of the Clean Air Act and its auto emissions standards. Ford executives criss-crossed the country delivering the message—from Fargo, North Dakota to Jacksonville, Florida; Norfolk, Virginia to Seattle, Washington. The aim of the campaign was to raise "honest doubts" about the law in the visited communities so that members of Congress would react to their constituents' concerns "back home," and reexamine the law. "I think we are going to get a gradual public questioning of the statutory provisions and that is all we ask," explained Ford's Will Scott, vice president for governmental affairs and planning.[23]

"Carrying the company's case to the constituents are about eight of its second and third echelon executives," wrote Tom Kleene in the *Akron Beacon Journal* describing the Ford program in Cincinnati, Pittsburgh, and Detroit. "For two months, they have been taking off in a company plane several times weekly to spread their message through meetings with the so-called thought leaders of local communities." The session typically included a Ford speech, luncheon, and discussion period for local educators, business leaders, and heads of civic associations, which numbered anywhere from 80 to 230 people. In some cases, though, Ford would hear from defenders of the law as well.

In Pittsburgh, for example, local citizens from GASP—Group Against Smog Pollution—asked quite bluntly, "If America can put a man on the moon, why can't you eliminate the pollutants from a car's exhaust?" And, "If the Japanese can produce cars that meet the standards, why can't you?" In Cincinnati, a group of professors challenged Ford on whether it was meeting its social responsibilities, building so many cars when the nation's real need lay in better mass transit systems. Why couldn't Ford produce mass transit vehicles, they asked?[24]

## JOHN DELOREAN

In the early 1970s, John DeLorean was a General Motors wunderkind. He ran the Pontiac Division in the late 1960s, leading it to record sales. He then managed GM's troubled Chevrolet Division and led it to a stunning turnaround. By 1971 he appeared on the cover of *Business Week,* and the following year, *Automotive Industries.* By 1973, he moved to the coveted 14th floor at GM headquarters, becoming a corporate vice president responsible for the entire North American division. John DeLorean was a rising star, on track to run the company. He was forty-eight, earned more than $600,000 a year, and held more GM turf than his peer Roger Smith, who would later become GM's chairman.

But John DeLorean was not exactly fitting in at GM. He was, in fact, the Joe Namath of the automotive industry; a guy with plenty of ability but a style that grated on the conservative, button-down ways of the industrial heartland. Higher-ups in the company would occasionally admonish him for not being focused on the needs of the corporation. Others complained about DeLorean's lifestyle—his hair, his cowboy boots, his women.

DeLorean, however, had begun his own critique of GM and the auto industry from the inside. "My concern was that there hadn't been an important product innovation in the industry since the automatic transmission and power steering in 1949," he would later write. In place of product innovation, DeLorean charged, the industry "went on a two-decade marketing binge which generally offered up the same old product under the guise of something new and useful." Year in and year out, he said, "we were urging Americans to sell their cars and buy new ones," but the only change was in style, or as he put it, "the new wrinkles in the sheet metal. . . ." DeLorean would also reveal poor quality in GM's cars and trucks, charging in 1972 that GM was spending $500 million annually in warranty repairs—a huge sum in the early 1970s.

"Soon, I found myself questioning the bigger picture, the morality of the whole GM system," he wrote. "The undue emphasis on profits and cost control without a wide concern for the effects of GM's business on its many publics . . ." Men of otherwise sound, personal morality, and responsibility, DeLorean would write, were as a group, making business decisions "which were irresponsible and of questionable morality."

By December 1972, sensing that he was on his way out, DeLorean wrote a nineteen-page single-spaced memo to his boss and former supporter Thomas Murphy, which recounted, in DeLorean's view, GM's failings and poor record on safety and pollution control. One small portion of that memo read " . . . In no instance, to my knowledge, has GM ever sold a car that was substantially more pollution-free than the law demanded—even when we had the technology. As a matter of fact, because the California laws were tougher, we sold "cleaner" cars there and "dirtier" cars throughout the rest of the nation."

"This approach of just doing the bare bones minimum to just scrape by the pollution law when GM could do much better by spending a few dollars is not socially responsible. With our virtual monopoly position in the industry we also, in effect, control our competitors—who would be economically devastated if they tried to do better socially but at a greater product cost.

"We of Chevrolet proposed to the EPG [Engineering Policy Group] that we make our cars cleaner than the law demanded—we were told that the other divisions did not need a $15.00 air pump to meet the law—we were told to take it off our cars. Our next proposal was to have all optional engines exceed the law (do the best we knew) since the customer would pay the extra cost anyhow—once again we were not permitted to do so for fear we would lose a few sales. . . .

"...Our corporation has lost credibility with the public and the government because each new emissions standard has been greeted by our management's immediate cries of 'impossible,' 'prohibitively expensive,' 'not economically responsible'—usually before we even knew what it involved. The remarkable thing is that with all of our resources and the amount we tell the government we are spending on emissions research that most of the significant developments in this field have come from someone else—for example, our first answer, the "Clean Air Package," was developed by a handful of engineers at Chrysler, the manifold reactor which meets the 1975 standard now (and should be in production) was developed by Du Pont with less than 10% of our facilities and manpower. The other 1975 answer, the catalytic converter with EGR, was developed by a small grant given by Ford, several oil companies and several Japanese manufacturers. Not a very good record for a corporation that professes to be vitally interested in emissions. When we tell government about our large expenditures for emissions controls we don't bother to tell them that very little is being spent on R and D and that most of our money is spent on adapting hardware to our wide variety of engines."

Murphy gave the memo back to DeLorean without any response or comment. In January 1973, after seventeen years of making his way to the top of the auto game, John DeLorean resigned from General Motors. He later founded an auto company of his own in Ireland—the Delorean Motor Co.—which produced a gull-wing sports car in 1978, but later went bankrupt. DeLorean's 1979 book on GM's inner workings, *On a Clear Day You Can See General Motors*, written with former *Business Week* Detroit bureau chief J. Patrick Wright, revealed a laundry list of GM misdoings—from industrial espionage and misleading advertising campaigns to attempted destruction of evidence of safety complaints from former Corvair owners. Hobart Rowan of the *Washington Post* called the book "a stunning account of the venality, narrow-mindedness- yes, even immorality—of one big American business."

In Portland, Oregon, Ford put on the ritz for some 175 guests, including, inadvertently, one from the Oregon Student Public Interest Group, who reported back to US PIRG in Washington that Ford "came equipped with packaged film clips for the TVs," and in the previous week "had sent cakes to several of the Portland media." Ford also provided the luncheon—"complete with hard liquor, a violin serenade, French wine, a stack of cigars at each table, and best of all, a little card at each place listing Oregon's congressional delegation."[25]

In some of its executives' speeches, Ford mischaracterized the Clean Air Act requirements by stating that its provisions required greater reductions than those mandated; overstated emission reductions achieved by 1973 models; and suggested that the required reductions were unnecessary because "America's air is getting cleaner." Ford argued that as older cars were cleaned up and retired, the problem would be solved. But Ford and the other automakers consistently dodged the problem of increasing vehicle travel: each year more cars were being driven, on average, more miles, outpacing pollution control. In fact, because of this, EPA was projecting that by 1985 there would be at least twelve air quality regions across the country that would still fall below air quality levels needed to protect public health—even if the 1975-76 auto emission standards were met.

Yet Ford's Thomas J. Feaheny told his Portland audience in June 1973, "New technical information and data . . . suggest that Congress went overboard. . . ." and that "some studies suggest that the threat of CO to human health may not be a serious as was thought back in 1970." He also claimed that Ruckelshaus had called for changes in the law. It was true that Ruckelshaus had called for a reexamination of the NOx standard based on health effects studies. But at the time Ford was making its presentations around the country, EPA was looking at the possible need for a *tighter* NOx standard, not a weaker one.

Ford also hammered away at pocketbook issues, calling the emission standards "unrealistic and unnecessarily costly to car buyers." Yet EPA had data showing that many luxury and other options already installed on many automobiles cost more than emission control devices—even those needed for meeting the most stringent standards. Ford executives, however, kept spreading the gospel as they saw it throughout 1973. But soon, they had help from another quarter: cities and states facing the possibility of EPA transportation controls.

## RETRENCHMENT

When the Clean Air Act of 1970 was originally adopted, it set two basic categories of pollution sources: stationary sources, like factories and refineries, and mobile sources, meaning most cars and trucks. The act also set deadlines for these sources, requiring, for example, that by 1975, automobiles reduce certain pollutants by 90 percent below 1970 levels (subsequently extended to 1976 by Ruckelshaus). The Clean Air Act also set pollution standards and deadlines for states and urban areas: by May 1975 states with the most polluted cities were required to submit to EPA pollution control plans that specified how they intended to meet the standards by the 1975 deadline (which could be stretched out two additional years, to 1977, with the right showing of need). One major element of these plans for auto-plagued cities came to be known as "transportation controls"—meaning measures to manage, and in some cases, restrict auto traffic and parking, or also promote mass transit, in the interest of clean air. It soon became clear that transportation controls would be political dynamite. By June 1973, EPA was finding that at least thirty cities would have to face traffic restrictions of some kind to meet clean air standards by 1975-1977 time frame. New York City was told its taxis would have to stop cruising, northern New Jersey might have to curtail traffic by 60 percent, and Los Angeles might have to remove nearly all autos by 1977.

"What is going on here is an unusual government charade," wrote reporter Gladwin Hill in the *New York Times*. "Federal bureaucrats whose job is to administer laws . . . are obliquely saying three things: they are telling states with big-city automobile smog problems to get down to brass tacks with pollution control plans; they are telling citizens that the crunch has come when air pollution abatement requires not merely expenditures of money by also some changes in accustomed patterns of life; [and] they are telling Congress that the Clean Air Act . . . needs some revision, particularly in deadlines."

Back in Washington, all of the rising state and local concern over the possibility of traffic restrictions and other transportation controls to meet clean air goals started to add up as a political negative for the act. Muskie's own subcommittee colleagues were raising concerns about the standards and deadlines. By this time too, energy shortages were beginning to loom as a possibility, and some members such as Senator James McClure (R-ID), also on Muskie's subcommittee, were beginning to talk about the need to reexamine national environmental laws in light of future energy needs.

Fearing a wholesale onslaught of the Clean Air Act, Muskie and his subcommittee charted a middle ground. In late June 1973, he decided to have his subcommittee and staff begin a thorough reexamination of the act. He included a request to the NAS for "an objective evaluation and review of current data on health effects of those pollutants which are related to emissions from automobiles. . . ." Asked by a reporter to give the single most important factor for the subcommittee's review of the health standards at that time, Muskie's chief of staff Leon Billings said, "It was the concern among members . . . for some way to rationalize the conflicting testimony on whether [the standards] were valid. There was a crisis of confidence, generated by the auto firms—mostly Chrysler."[26]

But Muskie's call for a thorough review was seen by some as a way to forestall major changes, which the auto industry was pushing. "There is no question that this is a shield," said one subcommittee staff member of the reevaluation and NAS study. The move was seen as a way to prevent a stampede to rewrite the act. Muskie, meanwhile, expected the whole matter to come back to Congress in about one year's time. But soon, the Clean Air Act would come under pressure from another direction, as half a world away the flow of petroleum to the United States and other nations was about to be disrupted.

# 6

## Energy, Cars & Jobs

We can't even begin to talk about mandatory fuel economy until we get some action on relaxing emission standards.

—*Elliott Estes, president, General Motors, May 1975*

In mid-October 1973, Arab ministers of the Organization of Petroleum Exporting Countries (OPEC), a relatively unknown organization outside of the international oil business, made a decision that shook the world. OPEC—in control of the Persian Gulf's huge oil reserves and then producing a third of the world's oil—decided to stop the flow of its oil exports to the West. The Arabs were at war with Israel, but were losing ground and needed some leverage. Imposing an oil embargo on the West would be a swift way to get the world's attention and specifically hit the United States, a key supporter and military supplier of Israel. At the time, the United States was importing about one-third of its daily oil supply.

The Arab oil embargo caught most analysts by surprise. It caused nearly instant turmoil in the United States. Oil prices rose precipitously—from $2.90/bbl in September to $11.65 in December. Gasoline prices followed suit. Gas lines and hoarding became part of the American scene as people scrambled for fuel. By early November, President Nixon addressed the nation, offering a range of strategies and new energy programs, including Project Independence, a huge federal program aimed at expanding production at home—a program that would pose dire environmental consequences if implemented. On Capitol Hill, most of the focus initially was on fuel supplies for electric utilities, and how the nation might shift to coal. Environmental laws, including the Clean Air Act, would soon come under heavy attack.

In Detroit, meanwhile, some auto industry officials thought the energy crisis would pass, and that they would soon return to business as usual. Thomas Murphy, then GM's chairman, described the mood of the country as he saw it, ". . . I think people in this country felt, well, okay, they're [the Arabs] having their fun. But it was not a real serious concern. It was a concern about the fact that they were dictating to us

## "False and Misleading"

In mid-December 1973, just as the House of Representative was passing its version of emergency energy legislation, GM's Chevrolet division began running an advertisement in the *New York Times* and other newspapers and magazines nationally. The ad urged its readers to write Congress and the president to relax auto emissions controls to save energy. "In the present emergency," the ad claimed, "by relaxing these controls to 1969 standards, we could save 5 billion gallons of gas"—savings that might mean "a 25% increase in your own gas mileage." The ad also advised its readers that "the change in your car could be made in minutes and RIGHT NOW."

The ad, billed as "a public interest message from your Chevrolet Dealer," created a firestorm of protest at the highest levels of government, as Russell Train, EPA administrator, asked the Federal Trade Commission to investigate the "false and misleading" advertisement. "We believe that action by the FTC is important in this case of a special interest group attempting to pursue its own goals at the expense of a vulnerable public during this energy crisis." Train further charged that figures in the ad were "grossly inflated and misleading." EPA, in fact, sent out a mailing to some media and environmental outlets around the country with the agency's rebuttal to the ad. "You may have seen in your area newspaper advertisements by 'Your Chevrolet Dealer' advocating the removal of auto emissions control systems," said EPA in its packet. "This advertisement contains several false and misleading statements, as is pointed out in the attached materials. We are sending this information to you in the hope that you may find it helpful in countering these arguments which threaten our hard-fought progress toward a healthier, more enjoyable environment."

At the same time that the Chevrolet ad was running, Representative Louis C. Wyman (R-NH) offered an amendment on the House floor on December 14 to allow car owners to take antipollution devices off their cars except in areas where air pollution posed "a demonstrable and severe" hazard to public health. Wyman argued that his proposal was a "common sense" policy to follow "as long as the fuel emergency lasts." The measure failed by a 210 to 180 vote, with Wyman vowing to try again in 1974.

John Quarles, EPA's deputy administrator, singled out advertising like the Chevrolet ad, which could feed into efforts like that of Representative Wyman's. If Wyman's amendment had passed, said Quarles, it would have rolled back the whole federal state effort to clean up the nation's air. "The risk to the country [of such advertising] is most severe when a crisis comes along requiring immediate legislation," he said. "Then Congress must act hastily. And any false information that is widely publicized is not likely to be effectively challenged.

"In normal times," he continued, "false information would fail the test of time because the truth has a way of getting out. But when there is a near-panic atmosphere to enact legislation to meet a crisis, one big blast of false advertising could send this country down the wrong path with statutory requirements that are very hard to change."

EPA estimates indicated at the time that fuel loss resulting from emission controls devices was "on the average about 10 percent," as opposed to the 25 percent savings claimed in the Chevrolet ad. Even a calculation of 10 percent was generous, according to the agency, since fuel economy losses were not tied solely to emissions control equipment, but also to related engine modifications made by the automakers in accommodating emission controls. EPA figured at the time that only five percent of fuel loss would actually be recovered with the removal of emission controls from 1970-1974 automobiles.

"The only certain result from removing the emission controls from vehicles," said Russell Train, "would be a major increase of pollutants from automobiles."

and were raising the price of oil. But I think people felt it was a phase and we'll get it behind us."[1]

In Washington, the auto industry remained focused on the emissions issue, where the battle revolved around its immediate concerns with the interim standards, and longer term, the viability of the catalytic converter. In this context, some auto industry officials did use the "fuel penalty" in their arguments against quick adoption of the catalytic converter. Ford and others stated that the nitrogen oxide standards for 1976 would cause a penalty in mileage. Ford had found a 13 percent decline in average fuel economy in 1973 cars (GM, however, had found a fuel savings).

In the Senate, the Public Works Committee held hearings in early November 1973 on proposals to further postpone emission control deadlines. Russell Train (who had by then replaced William Ruckelshaus at EPA), said he would not weaken the 1975 interim standards, which would have meant postponing the use of catalytic converters. Ford and Chrysler, however, continued their campaign to undo the interim standards and the use of catalysts. Ford's Herbert L. Misch, VP for environment, urged postponement until 1977. Chrysler president John Riccardo, also seeking postponement, said that the use of the catalyst would slow down Chrysler's effort to develop alternative engines. Without catalysts, he predicted, Chrysler could convert one-third of its production to stratified charge engines* by 1977. Riccardo also wrote to Senators

---

* Clarence Ditlow of the Center for Auto Safety, writing in a 1975 edition of the *Ecology Law Quarterly*, would note, "Since the domestic manufacturers rejected the stratified-charge engine at least fifteen years ago according to the Justice Department, there is little reason to have faith in the present auto industry and oil industry request to suspend the statutory standards to permit a shift to the stratified charge engine." In the late 1950s, Ralph Heintz, an inventor, developed and patented a stratified charge engine. This engine reduced HC, CO, and NOx emissions while also reducing gasoline consumption. It was believed by some that this engine could replace conventional internal combustion engines with little or no additional cost to consumers. The development of the engine was publicized generally at the time, so the automobile manufacturers knew of its existence and what it could do. According to the Justice Department, Victor G. Raviole, a former executive director of the Ford engineering staff, stated on several occasions in the early 1960s that the major auto companies were investigating such an engine, and on one occasion he predicted that it might be ready for production before 1965. However, nothing came of the US automakers' fleeting interest in the engine until Honda announced its work in 1973.

*This mid-December 1973 ad by GM's Chevrolet dealers was called "false and misleading" by EPA's Russell Train, who asked the Federal Trade Commission to investigate.*

Jennings Randolph and Howard Baker urging them to abandon the catalyst strategy in favor of stratified charge engine, suggesting that Chrysler would convert "our *total* engine production to the new [stratified charge] engine by the 1980 model year."[2] Muskie, for one, was not convinced. "I don't think a case has been made for postponing the use of catalysts in 1975.[3] . . . I hate to take steps backward. We now have some gains that are within reach, and I am reluctant to roll them back."[4]

General Motors had already announced plans to put catalysts on most of its 1975 cars and held to its commitment to use them—which significantly helped the political situation. GM, in fact, had become a booster of the catalysts, made the biggest investment in using them among the automakers, and contended the catalysts would improve fuel consumption—not a small matter given the Arab oil embargo. A year later, GM would run full-page ads explaining why it believed catalysts were "an answer to the automotive air pollution problem."

However, like his colleagues at Chrysler and Ford, GM's president, Ed Cole, did call for a three-year freeze on emissions standards—to keep them "at a level no more stringent than the 1975 interim California level." But Cole also countered Chrysler's contention that there would be other pollution problems with catalysts (e.g., sulfur and platinum), noting that GM's scientists had found that the pollution was "minor" and would not be a threat to public health.[5] Environmentalists opposed industry's call for a freeze on the standards. The Sierra Club said relaxing the standards any further could be a fatal blow to the program.

Meanwhile, the White House and Federal Energy Office under John Sawhill were also pushing to extend implementation of the final standards until at least 1978. In late December 1973, the Senate reported a bill to delay the standards until 1977. On the floor the bill passed 85-0, after defeating an amendment by Senator William Scott (R-VA) to try to extend the deadline to 1978. During the last-minute lobbying and debate over extending the deadline, some of the automakers tried to advance the argument that the lead-free fuel required by catalytic converters would result in the loss of one million barrels of oil a day. Muskie contended that the bill's one-year extension would allow enough time to evaluate the need for catalytic converters and to assess the impact of emissions standards on fuel economy. The House version—passed December 15—was even more generous. It postponed the final standards to 1978 and gave EPA the option of extending the deadline for two more years beyond that. The House-Senate conference did not complete its work before adjournment, but in early 1974 it did.

The final law, known as the 1974 Energy Supply and Environmental Coordination Act, delayed final auto emissions standards to 1977-78, and gave manufacturers a chance to apply to EPA for another one-year postponement for the CO and HC standards. Thus, the second major change in the Clean Air Act's auto emissions goals—the second in less than a year's time—had occurred with a window of opportunity for further deadline extensions. Senator Muskie, trying to put the best light on the changing politics of the moment, billed the changes as a one-time spe-

# General Motors believes it has an answer to the automotive air pollution problem...

## ...and the catalytic converter has enabled GM engineers to improve performance and to increase miles per gallon.

Starting with the 1975-models, General Motors will put catalytic converters on its cars. Our testing program, carried out at an accelerated pace over the last several years, shows that the converters work and that they reduce exhaust emissions to such a low level that as older cars not equipped with catalytic converters are gradually replaced, the automobile will cease to be a significant part of the air pollution problem in most areas of the country.

Catalytic Converter

Because the catalytic converter will be a part of the 1975-model GM car you buy, we would like to tell you here as much as we can in non-technical terminology about the catalytic converter and how it works.

### What is a catalyst?

A catalyst is a substance, in this case a metal, that speeds up a chemical reaction but remains unchanged itself by the process. For example some chemical reactions only happen quickly at very high temperatures. A catalyst can make them happen at lower temperatures.

### Why do cars need catalytic converters?

Automotive exhaust is composed mainly of nontoxic or harmless gases, those that we find in "pure" air. The parts of the exhaust that are called pollutants occur in very small quantities. They are usually measured in "parts per million."

The two pollutants that are changed by the catalytic converter are hydrocarbons and carbon monoxide. They are changed into harmless carbon dioxide and water vapor.

Automotive pollutants already are declining in the atmosphere because of the control systems we've been putting on cars for the past ten years. In most parts of the country, present controls are good enough to remove the automobile from the local air pollution problem. But some areas need more stringent state emission controls—and that's where the catalytic converter comes in.

### Why is GM using platinum and similar metals in its converter?

There are two basic demands made upon a catalyst: it must be efficient and it must be durable. GM scientists have determined that small quantities of platinum and palladium coated on pellets of aluminum oxide best meet these requirements.

Nearly a thousand other metals and combinations of metals were tested by GM scientists. Some needed very high temperatures in order to be efficient. Others were quickly rendered inoperable by the heat of the exhaust or some of the components of automotive exhaust. Platinum and palladium best met the specifications.

The next step then had to be to find a way to use these noble metals in the smallest possible quantities. GM scientists helped develop a bead

with a very rough surface. Because of the tiny hills and valleys on the surface of this bead (shown actual size), the real surface area of a single bead is over 25 sq. feet. The catalytic material is then spread on the great surface of the bead as sparsely as possible.

To give you an idea of how sparsely the catalyst is deposited on the beads, there are thousands of beads in a converter (actually 150,000 beads per GM converter) and all of them can be treated with less than a tenth of a troy ounce of platinum and palladium.

### How will the converter affect gas mileage?

In recent model years, we have had to compromise engine efficiency to "tune" the engine for low emissions. Since the catalytic converter treats the exhaust after it leaves the engine, we have been able to retune the engine for maximum efficiency and let the converter control emissions. Estimates based on preliminary tests indicate that 1975-model GM cars with catalytic converters will be more economical to operate than the current models.

Prototype 1975 cars tested on a simulated city/suburban driving schedule have averaged about 15% more miles per gallon over their 1974 counterparts. In addition, the results of the Environmental Protection Agency urban test generally confirm this improvement in gasoline economy.

### How will the converter affect performance?

The engine retuning allowed by the converter will also result in a noticeable improvement in the performance qualities of GM cars. The responsiveness to driver demands of our 1975 cars will be excellent.

The converter itself has very little effect on performance. Engine and drive train refinements, designs that are more aerodynamically efficient, even tires will play a role in the continuing improvement of the performance qualities of GM cars. And GM designers and engineers are working on ways to make cars lighter in weight without sacrificing safety features or passenger comfort.

### How long will a catalyst last?

If unleaded gasoline is used exclusively and normal engine maintenance is performed at recommended intervals, there is no reason why the catalytic converter should not last the life of the car. Lead in gasoline "poisons" the catalyst and therefore, our 1975-model cars have special fuel tank filler necks that allow only the smaller unleaded fuel pump nozzles to be used. However, in case of emergency, a motorist can use a few gallons of leaded fuel without significant or permanent effect on the converter, and of course, with no effect on engine operation.

In all, over 25 million miles of development testing have been completed, both at the GM Proving Grounds and in field experience. *Under normal circumstances, no maintenance or replacement of the catalytic converter is recommended.*

### Will unleaded gas be available everywhere?

Federal law required all large gasoline stations to offer unleaded gas by July 1, 1974. It has been estimated that 60% of all U.S. gas stations will offer unleaded gas by the time cars equipped with catalytic converters are on the road. As the public becomes aware that the use of unleaded gas lowers maintenance costs by

greatly increasing the life of spark plugs, engine oil and exhaust system components, the demand for unleaded gas should cause it to become available at most other U.S. gas stations.

### Will the converter remove 100% of all pollutants from automotive exhaust?

To scientists absolute or 100% effectiveness is strictly theoretical. For example, if you scaled down the earth to the size of a ball bearing, it would be an extremely smooth ball bearing. But one look at the Rocky Mountains or the Himalayas tells us that the earth is not extremely smooth.

The same kinds of questions occur in automotive engineering. There are laws of probability and physical limits to contend with. Machines can't ever be perfect. And the closer we come to perfection, the more expensive the process becomes.

The goal of anti-pollution systems is not perfection. It is to remove so much of the pollutants from automotive exhaust that the effect of the unremoved or uncorrected pollutants on the atmosphere will be insignificant. *We believe GM cars equipped with catalytic converters will achieve that goal.*

### What are hydrocarbons and carbon monoxide?

Hydrocarbons are the basis of all fossil fuel. An ideal engine would burn all of the hydrocarbons in gasoline. But there are no ideal engines. A very small part of the hydrocarbons in gasoline comes out of the engine unburned. The purpose of the catalytic converter is to oxidize (burn without combustion) these hydrocarbons.

Carbon monoxide is a byproduct of the combustion of all carbon-based materials. Cigarette smoke, for example, has a high carbon monoxide content. As with hydrocarbons, the catalytic converter oxidizes the carbon monoxide in engine exhaust.

### What happens to carbon monoxide inside the converter?

Oxygen comes into the converter along with exhaust gases as a result of excess combustion air or from air supplied by an auxiliary air pump. The oxygen sticks to the surface of the catalyst. As the carbon monoxide molecules pass over the catalyst, they also stick to the catalyst's surface and join together with the oxygen, to form carbon dioxide, the gas you exhale when you breathe.

### What happens to hydrocarbons inside the converter?

Hydrocarbons are more complicated than

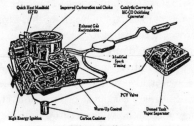

Quick Heat Manifold (LTF) — Improved Carburetion and Choke — Catalytic Converter/ HC-CO Oxidizing Converter — Exhaust Gas Recirculation — Modified Spark Timing — PCV Valve — High Energy Ignition — Warm-Up Control — Carbon Canister — Domed Tank Vapor Separator

#### 1975 Emission-Control System

carbon monoxide. They are generally made of a chain of carbon atoms, each of which is attached to several hydrogen atoms. As the hydrocarbons pass through the converter, they meet with the oxygen on the surface of the catalyst and begin to change. The oxygen pulls the carbon chains apart, forming carbon dioxide from the carbon atoms and good old-fashioned $H_2O$ (water) from the hydrogen atoms.

Catalytic Converter

The process by which certain hydrocarbons change into carbon dioxide and water is so complex that physical chemists still do not completely understand the exact order of the process. They can, however, measure what goes into the converter and what comes out, so they know it happens.

### Will the catalytic converter be the ultimate answer to the automotive air pollution problem?

Frankly, we don't think there are any ultimate answers to anything in science. Research at General Motors goes on; no matter how good a solution may be, there may be a better one somewhere down the road.

We're working with turbine engines, diesel engines, stratified charge engines, to name just a few of the projects now going on at the General Motors Technical Center.

There are mass-production problems with some kinds of engines. Vehicles powered by electricity stored in on-board batteries still require improvement. Other kinds of engines are low in one pollutant and high in another.

For the immediate future we believe the catalytic converter is the best answer to the problem of changing the very small amounts of hydrocarbon and carbon monoxide pollutants in automotive exhaust into harmless gases.

It is the practical answer. But the engineers and scientists at General Motors are looking for better answers all the time; that's their job.

GM cares about cars.
GM cares about people, too.

## General Motors
Chevrolet, Pontiac, Oldsmobile, Buick, Cadillac, GMC Truck

*GM's plan to use catalytic converters in 1975 was an important commitment in helping to advance the technology and in holding to the Clean Air Act's goals.*

cial circumstance, given the energy situation, "not intended to set precedents."[6] As later activity would reveal, however, a third extension would be granted in January 1975, prompting John Quarles, former deputy EPA administrator, to observe, "As a consequence of the three postponements, most cars produced for 1975, 1976 and 1977 are emitting or will emit roughly four times as much pollution per mile as the standards set by the 1970 Clean Air Act would have allowed. These higher emissions will continue as long as the cars remain on the road, well into the 1980s."[7]

In mid-March 1974, the Arab oil embargo ended, but the political and economic shock waves were just beginning. The US automobile industry, for one, was in for a long, rough ride. Within five months of the embargo, the automakers began to see that tighter oil supplies would have a serious impact on the economy and their business. By April 1974, car sales were down more than 35 percent. It was the worst slump in car buying since the 1958 recession. "Once President Nixon announced . . . that people should turn down their thermostats to save energy," recalled one auto executive, "we couldn't sell a big car to save our ass from first base."[8]

"The crisis hit General Motors, with its large, gas-guzzling cars, hardest of all," explains Wall Street analyst Maryann Keller. "Traditionally loyal customers were now demanding compact, fuel-efficient cars, and the sudden market shift rattled the company to the very roots of its big-car, cheap gas heritage. People were speaking a new language—a foreign language that GM didn't understand. It was called 'miles per gallon.'"[9] Motor vehicles then accounted for more than 40 percent of US energy use, and the average automobile got about fifteen miles to the gallon—an obvious target for saving oil.

## GERALD FORD'S DEAL

By early 1975, with President Gerald Ford now in the White House, Detroit's game plan shifted to take advantage of the national hysteria over energy—and specifically, the trade-offs that might be possible in the Clean Air Act. In January, the Ford administration and the Big Three made a deal: the automakers said they would make a 40-percent improvement in fuel economy if the government would ease auto emissions standards. In the president's State of the Union address of January 15, the administration said it planned to ask Congress to delay the auto standards deadline until 1982—essentially, freeze them for five years—in exchange for a promise by the Big Three to improve fuel economy 40 percent. The proposal brought a quick rejoinder from Capitol Hill.

"The president's proposal to undercut the national commitment to clean air through a moratorium on our efforts to clean up automobiles demonstrates either an unnecessary disregard for public health or a gross misunderstanding of the facts," offered Senator Muskie in February 1975. "Major gains can be made in fuel economy without compromising pollution standards." Environmentalists agreed, calling for separate standards. "The only way to insure improvement in fuel economy," said Rafe Pomerance of Friends of the Earth, "is to develop mandatory fuel-economy standards which will lead to light and more efficient vehicles. This can be done at the same time as pollution standards are met."[10]

Indeed, it was the view of some experts on Capitol Hill, EPA and, the Department of Transportation (DOT) that the automakers could achieve a 40 percent fuel economy improvement without any relaxation of auto emissions standards. By this time, in fact, data for the previous model year was already showing fuel economy improvement—running, on average, about 13.5 percent from 1974 to 1975. These gains, in part, were attributed to the use of catalytic converters then being used on some new cars. GM's fuel economy had increased by 28 percent. EPA and DOT officials also believed that fully half of the proposed 40 percent fuel economy target could be made simply by consumers buying smaller cars. Something else was going on as well. "Privately," wrote the *Wall Street Journal*'s Karen Elliott, "auto executives say their request that EPA freeze the emissions standards is simply part of a strategy to force Congress to compromise and accept the lower standards proposed by the president."[11]

### "The Federal Pinto"

Detroit at the time was feeling the bite of lower sales, and it turned to government regulation as the whipping boy. Leading the charge was Lee Iacocca. New standards, said Iacocca, "will give a big new push to inflation, depress sales and employment in our industry even further, increase gasoline consumption substantially—and do hardly anything for public health and safety."[12]

Iacocca, in fact, would complain publicly of money "thrown away" on past regulations, quoting statistics that showed Americans enjoying "one less day of coughing and chest discomfort every thirty-three years if smog were eliminated." Ford prepared a fifty-six-page press release outlining its case against further regulation and began meeting with the press and advertising executives to tell its story. Ford even put together what it called "the Federal Pinto," a car it would showcase at some of its briefings. The Federal Pinto, Ford said, would cost $820 more, get 30 percent less gas mileage, and weigh 426 pounds more. Ford was comparing its Federal Pinto to a deregulated Pinto, one that would include regulations as Ford saw them. Federal regulations, said Iacocca, would add $9 billion to the $50 billion or so people would spend on cars each year. Two million tons of additional material would also be required, he said, and 20 billion gallons of additional gasoline consumption.

"This is one of the most blatant power plays they've tried to pull in the last ten years," said Ralph Nader, charging that the industry's cost data on present and future standards were inflated, and that safety and pollution equipment actually played an insignificant role in the current auto slump. The automakers, he contended, "are hoping to find a scapegoat," which is why they were trying to link federal regulations to sagging auto sales.[13]

Two *Wall Street Journal* reporters, John Emshwiller and Albert Karr, had also investigated the Big Three's cost estimates of past regulations and found the automakers playing games with comparisons and not fully divulging the reasons for all cost increases. ". . . General Motors', Ford's, and Chrysler's estimates of the cost of past federal regulations range from $499 to $600 a car. In arguing for a moratorium on further regulations, the automakers quickly juxtapose those figures with the price increase the companies have effected in the last year or so (about $1,000 a car from 1973 to 1975 models), leaving the impression that the increases result largely from the rules. These higher prices are widely acknowledged to be one cause of the auto-sales slump."[14]

But Emshwiller and Karr also reported that the automakers' announced cost figures were "anywhere from 25 to 50 percent higher than those compiled by the federal Bureau of Labor Statistics"—an agency that used confidential data supplied by the industry itself. Nor was the industry much better when it came to projecting future costs, the reporters found, with estimates fluctuating wildly from month to month, and industry making adjustments to suit the moment:

> Some auto executives once warned that meeting then-pending 1970 pollution standards would cost $150 a car, but a few months later others were estimating $20 a car. And in current published material, GM attributes only $8 to 1970 pollution standards. Only last year, Chrysler warned that the total cost of all regulations through 1975 modes would hit $725 a car; now it said the cost is $571, some 20 percent less. Part of such differences may reflect development of new methods for meeting standards or tooling—amortization policies that could reduce costs, but the automakers don't discuss such potential gains in their public statements.[15]

The automakers would also try to leave the impression that the entire cost increase was coming from federal regulation, when actually, many other factors were also contributing to price increases, not the least of which were their own expensive "options." "About three-fourths of the nearly $1,000 in price increase on a typical Ford car between 1973 and 1975 models, Ford's own figures indicate, result from factors other than safety and pollution gear," reported Emshwiller and Karr. "A big factor—one that rankles some regulators—is the wrapping of expensive, highly profitable equipment that had been optional into the base price of new models. In 1973-75, Ford wrapped an estimated $150 worth of former options into its base price. . . ."[16]

## Sulfate Straw Man

During EPA's hearings to consider the second one-year extension offered in the 1974 Energy Supply and Environmental Coordination Act, the big issue of contention was sulfate emissions—an issue that became blown out of proportion and helped to delay implementation of the law by at least a year. A January 1975 EPA study found that cars equipped with catalytic converters produced about thirty-five times more sulfuric acid than cars without the devices. Using this study, Administrator

Russell Train extended existing interim standards for HC and CO—1.5 g/mi and 15 g/mi respectively—from the 1977 model year to the 1978 model year. The National Clean Air Coalition; the Public Interest Research Group (PIRG); Sierra Club; American Lung Association; League of Women Voters; American Medical Association; California Air Resources Board (almost all of the autos sold in California would be using catalysts in 1975); and the catalytic converter manufacturers all opposed Train's decision to grant the additional one-year extension.[17]

The catalysts, it turned out, oxidized sulfur in gasoline fumes causing sulfates to form, raising a new health issue that the automakers seized upon. EPA began fighting internally over how serious the problem was. Environmentalists advocated the use of low-lead, low-sulfur gasoline in catalyst-equipped cars to reduce sulfate emissions. The oil companies weighed in, too. Mobil said it could not remove sulfur from large quantities of gasoline and step up overall refining activities at the same time. Exxon said it would cost more than $1.7 billion to remove sulfur from all gasoline by 1980. EPA, meanwhile, said it was prepared to consider regulatory action on the sulfate matter if further study showed a definite health hazard.

Ford Motor first notified EPA of the sulfuric acid problem in early 1973. EPA's study followed in January 1975. But this study was soon found to be flawed and was contradicted by another April 1975 study that found much lower sulfuric acid emissions. This study was leaked to Clarence Ditlow of the Center for Auto Safety, who, in turn, made it available to the press. The issue was widely debated in the press and on Capitol Hill, as the sulfate matter also became a factor in the Ford administration's proposed five-year freeze.

Opponents maintained that the 1977 standards could have been met while eliminating sulfuric acid emissions by one of several options: blending gasoline stocks to cut sulfur content in auto fuel, installing desulfurizing equipment at refineries, or using three-way catalysts. The three-way catalyst was then the "next generation catalyst"—a catalyst not only capable of reducing CO and HC emissions, but also NOx. Engelhard and Matthey Bishop, Inc.—two catalyst makers—were also reporting that a three-way catalyst would emit virtually no sulfates. Robert S. Leventhal of Engelhard said that his company's three-way catalyst had been proven for 50,000 miles—the warranty period required under the Clean Air Act—and that Engelhard could produce enough of the catalysts to supply the 1977 California market and the entire nation by 1978. GM's Ernie Starkman said the three-way catalytic converter was too primitive for the auto industry to rely upon for the sulfate problem. He called the three-way catalyst "a theoretical possibility." EPA said it wanted more data on the catalysts' durability.[18]

In March 1975, California—supporting the original intent of the law—approved its schedule to adopt the 1977 standards on time. "EPA caved in to the oil and auto companies, and we are not about to join them in selling out," said CARB chairman Tom Quinn. "We are convinced that it is possible to eliminate the catalyst problems and at the same time crack down on other automobile pollutants."[19] Time would prove Tom Quinn right. By early 1977, the sulfate problem all but dissipated. General Motors, in fact, helped EPA with testing to produce the evidence that defused concern about sulfate emissions. By this time, the three-way catalyst was making its debut in California and was also making headway in reducing the more difficult problem of nitrogen oxides.

Yet, at the time of the sulfate scare, the politics were stacked decidedly against the catalyst makers. Russell Train, for one, was under the gun. First, President Gerald Ford, a native of Michigan and no stranger to the auto industry, was already proposing the five-year delay. Second, Train had to choose which economic interests to penalize: the oil companies, the auto industry, or the catalyst makers. Given the energy crisis and the state of the economy, the catalyst makers—the "new kids on the block" with new, uncertain technology—took the big hit. If it were not for GM's pro-catalyst position at the time, however feeble, and the quick action of opponents in pointing to sulfur-removal alternatives, the catalytic converter industry might well have gone under. Yet, in the final analysis, the sulfur was in the gasoline, not the catalyst. And in any case, the automakers should have anticipated the problem. "The sulfate question was predictable . . . ," said Senator James McClure in a June 1975 subcommittee briefing with Leon Billings. "I had only one year of chemistry. I can speak with as much authority on this as other people with no chemistry authority. The basic chemistry of catalysts required the production of sulfuric acid. It was just absolutely predictable. . . ."

EPA's Russell Train, however, had gone beyond the one-year extension, recommending Gerald Ford's proposal that final standards be delayed from 1978 to 1982.* But something else was brewing that political season; something which soon changed the dynamic of Clean Air Act politics—politics that were once neatly divided, liberal and conservative, Republican and Democrat.

## THE UAW FACTOR

In 1970, the Senate passed the Clean Air Act by a vote of 85-0. By 1975, however, there was a distinctly different mood on Capitol Hill and across the nation. "The buzz words of this year are not 'Vietnam' and 'ecology,'" wrote Bernie Asbell in his book *The Senate Nobody Knows*, "they are 'energy' and 'recession.'. . . We have been

---

* In Congress, Representatives George Brown (D-CA) and Richard Ottinger (D-NY), in reaction to Train's decision, introduced legislation (HR 4369) to implement the auto emissions standards as originally intended and extend them to trucks, motorcycles, and recreational vehicles. Under their bill, beginning in 1979, any internal combustion engine that could not meet the standards would have to be phased out. The Brown-Ottinger bill also proposed that auto manufacturers warranty their cars to meet emissions standards for 100,000 miles.

teetering all this year at the edge of a major depression. . . . So energy, unemployment and pollution control are all inextricably tangled. . . ."[20]

The UAW, which had supported the Clean Air Act in 1970, changed its position in the mid-1970s. Part of the reason was the energy crisis. "There is a big difference now," said UAW's Leonard Woodcock in a dramatic May 1975 appearance before Muskie's subcommittee. "I represent 170,000 people, indefinitely laid off, who are becoming increasingly desperate. They see foreign cars, because of the fuel economy problem, taking more and more of this market. . . . I'm not in the hip pocket of industry, as some in this Congress are now saying on the liberal side of the Democratic Party, I am representing desperate men and women and their children."[21]

Asked to specify how he thought meeting the auto emissions standards would affect unemployment of autoworkers, Woodcock replied he didn't have any specific figures. "All I'm trying to say, Senator, is that if we had no fuel economy problem the UAW would not be here today arguing for a pause. . . . I want to apologize to this committee for being so emotional, but I hope you understand I am in constant, increasing daily pressure and I have no answers for people."[22] Woodcock's appearance in the Senate committee room that day left an indelible mark on the senators present and the politics of clean air. It presaged political alliances to come and a significant move by labor away from the Democrats and traditional liberal politics, especially on energy/environment matters.

Several months later, in a private September 1975 meeting with Muskie in the senator's "hideaway" office, Leonard Woodcock, Henry Ford, and Pehr Gyllenhammar, president of Volvo (then planning an American assembly plant), came as a team to discuss the Clean Air Act. Woodcock attended with his aide and lobbyist Dick Warden. The auto executives, however, did most of the talking. Henry Ford and Volvo's Gyllenhammar both pressed Muskie for delay. "If the suggested legislation goes through," said Gyllenhammar, "it might rule out interesting alternatives, like the stratified charge, the diesel, the Stirling engine. It could result in our being stuck with the very thing that it would be best do away with—the piston engine. Perhaps we could go farther in perfecting these alternative ways if we had, say five years. . . ."* Later in the meeting, Henry Ford asked for a delay, too, throwing in

---

* Gyllenhammar's Volvos at the time were meeting California's standards—0.9 GPM for HC, 9.0 for CO, and 2.0 for NOx—which he proposed making the national standards after the five-year pause. "Indeed," he remarked at the time, "California standards for all cars would provide the guarantee that manufacturers would be hard pressed." He also suggested that instead of requiring 2.0 GPM as Muskie then wanted to do in his legislation, that "perhaps . . . the legislation might say something about going to 1.0 in the laboratory," during the five-year period, but not specifying when 1.0 would become an on-the-road standard. Gyllenhammar also suggested that emission control and fuel economy goals be tied together in a single policy "so we don't shoot for emission control first, then have to start all over on next year's fuel economy requirement. . . ."

both the high cost of emissions control and the jobs issue. "Do you know that, to meet the 1977 California standards, in our company we have to spend between forty and sixty million dollars? We have a terrible capital formation problem in this country," said Ford to Muskie. "I'm seriously perturbed about whether we can maintain the kind of employment we've had in the industry, with the possible exception of GM. If we could have a pause, we would see what's feasible, what's politically feasible, what's feasible in design."[23]

Muskie wasn't swayed by these arguments, according to Leon Billings. But what Muskie did take away from the meeting with Henry Ford was that industry responded to deadlines—reinforcing, for Muskie, the importance of the deadlines already in the act. Said Ford of his industry during the meeting, "without deadlines, we'd never produce a car."[24]

## THE ENERGY WEDGE

By this time, however, the auto industry had made clear its position on fuel economy vs. emissions controls. "We can't even begin to talk about mandatory fuel economy until we get some action on relaxing emission standards," said Elliott Estes, then president of GM, on Capitol Hill in May 1975.[25] Lee Iacocca said much the same, "Because of the long automotive depression, and because the prices can't be raised enough to offset the cost increases, we just don't have the money it would take to get the fuel economy job done and at the same time to meet statutory emission standards. Even if we could raise the money, we couldn't move full speed ahead on both jobs at the same time because the goals require the same kinds of engineers and scientists."[26]

Despite the industry's hard sell, Muskie had already concluded that auto emissions standards were not holding back the automakers on fuel economy, as he explained to one reporter in June 1975. ". . . What you have to understand is that people are worried about this mileage thing, and the [auto] companies are trying to make air pollution controls the scapegoat. But the problem in gas mileage *isn't* air pollution control. It's *weight.* The average automobile today consumes twice as much energy as the average automobile in 1947, and the principal reasons are weight and power. I bought one of the last cars sold before World War II and one of the first ones sold after World War II; power plants of only a hundred and fifty or so horsepower, and about a thousand to fifteen hundred pounds lighter than today's, and they were damned good automobiles, I tell you that. . . . Then the manufacturers began adding all that weight which they're now peeling off, not only on the small cars but on the big cars. One of the biggest sellers is that new Cadillac—what's it called?—the Seville. They've shortened it and they've peeled off the weight and they're going to keep on peeling off weight until they get the energy consumption reduction they've promised the president. . . ."[27]

Muskie also thought he heard auto executives tell him they were committed to making small cars, using new technology that would make those cars fuel efficient and cleaner. In fact, that was the crux of testimony when the automakers pleaded for more time. "Give us more time and we'll give you bigger energy and clean air rewards" was their pitch. In Congress, GM had announced it was making a $3 billion investments in new designs of cars that would be fuel efficient, cleaner, and provide strong competition against the Japanese and European subcompacts. Most observers, and policymakers like Muskie, assumed that GM meant it would also be producing small cars.

## MUSKIE-BUCKLEY PROPOSAL

In June 1975, Muskie and Senator James Buckley, ranking Republican on the Public Works Committee, then went to work on a compromise provision they thought would encourage fuel efficiency and small cars. Giving some ground on emissions deadlines and standards, but with the intent of extracting a measure of commitment from the auto industry on fuel economy, they offered the automakers a more lenient schedule and standards. Cars that achieved "twenty miles per gallon or more on the urban driving cycle" would be given to model year 1979 to meet somewhat less strict emissions standards. Cars that failed to meet the twenty MPG goal would have to meet the tougher statutory standards in 1978. This proposal, however, brought a swift response, both from Gerald Ford's White House—reiterating the administration's request for a five-year moratorium—and the auto industry. GM's lobbyist Bill Chapman called the Muskie-Buckley two-car strategy "the most destructive proposal I've ever seen." GM, it turned out, wasn't planning to do much with small cars afterall. "It's clear now that they had no intention of spending that three billion on small cars," said Leon Billings, briefing Senator Muskie in July 1975 before a scheduled meeting of the Public Works Committee. "They'll take a few pounds out here and there, pick up two or three miles per gallon here and there.* What they really want to do is build a base for an advertising campaign to say, 'Look, we've got a Chevrolet Impala that gets twenty miles to a gallon.' But it's still going to get just twelve to thirteen in the city."[28]

---

* GM's Richard Gerstenberg directed the company's "downsizing" plan—i.e., making large cars smaller in the wake of the '74 energy crisis. Downsizing consisted of just that, making all the larger models smaller, with lighter parts, selling them at higher selling prices. "Downsizing was a brilliant, stopgap measure for a company caught off guard by the energy crisis," says Maryann Keller. "It was a savvy financial move because the public was willing to pay more for the leaner, stylish cars. Compared to Ford and Chrysler, GM looked like a genius. The company was very successful with its seven-hundred pound lighter, foot-shorter big cars. The first small Cadillac, the Seville, proved to be very popular. GM was able to stabilize while Ford and Chrysler were suffering mightily at the hands of the Japanese. GM's downsized models elevated the company's market share while Chrysler's condition worsened and Ford was being scrutinized for faulty transmissions and exploding Pintos."

## "A Goddam Little Volkswagen"

Small cars were not considered good business in Detroit—in fact, for some, they were practically un-American. "Americans like to blast along over interstate highways at eighty miles an hour in big cars with every kind of attachment, windows up, air conditioning on, radio going, one finger on the wheel," said Henry Ford. "That's what they want, and that's what they buy, and that's what we manufacture...." Mr. Ford, in fact, was not a big fan of small cars, which by the late 1960s he was calling "little shitboxes" or "a goddamn little Volkswagen," a pejorative he used for any small European car.[29]

In the 1960s, in fact, something of a small-car boomlet had come to the US with foreign imports, mostly European. Volkswagen's little rear-engine car—dubbed the Beetle or "bug" as it came to be known—led the way. Imports claimed about 10 percent of the US market then, with the Beetle getting about half that market. At first, the VW's sales were tiny, climbing to about 20,000 in 1954. By 1965, however, 500,000 were being sold each year. And by 1973, the VW Beetle would surpass the fifteen-million mark in sales, making it the most popular single car model ever sold in the US, even surpassing Henry Ford's Model-T.*

Detroit, however, viewed the VW phenomenon as more of an agitation than a serious threat—certainly not a sign that anything might be wrong with the Big Three worldview. "...The fact that the bug captured 5 percent of the market Detroit took very seriously, but it seemed to be a peculiar 5 percent...," observes auto historian Harley Shaiken. VW buyers weren't "those people that turned out in droves to see the introductions of the new models every September. These were the people who were marching to a different drummer." The Beetle did become something of an antiestablishment statement for the rebellious youth of the 1960s, who bought the car, used and new, by the thousands. But the Beetle was also being purchased by mainstream Americans for its simplicity and thrift; a vehicle of basic transportation that eschewed the whole notion of new models and yearly style changes. VW advertising played on its plain and basic themes, emphasizing the fact that its body style never changed. The Beetle was also well made. But it wasn't just the VW bug

---

* Auto historian James J. Flink observes, "...The Beetle was built so tight that a window often had to be cracked before the driver could slam its door shut. The sheet of steel protecting the car's undercarriage made it virtually watertight: there are records of Beetles floating for miles after being carried off in floods. Air cooling solved the problems of freezing and hard starting in winter and of overheating in summer. The low-revving, short-stroke engine meant lower piston speeds, which lengthened engine life and permitted (with the 1,300-cc engine) a top cruising speed of up to 75 MPH to be maintained for hours. Rear mounting of the engine gave the car improved traction in mud, sand, and snow.... Four coats of paint were meticulously applied electrostatically and baked on, and no bare metal was left exposed on any part of the car. One out of every ten employees at Wolfsburg [Germany] was an inspector; and instead of spot checking, every car was inspected on 115 check points.... All this for a fully equipped car with a base price in the late 1950s of about $1,500!"

that was selling. American Motors was having success with a smallish, economical car called the Rambler, selling 217,000 in 1958, and twice that many in 1960.

GM and Ford also produced small cars in the 1960s and early 1970s, but none as successful or reliable as the Beetle. GM, for example, introduced the Corvair in 1959, which like the VW bug, had a rear engine that was air-cooled. But the Corvair was a doomed vehicle. In addition to having problems with its aluminum engine, the Corvair—especially those produced before 1964—also became a safety hazard. Ralph Nader's book *Unsafe at Any Speed: The Designed-in Dangers of the American Automobile* exposed very serious and deadly engineering problems with the Corvair,* especially its instability at highway speeds. A combination of factors caused the problems, including poor design and decisionmaking at GM. The Corvair had an inadequate suspension system in a rear-weighted car with a swing-axle design. At highway speeds, the axles—which were also too light—tended to break, sending the car into an uncontrollable spin, sometimes flipping over completely. Although some of the car's problems were corrected in subsequent models, GM allowed the Corvair program to wind down, finally canceling it altogether in May 1969. At Ford, production of the Pinto began in 1970 and would continue for the next six years. The Pinto was scored for a number of problems, not the least of which was its lack of power. "[The Pinto] was seriously underpowered with its standard four cylinder which, coupled with an astonishingly puny automatic transmission," says auto historian Timothy Jacobs, "produced a car that seemed to have the motive power of wet sponge." More dangerously, a defect in the Pinto's gas tank ventilation system caused the car to explode into a fireball when hit from behind, a problem Ford later corrected after lawsuits and a massive recall campaign. Other Ford models, such as Mercury Comets produced in parallel to the Pinto, suffered many of the same problems. Over at GM, the Chevrolet cousin to the Pinto was the Vega, whose first five years of production saw erratic fuel economy (23 MPG in 1971; 13 MPG in 1973), body rusting within a few months of purchase, a problem-plagued aluminum engine, and various brake, drive-train and rear-axle prob-

---

* According to David Lewis, who worked in public relations for GM, the Corvair's problems were serious and well known at GM. "There were many one-car accidents in Corvairs. And General Motors knew this definitely as early as 1961, but chose not to make a public announcement of it nor to have any recalls. I happened to be secretary of the Public Relations Planning Committee in 1961. At that time, during a meeting, the number two man in public relations, Bill Hamilton, rushed back from the GM tech center and said that GM engineers had confirmed what had been talked about, that Corvairs were inherently unsafe because of the design of the suspension system. And I remember that one of the people at the meeting asked, 'Well, what are we going to do about it?' And Hamilton said, 'The lawyers say we're not going to do anything about it. We're going to ride it out.' That information, however, was kept under wraps. There was no government mandate to recall the cars for safety reasons and so nothing was done. It was one of the most socially irresponsible acts by an industrial firm of the 20th century." Coffey and Layden, *America on Wheels*, pp. 207-209.

lems.[30] These shortcomings and others in GM and Ford small cars raised troubling questions about the US auto industry's engineering capabilities—a harbinger of things to come. It also brought forward for the first time in Detroit "the quality issue."

## BIG CARS, BIG PROFITS

Detroit's heart and soul—and its leadership—just weren't in the small-car business, a fact often admitted, and for some like Ford engineer Hal Sperlich, deeply lamented (see box). But like Sperlich at Ford, there were a few voices within the industry that tried to push efficiency and smaller car design well before the energy crisis. At General Motors, Ed Cole and John DeLorean, then head of the GM's Chevrolet division, had argued for smaller cars in the late 1960s. They pointed to the VW Beetle and the fact that much of the sales growth in the US since 1965 had been in the small car segment. Smaller families, congested roads, higher costs, and shifting values were also part of a trend toward a new market segment. But Cole and DeLorean were voices in the wilderness at GM; for they were up against the fundamental Alfred Sloan growth dictum of GM's success: trading up to bigger cars. By this rule, every American had a fundamental right (if not an economic obligation) to trade up to bigger cars—an idea that has never lost favor in management, even today. Cole and DeLorean—prodding GM to design smaller and lighter compacts and intermediates, while scaling down full-size cars—were bucking tradition. And they ran into GM's powerful finance committee, then dominated by executives who had served with Sloan, and who were solidly committed to the big-car world view.[31]

"Behind GM's reluctance to de-emphasize big cars," wrote business reporters Stephen Shepard and J. Patrick Wright in December 1974, "lies the essence of the Sloan strategy: bigger cars earn bigger profits. A Cadillac Coupe de Ville . . . cost only about $300 more to build than a Chevrolet Caprice, but the Caddy sells for $2700 more than the Chevy—yielding an extra profit of $2400 per car. Similarly, an Olds 88 returns about $1200 more profit than a Caprice. Even in the Chevrolet Division profits vary greatly with size: a typical intermediate, Chevelle, returns about $600 per car, the compact Nova about $450, and the sub-compact Vega only about $125." Bigger cars also meant more options, which were also highly profitable. Extra cost options such as air conditioning, automatic transmissions, vinyl tops, and power steering then returned profits of 40 percent or more. And at the time, 90 percent of all cars sold had automatic transmissions, 73 percent had air conditioning, and 87 percent had power steering. All of this, of course, required more power and bigger engines. Detroit, therefore, was in no hurry to abandon bigger cars. "Buying up to bigger cars is the fundamental concept of American life," said GM marketing president Mack Worden in late 1974. "You put a few more bucks into a car, enlarge it, and sell it for a lot more money," explained Leonard Piconke, Chrysler's director of marketing services.[32]

## HAL SPERLICH'S EPIPHANY

" . . . [Hal Sperlich of Ford Motor Co.] was above all else an engineer, with an engineer's passion for efficiency. Now [in 1971] he had an epiphany, which was that Detroit was a crippling place for engineers because it was deliberately inefficient. Slowly, without even realizing it, he had become subverted by that philosophy. He remembered how excited he had been fifteen years before when he had first seen the VW Beetle. It was so different from anything he had known before; it had the qualities that engineers worshipped. It was simple and it was efficient. It used a minimum of resources and produced maximum results. But the world of Detroit, the world of power and size for its own sake, had pulled him away from the elemental truths that the Beetle represented, and before long he had himself regarding the German import contemptuously. He wondered now whether Detroit's ethic was one of intentional excess because that was the American ethic, or whether Detroit led the country. It was as if for twenty years the Detroit companies had competed to see which could be the most wasteful. In Detroit everything had to be bigger than last year. . . .

The small cars that Detroit had produced, he believed, had been bad ones, reluctant efforts at best. If anything, the companies had brought out inferior unappealing cars to prove their own thesis that small cars were in fact inferior and unpopular. The cars were not very good, were weak and underpowered, and the companies had not pushed them, and that had proved, the industry argued, that Americans did not like small cars. When the market for big cars finally went sour in the late seventies, during the energy crisis, the Detroit people argued that it was not their fault, for they had produced small cars in the past and their customers had turned away. That was true, Sperlich believed, but it was far from the whole truth, which was that the industry had never given its customers *good* small cars. Rather, he was convinced, Detroit had produced its small cars in precisely the wrong way, not as a labor of love but as a defensive necessity, to fend off at least momentarily the European invasion. It had been done by men whose hearts had never been in it."

[Excerpted from David Halberstam, *The Reckoning*, pp. 512–513]

## WHAT DETROIT KNEW

Behind the scenes, however, GM and Ford were both investigating European engineering and efficiencies, and were discovering some remarkable things, such as the European's success with front-wheel drive. Front-wheel drive was known in the industry as an engineering technique that saved weight without sacrificing performance and that meant saving fuel as well. But neither Ford nor GM wanted to invest in new programs that would threaten their long tradition of big car-profitability. In 1971, Lee Iacocca sent Hal Sperlich to Europe to learn about front-wheel-drive cars. Sperlich test drove a Fiat 127 and found it to be one of the best handling cars he had driven in years. He concluded that customers in America would buy them. As an engineer, Sperlich also believed that front-wheel drive vehicles were superior. Others before him believed that, too. A Ford engineer in the 1950s named Fred Hooven advocated front-wheel drive. As did a GM engineer named Frank Winchell.

They were never taken seriously. Sperlich, however, after months of reconnaissance got the nod to move ahead with front-wheel drive at Ford Europe, only to be slowed "by an undercurrent pulling against the car" from within Ford Europe, the program later derailed in the wars that erupted between Iacocca and Henry Ford II.[33]

At GM too, front-wheel-drive small cars were studied in the early 1970s, but not pursued. In the spring of 1973, GM's Pete Estes, slated to become GM president, sent Tom Davis of Campbell-Ewald to Europe to learn about the new front-wheel drive cars, like the VW Rabbit. At the time, Estes was thinking of front-wheel-drive as an option for which GM could charge consumers more. Davis, however, thought this was an innovation more important than an option, but rather an improvement that should be incorporated into many vehicles. After Davis returned, he reported to Estes that the European cars with front-wheel-drive were better—better engineered and better all-around cars than those Detroit was producing. Front-wheel drive was a breakthrough of immense importance, he said. But Estes told Davis in so many words that it wasn't in GM's best interest to be first in the market with a new technology.[34]

> That was it, Davis thought later—the Detroit line, the symbol of the protected industry. Don't let GM do it first, let the other guy make the early, expensive mistakes. Right then, he was sure, at Ford and Chrysler there were people who were also deciding not to do it first because somehow someone else should do it first. It was, he thought, management by default. He knew there were businesses in America, typically smaller ones in various fields of technology and medical science, that were authentically competitive. There, companies lived on the edge, their survival depending on innovation and technological advantage. But in the auto industry, as in most big industries, it was not like that. It was a protected world, the shares of the market already apportioned, GM big, Ford moderate, Chrysler small, with the government watching to see that GM did not put either of the others out of business. It was not a vibrant industry anymore, he thought, because the top people were no longer doing things simply because they were the right thing. . . . [35]

As David Halberstam would observe of the Ford-GM reluctance on front-wheel-drive, "the manufacturers had squandered a decade in which they could have created cars suited to the new nature of the industrialized world."[36]

## ATTACKING MUSKIE-BUCKLEY

Meanwhile, back in Washington in June 1975, as the US Senate was considering the Muskie-Buckley proposal to give some ground on tougher auto emissions standards in return for Detroit producing smaller, high-mileage cars, the automakers wanted nothing to do with it. In late June 1975, Lee Iacocca wrote to all members of the Senate Subcommittee then considering the Muskie-Buckley proposal, "As you know, Ford Motor Company has consistently urged a five-year moratorium . . . as being the most reasonable course of action because of the energy crisis and the economic situation." Calling the Muskie-Buckley proposal for twenty-MPG-cars "a massive government 'give away' to the foreign imports," Iacocca said that "only Ford Pintos or similar vehicles with our small engines, which are estimated to be less than 24 percent of our product line, could meet that fuel economy standard. . . ." He explained further that "the Volkswagens, Toyotas, Datsuns, Hondas, and other foreign imports would get the benefit of less stringent emission standards and, as a result receive major cost benefit. . . ."[37]

"A law weighted so heavily in favor of foreign imports," said Iacocca, "obviously would be damaging to domestic automobile manufacturers and certainly would be injurious to American working men and women who are in direct competition with foreign workers for jobs." Ed Muskie by now was furious, and he let the fur fly in one committee meeting.

> I'm not wedded to the two-car strategy. But it's clear from industry's reaction to this proposal that their answer to the energy problem is not the small car. It's reducing the weight of the big car. They are going to avoid any new technology. They just want to continue to feed the present habits of the American automobile owner. Mr. Iacocca had a meeting with me and Senator Buckley and three other company presidents. They told me that they were committed to a small car strategy. Once we surfaced this proposal they backed off from that. They didn't back off from it, they never *meant* it. . . .
>
> All along . . . they have urged changes in the Clean Air Act that will minimize the pressure on them for achieving technological breakthroughs. I am prepared to be sympathetic, because the health of the American economy is at stake, the jobs of American workers are at stake. But I don't think that surrender to *them* and to *their* version of what the policy ought to be is the answer—even the answer in *their* interests. My own feeling is if they pursue their own policy lines of foot-dragging against the future, the result will be an increasingly vulnerable American automobile industry, not a healthy one.
>
> *Now* is the time for them to address themselves to two points: the American people want more energy-efficient automobiles. They don't want some half-baked technological compromise. They want an energy-efficient automobile. I think the American industry can produce that, and that when it begins to, it will begin to be healthy again, economically. I think that is consistent with cleaning up the air.
>
> What was the statistic they kept throwing at us all that day. . . ? Twenty-one per cent. Twenty-one per cent penetration of foreign imports into the American market. They kept waving that number in front of us and I was impressed with that number. But they made their point more effectively with me than they did with themselves. They were using it to influence us, [but] *they* were not influenced by it. . . . [38]

The Muskie-Buckley proposal was subsequently abandoned in committee. The automakers, however, continued to use the fuel economy issue to slow and threaten the Clean Air Act.

*Detroit automakers spent $750,000 to run this ad in 1800 daily newspapers, but its contentions brought a rash of criticism and examples of technology that could meet the standards.*

## "You'll Be Paying the Bill"

In September 1975, Detroit's big automakers began a full-court press to push Congress into giving them their five-year freeze. At the center of this effort was a nationwide advertising campaign to persuade citizens to write their members of Congress. A full-page ad, placed in some 1,800 daily newspapers at an estimated cost of $750,000, used the headline: "You'll be paying the bill, so let Congress know your choice!" The ad purported to give the reader two choices: Choice 1 essentially outlined the case for the Ford administration's five-year delay; Choice 2 (not exactly a choice) explained that present law then called for stricter standards on 1977-78 cars. "To our knowledge," claimed the ad, "no auto manufacturer yet knows how to meet the 1978 standards on a mass production basis." The automakers added that their current "best effort" experimental control systems indicated: 1.) "your gas mileage could be reduced by 5% to as much as 30% . . ." and, 2.) "the cost of your car could increase by an estimated $150 to $400." The ad generated queries to EPA and a few sharp responses from members of Congress and environmentalists.

Brian T. Ketcham, vice president and staff engineer with Citizens for Clean Air, Inc., of New York City, who had tested catalyst systems on Ford cars, wrote to members of Congress about the automakers' ad. He found it highly misleading and offered the following observations:

> First, they claim that auto emission controls are working. Clearly this is not the case: auto pollution controls are not working effectively in congested urban centers. Data collected by New York City's Department of Air Resources shows that automotive pollution—specifically carbon monoxide—actually increased more than 20 percent in midtown Manhattan over the past three years.
>
> Second, the industry claims they don't know how to mass produce an effective emission control system. In fact, technology that can meet the 1978 emission standards has been available for at least three years. It is reliable and easily mass produced. Dual-catalyst technology, the system successfully tested by Citizens for Clean Air, Inc.(CCA), differs very little from the production of a simple muffler.
>
> Third, the industry claims a significant fuel economy penalty associated with any system designed to meet 1978 standards. *Properly designed*, a dual-catalyst emissions control system need not demonstrate a loss in fuel economy. CCA's dual-catalyst Ford Pinto demonstrated a 20 percent improvement in fuel economy against the same stock Ford vehicle.
>
> Fourth, the industry claims that the consumer will pay from $150 to $400 extra to meet 1978 standards. . . . The dual-catalyst system designed for the Ford Pinto has been costed out at less than $40 to manufacture.
>
> Thus, contrary to Detroit's slick ads, low cost, effective and efficient auto pollution control systems can be produced in time for the 1978 model year cars. I can make these observations because, as a member of a 3-man team of volunteer engineers, I helped to equip and test an effective dual-catalyst emission control system. As installed on the 1974 Ford Pinto mentioned above, this system not only meets 1978 emission standards

at low mileage, but gets a 20 percent improvement in fuel economy as well (from 17.6 MPG for the stock Ford Pinto to 21.2 MPG for the dual-catalyst installation). We were able to accomplish this task in a matter of days and with virtually no budget (contrary to auto industry claims, billions of dollars are not required to meet 1978 standards)....[39]

Mr. Ketcham, however, wasn't the ad's only detractor. EPA took the unusual step of issuing a four-page fact sheet in reply to the ad, noting that it had received "many inquiries" about the ad and its claims. EPA diplomatically noted, "This advertisement tends—as is perhaps inevitable in such communications—to oversimplify the issues involved." The agency also went through the ad's claims, noting where it wrongly stated facts, omitted information, or failed to present context.[40]

"Of course the car buyer will pay for the cost of emission controls on the car that he buys," said EPA, "just as he pays the bill for the air conditioner, chrome trim, carpeting and vinyl roof that may be installed. . . ." And while car buyers will be "paying the bill" for the cost of emission controls, added EPA, "each citizen is and will continue to be 'paying the bill' for the damage to public health that is caused by automotive air pollution. . . ." The bill for emission control on a new car, which EPA estimated* to be between $50-$100, "is low compared to the cost of the many luxury items on new cars that are sold as options, and represents a far better bargain for the Nation than do many of such items of optional equipment." EPA also found the automakers overstated NOx reductions by about 30 percent when comparing pre-controlled cars to current standards.**

But perhaps the most outrageous claim made in industry's ad was that "no auto manufacturer yet knows how to meet the 1978 standards on a mass production basis." The automakers were, of course, referring to all three standards when they made this claim—HC, CO, and NOx, the last of which was causing the most consternation. However, General Motors was already using the technology to meet the HC and CO standards and had, in fact, installed it on millions of vehicles. In fact, in an advertisement only a month earlier, run in *Harper's*, GM had sung the praises of the catalytic converter and what a good job it was doing. According to that ad, the catalytic converter "helped GM engineers to increase gas mileage in city driving by 28% on a sales-weighted average."[41]

---

* EPA explained, "The cost estimates in the advertisement are . . . for meeting all three emission standards [i.e., CO, HC, and NOx]. The costs of meeting only the statutory HC and CO standards at an NOx control level of 2.0 grams per mile would not be so high; instead of from $150 to $400, as stated in the ad, the increase in costs would range from $50 to $100."

** Said EPA, "The industry's 40% reduction estimate appears not to be based on NOx emissions from pre-controlled cars, but rather on the substantially higher level of NOx emitted from earlier models of cars that were controlled for HC and CO but were not required to be controlled for NOx." Nor did the automakers bother to tell the ad's readers that prior to the government's imposition of NOx controls beginning in 1973, "the industry allowed NOx emissions to rise sharply from what they had been on uncontrolled cars."

## BEYOND "TREE HUGGERS"

By the 1975 model year, catalytic converters had made their debut on most cars sold in America. US automakers, however, were ready to abandon the device if Congress or EPA showed any signs of wavering. Whenever uncertainty or controversy would crop up about the device—whether the issue was sulfates, fuel economy, or if a new three-way catalyst could control NOx—the automakers would milk those concerns for whatever they could. Environmental and public interest organizations tried to counter industry's assertions, but their arguments never quite carried the political clout of the automakers. "They never met a payroll" was a common epithet often hurled at environmentalists.

The catalyst makers, however, representing companies such as Corning Glass, W.R. Grace, Matthey Bishop, and Engelhard, couldn't be dismissed so easily. By the mid-1970s, these companies had their own full-time people in Washington following the new law. In 1973, for example, Corning chose John Blizard to be its man on Capitol Hill. A mechanical engineer by training and then working in new product development at company headquarters, Blizard was recruited for his directness and no-nonsense problem-solving. His charge, in part, was to counter the negative, anticlean air and anticatalyst propaganda the auto companies were spreading. The automakers, for example, were happy to portray catalysts as untried, impractical, and unsuitable for a family car. They charged the devices would start fires, waste fuel, and create noxious gases—and were an unnecessary expense.

Blizard, working with others in the catalyst industry, began convening strategy meetings at Washington's International Club with congressional staff, environmentalists, and interest groups such as the American Lung Association, AARP, and League of Women Voters. By 1976, he and the catalyst makers had also founded MECA—the Manufacturers of Emission Controls Association. Blizard became MECA's first director. "Tree huggers were one thing," said Blizard years later, referring sarcastically to the term some businessmen used for environmentalists, "but when Grace, Engelhard, Corning, and others got involved, the automakers knew they couldn't just say anything. They were very unhappy with people who knew the facts." From then on, it was no longer just environmentalists vs. the auto companies; now there was a business interest in clean air. The catalyst industry and MECA helped to level the economic playing field in the Clean Air debate.

Meanwhile, environmentalists and catalyst makers forged a continuing relationship of mutual interest. In fact, during the mid-1970s on more than one occasion, some of the catalyst makers would make sizeable donations to the Sierra Club and other environmental organizations, with the money sometimes used to bring grassroots activists to Washington to plead the case for a tougher Clean Air Act.

John Blizard, at the same time, became an effective critic of the auto industry's position. When asked by author Bernie Asbell in July 1975 about the automakers' contention they could not meet the clean air standards, Blizard offered these comments:

> ... [T]hey claim it can't be done because they don't want to have to change anything.
> They have an enormous investment in tooling and capital equipment that makes the

*car the way it is today. And they don't want to have to obsolete that equipment by making the car in some different way. They're delighted to add anything to the car that sits on the outside and make people in the showroom say, 'There is a sexy, interesting car.' Like the disappearing headlights, or the vinyl top, or the opera window, or the engraved designs on the opera window. You don't see a catalytic converter. People don't mind when these other things, these sexy, visible things, make the car cost more, as the catalytic converter does. In fact, these things are usually optional, and people gladly buy them. Actually the catalytic converter can make the car cost less in the long run because it uses less fuel if [the automakers] put in the proper type of equipment. But if the automakers do it in a halfhearted way, with the least possible addition of technical equipment to the engine, it uses more fuel. So in that way, the automakers can hold down the sticker price slightly, making it easier to sell, but they thereby increase the lifetime cost of the car.*

Blizard would be summoned to Detroit on occasion to hear about the error of his ways and why he and MECA should tone down their act. "They wished the catalytic converter people would go away," said Blizard. But the education sessions never seemed to work. In 1977, MECA mounted a public relations-public education campaign of its own, sending its lobbyists around the country on speaking tours to explain to high school students and the public what catalytic converters were all about, why they worked, and how they were being improved. Blizard, meanwhile, continued to draw the ire of Detroit. In fact, in 1980, after one GM lobbyist discovered Blizard's strategy luncheons, Roger Smith, GM's chairman, called Corning president Amory Houghton to complain about Blizard's activities. Smith suggested to Houghton that he should "get that son-of-a-bitch Blizard out of Washington." Yet, when John Blizard left his Washington desk at MECA and Corning in October 1982, it was on his own terms. When colleagues later gave him an award for his years of service in the clean air wars, the inscription read: "A friend dedicated to the finer principles of life and responsibility—pioneer of air pollution control; holder of the highest ethics in the political environment. . . . We are happy to salute you."

GM's Elliott Estes had also testified before Muskie's subcommittee in May 1975, noting, "We are pleased with the performance of the catalytic converter on our new 1975 automobiles. It enables us to improve gas mileage from 15 to 28 percent compared to 1974 and greatly improves the driveability of our cars while also significantly reducing exhaust emissions." ( A year later, however, other GM officials, such as Cadillac's E.C. Kennard, were lobbying key members of the House with telegrams, insisting that new emissions standards would mean a 30 percent decline in fuel economy.)

On Capitol Hill, Ed Muskie used the automakers' "You'll-be-paying-the-bill" ad to make his own points about fuel economy, cost, and public health. First, he cited a National Academy of Sciences study, completed a year earlier, which reviewed the

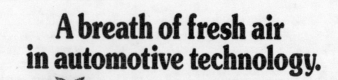

# A breath of fresh air in automotive technology.

The catalytic converter is a device for people and flowers and trees, for every living thing. It reduces exhaust emissions of hydrocarbons and carbon monoxide by about 50% from the already lowered levels of 1974.

The converter is also a device for pocketbooks and for energy conservation. According to EPA figures, it helped GM engineers to increase gas mileage in city driving by 28% on a sales-weighted average.

Not only will the converter save you money in fuel bills and maintenance costs over the years, it's one of those extraordinary technological advances that won't cause you any trouble under normal operating conditions. After a billion miles on the road, it's proved dependable. If you use unleaded gas and maintain your engine properly, the converter will last the life of your car.

Catalytic converters do add to the basic cost of a GM car. Part of that money goes for insulation that keeps the outer skin temperature of the converter in normal operation about the same as that of an ordinary muffler, and far lower than the temperature of the exhaust manifold.

A fuel-saving catalytic converter comes with most 1975 and 1976 GM cars as standard equipment. It's a breath of fresh air from GM, a world leader in automotive pollution control technology.

## General Motors

Chevrolet, Pontiac, Oldsmobile, Buick, Cadillac, GMC Truck

Catalytic converter, standard equipment on most 1975 and 1976 model GM cars.

*This August 1975 GM ad touting catalytic converters carries a message in sharp contrast to other industry claims that no automaker had the technology to meet emissions standards while saving fuel.*

air quality standards and "found no substantial basis for changing them." In fact, he said, "they pointed out that the margin of safety provided by the air quality standards is uncomfortably small." The academy found no new evidence to justify a relaxation of the hydrocarbon or carbon monoxide standards. Rather, they found that attainment of these standards was technically feasible. The economic benefits of cleaning up auto emissions alone, he said, were between $2.5 billion to $10 billion per year.[42]

Muskie also pointed to some worsening pollution evidence. "There have already been over 60 alerts for [photochemical] oxidant this year," he noted. "The problems of Los Angeles are well known, but regions from Massachusetts to Oregon, to Florida also had alerts. Detroit had its first air pollution alert ever for oxidant, as did Louisville and Kansas City. Nor is this just an urban problem. The entire state of Iowa celebrated the 4th of July with a record levels of air pollution and its first alert ever. . . . A recent study by EPA shows that clouds of oxidant can be carried 50 to 75 miles or more from cities to rural areas. . . ." As for fuel economy, a joint EPA and Department of Transportation study reported possible gains of 60 percent for 1980 model year cars with emission standards close to the 1975-76 statutory level. "Their analysis suggests that automobile weight, not emissions is the most important factor in fuel economy," said Muskie. An NAS report supported that same conclusion. And still another study, prepared for Ford Motor by the Jet Propulsion Laboratory at Cal Tech, found that emission reductions and fuel economy goals over the next five to ten years could be met through vehicle and engine improvements.[43]

### 1975–1976

Congress, meanwhile, took no final action to alter the Clean Air Act in 1975. Nor did the Ford administration's omnibus energy bill emerge that year. In the following year, Muskie's committee and the full Senate finally adopted a bill that included a one-year extension for 1978 models only. The House adopted a weaker version, essentially incorporating the five-year, delay-to-1982 schedule originally proposed by EPA's Russell Train. In the House-Senate conference that completed its bill in late September 1976, the Senate version prevailed. But there was still one more step. The bill as finally adopted by the House-Senate conference committee had to be approved by each chamber.

Environmentalists, not happy with all the provisions, supported the final version. So did the UAW. Electric utilities, oil, paper, and chemical companies opposed the bill for other reasons. The auto industry issued a press release saying that it also opposed the bill. This came as something of a surprise to both House and Senate conferees, since by killing the measure, the auto companies would then be subjecting themselves to illegal production. Their 1978 models were only nine months away from production (i.e., the fall of 1977), and if the bill died, they would not have the benefit of the law's one-year extension. The auto industry was gambling that after killing the bill in this session, they could come back the following year and force a quick remedy in the next Congress to "legalize" their 1978 vehicles.

On the floor of the Senate a few days later, in the midst of a filibuster on the Clean Air Act with Congress about to adjourn for elections, Senator Muskie, frustrated by not being able to get a vote on his bill, vented his anger at the auto industry. ". . . [I]t's clear to me, from every evidence of the reaction of the automobile industry to this bill, that they are doing their best to kill it, notwithstanding the fact that if they kill it they will be manufacturing automobiles illegally before another law is likely to be passed. And what is the industry attitude? Their attitude is, 'Well, Congress wouldn't dare hold us accountable for failing to meet the law. We're too important. There are too many jobs involved. We're above the law. We'll break the present law and dare Congress to do anything about it.'"

## "PUT ME IN JAIL"

In fact that same day, GM's president, Elliott Estes, said as much in a statement to wire service reporters. "They can close the plants. They can [put] someone in jail—maybe me. But we're going to make [1978] cars to 1977 standards."

"If they think they can come back in the early months of next year and get a quick fix from the Senate to make them legal," said Muskie on the Senate floor still trying to get a vote on his bill, "they better take a lot of long careful thought about it." But the Clean Air Act died. And just as Muskie predicted, the automakers did come back for a fix. The following year, the Big Three came to Capitol Hill saying they must have quick legislative action to "legalize" their 1978 models.

In January 1977, after the smoke cleared, Muskie aide Leon Billings said there probably would be legislative action that year addressing the 1978 model issue. But there was still some simmering residue about the way industry was threatening Congress, "Right now the Congress only has a 'nuclear' deterrent—the power to block car sales altogether [i.e., shut down]—which Detroit knows we can't use. As a result, we have a situation in which Detroit is challenging the credibility of the Congress as an institution. Firms like General Motors and suppliers like United States Steel, are so big they think they are above Congress and can force it to change. . . ." Congress would be willing to give more time to accommodate the development of technologies, said Billings, but the Senate would be reluctant to yield any more ground on emission goals. "We can't compromise on public health standards," he said.[44]

# 7.
## *The 1977 Amendments*

Environmentalists are calling it a victory for Ed Muskie and Paul Rogers and a defeat for John Dingell. Nevertheless, Detroit's automakers now have until 1981 to meet what was originally a 1975 clean air deadline.

*—Dick Kirschten,* National Journal
*August 1977*

Paul Rogers had been in Congress for more than twenty years when the Clean Air Act came to his subcommittee in 1977. A tall, genteel man with a reputation for mastering his material, Rogers represented the 11th congressional district of Florida, which included the northern end of the famed Gold Coast stretching from Pompano Beach to West Palm Beach—a district in transition, moving from southern traditionalism to newer values imported by northern retirees. Rogers had more or less inherited this seat from his father, who had held it from 1944 until his death ten years later.

Arriving in Washington in the mid-1950s as a young bachelor, it took Paul Rogers a few years to find his niche. By the 1960s, however, he began to focus on public health policy and soon became chairman of the House Commerce Committee's Health and Environment Subcommittee. Rogers used that forum to oversee and investigate health and environmental issues. He would later be tagged "Mr. Health" for his concern on issues ranging from hospital cost containment to worker exposure to radiation. Rogers also became keenly concerned about air pollution and public health. In the 1960s he initiated oversight on the nation's early clean air laws and in 1970 helped author the Clean Air Act. Now came the fight to reauthorize that law.

## A NEW POLITICS

By 1977, the political landscape in Washington had changed quite dramatically from even a year earlier. The national elections of November 1976—the first presidential election to follow the convulsing events of the Watergate affair, the articles of impeachment against Richard Nixon, and Nixon's subsequent pardon by Gerald Ford—brought Jimmy Carter, the first in a new wave of southern Democrats, to the White House. Two years earlier, in the 1974 midterm elections, a new crop of some seventy-five young, mostly white male Democrats, dubbed the "Watergate babies," had been swept into the US House of Representatives. They had already begun a revolution in Congress, shaking up their own party's seniority system. They were also eager to make their mark on national policy, especially energy and environmental policies. Many sought seats on the House Commerce Committee, which had a wide swath of jurisdiction over such matters. These feisty new Democrats would become pivotal votes on the fight over the 1977 Clean Air Act Amendments, especially in subcommittee and full committee.*

Paul Rogers, meanwhile, saw the auto industry in something of a bind politically, especially since the Big Three had lobbied to kill the Clean Air bill in 1976. Detroit had also bet on Gerald Ford. "They gambled on the reelection of President Ford and some changes in the composition of the House that would have put them in a more favorable position. They lost." Rogers now saw Jimmy Carter as a key factor in helping write a better Clean Air law. "Gov. Carter is a strong environmentalist from all that we hear," said Rogers in December 1976 preparing for the fight ahead. "I doubt that we'll have an EPA administrator who will endorse a five-year delay [on the auto standards]," which is what EPA's Russell Train had called for in 1976.[1]

Yet, even though Jimmy Carter and Watergate babies signaled strong support for the Clean Air Act, the auto industry still had powerful friends on Capitol Hill—and one in particular, Representative John Dingell (D-MI).

## DETROIT'S MAN

Dingell, like Rogers, had been a member of Congress for twenty-two years, since 1955, when he took the congressional seat his father held dating to the days of the New Deal. Representing a congressional district of auto industry plants and auto workers—from Ford's sprawling River Rouge plant to the suburbs of Dearborn—John Dingell was then (and is now as this book goes to press) ever-attentive to any issue that may affect the automobile industry, from trade to taxes. Dingell had been especially tenacious on the Clean Air Act, even in the earliest fights of the mid-1960s. He authored a controversial amendment during the 1967 Clean Air Act debate, which preempted California from setting its own standards. At the time, Senator George Murphy (D-CA) had secured a provision allowing California to craft its own stricter air pollution control program, exempting it alone among all states from federal standards. Dingell, on the House side, pushed through an amendment in

---

* Among the incoming post-Watergate members who served on the forty-two member House Commerce Committee in 1977 were, for example, Doug Walgren (D-PA); Toby Moffett (D-CT); Andy Maguire (D-NJ); Dick Ottinger (D-NY); Phil Sharp (D-IN); Marty Russo (D-IL); Barbara Mikulski (D-MD); and Henry Waxman (D-CA), representing Los Angeles.

committee to delete Murphy's provision. Dingell's amendment was linked directly to the auto industry, and his efforts on behalf of Detroit were publicized heavily in California. The smog problem there was being called "Dingell's dust." A major battle ensued on the House floor over the provision, with California lobbying furiously for its exemption and eventually prevailing over Dingell.[2]

But by the 1970s, Dingell was a much more powerful member, and he was the industry's leader in monitoring the federal clean air act. In the 1976 session of Congress, Dingell succeeded in incorporating the Ford administration's five-year delay into the House bill, plus a provision for a future unspecified NOx standard left to the discretion of the EPA administrator (or leaving it at 2.0 g/mi, a weaker standard). Dingell's handiwork in 1976, however, yielded to the stronger Senate version in conference, as Ed Muskie had the votes. But the Muskie bill died in Congress. Dingell, meanwhile, had no kind words for the Muskie-Rogers alliance that did him in. "The only beneficiaries of the Muskie-Rogers position are the Arabs," he said, alluding to the "waste of fuel" that would occur in his view because of the tighter standards.[3] When asked in late 1976 about a new three-way catalyst that could make attainment of stricter auto emissions standards possible without compromising fuel economy, Dingell used the opportunity to slam Engelhard. Engelhard, he charged, "was throwing money around to buy themselves a $2 billion to $3 billion market." By doing so, Dingell charged, "they are literally freezing out other technologies, including the diesel passenger car."[4] The diesel, however, had its own problems, as time would tell.

In 1977, Dingell teamed up with ranking Commerce Committee Republican, James T. Broyhill—also his ally in 1976—to fashion a clean air bill that would protect the interests of the Big Three automakers. The congressmen's plan was to weaken the standards and push back the timetable—even for achieving weaker standards. In early 1977, Dingell and Broyhill—joined by Leonard Woodcock of the UAW labor union and Senator Don Riegle—made plain their intentions at a major press conference in the Rayburn House office building's huge Commerce Committee meeting room. They would offer their own bill with new standards and a new compliance timetable.

## ENERGY & GROWTH

Although the 1973-74 Arab oil embargo was history by the time Jimmy Carter took office, America was still deeply mired in the energy debate. There was no national energy plan. The nation's dependence on foreign oil was still a major political issue, and the Carter administration had energy policy as a center point in its planning. Carter was expected to devise a national energy plan that would shift the nation to more abundant and more secure energy sources, chiefly coal. But Carter wanted to make these changes while protecting environmental quality. Yet, moving to coal meant more air pollution, especially more sulfur and nitrogen oxides. Early reports showed that by 1985 increased NOx emissions attributable to industry and utilities switching from natural gas or oil to coal could rise from 5 percent to 10 percent in major cities such as Denver, New York, Philadelphia, Chicago, Baltimore, and Salt Lake City. The other major source of NOx emissions was the automobile, of course. So Carter's team figured that holding firm on automobile NOx would be easier and less politically volatile than forcing thousands of industrial and utility plants to tighten down on their emissions.

The other difficult issue in the clean air debate was urban growth and industrial expansion, particularly in metropolitan areas struggling to meet clean air goals. EPA by this time had already threatened to stop federally funded projects and new construction in urban areas that were not meeting clean air goals. The automobile was also a target on this front as well. "If the auto continues to be dirtier than necessary," explained EPA administrator Doug Costle, "then controls on industry—especially new industry—will have to be that much more restrictive."

The Carter administration was also hearing that the auto industry could make progress on emissions, and that it could do so while increasing fuel economy—a major consideration in the ongoing energy debate.


## VOLVO & CALIFORNIA

California's Tom Quinn, chairman of the state's Air Resources Board, had written the White House about a number of vehicles that were meeting California's tougher standards. "It is clear from the performance of the 1977 Volvo that the statutory emissions standards can be achieved with excellent fuel economy and driveability," wrote Quinn in a February 1977 letter to President Carter. "Not only did the Volvo certify at less than one half of the statutory NOx standard, which has been so strongly opposed by the American companies, but Volvo achieved 21.6 miles per gallon, 10 percent better fuel economy than the company's comparable 1976 models." Quinn disputed the American automakers' contention that they could not duplicate Volvo's success in American cars.[5] Quinn, in fact, urged the Carter administration to adopt California's 1977 standards—0.41 HC, 9.0 CO, and 1.5 NOx—as the national standards through 1980. There was somewhat lower fuel economy in California cars with these standards, Quinn explained, but "the major reason for this is not some inherent conflict between low emissions and good mileage, but rather a lack of maximum effort by the manufacturers [on fuel economy]." Adoption of the California standards as an interim federal requirement, Quinn argued, "has a major advantage over other approaches: the manufacturers cannot argue that those standards are unattainable since cars meeting those requirements are now being manufactured and sold." American automakers, Quinn concluded, can "easily produce much cleaner cars," and do so by the 1978 model year.

"Our experience in California shows that industry generally overstates its difficulties in meeting new standards and then makes a maximum effort to comply once the requirements are set," Quinn said in his letter to Carter. "In 1973 when California adopted stringent 1975 standards, the industry warned of catastrophic fuel penalties and other problems. But when those 1975 cars came along, the first automobiles equipped with catalysts, we saw the greatest improvement in fuels and driveability ever achieved."[6]

Industry, however, was sticking to its guns, reiterating its 1976 shutdown position rather than produce 1978 models that could not meet the standard. "We would close down rather than flout the law," said Ford Motor's vice president Herbert L. Misch at the February 1977 Senate hearings.[7] But the automakers were finding it increasingly difficult in the emission-fuel economy debate to hide behind the "we-don't-have-the-technology" argument, as it was becoming obvious with Volvo and others that the standards could be met without a fuel penalty. So now the Big Three turned their arguments to production difficulties and related economics. "While it is true that some more stringent sets of standards appear to be achievable in 1979 or 1980 with minimal losses in fuel economy," said GM's vice president David S. Potter at the Senate hearings, "they will still require new design, testing, and hardware, with the unavoidable costs that follow."[8] In other words, the job could be done, but at a cost to consumers—which ranged anywhere from $200 to $400 per car.

### "Unequivocal Evidence"

At the Senate's opening hearing on the Clean Air Act in February 1977, Senator Gary Hart, a young Colorado Democrat who had served as George McGovern's 1972 presidential campaign manager, would play an important role on the clean air bill in committee. Hart was chosen by Ed Muskie to handle more of the day-to-day legislating on the bill, as Muskie was being drawn away to his duties as chairman of the Senate Budget Committee. But Hart showed from the outset that he expected the automakers to provide clear and certain evidence of any need to change the standards. "Although the National Academy of Science has given strong support to the auto standards enacted by Congress, critics still complain that the standards are too stringent. I disagree. Before we even think about relaxing the standards on carbon monoxide . . . and on nitrogen oxides, we must ask for unequivocal evidence that the American public's health and welfare would not be damaged by such relaxation. No evidence seems to exist to sustain that point."[9]

Paul Rogers, meanwhile, was already moving his bill through subcommittee on the House side, and then to the full Commerce Committee where John Dingell was waiting with his amendments and weaker bill. The Carter administration was slow in getting its package together, but Rogers was talking with White House officials about the possibility of using their bill. When EPA's Doug Costle offered the administration's package of Clean Air Act amendments in April 1977, it was not everything environmentalists, some state officials, and many in Congress had hoped it would be. The Carter package was weaker than both the House and Senate versions, both of which included tougher CO and NOx standards.

The administration's bill called for a one-year delay for some standards, up to three years for others. At the time, new 1977 cars were required to meet standards of 1.5 g/mi HC, 15.0 g.mi CO, and 2.0 g/mi NOx. All parties agreed that these standards should be extended to 1978 model years, conceding to industry's "we'll-shut-down-rather-than-be-illegal" stand. The other key issues were the CO and NOx standards—what levels should be set and how soon they should go into effect. The administration's package both weakened the standards and allowed the timetable to slide. The hydrocarbon standard was delayed until 1979 and the carbon monoxide standard until 1981. A final decision on the NOx standard was also delayed until 1980, establishing a 1.0 level by 1981 and giving the EPA the right to go to 0.4 level by 1983, if the agency found that such a standard was needed to protect public health.* "We believe the technology necessary to meet the 0.4 gram [NOx] level will be available by 1983," he said. Costle, in fact, recommended a tax on manufacturers who failed to adopt the technology. Yet, the administration did allow for waivers of the NOx standard for diesel cars.[10]

David Hawkins of NRDC, especially unhappy about the administration's NOx standard, called the Carter package "a big disappointment. . . . We thought Carter was on our side." Senator Gary Hart also criticized the Carter package, noting that the standards were substantially weaker than recommended. "The delay is unnecessary," said Hart, vowing to press for a tighter schedule.[11] Rogers was somewhat more optimistic. Even though his own bill was tougher than Carter's, Rogers saw the administration's package and White House lobbying muscle as important elements in staving off more drastic versions in the fight ahead with John Dingell and the auto industry.

## CARTER PLAN HIT

The auto industry, meanwhile, noting that President Carter was about to give a major address on national energy policy, attacked the administration's auto emissions plan for its energy costs. Chrysler's John Riccardo, calling the proposal "environmental overkill of the worse kind," honed in on energy.[12] "On the same day that President

---

* The provisions of the Carter package included the following:

|  | HC | CO | NOx |
|---|---|---|---|
| Original standards | 0.41 | 3.4 | 0.41 |
| Existing 1977 | 1.5 | 15.0 | 2.0 |
| Carter 1978 | 1.5 | 15.0 | 2.0 |
| Carter 1979 |  | 9.0 | 2.0 |
| Carter 1981 |  | 9.0 | 1.0 |
| Carter 1983 |  | 9.0 | 0.41[†] |

† option for EPA after determination

Carter is going to tell us to sacrifice and save energy," said Riccardo, "the administration comes out in favor of automobile emissions standard that would waste energy on the order of billions of gallons of gasoline a year, cost hundreds of dollars per car and produce no measurable difference in air quality."

"We find the EPA's proposed auto emission standards unnecessarily drastic and completely inconsistent with the president's position on inflation and energy," said GM's chairman, Thomas A. Murphy. "It's perplexing to us because it proposes standards that can only result in more gasoline consumption." Costle, however, had made clear in his remarks that clean air was not as he put it "an aesthetic luxury." Rather, he said, clean air is "a public health necessity."

"The president and I are committed to the principle that our nation must have a strong environmental program as a necessary prerequisite to future progress in solving our energy and economic problems," said Costle.[13]

After Carter unveiled his energy plan in April 1977, Chrysler's Riccardo appeared in a televised spot outlining the company's reaction. Riccardo indicated he was more concerned about the administration's position on emissions and safety standards than he was about proposals for increasing automotive fuel economy. He argued, however, that auto emissions standards were inconsistent with fuel economy goals. They would impose a fuel penalty of "three miles per gallon" he said, and "go far beyond health needs." Riccardo especially singled out the CO and NOx standards.[14]

## ROGERS-DINGELL SHOWDOWN

Meanwhile, a key showdown was about to begin in the House Commerce Committee. The Rogers forces, in adopting the Carter package, now had the backing of the White House. The auto industry was putting its full support behind the Dingell-Broyhill bill. The differences were significant, as Dingell-Broyhill proposed to delay the statutory HC standards until 1980, drop the original CO and NOx standards, and weaken key provisions for pollution control equipment warranties, parts certification, production-line testing of new models, and inspections.

When Dingell finally offered his package in the full Commerce Committee as a substitute to the Rogers-Administration bill, the resulting roll call vote on the move produced a tense drama. The Commerce Committee was a large House committee, consisting of forty-three members. As the roll call proceeded, a number of the freshman "Watergate babies" who had been fiercely lobbied by both sides, some with loyalties both to labor and the environment, for example, agonized over their vote. Doug Walgren, a young Democrat from the Pittsburgh area, who earlier admitted that the auto dealers and United Auto Workers had helped him get elected but who admired Paul Rogers and wanted to support the environment, nonetheless voted with Dingell. On the Republican side, a key, pivotal vote for Rogers was cast by veteran Republican Tim Lee Carter from Kentucky, a physician who felt strongly about protecting public health. As the final tally approached, Rogers lost a proxy he thought he had from Commerce Committee chairman Harley Staggers (D-WV), who left the room without leaving his proxy with the committee clerk. Dingell, seated next to Rogers in the committee's formal seating arrangement, grinned broadly with that development and slapped Rogers on the back thinking he had won. But Dingell had miscounted. The final tally indicated a tie vote, 21-to-21, which meant Rogers had won. That brought a big smile to Rogers and elation among his supporters.[15]

Leaving the committee room following the vote, however, Dingell indicated to a *Wall Street Journal* reporter that his forces would prevail on the House floor. An all-out lobbying campaign began around the Dingell effort to defeat the Rogers-Carter administration bill. In this battle, both Republican and Democrat would be lobbied hard by the Dingell-auto industry coalition, with the auto dealers and Big Three focusing on the Republican side, and the UAW going after Democrats.[16]

## CHRYSLER'S MAILGRAMS

The auto industry wasted no time in rallying a vast network of dealers and suppliers to bring its message to Capitol Hill. Senator Gary Hart, in fact, angered by some Chrysler lobbying, circulated a "Dear Colleague" letter to the Senate singling out a solicitation Chrysler was using to enlist its suppliers' support. "The enclosed letter from the Chrysler Corporation to companies with which it does business was sent to me by a concerned constituent. Chrysler has verified that the letter is official, and I expect that it will generate a significant amount of letters and telegrams to members of Congress. Although there is nothing wrong with a corporation using its financial power to exert pressure on Congress, I urge you to make your staffs aware that much mail you receive is the product of a concerted, well-financed industry campaign."[17]

But Chrysler officials, it turns out, not only went to their suppliers, they also used their employees. An internal Chrysler memorandum dated March 23, 1977 from J.C. Moore, the company's manager for public relations, asked all plant managers and their staffs to give the company the legal right to send mailgrams to Congress under their names to support legislation to delay and weaken auto emission standards. The memo included a sample mailgram and explained that Chrysler needed the workers' authorization to "give us the flexibility needed to get maximum impact on the outcome of legislation." An attached authorization form gave Chrysler the right to send mailgrams out under employees' names "when it was determined by Chrysler to be appropriate to do so." The form also specified that Chrysler might change the wording of the mailgram "to provide some variety," though the "substance of the message will remain the same."

Two years later, in March 1979, when Congressman Benjamin Rosenthal (D-NY) learned of Chrysler's mailgrams, an investigation was begun to determine whether the company infringed on the political rights of its managers and their staffs by seeking their authorizations to send the messages to Congress. "Those forms eliminate

CHRYSLER
CORPORATION

March 25, 1977

Dear Mr.

As a supplier to the auto industry you are no doubt aware of the importance the motor vehicle emission legislation, currently being considered by the U. S. Congress, has on the future of our business and its possible disastrous impact if requirements become unreasonably restrictive.

The various groups directly interested in this matter are backing the Broyhill-Dingell Bill in the House and the Riegle-Griffin Bill in the Senate. The motor vehicle manufacturers, the United Auto Workers (UAW), the National Automobile Dealers Association (NADA), and others feel the requirements contained in this legislation are the most reasonable compromise between health protection, fuel economy, driveability, low cost, and protection of jobs.

You were extremely helpful during the last session of Congress in getting the Broyhill-Dingell Bill through the House, and we would like to ask for your assistance again. There are two things you can do which we would very much appreciate. First, contact your U. S. Representative and let him(her) know how important it is to all of us connected with the motor vehicle industry that he(she) support the Broyhill-Dingell Bill. Then contact your U. S. Senators and seek their support of the Riegle-Griffin Bill. <u>Second, authorize us to send your Representative and Senators a mailgram over your name urging support of these Bills as they come up for vote.</u> When the Bills come up for crucial floor votes, we will not have sufficient time to alert you. Your authorization for the mailgrams, will give us the flexibility needed to get maximum impact on the outcome of the legislation. We have attached a sample mailgram and the authorization form which we would appreciate very much your signing and returning as soon as possible.

I hope we can count on your support for this legislation because it is important that the issue be resolved in a manner that allows all of us to remain healthy and profitable. Unnecessary and unrealistic requirements could have a very negative affect on our business.

Please take action today.

Sincerely,

J. T. Watson
Purchasing Agent,
Chassis Parts, Hard Trim,
& Stampings
Corporate Purchasing Office

Attachment

*This March 1977 Chrysler memo to the company's suppliers illustrates how the automakers tapped into a wide array of allies to generate political pressure.*

any semblance of employee political autonomy," said Rosenthal, "and are designed to mislead legislators into thinking that proposed legislation has widespread support or opposition." R. Michael Cole, legislative director for Common Cause, added, "In our view, that authorization form constitutes a power of attorney. It is a very unusual example of the many ways in which corporations are orchestrating political pressure." A Chrysler spokesman denied the forms gave the company power of attorney and said they were "merely an authorization request for support of a specific program." But there was another issue as well.

The Internal Revenue Service (IRS) at the time allowed that direct lobbying was tax deductible, but prohibited deductions for indirect, or grassroots, lobbying. Rosenthal believed that Chrysler was engaged in the latter and therefore might not be entitled to deducting those costs as expenses. A Chrysler spokesman said the company had not engaged in grassroots lobbying and that handling the costs as business expenses was proper. Rosenthal, however, had obtained two other Chrysler documents from 1976 that encouraged not only Chrysler employees to support the legislation weakening the standards, but to encourage their friends to do so as well. At the time, the IRS defined grassroots lobbying as "attempts to influence the general public or segments thereof with respect to legislative matters, elections, or referendums."

## HOLDING BACK

As the Rogers-Carter administration bill headed for its final showdown on the House floor, the Commerce Committee released its final report on the bill. Like many such reports, there is often a very good summation of facts and issues compiled so members can make informed decisions on the bill when it arrives on the floor. The report on H.R. 6161 included some well-documented history on the slow progress in cleaning up auto emissions,* why fuel economy would not suffer with tighter emissions standards, and why the "expeditious achievement" of the Clean Air Act's original 90 percent reduction in new car emissions—specifically required by the 1970 statute**—was needed to protect public health. The report also made important rev-

---

* "It must be understood," said the report, "that actual changes in light duty vehicle emissions have not been nearly as significant as some have implied when they have cited the 40 to 80 percent reduction . . . since 1967. Actually, total vehicle emissions have been reduced very little and, in the case of nitrogen oxides, total NOx emitted from automobile on the road have increased over the last 7 years. For example, the latest EPA analysis shows that since 1970, the total hydrocarbons and carbon monoxide emissions from all automobiles on the road had decreased by a mere 14 percent and 16 percent respectively. In the same period total automobile nitrogen oxide emissions have increased by 16 percent."

** This reduction, it should be remembered, was "statutorily-required," which means written into the law itself, not relegated to EPA rulemaking or administrative discretion.

elations about how the auto industry was also holding back, slowing down, or not going ahead with key technologies it knew would do the job—especially the dual and three-way catalyst systems.

The automakers' delay tactics even caught the attention of National Academy of Sciences' president Philip Handler, who had noted previously in 1975, "There has been an apparent reluctance on the part of the manufacturers to assemble in a demonstration vehicle the component emissions-control technologies which the manufacturers have in hand. In this way they can maintain with some consistency that the required technology 'has not been demonstrated.'...." Even as test cars and demonstrations in California were showing that these systems could meet the original statutory standards, including a 0.4 NOx standard, EPA found evidence in 1976 that industry slowed development efforts on these technologies anticipating that Congress would move to relax or abolish the NOx standard. The automakers also held back their information on these technologies, not reporting to EPA. As the House Commerce Committee report explained:

In order to evaluate the capability of automobile manufacturers to meet emissions standards, EPA solicits information from domestic and foreign manufacturers as to the development of new emission-related technology.

But recently the Agency has reported a lack of complete response on the part of manufacturers, indicating the manufacturers have been withholding information which would have dramatic impacts on both emissions and fuel economy.

In some cases the omission of information was so gross as to exclude the development of entire engine lines and development of five and six-cylinder diesel engines.

In another area which promises benefits in both emission control and fuel economy, General Motors began development of electronic controls in 1970 but failed to report this work until they asked for a suspension in 1975.

Testimony before the committee, reports in the trade press and articles in professional journals, indicate potential savings of 15 percent in fuel through improved transmissions. But little information has been reported to EPA.

Most significant is the fact that GM reported the possibility of an improved catalyst, but when EPA requested the data from these tests, General Motors said that the data . . . would not be provided until they were analyzed by General Motors.

This would indicate that EPA is given only limited information on which to base its projections of emissions control. And without this information, the only data forwarded to EPA is that which the automobile manufacturers determines will best serve their own purposes.[18]

---

Essentially, this meant that such goals were elevated by Congress to a higher level of public policy importance than might otherwise be the case, and in the House committee's eyes, were still at that level of importance.

## FUEL ECONOMY

Throughout the 1977 debate, the Big Three, John Dingell, and their allies continued to assert that the emissions standards would negatively affect fuel economy. But
Congress had already voted in separate legislation—the Energy Policy and Conservation Act of 1975—to require specific fuel economy goals for automobiles by 1980
and 1985. And in the federal government at the time, a time when national energy
concerns were very much in the forefront, there was generally broad agreement that
the auto industry could meet the House version of the emissions timetable while
still meeting or exceeding the congressionally required fuel economy goals. In fact,
National Academy of Sciences president Philip Handler stated in July 1975, "it is
common knowledge and a fact of the marketplace that fuel economy gains are being
made largely by virtue of changes that have nothing to do with the engine system."
Looking out to the 1985-required fuel economy goals, the Federal Energy Agency
and EPA concluded those goals could be achieved "almost totally by non-emission
control related changes such as weight reduction, model-mix shifts, driveline
improvements, and the use of diesel engines."

After reviewing the findings of an April 1977 EPA report on emissions standards
and fuel economy levels, the House Commerce Committee concluded in its report
that it was possible for manufacturers to meet emissions standards of .41/GPM HC,
9.0/GPM CO, and .40 GPM NOx, and achieve up a 4 percent fuel economy improvement while doing so, "if the manufacturers choose to work hard to maximize fuel
economy." The EPA analysis, said the House report, "again confirms the long-held
Committee view that the fuel economy effect of any particular emission standard
largely rests with the manufacturer. If they choose to apply available, advanced technology there need be no permanent fuel penalty whatsoever at any standard."[19]

On May 19, 1977, the Rogers bill got a big endorsement from editors at the *Washington Post*, who specifically mentioned the auto emissions-fuel economy question.
"Until recently . . . ," wrote the editors, "we at this newspaper believed that there
was a substantial trade-off between clean exhausts and fuel efficiency. If you wanted
less pollution, according to that wisdom, you would have to settle for fewer miles
per gallon. That's still true, Mr. Dingell argues. But last month the federal Environmental Protection Agency told Congress that present technology permits the
tighter standards of the Rogers bill without any penalty in fuel. . . ."[20] Still, whenever any positive signs would surface that fuel economy and emissions might be
improved simultaneously, such arguments would be quickly quashed or heavily qualified. Consider what happened to Senator Muskie.

## THE MITSUBISHI LETTERS

On April 27, 1977, Senator Muskie received a letter from Tomio Kubo, president of
the Mitsubishi Motors Corp. Mr. Kubo explained that his firm had developed an

engine that met all of the original "Muskie standards" [i.e., the 1970 statutory standards] with improved fuel economy. Kubo further stated that his firm's new engine "does away with the old idea that gas mileage must suffer if NOx is reduced."[21] For Muskie, this was a very encouraging statement, indeed. However, about two weeks later (May 17), a short, second letter from Mr. Kubo went out to Muskie. It included this caveat, "[L]est there be any misunderstanding, I would like to make clear that given a more reasonable NOx standard, fuel economy improvements could be even greater."[22] This letter was cited in a May 23 article in the widely circulated auto industry trade newspaper, *Automotive News*. The only problem, however, was that Muskie had not released the letter to *Automotive News*. In fact, Muskie had not even received the letter by that date.

"I did not release the letter," Muskie said, "because it had not even arrived at my office. It was released by the Chrysler Corp., for whom Mitsubishi makes the Plymouth Arrow and Dodge Colt. This smacks of the same intimidation tactics used five years ago by the auto companies on their catalyst suppliers. The threat then was cancellation of supply contracts if the catalyst manufactures spoke out regarding the true capability of catalysts to reduce auto emissions.

"I am greatly disappointed that an American company feels the necessity to downplay its own supplier's accomplishments, rather than welcoming the technological achievement as a means of getting on with the cleanup jobs."[23]

The Big Three continued to soldier forward with their "tighter-emissions-means-less-fuel-economy" argument throughout the 1977 legislative season. Posturing for the weakest possible measure to come out of the House-Senate conference, GM chairman Thomas A. Murphy stated in mid-June 1977, "It's going to be tough for us to meet the House-passed legislation and it will be extremely difficult to meet the Senate numbers without having some loss in fuel economy. We're trying to do two things here and to some degree they're in conflict. We're trying to control emissions at the same time we're trying to improve and conserve fuel. These two aims in a way are mutually exclusive. But if anybody can accomplish this, General Motors can and will. We don't want to add to our cost either in the original equipment or in the fuel that's consumed by the vehicle over time."[24]

Three weeks earlier GM had announced that it would put three-way catalysts on all of its cars with a "minimal" loss in fuel economy—but not until the 1982 model year. This announcement dovetailed with the Dingell-Broyhill schedule of weaker standards. GM claimed it couldn't bring the three-way catalyst any sooner because it was "a very sophisticated system" that needed more time to phase in.

However, Volvo was already selling cars with the same three-way catalyst in California even as GM's Thomas Murphy was complaining in Washington about how difficult that would be. Ford Motor, too, indicated it could put three-way converters on some cars by 1979, and on most of its production by 1980 "with some risk" if it had to. In fact, Ford projected it could develop a three-way catalyst that would yield fuel economy gains while meeting emissions standards. Ford even showed one scenario with a three-way catalyst system that would meet emission standards tougher than proposed in the Dingell-Broyhill bill while yielding a 1 percent fuel advantage.[25]

## MUSKIE'S EVIDENCE

In Senate debate, Ed Muskie hastened to point out what the automakers were already doing. Existing cars had improved fuel economy under the tightened emissions standards, Muskie explained, even though the automakers had predicted certain decline or minimal improvement. "The most significant tightening of auto emissions standards to date occurred in model year 1975," Muskie noted in his June 8 floor statement. "Although Chrysler testified that these standards would cause a fuel penalty, their cars realized a 12 percent fuel economy gain." General Motors estimated a substantial gain, and its actual experience, said Muskie, "was twice the fuel economy improvement predicted."[26] He also cited 1977 models, which were required to meet a new NOx emission standard that had been tightened by 33 percent. "The auto industry has always claimed that this [NOx] standard would cause the greatest fuel economy penalty. Chrysler estimated a 7 percent fuel economy loss; the actual loss was zero. General Motors estimated a 5 percent loss. The actual change was a 9 percent improvement between 1976 and 1977 model years."[27]

The automakers were simply using the energy crisis and "fuel penalty" line as a ruse to weaken, delay, or dismantle the auto emissions standards. And their rhetoric on the issue continued, despite evidence to the contrary.

Other issues surfacing in the 1977 debate centered on the performance of emission control equipment and on how these systems worked once cars were out on the road. It was one thing for a new car fresh from the factory to pass an EPA emissions certification test. It was quite something else for that same car to keep controlling emissions at the certified level for many years thereafter. In fact, the president's Council on Environmental Quality (CEQ) had reported in 1976 that "pre-production prototype" cars being used to meet EPA's certification tests—which were especially assembled by the automakers to meet those tests—were "not necessarily representative" of models then in use. And for some automakers, the cars coming off their assembly lines for public use were a lot worse. "Eighty-seven percent of the vehicles produced by one manufacturer failed to meet the carbon monoxide standard," reported CEQ.

EPA was recommending that Detroit's production be monitored through assembly line testing, that more support be given to EPA's program to recall vehicles for equipment problems, and that the auto manufacturers be required to warranty their pollution control equipment for five years or 50,000 miles of operation. CEQ also underscored the importance of a newer approach to address the performance of existing vehicles: emission inspections. Only four metropolitan areas at the time were required to use emission inspection programs in an effort to reduce auto emissions as part of their overall cleanup programs. But in the House and Senate bills that later emerged, proposals to cover some of the warranty and emissions inspection issues were added. The Senate bill, for example, included a five-year or 50,000-mile pollution equipment warranty, but Dingell was pushing a proposal to weaken that to eighteen months or 18,000 miles. Rogers' bill incorporated extending emissions inspections programs to all twenty-nine metropolitan areas then exceeding federal air quality standards. The *Washington Post*, for one, agreed. "Americans accept the idea of regular inspections of automobile brakes and lights," wrote the *Post's* editors in May 1977, endorsing mandatory auto-exhaust checkups. "It is now time to add exhaust pipes to the list, for the same reason: the protection of people who want to keep breathing while they keep driving."[28]

## House Floor Fight

In late May 1977, as Dingell had vowed, the full House was faced with a showdown vote on the Dingell-Broyhill amendment, in effect, a bill to substitute for the Rogers-administration bill. Labor, the auto companies, and the auto dealers had all been lobbying furiously on behalf of the Dingell-Broyhill substitute for weeks. The bill not only pushed back the deadlines to 1980-81, it also altered the statutory levels for carbon monoxide and NOx that were set in 1970—doubling the amounts previously allowed. The bill also weakened the provisions for car warranties, parts certification, production-line testing of new models, and emission inspections.

Dingell and his supporters argued that changes in the standards were necessary to give the manufacturers more time to develop new technology, prevent loss of jobs, and to give more emphasis to fuel conservation in car design. Emission controls, said Dingell, would add more than $500 to a car's purchase price and cause added fuel expenses.[29] Paul Rogers countered that Dingell's cost estimates were too high, that the manufacturers were already meeting tougher standards in California, and that jobs had increased nationwide because of environmental laws. Fuel economy had increased, too, he explained, even as emissions standards were tightened. But it was the cost to public health that Rogers kept hitting at. "Health effects do mean something," he said during the floor debate. "It has been shown that 80 percent to 90 percent of cancer comes from the environment as well as heart conditions and lung disease. We know what can be done and we should do it." Dingell charged that those pushing for stronger controls could show "no quantifiable health benefit."[30] Yet the House Commerce Committee report on the Rogers bill was full of examples from EPA, the American Lung Association, and the National Academy of Sciences showing "quantifiable health benefits."[31]

Still, on the House floor, Rogers knew he was in trouble, even with White House support. He had prepared a fallback position with colleague Richardson Pryer (D-NC). Pryer offered an amendment he described as a compromise between the Dingell and Rogers bills, but was actually an attempt to hold to the tougher standards in the Rogers bill using Dingell's more relaxed schedule. A roll call ensued, but the

Pryer substitute failed by a 190-to-202 vote, with a mere seven votes accounting for the difference. The Dingell-Broyhill amendment was now assured, and its adoption followed by a vote of 255-to-139. This weaker auto emissions package then became a core part of the House clean air bill.

Seated in the House gallery, peering down on members as they cast their electronic votes, were the UAW's Leonard Woodcock and Douglas Fraser. One House member during the voting remarked that it was difficult to pass up the opportunity to cast a vote that pleased both big business and big labor at the same time.

## The UAW Effect

The UAW, in fact, played a key role throughout the House fight, mobilizing the entire AFL-CIO to its side. The autoworkers flew senior UAW officials to Washington from around the country to lobby House members. UAW lobbyist Howard Pastor said the union believed the environment and public health were adequately protected under the weaker standards, and that there was no public health trade-off—only elimination of "unnecessary margins of safety" that might cost jobs. With the UAW, the Big Three, the Business Roundtable, and local automobile dealers* all linked arm in arm, even the White House had an uphill fight. "What are you going to do," observed one supporter of tougher standards, "when you have Henry Ford and Leonard Woodcock on the same side?"[32]

During the floor debate, Dingell argued that the Rogers-Carter administration standards would cost between 20,000 and 100,000 auto industry jobs; would cost car buyers an additional $350 for new cars; would decrease fuel economy by about 10 percent; and require an additional 145,000 barrels of oil each day. Supporters called Dingell's assertions inaccurate or overstated and charged that industry was dragging its feet, having already improved fuel economy by 50 percent since 1974 with tougher emissions standards.

"In deciding how to vote," observed the *Wall Street Journal*'s reporter, "most members probably relied less on the confusing statistical barrage than on the weight of lobbying pressures from car dealers in their home districts on the one hand, and from environmentalists on the other." Yet, in this battle, environmentalist were clearly outgunned.

---

* The importance of auto dealer lobbying during one 1976 House floor amendment was captured by author Bernie Asbell. "[I]n a campaign by 'local, independent' businessmen, quietly inspired by Detroit, the corridors of House office buildings have been so alive with local-franchise auto dealers, you'd think the new models were being shown there." An auto dealer, observed Asbell, "is often a community leader and quite likely to be among a congressman's leading campaign contributors." And dealers' effect, he observed, is often more direct. Unlike more diffuse, hard-to-pin-down corporate influence in Congress, where direct cause-and-effect voting is not always apparent, "the Congressman does heed the song of his local Dodge Boys."

## PROFITS OVER LUNGS

"The House today has chosen to protect the $4-billion-a-year profits of the American automobile industry rather than the lungs of the American people," charged the National Clean Air Coalition in a sharply worded statement critical of the House vote. "It is now up to the Senate to protect the breathing public."[33] Representative Andy Maguire (D-NJ), reacting to the House vote, called the auto industry's record on auto emissions "miserable," and charged Congress with coping out for "a compromise of a compromise, of a compromise. . . ."[34]

EPA administrator Doug Costle viewed the House vote a "needless setback for public health for at least the next decade," especially since technology was available to meet the standards at a reasonable cost." The automakers, in Costle's view—turning out cars that would be dirtier than they should be given the available technologies—were, in effect, penalizing other industrial sources that did not have the cleanup technology Detroit had. New plants—and jobs—would be lost in some areas because dirty automobiles would either push new areas into noncompliance, or keep already noncompliant areas violating the law. Thus, Detroit's capacity for dirtying the air under the House-adopted version was coming "at the expense of everyone else."[35] "If they had spent the money to meet the standards instead of lobbying," added Henry Waxman, "we wouldn't be here fighting this fight, and we'd have healthier people across the country."[36]

On the Senate side, Muskie's bill, which came out of committee with Gary Hart's help in May, was generally stronger than the House-passed bill, although it too faced weakening amendments on the floor. The Muskie bill had given some ground on deadlines, extending them until 1980. President Carter, opposing any further delays, lobbied the Senate to hold on to key provisions, citing public health and worsening urban air pollution. "More than 96 million people in at least 48 of our cities breathe air which exceeds the federal health-based air quality standards," Carter said in a letter to Senator Muskie. Another administration letter signed by Transportation's Brock Adams, EPA's Doug Costle, and Federal Energy administrator Jack O'Leary stated that the Muskie bill's auto emissions goals could be achieved with "little or no fuel economy penalty . . . if the industry employs the optimal fuel economy technology."[37]

On the Senate floor, Michigan's two senators, Donald W. Riegle (D) and Robert P. Griffin (R), had a package of amendments ready to use similar to those of Dingell-Broyhill on the House side. Like Dingell, Riegle and Griffin argued that forcing the auto industry to meet the standards by 1980 would mean among other things the loss of 134,000 barrels of oil a day over the next six years and raise car costs to consumers with very little added benefit in reduction of tailpipe pollutants. Muskie and the administration countered that holding to 1980 would force the industry to use a higher level of technology sooner, such as the three-way catalyst, diesel engines, and the Honda-type stratified charge engine. Muskie, in particular, kept public health in the forefront, repeatedly citing a 1974 National Academy of Science study that found 15,000 people dying each year from lung and other diseases either caused or aggravated by air pollution—4,000 of which were attributed to automobile air pollution.[38]

In the ensuing debate, Senator Howard Baker (R-TN), offered a compromise amendment—a proposal that retained the committee's 1980 deadline but softened intermediate requirements for 1979. Riegle-Griffin gave way to Baker, and the compromise was adopted. The final Senate bill was approved on June 10 by a 73-7 margin. In the end, the Senate had pushed deadlines back to 1980 while the House had delayed them to 1982. The House-Senate conference, however, was sure to be contentious, especially on the auto emissions standards.

## BAD AIR, 1977

Out in the country, meanwhile, millions of people were still breathing bad air. In June, the city of New York, under order from Mayor Beame, initiated an automobile parking ban in Manhattan to help clean up the air. New York had made some progress with its dirty air since 1970, reducing carbon monoxide (CO) by 17 to 22 percent in the central business district. But it still had an air pollution problem. Carbon monoxide levels in the city were still above the allowable federal standard of 9.0 parts per million (PPM). And at some locations, such as the entrance to the Queensborough Bridge at 59th Street and 2nd Avenue, CO levels were as high as 17.0 PPM. The city also had about fifteen days per year in which ozone pollution was a problem. Not far away, the state of Connecticut was exceeding the .08 PPM ozone standard about thirty days per year—four days of which typically exceeded .20 PPM.[39]

In Senate debate, Ed Muskie pointed to other examples. EPA had projected that CO and HC emissions would go down in Baltimore by 1977, he said. But in fact, just the opposite occurred. By mid-1977, total hydrocarbons and carbon monoxide from vehicles in Baltimore had grown more than 200,000 tons, a combined increase of 35 percent.[40]

Across the US, in fact, cities were recording ozone violations regularly that summer—typically an indicator of high auto emissions. Los Angeles and San Diego were among the leading violators of the federal ozone in the summer of 1977, exceeding the .08 PPM level practically every day. Houston wasn't far behind, recording forty-seven days in the ninety-two day period from June 1 to August 31, 1977, in which it violated the federal standard. St Louis would report thirty-three such days that summer; San Francisco about eighteen. Chicago would report about twenty days above its own citywide ozone standard, which was a bit tougher than the federal standard. Philadelphia reported twenty-three "unhealthful days" and Boston thirty-six such days under their air quality indexes (AQI). Cleveland noted twenty-eight "unsatisfactory days" and another eleven that were "poor/very poor or extremely poor" under its AQI. Cincinnati recorded sixty-seven days in the "poor/very poor or extremely poor" category that summer. Washington, DC's Metropolitan Council of Governments would report thirty-six "very unhealthful days" and another twenty "unhealthy days" that summer under its AQI.[41]

The auto industry, for its part, maintained it had made great strides reducing emissions since the late 1960s, claiming reductions in the 40-to-80 percent range. "Actually," explained the House Commerce Committee in its May 1977 report, "total vehicle emissions have been reduced very little and, in the case of nitrogen oxides, total NOx emitted from automobiles on the road have increased over the last seven years." In addition, EPA had found that since 1970, the total hydrocarbon and carbon monoxide emissions from all automobiles on the road had decreased by a mere 14 percent and 16 percent respectively. EPA also found that total automobile NOx had gone up by 16 percent. "[T]his poor performance in actual emissions control," concluded the House Commerce Committee, "is strong evidence of the need for moving to tighter emission standards as quickly as practicable."[42] But with the House bill now reduced to the Dingell-Broyhill provisions at mid-year 1977, proponents of tighter standards were worried about holding on to the Senate version.

Even the otherwise conservative *Washington Post* columnist George Will excoriated the House in a June 1977 column for making "an unacceptable choice against the health of Americans who breathe." Will was especially upset that the House version would allow "a five-fold increase in nitrogen oxide emissions over what would be required under existing law." And he took the opportunity to single out the automakers:

> The automobile industry says it does not know how to meet the present, unrevised standards. But the industry has a dismal record of asserting what can't be done, and an admirable record of doing what it is forced to do. The lash of necessity concentrates the mind.
>
> Automobiles should be the focus of the fight for clean air because they are the most pervasive source of pollution. And it is easier to shape the decisions of four automobile companies than it is to deal with scores of thousands of fuel-burning industries. But advocates for the automobile industry say that unless pollution standards are relaxed, jobs will be lost because automobile prices will rise unreasonably, and production may be disrupted.
>
> The House bill is an attempt to secure jobs at the expense of the health of millions, especially children and the aged. But more permissive automobile pollution standards will be an obstacle to industrial growth in many areas.
>
> Where pollution already is the maximum permitted, only a decrease in automobile pollution can make possible increased industrial pollution. So the House bill sacrifices other industries, as well as the breathing public, to the automobile industry.
>
> Some advocates for the automobile industry seem to have learned their science from the tobacco industry. They argue that there is little "scientific proof" of the connection between automobile pollution and particular diseases. Such arguments deny the undeniable: statistical patterns that demonstrate a correlation between high pollution and high disease rates. . . .[43]

## ILLEGAL CARS CLOSER

By July 1977, the House-Senate conference had not yet convened, and the automakers began reminding Carter and Congress that their 1978 models, scheduled to begin rolling off the assembly lines, would be illegal unless Congress soon approved its Clean Air Act amendments. The Big Three reiterated their 1976 stance that they would shut down. "Under current circumstances," said GM's Thomas Murphy in a letter to Carter, "General Motors will be unable to sell and accordingly, as a practical matter, will be unable to produce its 1978 model automobiles." Chrysler's John Riccardo said it was "imperative that the bill be passed" before it could begin producing '78 models.[44]

"I don't find their arguments persuasive," said Gary Hart, harkening back to the previous year. "They charge uncertainty, but they had a bill last year which gave them another year of grace, but they at least tacitly allowed it to be killed." But now the Big Three were charging Congress with delay, and Hart found that objectionable. "Every time the industry doesn't get exactly what it wants from Congress, it charges Congress with foot dragging. It confuses getting a bill with getting the exact bill it wants." Hart added that if the automakers had started working on the problem in 1970 rather than fighting for delays over the last seven years, they could have met the original standards by this time.[45] But the Big Three were pushing hard, waving around high unemployment numbers if they were forced to shut down. One House staff member even reported receiving a telephone call from a Federal Reserve Board economist worried about the impact a closure would have on the nation's economy.[46] And in the final legislative showdown to come, the auto industry still had John Dingell.

## HOT CONFERENCE

The House-Senate conference began in late July, just before the normal monthlong congressional recess in August. The conference committee had been slow to form, partly over the naming of conferees. The Senate, with the tougher version, was in no hurry to act. Muskie at one point said the Senate didn't need to act. "We don't need a bill," he said, goading the industry. Auto executives again threatened to shut down their lines rather than produce illegal cars subject to fines of up to $10,000 each. President Carter, however, intervened, pressing Congress to act before its summer recess.[47] The recess was then postponed, and the conferees met for eight days, culminating in a seven-hour marathon session on August 2 that ended at 2:20 AM.

As the conferees tried to hammer out their differences in a large committee room of the Rayburn House Office Building, the final session of August 2 proved to be the most testy. About midnight, just as the House side was under pressure to accept the more stringent Senate version, Representative Dingell, trying to buy time for his position, called for an overnight recess. Representative Henry Waxman (D-CA) objected, saying the bill already had too much compromise and too much extension. "We have a commitment to protect the health of the American people," said Waxman, "and not be faced with the blackmail that the auto industry had threatened us with." Dingell replied there was "no effort by industry or labor or anybody else to blackmail."[48]

After a brief recess, the House side offered a proposal that would have retained a weaker CO standard—9.0 GPM rather than 3.4. It was now about 1 AM. Dingell, defending the proposal, said there was no quantified evidence of health hazards from automobile CO in the open air. That brought spirited replies from some senators, and one in particular. "We have [polluted] air we can see," said Senator Wendell Anderson (D-MN) in a raised voice to Dingell, alluding to the polluted air in Washington that evening.[49] Anderson had been a fairly quiet participant up until this point.[50]

"Driving in from Virginia," Anderson said, referring to his own commute, "I can't see the Washington Monument." Even on the short walk from his Senate office over to the Capitol, Anderson said his eyes hurt on polluted days. "There is a health problem," he said emphatically, pounding on the table. "I don' see how a responsible parent could bring children from Minnesota to Washington, DC," he added.[51] When Dingell moved to reply, Anderson held his ground, "Don't point your finger at me! I've been listening to you for two weeks, now it's your turn to listen to me!"[52]

"We're told there's no health problem," Anderson continued. "I don't accept that."[53] Gary Hart (D-CO) then added that many areas across the country were still not in compliance with the 1970 Act. The Senate conferees then rejected the House proposal unanimously.

At that point, Ed Muskie, who had been "unusually quiet throughout the conference" according to one account, added his voice on the CO question.[54] Muskie called CO "the most lethal, most harmful of pollutants emitted by automobile" and said the manufacturers had not asked to relax CO standards until Congress appeared ready to back away from the NOx standard. "Every time we give way to the industry they move for more relaxation. I'm convinced the industry can meet these standards within the confines that we've laid out. And I think it is time the Congress told industry just that."[55] The conferees then agreed to a 3.4 CO standard with proviso for a waiver.

In the final analysis, the House-Senate conference agreed to a bill that was closer to the Senate version, but one which yielded final standards that were weaker than

---

* The auto emissions standards were now extended two more years, through 1979 models, which were required to meet the following standards: 1.5 g/mi HC, 15 g/mi CO, and 2.0/g/mi for NOx. The 1980 model year standards were tightened as follows: from 1.5 g/mi to .41 for HC; from 15 to 7 for CO, and for NOx, remained at 2.0 g/mi. For 1981 and beyond they were set at .41 for HC, 3.4 for CO, and 1.0 for NOx. However, the CO standard for 1981 and 1982 could be waived up to the 7 g/mi-level by EPA if public health did not require adherence to the statutory standards and if technology to meet it did not exist. In addition, other waivers were also permitted. An "innovative technology" waiver of 1.5 g/mi NOx was extended to any company for up to 50,000 vehicles or engines incorporating the technology in any four-year period after 1980. A four-year waiver was also granted for light-duty diesel engines, allowing NOx levels of 1.5 g/mi for model years 1981-1984. American Motors, then dependent on

those required under the 1970 Act.* Both the full House and Senate approved the final measure and conference report by voice vote on August 4 and sent it to the president. John Dingell, however, refused to sign the conference report. Nor was everybody in the auto industry happy with the new law. "We are still concerned about the extreme cost and fuel penalty of standards which are more stringent than required to protect health," stated Chrysler after the conference agreement was reached. The standards, said Chrysler, "go beyond health needs" and "will unquestionably waste fuel." The UAW's Douglas Fraser, noting that the automakers got the extension they needed for continued production, was more upbeat about the future. "Now that this reasonable agreement has been reached," said Fraser, "we would hope the companies never again would go to Congress seeking to postpone or weaken these clean air standards."[56]

On August 7, 1977, when President Carter signed the bill, he said it would permit economic growth that was environmentally sound. He also promised that the new auto emissions timetable would be strictly enforced. The law, he said, provided automakers a "firm timetable for meeting strict, but achievable, emissions standards."[57]

---

emissions technology from other companies, was given a two-year waiver until 1983 to meet the 1.0 g/mi NOx standard. The original .4 g/mi NOx was retained, but only as a research objective. There were also waivers and special provisions for high-altitude vehicles, trucks, buses, and motorcycles.

# 8

## Enforcement Wars

As a record of compliance with the law, and as an expression of concern for public health, this marks a dismal showing by automakers.
*—Barbara Blum, EPA deputy administrator,*
*May 1978, commenting on 12 million autos recalled*
*for emission system defects[1]*

Charles E. Archbald II, of Mantoloking, New Jersey, was having a surprisingly good effect with his new car—a 1973 Plymouth Fury V-8 issued to him as a New Jersey state employee. After he made a little adjustment at the dashboard, setting the heating indicator to defrost, he discovered the car was suddenly getting better-than-expected gas mileage. But there was a catch to Mr. Archbald's good fortune—a catch so strange that Mr. Archbald decided to bring his tale to Ralph Nader in a 1974 letter.

"This car, when I acquired it last June, produced average gasoline mileage for its size, perhaps 14 to 16 MPG, depending on driving conditions. I was advised by a friend that if I put the heater lever on 'Defrost,' the mileage would improve. It did." Mr. Archbald's car was now getting between 18 and 25 MPG.

Mr. Archbald explained that his friend— who had purchased his Plymouth Fury in 1972—learned about the special defrost trick after he complained "regularly and loudly" about the car's poor mileage. "The service manager, I suppose to quiet his complaints, told him about this trick and claimed that it would 'balance' the emission control system. He also stressed the confidentiality of this information and even went so far as to tell him only after leaving the . . . premises on a test drive. He was urged not to tell anyone else. . . . He did, however, violate this confidence. I have compounded it by informing the head of our state motor pool, which has several hundred similar vehicles. . . .[2]

The "balancing" of the emissions system described by the service manager in Mr. Archbald's letter meant essentially disabling it. When the heater lever was moved to defrost, the mileage improved, but the emissions controls no longer worked. The defrost option, in the argot of auto emissions specialist and the EPA, amounted to a *defeat device*, a mechanism linked to the automobile's engine that shut off or circumvented the emission control system.

The term *defeat device* was coined by Big Three engineers to describe mechanisms in their engines that would override or disable emission control systems only temporarily, they claimed. Such valves, switches, or sensors could be used to deactivate pollution control systems, such as the exhaust gas recirculation system (which then captured pollutants and recirculated them to the engine to burn again). But such defeat devices, they said, would only be activated for short periods of time, such as during engine start-up when certain pollutants such as nitrogen oxides weren't a problem.

EPA, however, found a more widespread pattern of abuse with the devices during normal vehicle operation and advised the automakers in 1972 the devices could be illegal.* EPA's warning to manufacturers was clear about what was expected. "[I]f your company plans to use sensors or devices in 1973 model vehicles which may adversely affect emission control under conditions or during operations likely to occur in actual use," wrote Ruckelshaus, "I strongly urge that you promptly undertake the necessary technical work that will allow you to remove such sensors or devices . . . or to render them inoperative . . . if they cannot be physically removed. . . ."[3] Yet as Mr. Archbald discovered, some of these devices were not removed or rendered inoperative. More than twenty years later, the defeat device issue would come up again.

## FAST FORWARD, 1995

On November 1995, US Attorney General Janet Reno held a press conference in Washington, DC, announcing a Department of Justice settlement with General Motors. The major TV news networks were there, cameras rolling, ready to feed the evening broadcasts. GM, it seems, had some Cadillac engines that were modified in a such way that the engines "defeated" their air pollution control system. The result was nearly a half million 1991-95 Cadillacs spewing carbon monoxide into the air in excess of federal air pollution standards. "Since 1991, these cars have poured carbon monoxide into the atmosphere at two to three times the legal limit," said Reno, announcing the settlement and consent decree. "It's simply not fair to burden people's health to improve sales appeal of automobiles."[4] EPA officials estimated the devices caused enough additional pollution to blanket downtown Washington, DC with a ten-foot-thick layer of carbon monoxide. Carbon monoxide (CO) is a colorless, odorless gas, which does its health-effects handiwork on the human body

---

* "Two general classes of devices that some manufacturers are planning to install in 1973 vehicles warrant special scrutiny," wrote EPA's William Ruckelshaus to auto manufacturers in July 1972. "I am referring to *ambient temperature* related devices which are designed so that the entire emission control system is operative when the car is tested under the standard 68-86 [degree] F. test conditions, but which modify or disable such control systems when the vehicle is outside that range; and to *accessory* related devices which do the same thing when accessories that are not operative during the official [EPA certification] test are turned on."

by replacing oxygen in red blood cells. It can cause headaches, dizziness, impaired vision, and heart problems—and in extreme cases, unconsciousness or death. It can also lead to deterioration of learning skills.

Under the terms of the Justice Department settlement, GM was fined $11 million for violating EPA pollution rules; was required to spend $25 million to recall and fix the 470,000 Cadillac Fleetwoods, DeVilles, Eldorados, and Sevilles; and would pay an additional $8.75 million in a community service penalty, offsetting pollution through old car buybacks and retrofitting school buses to run more cleanly. Justice called the settlement—which totaled $45 million—the "largest ever" filed under the amended Clean Air Act.

GM's problems began in 1990. That's when some of its customers who had bought Cadillac Sevilles and DeVille models—those equipped with the big 4.9 liter V-8 engine—began complaining that their cars tended to sputter and stall when the heater or air conditioner was running, referred to as the *climate control system* in auto parlance. As remedy, GM technicians turned to the PROM chip—PROM, for "programmable read-only memory"—in the Cadillac engines. Computer chips are a fact of life in the operation of today's cars and trucks, found everywhere, including the engine. Every car, truck, and SUV today has a controlling engine PROM. These chips contain varying instructions, which in turn, can change the way an engine performs, including how much pollution it emits. When the problem-plagued Caddys rolled into GM, the company's technicians rewrote the computer codes for the PROM chip to correct the stalling problem and installed the new chip.[5] "We simply recalibrated the engines to avoid stalling when the air conditioner runs," said one GM official.[6]

That change, in effect, told the engine to increase the idle speed by burning richer—i.e., consume more fuel than air in combustion—when the air conditioning was turned on. This solved the stalling and sputtering and pleased Cadillac customers. But it also changed something else. By increasing the fuel flow to the combustion chamber, the car's catalytic converter was "overwhelmed," according to EPA's Bruce Fergeson. This allowed more carbon monoxide to escape—in fact, two to three times the level allowed under EPA regulations. Instead of the permitted level of 3.4 grams per mile, the "fixed" Caddys now emitted 7 to 10 grams per mile—levels equivalent to what cars were spewing out thirty years earlier.[7]

EPA discovered GM's chip change and the resulting pollution problem in September 1993 quite by accident. GM had loaned EPA one of its 1993 Cadillac Seville models with a 4.9 liter engine to help EPA in revising its emission systems testing procedures. The model loaned had the new controller chip, and that's when the agency discovered the increase in the Cadillac's carbon monoxide emissions. EPA then began an enforcement proceeding against GM for violating the Clean Air Act. EPA charged that GM knew about the emissions increase in the Cadillacs, but did not report the problem promptly to the government. As a result, more than 100,000 tons of carbon monoxide in excess of the standard were released from the ill-equipped Cadillacs during the 1991-1995 period.[8]

Technically, the Cadillacs at issue met EPA emissions standards because the test procedures EPA used only tested the car's performance when the air conditioning was turned off. However, that made no difference to EPA and Justice Department officials, who equated GM's chip change to the installation of a defeat device. "We strongly disagree with the allegations made by the federal government," said GM in a statement. "This is a matter of interpretation of current regulations regarding the complex issue of off-cycle emissions."[9] GM said it had discovered the emissions problem and developed a new chip to lower them again. But EPA and Justice alleged that GM deliberately installed the device to circumvent the emissions control system.

When Janet Reno announced the settlement, GM officials were furious. They felt betrayed and blindsided by the Justice Department's press conference, which made the evening TV news broadcasts nationally. GM had worked with the federal agencies for thirteen months in the course of reaching the settlement and thought they had reached an understanding. "This was going to be a circumstance where a collaborative resolution had been reached and we had fully expected . . . to participate in the messages," said Dennis Minano, then GM's VP of corporate communications. Another GM attorney added, "I'm concerned about the disincentive it creates to negotiate with the government. Why try to work things out when in the end you'll be treated as if you were a major wrongdoer?"[10]

Still, in EPA's eyes, there was wrongdoing. GM should have known how the new chip would change engine emissions and should have informed the agency of that fact. GM's Minano charged the government's case hung on slender thread of regulatory interpretation—"how you interpret the regulations, the circulars, and the practices out there and apply it to an off-cycle situation when you have no test procedure."[11]

EPA replied there was ample notice and agency guidance, which if not exactly fitting the GM/Cadillac situation, was parallel enough for GM to know it had an obligation to inform. In 1978, in fact, EPA had sent an advisory to all automakers informing them in some detail that computer coding could be considered a defeat device. That circular, however, did not apply specifically to carbon monoxide, but another pollutant, oxides of nitrogen.[12] But the parallel was clear, nonetheless.

The GM case, however, only highlighted a much bigger problem regarding how pollution control systems in the nation's cars and trucks were being certified in the first place, and more importantly, how those systems actually performed in the real world.

In 1991, the National Academy of Sciences (NAS) issued a short research paper that made some fairly astounding observations about EPA's Federal Test Procedure (FTP)—the singular testing process the federal government uses to calculate the likely rate of pollution from new automobiles. First, the NAS charged that the vehicles EPA used to calculate auto pollution were cleaner than most of those that would actually be used on the road. Second, the way the EPA corrected for certain variations in automotive speed and evaporative emissions in the test procedure was inaccurate. And finally, the current inspection and maintenance (I & M) programs envisioned by the Clean Air Act and EPA as a way to bring emissions down were also not working and not leading to reductions anticipated. Consequently, concluded NAS, automotive emissions of smog-causing pollutants were probably two to four times greater than EPA projections.

## MAKING THE LAW WORK

When Congress enacted the 1970 Clean Air Act and amended it in 1977, it gave EPA certain enforcement powers to insure that the nation's auto manufacturers would produce vehicles capable of meeting the auto emissions standards. Under Section 207(c) of the act, Congress established four powers: certification, testing, recall, and warranty. Motor vehicles are certified through testing that their emissions control systems will perform to meet the federal standards. Motor vehicles can be recalled by EPA or the manufacturer when they are found to exceed the standards for one or more reasons relating to the performance of an emissions control system or a flawed design or defect in emissions control equipment. Warranty provisions that require pollution control equipment to function over certain time period—initially five years or 50,000 miles, but later extended—can also serve as enforcement mechanisms, triggering recalls or agency investigations when pollution control devices fail to perform as specified during the warranty period.

Experience under the earlier and weaker 1965 and 1967 federal air pollution laws had shown that auto manufacturers were practically custom-building their test cars—cars that would be certified with flying colors. It was soon learned that actual production-line cars of the tested models would not necessarily perform at the same level. In April 1970, Nixon administration officials preparing legislation for Congress on the Clean Air Act, noted that the existing law, the Air Quality Act of 1967, contained loopholes regarding pollution control testing of "production-line" automobiles. In fact, there were no provisions for such testing under the law. The testing that did exist—then voluntary for the automakers—was a certification that a manufacturer's cars were meeting the emissions standards of that day. Even industry acknowledged that test cars were practically custom-made and more finely tuned than "production-line" models.[13]

It was no surprise then, that when EPA's predecessor, the National Air Pollution Control Administration (NAPCA) actually tested rental cars that had been driven an average of 11,000 miles, 50 to 80 percent of those cars failed to meet the federal standards. "Cars are being cleaned up," assured NAPCA's Kenneth Mills in April 1970. "But we still have to recognize that the average cars are not meeting federal emissions standards. There is definite improvement, but it's not as good as it should be.

"The manufacturers may not have translated faithfully their prototype designs to production cars," Mills explained. "There is a distinct possibility that they cut corners, made some compromises for the production line," and "there may have been a lack of quality control at various stages of manufacturing."[14] The automakers also maintained large test fleets and backup vehicles in order to assure their cars would make the grade at certification time. "Choice of those [vehicles] to be reported for emissions test certification . . . are at the manufacturers' option," said federal investigators in one October 1969 report. "Further, it is reasonably certain that multiple tests are run on test vehicles at required mileage intervals, but only the required single test results are reported in applications for certification."[15]

The certification of vehicles, in fact, was a very weak point in the system. The automakers provided the data and performed the tests. As it became increasingly clear the automakers were honing the emissions-control performance of test cars, as compared to those that might come off the line unattended, regulators began to look for what they called "unauthorized or prohibited maintenance" on those cars. And soon, a very interesting case emerged.

In May 1972, Ford Motor withdrew its application to EPA for certifying some of its cars, admitting that it discovered inaccuracies in its own test data. In the Senate, when Senator Ed Muskie questioned EPA administrator William Ruckelshaus about this, Ruckelshaus said that Ford had performed prohibited maintenance on the vehicles being tested for certification. Muskie also learned that EPA really had no secure way to check the data that was being submitted by the auto companies in the certifications process. So he asked the General Accounting Office (GAO) to investigate.[16]

GAO found that Ford had conducted "unauthorized maintenance" of the test cars—tinkering that was not reported to EPA. It also found that EPA did not have "reasonable assurance" that the auto companies generally had complied with federal regulations related to maintenance. EPA staff were not available to monitor the testing the automakers were doing at their plants. "EPA has generally accepted at face value the information submitted by the auto companies," reported GAO. "When prototype vehicles are delivered to EPA for testing, the EPA staff makes visual observations of the vehicles; however, EPA officials told us that there is no practical way to inspect the vehicles to determine whether unauthorized maintenance had been performed."[17]

Ford, for one, had worked over its cars ahead of time to assure they would be certified. According to GAO, "Subsequent investigation by Ford disclosed that Ford personnel, in addition to performing unauthorized maintenance, had made unauthorized inspections and had conducted unauthorized diagnostic emissions tests. Ford identified 442 instances of unauthorized maintenance performed on 26 test vehicles." Computer records at Ford produced in May 1972 revealed the illegal actions.[18]

When Ford "turned itself in" to EPA for unauthorized maintenance of its test cars, it said the problem was due to a lack of proper management control over the testing process and it was seeking to remedy the problem by shifting the testing from its Engine and Foundry Division to a new Environmental and Safety Engineering Staff.

But actually there was a lot more to it than that.

## OPERATION "LEMON JUICE"

Ford Motor was actually found to have kept the equivalent of two sets of books—one for itself and one for EPA—in certifying its engines. The incident was uncovered by an operations director of Ford's Engineering Technical Services, Harley Copp.[19] Mr. Copp had received some complaints from engineers about inadequate computer support in the engine testing shop. He didn't think much of the complaint at the time, but ordered a full audit and review of what the division was doing in its engine work and emissions certification testing.

A few days later, one of Copp's staff, Bill Hieney, called to report that the review had turned up two sets of computer programs—one for Ford and one for EPA. Ford, it turned out, was putting into the government computer file engine adjustments that were permitted by law, and into its own file all the adjustments they were making to the engine—legal and illegal. Some of Ford's employees called the operation *lemon juice,* taking its name from the old practice of writing secret messages in lemon juice on white paper, only legible if read over a candle. Copp, however, was appalled, recognizing immediately the legal ramifications. With computer printout in hand, he reported the matter to a Ford vice president, who encouraged Copp "to look into it some more." Not long thereafter, however, Copp was told the matter should not surface publicly, as it would surely embarrass Ford. But Copp persisted, arguing that the company should go straight to EPA and inform them. Soon thereafter, some Ford officials did go to EPA in Washington, admitting there were "irregularities" in its certification process for its 1973 engines. But by then EPA had referred the matter to the Justice Department. Meanwhile, before the federal investigation reached Ford, Copp was visited by a Ford attorney, who asked him about a strongly worded letter he had written to higher-ups in the company about the incident. The Ford lawyer also wanted to know the names of those who received copies. According to Copp, this letter disappeared from Ford files and was replaced by a fraudulent, unsigned version not written by Copp. Copp, however, was never interviewed by Justice, but Ford was required by EPA to recertify its engines under the eye of special EPA task force in September 1972.

Meanwhile, Henry Ford II, working on damage control, told one audience "some of our people withheld maintenance information that should have been submitted to the government" for the company's 1973 models. Mr. Ford explained that as soon as he and other members of top management learned of the failure to report, "we promptly notified [EPA] and withdrew our applications for certification." Mr. Ford also acknowledged "discrepancies in 1972 model certification," which were also "promptly reported" to EPA. Ford said his company had firmly established policies on these matters and adhered strictly to all government rules and regulations.[20]

In the end, the Justice Department charged Ford with both criminal and civil violations of the Clean Air Act. Ford pleaded no contest to 350 separate counts, and the judge imposed the maximum penalty—$3.5 million in the criminal case and $3.5

million in the civil case, a record at the time.[21] Still, Harley Copp and others felt Ford got off easy. "The $7 million settlement was an exchange for not imposing criminal penalties on Ford officials," charged Clarence Ditlow of the Center for Auto Safety—officials who, in Ditlow's view, "had willfully falsified records submitted to EPA or who had approved such falsification."*

As Congress and EPA tightened up the certification and testing process under the 1970 Clean Air Act, a decade or more of battling with the automakers began to enforce those provisions. Among EPA's key powers was the recall—to have a manufacturer bring back for repair vehicles whose emissions systems were not meeting the standards. (See appendix A.)

## THE CHRYSLER RECALL

In March 1974, EPA administrator Russell Train ordered the Chrysler Corporation to recall 825,000 of its 1973 model Chryslers, Plymouths, and Dodges to correct a defect in the air pollution control system. It was EPA's first major recall for a pollution control defect and at issue were some of the defeat devices that former EPA administrator Bill Ruckelshaus had warned the manufacturers about in July 1972. The problem device was a tiny temperature sensor valve located inside the radiator, which cost about two dollars retail. The sensor was supposed to signal and turn on the exhaust gas recirculation system when the engine water temperature reached sixty degrees. However, the sensor was failing to do that, thus allowing excessive nitrogen oxide pollution to build up and pollute the air. EPA had first notified Chrysler that it considered the problem serious enough for a recall and invited the company in for a conference. Chrysler, however, declined to meet, and the order was issued. In the agency's letter to Sidney L. Terry, Chrysler vice president for environmental and safety relations, Train estimated that within the requisite 50,000-mile warranty period for pollution control systems, "virtually all" the Chrysler vehicles equipped with the sensor would "emit nitrogen oxides considerably above the federal emissions standard." The problem was verified by Chrysler testing.[22]

Laboratory and durability tests by the company showed that after a time the sensor began activating the pollution control system at higher and higher temperatures. Tests of 578 vehicles indicated sensors in 47 percent were functioning at higher than specified temperatures, and according to EPA, all vehicles with more than 10,000 miles on them were exhibiting problems. EPA concluded that the devices seemed

---

* Nor was this the first time that Ford had faced EPA and Justice in a showdown over vehicle certification. In 1971, Ford had shipped about 200,000 1972-model vehicles to its dealers before the vehicles were certified by EPA. EPA considered the shipments illegal and requested the Justice Department to take action against Ford. In this case, though, a settlement was reached, and Ford signed a consent judgement, paying a $10,000 fine, or about 5 cents per vehicle.

to worsen with time, to the point where they wouldn't activate until the engines reached full operating temperatures of 190 to 225 degrees.[23] Chrysler cooperated in the recall and did not appeal. Chrysler, in fact, had developed an improved sensor, installed in 1974 models, that was working satisfactorily.*

## ASSEMBLY LINE TESTING

In January 1977, in response to increasing evidence that auto emissions systems in new cars were not actually performing at their certified levels once they reached the highway, EPA began conducting random assembly line tests. In one such spot check at a Ford assembly plant, EPA found that certain models of Ford Granadas and Mercury Monarchs—although certified in earlier prototype submissions to EPA— emitted about twice the allowable level of carbon monoxide. In the month following the inspection, EPA ordered Ford to recall 54,000 of those models so that adjustments could be made to their carburetors. But there was something else, too.

EPA's order also called for production to stop on the Granadas and Monarchs within several days unless the design modifications were made in the production lines to remedy the problem. It was the first time the agency had threatened to shut down an automaker in an auto emissions enforcement action. A Ford spokesman at the time acknowledged "a quality problem in the carburetors . . . resulted in high carbon monoxide emissions." Ford avoided the shutdown by agreeing to an EPA-approved modification of its design and production processes.[24]

"We have long suspected that cars coming off the assembly line do not meet pollution control standards," said acting EPA administrator John Quarles at the time of the Ford assembly line check. "Until now, we had no concrete evidence." It is "significant and disturbing," he said, that EPA's early assembly line tests had found "such substantial violations." Some of the cars tested from the assembly line emitted four times the permitted level of carbon monoxide. "This provides documentation of the concern that a significant number of cars coming off assembly lines may fail to meet auto emission standards."[25] The year before assembly line testing was initiated, EPA had recalled 1.5 million vehicles for overpolluting. With assembly

---

* Chrysler did, however, place part of the blame for the problem on EPA. Originally, Chrysler had located the sensor on the firewall of its models, and not in the radiator. In mid-1972, when EPA was reviewing this and other devices, it required Chrysler to move the sensor to the radiator, taking the position that installing the device on the firewall would not allow it to activate the pollution control system in colder climates. Chrysler said the change caused it to hastily deploy the sensor at the new location without extensive testing. Chrysler warned the agency in January 1973 that this might create problems. Although some difficulty may have been caused by the eleventh-hour decision, the issue was more about the internal workings of the sensor itself, which appeared to be remedied by the new sensor Chrysler was using in its 1974 models.

line testing, EPA hoped to catch many of the underperforming vehicles before they were sold and put into use.

But within months of EPA's first showdown with Ford in 1977 over its Monarchs and Granadas, the agency was soon back at the company again. In this case, the problem began in September 1976, when assembly line testing on Ford Bobcats, Pintos, and Mustangs indicated that those 1977 models were exceeding NOx standard due to problems with the engine's ignition spark timing. Within a month, Ford had approval from EPA to make a design change in the engines and on the assembly line to remedy the problem. But two months went by, and no action was taken by Ford. By April 1977, EPA notified Ford it was coming to test vehicles under the selective enforcement audit program. EPA's audit indicated that 55 percent of one of the engine classes would exceed the NOx standard by 0.20 grams/mi, and 61 percent of another engine family would exceed by 0.35 GPM. The following day, Ford agreed to a voluntary recall. But EPA moved in June 1977 to make it an official agency-ordered recall.

"... Ford became aware of this emissions problem in September 1976," wrote EPA's new administrator Doug Costle in a June 7 letter to Ford VP Herbert L. Misch, "and received approval to implement a corrective design change on October 15, 1976. Almost two months elapsed before a decision was made to proceed with the design change on production vehicles, and then the change may never have been implemented .. . if not for the [line audit] notification.

"Of greatest concern, is that there is no indication that Ford intended to remedy the nonconformity known to exist in vehicles already sold to the public. I believe that the least a manufacturer should do upon identification of an emissions non-conformity is to recall and remedy the nonconforming cars already in the field while simultaneously expediting an acceptable change for vehicles in production."[26] Ford, for its part, said that a "production scheduling error" had led it to continue producing the bad vehicles through January 3, 1977. At the point, the company said it began making the design change on the assembly line. On the recall of existing vehicles, Ford said it would begin the recall as soon as EPA approved the plan and as soon as the necessary parts had been supplied to dealers. The cost for the corrections to cars in the field would be approximately $10, including a new spark relay valve, a fuel separator, and vacuum hoses and connectors.

## Working the Loopholes

During the mid-1970s, EPA returned to an issue of earlier concern: how cars' emissions systems perform after they had been in use for a while? Could they still meet the standards? EPA's Eric Stork, deputy administrator for Mobile Source Pollution Control, noted the high rate of failures in testing such cars. "When we test these cars in the condition we receive them from their owners, we find that an appalling number of cars, even relatively new cars, fail to meet one or more of the standards. On average, about 60 percent of the cars we test fail to meet one or more of the standards.[27]

"In another program," he continued, "we still found 60 percent out of compliance in an as received condition, but we found 80 percent in compliance after relatively simple repair and tune up." The most significant adjustment Stork noted in meeting compliance at the time for these engines was essentially a function of a single screw on the carburetor, i.e., "the proper adjustment of idle mixture and idle speed." But the manufacturers were at the root of this problem, and EPA expected to change that.

"It makes very little sense to force the industry to design a car to be clean and then let them stick a big screw on the carburetor which you can reach with your fingers and give a half a twist and then that car's as dirty as if it were never designed to be clean," explained Stork. "That just makes no sense. So we're pursuing this and we expect, beginning with the 1980 models, to get some of these easy adjustments, especially idle mixtures and choke adjustment, off the cars." Stork explained that some of the auto companies were indicating to EPA they could remove those easily tampered-with features from their cars' engines. "But when we propose it in the *Federal Register*," he said, "I would expect strong opposition from the auto industry because we get strong opposition [from the auto industry] to almost everything we do."[28]

In fact, recounting the agency's track record, Stork explained just how difficult it had been to deal with the industry. "In the first regulations we published, the industry didn't have much trouble finding loopholes. Then, they started driving right through the loopholes. So then we learned about that and we closed the loopholes. Then, they found loopholes in the loopholes. And then we closed those. But they've got so many very smart people, always looking for new loopholes.

"So there's a never-ending process. What it means is that the regulations get more and more complicated. I'm not blaming industry. If I worked for the industry I'd do a better job at finding loopholes than they do. My job is to close the loopholes and that's what we do. . . ." Asked about the agency's progress in controlling auto emissions at the time, Stork replied, "We're making enormous progress. Are we winning the battle? Probably not. If you describe 'winning the battle' in terms of making sure that every place in the United States has clean air, we've got a long way to go to win that battle. We've got a long way to go in getting cars that are designed and built to be clean."[29]

In fact, EPA was then engaged in a key court battle with Chrysler over an engine adjustment issue that was much more than that. The case became a battle royal—taken all the way to the US Supreme Court—and a landmark case on the manufacturer's responsibility for designing durable emissions control systems that met the law.

## MANUFACTURER RESPONSIBILITY

On December 10, 1976, EPA administrator Russell Train announced the agency was ordering Chrysler to recall 208,000 automobiles, or nearly one-fourth of its 1975 production. The recall covered 1975 Chrysler Cordobas and Newports, Plymouth Furys, Dodge Monacos, Chargers, and Coronets, among others. At issue was Chrysler's easily accessible idle adjustment, made with one screw on the carburetor. The carburetor design, said Train, was "routinely" causing Chrysler dealers and other mechanics to make adjustments that produced excessive pollution. EPA felt Chrysler should correct this problem at the design stage and recognized that recall was a first-of-its-kind. "This precedent-setting recall is the first based on improper design and adjustment procedures, which are the responsibility of the manufacturer. . . ." said Train. Chrysler denied responsibility and said it would challenge the EPA order, pinning the blame on owners and mechanics who made the adjustments. "By this order, EPA is trying to require Chrysler to be responsible for the actions of private individuals," said Chrysler. "We cannot accept that responsibility nor the precedent it sets. The law states that the manufacturer is responsible for remedying nonconforming vehicles that have been 'properly used and maintained.'"[30]

In a letter to Chrysler's president John Riccardo, Train said that EPA had found "a substantial number of (the recalled) vehicles violating the CO standard," then set at 15 grams per mile. "The data indicate that in the first year of operation of these vehicles, carburetor misadjustments are routinely performed by Chrysler dealerships . . . (and at) nondealer service facilities as a result of Chrysler's carburetor idle system design and carburetor adjustments procedures. In particular, we have found that the idle system is sensitive to small adjustments of the idle mixture screw and engine temperature which facilitates improper adjustment." But it was really more complicated than turning a single screw; that was only the end-result remedy employed when the car began running rough and would be brought in for an adjustment.[31]

Chrysler, in effect, had designed a system that was guaranteed to pollute, because it could only be properly calibrated with the use of sophisticated equipment*—such

---

* In 1975 automobiles, the catalytic converter was the key device used to control pollution. Attached to the exhaust system, the converter would reduce carbon monoxide and other pollutants by promoting a chemical reaction. Key to this reaction, however, was oxygen—and specifically an adequate supply of oxygen in the exhaust stream in order to oxidize the emissions. Without enough oxygen, the converter would not work properly and possibly stop working altogether. At the time, there were two ways to supply sufficient oxygen to the exhaust stream: either by an auxiliary air pump or through a precise adjustment of the air-fuel mixture at the carburetor. Chrysler engineers knew that air pumps generally decreased emissions more effectively than the air-fuel adjustment technique. Air pumps also cost more, about $50 a car and had a slight fuel economy penalty. Still, Chrysler chose the air pump route for its cars in California to meet those standards, but not the rest of the nation. For those cars it

as infrared analyzers not typically found even at the average Chrysler dealership. When cars came in running rough or receiving poor fuel economy, the common "fix" was the idle adjustment—really a misadjustment for the pollution control system—which made the car run smoothly, but also made it a bigger polluter. It was EPA's conclusion, therefore, that Chrysler had designed a system that was so complex it was unlikely to be properly maintained, and therefore, guaranteed to pollute—so EPA ordered the recall.

Chrysler, however, decided to begin the appeals process, first within the agency itself. After four prehearing conferences and a lengthy public hearing in which Chrysler and EPA were the only parties, administrative law judge Edward B. Finch reviewed the case in February 1978 and sided with EPA. "This recall demonstrates that the responsibility of a manufacturer to design and manufacture vehicles that meet emissions standards doesn't stop at the assembly line," explained EPA's Marvin B. Durning, an enforcement official reacting to Finch's ruling. "Vehicle design must take into account the realities of the use, service and maintenance the vehicle is likely to receive throughout its life in the hands of consumers."[32]

Chrysler then appealed the decision of the administrative law judge to the EPA administrator, Doug Costle. Costle upheld the administrative law judge's decision on November 20, 1978. Chrysler then brought its case to the US Court of Appeal for the District of Columbia. But Chrysler struck out there, too, as the appeals court agreed with EPA. The appeals court did not dispute Chrysler's contention that its pollution control system was capable of meeting the Clean Air Act standards. But the court did find, reviewing the record and intent of Congress, that the Clean Air Act placed the burden on the auto manufacturer not only to design vehicles that

---

relied on the carburetor idle adjustment method, specifying a certain "lean" setting at the factory, meaning a low proportion of fuel to air in order to meet federal CO emissions standards. But what was set at the factory didn't last long once the vehicle was in use. And bringing the vehicle back to its original setting entailed more that just getting the right idle setting. First, the adjustment screws themselves were highly sensitive. A tiny 1/20 turn of a mixture screw above the original specification meant a substantial increase in carbon monoxide. A full rotation of the screw would produce CO at idle equal to about twenty-three times Chrysler's original specification. Second, the entire system could only be properly calibrated with the use of sophisticated laboratory equipment. Third, it was unclear that even Chrysler dealership mechanics understood what they were doing, as one EPA survey of twenty-seven mechanics determined that only six of those surveyed realized that a "rich" idle mixture would cause the catalytic converter not to work at idle, while thirteen stated the exact opposite—that a rich mixture would make the catalyst work harder. And finally, because a rich adjustment actually made the car run smoother at idle than a lean setting, mechanics were typically making the setting on the rich side, with many admitting that it was not possible to achieve "acceptable engine smoothness and driveability" when the idle mixture was set to Chrysler's specifications.

comply with federal standards initially, but also to design systems less susceptible to faulty maintenance. In reviewing Congress's intent the court found "... The primary responsibility for emission control was left with the manufacturers; they were expected to solve the maintenance problem by designing a system that would be less susceptible to faulty maintenance." Admittedly, said the court, Congress did not intend liability to rest on the manufacturer if the condition of poor maintenance could be attributed to owners or mechanics. "If, however, design defects of the manufacturer proved to be responsible for the condition of poor maintenance, the legislative history would indicate that Congress did indeed intend responsibility for remedy to rest on the manufacturer."

In rendering its decision, the appeals court agreed with EPA, finding substantial evidence in the record to support EPA's conclusion that misadjustments to the Chrysler cars "were encouraged or fostered by the design of Chrysler's emission control system and its carburetor adjustment procedures." The mechanics' contributions to the problem were seen as "the inevitable byproduct of Chrysler's emission system design and service procedures."

"Chrysler chose to employ cheaper and less effective emission control equipment," said the court, which meant that "misadjustments serious enough to cause widespread nonconformity were likely." Chrysler "thus took a gamble that the idle adjustment methods of providing sufficient oxygen to the catalytic converter would work, or that EPA would be unable to prove its case for a recall. The statute demands that Chrysler bear the consequences of its decision."[33] Chrysler then appealed to the US Supreme Court.

In its plea to the Supreme Court, Chrysler argued that Congress intended in the Clean Air Act that owners and mechanics were responsible for the proper maintenance of emission control systems, and that the appeals court had erred in shifting that burden to the manufacturer. The Supreme Court, however, did not agree and refused to hear the case, letting the appeals court ruling stand.[34] It was a huge victory for EPA. The decision meant that auto manufacturers had to produce vehicles that not only complied with the Clean Air Act initially, but that would continue to do so even after maintenance was performed at a typical mechanic's shop. In effect, the decision said that the automakers, under the law, were required to "manufacture in" continued emission-system performance over time; systems that would not go out of kilter in the context of normal maintenance.

## GM FIGHTS SPOT TESTING

Another key contest between EPA and the automakers came over the agency's right to make unannounced factory visits. In December 1977, EPA received an anonymous letter from a person at General Motors' Flint, Michigan auto assembly plant alleging that cars used for federal emissions testing at the plant, specifically Buick LaSabres, had been preselected and modified by GM specifically to pass the tests.

The following month, January 1978, EPA informed GM of the allegations it had received. GM, said EPA, may have presented unrepresentative cars for testing or may have changed carburetors and pollution-control equipment on the test cars to make them do better in the tests. EPA soon sent investigators to the plant, who began questioning assembly line workers about the charge.[35]

By March 1978, GM filed an action in federal court challenging EPA's authority to conduct a criminal investigation of its employees at the assembly plant, arguing that criminal investigations were the province of other federal agencies. EPA said its inquiry at the Flint plant hadn't yet become a criminal investigation, but conceded it could become one. Not long thereafter, EPA referred the matter to the Justice Department, which began a review of the case.[36] GM, later amending its federal court complaint, called EPA's methods "unreasonable, arbitrary and capricious" and an abridgement of the company's constitutional rights. GM also sought to prevent EPA from spot-checking assembly line cars.

Assembly line checks were crucial to EPA's program, used to predict whether cars would perform at the legally required emission control levels after 50,000 miles. In early 1977 EPA had begun assembly line spot checks instead of testing actual vehicles in use, calculating emission system performance by way of a "deterioration factor" to arrive at an expected 50,000-mile performance value. GM claimed the practice was illegal and would, in effect, require manufactures to comply with more stringent emissions standards than those mandated by Congress. Further, GM said EPA's switch to a spot-checking and judgement-by-deterioration formula, amounted to "an abdication by the EPA of its responsibilities to conduct actual use tests and the unwarranted substitution of arbitrary and capricious formulas." EPA, however, said it had found the spot test to be "the only means the agency has to check to see if the cars are actually being built the way they were designed and approved."[37]

The US Justice Department, meanwhile, announced on May 5, 1978 that it would begin a criminal investigation of GM to determine if the company had violated the Clean Air Act by changing equipment on its assembly line. James K. Robinson, US Attorney for Detroit, said that an initial review of the evidence submitted by EPA "indicates that further investigation is appropriate." He cautioned, however, that an investigation did not indicate that there was necessarily evidence of wrongdoing. FBI agents were assigned to the case. GM spokesman at the time, Clifford D. Merriott said, "GM is aware of the investigation. We are confident that when the investigation is concluded, GM will be cleared."[38] In the end, GM paid a nominal fine and the case was settled, but all the automakers got the message that EPA would go to the mat over the right to spot check.

### "DISMAL SHOWING," 1978

In May 1978, as EPA opened a new auto emissions testing facility in Springfield, Virginia, EPA deputy administrator Barbara Blum used the occasion to recap the industry's track record on recalls. Since 1972, EPA calculated that one in every five cars and trucks sold in the US had been recalled because of emission control system defects—10 millon of which were recalled on EPA orders and 1.8 million of which were recalled by the manufacturers. "As a record of compliance with the law, and as an expression of concern for public health, this marks a dismal showing by automakers," said Blum. "Auto exhaust remains the No. 1 air pollution problem in our nation's urban areas. The carbon monoxide, hydrocarbons, and nitrogen oxides emitted from auto tailpipes make people ill, shorten their lives, lead to lost workdays, and unnecessary suffering."

At the time, EPA announced it had another 11 million cars under investigation for possible future recall, covering some thirty different model types. "'Recall' is not a pleasant word," Blum offered. "But as long as polluting cars continue threatening public health, 'recall' is word EPA will continue to utter and act upon. . . . The fact that a class of vehicles is under investigation is not reason to conclude that a recall necessarily will be ordered. . . . It does mean however, that emission data indicate a potential violation of emissions standards or that some defect related to emissions controls may exist. . . ."[39]

The day before Blum made her remarks about recalls, American Motors Corporation (AMC) attempted to beat EPA to the punch on a recall of 310,000 Jeeps and other vehicles. AMC announced it was making a recall of the Jeeps for emission system defects. The defect was similar to an earlier Ford problem involving an inadequately brazed joint in the exhaust-gas recirculation system that allowed NOx emissions to escape without treatment. In its announcement, however, AMC did not mention EPA.[40] AMC was trying to end run EPA by announcing its intention before the agency did because an EPA order carried more legal clout. It didn't work. EPA ordered AMC to make the recall anyway.

"There is a world of difference between a car company making a recall and EPA ordering one," noted an EPA spokesman at the time. Under an EPA-ordered recall, the company must submit a corrective action plan to the agency for its approval. However, that is not the case with a company-announced recall. Under an agency recall, the company is also required to send a letter to all owners of the vehicles, warning them of the problem. A company recall can be made simply by making an announcement to the press.[41]

AMC's executive director for vehicle emissions, George Brown, said his company had been working with EPA on the problem since July 1977 and had voluntarily announced it would recall 157,500 of the vehicles for repairs. "We told the EPA we couldn't make the necessary tests, do the designing, and get the necessary parts until August and September [1977]. We were well along the way and they knew it. Then they sent us a letter today [May 9, 1978] ordering the recall. They didn't need the recall to get the right action. We had agreed to do what they are now ordering us to do." Asked by a reporter why he thought EPA resorted to the order, Brown replied, "They had their reasons to announce this at their new testing facility which they want to publicize [i.e., Springfield, VA]. It will get them good headlines, I guess."[42]

But EPA, although willing to give credit for company recalls, said there were other considerations with AMC. "It is EPA's policy to encourage voluntary recalls and give public credit for such actions when a manufacturer promptly takes the investigative initiative as soon as the problem is identified," said Blum. "In this case, however, EPA had to expend significant resources to quantify the extent of the problem after AMC was notified. Further, there is some doubt as to whether AMC's corrections would be sufficient to ensure that the vehicles' emissions will be within the standards mandated by the Clean Air Act."[43]

## NEW DEFEAT DEVICES

As EPA was using its muscle to take Detroit to task for not meeting emission control standards, California authorities were writing the agency to warn of "a new generation of defeat devices." Thomas C. Austin, then deputy executive director of CARB, noted in a February 1978 letter to EPA that Chrysler and Ford had cars with emissions that were not being caught in EPA's certification testing. The cars in question had elements that came into play in the "highway cycle," meaning highway driving.[44]

"The 1978 California model Chrysler vehicles using 'electronic spark advance' (ESA) controls exhibit NOx emissions on the EPA highway cycle which are approximately 2.2 times greater than [the certified test] NOx levels," said Austin in his letter. In this case, the particular Chrysler system at issue emitted its highest NOx when the spark was advanced at cruise speeds—a driving phase and technological adjustment not measured in the test procedure. Mr. Austin and California took the position that this Chrysler technology qualified as a defeat device, and that EPA's Advisory Circular 24 (AC 24)—the notice circulated to manufacturers instructing them on such devices—did not adequately cover the changing technology. Nor did EPA's stated NOx emission levels for certain phases of the highway cycle test.

California also found potential problems with a Ford lean-burn combustion control system (LCC) then being designed for 1979 models to work with a three-way catalyst. "The LCC system changes a three-way catalyst into a 'lean burn' system during high speed, quasi steady state operating conditions, causing not only an increase in NOx emissions from the engine but a total loss of the catalyst's ability to reduce NOx emissions at the tailpipe. . . . Data on the Ford LCC system indicates that it will cause highway cycle NOx levels to be nearly three times those measured on the [certification test]."

To remedy the situation, CARB adopted a NOx ceiling and formula for emission levels in the highway cycle (a move Ford opposed), to be applied to 1980 and subsequent models. CARB urged that EPA do the same for the rest of the country. "In order to prevent the use of new generation of 'defeat devices' in the 49 states, we suggest that EPA consider an immediate modification to AC 24 to include consideration of highway cycle NOx emissions [i.e., incorporating a highway cycle NOx emission ceiling] in determining the acceptability of emission control systems."[45] Making the certification process and testing more accurately reflect real world driving and use would be a continuing issue for EPA. Back in Washington, however, the agency's enforcement program was being attacked on Capitol Hill.

In January 1979, the GAO, responding to a request for information made nearly fifteen months earlier by Senator Muskie, reported that EPA was estimating that 80 percent of the nation's automobiles on the highway—about 100 million vehicles—were not meeting the federal air quality emissions standards. More significantly, nearly one half of these vehicles exceeded the limits within one year of manufacture, and the failure rate increased with the car's age. The reason for the failures was given over to "improper maintenance and adjustments" by owners and service stations after they left the factory. GAO concluded, therefore, that car inspection and maintenance programs requiring at least an annual inspection would remedy the problem, both by identifying potential problems and the needed fixes to correct the emission problems. Establishing I & M programs, as they would come be called, was easier said than done. I & M programs became highly contentious in many states well into the 1990s, and the move toward I & M programs also helped shift responsibility away from the manufacturers.

## GM & OFFSETS

By 1982, with the more industry-receptive Reagan administration in Washington, some GM officials, in particular, began talking with EPA about altering the agency's recall program. GM was generally feeling the bite of EPA recalls. Between 1975 and 1981, the company had nearly 6 million vehicles recalled for emission-system problems. "The result has been a significant increase in the manufacturer's potential liability for recall costs," explained GM's T. M. Fisher, director of Automotive Emission Control, in a February 1983 letter to some local pollution control officials enlisting their support to change EPA's program. "This potential for increased liability is occurring despite the substantially declining public health risk as we approach and meet the Clean Air Act air quality goals," argued Fisher, suggesting that such measures would not be needed. "We believe the EPA Administrator should be authorized to consider and approve [alternatives to recall] on a case-by-case basis."[46]

In 1981-1982, EPA had ordered the recall of some 700,000 General Motors automobiles—1979 Buicks, Oldsmobiles, and Pontiacs—that were then exceeding the federal emissions standard for nitrogen oxides (NOx). These cars were emitting NOx at about 2.7 GPM, although they had been certified to meet the NOx standard of 2.0 GPM. After EPA ordered the recall, GM said it could not figure out what was causing the excessive NOx. The company did, however, propose a way to bring down the NOx level—by altering the engine timing and installing vacuum regulators. But taking this route, GM warned, would reduce fuel economy by 0.7 miles per gallon.

Not going through with the recall, GM calculated, would therefore save car owners 26 million dollars in gasoline costs over the coming years. GM itself would save 12 million dollars by foregoing owner notification costs. In fact, with this case, GM began lobbying EPA to allow for an alternative to EPA's recall program generally; an alternative labeled "offsets"—trading old-car emissions infractions for new-car emissions improvement.

In exchange for nixing the recall of 1979 models, GM proposed it would build 1982 and 1983 models that would pollute less than the law stipulated, thus offsetting the amount of pollution from the older cars. EPA agreed to the proposal and announced in July 1982 that GM would produce 2.3 million 1982 and later model year cars that would comply with a tighter NOx standard (i.e., 0.90 GPM) than required by law (i.e., 1.00 GPM) to compensate for the 1979 models that were exceeding the standard. GM and the other automakers had been pushing this idea for years. On Capitol Hill, however, Senator Robert T. Stafford noted that although some flexibility might be needed in the agency's program, "the law does not presently allow this approach as a means of complying with the tailpipe emissions standards." Stafford also said that the potential air quality implications of such a change were so great that it should not be undertaken without "the closest possible examination" of the GM case and the broader implications of a "mobile bubble" policy.

David Hawkins of NRDC called the entire action a "sham" and said GM had given up nothing to win a reprieve from the recall, explaining that the company was already producing the same vehicles at less than 0.90 GPM in 1981. Senator Stafford added, however, that GM was in effect admitting it could do a better job than the law required. "Clearly, the most encouraging aspect of this massive failure is the evidence, for the first time, that a motor vehicle manufacturer can reduce emissions . . . at extremely small cost and with little inconvenience." Still, the prospect that this approach was not specified by the Clean Air Act, and that EPA was signaling its use on a case-by-case basis, brought a court challenge. In October 1982, the Center for Auto Safety and Representative Toby Moffet (D-CT) filed suit to overturn EPA's action.

GM, meanwhile, was pushing the idea of alternatives to recall in Congress and had made the issue part of its lobby campaign. The company was also preaching the benefits of offsets to local air pollution control officials, hoping they would help lobby for the change in Washington. "The air quality benefits of recall are virtually nonexistent since the exceedances corrected are generally very small and occur well into a vehicle's life," argued GM's Fisher in his February 1983 letter to local pollution control officials. Fisher also ticked off other problems, such as customers disabling the corrective action and losses in fuel economy, concluding that the "limited benefits" could not justify the recall costs.[47] But the purpose of the recall program was not to be justified on cost in any case; it was to serve as an EPA enforcement tool and economic deterrent to manufacturers turning out poorly performing and badly designed emission-control systems. Back in court, however, GM's bid to circumvent the recall program was dealt a fatal blow.

In an October 1984 ruling, a three-judge federal appeals court panel ruled the GM-EPA "offsets" deal could not be used as a substitute enforcement mechanism for recalls. The legislative history of the Clean Air Act, the judges ruled, clearly intended the use of recalls as an enforcement device. "[N]either GM nor the EPA has been able to refer us to a single passage in the legislative history indicating that Congress had in mind any other remedy than recall when it enacted" the enforcement provisions of the 1970 act.[48]

## THE "USEFUL LIFE" FIGHT

Under the Clean Air Act in the late 1970s, an automobile's "useful life" was established as "a period of five years or 50,000 miles, whichever comes first"—a definition that also pertained to emission-control systems and the auto industry's liability for them. In 1977, EPA ordered GM to recall and fix free of charge 202,000 Cadillacs that exceeded federal clean air limits. At first, GM agreed to make the recall and conduct the repairs. But in negotiations with EPA, which dragged on over a year or more, a heated difference of opinion emerged over the "useful life" definition. GM saw that by the time it got around to repairing the 1975 vintage vehicles under recall, the "five-year clock" would have run out on many of the cars, and therefore, it would no longer be responsible for the repairs. EPA, in effect, said no, it doesn't work like that. The recall, said EPA, would cover the *entire class or category* of vehicle that had the problem, regardless if some individual cars in that class may have subsequently gone beyond the 5-year/50,000 miles use period. EPA formalized this interpretation with a ruling in May 1980. GM, sticking to its position, appealed, pushing the case back another few years. The court's decision, when it came three years later, only muddied the waters further.

A three-judge District of Columbia Circuit Court panel ruled in favor of GM 2-1, but in the process, raised unusually strong opinions about the potential of automakers to use delay to avoid responsibility in the recall process. Senior Judge David Bazelon, who in fact voted in favor of GM's motion, nevertheless raised the prospect of the industry's using delay tactics. The flaw or exceedance "may be discovered only late in a vehicle's useful life," Bazelon wrote, "and only an unusually uninventive lawyer will be unable in the context of today's backlogged court dockets to prolong administrative and judicial appeals for at least several years." The recall system, under such delays, he said, could thus be rendered useless. Judge Patricia Wald, the dissenting vote in this case, picking up on Bazelon's point, added "disturbingly, it permits the automobile manufactures to circumvent in large part . . . [the] recall and repair obligations through a strategy of engaging in prolonged litigation."[49]

By the time this decision was rendered in December 1983, many of the Cadillacs at issue were nine years old. EPA, meanwhile, had gone through a major change in management, as Bill Ruckelshaus was brought in, as administrator, and the case received a fresh look. Finding language enough in the three-judge opinion to believe it might win on appeal, EPA did just that. The agency petitioned for a rehearing by a full panel of judges—eleven rather than three. In September 1984, the full court ruled 8-3 in favor of EPA. It found the agency had properly interpreted the act, and it did have the authority to order recalls of cars that had passed the "useful life" period.

Judge Patricia Wald—who dissented in the earlier panel, charging that GM's position would have gutted the recall program—wrote the new opinion. Wald found that the Clean Air Act did not exempt "older members of a recall class" from EPA action. "[N]o matter what their age at the time of recall," she wrote, "nonconforming cars have been riding the roads in violation of pollution standards."[50] *Wall Street Journal* reporter Andy Pasztor called the decision a major victory for the EPA, validating an important part of the agency's recall program.[51]

GM, however, wasn't finished. The company decided to take the case to the US Supreme Court. But the Supreme Court refused to hear the case. In April 1985, it allowed the appeals court ruling to stand. EPA had won. "We are disappointed that the court didn't take the case because the EPA ruling substantially expands the manufacturer's liability for emission recalls," said GM in a statement.[52] Indeed it did, and that was the whole point of the law and its enforcement: to create a powerful deterrent so automobile manufacturers would turn out cars and trucks that would perform within the bounds of the law and wouldn't have to be recalled in the first place.

On balance, the enforcement wars of the 1970s and 1980s came out in EPA's favor. The auto emissions enforcement provisions of the Clean Air Act were successfully defended. Former EPA enforcement officials say they were determined to marshall the resources to win when key parts of the program were challenged. "We would make sure we had all the resources needed to win—engineers, lawyers, and testing," said one former enforcement official. "Soon, the manufacturers understood that these would be costly challenges for them."

"Durability was always a key goal," he said. "We wanted good, in-use performance. That was the goal." To a degree they succeeded, at least establishing the foundation. Still, the industry challenges did eat up EPA resources, and that in part, is one reason why the automakers brought a steady stream of lawsuits, trying to wear the agency down, whittle away at the act, and buy a little more time. That in fact, is a hallmark of the industry's style over many years.

## CLEAN VEHICLES ELUSIVE

Despite the hard-won battles in building the credibility and effectiveness of EPA's enforcement program, assuring the production and operation of cleaner cars and trucks would remain elusive well into the 1990s. In 1991, for example, the National Academy of Sciences (NAS) issued a paper that made some fairly astounding observations about EPA's Federal Test Procedure (FTP)—the singular testing process the federal government uses to calculate the likely rate of pollution from new automobiles.

First, the NAS charged that the vehicles EPA used to calculate auto pollution were cleaner than most of those that would actually be used on the road. Second, the way the EPA corrected for certain variations in automotive speed and evaporative emissions in the test procedure was inaccurate. And finally, the vehicle I & M programs, envisioned by the Clean Air Act and EPA as a way to bring emissions down, were also not working and not leading to anticipated reductions. Consequently, concluded NAS, automotive emissions of smog-causing pollutants were probably two to four times greater than EPA was projecting.

By the mid-1990s, a separate group of scientists from the University of Michigan, Argonne National Laboratory, and the Lawrence Berkeley Laboratory, also investigating emissions testing, found that "real world emissions" were actually a lot higher than what was commonly claimed by automakers and government officials when measured by using the FTP and the federal standards. In other words, claiming that cars were actually performing at the level of the emission standards, which were based on the federal certification test, was not really accurate. There was much more pollution being generated than the tests would indicate.

"The large discrepancy between the regulatory tests, called the Federal Test Procedure (FTP), and real-world emissions is well known," they wrote. But there were two additional loopholes in the process that were not catching other categories of emissions, namely, driving at higher power and malfunctioning emission-control systems. "Primarily due to these loopholes," they wrote, "average emissions of CO and HC by cars on the road are about five times greater than the . . . standards, and NOx emissions are estimated to be about twice as high."[53]


## "Flooring It"

Marc Ross, a professor of physics at the University of Michigan and one of the investigators in the study, would later show that the high-power, "pedal-to-the-metal" option—i.e. flooring it, running at wide-open throttle—was responsible for a lot more auto pollution than generally realized. But not only was this pollution being missed in testing, it was also being missed by the automakers in their design of pollution control technology. And according to Ross, the automakers—at least as of 1994—could have been building cars with existing technology to dramatically reduce emissions.

Instead, most American cars were then using an "excess fuel" approach to obtain their high-power needs. The only problem with that approach, however, is that it puts the pollution control system out of kilter, since it makes the catalytic converter ineffective. The converter is located in the exhaust line, but in order for it to work properly, it has to be coordinated with what goes on in the engine. The fuel-air mixture delivered to the engine must have the chemically correct ratio; with that, the catalyst can work best on the resulting exhaust. Cleverly, the automakers have placed an oxygen sensor in the exhaust line, and its signal is used to adjust the mix of fuel and air entering the engine. However, in most American cars, that is negated by a high-power surge—when the pedal is pressed to the floor. When that happens, the sensor is overridden, and excess fuel floods into the cylinders—"20 to 30 percent more than is needed to chemically balance the oxygen," says Marc Ross. The flood of fuel "raises by orders of magnitude the emission rate of carbon monoxide and hydrocarbons." In fact, explains Ross, "each second of driving with the pedal down corresponds roughly to *30 minutes* of carbon monoxide emissions and 1 minute of hydrocarbon emissions" under more normal driving circumstances. Ross adds that such high-power surges are more common than one might think, especially for small cars, in which drivers often find themselves in hill climbs or in expressway traffic, driving for long stretches at wide-open throttle.

"The design that relies on excess fuel for high power," says Ross, coming back to the automakers' role, "is a vestige of the days of carburetor engines. . . . With simple changes in engine design, cars could probably achieve high power much more cleanly." In fact, some European makers by then had done just that. Volvo modified its software controls on the air–fuel mix to enable its cars to get high power with a third to a half of the emissions. "With rare exceptions," says Ross, "US automakers appear not to have seriously studied such approaches, much less implemented them."[54]

# 9
## *Help from Their Friends*

We were lucky that when push came to shove, we had appealed to a Democratic administration. . . .
—*Lee Iacocca, on the $1.5 billion Chrysler bailout, December 1979*[1]

The United States of America in 1980 was in a difficult time between Jimmy Carter and Ronald Reagan. Interest rates were hitting the roof, inflation was ravaging capital and savings, and unemployment was growing. Another energy shock was rippling through the world's oil-dependent economies. In January 1979, Iran's American-backed shah was deposed and fundamentalists under the Ayatollah Khomeini seized power. Hostages were taken at the American embassy in Teheran and another oil embargo ensued. Within a few weeks, gasoline prices doubled and the US auto industry began to feel the consequences.

Americans clamored for more efficient automobiles, but Detroit, for the most part, didn't have them. Americans turned in droves to Japanese models, which soon captured 20 percent of the market, mostly at the expense of Ford and Chrysler. Total US vehicle sales slipped below 9 million units in 1980—down from 10.6 million in 1979. When the 1980 financial numbers came in for the Big Three, there were record losses. GM experienced its first operating loss since 1921, reporting $762 million in red ink. Ford also lost big, posting $1.7 billion in the red. But for its size, Chrysler suffered the most, bleeding $1.8 billion, the largest loss in US business history. Help soon arrived, however, not only for Chrysler, but for all the automakers in one form or another—ranging from high-level US jawboning to slow down Japanese exports, to special "regulatory reform" packages designed to ease up on the beleaguered auto industry. In the process, some very significant shifts began to occur in Washington politics; shifts that would blur the lines between business and government and alter some key, long-standing loyalties of Democrat and Republican and their respective labor and big business constituencies. The US auto industry, for one, and environmental politics for another, would take new forms. And one of the first key indications of the changes at hand came with the politics and maneuvering required to bail out Chrysler.

## THE CHRYSLER BAILOUT

Chrysler's troubles had been building since 1978, when its "sales bank" system of keeping cars on hand without orders started clogging up. An enormous backlog of unsold cars began to pile up as the market went south. Chrysler's economic performance began to nosedive, and CEO John Riccardo resigned. Lee Iacocca, who had risen to become president of Ford Motor on the success of the 1964 Mustang, had been fired by Henry Ford II in 1979. Ford and Iacocca had a long internal feud that finally boiled over. Shortly thereafter, Iacocca was hired to replace Riccardo and rescue Chrysler. His first job as Chrysler's CEO was to convince Democrats in Congress—a party then not typically inclined toward big corporate favors—that the federal government should extend his near-bankrupt company $1.5 billion in loan guarantees. But Congress had its share of skeptics, Democrat and Republican. Representative John Heinz (R-PA) thought the company should issue more stock. Senator William Proxmire (D-WI) was also a critic, until Iacocca reminded him that American Motors Corporation, headquartered in Wisconsin, had received government help in the past. Representative Norman Shumway (R-CA) wasn't convinced Chrysler's management problems had been resolved. Iacocca told Congress that Chrysler's problems were due to "a combination of bad management, excessive regulation, the energy crisis and the recession." Chrysler's management mistakes of the past would not be repeated, he said. He had assembled a new management team—the best automobile men in the United States. "You just watch us," he said at one hearing. "You will see a lot of action at Chrysler. You will see better cars and you will see better service and better quality. And that in the end, is all that is going to matter."[2] But much of the action was in Washington, at least initially.

Iacocca understood his company needed both the White House and the party leadership in Congress to gain final approval of the loan guarantee bill. On Capitol Hill, he went right to the top—to Tip O'Neill (D-MA), Speaker of the House. O'Neill "was our real point man in the Congress," says Iacocca. O'Neill set up "a Speaker's task force" to help lobby the bill in the House.[3] The task force consisted of a group of about thirty other House members who lobbied their colleagues. In Congress, member-to-member lobbying is a most persuasive technique. O'Neill also spoke on behalf of the Chrysler bill during the House debate—a move by the Speaker usually reserved only for the most important issues. "Tip used raw emotion to sell his guys in the House," says Iacocca. "Once you've got the Speaker . . . you have a lot of clout." Indeed, when the vote came in, the House agreed 271-to-136 to help Chrysler.

Iacocca, however, had covered all the bases. He met, for example, with Congressman Parren Mitchell (D-MD), leader of the Congressional Black Caucus. "In 1979, 1 percent of the black payroll in the entire United Sates was paid by . . . Chrysler," explained Iacocca. "Blacks comprised an important part of the coalition that made the loan guarantee possible. . . ." Coleman Young, the black mayor of Detroit, had also come to Washington several times to testify on behalf of Chrysler. Iacocca even appealed to what he called "the Italian caucus." Representative Peter Rodino (D-

NJ) "brought me in and said: 'I want you to talk to my pals here.' There were thirty-one guys, (well, actually, thirty guys and Geraldine Ferraro . . . ), and all but one voted for us." Said Iacocca, "We . . . had to play every angle. It was democracy in action."[4] Chrysler's Washington office organized a massive lobby effort of its dealers. Groups of Chrysler and Dodge dealers came Washington regularly during the bill's consideration. Wendell Larsen, Chrysler's vice president of public affairs, would brief the dealers, "telling them which congressman to talk to and what to say. . . . " Chrysler had delivered to each congressman a computer printout of all the suppliers and dealers in his district who did business with Chrysler. "We outlined exactly what the consequences for that district would be if Chrysler went under," says Iacocca. "As I recall, there were only 2 districts out of the entire 535 that had no suppliers or Chrysler dealers. . . ."[5]

Chrysler also waged a public relations battle, not only with the general public, but also with members of the House and Senate who were not convinced Chrysler should receive government help. Recalls Iacocca,

> Instead of our regular advertising, . . . we ran a series of editorials . . . Instead of promoting our products, we were promoting the company and its future. . . . [I]t was time to advertise our cause instead of our cars. . . . In these ads, which K & E [Kenyon & Eckhardt] began to refer to as "paid PR," we set the record straight. . . . We were not building gas guzzlers. We were not asking Washington for a handout. Loan guarantees for Chrysler did not constitute a dangerous precedent. . . . [W]e asked—and answered some pretty tough questions: "Doesn't everyone know Chrysler cars get lousy gas mileage? Aren't Chrysler's big cars too big. . . . Isn't Chrysler building the wrong kind of cars?. . . Does Chrysler have a future?". . . The ad campaign was a major success. I'm pretty sure it played a role in the massive effort to convince Congress. . . . [Y]ou never really know what finally makes a difference in the battle for people's minds. But we heard reports of people in the Carter administration and in the Congress running from one office to another with these ads in their hands. . . .[6]

But in the end, one of the key alliances Iacocca and Chrysler had struck was with organized labor. Clearly, jobs were on the line if Chrysler went under. And labor and the UAW worked hard for the package. Doug Fraser, then head of the UAW "constituted a lobby effort of his own," says Iacocca. "Fraser testified brilliantly. He talked vividly about the cost in human lives and suffering if the loan guarantees were not passed. . . . Fraser was a tireless and effective lobbyist who met individually with a number of congressman and senators. He was also a good friend of Vice President Mondale, and he paid a couple of important visits to the White House."

A couple of weeks after the Loan Guarantee Act passed, the Republicans came to power. The Reagan era had begun, and Iacocca knew he had just pulled off a coup not possible with Republicans.

We were lucky . . . we had appealed to a Democratic administration that put people ahead of ideology. Democrats usually do. They deal with labor, they deal with people, they deal with jobs. Republicans deal with trickle-down theories of investment. . . . I'm the first to admit that . . . when I've made a lot of money, I've always favored the Republicans. But ever since coming to Chrysler, I've leaned toward the Democrats. Overall, I'm for the commonsense party, and when the chips are down, that's usually the Democrats. There's no question in my mind that if there had been a Republican administration in 1979, Chrysler wouldn't be around. . . .[7]

## "Special Bond"

After Chrysler got its loan, Iacocca used one of the company's new ads to thank the America people for saving the company. "The Congress of the United States has passed the Chrysler Loan Guarantee bill. The New Chrysler Corporation is in business to stay. The jobs of 600,000 workers have been saved. And with that act a special bond had been created with the American people. . . ." However, some Washington insiders, such as Ed Muskie's aide, Leon Billings, felt Chrysler's "special bond" was with the Democrats, shifting traditional Democratic alliances and loyalties on key issues like the environment for years to come. "They changed the political dynamic," says Billings. "They hired Tommy Boggs, the auto industry's first hire of an established Democrat."[8] Boggs was then, and for years later, a recognized lobbyist and power broker for the Democratic side and a key player in Washington politics.

Chrysler was the first of the Big Three to get into big financial trouble as the second energy shock reverberated throughout the economy. Ford and GM were also hard hit, but they did not begin to bleed as quickly or as deeply as Chrysler. All three, however, were watching their sliding market share with increasing concern, and the fact that the Japanese were taking more and more of it.

## "An Economic Pearl Harbor"

The rise of the Japanese automakers as major factor in the US market began slowly in the mid-1960s with a few Toyota Coronas and small Datsun and Toyota pickup trucks. In 1969, the Datsun 240-Z sports car was named Sports Car of the Year by *Road Test* magazine. And by 1975, both Datsun and Toyota had surpassed Volkswagen as leading foreign importers. On the heels of the energy crisis, however, Japanese cars took off. Imports of Japanese vehicles rose to 1.37 million in 1976 and 2.4 million by 1980.[9]

Calling the impact of Japanese imports an "economic Pearl Harbor," Henry Ford II said, "We just can't stand for it. We can't degrade this country the way it's been degraded by the way the Japanese are treating us." UAW president Douglas Fraser told his rank and file, "The Japanese are not exporting cars to the US. They are exporting unemployment."[10] The Big Three and the UAW joined forces to seek protection from Japanese imports, unless the Japanese began to manufacture in the US. Auto executives went to Congress seeking legislation to limit Japanese imports. Meanwhile, laid-off auto workers in places like Mount Clemens, Michigan, were taking sledge hammers to Japanese imports in public displays of frustration and anger. A white sign with red lettering posted on the guard booth at the UAW parking lot in Detroit read "300,000 Laid-Off UAW Members Don't Like Your Import. Please Park It in Tokyo."

In 1980-81, first Congress, and then Ronald Reagan attacked the Japanese and threatened a trade war. The intention of the administration in calling for trade restrictions, as well as free traders in Congress, was to "buy time" for the US automakers to tool up to produce small, fuel-efficient cars to compete with the Japanese.[11] In Tokyo, meanwhile, the Japanese got the message. Japan's Ministry of International Trade and Industry (MITI) established the Voluntary Restraint Agreement, which went into effect in 1982. Japanese car sales were to be kept at the 1979 level. The limitations worked out to 1.68 million vehicles in 1982, 1.81 million in 1983, and 1.85 million in 1984. But in addition to the sales, the Big Three also claimed they were being disadvantaged by cheap foreign labor.

In January 1981, however, the outgoing Carter administration secretary of transportation, Neil Goldschmidt, issued a report to the president entitled, "The US Automobile Industry, 1980," which took issue with industry's claim that "cheap labor" accounted for the Japanese advantage. Goldschmidt found that only about one half of Japan's $1,500 per car cost advantage was attributable to wages. "The greatest source of Japanese advantage," he wrote, "is structural: process and product technology that yield major productivity gains." Goldschmidt's charge to US management was to commit "major resources to matching these productivity accomplishments if our industry is to regain competitive health."[12] But the Goldschmidt report also criticized the federal government for imposing environmental and other regulations on the industry without regard for their cumulative impact. The automakers had pushed the White House and the federal agencies during the Carter years to ease up on environmental and safety regulations, with some results.

The Carter administration's OMB, for example, responding to the industry's charge that federal regulations were a significant cause of its cash shortages, began a May 1980 inquiry into the economic effects of various regulations on the auto industry. A meeting was held with Carter, some of his cabinet, and the CEOs of GM, Ford, Chrysler, AMC, and Volkswagen of America to discuss the industry's problems. The administration asked the automakers for a list of their major problems, and the MVMA promptly replied. Suggested changes sent to Carter included: across-the-board waivers of the 1982-83 CO standard for light-duty vehicles; withdrawing the proposed high-altitude emissions standards; revising the ozone national ambient air quality standards to allow five exceedances on a yearly average; dropping transportation control programs from state implementation plans; and other additional proposals for heavy- and light-duty trucks. However, the Carter administration was

## "Our Japanese Strategy"

In 1980, as some auto executives and labor were bashing the Japanese, GM's Roger Smith had quietly asked Isuzu (which GM had partly owned since 1971) to calculate what it would cost to build a car comparable to GM's proposed S-car. The S-car was a small car line GM was planning to launch in the 1985 model year. When Isuzu's comparative cost analysis came back, Smith was stunned: Isuzu could do it for $2,857 compared to GM's $5,731. GM wasn't even in the ball game with those numbers. Smith then decided to kill the S-car project and begin looking for a Japanese business partner to build small cars. As Smith put it a few years later, "It was terrifying when you saw what gasoline was selling for—and everybody saying it was going to be three bucks a gallon. Our market study said if you asked the average housewife, she didn't care if she went to the store once in the Cadillac . . . what she wanted to be able to do was go to the store *three* times. We all of sudden said 'Boy are we in a pile of trouble here.' . . . [P]eople wanted to get the maximum mileage. And we were not in that game, so we said we better find out what to do, and that's where our Japanese strategy came from." GM began looking for a Japanese partner.

In early 1981, GM used its connection with Isuzu to try and make a deal with Honda, but Honda rebuffed GM. Shortly thereafter, GM acquired a 5 percent position in Suzuki. By this time, in fact, the US automakers had a number of contracts with Japanese automakers and other suppliers. In addition to GM, some were also talking mergers and/or joint ventures with the Japanese. Ford at the time was talking about a merger with Toyota, but a deal never materialized. By December 1981, GM began talks with Toyota, and two years later, in March 1983, reached an agreement in principle to begin a joint venture to produce Chevy Novas in California. The 50-50 venture was called the New United Motor Manufacturing, Inc., or NUMMI. The GM-Toyota deal came at the height of America's Japan-bashing hysteria and was not a popular move. GM's Roger Smith, however, defended the deal on the basis of costs and as an interim strategy to get to a genuine American small car, built in America, by Americans that would compete with the Japanese. That car would become the Saturn—but not until the 1990s.

Chrysler went to court to try to stop the GM deal with Toyota, but when it later settled with GM, Chrysler began its own collaboration with Mitsubishi. By 1989, Ford had given almost all of its small-car development to Mazda.

fairly judicious in granting regulatory concessions to the industry, although some were made.* As of September 1980, heading into a national election, the Carter administration said its regulatory reforms had resulted in automaker cost savings of about $600 million. But after the 1980 national elections, Jimmy Carter was gone, and the auto industry saw much bigger opportunities.[13]

* For example, Carter announced in July 1980 as part of this economic relief plan for the auto industry that the administration would interpret the Clean Air Act's high-altitude emissions standard to apply to cars sold at altitudes below 6,000 feet (except for CO and ozone nonattainment areas, which meant Denver, Albuquerque, and Salt Lake City were still

## The "Auto Package"

When Ronald Reagan came to Washington in 1981, "regulatory relief" for many of the nation's industries was high on the new administration's agenda. OMB director-designee David Stockman, former Michigan congressman, and Representative Jack Kemp (R-NY) drafted a paper for Reagan entitled, "Avoiding an Economic Dunkirk," in which they recommended several changes in the auto emissions program: granting CO waivers for the 1982 model year; simplifying the new car certification program; canceling EPA's fuel additive testing program; and relaxing 1984 heavy- and light-duty truck standards. Eric Stork, former EPA deputy assistant administrator for mobile source (i.e. motor vehicles) program, helped Stockman with the recommendations. Stork polled large corporations and industry groups on the changes they wanted at EPA and compiled these for Stockman's office.[14] Between November 1980 and January 1981, other groups also contributed to the Reagan administration's reform proposals, including the Heritage Foundation. The automakers had also been doing their own lobbying, sending the administration materials and suggesting changes in a number of regulations. Included on a list of seven environmental and safety regulations identified for elimination or other modification by GM's William Chapman in a January 1981 letter to OMB's Jim Tozzi, then assistant director for Regulatory and Information Policy, was a proposal to "relax the definition of 'attainment'" for the ozone standard under the National Ambient Air Quality Standards, ozone being the key smog standard.[15] By the time OMB's final list of auto industry regulatory reforms was released, it had about thirty items.[16] OMB's efforts were soon buttressed by the President's Task Force on Regulatory Relief, chaired by Vice President George Bush.** With assistance from OMB's David Stockman, and Boyden Gray, the vice president's counsel, the task force went about its mission: to "cut away the thicket of irrational and senseless regulation" and review pending and past regulations "with an eye toward revising them."[17]

## The GM Hit List

"The big push," at the time, according to acting EPA administrator Walt Barber, was, "What could we do to provide some monetary relief to the auto industry?" The

---

protected). The administration had also granted the automakers nineteen of sixty-two requests for waivers from the 1981 CO standard were granted. In August 1980, EPA dropped the requirements for all 1982 and later models to meet emissions standards at all possible idle speed settings. In September 1980, additional regulatory reforms for the auto industry were announced, primarily for light- and heavy-duty trucks, as well as a reevaluation of EPA's certification program.

** A week after setting up the task force, Ronald Reagan issued a sixty-day "freeze" on pending final regulations—some of which had been turned out in the waning days of the Carter administration. By mid-February 1981, Reagan had signed Executive Order 12291, which made OMB and the task force the central powers involving regulatory relief and also required federal agencies to do a "regulatory impact analysis" before proposing a new rule.

answer, essentially, was found in a General Motors "hit list" of thirty or more environmental, health, and safety regulations the company had circulated in Washington a year earlier. This list, with some reworking, became known as the "automobile package" inside the task force, and was essentially adopted by the administration. "If you take a look at the automobile package," explained Boyden Gray at the time, "it is a pretty good overview of how we hope to proceed."[18]

By March 31, 1981, GM, now aiming at Congress, called a press conference in Washington announcing its plan to seek amendments to the Clean Air Act. Repeating its call for some of the same changes sought through the administration—including the roll back of the CO and NOx standards—GM laid out a proposal for other sweeping changes for the act, its auto emissions standards, and EPA's mobile sources program. First, GM wanted to average emissions on a fleetwide basis rather than using car-by-car standards. Second, GM proposed that a system of emission "credits" be established for auto manufacturers, with the automakers able to buy, sell, or trade such credits depending on whether individual engine families were above or below specified emission levels—based on GM's proposed fleet average standard. This meant, for example, according to Dr. Craig Marks, director of GM's Clean Air Act Review Task Force, that if a manufacturer's fleet average failed compliance requirements, the company could use its own emissions credits or purchase them elsewhere to avoid an expensive recall. Third, GM wanted to replace the current system of vehicle inspections before and after manufacturing, using instead a single test that would be given three or four years after cars were on the road. This, said Marks, would eliminate "redundant" tests that usually produce "conflicting data."[19] David Doniger of the NRDC, reacting to GM's announcement, said the company's plan was to "weaken" the standards and then "not let you know if they were meeting even those [weaker] standards until three or four years down the road."[20]

On April 6, 1981, a list of eighteen actions "to help the US auto industry" was announced by George Bush and the Task Force on Regulatory Relief. "The industry must solve its own problems," said Bush, reading from a statement by the president, "but the government must not unnecessarily hamper its effort through excessive regulation and interference."[21] The list included the following EPA actions:

- revise the 1984 model year HC and CO standards to a level that would not require the installation of catalysts on gasoline-powered heavy trucks;
- relax the 10 percent Acceptable Quality Level (ACL) to 40 percent for assembly line testing of light trucks and heavy-duty engines;
- delay the implementation of the Selective Enforcement Auditing (SEA) program for heavy-duty engines for two years;
- affirm EPA's intention to relax the statutory NOx emission limits for heavy-duty engines for three years to the level that can be achieved by diesel engines;
- adopt an emission averaging scheme for manufactures to meet the NOx emission requirement for light- and heavy-duty trucks;

- propose alternative particulate "averaging" scheme to replace the individual vehicle standard currently in place for 1985 model year passenger cars and light trucks;
- request that Congress eliminate the requirement that passenger cars meet the 1984 emission standards at all altitudes, while preserving EPA's authority to require proportional standards for light and heavy trucks, as well as passenger cars;
- adopt a self-certification program for vehicles to be sold at higher altitudes while continuing to monitor in-use emissions at high-altitude; forgo assembly line testing at high altitudes;
- initiate consolidated proceedings to waive the statutory NOx standard from 1.0 to 1.5 GPM to the maximum extent permitted by law for all light-duty diesels through the 1984 model year;
- initiate consolidated proceedings to waive the statutory CO standard from 3.4 to 7.0 GPM to the maximum extent permitted by law for classes of 1982 model year light-duty vehicles not previously produced to meet the 3.4 GPM standard;
- adopt equivalent non-methane hydrocarbon standards as an option for all vehicles;
- [abandon proposed] onboard technology for the control of hydrocarbon emissions resulting from refueling motor vehicles;
- further streamline the motor vehicle certification program by reducing paperwork and increasing industry flexibility;
- relax test vehicle exemption requirements to reduce administrative burdens presently associated with this program;
- reduce the annual number of Selective Enforcement Audit test orders to the maximum degree consistent with maintaining approximately the current level of compliance; explore deferral of standards for automobile paint shop operations; and,
- affirm EPA's intention to provide sufficient leadtime for compliance with emission regulations, as measured from the date of promulgation of regulations.[22]

In addition to these actions and proposed rulemakings, there were another thirteen "items for further EPA study" also proposed; any one of which could lead to additional regulatory and/or statutory changes.* "On balance," said acting EPA admin-

---

*These included, for example, the following: "Whether to reduce reliance on (or even phase out) certification and selective enforcement auditing, linked to adoption of a stronger program for identifying and resolving poor in-use performance. EPA will also consider use of emission fees paid by the manufacturer as an alternative to recall for vehicle classes which do not meet in-use requirements. Whether to apply emissions-averaging to all compliance programs. Whether to make administrative and legislative changes in the design and defect and performance warranties. Whether to eliminate the testing requirement for meeting the heavy-duty evaporative emissions standard, requiring instead that manufacturers attest to EPA that vehicles, as designed, comply with the standard. Whether there is a need for the passenger car CO standard of 3.4 GPM and NOx standard of 1.0 GPM. This review will allow the Administrator to make appropriate recommendations to Congress. Whether the 1985 particulate standard for diesel cars and light trucks is technologically feasible and whether the timing

istrator Walter Barber at the April 6, 1981 press conference announcing the proposals, "we don't see any environmental degradation as a result of the package."[23]

"[T]he agencies are being given the signal that the results should come out a certain way before the necessary analysis has even been begun," explained GM economist George Eads at the time.[24] Indeed, that's exactly what EPA's Mike Walsh discovered in a meeting with OMB's Jim Miller in the spring of 1981. Walsh, then directing the agency's mobile source office, had come to brief Miller and his staff on changes in the regulations, "We had developed a set of proposals that provided substantial relief to the industry without gutting the program, and still keeping health protection more or less intact. Miller and his staff made it clear that the industry, and GM, wanted much more."[25]

## "REMOVE THE EQUIPMENT"

Meanwhile, on Capitol Hill, it became abundantly clear what the auto industry really wanted—a rollback of both the CO and NOx standards that would in effect allow them to quit installing pollution control equipment they were already using on existing models. These changes would also ease the way for bringing other engines into production—notably diesels that GM wanted. If the CO and NOx standards were relaxed, said the automakers, they could remove $360 worth of pollution control equipment from the cost of a new car—$60 worth for CO controls and $300 for NOx controls. GM's chairman Roger Smith promised Congress in that the savings from no longer installing the devices would be passed on to consumers "dollar for dollar," thus lowering sticker prices on new cars. "The air will keep getting cleaner and cleaner, and car prices will go down," said Smith. "That's the best way I know of affecting sticker shock right now."[26]

Industry claimed, along with the Reagan administration, that most US cities could still meet the national clean air standards even if the CO and NOx standards were relaxed. As old cars were retired from service, they said, the air would improve enough to make up the difference. Making the changes would save the industry $1 billion according to the White House.

---

and level of the standard is appropriate. Whether the National Ambient Air Quality Standards should be revised.... Whether future additional regulations of the chlorofluorocarbon emissions is needed and how the automotive industry would or should be affected by such requirements. Whether the 1984 heavy-duty truck requirements should be further revised based on the results of manufacturers' current heavy-duty transient test programs. Whether heavy-duty engines and light trucks should meet standards for their full useful life or just for their half life as is the case with passenger cars. Whether the current requirements relating to unregulated pollutants impose unnecessary reporting burdens and should be revised...."
The White House, *Actions to Help the US Auto Industry*, April 6, 1981, Attachment A: Regulatory Relief for the Auto Industry, "Items for Further EPA Study," pp. A-28-29.

By this time, the catalyst makers, represented in Washington by the Manufacturers of Emission Control Association (MECA), an organization of thirteen companies employing 2,500 workers with a $54 million-dollar payroll, did not like what they were hearing in the Reagan administration or the automakers' calls for removing pollution control equipment. They had invested $100 million to develop and refine their catalyst systems. MECA's executive director, John Blizard, in May 1981 testimony before a House Government Operations subcommittee, warned that the Reagan administration proposal would not bring significant economic relief, but would penalize his industry and set back the effort to clean up the air.

MECA opposed the administration's proposals, including those aimed at relaxing the CO and NOx standards for 1983 and later model year passenger cars, as well as those targeting diesels and heavy truck standards. Eleven MECA companies had invested heavily to perfect the trap oxidizer to control diesel particles, Blizard explained, and if the standard were relaxed, the technology, which was then nearing completion, would be lost. Blizard also addressed the issue of fuel economy, explaining that the new three-way catalyst for passenger cars allowed 1981 models to get, on average, 22 MPG, and that this technology, in combination with engine sensors controlling fuel/air mixtures, was helping to advance and clean up the combustion process while making it more efficient. Increasingly, he explained, catalyst technology and improved fuel economy were "inextricably bound." Blizard also reminded his listeners that the US was beginning to carve out an export business in pollution control technology and that backing off that technology now by changing the rules would undermine that economic advantage. "Let us not move too impulsively," Blizard counseled, noting also that retaining standards like those for carbon monoxide would also help 145 counties throughout the United States that were then exceeding CO standards.[27]

In August 1981, the administration, rather then sending a clean air bill up to Congress, announced a set of eleven principles offering a "framework" for revising the act. EPA's Anne Gorsuch announced the administration's package, noting for example, that the NOx standard could be relaxed to 1.5 GPM or even 2 GPM "without affecting air quality goals." The CO standard would also be relaxed, said Gorsuch, from 3.4 GPM to 7.0 GPM. Another of the administration's "principles" called for eliminating mandatory federal sanctions for states not in compliance with federal requirements for automobile inspection programs.[28] Industry was claiming that the standards were not necessary to meet the clean air goals and therefore should be rolled back. David Hawkins of the National Clean Air Coalition and former Carter administration EPA official said the industry's assertions about meeting national standards with a relaxed CO standard were based on overly optimistic predictions about on-the-road performance of pollution control equipment. Industry also wanted to eliminate mandatory auto emission inspection programs, which would mean that violations of the national CO standard would likely double in the 1984–1990 period.[29] "It appears the auto companies want everything or nothing," explained Leon Billings, "and the usual result of that approach is you get nothing."[30]

## "THEY KEEP COMING AT YOU"

Mike Walsh is a veteran of the auto pollution wars in Washington and at EPA. For nearly thirty years Walsh fought the good fight in and out of government—from hands-on testing of emissions control equipment and alternative engines for New York City in the early 1970s, to working in and later heading up EPA's Office of Mobile Sources in the 1974-1981 period. "After a few [difficult] meetings with Anne Gorsuch," he says of his bid to remain at EPA after the Reagan administration arrived, "I left."

Today, Mike Walsh is an international air pollution consultant who travels the world advising clients such as the World Bank and the national government of China. He has also served as a consultant for California, MECA, and other organizations. He appears regularly before congressional committees as an expert witness. His articles are found in the journals and technical papers of the Society of Automotive Engineers.

Looking back on his career at EPA, Walsh remembers in particular how some auto industry officials would present their case for changing or eliminating rules that did not suit them. He remembers one 1978 meeting between GM's Pete Estes and EPA administrator Doug Costle, in which Walsh, then head of the OMS, was also present. Estes essentially said that GM was going to build cars the way it wanted to, regardless of EPA's rules. The issue at the time was EPA's forthcoming rule for diesel (particulate) emissions. Walsh remembers Estes, laughing and arrogant, saying to Costle, "I don't care what you do. We're going to build our [diesel] cars our way.... We're going to roll over you.... It's necessary for jobs. It's necessary for energy...." EPA, however, held its ground on the diesel rule, but once it was issued and GM started producing its "cobbled together" diesels as some viewed them, the company then proceeded to blame EPA's rule for the problem-plagued engines and consumer lawsuits that followed.

Then there was the time in the late 1970s when Ford Motor Co. helped persuade the House Appropriations Committee to call Walsh on the carpet for allegedly "misallocating" EPA monies. Walsh, then heading up the Mobile Sources office, was called to Capitol Hill to explain a shift in activities within his office. Walsh, responding to industry criticism that the auto emissions certification process was too burdensome, proceeded to shift personnel away from certification, and into additional monitoring of "in-use" performance of automobiles—how they were actually performing on the road. That apparently rankled Ford and other automakers even more. Ford lobbyists, knowing how Congress disliked any hint of a federal agency taking liberties with its appropriations power, played up Walsh's "misallocated" priorities for all it was worth, riling committee staff to the point where a hearing was held to focus on Walsh's actions. Yet, in defending his reallocation of staff, Walsh explained he was only responding to industry's original critique. He was trying, he explained, to focus agency effort where he believed it would do the most good.

These and other instances are emblematic of a pattern Walsh has seen over the years. "It's like a giant glacier," he says of industry's persistent lobbying. "They keep coming at you. First, they fight the proposal in Congress. Then they come at you through the regulatory process at EPA. If that doesn't work, they go to the White House, OMB, or Commerce or some other place where they have leverage and friends. They'll end run you. Then, after all that, they'll go to the courts."

"With every rule making," he says, "they'll milk everything they can out of you, then after it's promulgated, they'll sue you anyway. They fight for every inch. They keep coming; keep coming—keeping you busy and slowing you down. . . ."

Walsh is not a naysayer, however, and he does admit to much technological progress, taking almost personal pride in the fact that catalyst technology has been so widely adopted globally—nearly 90 percent of all new cars produced globally come equipped with catalytic converters. American automakers, he says, have much cleaner, more efficient, better-engineered cars today than they ever had, and he calls industry's engineers today "top-notch." But the Big Three, he says, could have made things happen a lot quicker than they did. He points to a chart which shows the dramatic progress made in reducing auto emissions since 1970, even though vehicle miles of travel have risen precipitously upward in that same time frame. Still, this reduction could have taken place in half the time, he says, had industry put more effort into engineering and improved compliance rather than fighting the requirements at every turn.

"It's not over," he warns, pointing to problems with trucks, off-road vehicles, and sport utility vehicles (SUVs)—and especially the trade-in-the-making that would bring more diesels back into the picture as a supposed fix. "It's a bad deal," says Walsh, pointing to a 12 percent reduction in carbon dioxide in trade for a doubling or tripling of NOx and an eight-fold increase in particulate that diesels would bring to urban areas. That, he says, "would be unfortunate and unnecessary."

## THE LOU HARRIS POLL

By late 1981, the Reagan administration's proposed deregulatory attack on the nation's environmental laws began to come up against an unexpected obstacle: public opinion. Reagan was slow to make his appointments, and when he did, those like Secretary of the Interior James Watt, and Anne Gorsuch at EPA—conservatives who challenged the activist government role in resource stewardship—galvanized the environmental community into opposition and highly visible campaigns. Public opinion at the time was moving positively in the environmental direction as well. In fact, when asked what was holding up the auto industry's antiregulatory lobbying campaign in late 1981, J.R. Kingman, a Washington public relations manager for GM, replied, "the Lou Harris poll."[31] Public opinion pollster Lou Harris had found that 80 percent of the American public did not want *any* relaxation of existing federal regulation of air pollution. In fact, 86 percent favored either the current or more stringent controls. Respondents also indicated by a 54-42 percent majority that they opposed pushing back auto emission deadlines.[32] Lou Harris himself went to Capitol Hill to testify before Henry Waxman's subcommittee in October 1981, and he told the members in no uncertain terms that they risked their political futures by weakening environmental laws:

. . . Mess around with the Clean Air and Clean Water acts, and you're going to get into the deepest kind of trouble. . . .

. . . I am saying to you as clear as can be, that clean air happens to be one of the

sacred cows of the American people, and the suspicion is afoot that there are interests in the business community and among the Republicans and some Democrats
who want to keelhaul that legislation.

And people are saying, "Watch Out. We will have your hide if you do it." That is
the only message that comes out of this as clear-cut as anything I have ever seen in
my professional career.[33]

The auto industry, however, was undaunted and persisted with HR 4400, a bill
sponsored by Representatives Bob Traxler (D-MI) and Elwood Hillis (R-IN). This
bill essentially comprised a "wish list" of industry changes, extensions, and relaxed
standards—and in particular, the CO and NOx standards. "The Traxler-Hillis bill
calls for slight revisions in two of the three vehicle emissions standards in the act,"
said GM's Roger Smith in a September 1981 speech before the Engineering Society of Detroit. "These proposed revisions would allow manufacturers like General
Motors to remove some of the hardware from our cars without jeopardizing the
achievement of national air quality standards or the public health."[34]

The protections then called for in the act were, in Smith's view, "not necessary to
meet public health objectives." Smith contended that CO emissions were declining "faster that any other pollutant," and that there was "no danger of its building
up in the atmosphere because it reacts in soil and actually helps make the soil more
fertile." Smith further asserted that controlling NOx was very expensive, arguing
that most cities outside of southern California were then in compliance with the
nitrogen dioxide standards, and that decreasing NOx further "could actually cause
smog to get worse instead of better." He also pitched industry's call for averaging
emissions. "We're suggesting that auto manufacturers should be allowed to meet
the regulations with a fleet average emissions number, not unit-by-unit." He concluded, "The sooner Congress acts in revising the Clean Air Act, the sooner General Motors can begin to make the engineering and production changes necessary
to take some emissions control equipment off of these cars. We might be able to
remove some $300 worth from our base cars."[35]

However, industry's proposal to roll back standards became a hard sell in Congress. "In 1977, if certain changes weren't made, cars weren't going to be produced,"
explained Timothy MacCarty, lobbyist for the MVMA. "It's a harder job selling a
rollback. Now we're talking about standards that we're meeting...."[36] Still, through
rule-making and other executive branch actions, the Reagan administration helped
the auto industry on several fronts.*

---

* By May 1981, the Reagan administration began revising some EPA rules based on the
auto industry's recommendations, publishing, for example, relaxed procedures for compliance with high-altitude emission standards. Not long after this rule was adopted, in response
to a request from Ford Motor Co., EPA began allowing cars certified for sale in high-altitude areas also to be sold at low altitudes. In October 1981, an EPA interim rule shifted some
responsibility for the new car certification program to manufacturers. Final rules streamlining

Back in Congress, John Dingell was doing what he could to move the Traxler-Hillis bill, but Democrats resisted, seeing defense of clean air as a political plus for the upcoming 1982 elections, then nine months away. On the Senate side, Senator Robert T. Stafford (R-VT), the moderate chairman of the Environment and Public Works Committee, adopted a fine-tuning approach to the act, making few changes at the committee level. Stafford had sent a warning to major corporations in early May 1981 that if they persisted in trying to "rewrite the fundamentals" of the act, they would precipitate a bloody, "15-round political prizefight," likely to drag on for several years.[37] Some Democratic senators vowed they would fight the industry-backed changes. "If anything approaching the Traxler-Hillis abandonment of automobile standards is adopted by this committee," threatened Senator Daniel Patrick Moynihan (D-NY), "there will be no Clean Air Act this year." Moynihan was talking filibuster.[38] By December 1981, there was also strong support for the auto emissions standards coming from state and local officials, and most notably the National Governor's Association and state and local air pollution officials represented by two key organizations—State and Territorial Air Program Administrators, and the Association of Local Air Pollution Control Officials—known jointly as STAPPA-ALAPCO. These three bodies reported to Senator Stafford that relaxing the CO standard, for example, would increase levels of that pollutant by 4 percent for 1987 and by 14.9 percent for 2000. Relaxing light- and heavy-duty truck standards would make the numbers worse, they added, pushing at least a dozen cities and states into CO nonattainment. "As you know," wrote West Virginia governor Jay Rockefeller, then chairman of NGA's Energy and Environment Committee, "the National Governors' Association opposes any relaxation of the existing standards for mobile sources under the Clean Air Act." Rockefeller also added that STAPPA had "voted overwhelming this week to join the Governors in opposing any change" in the auto emissions standards.[39]

By year's end, however, there was little movement of any bill in Congress. The House Energy and Commerce Committee had deadlocked, and the Senate Public Works and Environment Committee had only begun its consideration. The automakers, and GM in particular, however, would return in 1982, using the economy and jobs to continue their attack.

---

the certification program were issued in October 1982. Another rule eased the strictures on automobile assembly operations with paint shops, known to be especially significant contributors to volatile organic compound (VOCs) emissions. In December 1981, EPA delivered a promised rule change establishing nonmethane hydrocarbon standards for light-and heavy-duty engines. In January 1982, it issued a standard approving the averaging of particulate emissions for light-duty diesel vehicles, and in November 1982, it announced its proposal to delay for two years the 1985 diesel particulate standard for light-duty vehicles. See, for example, Melissa Merson, "Environmental Regulation of the Automobile," *Environment Reporter*, monograph no. 31, vol. 13, no. 33, December 17, 1982, p. 51.

## ALBUQUERQUE BLUES

In December 1981, as various proposals were being offered in the House and Senate to weaken the auto emission standards, one amendment of particular concern to the environmental community was that sponsored by Senator Steve Symms (R-ID). Symms, who had come to the Senate after a number of years in the House, was no friend of the environment. He had been the target of Environmental Action's "Dirty Dozen" campaigns in the 1970s, a designation highlighting a poor environmental voting record intended to help expose those unfriendly to the environment. In Symms case, however, it made little difference as Idaho voters appeared satisfied with his positions. He became a senator in 1980.

COALITION V. EPA   Symms' proposed amendment to the Clean Air Act sought to weaken the carbon monoxide tailpipe standard, doubling the allowable amount of CO emissions from 3.4 GPM to 7.0 GPM—a proposal the automakers heartily supported. On December 3, Symms offered his amendment in the Public Works Committee. However, the measure failed to come to a vote as some senators wanted more time. The next session was scheduled for December 11. In the interim, on December 8, the National Clean Air Coalition (NCAC) released a national study that found that with the Symms amendment as law, sixteen major metropolitan areas would never meet the national ambient air quality standards for CO established under the Clean Air Act. In making this claim, NCAC had challenged EPA's projection of a much improved CO situation by 1999 with the relaxed standard. NCAC charged that EPA forecast was incorrect and based on faulty data. EPA assumed that auto emission systems would deteriorate less under the relaxed standard—at a rate of 54 percent rather than 59 percent, the traditional rate—thus making a "very optimistic" projection about CO compliance. Applying the higher and more accurate 59 percent deterioration rate for auto emission systems, said the coalition, would mean that sixteen metropolitan areas would never meet the national standard for CO. NCAC held a national press conference on its findings and made a special effort in the affected metropolitan areas—one of which was Albuquerque, New Mexico, a major city represented by Senator Pete Domenici (R-NM), a key member of the Senate Public Works Committee, and it turned out, a very important vote on the Symms amendment.

DOMINICI KEY   The Symms amendment was receiving serious consideration in part because the National Commission on Air Quality report (NCAQ) had recommended a similar change. However, the NCAQ recommendation came with some important caveats: principally that mandatory inspection and maintenance programs be established in severely affected cities, and that the original standard be applied to trucks and in high-altitude areas. Senator Gary Hart (D-CO), who chaired the NCAQ, opposed Symms' amendment because it did not include these caveats, and Republicans could give no assurances the stipulations Hart wanted would remain intact during floor debate. All of this meant that Domenici had become a key vote, especially since the committee was evenly divided on the question.

EVENING NEWS   Meanwhile, the NCAC report was a lead story on the evening news and received prominent play in many newspapers. Senator Domenici, usually a mild-mannered member of the Senate, conducting his affairs in a gracious and diplomatic style, was especially upset about the study and its coverage in New Mexico and Albuquerque in particular — which he described as being in "near panic" over the news. As the Public Works Committee convened on December 11 to proceed with its markup, Domenici had no kind words for the Clean Air Coalition study, remarking that the group had "sunk to a new level of lobbying" in releasing the report days before a scheduled committee vote on a key amendment. Domenici even singled out David Hawkins, former Carter administration official and then at NRDC, a founding member of NCAC. "You should know better, David Hawkins," he said, excoriating the environmentalist for his tactics.

NCAC TARGETED Domenici then proceeded to ask for a delay in the vote, noting, of course, that he did not intend to support the Symms proposal in the first place, but that he wanted to be sure there were no "new startling facts" out there. Domenici then requested committee staff to review the issue, including an investigation of the NCAC study. David Hawkins stood by the veracity of the coalition's report, saying he welcomed the committee's inquiry. By the time the Senate committee convened in late January 1982 to consider the staff's findings—and memorandum that had been specifically prepared on the NCAC study and EPA's numbers—there was no outright condemnation of the coalition's report. Rather, the staff review found that although certain of the coalition's assumptions were "pessimistic," they were still "defensible." Moreover, on the matter of deterioration rates for auto emissions systems, committee staff found that it was "simply not possible to state with certainty where either estimate [i.e., EPA's or the coalition's] is correct because sufficient in-use data has not yet accumulated." When the Senate Public Works Committee finally approved S.3041 in August 1982, it retained the existing CO standard of 3.4 grams per mile. Although the bill was reported to the full Senate in November 1982, no floor action was scheduled.

## GM's "CRIPPLING EFFECT"

"Certain amendments being proposed by Senators Hart and Stafford and Representative Waxman would, if enacted, have a crippling effect on the automobile industry and severe adverse effects on the entire economy," began a five-page lobby sheet handed out by GM lobbyists in March 1982. The amendments at issue, explained GM, "would stop production of diesel cars and diesel light-duty trucks, both gas and diesel heavy trucks, as well as many of our most fuel-efficient small gasoline cars...." The second paragraph of the handout continued in capitalized format. "The promotion and support of amendments so potentially disruptive as these by Senate and House members create debilitating uncertainty throughout the industry, causing unproductive expenditure of scarce resources and, in a very real way, add to the current economic problems of the whole country." The amendments, said GM, using more capitalized and underlined emphasis, could result in *permanent losses at General Motors alone of 31,000 to 42,500 jobs by 1996. Our suppliers, our dealers and many related enterprises also will suffer severe employment problems."[40]

Under the Clean Air Act, EPA had authority to defer the 1983 deadline and weaken the standard for heavy trucks, which EPA's Anne Gorsuch was planning to do. The original standard, however, required heavy trucks to reduce HC and CO emissions by 90 percent, essentially requiring the use of catalytic converters. The Reagan administration and the automakers wanted to exempt trucks from having to install converters. In late 1981, Senator Gary Hart had pushed an amendment through committee requiring that heavy trucks meet the tougher standard and, therefore, install catalytic converters, by 1984. Hart took his action to prevent EPA's Gorsuch from loosening the standards. Even at the 90 percent reduction level he was defending, Hart said, heavy trucks would still contribute a third of the CO produced by all vehicles in 1985.[41] On the House side Representative Henry Waxman had a similar amendment. GM persisted with its shutdown threat. "Since GM knows of no technology available to produce vehicles to meet . . . these standards" all heavy-duty truck production "would cease." The halted production would result in "a permanent job loss" of about 20,000 workers.[42] EPA, under Gorsuch, was also proposing to roll back the HC and CO standards for pickup trucks and vans. A second Gary Hart amendment, adopted in committee by 13-0, was designed to prevent that change from occurring as well.[43] Again, for this issue as others, GM repeated its mantra that "technology was not available" to meet the standards, and therefore, production for the models at issue would cease if the provisions were enacted.[44] GM was also attacking a Waxman provision that would have retained the current law's provision requiring that all cars, including those operating at higher altitudes, meet the federal standard beginning in 1984. GM objected as well to amendments from Hart and Stafford pertaining to diesel cars that would have tightened NOx and partic-

* GM, already a diesel engine producer for heavy trucks, saw diesel for cars as a way to stay in the large-car and pickup truck markets and as a way to gain ground on Ford and Chrysler. Diesels, however, had and still have problems. In March 1979, the Congressional Office of Technology Assessment (OTA) reported that diesels emitted 2-to-4 times more NOx per mile than conventional engines as well as higher levels of particulates. "Additional testing is needed before diesels can be given a clean bill of health," said OTA at that time. "Diesel particulate emissions are of special concern because of their possible carcinogenic properties." It was also learned that diesel particles were very small—the kind that could be inhaled and lodged deep in the lungs, reaching the most sensitive lung tissue. This was especially problematic because the tiny particles themselves were only part of the story. Thousands of chemical pollutants, it turned out—some carcinogenic—could attach to the particles, hitchhiking to wherever the particles traveled. In February 1980, when EPA administrator Doug Costle issued the agency's first particulate emissions standard for diesel-powered cars he noted that diesels emitted 30-to-70 times more particulate that gasoline engines. EPA's small particle rule, however, required that by 1982, passenger cars and light trucks meet a standard of 0.6 GPM. It further scheduled tightening the standard to 0.2 GPM by 1985. Diesels had already been the beneficiary of a provision from the 1977 Clean Air Act amendments, providing four years of waivers from the 1.0 GPM NOx standard. All 1981 and most 1982 diesel models were

ulate standards.* GM concluded that such amendments would cause "production stoppages" in about half of its diesel engine passenger car production for 1983 and 1984 models. Further, said GM, "The effect of these amendments favors Japanese manufacturers because they would permit production of only the smallest cars for one year longer than larger diesel cars"—the cars GM was making.[45] But GM's claims of emissions regulation slowing the auto economy, taking jobs, and favoring the Japanese were overblown to say the least. One Michigan congressman at the time, William Broadhead (D-MI), conceded that regulations on tailpipe exhaust had a minimal impact on the auto industry compared to high interest rates and a sluggish economy. And a Congressional Research Service report concluded that relaxing auto standards could have the effect of encouraging sales of dirtier diesel cars—those sold then by GM and Volkswagen—at the expense of Ford, Chrysler, and American Motors, companies not planning to sell diesels.[46]

By March 1982, GM was lobbying for the Luken-Madigan bill, H.R. 5252, which essentially contained the provisions that would cancel the various amendments that Hart, Stafford, and Waxman were advancing.[47] But enactment of that bill, or any bill for that matter, was not in the cards for 1982. Although the Senate Environment and Public Works Committee reported its bill in August 1982, with the Hart and other amendments included, the bill faced dozens of other amendments on the floor, which is one reason why Senate leaders had no desire to schedule it for floor action. The House versions meanwhile, whether Waxman's or Luken-Madigan, never emerged from committee. Consequently, in the 97th Congress, no final action was taken on the Clean Air Act rewrite.[48]

## KILLING THE SMOG DECREE

The Reagan administration also addressed another important concern of the Big Three: the Justice Department's 1969 settlement decree in the "smog conspiracy" case. Originally, the decree was written to keep the Big Three competitive, and, it was believed, to keep them working toward pollution control technology, but on separate research tracks. The decree imposed stipulations on the exchange of research and technical information among the Big Three, and also prohibited them from filing jointly authored statements to federal agencies regarding emission standards or regulations.

In reviewing the decree at its ten-year mark, the Carter administration recommended

---

allowed to emit up to 1.5 grams of NOx per mile. GM wanted this waiver to extend through 1984, and it was preparing to challenge EPA's plan to enforce a particulate standard—a standard not specified by law like NOx and CO. And on Capitol Hill, GM was backing a 2.0 GPM particulate standard—which would allow ten times the pollution proposed by the EPA standard.

that it should be renewed and extended ten more years. The automakers opposed the extension, citing changed circumstances, which in their view made the prohibitions "inequitable and inconsistent with the public interest." The automakers argued that the high cost of research and development for improved emissions control and fuel efficiency required their "combined efforts." But in March 1979, the US District Court in California, where the smog case originated, renewed the decree for ten more years.[49] Two months later, however, the renewal was challenged and overturned in one court, then upheld on appeal.[50] That's when Ronald Reagan weighed in.

In late May 1981, as his administration moved to demonstrate how it was taking action to address the economic woes of the auto industry, Reagan asked the attorney general to consider vacating the decree altogether.

A few months later, the deed was done. On September 4, 1981, Assistant Attorney General William F. Baxter formally announced removing the decree's restrictions, which had been in effect for twelve years.[51] Although the Center for Auto Safety, California, and others fought furiously to prevent the final unraveling of the smog decree, by August 1982 the matter was finally resolved in favor of the auto industry.[52] Still, during the four-year fight, the decree's proponents repeatedly expressed the view that its restrictions had positively affected competitive research on auto pollution control technology. EPA, Justice, and the State of California argued on behalf of the decree as an effective regulatory and competitive instrument.[53]

"Advances that have been made in auto emission control technology are in many instances, directly attributable to the prohibitions imposed by the expiring provisions, . . ." stated the Justice Department. "Elimination of the provisions from the decree would cut off prematurely relief that has by all accounts been very effective in preserving competition. . . ." CARB provided specific examples where "factual information received from one or more [of the automakers] . . . contradicted the testimony of the others, but which convinced us that [certain] regulations were feasible for the industry as a whole."[54] CARB's 1982 arguments against dissolving the decree noted that joint statements by the automakers would "never represent the position of the industry forerunner. . . ." Rather, it would "inevitably reflect a median or lowest-common-denominator position. . . ." If the manufacturers are permitted to submit only a joint statement, or to coordinate their statements in advance, warned CARB, the information received by regulatory authorities "will be unduly pessimistic," and would likely result in an unnecessarily conservative standards.[55] Congressman Henry Waxman, in his arguments for continuing the decree, noted that the automakers always lobbied Congress for "the same pollution control program" even though his subcommittee had found "that different manufacturers were capable of achieving differing degrees of emission limitation." In order to legislate fairly and regulate effectively, he said, "the ability to obtain information separately from affected interests is indispensable. . . ."[56]

Others, like Clarence Ditlow of CAS, argue to this day that the catalyst technology of the 1970s would not have advanced as quickly as it did, nor would the

> ## Memo for the Attorney General
>
> *As you are aware, the Task Force on the Problems of the Auto Industry has completed its assessment of the crisis that has beset this important sector of our economy. It has recommended a number of policy initiatives in addition to the Economic Recovery Program which would be effective in providing relief to the industry and would be consistent with the economic philosophy of this Administration.*
>
> *One of the most important recommendations of the Task Force is to provide meaningful relief from the Federal regulatory requirements that have been imposed on the industry. Many of these are unnecessarily restrictive. In most areas where regulations are not necessary for safety, or essential to the presentation of a reasonable environmental standard, rule making or legislative initiatives will be taken immediately to roll them back.*
>
> *Consistent with this objective, the Task Force also examined measures to reduce the burden on the industry of complying with necessary Federal regulatory requirements. The consent decree entered in United States v. Automobile Manufacturers Association in 1969 imposes an additional burden on certain motor vehicle manufacturers in their attempts to comply with federal safety and emission requirements. Accordingly, the Department of Transportation and the Environmental Protection Agency have agreed to adopt new policies regarding the waiver of the decree's prohibition on joint statements to the agencies, in an effort to reduce the cost and burden of responding to their regulatory initiatives.*
>
> *In addition, the manufacturers party to the decree have asked you to consider whether it would be appropriate to vacate the consent decree. Although this may not result in relaxation of the constraints imposed upon the industry, the time has come for a fresh look at the parameters of those constraints. In light of the foregoing, I ask you to expedite your consideration of this request, once the pending appeal concerning the decree had been concluded.*
>
> Signed: Ronald Reagan, May 20, 1981.

standards of the Clean Air Act of 1970 have held up as long as they did, without the decree's stipulations being in effect. "The decree kept the Big Three apart," says Ditlow. "They couldn't lobby together, and they didn't know the details of each other's research programs. They conducted their R & D independently of one another because of the decree. . . . So, GM went further than the others, and helped push the catalytic converter along."[57] However, by 1982, with the last remnants of the smog decree lifted, the industry was free to begin joint ventures and "cooperative R & D." By 1984, the National Cooperative Research and Development Act became law, allowing specifically for companies to work together on "pre-competitive" technologies. Additional laws, and other government-sanctioned ventures encouraging industry/government research and new partnerships would follow. A new era of "cooperation" was unfolding.

# 10

## *Missed Opportunities*

... [T]he money wasn't being spent as well as it should have been. We just didn't have the right focus or, to be honest, the right kind of passion for cars and trucks.
*—Robert Lutz, former Chrysler president,*
*describing the company in the 1980s*[1]

Throughout 1982 and 1983, gasoline prices in the United States began a steady decline and consumers began buying bigger cars with larger engines and features such as turbo charging. Large car sales at GM, for example, rose from 55 percent of sales in 1980 to 61 percent in 1983. The move back to large cars pushed GM's profit to a record $2.8 billion in 1983. Ford, Chrysler, and AMC sales improved as well. In 1983 and 1984 Detroit's automakers each turned a profit and Chrysler paid off its $1.5 billion federal debt seven years ahead of schedule. By 1984, Chrysler earned $2.38 billion and in the following year, $1.64 billion.

Suddenly, the Big Three were flush with cash. GM alone ended 1984 with $8.6 billion in cash. Fueled, in part, by Ronald Reagan's tax cuts, Americans bought 14.5 million vehicles in 1984, 15.7 million in 1985, and 16.3 million in 1986—an all-time record. Cash continued to flow into Big Three coffers. Apart from tax cuts, the federal government had helped Detroit in more direct ways, too: bailing out Chrysler, imposing import restraints on the Japanese, and relaxing environmental and safety regulations. All of these benefits and special allowances were made in the shadow of worsening economic times to protect American jobs and give American automakers time to retool. But what did the automakers do with these special protections and benefits given them by the American people? How did they improve their businesses and products? What did they give back to society? Would the Big Three emerge in the 1990s better positioned as a result? Would the environment benefit? How about workers? And most of all, how did the Big Three put their new found profits to work?

### GM's SPENDING SPREE

Under Roger Smith in the 1980s, GM embarked on an ambitious program of expansion, capital spending, and restructuring. It initiated a corporate reorganization in

North America; began a string of acquisitions outside the auto business; embarked on a factory modernization and retooling campaign; and started a new car venture called Saturn. First announced in 1983, Saturn was to be America's small car answer to the Japanese, but it wouldn't hit the pavement until 1990. In the meantime, Roger Smith began buying up other companies. In June 1984, Smith spent $2.55 billion to acquire Electronic Data Systems Corporation (EDS) of Dallas, Texas, one of the world's leading data processing companies, owned by Ross Perot. But EDS was just the beginning. In 1985, working under the project code name "Star Trek," GM went after the Hughes Aircraft Company, bidding against both Boeing and Ford for the prize. In the end, through a complicated cash and stock transaction,* GM acquired Hughes for an estimated $5 billion in June 1985.

Smith saw Hughes making GM a "computer integrated industrial enterprise." He had pitched the deal to his board envisioning that Hughes' advanced technologies would bring new advantage to automotive manufacturing and the automobile itself. "The automobile is in the process of making a rapid transition from a mechanical product which incorporates a few electrical subsystems, to one with electro-mechanical and electronic elements within the next decade," he told them. Smith also envisioned GM making cars equipped with electronic gadgets that would allow drivers to see through fog and avoid collisions.[2] GM even initiated a secret program called the Trilby Project, aimed at using defense-era "systems engineering" approaches in designing and manufacturing automobiles. But it was the electronic advantage Smith was seeking to regain GM's position relative to the Japanese, "I am a firm believer that the major gains in the automotive industry are going to come in electronics," Smith said in early June 1985. "The automobile, in some respects, is still in its infancy. . . . The big thing left is electronics. It's the next frontier."[3] In the end, however, Hughes brought very little of this to GM's automotive business. And the Trilby Project eventually died as well.

"I think there was a misconception on the technology," explained GM's Donald Atwood. "People in general wondered . . . 'When am I going to find a Hughes gadget in the car?' And the answer is *never*. Hughes doesn't make gadgets for cars. Hughes does basic technology work which they apply to their products, and it's the basic technology which we want to apply to the automobile—basic technology being the underlying technology in instrumentation. They make instruments for aircraft cockpits, but it's the *technology* that gets transferred, not the cockpit instrumentation. . . ." Wall Street auto analyst Maryann Keller concluded, "In many respects, Hughes was just another example of the acquisition-happy mood around GM at the time. The company had money to spend, and ambitious executives on the finance staff real-

---

* In the last few days of the bidding for Hughes, and due in part to difficulty interpreting GM's offer, Ford Motor was sure it had won the prize. Ford had even prepared a press release describing the deal and had also dispatched press agents and company officials to Los Angeles to announce the acquisition.

ized they could make a name for themselves by initiating high-visibility deals comparable to the Toyota joint venture or the EDS acquisition. . . ."[4]

## ROBOTS RUN AMOK

GM also poured money into factory modernization—and in particular three megafactories with completely automated lines run by industrial robots.* Between 1980 and 1985, GM spent $42 *billion* on new factories, tools, equipment, and products. Roger Smith was infatuated with high technology and believed it would give GM a competitive edge, even if common sense suggested otherwise. "When [Roger Smith's] staff proposed a factory in Saginaw, Michigan that would build axles entirely with robots—no people on the shop floor at all—Smith approved the plan even though the axles would cost more than those assembled by UAW hands in an older plant."[5] In 1985, when GM's "industrial showcase" factory in Hamtramck, Michigan came on line—complete with the latest robots—costly mistakes became legion, increasing downtime and raising maintenance costs.

". . . As Hamtramck's assembly line tried to gain speed," observed the *Wall Street Journal's* Paul Ingrassia and Joseph B. White, "the computer-guided dolly wandered off course. The spray-painting robots began spray-painting each other instead of the cars, causing GM to truck the cars across town to a fifty-seven-year-old Cadillac plant for repainting. . . ." Other computer-controlled welding machines would occasionally smash a car body, or just stop dead in their tracks. When that happened, "the entire Hamtramck line would stop," explained Ingrassia and White. "Workers could do nothing but stand around and wait while managers called in the robot contractor's technicians." Adding to these robot and assembly line woes was the design of GM's cars—"over-loaded with electronic gadgets and hard to build." The front and rear bumpers of Cadillac Sevilles had more than 460 parts and took thirty-three minutes of labor to put together. Although Hamtramck was supposed to be a state-of-the art plant, a model of productivity, it was still miles behind the Japanese. In 1985, the year the plant started production, GM's spending on maintenance and repairs jumped 18 percent to $5.4 billion from the $4.6 billion the year before.[6]

"Infatuated with technology and given a nearly bottomless checking account, Smith spent the company dry and got almost nothing to show for it, . . ." says *Fortune's* Alex Taylor about GM in the 1980s. "He promoted a culture in which no one acknowledged problems publicly and bookkeepers improved results by manipulating the numbers. . . ."[7]

---

* In fact, GM acquired five small companies that were developing vision systems to enable robots to "see" what they were working on by recognizing specific shapes and parts. These were View Engineering Inc.; Automatix Inc.; Robotic Vision Systems Inc.; Difracto Ltd.; and Applied Intelligent Systems, Inc.

## CHRYSLER GOES SHOPPING

Chrysler, like GM, also used its 1980s profits to expand its empire. In the summer of 1985, Chrysler teamed up with Allied-Signal and made a joint bid of $3 billion for Hughes, which like Ford, lost out to GM. Undeterred, in June 1985, Chrysler spent $637 million to buy Gulfstream Aerospace Corp., a maker of executive business jets. Lee Iacocca said acquiring Gulfstream was a way to move into "high tech industries like aerospace and electronics," but Gulfstream wasn't in the same league as Hughes. In any case, Iacocca was looking beyond the auto business. He reorganized Chrysler into a more conglomeratelike structure, forming a holding company with three divisions—Chrysler Motors, Chrysler Financial, and Chrysler Technologies. He wanted to emphasize diversification and move away from autos. Chrysler soon shelled out $400 million to buy FinanceAmerica, a consumer-lending subsidiary of Bank of America, which was added to Chrysler Financial, the company's consumer and auto-dealer financing arm. Chrysler Financial's assets doubled in the mid-1980s, from $7.2 billion to $14.4 billion, becoming a financial services supermarket.

Meanwhile, within Chrysler, Hal Sperlich, Iacocca's friend and engineer who had come with Iacocca from Ford to Chrysler, was finding it more and more difficult to get the money he needed for auto development funds. Sperlich was chief of operations and he wasn't getting the money he needed to improve cars. Iacocca would say the cars only needed some new "skin" or a new dashboard, and that was all.[8] When oil prices collapsed in 1986, it was more good news for Detroit. Sales continued to do well, and more cash rolled in. In 1986-87, Chrysler bought Lamborghini, one of Italy's premier sports car manufacturers, and paid $367 million for Electrospace Systems, a Dallas defense contractor. Iacocca also gathered up four rental car companies—Dollar, General, Snappy, and Thrifty—which insured a captive market for some of Chrysler's auto production, while keeping those companies away from the other automakers.[9]

In March 1987, Chrysler set its sights on American Motors, first buying up Renault's ownership stake in AMC, and a few months later, laying out $1.1 billion in cash and Chrysler stock for the rest of AMC. With AMC under its belt, Chrysler had suddenly become a 20 percent larger car company. Iacocca, however, was still thinking big. At one point he wanted to relocate company headquarters from Michigan's Highland Park to Manhattan, "where he liked to hang out in the corporate suite at the Waldorf Towers and socialize with the likes of New York Yankees owner George Steinbrenner." According to one Chrysler executive, "a corporate identity consultant even devised a name for the new conglomerate: ChryCo." In 1987, in fact, Chrysler thought about making a run for E.F. Hutton, but in March of that year, Chrysler's executive committee voted it down.[10] Iacocca also flirted with the idea of trying to take over GM in 1987, but is said to have concluded that "it would be easier to buy Greece."[11]

## HIGH-FLYING FORD

Ford Motor Company, which had slowly but successfully integrated some of the efficiency principles of management guru W. E. Deming into its operations, began a significant turnaround about the time its new Taurus and Sable models came out in 1985 and 1986. Huge amounts of cash began rolling in. In 1986, for the first time since the Model-T, Ford's profits exceeded GM's, hitting $3.3 billion. In 1987, it posted an even better year at $4.6 billion, an automaker record. Soon, the company began spending.

During 1985-89, Ford spent $4.2 billion buying back its own stock. Million-dollar bonuses were paid to forty-four executives, and shareholders were rewarded handsomely with new dividends and a stock split. Ford also began buying up other companies, focusing on financial services. Ford acquired a California savings-and-loan, a Philadelphia consumer-lending concern, and another big consumer lender in Dallas. It also bought some auto businesses: Aston Martin and AC in 1987. Before the dust settled, Ford would spend some $6 billion on acquisitions. But Ford was still nursing its loss to GM in the 1985 bidding over Hughes and wanted an aerospace company of its own. In 1988 Ford posted profits of $5.3 billion, and by year's end had $10 billion in accumulated cash on hand—enough for then-CEO Donald Peterson to think about even a bigger Ford empire.

In March 1989, Peterson proposed to his board that Ford launch a $3.5 billion bid for Lockheed Corporation, the LA-based aerospace and defense giant. The board, however, nixed Peterson's proposal. Peterson and the board did agree to go after Jaguar, the British luxury car maker, which after a brief competition with GM, Ford acquired in October 1989 for $2.5 billion, a stunning amount. At the time, in fact, Jaguar had tangible assets only valued at about a quarter of the bidding price and had posted a loss of nearly $2 million in the first half of the year.[12]

## WASTED RESOURCES

One by one, each of the Big Three soon began to discover that throwing money around would not solve their underlying problems. "[A]s Ford focused on diversifying, it started to coast in the car business. . . ," observed reporters Ingrassia and White, ". . . the quality and reliability of Ford cars, which had improved steadily throughout the 1980s, suddenly plateaued in 1988 and 1989. . . ."[13] Ford "had skimped on new product programs as well as on plant and equipment in the eighties," says *Financial World's* Robert Wrubel, "and instead bought Britain's Jaguar and the Associates," a finance and insurance company. Ford missed an opportunity to push ahead in designing more efficient engine technologies for its passenger cars. In the mid-1980s—a time Ford faced the prospect of paying millions in fines for missing federal fuel economy standards—Ford management decided to push more heavily into trucks and SUVs rather than spend more money on upgrading its car engines. Toyota and Honda were then manufacturing multivalve engines, but Ford had none close to production.

"[W]hat we've got to do is move our spending to trucks," explained Ford's chief technical executive Louis Ross at an August 1986 meeting with the top brass, including CEO Don Peterson and president Red Poling. "We want to spend 70 percent more on truck programs [i.e., pickups, minivans, sport utilities] in the next five years than we have in the last five...." Ross pointed out that there was a 25 percent import tax on two-door trucks, "which holds back the Japanese." So, he concluded, "why the hell don't we, as a company, redirect our resources substantially to our trucks?"[14] And Ford did exactly that. Ford's committees approved the truck push, but also decided to increase spending on engines and transmissions over the next five years, but at a lesser rate than its truck/sport utility push. Ford pickups were America's No. 1 selling vehicle in the 1980s, and today Ford trucks hold more than 30 percent of the market. Ford minivans became hot sellers as well.

## HONDA'S CONNECTING RODS

Some Big Three factories, particularly at GM, were facing basic production and engineering problems that had cost them market share in the past—problems that were still not fixed in the mid-1980s, despite new factory robots and company overhauls. In fact, some observers, like Paul Ingrassia and Joseph P. White, would write that by then, "GM was producing some of America's worst cars."[15] The key issue was not, as Roger Smith had maintained, building futuristic, robot-filled factories-of-the-future. Rather, it was basic automotive engineering, and in 1986 the Japanese were winning that battle simply by doing the little things right.

To illustrate this point to GM engineers, Alex Mair, a company VP at GM's Technical Center, took two connecting rods—one from a 1.8 liter GM engine that was used in the Chevrolet Cavalier, and the other from a similar Honda engine. Mair's point would be to show how a small engine part could make a big difference. The connecting rods Mair held up for inspection did not appear all that different. The Honda rod was a bit smoother, lighter, and cleaner looking than GM's. But the GM connecting rod had something else: little weight pads at the bottom and on the top. Honda's did not have the weight pads. Not only did GM have a cumbersome manufacturing system for producing and refining the connecting rods as compared to Honda's, the rods themselves actually made a big difference in the engines and the cars that grew up around them in the manufacturing process.

Connecting rods are key players in the internal combustion engine, connecting the pistons inside the engine's cylinders to the crankshaft below that delivers the engine's power to the driveshaft, which distributes the power to the axles and wheels. But inside GM's Cavalier engines, because of the added weights on the connecting rods, the pistons would have to be higher than the corresponding Honda pistons—

by about a quarter inch. That might not seem like a lot, but here's the rub: because GM's piston was higher, the engine block and the engine had to be that much higher as well, and so did the hood. All of that meant extra material, extra weight, and extra height. This was the "domino effect" of the weight pads, explained Mair, and it was at work on the entire vehicle—and most importantly, on the *performance* of the car as well. GM's Cavalier was heavier, less responsive, slower accelerating, and less efficient than the Honda.

"When customers complained, as they often did, that the Chevy Cavalier couldn't seem to get out of its own way," wrote Ingrassia and White, "[the connecting rod] was at the root of the problem. Everything about the Cavalier was heavier and clumsier—the flywheel, the clutch, the action of the gearshift lever, the tires, etc. Quality suffered, too. The Cavalier's clunky clutches generated three to four times the number of complaints as Honda's lighter, smoother, mechanisms." Meanwhile, Mair estimated that GM added about $145 per car to its costs because of decisions traceable to the way it manufactured and accommodated its connecting rods. Spread over GM's 4.7 million cars at the time, the extra cost amounted to a hefty $681 million, money that obviously could have been used to better effect.

GM wasn't alone. With the $4 billion that Chrysler had on hand in 1984-85, there might have been some investment in new auto plants, for example—or perhaps even a new-car platform or two that might have tried to advance the ball on emissions control or fuel economy. But by this time, Lee Iacocca had become a national figure, publishing the best-selling autobiographical book *Iacocca* and appearing on the covers of *Time* and *Business Week*. Iacocca had grander ideas than just being a car company executive. Although he had an option to buy an Western Electric factory in Indianapolis and convert it to an assembly line, he allowed the option on that facility to lapse in March 1985. Three months later he spent more than $600 million for Gulfstream Aerospace.[16] But as Chrysler and Lee Iacocca would later learn, they couldn't compete in the defense industry, and sold Gulfstream five years after they bought it. Chrysler's car business, meanwhile, began to falter. "Every model introduced after the K-car line that started in 1980 flopped...." wrote *Fortune's* Alex Taylor of Chrysler's troubles. One executive explained, "Where we got betrayed, where we blew it was on execution."[17] Even Iacocca would later admit of his own grandiose conglomerate dreams for Chrysler. "We wasted a lot of time, a lot of effort, setting up a holding company. I was never a conglomerate type of thinker anyway...."[18]

"...[T]he money wasn't being spent as well as it should have been," says former Chrysler president and vice chairman Bob Lutz. "We just didn't have the right focus or, to be honest, the right kind of passion for cars and trucks." Chrysler, in fact, was essentially duping consumers with its K-cars, built on an older platform used for larger cars when gasoline prices fell. Using the K-car platform, Chrysler made handsome profits on luxury versions that were little different from economy models. Rather than redesigning, Chrysler simply installed various body types onto the same platform. The practice continued into the early 1990s. "[U]nder the sheet metal," explains Lutz, "the basic underpinnings and mechanicals of the 1991 Chrysler Imperial priced at $27,000, were virtually identical to that of the 1991 Plymouth Acclaim, priced at $13,000—and with the exception of a slightly more powerful engine, neither one of them was a whole lot different from the $7,000 Dodge Aries of just a couple of years earlier." Lutz acknowledges that "consumers quickly saw through our attempts to puff up higher profit margins by simply stretching and gussying up the original K-car platform."[19]

## DID RESTRAINTS BUY TIME?

In the mid-1980s, the Japanese were still holding their own in the US auto market, despite limitations on the number of cars they were allowed to import. In the early 1980s, Congress and Ronald Reagan attacked the Japanese on free trade and threatened a trade war. Japan's Ministry of International Trade and Industry (MITI) got the message, and in 1981 signed the Voluntary Restraint Agreement, which went into effect in 1982, limiting the number of cars they would export to America.

US automakers, of course, were not on the sidelines in all of this. "In the early 1980s, Lee A. Iacocca . . . led the political lobbying for barriers against Japanese vehicle imports," writes Peter Passell in the *New York Times*. "The 'voluntary restraints' that were negotiated protected the Big Three's core market even as the domestic steel, electronics, machine tool and earth-moving-equipment industries were mercilessly battered by Japan's high-quality goods and the strong dollar. American consumers, meanwhile, paid extra for the Japanese cars they so dearly wanted—or could not get the models they wanted at all. . . ."[20]

"The import quotas were critical," observed Maryann Keller in February 1984 as GM reported record $1.3 billion profits for the previous quarter. "Without the quotas, there would not be any record earnings, because the Japanese would be pursuing their usual volume-based strategy and holding down prices. Without the quotas GM's revenue per unit would have been significantly lower."[21]

Under the Voluntary Restraint Agreement, Japanese car sales were kept at the 1979 level. The limitations worked out to 1.68 million vehicles in 1982, 1.81 million in 1983, and 1.85 million in 1984. As the agreement expired, with the Reagan administration not renewing it, MITI established its own program, dubbed Voluntary Export Restraints, which operated somewhat more loosely between 1985 and 1994 when all restraints were lifted.[22]

Both Lee Iacocca and Ford's Donald Peterson criticized the Reagan administration for not renewing the Japanese restraint agreement in 1985. Iacocca later canceled plans to build a new auto assembly plant and increased Chrysler's share of Mitsubishi Colt imports from 87,500 annually to 287,5000. GM, noting that "the time has come to return to free trade," welcomed the lifting of restraints. Raising Japanese export quotas allowed GM to import 300,000 Isuzus and Suzukis annually into the US to be sold as Chevrolet Sprints and Chevrolet Spectrums.[23] Iron-ically though, the import restraints that Ford and Chrysler clamored for only made the Japanese stronger.

All along, the restrictions were rationalized by free-market Reaganites as a tem-porary measure to give Detroit time to get into competitive form. But in the final analysis, the Japanese used the time more effectively than did the Big Three. First, the Japanese began producing more cars in America. Honda was the first in 1982 with its plant at Marysville, Ohio. But others soon followed. By 1985, Nissan was turning out 150,000 Sentras and pickup trucks a year at its plant in Tennessee. Toy-ota began building its first plant in Kentucky in 1986. "Toyota's plant in George-town, Kentucky is a monument to automotive protectionists," said one American who worked closely with Toyota in the early 1990s. "Toyota would not have made anything like that $1 billion plus investment without the [trade quota] agreements."[24] By 1990, the Japanese were building 1.2 million cars and trucks in the United States. They were also importing light trucks not covered by import restrictions.

The second move the Japanese made in response to import restrictions was to go after the luxury car buyer. Since the Japanese importers were laboring under restric-tions, they decided to go for higher profits from each unit sold by targeting the lux-ury car market, traditionally an American bastion dominated by GM. Luxury cars can earn gross profits of up to $11,000 per sale. In 1985, Honda came into the market with its Acura. By 1992, the Japanese had established three other luxury divisions, all in the United States. Mazda would follow later with its Amati division. By 1992, the Japanese were selling $3.5 billion worth of Acuras, Lexuses, and Infinitis every year.[25]

"Clearly, Detroit would have been much better off had it confronted the Japa-nese directly in 1981 rather than hidden behind import restraints," observes *Fortune's* Alex Taylor. "It would have been faster to adopt Japanese production methods and to rationalize its own factories. Instead Detroit effectively conceded a permanent share of the US market to the Japanese, who reinvested in more American plants."[26]

Micheline Maynard, *USA Today's* Detroit bureau chief, also observes that GM executives during that period "weren't convinced the problems were real." They thought with time their sales would recover. "Long into the 1980s, the prevailing mindset within GM was that the young buyers might try imports while they were single, but when they began raising families, they would want the big cars GM sold," says Maynard. The company didn't need to change, went the logic, as buyers would come to it. "GM thought it could rely on its huge stable of customers to come back for new GM cars and sustain the automaker's market share. But even the most loyal GM buyers had run out of patience. They began to desert the company in droves midway through the decade, buying aerodynamic Ford Tauruses, reliable Honda Accords, and appealing Toyota Camrys." Though GM's market share was clearly shrinking, notes Maynard, "the loss of customers did not spark a crisis within the huge company."[27] However, one major project that GM did initiate to take on the Japanese was the Saturn car company.

## SATURN SQUANDERED

GM's much ballyhooed Saturn—the visionary "little red car" of the future that Roger Smith said would beat the Japanese—could have been a revolutionary automobile for GM and the US auto industry. Had the company's leaders had used their resources more wisely, things might have turned out differently. However, when Saturn finally came to market in 1990, it missed "visionary" by a long shot and barely scraped past mundane.

Conceived in June 1982, nearly ten years after the first energy crisis and only a year after the second energy crisis, Saturn was the code name given to GM's small-car program aimed at taking back market share from the Japanese. The name Saturn was adopted from the US rocket program that leapfrogged the Soviets in the space race. "The name signified [GM's] intention to launch a futuristic plan in the automotive industry that would be comparable to the space program," says Maryann Keller.

Keller recounts a November 1983 news conference in which Roger Smith envisioned the new project. "Saturn, he told the media, was not just the design of a new product, but also the creation of a new manufacturing, engineering, and assembly system to produce it. It was, Smith said, a project of 'cosmic proportions.' The end product would be the car of the future. . . . And to build it, GM would design the factory of the future. The more Smith spoke, the more magnificent his vision appeared. The press was dazzled and they rushed to tell the world about this wonderful new idea. . . . It represented Roger Smith's dream come true for the corporation, the first entirely new nameplate for GM since the days of Billy Durant. . . ."

When Saturn was first launched, GM announced it was prepared to spend $5 billion on the project, a huge sum in an industry that normally spends about $1 billion to develop a new model. But Saturn was to be different—in more ways than one. First, GM assembled a "team of 99" from its managers and workers to think through the whole process. Labor and management were to function as a team, emulating the Japanese; workers and managers were hand picked from throughout GM, given the promise of lifetime employment. Saturn was "the key to GM's long-term competitiveness, survival and success," said Smith in July 1985. Then GM launched, in effect, a national bidding contest among the states for the first Saturn assembly plant (Maryann Keller called this ploy "a nationwide *The Price is Right*" contest. At one point Smith appeared on the Phil Donahue show with seven governors all competing with promises to convince GM to pick their state). Along the way, GM had been offered all manner of inducements, from tax abatements and utility rate reductions, to free land and new highways. The suspense ended when GM's board approved $1.9 billion in December 1987 for a site in Spring Hill, Tennessee.

Then, in another contestlike gambit, GM announced it would award 100 franchised Saturn dealerships nationally, and even hired architects and designers to assure the new facilities would be, among other things, "consumer friendly." Advertising was the next big prize. Estimated billings for the Saturn account were expected to exceed $100 million a year and that touched off another frenzy on Madison Avenue.

All the while, Saturn and GM were in the news. John Russo, Youngstown State University director of labor studies, watched all the Saturn huckstering and state bidding. "Overall, Saturn's influence on the public consciousness is indicative of how easily global corporations can shape the national economic debate, using sophisticated public relations . . . with a measure of old fashioned economic blackmail."

In the end, Saturn's eight-year sojourn was more about process than it was a revolutionary new car. Originally in 1983, Smith had called for a 60-mile-per-gallon automobile that wouldn't cost consumers an arm and leg, priced at $6,000. But in the end, Saturn's cost nearly doubled, and its MPG rating came in at 25 city-35 highway. While there were some advances in labor-management relations and commendable manufacturing innovations, the central product—the car—missed its intended mark. "The Saturn has become a cult car," observed Maryann Keller in December 1993. "But from a manufacturing standpoint, it hasn't even come close to its original goal, which was to produce a small car at a cost competitive to, or better than, the Japanese."

Given the huge and extensive commitment of corporate time and energy GM put into this project—the money, advertising ballyhoo, professional resources, new tooling, technological rethinking, etc.—the company might have received more return on its investment had it really set its sights on building a quality, fuel-efficient, environmentally clean automobile for the future. Rather, as Saturn was being conceived and rolled toward production in the 1980s, Roger Smith and GM were doing their best to dismantle pollution control laws in Washington and elsewhere.

While there is no question that Saturn has carved out a place for itself in the annals of automotive history, it is not a significant departure in making quality automobiles that are cleaner, fuel efficient, and economic in operation. Yet, had GM really embarked on an all-out crusade to build clean, energy-efficient, quality cars—pushing the boundaries of available technologies as it went—it might have succeeded in "leapfrogging" the Japanese rather than following them, setting a higher standard of performance in the global car race.

## Money Well Spent?

The biggest questions of the buying and spending binge that consumed the Big Three during the 1980s are what did it buy? Did it make any of the Big Three a fundamentally better car company? Did any of the investments really advance the ball for environmentally improved automobiles—vehicles that incorporated the best "clean car" technologies possible; cars and trucks that were truly fuel efficient? In short, was there any attempt on the part of the Big Three during these years to infuse into the notion of "quality product" broader social values, such as environmental protection or minimizing resource use? Were such considerations ever elevated to marketing targets or goals? Were they ever made a part of strategic planning?

Clearly, energy, environmental, and safety issues were all established social concerns by the 1980s—all very much worthy of corporate attention. Yet huge amounts of money passed through the fingers of Big Three executives and their boards of directors on diversions and projects of little-to-no lasting business value. At the time, however, there doesn't appear to have been any farsighted leaders in the industry to push environmental and energy issues forward as part of a new kind of strategic thinking; no one to advocate the value of advancing and incorporating these considerations as goals in the making and selling of cars—not to mention, as factors that might have enhanced competitive advantage.

Given the large amounts of money squandered by the Big Three in the 1980s, any one of them might have at least tried an earnest, multiyear "skunk works" for an environmentally superior car or a super-efficient automobile.* Arguably, taking this gamble would have had as much societal payoff as any one of the other ventures the Big Three bankrolled in the eighties. The Big Three might have focused on efficiency and environmental values as part of a "total quality" package. Certainly the multimillion dollars spent advertising other products could have been used to feature and sell clean, efficient cars as desirable social and economic products worthy of the consumer's attention.

While there were quality improvements in some car lines, on the whole, a decade was squandered, money was misspent, and opportunities to set the course for a new kind of car was lost. Instead, each of the Big Three was distracted by empire building, whiz-bang technology, and/or cleaning up past mistakes. They were all too distracted to have any real vision, to see how taking the lead on environmental and safety issues might have redefined quality in a new way, providing new economic advantage in the process.

## On the Hill

In Washington, too, the automakers missed opportunities to be more creative about their legislative and regulatory strategies. In many ways, they were still fighting the battles of the 1970s, making their anthem and plea to Congress something like this: "Environmental, safety, and fuel economy regulations are still holding us back, and here's what you can do to help us." But this strategy, too, would prove costly and counterproductive, but it might have been turned to opportunity had industry leaders been more perceptive.

In June 1983, after failing in the previous year to alter the basic health standard of the Clean Air Act, the MVMA adopted four "priority revisions" for the Clean Air Act: weakening the carbon monoxide standard from 3.4 GPM to 7.0 GPM for pas-

---

* GM, however, would begin work with electric vehicle subcontractors in 1988 and start an in-house EV program in 1990. However, this undertaking would prove to have its own shortcomings, be turned on and off by management, and was not on the same scale as Saturn, though launched seven years after it.

senger vehicles; weakening the NOx standard for light-duty diesel-powered passenger and other vehicles from 1.0 GPM to 1.5 GPM; removing the mandatory 90 percent HC and CO reduction requirement for heavy trucks (which meant not installing catalytic converters); and, modifying the high-altitude provisions of the Clean Air Act, creating a separate standard for cars sold in areas above 4,000 feet in altitude (as opposed to one national standard).[28] Also, earlier that year, General Motors had outlined much the same list in a lobby paper entitled "Modifying The Clean Air Act—The GM Position,"[29] which targeted three provisions in a pending Senate bill it wanted deleted.* In a February 1983 letter, GM lobbied local air pollution officials seeking their help on five provisions it wanted changed in the Clean Air Act, as well as certain provisions targeted in Senator Robert Stafford's committee bill.[30]

EPA meanwhile, at the prodding of Vice President George Bush's Task Force on Regulatory Relief—which was still working with the GM-derived hit list that became the basis for the administration's "auto-package"—went about issuing some delays for the auto industry in 1983, among them: a two-year delay of diesel particulate standards for cars and light trucks; a delay of the 1984 HC and CO standard for heavy trucks; and a delay of the NOx emission limits for post-1984 model year engines.[31] But the political climate was changing, and both the administration and the auto industry had misread, or thought they could ignore, public opinion.

The Reagan administration's environmental team—such as it was—began to self-destruct in 1983. In March, Rita Lavelle, head of EPA's superfund program for cleaning up toxic waste, was fired by Reagan after investigations into mismanagement and conflict of interest. Lavelle would later be convicted of perjury. Also in March, EPA administrator Anne Gorsuch, found in contempt of Congress, was forced to resign. In October, Interior Secretary James Watt was also forced to resign under a cloud of controversy after his insensitive remarks about minorities in his department. In trying to repair the damage, the White House turned to former EPA administrator William Ruckelshaus (then nicknamed "Mr. Clean") to help revive a demoralized agency and Judge William Clark to take over at Interior. Ruckelshaus served for nearly two years and managed to get EPA on its feet again, initiating several enforcement programs. In early 1985, upon his departure, Ruckelshaus observed that "industry thought it had the upper hand," in the early years of the Reagan administration on environmental matters. However, he added, industry's effort to roll back environmental regulation was "stopped in its tracks."[32] Perhaps that was true at EPA for the moment, but industry was not about to roll over on Capitol Hill or elsewhere in Washington. It was time for a new strategy.

---

* The bill, pending in the Senate Environment and Public Works Committee, included a provision tightening the heavy-duty truck standards for NOx; a provision establishing a statutory standard for light-duty trucks (i.e. pickups, vans, etc.); and a statutory standard for particulates.

## ENVIRONMENT AS SOCIAL POLICY

What had become clear to pollsters, if not to the auto industry and the Reagan administration, was that an important political divide existed on matters of regulation. Some regulations were seen as dealing more purely with the economy, while others, like environmental and public safety regulations, were viewed in a broader societal context. While deregulation in telecommunications and transportation may have been publicly supported for economic reasons, dismantling environmental laws was opposed by the public because of the key role these laws played in protecting the general welfare—as Lou Harris had found in his 1981 polling.

As Reagan administration officials like Watt, Gorsuch, and LaVelle vigorously attacked environmental laws in the early 1980s against a continuing backdrop of environmental contamination and toxic dangers—Love Canal, Times Beach, Bhopal—public concern about the environment only grew stronger. It was no time for trashing the nation's environmental laws. The public wasn't buying the Reaganite rhetoric. Even the auto industry was beginning to get the picture. "Nobody in industry sincerely believes the EPA's agenda is going to include the more important deregulatory moves we've been pushing for the last four years," said one auto industry lobbyist in early 1985. "The real question is how much effort the environmentalists will make to push the laws further in the opposite direction."[33]

Environmental groups were certainly fighting to protect and implement existing laws and regulation. But what was beginning to become clear in the mid-1980s—as had been true in the early 1980s with Clean Air Act gridlock in Congress—was that neither side would make much progress during the remaining Reagan years. Legislative stalemate would remain a fact of life on Capitol Hill, particularly as the Clean Air Act became embroiled in the acid rain issue.


## WHERE'S THE VISION?

Back in Detroit, meanwhile, auto executives were quietly cleaning up after their economic misadventures, some about to face major showdowns with their boards of directors who were beginning to realize the Big Three really hadn't made a whole lot of progress in the 1980s—a criticism that would soon be heard elsewhere. "The American auto industry is clearly a dinosaur on the way out," Representative Claudine Schneider (R-RI) would say a few years later, near the end of the decade. "The Congress is getting tired of industries that fail to learn when the handwriting is already on the wall. The industry has had enormous profits since the early '80s. But where our competitors have invested those profits, our industry has been sitting on them. We have very little sympathy for their failure to have any vision."[34]

# II

# Bad Air, 1987

Seventeen years after the passage of the Clean Air Act there are still 80 million people living in areas with unhealthy air.

—*David Doniger, NRDC, April 1987*[1]

In 1987, when the US Environmental Protection Agency (EPA) reported on the state of the nation's air, the numbers were not good. About seventy-five cities were not making the grade for meeting smog standards, measured by ground-level ozone. Los Angeles had 129 days in violation, Houston had 21, New York and San Diego each with 34, and St. Louis with 12, among those listed. On some summer days in Boston, the ozone level went 50 percent above the standard, as it would in New York's Connecticut suburbs.[2]

More than fifty cities were not making the grade for carbon monoxide. Denver was among the leaders in this category. In November of 1986, Denver experienced the year's highest single reading of carbon monoxide, reaching a stunning 25.9 parts per million (PPM), nearly three times the federal standard, then set at 9.0 PPM. Los Angeles had the next worst single day at 18.1 PPM followed in order by Las Vegas, Phoenix, Fresno, New York, Fairbanks, Provo, Sacramento, and Raleigh-Durham. In fact, eight of the ten cities with the worst carbon monoxide levels were in the West.

"Air quality is fast becoming the most important single issue confronting the West," said Senator William L. Armstrong (R) of Colorado in November 1987. "Not only is it a serious health hazard, it is a major factor in business and industry plant-location decisions."[3]

"I think Western cities are finally discovering that people don't want to bring their conventions to polluted cities, that businesses don't want to move to polluted cities and that even residents themselves don't like to live and raise their children in the middle of a brown cloud," said Steven Howards, executive director of the Denver Metropolitan Air Quality Council.[4] Even in Nevada, people were voting to require tougher emissions testing. "The people in Nevada are fiercely independent," said

Terry Callison, supervisor of the emission control office for the state DMV. "But all of a sudden, people woke up and decided to do something."[5]

## THE BROWN CLOUD

Denver once drew people from all over the world who were suffering from various respiratory ailments. Sanatoria to treat patients with tuberculosis were once found scattered throughout the city. Over the years, however, the sanatoria disappeared, though Denver became something of a research center for pulmonary disorders. By the 1960s, "the brown cloud" became synonymous with Denver, a high-altitude variety of urban smog that was particularly noticeable in the winter months. In high altitudes, car engines have less oxygen and burn gasoline less efficiently than at lower altitudes, spewing out more pollutants. In Denver, combined with stagnant air, the brown cloud built to epic proportions. Especially problematic was carbon monoxide. In 1975, Denver violated the federal clean air standard for carbon monoxide 177 times.

By the winter season of 1984-85, Denver had made improvements, but still exceeded the federal standard for carbon monoxide on 45 days. In the 1985-86 season it was 36 days. Still, there was little room for complacency. In November 1987, at the start of Denver's annual pollution season, the Denver Better Air Campaign kicked off its fourth annual drive to encourage people to leave their cars at home one day a week and either carpool or take a bus. The Better Air Campaign had a goal of reducing Denver's CO pollution by 10 percent. Downtown at the kickoff, children were costumed with antipollution slogans parading in the streets while adult volunteers waved placards promoting clean air. Governor Roy R. Romer rode the bus that day. "For the first time," said Anne Grady, coordinator of the Denver Better Air Campaign, "we have the business and political leadership we need to draw serious attention to this very serious problem." A few weeks later though, in late November 1987, Denver had another one of its ugly bad air days. The brown cloud was all too apparent.[6] In 1988, Denver began using oxygenated gasoline in the winter months to help cars burn their fuel more completely, but the city still had a ways to go before the air would improve.

## PHOENIX TOO

In October 1987, Phoenix, Arizona, began a voluntary "no-drive" program aimed at getting commuters out of their cars. Up to one-third of the city's smog problem was then owed to motor vehicles. "Part of the problem is that Arizona has the one-man, one car syndrome," said Kevin DeMenna, a public affairs officer with the Phoenix Chamber of Commerce. But now that had to change. "Five years ago," said Patricia Fullinwider, coordinator of the Phoenix Better Air Campaign, "it seemed like only the experts were talking about the problem. Now people seem more aware that we've got a pollution problem and that we need to do something."[7]

Phoenix had also begun talking about a light rail system and its metropolitan area government was recommending that the state require the use of fuels with added oxygen during the winter months to help gasoline burn more cleanly. "What we're saying is we are not going to wait until this is another Los Angeles," said Patricia Fullinwider. "We're going to do something now."

Phoenix, like Denver, once attracted people for its clean, dry air. In 1952, Bernie Bernstein left Chicago and settled in Phoenix at the recommendation of his doctor. He was thirty-five years old. In Chicago, Bernstein had sinus problems, and his doctor advised him that the dry, clean air in the southwest would help relieve his condition. But over the years, Phoenix gradually succumbed to "the brown cloud," too, pollution that began to hang over the landscape so thick it was visible for miles. By 1989 Bernie Bernstein, now seventy-two, was not happy about the change in the air, asking, "where can I go for clean air?"[8]

By this time, Phoenix was no longer being touted by physicians as a therapeutic location. "It would be difficult for me to recommend [Phoenix] for people with lung disease," said Joanne Gersten, an epidemiologist with the Arizona Department of Public Health in June 1989. "I have a suspicion they die at an earlier age here because of the pollution assault."[9] Indeed, studies by the Arizona health department at the time showed that Phoenix's death rate from respiratory disease was significantly higher than less polluted parts of the state, and that cardiac deaths in one Phoenix neighborhood rose significantly when carbon monoxide levels rose. Residents in another especially polluted part of Phoenix, when compared with residents of a community with cleaner air, were found to suffer 20 percent more headaches, coughing, sore throats, malaise, and shortness of breath—all symptoms typical of carbon monoxide and particulate exposure. "It affects the well-being of everyone in the valley," said Phoenix pulmonary specialist Bernard E. Levine of the city's air pollution.[10]

Across the country, meanwhile, some state regulators began asking the federal government to set stricter standards. "There are some fairly significant reductions out there," said Nicholas Nikkila, Missouri's chief air pollution regulator in April 1987, "but to get them we need national guidance."[11] However EPA at the time wasn't offering much help.

## Clean Air Gridlock

For two years, EPA had delayed a decision about requiring some kind of device—either on cars or at gasoline pumps—to capture gasoline fumes that escape into the air during refueling, one source of smog-forming pollutants. The oil and auto industries both opposed any action on the problem. EPA was also reluctant to enforce sanctions on cities not meeting their deadlines. By late November 1987, however, with deadlines looming, EPA administrator Lee Thomas announced that EPA would relax the deadlines—stretching out compliance for as long as fifteen years, but only if cities adopted tougher control measures, including vehicle emission-inspection programs and the use of cleaner fuels like compressed natural gas for vehicle fleets, as well as tougher controls on industrial pollutants. Environmentalists had advocated a strategy similar to this, hoping to link deadline extensions to new controls on acid rain, toxic fumes, and auto exhausts.

In Congress, there was still an effort underway to update and reauthorize the Clean Air Act. But gridlock was pretty much the order of the day. On the House side, the ongoing feud and power struggle between Representatives Henry Waxman and John Dingell and the interests they represented—Waxman pushing for tighter emissions standards and improved compliance, Dingell for more lenient or status quo levels at best—would keep proposed improvements to the act from making much headway. Bills would move out of subcommittee only to be bottled up in full committee, or kept off the floor by one maneuver or another. On the Senate side, Senator Robert Stafford (R-VT) chairman of the Senate Environment and Public Works Committee, was not inclined to change the Clean Air Act. There too, although bills or amendments moved out of committee on occasion, none made it to final consideration.

The auto industry was especially hot about one bill proposed by Senator George Mitchell (D-ME). Mitchell's bill, among other feature, proposed tightening emission-control standards for cars and trucks, doing away with vehicle averaging to meet emission standards, and doubling the vehicle "useful life" requirement under which emission-control systems would be required to work. Fred Bowditch of the MVMA was advocating "fleet turnover" rather than the tighter provisions of Mitchell's bill. When asked about the cost of complying with Mitchell's standards, Bowditch replied, "We don't know how to estimate them because we don't know how to make these improvements."[12]

GM sent a special letter to some 150,000 of its shareholders asking them to write their senators to oppose the bill. GM's letter said Mitchell's bill "would cripple the US economy" and cost billions of dollars. "There are no technological breakthroughs of a comparable magnitude on the horizon," wrote GM vice president James Johnston to the shareholders, explaining why GM couldn't meet the proposed standards. "Any further improvements will likely come from very costly refinements of the current system, and it is not at all clear that the proposed standards could be met even if these refinements could be implemented." Johnston added that complying with those standards would also hurt US automakers' ability to compete in the international auto market by forcing them to divert engineering resources.[13] But neither Mitchell's bill, nor any other, was going anywhere, as a legislative stalemate had set in.

## ELECTION YEAR POLITICS

In late 1987, however, with national elections a year away, politicians in Congress began maneuvering to use lack of action on the Clean Air Act as a vote-getting issue. Reading the public opinion polls, Democrats were anxious to strengthen the law to enhance their chances both in congressional elections and potentially the White House as well. John Dingell, however, fought to keep the bill in committee. By September 1988, it was clear Dingell would not give up the bill, even though a near revolt of Democrats sought its release (however some Democrats, like Henry Waxman, were not entirely sad to see the bill die, as they were beginning to believe they might get a stronger measure in the next Congress). On the Senate side, despite eleventh-hour negotiations by Senate majority leader George Mitchell (D-ME), the Senate's bill was also blocked by Senator Robert Byrd (D-WV), concerned about what the bill's acid rain provisions might mean for his coal-mining state.

Yet the politics of clean air was changing, and even John Dingell got the message. In December 1987, the House voted by continuing resolution to extend the Clean Air Act to August 1988—months before the national election—at which point the House agreed to finally take up the reauthorization of the act. Dingell had tried to put the measure over until 1989, but he lost to Waxman on a floor vote. Business groups were stunned that Waxman had won on the floor.

John Dingell was so concerned, in fact, that he "summoned more than dozen leading corporate lobbyists to his Capitol Hill office." Dingell "was very frustrated by industry's inability to influence the vote," said one of those attending the meeting. "He said that he needed better help from business interests if he was to prevail when the House had a full-fledged debate. And he said we had not done as good a job as had the environmentalists." The lobbyists got the message and in January 1988 incorporated the Clean Air Working Group [CAWG].[14]

CAWG, which had been meeting informally since 1981, emerged as a new industrial fighting force, backed by nearly 2,000 members representing Fortune 500 companies and industrial trade groups in the auto, oil, steel, chemical, and coal industries, among others. Bill Fay, a vice president of the National Coal Association became CAWG's executive director, and Earl Mallick, of USX in Washington, its chairman. At the peak of its operations in subsequent congressional battle, CAWG's weekly meetings were being attended by more than 100 corporate lobbyists.[15] Environmentalists and consumer groups would later cite CAWG's multimillion dollar "outreach" projects and national publicity campaigns with spreading misleading and false information about the clean air law. Some of the CAWG's propaganda predicted a "quiet death for businesses across the country" if the clean air legislation was passed.[16]

Meanwhile, environmental concerns had only heightened during 1988. Beach pollution, episodes of bad air in many big cities, a very hot summer, and emerging concerns about global warming all contributed to raising environmental awareness to a new level. During the presidential election campaign, environmental issues became a major focus of both Vice President George Bush and Democratic nominee Michael Dukakis.

## THE GREENING OF GEORGE BUSH

George Bush, as the Reagan administration's point man on the Regulatory Relief Task Force, had generally not endeared himself to the nation's environmentalists. But in his campaign, Bush went through a rather amazing metamorphosis on environmental matters. Bush's handlers and advisors deftly used his more moderate environmental leanings and his hunting and fishing outings to transform him into a presidential candidate who could garner suburban and sportsman "environmental" votes. Bush had reportedly told some advisors early on that he believed the nation should do more about pollution and that he would differ from Reagan on the issue. By early 1988, Russell Train, William Ruckelshaus, New Jersey governor Thomas Kean, Nicholas Brady, campaign strategist Robert Teeter, and C. Boyden Gray were all helping craft Bush's environmental message. At a May 1988 campaign stop in Seattle before a business group, Bush broached the topic of clean air, noting that while progress had been made, "nearly 80 metropolitan areas are flunking clean-air standards."[17]

During his campaign, Bush would plant the seeds of a new approach to cleaning up air pollution that would later become part of a national program: using cleaner burning alcohol fuels in automobiles, also called alternative fuels. Bush had begun to venture out on alternative fuels as chairman of Ronald Reagan's Regulatory Reform Task Force. Boyden Gray, chief counsel to Bush, was also a vocal supporter of increased methanol use and headed up the federal agency working group writing the methanol fuel recommendation for the states. By the time he ran for president, Bush and his advisors—principally Boyden Gray and a former Ford administration energy official, Bill Rosenberg—began to see the political and economic value of alternative fuels. Rosenberg, for one, who would later become Bush's nominee to EPA as assistant administrator for Air and Radiation, saw alternative fuels as a new market; a way for some businesses and possibly farmers to benefit. While campaigning in the Midwest, Bush made alternative fuels a part of his platform.

Then, in a campaign speech at Lake Erie on August 31, 1988, Bush asserted, "I am an environmentalist. Always have been, from my earliest days as a congressman, when I first chaired the House task force on earth resources and population. And I always will be, to my last days as a president of this great and beautiful country. That's not inconsistent with being a businessman. Nor is it with being a conservative. In fact, it is an essential part of the thinking that should guide either one." By this time, Bush was adding acid rain and ozone depletion to issues he would address as president.

"Talk about an election year conversion," Dukakis would say of Bush's new environmental promises. Still, the issue helped Bush win the election, especially after he went to Boston Harbor in September 1988 and made national TV news criticizing Dukakis' failure to clean up the harbor while governor. The Dukakis people were slow to respond. Frank Blake, a Bush environmental campaign advisor couldn't understand why "Dukakis gave us the issue." Leslie Dach, Dukakis' campaign spokesman and communications director, later explained, "We screwed up the environmental issue. Any campaign has limited space and time. We didn't think we could use the environmental issue to get new votes. So we decided to focus on the economy. It was probably a mistake that we did not first occupy the turf on the environment."[18]

Once in the White House, Bush's team began to see a new Clean Air Act as a political tool to help win the *next* presidential election, in 1992—especially in California, which would comprise 20 percent of the electoral votes needed to win.

# Fuels on the Fire

Until we began discussing an alternative fuels mandate at the White House level, I had never even heard the term reformulated gasoline. No oil company executive had ever given the EPA the slightest hint it could be done.

—*William K. Reilly, administrator*
*Environmental Protection Agency*[1]

It was June 1989 at the White House, and George Bush, newly elected president, was introducing the broad outlines of a proposed Clean Air bill for Congress. "Twenty years from now," he said, "every American in every city in America will breathe clean air."

After nearly a decade of congressional gridlock over the Clean Air Act, and eight years of Reagan administration regulatory attack, the fact that Bush was taking the initiative at all was a welcome sign. Environmentalists were cautiously optimistic. Bush's program sounded good, zeroing in on urban pollution. All but three of eighty-one cities then failing to meet the clean air standards would meet those standards by the year 2000, he promised. Only Los Angeles, Houston, and Denver would be given more leeway.

Key to Bush's plan on urban smog was the use of cleaner, nonpetroleum fuels—alcohol fuels and other so-called alternative fuels, which would soon come to embrace a range of options from methanol and ethanol to reformulated gasoline and compressed natural gas. Under the president's initial proposal, however, the auto industry would be required to produce one million cars annually capable of running on methanol by 1997. These methanol-fueled cars would be used in the nation's nine most polluted cities: Los Angeles, Houston, New York City, Milwaukee, Baltimore, Philadelphia, greater Connecticut, San Diego, and Chicago.[2] In earlier discussions, EPA had gone even further, proposing that half of all new cars run on methanol by the year 2000 in twenty-five cities.[3] But in the end, EPA was overruled. Still, for the Bush administration, and for the Congress, venturing into alternative fuels and cars that ran on them was major new ground—especially on the scale Bush proposed. By introducing both the fuels provision and the "million-car mandate," as it would be called, the Bush administration got the immediate attention of both the Big Three and Big Oil. A new politics was forming and a new route to cleaning the air was taking shape, but it would turn out to be much more contentious than first envisioned.

Proposals to advance nongasoline motor vehicle fuels had been around for more than thirty years, brought to the fore typically by energy crises. Alternative fuels plans would surface from time to time whenever there was an energy scare or tightening of supply. By the late 1970s and early 1980s, some alcohol fuels pilot programs were adopted by the government, with subsidies for the production of "gasohol"—an ethanol (10 percent) and gasoline mixture. But with the collapse of oil prices to $15 a barrel in 1986, interest in a major push for alternative fuels all but evaporated.

By the late 1980s, however, intractable urban air pollution began to raise the prospects for alternative fuels. No longer viewed solely as an energy strategy, alternative fuels were now being considered from an environmental and public health standpoint—as a way to reduce urban smog. The internal combustion engine, some argued, was "maxed out" in terms of gaining any additional pollution control—"like getting blood out of turnip," said one auto lobbyist. But burning cleaner fuels could bring down tailpipe emissions. The problem all along, some would say, was dirty gasoline—"garbage in, garbage out." The oil industry had gotten a free ride, some said. It was time to bring in cleaner alternatives to gasoline.

State officials were among the first to move toward alternative fuels as an air pollution strategy. California, as usual, was setting the trend. In May 1987, the state committed to purchasing 100,000 cars that could use alcohol fuels such as methanol by 1991-92. Methanol could be derived from natural gas or coal. When refined as a fuel, methanol burned fairly cleanly, offering reductions in smog-forming pollutants. California was also making a modest commitment to help fund the public and private purchase of 5,000 vehicles that would run on methanol. But there was also a larger plan in California's sights: replacing 30 percent of the state's gasoline consumption with methanol by the year 2000. The oil company ARCO agreed to market methanol fuel at seventy-five of its California gas stations in the same period. The California program, according to California Energy Commission chairman Chuck Imbrecht was designed to overcome "the chicken and egg problem"—the refusal of auto companies to build methanol-burning vehicles because there was no way to fuel them, and the oil companies' refusal to produce the fuel because there were no vehicles to use it. Now California had taken the first step to insure both. Imbrecht believed this would be the beginning of a national program.[4]

In Washington, meanwhile, there was already action underway on alternative fuels. A Reagan administration working group was preparing a report that would recommend that states adopt methanol programs as a way to comply with federal air pollution standards. On Capitol Hill, legislation introduced by Senator John D. "Jay" Rockefeller (D-WV) and Representative Phil Sharp (D-IN) would become the Motor Fuels Act of 1988, creating incentives and experimental fleets for "flexible-fueled vehicles," or FFEs, vehicles capable of burning either gasoline or various alternative fuels.

## THE BUSH PLAN

Bush's original alternative fuels plan unveiled at the White House in June 1989—which had grown out of his earlier campaign promises to farmers and the influence of key advisors Boyden Gray and Bill Rosenberg*—called for 100 percent methanol (or its equivalent in other fuels like compressed natural gas) to become the standard, known as "M-100" during the debate. But the plan calling for 1 million alternative-fueled vehicles using the M-100 standard, shook up both the oil and auto industries. The automakers, for their part, preferred methanol if there had to be alternative fuels. For Detroit, methanol meant fewer changes would be needed in conventional engines. Indianapolis race cars, in fact, already used M-100. Much of the oil industry, on the other hand, viewed the proposal as a major threat to its preeminent position in gasoline. By September 1989, the Mobil Oil Corporation was running quarter-page "advertorials" attacking methanol as a "panacea with problems."

The American Petroleum Institute (API) called the Bush proposal "an extremely costly and inflexible step, which would provide highly uncertain environmental benefits." Reacting to EPA's earlier, tougher proposal calling for even more alternative-fuel vehicles, the oil industry warned that it would cost $18-to $24 billion to build 60 new methanol plants and that extra natural gas needed to make the methanol would have to be imported from the Middle East. The auto industry, for its part, was cool to the idea, although it had shown off its methanol-powered cars at auto shows and elsewhere and was also developing "flexible-fuel" engines capable of burning methanol, ethanol, and gasoline interchangeably. Ford Motor Co. called the Bush proposal "bold," but reiterated its support for an earlier auto industry proposal for a smaller pilot program rather than the administration's more ambitious program.[5] The auto industry would remain somewhat tepid on alternative fuels as the Clean Air Act debate unfolded, described by one EPA participant as wavering "between weak opposition and ambivalence."[6]

## EMISSIONS DEAL?

Behind the scenes, however, there was some speculation that a deal was being discussed with the auto industry: in return for industry's agreeing to manufacture some methanol-burning engines, there would be no new requirements in the administration's bill on conventional gasoline engines. Representative Henry Waxman (D-CA), for one, was watching the initial negotiations within the administration as it worked to formulate its package. Waxman made it clear that he

---

* After Bush was elected in November 1988, Bill Rosenberg, with the help of EPA staff in Ann Arbor, Michigan, pulled together the alternative-fuels program Bush would use in his Clean Air Act announcement.

was looking for tighter provisions for cleaner burning gasoline cars as well as alternative fuels.*

By late July 1989, the president's initial Clean Air Act package had been changed from the one he presented in June. One of the proposals now included a provision for averaging the emissions from new vehicles to meet the standards, which brought a swift reaction from Capitol Hill. "[T]he administration bill cut a sweetheart deal with the automakers that relaxes many of the current motor vehicle standards," charged Waxman. "The bill eliminates the requirements that each car meet pollution standards in favor of a program that would allow car makers to 'average' the performance of vehicles...." Auto emissions, Waxman said, "would actually be allowed to increase from today's levels."[7] Under the "averaging" provision—an old idea that had appeared in earlier debates—any of the automakers could produce a model line of cars that polluted above the standard, so long as another model line produced below it. The idea sounded good in principle. But on closer inspection, it was found that averaging would actually cause auto pollution to rise. Michael Walsh, former New York City and EPA air pollution official, wrote a memo for Congress and others which explained that auto manufacturers were then producing cars with a margin of safety built into their vehicles to insure they met the standards. Allowing fleet averaging, he said, would eliminate the margin, and permit pollution to rise to the maximum permitted levels.[8] Averaging, in other words, was a step backwards and would cause the aggregate level of pollution by automobiles to rise.

By October 1989, when the Bush and Waxman measures were to be considered by the House Energy Subcommittee, the first showdown came. As the subcommittee began its work on the bill, it appeared the old "going nowhere" contests between John Dingell, representing the auto industry, and Henry Waxman, representing Los

---

* In May 1989, Waxman and Jerry Lewis (R-CA), introduced their bill for alternative-fuel cars by 1993, which also required a tough regimen of emission standards. Waxman-Lewis proposed to extend deadlines for curbing smog in violating cities, with a gradual phase-in of alternative-fuel vehicles according to the severity of the pollution, determined by how a city was classified. Under a *moderate* designation—violating the ozone standard up to 20 percent of the time—a city would have four years to comply. However, it would have to establish enhanced auto inspection and maintenance programs and any buses purchased after January 1, 1992 would have to run on cleaner, alternative fuel. Cities in the *serious* (20 percent-50 percent violation rate) and *severe* (50 percent-100 percent) categories would be given more time as well (eight and twelve years), but would have tougher, graduated stipulations, with increasing proportions of centrally-fueled and new-car fleets designated for alternative fuel use by specific deadlines. "Extreme" cities—Los Angeles and Southern California primarily—would get another sixteen years. In these cases, ten percent of all new vehicles would have to burn alternative fuels by 1994, 30 percent by 1996, 70 percent by 1998, and 100 percent by the year 2000. William Fay, director of CAWG called the bill a giant leap backward," noting in particular that "some of the demands...for the auto industry just can't be met." Thomma, "Bill in Congress," *Detroit Free Press,* May 12, 1989, p1A.

Angeles and pushing for a stronger Clean Air Act, would take center court once again. And they did, for awhile. But a key breakthrough occurred that surprised many House members: a bill was voted out of subcommittee. Dingell and the auto industry lost two key votes in subcommittee: one on averaging, which was defeated in favor of car-by-car standards, and a second on installing special canisters in cars to capture gasoline fumes during refueling. Those losses signaled to Dingell that politically, a compromise was in order. And there were other realities as well, not least of which was a more aggressive posture by some states.

## STATES GET TOUGH

On August 10, 1989, eight northeastern states agreed to adopt California's 1993 auto emissions standards. Under the Clean Air Act, states could pre-empt federal standards when they adopted the California program. By taking this step, the northeastern states would go beyond the Bush bill, putting pressure on Congress to get tough. California's standards for hydrocarbons and NOx were tougher and under the NE plan would come into effect years sooner than the Bush proposal. Adopting the California standards would also put the northeastern states well beyond the administration's "fleet averaging" proposal, also barred in California. "What we are saying," explained New York governor Mario Cuomo of the eight-state move, "is that if Washington refuses to, we will do what we must to protect the health of our people. But . . . it would be better for the nation if Washington would recognize its special responsibility."

General Motors was not happy with what was taking place in the states. "If auto manufacturers are forced to respond to a patchwork of different emissions standards throughout the nation, production, distribution, and sales of vehicles will become increasingly complex and costly to consumers." Madeline Lewis, speaking for New York environmental commissioner Thomas Jorling, said the average cost of adopting the needed pollution control equipment would be about $100 to $150 per car, or "about the price of a hubcap." She also called the Bush administration's averaging provision "very inadequate," adding, "Each car should be controlled and inspected. Once you start averaging, you lose control of that." The northeast states also wanted other provisions: warranty requirements for pollution control equipment that would last for 100,000 miles as opposed to 50,000; an aggressive recall program; and blocking imports of higher-polluting vehicles. On the West Coast, Los Angeles air pollution officials had proposed earlier that year an even more ambitious antismog effort with tougher provisions, to be phased in over the 1993-2007 time frame. Los Angeles' plan also proposed charging a premium to families owning more than one car; significantly tightening regulations on the oil, auto, and utility industries; and also advancing new automotive technologies, such a electric cars. Meanwhile, across the nation, public opinion was rising in favor of tougher environmental restrictions.

## "RED SEA PARTED"

Back in Congress, with all of this bubbling up, it was clear to John Dingell that a new approach to auto emissions standards was in order. Dingell and Waxman agreed to support a compromise measure—at least on the auto emissions part of the bill. The Waxman-Dingell agreement essentially adopted the California standards for the forty-nine other states—that is, it made the standards then in effect for California the national standards for the next five years. The key parts of their bill included: a phase-in of California emissions standards from 1994 through 1996; 100,0000-mile or ten-year pollution equipment warranties; an EPA review to determine the feasibility of second-round standards in the years 2003 to 2006, and whether more stringent standards might be needed by then; and a program to control emissions of toxic air pollutants from motor vehicles and motor vehicle fuels.* The agreement would hold, said Waxman and Dingell, all the way through to final consideration, even on the House floor (the alternative fuels portion of the bill, however, was another matter, outside of the agreement).

"The Red Sea has parted," commented Representative Gerry Sikorski (D-MN), referring to the long-standing impasse between Dingell and Waxman.[9] The automakers, however, were "unenthused," according to Dingell, who called the bill a "fair compromise, honorably achieved." Waxman thought the provisions "[let] automakers know what might be coming, and gives them time to plan properly and research new emission reduction options."[10] Still, the automakers weren't buying. "We're disappointed that they went as far as they did in their proposal," said Tim-

---

*The details of the subcommittee-approved bill were as follows: Beginning with 1994 models, cars and light-duty trucks could emit 0.25 GPM of nonmethane hydrocarbons for five years or 50,000 miles, whichever came first; and 0.31 GPM after that up to ten years or 100,000 miles. The federal law then in effect set that standard at 0.41 GPM. For carbon monoxide, the limit would be 3.4 GPM in the five-year, 50,000-mile period (same as then-current law) and 4.2 GPM after that up to 10-years or 100,000 miles. Beginning with 1994 cars and 1995 light-duty trucks, NOx emissions would be held to 0.4 GPM, then the California limit. The standard would be phased-in over two years, 40 percent the first year and 100 percent the second year. The existing NOx limit at the time was 1.0 GPM. EPA and the Congressional Office of Technology Assessment were each required to complete a study on whether to tighten the requirements further in the future. The EPA administrator would also be required to make a decision on whether to tighten requirements by December 31, 1999, taking into account cost and other considerations. If the administrator decided to tighten at that time, EPA could impose new requirements as early as January 1, 2003, but no later than model year 2006. Pollution control equipment would have to be built for a useful life of 100,000 miles, twice the existing standard, and if the equipment failed before 75,000 miles autos could be recalled. Within eighteen months the EPA administrator would also complete a study on the need for controlling other toxic air pollutants from vehicles not then regulated, and if needed, issue regulations for those pollutants within fifty-four months.

othy MacCarthy, of the MVMA. MacCarthy said the provisions were tougher than needed and would result in higher auto costs, loss of fuel economy, a shortage of models, driveability problems, and more recalls. He also indicated that EPA had calculated $500 per car costs for Waxman's original bill. A statement from GM officials indicated the bill "goes to an extreme that will bring virtually no significant benefits over what the [White House] bill provides." Harold Poling of Ford Motor said Waxman-Dingell went "well beyond" the Bush bill, which Ford Motor had supported—adding, however, the Bush plan "would have put a severe strain on our human and technological resources."[11]

This was only one step—although an important one—in the tortuous legislative gauntlet of the 1990 Clean Air Act fight.

## ARCO's "New Gas"

Not long after George Bush floated his first Clean Air Act proposal with the million-car mandate, the old Atlantic-Richfield oil company, now called ARCO, made national news with a new kind of gasoline. On August 16, 1989, the *New York Times* ran a front-page story with the headline: "ARCO Offers New Gasoline to Cut Up to 15 Percent of Old Cars' Pollution." ARCO, it seemed, had come up with a way to reformulate some of its gasoline—aimed initially at older cars in southern California—that would reduce some kinds of emissions. According to ARCO, NOx would be reduced by 5 percent, reactive organic gases by 5 percent, CO by 9 percent, and sulfur dioxides by 80 percent. Similar fuels for other cars would follow, said the company.[12]

But in a stunning admission, ARCO officials acknowledged that the chemistry and refining involved in making cleaner gasoline was really quite simple and could have been done years sooner.[13] James Morrison, an ARCO vice president, would later say that ARCO could have produced reformulated fuels years before, "but we were already selling all the gasoline we could make and there was no government requirement for a low-pollution product, so where was our incentive?"[14] However, with the Bush proposal in the wings, ARCO was now worried about the potential competition from alternative fuels, and potentially, tighter restrictions on gasoline.

"We're making this heavy investment because we believe the dominant fuel of the future will be gasoline, rather than the alternatives you've been hearing about," said ARCO chairman Lodwrick M. Cook.[15] ARCO was also responding to an air quality management plan by California's South Coast Air Quality Management District (AQMD), the air quality authority that governs the "gasoline gold mine" that is the Los Angeles Basin, a market dominated by ARCO. The AQMD had proposed a twenty-year plan, later approved, that would eliminate gasoline-powered cars in favor of vehicles using methanol, ethanol, compressed natural gas, and electricity. With such prospects in the offing, ARCO instructed its chemists in March 1989 to formulate a cleaner-burning gasoline. Within three months, the company's scientists had a formula that reduced smog precursors by 37 percent.[16]

When ARCO made its announcement in Los Angeles, its executives appeared alongside officials from CARB and the AQMD. These state officials, however, were cautious, encouraging the ARCO development, but adding their concerns. "We've still got to go further than this," said James M. Lents, executive director of the AQMD. "We believe . . . that methanol and natural gas, electricity, and those kinds of fuels are the kinds that are needed. We're skeptical that gasoline can ever be as clean as some of these fuels, but we think they deserve the chance and our support. . . ."[17] Other oil companies soon followed ARCO. "Everybody is looking at reformulated gasoline right now," said Gere Smith, a spokesman for Phillips Petroleum in Bartlesville, Oklahoma. "Everybody is looking at whatever it's going to take."[18]

ARCO's move—although it initially divided the oil industry on strategy—would subsequently help to blunt the Bush administration's call for a strong move into alternative alcohol-based fuels and alternative-fuel vehicles. "Until we began discussing an alternative fuels mandate at the White House level," recounted EPA administrator William Reilly, "I had never even heard the term reformulated gasoline. No oil company executive had ever given the EPA the slightest hint it could be done."[19] By October 1989, ARCO was using full-page newspaper ads to tout its new discovery nationally under the rubric of "The Clean Air Agenda," explaining why reformulated gasoline was the best "alternative fuel."

Bill Rosenberg of EPA would later marvel at "the immediate market response to develop and sell cleaner gasoline." He added that ARCO and the other companies that followed with their cleaner gas "verified that fuels could play a big role in the clean-air debate. They showed that cleaner fuels were feasible and economic. That cut the pins from under the American Petroleum Institute's argument against stronger fuel standards."[20] Ed Rothschild of Citizen Action put it a little differently. "The oil industry knows how to reformulate gasoline," he said. "It's not a matter of technology. . . . The fact is, the oil industry does not want competition."[21]

## CAR PLAN KILLED

On Capitol Hill, meanwhile, the auto and oil industries had teamed up with John Dingell and Representative Norman Lent (R-NY) to oppose the Bush plan for one million alternative-fuel cars by 1997—which they succeeded in killing during subcommittee consideration. An amendment drafted by Dingell and Lent to block the Bush plan was circulated and sponsored by the oil state's Ralph Hall (D-TX) and Jack Fields, Jr. (R-TX). It proposed to make the plan "fuel neutral" by lowering the alternative fuel standards to "M-85," which meant 85 percent methanol or its equivalent rather than 100 percent methanol. This opened the door to a whole host of other alternative fuels—including, most importantly, gasoline which could be formulated to run at an M-85 equivalent standard. The auto industry liked M-85, too,

# THE CLEAN AIR AGENDA.
## Why the best known alternative to gasoline is reformulated gasoline.

### WE CAN BEGIN CLEANING UP OUR AIR, STARTING TODAY.

Over the years, ARCO has experimented with various alternative fuels, advancing its understanding of gasoline technology. These efforts have led us to an important new development, a reformulated gasoline that we believe is an important step toward solving today's air pollution problems.

We call it EC-1 Regular, the first Emission Control Gasoline.

All of our tests indicate that reformulated gasoline like ARCO EC-1 will be one of the most effective pollution control measures since the catalytic converter was put in cars 15 years ago. Effective and less costly to motorists than other potential alternatives.

To make ARCO EC-1, we eliminated all lead; eliminated one-half of the benzene and up to one-third of other aromatics and olefins; reduced sulfur by up to 80 percent; and reduced vapor pressure by a full pound per square inch below the California standard, the most stringent in the nation.

For now, because of refinery limitations, we plan to market ARCO EC-1 only in Southern California, from Santa Barbara to San Diego. Our first target, the heaviest polluters in the area—pre-1975 cars and pre-1980 trucks without catalytic converters that now run on leaded gasoline. While these cars and trucks represent only about 15% of the on-road vehicles in Southern California, they are responsible for over 30% of the vehicular air pollution.

### REDUCING AIR POLLUTION, WITHOUT RAISING COSTS TO THE CONSUMER.

With ARCO EC-1, tailpipe and evaporative pollution from older vehicles will be cut substantially without affecting performance. With the same 88 octane rating as ARCO leaded regular. And without an increase in price to our dealers.

The cost to the consumer in using ARCO EC-1 is substantially lower than proposed alternatives. It does not require engine modifications. It does not require changes in the refinery-to-station infrastructure that would inevitably affect the price of fuel. In fact, ARCO EC-1 requires no changes at all by the consumer. And no other suggested alternative fuel can make that claim.

Our tests show that if all leaded gasoline users in Southern California switched to a reformulated gasoline like ARCO EC-1, about 350 tons of pollutants would be removed from the air each day. The impact would be equivalent to permanently removing 20%—or more than 300,000—of these high polluting, pre-catalyst-equipped vehicles from Southern California highways.

### WE'RE NOT STOPPING HERE.

Having worked with the South Coast Air Quality Management District and the California Air Resources Board—sharing our progress and test results—we consider ARCO EC-1 a public-private partnership. It is a partnership that begins to reduce air pollution today, not at some uncertain future date, as suggested by alternatives.

But we know there's much more to be done. At the top of our agenda is more research into other reformulated gasolines. Our intent?

To make all our gasoline with the EC formula. Cleaner-burning gasoline for all of our customers. And reformulated, emission control gasoline for future vehicles.

Today, ARCO EC-1 is one pure and simple solution to our pollution problem. Others will follow.

**ARCO ◆**
Searching for Clean Air Solutions.
For more information, please contact: ARCO, Public Affairs AP 6412
515 South Flower St., Los Angeles, CA 90051

*When Congress and the White House started talking about alternative fuels for cars and trucks, the oil industry suddenly "discovered" it could make cleaner gasoline.*

since that meant fewer alterations to conventional engines. EPA, however, said M-85 was a poor substitute for pure methanol from an air pollution standpoint, since it would release 30 percent more of the pollutants that caused smog.[22] But the real kicker in the Hall-Fields amendment was that it did not require *any* production of alternative-fueled vehicles, merely an EPA certification that automakers had the "capacity" to produce such cars. During debate on the measure, there were mixed signals sent over from the White House, with EPA's Bill Reilly telling Waxman that the administration opposed the amendment, while John Sununu reported to Lent that the administration was "neutral" on it. In the end, over Henry Waxman's strong objection, the Hall-Fields measure was approved in October 1989 by the House Energy and Commerce subcommittee by a 12-10 vote.[23] Republicans joined John Dingell and moderate Democrats to carry the vote. Environmentalists were not happy. "By abandoning President Bush, the Republicans have given a giant gift to General Motors and Exxon so they don't have to produce the cars and fuels that will lead to clean air," charged Sierra Club lobbyist Dan Weiss.[24]

### Auto Industry Digs In

By November 1989, the Senate Committee on Environment and Public Works—regarded by industry as "a wholly owned subsidiary of the environmental community" and one industry lobbyists typically sought to thwart—passed a version of the Clean Air Act with auto emissions provisions tougher than the House version. This bill also included one of the first attempts to get at the automobile's contribution to global warming by requiring fuel economy measures of 33 miles per gallon for 1996-1999 model years and 40 MPG by the year 2000 (later dropped). Automakers complained that meeting the proposed emissions standards set for future years would not be technologically feasible. Ford Motor Co. denounced the bill, saying it placed impossible burdens on the industry and "unnecessarily high costs [on consumers] for minimal air quality benefits."[25] The Senate committee bill, however, contained no alternative fuels provision. Senate Republicans on the committee favored alternative fuels as a means of controlling air pollution rather than stricter auto emissions standards and had a proposal similar to the Bush plan, one version of which would have knocked out Tier 2 standards (emissions standards to come after 2003) in favor of wider alternative fuel use. These proposals were either defeated or not taken up by the committee.

Detroit had all along preferred the administration's bill as the lesser of two evils and mounted a campaign to adopt the Bush bill and not the Senate committee bill. Advertisements in major newspapers began to appear, trying to persuade the public that certain provisions—especially those in the Senate committee bill—were not needed. New car technology was already doing the job, industry claimed, and the air would become cleaner as more new cars replaced older ones—an argument made by the industry since the 1960s.

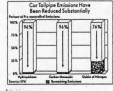

*This Big Three ad, run nationally in November 1989, was aimed at beating back a tougher clean air bill drafted by the Senate Environment and Public Works Committee.*

## BEHIND CLOSED DOORS

By January 1990, after the Senate Public Works Committee had sent its tougher bill to the Senate floor, Republican senators such as Steve Symms and Alan Simpson began voicing their objections, indicating a possible filibuster. It became clear after one day's debate that the Democrats lacked the sixty votes needed to end a filibuster. That's when Majority Leader George Mitchell, in a somewhat unusual and controversial move, pulled the bill in favor of beginning private talks to negotiate a compromise bill with a "group of fifteen" senators and White House negotiators—including John Sununu. This White House/Senate "summit" soon raised the ire of environmentalists, who saw their best provisions being whittled away.

"Every day that bill is negotiated it's getting weaker," claimed Casey Scott Padgett, legislative counsel for Environmental Action. Dick Ayres, director of the National Clean Air Coalition, wanted the bill debated on the Senate floor, in the open. "That kind of sunshine [i.e., debate on the floor] gets us those final 'yes' votes," contended Gene Karpinski, executive director of the US Public Interest Research Group. Industry, however, preferred the negotiated route. "This is an issue that needs to be resolved behind closed doors," said Bill Fay, administrator of the industry-funded Clean Air Working Group. Fay said the volatility of the issue made it difficult for senators to publicly offer amendments without being subject to "activist vilification" by environmental groups in their home states.[26]

When the measure finally emerged, Dick Ayres charged that it was "negotiated in secret" with the public given only "euphemistic summaries." Ayres was upset with a number of changes, including those for auto emissions standards and alternative fuels. The administration's original proposal for alternative-fuel vehicles he charged had been "watered down and skewed" to favor reformulated gasoline.[27] "The back room dealing has generated bad deals for the American people," he said. In some respects, the bill was even weaker than existing law. Ayres assured the press that environmentalists would organize to oppose it. Industry, however, seemed content with the outcome. "The movement's in the right direction," said Bill Fay, for the Clean Air Working Group.[28] George Mitchell made clear that amending the deal could bring the whole package down.

Nevertheless, there were a couple of major "showdown" amendments being planned that would strengthen the auto emissions title and give alternative fuels a chance in the Senate. Throughout this whole legislative process, however—which ran from mid-1989 to late 1990—there was much maneuvering and heated fighting over other parts of the Clean Air Act, principally over the acid rain provision and how it would affect the coal industry, jobs, and the electric utilities. In addition, controls over stationary sources, such as those involving major industries such as steel and petrochemicals, were also intensely fought out. The auto emissions and alternative fuels sections of the legislation would become entangled in these fights, or in legislative maneuvering designed "in trade" for some consideration made in deference to one or more senators or representatives.

## THE WIRTH-WILSON SHOWDOWN

On March 8, 1990, Senators Tim Wirth (D-CO), John Kerry (D-MA), Brock Adams (D-WA), Alan Cranston (D-CA), and Frank Lautenberg (D-NJ) announced they would offer amendments to restore some provisions that had been dropped from the bill.[29] A week later, Wirth and Pete Wilson (R-CA) teamed up to propose a package of motor vehicle amendments that would require an aggressive alternative-fuels program: specifically, requiring the use of cleaner burning gasoline blends by 1993 in all smog-ridden cities—sixty to seventy cities, not just the nine worst—and tough, second-round, Tier 2 emission standards that would begin in 2002, unconditionally. Environmentalists began gearing up to make the Wirth-Wilson vote their top priority—"the Key Environmental Vote of 1990," according to one Sierra Club flier. The League of Conservation Voters (LCV) had already set Wirth-Wilson as one of its key indicator votes for its annual scorecard tabulating how senators vote on environmental legislation. "If folks who traditionally score highly want to take a walk on the Clean Air Coalition, ..." said LCV director Jim Maddy, "they're going to pay the price on our scorecard."[30]

When the Senate vote on Wirth-Wilson came on March 20, the measure was defeated by a tabling motion, 52-46. But the votes were all over the lot and not easily accountable along strictly pro-environment or pro-industry lines. Farm-state senators voted for the measure because they thought ethanol would get a boost. Others thought small business would be protected while oil companies and auto manufactures would bear the brunt of the clean-up costs. A number of senators sided with George Mitchell, believing that amending the deal would jeopardize the whole package negotiated with the White House. Conservative, normally anti-environmental senators voted for the measure. Liberals, typically with environmentalists, voted to table Wirth-Wilson. "You got Helms!" exclaimed one oil company representative devilishly to a Sierra Club lobbyist, referring to North Carolina's conservative Republican Jesse Helms. "I think I'll reconsider my position," he said, sarcastically. Senator Helms, meanwhile, said of his vote in support of Wirth-Wilson, "You had to choose between big business and the little guy, and I made my choice." Senator Jake Garn, another conservative Republican, said he supported the amendment because "Salt Lake City's major pollution problem is the automobile." Still, others believed the conservative republicans like Garn and Helms hoped that Wirth-Wilson would win, so the whole Clean Air package and pact with the White House would go down in the process. An aide to Senator Steve Symms (R-ID)—who also voted for Wirth-Wilson—freely admitted that Symms' intention was to scuttle the whole White House deal.[31]

At this point, the Senate bill had no provision whatsoever for alternative fuels. But that's when Senator Tom Daschle (D-SD) stepped in. Daschle, like the other senators, had been warned that his amendment might cause the White House-Senate deal to fly apart. But still he persisted and went to the floor with his package. Daschle's alternative-fuels amendment dropped the million-car mandate, added more fuels to the list of those eligible, including ethanol and reformulated gasoline, and required the fuels to be used by *all* vehicles in the nine most polluted cities, not just *new* vehicles. Daschle's proposal brought supporters like the Republican minority leader, Bob Dole, to the cause, while peeling off the auto industry's opposition. Daschle's amendment also specified an oxygen component to help fuels burn cleaner and also called for a reduction of certain toxic components in gasoline such as benzene. The latter issue became an important new element in the debate, as Daschle would later explain, with evidence that toxics in gasoline were being missed by traditional emissions regulation. "It does not matter how many levels of tailpipe standards were required if the technology cannot handle the gasoline," he would say.[32] Daschle's amendment was adopted in late March 1990.

"The Wirth [-Wilson] amendment organized the opposition of the automobile and oil industries," said Citizen Action's Ed Rothschild. "The Daschle amendment passed because the auto industry wasn't threatened by it."[33] Others thought Bob Dole and the Senate's generally more prominent agricultural interests might have helped, too. "We never thought that it would pass...," said Chevron's Dale Brooks of Daschle's amendment. "We got blindsided."[34]

The oil and auto industries were somewhat at odds with each other during these fights, not above finger pointing when their interests were threatened. "There is a hell of a lot more difference in the automobiles than there will ever be in the fuel," said the American Petroleum Institute's Charles DiBona, suggesting more work on the engine to solve the problem. DiBona charged that the various alternative-fuels proposals being offered by Congress had "absolutely nothing to do with clean air." He argued that alternative fuels generally, and ethanol in particular, had "a negative contribution" to clean air. "It is in there," he said, "simply to increase the subsidy to ethanol by mandating its use."[35] Over at GM, meanwhile, Joseph Colucci, head of the company's fuels and lubricants department, issued a report saying that cleaner fuels were the way to go, nearly matching provisions in the bills then pending before the House and Senate.[36] Still, despite their differences, the auto and oil industries had joined in a $14-million joint venture to research and test a variety of reformulated gasoline formulas and additives.

"The oil and auto industries said they're working together to solve this problem," remarked ethanol industry lobbyist Eric Vaughn of the Renewable Fuels Association. "But behind their backs, they're pointing at each other and saying, 'Well, you know, if that catalytic converter could just be a little bit bigger or better' or 'If that gasoline just had a little bit less [toxic] content.' I think it is an unfriendly, unhappy marriage."[37]

## "GOVERNMENT GAS"

On April 4, 1990, the Senate passed its version of the 1990 Clean Air Act by a vote of 89-to-11. Over in John Dingell's House Energy Committee, meanwhile, there had been fierce fighting on alternative fuels and some reformulated gasoline proposals. In late March 1990, Representative Bill Richardson (D-NM) offered an amendment to require reformulated gasoline (RFG) to replace conventional gasoline in thirty of the nation's most polluted cities. Richardson's amendment also specified formula for the RFG to maximize its clean air potential. The oil industry and the Bush administration fiercely opposed the Richardson amendment, citing its "blending dictates," high costs, and allowance for alcohol additives, specifically ethanol. Richardson's amendment lost in a tight 22-21 committee vote. He vowed to return on the floor with an even stronger version.

"We're seeing dramatic success stories from people using alternative-fuel cars," said Richardson. "Promoting alternative fuels is good for clean air, and it's good energy policy.... Unless you give the oil industry specific targets and you give them incentives, the oil industry is not going to clean up gasoline. I am not confident that the existing structures that control fuels—auto and petroleum—have the political will to produce cleaner fuels, because it cuts into their pocketbook.... I think government can be a catalyst to clean up the air."[38] The oil industry, meanwhile, began running newspaper ads on "government gas" charging that alternative fuels would not cure the smog problem, but that "answers" were just "months away," as the auto and oil industries were "running thousands of tests" on clean-burning gasoline. Back in the House, in negotiations before the final Richardson floor amendment was to be offered, a compromise targeted nine cities to use RFG, allowing others to opt in later. The compromise was adopted by voice vote on the floor and was refined later in the House-Senate conference to become the final law.[39] Still, in the House floor debate, there was one last chance for alternative-fuel vehicles.

## MILLION-CAR ATTEMPT

In late May 1990, Henry Waxman had drafted a floor amendment to resurrect the Bush administration's original "million-car mandate." Waxman's amendment would require automakers to produce one million alternative-fuel cars annually beginning in 1995, with tighter emissions standards taking effect five years later. A second part of the package proposed that large fleets of vehicles—taxis, delivery trucks, etc.— be converted to alternative fuels. In its later years, Waxman's proposal would move more vehicles toward the use of natural gas and electric power. But even the natural gas industry, a supporter of the idea generally, worried about supplying the infrastructure necessary to support a large surge in alternative-fuel cars. Ethanol and methanol makers worried that forcing clean cars on the market might boomerang if they came too fast and did not work properly, and the automakers played that tune as well.

"To try to shove a lot of alternative-fuel vehicles down the consumers' throats might result in an adverse reaction to alternative fuels," said Timothy McCarthy of the MVMA.[40] Waxman, however, said the industry would always take that position. "They've always looked to protect the status quo," he said. "But they have a

# It Won't Cure The Smog Problem.
# It Will Cost You More.
# It Will Cut Auto Efficiency.

*In May 1990, oil industry opposition to congressional proposals for new clean fuel formulations brought this American Petroleum Institute ad.*

deteriorating status quo right now. If they would push to develop clean-burning cars, I think they could become the world leader again of the automobile industry."[41] Fifteen years earlier, Ed Muskie said much the same thing.

John Dingell, however, opposed the Waxman clean-car mandate, and a major floor fight loomed. Dingell and Waxman began talking and reached agreement on some points. But when the measure came to the floor, there was still an impasse. Speaker Tom Foley (D-WA) intervened, forcing Waxman and Dingell to resolve their differences. Foley sat with the two members in one part of the House chamber surrounded by staff until they reached a compromise. Foley wanted the Clean Air Act passed that year and was mindful that John Dingell could resort to maneuvers that would eat up the clock. "Seated between them ... Foley listened," recounts Richard Cohen of the *National Journal*. "Foley did not suggest or explicitly demand a solution. But through his body language and his tone of voice, he made it clear to [them] he wanted the conflict settled then and there. . . . The message got through. . . . With quiet strength, Foley provided the last push needed to reach a compromise."[42] A substitute amendment was adopted in place of the million-car mandate—this one supported by Dingell that would require automakers to manufacture 150,000 clean-fuel vehicles by 1996 and another 300,000 by 1999—but only as a pilot program in Southern California. The substitute also required that in dirty air regions, fleets use alternative fuels.[43] The MVMA disliked even the compromise amendment, calling clean-fuel cars "an automotive technology not ready for consumer use." Mandating such vehicles before they are ready for market, said the MVMA, "could cause consumer backlash and set back acceptance of those vehicles."[44] Nevertheless, on May 23, 1990, the House version of the Clean Air Act was approved by a 401-to-21 vote, with Waxman's alternative-fuels pilot provision.

## CONFERENCE WARFARE

Having run the gauntlet of both House and Senate, the final hurdle for the Clean Air Act Amendments of 1990 was the negotiations over differences in each version that would occur in the House/Senate conference. The conference committee that finally convened was huge, comprising, for example, 140 House members from the various committees involved in writing their version of the bill. There were battles and infighting over the naming of conferees even before the negotiations began. It would take this committee the better part of three months to reach final agreement. As the conference opened in mid-July 1990, amidst a beginning process of back-and-forth offer and counter-offer, there was still intense politicking over which version would prevail, as well as some entirely new elements that entered the debate.

"We need a tough, comprehensive mobile-source program with the strictest standards for tailpipe emissions," said New York City's Environmental Protection commissioner Albert F. Appleton lobbying the conferees by letter. New York City was facing a perennial smog and carbon monoxide problem, which came primarily from motor vehicles: half of New York's hydrocarbons came from motor vehicles, as did 90 percent of its CO. New York City mayor David Dinkins pressed the New York delegation to push for the toughest possible provisions.[45]

As the House-Senate conference was proceeding, New York State moved to adopt California's tailpipe standards under existing law. "By adopting the California standard for motor vehicle emissions," said New York State's environmental commissioner Thomas Jorling, "New York State is adopting the single most cost-effective program of emissions reduction that can be applied." He also added that the California standards—which would be applied to the 1993 model year—as "qualitatively superior" to any new clean air program that Congress was considering.[46] In the House-Senate conference, in fact, John Dingell had proposed that the state option to enforce the California program be assigned to EPA, essentially taking it away from the states. Automakers, behind the move, were concerned that as more states followed California, they would being forced to produce a "third car"—one for California, one to meet national standards, and another version to satisfy what other states might adopt under the California option. Opponents saw the Dingell amendment as a clear threat to the rising state initiative on clean air.

William Becker, executive director of two important state and local government organizations—STAPPA/ALAPCO, State and Territorial Air Pollution Program Administrators and the Association of Local Air Pollution Control Officials—maintained that state authority to enforce the program was critical for states and local governments that might opt for the California standards, or the clean-fuel pilot program that also became part of California's program. The conferees had adopted the House provision requiring automakers to produce 150,000 ultra-clean cars for Southern California in 1996, and 300,000 in later years. Becker thought that some states and local governments, dissatisfied with what they found to be weaker federal emissions standards, might opt instead for the tougher California provisions. "Don't be surprised if there is a flurry of activity over the next several years as states opt in to the [California] program," he said, predicting in fact, what would later become a major development in clean air politics. Back in the conference, under pressure from Senator Daniel Patrick Moynihan (D-NY) and others, Dingell dropped his amendment in exchange for assurances that automakers would be required to design only two types of cars.[47]

The 1990 Clean Air Act, in fact, would set in motion a new round of state-based politics with a regional body called the Ozone Transport Commission (OTC). The OTC, created by the act, was an organization of governors from twelve northeastern and mid-Atlantic states and the District of Columbia. It would be empowered, after consultation with EPA, to adopt regionwide strategies to attack ozone pollution, increasingly becoming an interstate problem. Prevailing winds would carry the pollution into Maine from Maryland, or from New York into Connecticut. The OTC would later prove to hold very big implications not only for fuel formulation and vehicle emissions standards, but also for pushing automotive technology beyond the ICE. And one big reason would be market share: the combined possibility of California plus the Northeast seeking the same standards would make for a huge market, thereby becoming a significant force in pushing company planning, investment, and "best technologies" forward not only to satisfy those regional markets, but for the whole nation.

In the end, the Clean Air Act Amendments of 1990 produced tougher provisions on emissions standards than anything proposed in the previous eight years. Ironically, had any of the Democratic bills of the Reagan era become law, they would have put in place weaker standards. The 1990 bill established first-round standards, also known as Tier 1 standards, that were scheduled to go into effect by 1994. These required NOx emissions to be reduced by 60 percent and hydrocarbons by 40 percent. Second-round, or Tier 2 standards, reducing emissions by another 50 percent, would come into play in model year 2003, unless EPA found they were not needed or infeasible. The new law also required that pollution control equipment be durable enough to meet new emissions standards for ten years or 100,000 miles. New cars would also carry special canisters to trap VOCs during refueling—by 1999, all new cars would have them.[48]

Although the auto industry complained that some of the standards were "extremely technology-forcing" and beyond its current capabilities,[49] the intention of the Clean Air Act established by Congress twenty years earlier was precisely that. Going into the House-Senate conference, for example, the automakers opposed Waxman's provision requiring the automakers to produce 150,000 ultra-clean cars for Southern California in 1994-1996, and 300,000 by 1997. The Big Three said it imposed an impossible schedule on them for producing and selling a whole new generation of cars that ran on natural gas or methanol — or they would have to use electrically-heated catalytic converters, an unproven, expensive technology. Yet Ford Motor, for one, had experience dating back to 1980 with producing propane passenger cars, and again in 1982 and 1984 with smaller runs of CNG vehicles.[50] The Waxman provision was adopted, but with some deadline adjustments. Waxman, in fact, was pleased with the final auto emissions title. "This is the most aggressive air pollution control package for cars and trucks," he said during the conference. "We are going to make tremendous advances, especially in California which will benefit the rest of the country after these goals are technologically met."[51]

In the fuels arena, the oil industry tried to undo previously agreed-to provisions in conference. The reformulated gasoline strategy was adopted by the industry as the lesser of two evils; as the preferred alternative to Bush's million-car mandate and methanol requirements. But during the House-Senate conference, Chevron lobbyist Dale Brooks charged that both the House and Senate went overboard with provisions to mandate both tough emissions standards and technically infeasible gasoline formulas. Working with the administration, the industry tried to introduce more flexible language into the final bill allowing fuels that would provide "equivalent benefits to be used in lieu of the mandated formula."[52] The conferees, however, didn't buy it.

The final negotiations on alternative fuels and reformulated gasoline, in fact, were quite extraordinary, involving "a two-day, around-the-clock meeting to resolve the final details with several chiefs of the US oil industry." In closed-door sessions in a congressional committee room, the meetings included top officials from Exxon and Mobil, plus the lobbyists from Amoco and the American Petroleum Institute to hash out the final details, which specified technical language for the cleaner fuels to be used. In the end, provisions were adopted in the bill to define the fuels—or at least the "base gasoline" to be used in building the standards—and included specifications ranging from API gravity and sulfur content to the percent of benzene contained.[53]

The plan that finally emerged required the oil industry to sell reformulated fuels that would cut ozone and toxic emissions by 15 percent in the nine smoggiest cities—but by 1995, not 1992 as originally sought. Another requirement for reformulated gasoline included 2.7 percent oxygen content for the forty cities that did not meet federal carbon monoxide standards. EPA, however, was given some leeway over deadlines and other considerations.

## NEW FUELS REGIME

When ARCO first came forward with its "new" reformulated gasoline in 1989, offering it as the substitute for new alternative alcohol fuels that George Bush had put forward, little did it realize what a big window it had opened up. The Bush administration started the ball rolling, but the oil industry certainly gave it a big push. "We put the quality of the gasoline into play in the clean-air debate," Bill Rosenberg would later observe. "That was fundamental." Indeed it was. Not only did politicians begin to see and understand that gasoline was part of the auto emissions problem and urban smog, they also began to see a whole new disturbing world of fuels toxicity. Industry asked for reformulated gasoline, and Congress gave it to them. What followed in the Clean Air Act, however, was the beginning of a whole new regulatory matrix devoted exclusively to gasoline and other automotive fuels.

With the exception of removing lead from gasoline in the 1970s, no regulatory action on the automobile's fuel had been taken. But that had changed. In addition to bringing detailed requirements for reformulated gasoline—including performance standards and specifications aimed at among other things, how much oxygen or benzene it contained, its potential to form nitrogen oxides and where certain formulas were to be used—the Clean Air Act Amendments of 1990 also identified automotive fuels as a key source of hazardous air pollutants (HAPs). "Most people, when they think of toxic chemicals, imagine them spewing out of plants and factories," explained EPA Mobile Sources director Dick Wilson in April 1990. "But it turns out that over half of the cancer incidence is caused by air pollution coming from cars."[54] Indeed, even the auto and oil industry would admit there was more chemistry involved than even they knew. "The gasoline power automobile has been around for a century now," said GM's J.M. Colucci and Mobil's J.J. Wise in launching the second phase of the joint auto-oil air quality research program in December 1990, "but we still know very little about the specific compounds that come out of the tailpipe."[55]

With the Clean Air Act's new fuels requirements, Congress, EPA, and state governments embarked on a continuing process of cleaning up gasoline. Shortly after the Clean Air Act was passed, California moved to tighten its reformulated gasoline, with tougher rules to go into effect in 1996. And as was shortly discovered in the battles that followed over standard-setting and rulemaking for reformulated fuels—including a very protracted and very bitter "Reg-Neg" (regulatory-negotiation) process—no one fuel was perfect. All had drawbacks of one sort or another.

Methanol and ethanol burn more completely than gasoline and release fewer hydrocarbons. They do not require some of the toxic aromatic additives that gasoline does. Cars run well on methanol, but the fuel contains only about half the energy of gasoline, is corrosive of engine parts, and releases formaldehyde, a possible carcinogen. Methanol fuels at 100 percent bring down emissions, but made from natural gas they become a global-warming worry. At certain mixtures (M-50 and M-25), methanol fuels would be highly evaporative and even worse than gasoline in ozone formation. Ethanol emits acetaldehyde and is heavily subsidized in its current use. If harvested from agricultural crops on a huge scale, ethanol could adversely affect land resources or compete for food crops. Fuels with higher oxygen content reduce carbon monoxide, but can also raise VOCs, NOx, and other toxic components. Oxygenated fuels also yield poorer fuel economy and do not always perform well in cold weather. CNG vehicles are low polluting, in fact perform better than both gasoline or methanol-powered vehicles in emissions and greenhouse gases, but have limited driving range, require large tanks, and expensive conversions.

"While none of these alternatives merit priority consideration in a long-range sustainable transportation plan," says Daniel Sperling, "alternative fuels for internal combustion engines can yield substantial reductions in urban air pollution, and in some cases less greenhouse gas emissions, thereby acting as bridge to hydrogen and fuel cells." Yet Sperling also adds, "the most powerful argument against these fuels is that because society can be expected to embrace a transition to a new fuel only once in a great while, pursuing alternative fuel may well divert attention from electric propulsion [including hybrid and fuel cell technologies], which promises greater and more lasting benefit."[56]

In addition, reformulated gasoline, for one, essentially shores up the internal combustion engine, especially since it "reinvests" in the ICE fueling infrastructure. Just as the 1970 Clean Air Act emissions regulations for the ICE itself had the effect of continuing the engineering emphasis on and investment in that engine technology, so too would the 1990 RFG rules and specifications do for the fuel system that serviced it. Certainly, there would be a public health benefit in all of this, as the air would become cleaner. Yet this 1990 congressional and White House battle over automotive fuels shows how difficult it is for society to disengage from an entrenched and dominant technology like the internal combustion engine. The ICE's fuels, however, would be cleaner, no question—but they would get even more political and regulatory attention in the future.

## BIG HEAT LOOMS

Although the environmental community had supported alternative fuels in the interest of cleaning up smog and pushing the development of cleaner cars, there was clearly apprehension about various fuel packages, and particularly the recognition that most of the alternative fuels—and especially RFG—would do little to address the carbon dioxide problem, at the heart of global warming.

"The bottom line," wrote Steve Nadis and James MacKenzie of the World Resources Institute, "is that clean gas is not a long-term solution, despite the environmental advantages it offers now. Since any form of gasoline contains the same amount of carbon as another other, changing the formula of gasoline would not lesson the greenhouse effect . . . nor would it help cut back significantly on oil imports." Nadis and MacKenzie added, "we should do everything possible to improve gasoline as long as we use it, keeping in mind that we will eventually have to switch to something better."[57]

Yet for both global warming and urban smog, there was a solution that had been around for a very long time: improved fuel economy—simply using less fuel in the first place, regardless of brew. But on that front, the legacy of resistance from the automakers was particularly deep and tenacious, with the biggest battles still ahead.

# 13
## Gas Guzzling

They spend all their money lobbying saying why they can't do it, and the Japanese go
ahead and do it.

—*US Senator Patrick Leahy (D-VT), 1991
on the Big Three and fuel economy*

On August 2, 1990, Saddam Hussein's Iraqi army invaded and annexed oil-rich
Kuwait. Within twenty-four hours of taking Kuwait, the Iraqis began massing on
the Saudi Arabian border, raising the specter that 45 percent of the world's oil reserves
might soon be controlled by Saddam Hussein. Five days later, American troops began
arriving in Saudi Arabia under operation Desert Shield to protect the Saudi oil fields
from possible Iraqi attack. On January 15, 1991, after Iraq failed to meet a United
Nations deadline to pull out of Kuwait, allied forces, led by the United States, launched
an air assault on Baghdad. A month later, Operation Desert Storm, the allied ground
assault, swept into Iraq and liberated Kuwait in less than four days.

With the opening shots of the war in August 1990, gasoline prices in the United
States rose 20 cents a gallon overnight. Crude oil prices remained volatile throughout the war and reached $40 a barrel in October 1990. The US stock market became
jittery with fears of energy driven inflation. At the time, America was consuming
about 16 million barrels of oil a day, or about 28 percent of world production. Nearly
half of US oil consumption, roughly 46 percent, was then imported. Cars and trucks
consumed the equivalent of about 80 percent of the imports—roughly 6 million barrels a day. Before long, automotive fuel economy became an important concern in
Washington, just as it had in the previous Middle East crises of the 1970s.

### FALTERING MPG

On one level, the automakers appeared to be making progress. Between 1974 and
1990, Detroit had raised the average gas mileage of its cars from about 13.2 MPG to
26.9 MPG. Yet the direction since 1986 had been in reverse. A rollback of the federal
fuel economy standards was sought by, and given to, the automakers by the Reagan

administration. By 1988, automotive fuel economy, on average, was going down by about 1 MPG a year.

As it happened, just as the Gulf War erupted, there was a bill in the US Senate that proposed to reverse the slide in fuel economy and, in fact, require much tougher national standards. The bill, S. 1224, sponsored by Senator Richard Bryan (D-NV), sought to reach 40 MPG by the end of the 1990s. Although the US automakers opposed the bill, with the Gulf War raging, the bill's proponents felt they had a good chance at passage—and making the first major improvements to the law in many years.

At the time of the Gulf War, the average fuel economy for American-made passenger cars was 26.9 miles per gallon. That was certainly better than it was at the time of the first Arab oil embargo of 1973-74, when the average American car got 13.2 miles to the gallon.* The improvement over the intervening seventeen years amounted to a doubling of fuel economy, but this averaged out to only about an 0.8 MPG improvement each year. The improvement, nonetheless, was owed largely to the Energy Policy and Conservation Act, or EPCA, passed by Congress in December 1975. EPCA established "Corporate Average Fuel Economy" standards, or CAFE standards (pronounced as in the French *café*).

## CAFE History

Under the law, each automaker's fuel economy level was the average rating for all of its cars, referred to as its corporate fleet average. That meant that if GM's Cadillacs got less than the requisite MPG for a given year, some other GM model would have to balance that, and so on through all models, yielding a fleet average that met the standard. Under EPCA, the initial CAFE standards were written into the law itself, set at 18 MPG for automobiles by 1978, 19 MPG in 1979, 20 MPG in 1980, rising to 27.5 MPG by the 1985 model year. However, after 1980, the Department of Transportation, through its National Highway Transportation Safety Administration (NHTSA, pronounced *nitsa*), was charged with setting the specific 1981-1984 MPG standards, as well as the 27.5 MPG standard for model years 1985 and beyond, unless the agency decided to modify it.**

In the first year of the program, 1978, GM became the leader, achieving 19 MPG— 1 MPG better than the standard. GM reduced the size of its cars. It took 9 inches off its wheelbase spread in luxury models, for example. Full-size models became midsize models, and midsize models shrank to compacts. For the next year, 1979, GM

---

* The 1974 new car average fuel economy for GM-made cars at the time was 12.2 MPG; for Ford, 14.2 MPG; and for Chrysler, 16.3 MPG. The imported fleet MPG average was then 22.2.

** When the 1975 law was enacted it allowed the secretary of transportation to adjust the 1985 target, reflecting a "maximum feasible" level depending on available technology, "economic practicability," and other factors, including the nation's energy needs. However, the secretary was required to set annual targets for 1981 through 1984 to ensure that automakers made steady progress toward the 1985 goal.

had plans for front-wheel drive, a manufacturing shift that would require no small change in related parts—new transmissions, braking systems, and axles. At about the same time, NHTSA had set the 1981-1984 CAFE standards at 22, 24, 26, and 27 MPG. GM and Ford promptly filed protests, contending the standards would require new, unproven technologies and would deprive customers of the utility and acceleration demanded in new cars. In January 1979, however, NHTSA rejected the automakers' protests, concluding they could meet the standards without significant change in the mix of car sizes then being sold.

During 1979 and 1980, the second oil embargo in a decade—this one brought about by the Iranian Revolution—sent America into another energy tailspin, pushing American drivers increasingly toward more fuel-efficient Japanese cars. The Big Three lost a 3.8 percent market share to the Japanese between 1979 and 1980. Still, GM met the 1980 CAFE standard, as its production of new fuel-efficient compact and subcompact models helped it do better than Ford and Chrysler. But all three automakers suffered big bottom-line losses due in part to the shifting market. The "import problem" suddenly became a national obsession, and the Japanese—under intense pressure from the Reagan administration and Congress—agreed to limit their US exports. The Big Three, meanwhile, had each added new kinds of domestically built small cars to their model lineups. But that's when a new round of fighting broke out between the automakers and consumer advocates over NHTSA's next level of fuel economy standards.

### CLAYBROOK'S 1981 NOTICE

Under EPCA, the CAFE standards set for model years 1985 and beyond would be 27.5 MPG unless NHTSA decided to modify it. The timing for NHTSA's review of this post-1985 requirement came precisely in the middle of a political sea change in Washington. Jimmy Carter had lost in a landslide to Ronald Reagan in the 1980 November elections with Republicans also taking the US Senate.

Joan Claybrook, a former Ralph Nader associate who had been NHTSA's administrator under Carter, issued a notice in January 1981 for a tough new set of post-1985 CAFE standards—reaching 48 MPG over the next decade. Claybrook's notice—issued in the waning days of the Carter administration—called for public comment and new information, and it also offered NHTSA's analysis detailing how additional gains in fuel economy could be made.[1]

First, Claybrook's notice found that the auto industry itself had projected on two earlier occasions—once in 1979 and once in 1980—that it would attain significantly higher fuel economy in the post-1985 period, reaching levels in excess of 30 MPG by 1985. Other automakers were also demonstrating significant gains with new models. Volkswagen, for example, had a four-seat turbocharged Rabbit with a diesel engine that achieved 60 MPG in a combined EPA test cycle. Assuming industry's 30 MPG post-1985 levels would continue to rise into the 1990s and using the industry's own 1985 plans and financial assumptions, NHTSA proceeded to sketch out a product development/new model scenario for the Big Three. The agency projected that average fuel economy for GM, Ford, and Chrysler could rise to more than 40 MPG by 1990 and over 48 MPG by 1995. Claybrook and NHTSA suggested these gains could be made through a number of production and technological improvements, including the mix of vehicle sizes; utilization of front-wheel-drive; weight-saving body construction; engine enhancement; transmission improvements; and other changes. Claybrook and NHTSA sought public and industry feedback on these findings.

Not surprisingly, the incoming Reagan administration withdrew Claybrook's notice three months later. "This action is being taken in recognition of the market pressures which are creating strong consumer demand for fuel-efficient vehicles and sending clear signals to the vehicle manufacturers to produce such vehicles," said Diane Steed, Claybrook's replacement at NHTSA. "It is expected that the market will continue to act as a powerful catalyst. Information available to this agency concerning the vehicle manufacturers' product plans for future model year vehicles demonstrate a strong commitment to improving fuel efficiency."* The Reagan administration, in fact, would later try, unsuccessfully, to abolish CAFE standards altogether.

## BACKSLIDING BEGINS

By 1982, with gasoline prices in a steady decline, consumers turned again to bigger cars with larger engines. Large car sales at GM rose from 55 percent of sales in 1980 to 61 percent in 1983—helping push the auto giant's profit that year to a record $2.8 billion. Yet, as GM responded to the big-car market its progress on fuel economy stalled. GM's CAFE dropped from 24.6 MPG in 1982 to 24 MPG in 1983—2 MPG below where it should have been. It slipped again in 1984 to 24.8 MPG, missing the goal of 27 MPG, facing the prospect of paying fines for its shortfall.

Under EPCA, failure to meet the MPG deadline in a given year meant stiff penalties: $50 a car for every one MPG a company's fleet fell below the standard, calculated in one-tenth MPG increments. But EPCA also provided some wiggle room: if a manufacturer's CAFE exceeded the fuel economy standard for a given class of vehicle in a particular year, the automaker could earn a "credit" for MPG achieved beyond the standard for that same vehicle class for up to three years in the future, or three years in the past.** Such credits could then be applied against any penalties

---

* The Center for Auto Safety (CAS) challenged NHTSA's withdrawal in May 1981. In September, NHTSA denied CAS's formal petition, afterwhich CAS took NHTSA to court. The court case, however, decided in June 1983, was dismissed (see, US Court of Appeals, District of Columbia Circuit, *Center for Auto Safety v. National Highway Traffic Safety Administration*, No. 81-2245, June 21, 1983).

** Originally, companies could use the MPG credits from one year in which they exceeded the goal and apply them to a shortfall in the year before or after. In 1980 Congress extended that to three years in either direction.

or fines that might be levied or threatened. GM had accumulated credits from previous years, so it didn't have to pay penalties for its 1984 models. However, by late 1984, GM realized it would not be able to meet the 1985 CAFE standard, and it was fresh out of accumulated credit. It had no penalty cushion. Ford faced a similar situation. At the time, GM could face as much as $500 million in fines and Ford $150 million.[2] The two companies' 1985 models would fall short of the 27.5 MPG standard: GM's cars to average 25.1 MPG and Ford, 25.5 MPG. "If we have to pay fines," said one GM spokesman at the time, "it will be with the capital that we need to develop more fuel-efficient cars." Ford mused that it might have to curtail production of its larger cars to raise its overall fuel economy average, "which would deprive our customers of a product they want."[3]

In June 1985, just as Ford and GM were about to be fined hundreds of millions of dollars for their expected CAFE shortfalls, EPA made an "adjustment" in its fuel economy testing procedure which, in effect, gave retroactive credits to Ford and GM for their 1981 through 1985 models.[4] This proved to be an especially timely rescue for the two automakers, although they maintained at the time the adjustment was just a coincidence, the result of legal action begun years earlier.* Others, however, saw it as a bailout. "EPA has adjusted upwardly by 0.3 to 0.8 MPG the CAFE's achieved by the auto companies from 1981 through 1985," explained Clarence Ditlow at an August 1985 public hearing at DOT. "[T]hese adjustments have effectively made the 27.5 MPG standard a far easier task for 1985-86." With the change, Ford went from owing a $112 million penalty at the end of the 1984 model year to having a $130 million credit, which more than made up for any deficit in the 1985 model year.[5] GM had a similar windfall. But the automakers wanted more.

## CHRYSLER TO THE RAMPARTS

Ford and GM had both petitioned NHTSA in March 1985 to reduce the 1986 CAFE standard to 26 MPG—1.5 MPG below the standard.** The two automakers claimed they hadn't anticipated the brisk sale of bigger cars, thus dragging down their CAFE levels. Chrysler, however, had mostly smaller cars in its fleet and opposed the reduction. The company had invested $5 billion in factories to build more fuel-efficient

---

* EPA actually recalculated the fuel economy ratings for passenger cars made by twenty-five manufacturers. The new ratings came about because of a 1981 decision made by the 6th Circuit Court of Appeals ordering EPA to recalculate the ratings to reflect changes in the fuel economy test procedure that had been made over the years.

** GM and Ford weren't the only automakers having trouble meeting fuel economy standards. In 1985, Mercedes could manage only 23.6 MPG, several points off the 27.5 MPG standard. During 1986-88, when Mercedes began introducing its gas-guzzling S-series, fuel efficiency dropped even farther from the US standard, to 21-22 MPG. Daimler-Benz paid $26 million in US fines for its violations.

cars, those with front-wheel drive, lighter parts, and some turbocharged four-cylinder engines. Chrysler's first quarter 1985 sales indicated the company was not being hurt for its commitment: its market share that quarter was up nearly 2 percent. But a CAFE rollback now for 1986 models would mean rewarding Ford and GM, thereby penalizing Chrysler. "Chrysler made the hard choices necessary to comply with the law," said Robert A. Perkins, a Chrysler VP in June 1985. "GM and Ford chose a different course. They should not be relieved of the consequences."[6] Chrysler was fighting for its life, having made a huge capital commitment to small- and medium-size cars.

In Washington, Chrysler officials urged the government to hold firm on CAFE. At an August 1985 NHTSA public hearing, for example, Chrysler's John D. Withrow, VP for product development, challenged GM's and Ford's contention that their CAFE problem was due to unforseen events and consumer demand that just "snuck up on them":

> ... by mid-1983 both GM and Ford were well aware that they would have trouble meeting both the 1984 and 1985 standards, given the technological paths they were then on. One has to ask: If GM and Ford knew in 1983 that they were going to miss the 1985 standard, how could NHTSA conclude that it took these companies until almost March 1st of this year [1985] to figure out that they were going to miss the 1986 standard?
>
> ... At Chrysler, we hold meetings almost monthly in which we project the company's future CAFE up to five years out, and when we see the market shifting, we take remedial action immediately to make sure we continue to meet the law. How is it that GM and Ford failed to recognize the same signals that we've been reading loud and clear for the last three years?. . . [7]

Chrysler's Robert S. Miller, Jr., executive vice president for finance and administration, charged that Ford and GM "failed to adequately reduce the weight of their cars and hung onto too many gas-wasting big engines and older transmissions."[8] Chrysler mounted a brief advertising campaign, featuring Lee Iacocca, touting its support for holding the line on existing CAFE standards, slamming GM and Ford.*

## "SHELL GAME"

Clarence Ditlow of the CAS, testifying at DOT's August 1985 hearing, pointed to past statements by both Ford and GM in which they had projected meeting and

---

* Chrysler, however, was no innocent. The company clearly did not support *increasing* the CAFE standards, and in earlier years, had petitioned NHTSA successfully for a reduction in light truck standards. It also paid a gas-guzzler tax on its bigger luxury cars. Still, Chrysler spent $225,000 on its pro-CAFE ads.

going beyond the 1986 CAFE standards. Now they were conveniently abandoning those projections. Ford stated in 1984 its cars would achieve 28.5 MPG by 1986; GM had stated its models would reach 27 MPG in 1986 and exceed 27.5 MPG by 1987. In addition, Ford and GM were also the beneficiaries of the June 1985 EPA adjustment in the mileage test rating and credits forthcoming under that change, which would also help them meet the standard. But now, charged Ditlow, Ford and GM were playing an elaborate shell game, adjusting sales mixes, extending old models and delaying new ones, and generally using "accounting tricks" to deflate their earlier MPG projections. Ditlow also charged that GM and Ford's use of a confidentiality proviso was hiding these adjustments from public view. Even *Automotive News* reporter Helen Kahn conceded, "While all of this is perfectly legal and may be both truthful and justified, the requests for confidentiality . . . do raise questions about why the companies' most recent filings find their CAFE numbers so much worse than only a short while before."[9]

Ditlow added that GM had clung to old rear-drive models, did not install fuel injection on many models as planned, and restricted the use of overdrive in other models—all of which would have added up to MPG gains. The Environmental Policy Institute, also appearing at the DOT hearings, found technological backsliding at Ford and GM in the early 1980s, the first years the automakers began to miss CAFE goals, with the average fleet weights increasing from 1982 to 1983, and fuel economy for several models decreasing. GM's Chevette, for example, dropped from 38.2 MPG in 1982 to 33.2 MPG in 1983. The Deville went from 18.6 MPG to 15.1 MPG.[10]

Ditlow argued that since 1976, CAFE and its enabling law EPCA had done their job well. Energy consumption was down, and so were foreign oil imports—saving $3 billion in 1980. Consumers were saving money, too; a 1985 new car buyer saved $3,300 in gasoline costs due to the CAFE standard. Now, GM and Ford were saying all of that was unimportant. All that mattered now, with low gasoline prices, was the sale of large cars. Consumers were clamoring for them. Yet there was more to it than just consumer demand, asserted Ditlow. The reason Ford wanted to keep cranking out its lumbering old rear-drive Ford LTDs and Crown Vics, and GM its Chevy Malibus and Caprices, was profit, pure and simple. The capital investment sunk into the production of these vehicles had already been recovered, with each car generating as much as $1,500 in profit in 1985. These big cars were cash cows, and the automakers were not about to give them up. They would maneuver in whatever way they could to keep them coming.[11] Ford and GM said they would have to close plants if they did not get relief from CAFE, putting 100,000 people out of work. In fact, domestic producers, they said, could be forced out of the large car market segment completely—a segment which the US producers led. But others, including Lee Iacocca, thought this reasoning disingenuous. "GM said they'd have to shut plants," observed Iacocca. "So why are they offering a 7.7 percent financing program [a very low rate at the time] on their big Cadillacs? That's taking $2,000 out of the price of those cars, and they're giving them away. I thought the public was demanding those cars."[12]

# "Dialing back fuel standards on cars will set up the American people to be energy hostages again and again."

*Lee A. Iacocca*

### Either some pages fell out of our history books, or some people just refuse to read them.

After the first energy crisis in 1973, the government established Corporate Average Fuel Economy standards (CAFE). The law required American car manufacturers to meet increasingly stringent mileage standards for the cars they sell in the U.S.

CAFE is saving billions of gallons of fuel a year. It's a conservation program that works.

But now, the U.S. Department of Transportation, at the urging of GM and Ford, has decided to roll back mileage standards for passenger cars. If we let it happen, America will be making a tragic mistake.

### America: Still hooked on oil.

America's economy still runs on oil, and three out of every ten gallons we use is imported. The nearly $60 billion we paid for foreign oil in 1984 was the single biggest item in our record trade deficit.

In 1979, our gasoline stocks dropped only 5 percent and almost caused panic. And the news is full of evidence that the foreign oil pipeline could be blown up tomorrow.

### Chrysler obeyed the law.

Chrysler Corporation obeyed the law on fuel-efficiency standards, and we did so at a time when we were on the verge of bankruptcy. We invested a record $4.8 billion to convert the overwhelming majority of our fleet to fuel-efficient, front-wheel drive powertrains.

On the other hand, why shouldn't people who prefer cars that are less fuel-efficient pay a tax for the privilege?

### Ignoring the law.

General Motors fell short of the 1984 standard by 2.2 miles per gallon. It produced 4.7 million cars in '84, and that means their fleet will use more than an extra 220 million gallons of fuel in the first year of driving alone. Over ten years, that fleet will consume more than 1.7 billion extra gallons of gasoline. And Ford's '84 fleet could waste almost another 500 million.

But if every car on the road in America averages 27.5 miles per gallon—the 1985 standard that Chrysler will meet—the U.S. would save more than 20 billion gallons of gasoline each year, or about four months of imported oil at current import levels.

Chrysler proved that the American auto industry can design and build vehicles that conserve energy without compromising performance, comfort or choice. Example: Chrysler pioneered the most fuel-efficient people mover of all, the mini-van. And the public response proves our point.

Chrysler is not depriving the American consumer of family-size sedans. As a matter of fact, Chrysler's percentage of mid-size or larger cars is higher than Ford's. And yet, Chrysler will meet the CAFE standard of 27.5 miles per gallon, but Ford won't.

### CAFE benefits you, the consumer.

The American consumer and the American public stand to benefit most from keeping CAFE.

CAFE holds our trade deficit down by reducing our dependence on foreign oil from unstable regions of the world.

CAFE gives the American automotive consumer a broader choice of fuel-efficient American cars.

### CAFE saves jobs.

And CAFE protects American jobs. If CAFE is weakened now, comes the next energy crunch American manufacturers will not be able to meet the demand for fuel-efficient cars...again. Americans will turn to fuel-efficient imported cars...again. And American workers—both in the auto industry and in the other industries that serve it—will be out on the street. Many of their jobs—as was true the last two times around—will disappear forever.

### The penalty for dialing back CAFE.

A CAFE dialback would penalize a company for obeying the law and reward those who ignored it.

And in the long run—when the next energy crisis hits—the CAFE rollback will penalize all of America.

### What's good for America.

The CAFE standard for passenger cars is the last vestige of an effective U.S. energy policy. Despite current supplies, America's energy future is still vulnerable. The choice is ours. We can open ourselves to yet another energy crisis, or we can keep an energy conservation program that works.

CAFE is good for America—and what's good for America should be good enough for America's automakers.

If you believe that energy conservation and fuel standards are important for America, please write to your U.S. Senators and Representatives and Mrs. Elizabeth Dole, U.S. Secretary of Transportation. You have only 10 days to make your opinions known in Washington.

## CHRYSLER CORPORATION

*Chrysler and Lee Iacocca, after making substantial investments in fuel-efficient cars, offered this 1985 response when Ford and GM moved to roll back CAFE standards.*

In the end, GM and Ford had their way. On October 1, 1985, NHTSA agreed to reduce the 1986 standard to 26 MPG.[13]

## FORD'S THREAT

No sooner had the NHTSA ruling relaxing the 1986 CAFE standards been issued, that Ford and GM, and their representatives in Washington, began agitating for relief beyond 1986. "One year of relief is not enough," said Jeffrey Conley, executive director of AutoChoice, a lobbying group working on behalf of the automakers. Conley argued that another rollback for the 1987 through 1989 model years was necessary "to avoid economic hardship to the domestic auto industry."[14] Ford Motor Co., however, was working another angle.

In November 1985, Ford chairman Donald Peterson in effect presented a threat to Elizabeth Dole, the secretary of transportation. If NHTSA did not lower CAFE standards for the 1987-1989 model years, Peterson explained, Ford would have to consider putting more "foreign content" into some of its big cars, namely its best-selling Crown Victoria and Lincoln Mercury Grand Marquis. Such a move would mean a loss of US jobs as well. Yet it was necessary, according to Ford, and perfectly legal. Under the law, a vehicle that had 75 percent US-Canadian content was considered an import, and imports were not subject to the same fuel economy standards as domestic cars were. Both the Crown Victoria and the Grand Marquis had an EPA rating of 16 MPG city, 23 highway, making them one reason why Ford would have problems meeting CAFE standards.[15]

Three months earlier, another Ford official, Louis Ross, executive vp for North American operations, said Ford was prepared to move engine production for its Crown Vic and Grand Marquis models to Mexico to avoid classifying these cars as domestically made.[16] In September 1985, Ford's board of directors voted to cut domestic content of the cars to at least 74 percent. "Our people hate like hell to implement that plan," said Peterson about the time he visited with Dole. "They obviously hope that, despite the board's action, they won't have to."[17] Ford, however, was still facing violations of the law in 1987 and beyond.

GM was also facing violations. GM cars would only achieve 26.3 MPG by 1987 and 26.9 by 1988. And once again, GM threatened to close its big-car plants rather than pay fines. GM had its workers write to DOT expressing their support for a further CAFE rollback—over 12,000 letters poured in. GM shareholders and dealers were writing, too. On Capitol Hill, nearly 100 congressmen, mostly those with auto plants in their districts, had also written DOT supporting further CAFE rollbacks. However, others on Capitol Hill were fighting the relief move. Senator Ernest Hollings (D-SC), one of EPCA's original sponsors, was concerned about weakening the statute. Senator Dan Evans (R-WA) said if further rollbacks occurred, he would seek legislation preventing the automakers from using mileage credits to offset penalties. In 1985, a similar bill Evans sponsored had passed the Senate but died in

## CLARENCE M. DITLOW

"I frankly don't think there's any place in America for a car that gets 15 miles per gallon," Clarence Ditlow told a reporter in the heat of a legislative battle over CAFE. For the last twenty-five years, Ditlow has been at the center of many fights with Detroit over fuel economy and other issues. He is head of the Center for Auto Safety in Washington, a nonprofit group founded by Ralph Nader and Consumers Union in 1970. Ditlow is a also a crusader for what might be called the "inherently safe" vehicle—a vehicle regardless of size that is engineered to protect its occupants in a myriad of clever ways.

The son of a Chevrolet service manager, who grew up in south-central Pennsylvania near Harrisburg, Ditlow went off to Lehigh University to study chemical engineering. Law degrees from Georgetown and Harvard followed. But it was what Ditlow saw first-hand as a engineering student in early 1960s Pennsylvania that stuck in his mind. On field trips to steel mills and chemical plants, he saw first-hand the daily safety and environmental risks faced by workers and nearby communities. Following law school in 1965, he came to Washington and went to work as an examiner in the US Patent Office, where he sharpened skills that would later serve him in challenging auto industry safety submissions. In 1971, he began working with Ralph Nader's Public Interest Research Group (PIRG) where he became one of the early activists prodding EPA on auto emissions standards. Five years later he became executive director of CAS and has been there ever since.

With his colleague, friend, and fellow Naderite, Joan Claybrook, head of Public Citizen, Ditlow has been involved in all the key auto safety fights of the last thirty years or so, including standard seat belts, three-point lap and shoulder belts, air bags, passenger car safety standards for light trucks and vans, child safety standards, and SUV safety. He has played a major role key legislation, such as the Magnuson-Moss Warranty Act, which holds manufacturers liable for certain repair costs, and the Energy Policy and Conservation Act, which established CAFE standards.

Ditlow has also pushed EPA and DOT enforcement actions and has played a major role in many recalls, such as 6.7 million Chevrolets for defective engine mounts; 1.5 million Ford Pintos for exploding gas tanks; 15 million defective Firestone 500 steel-belted radial tires; and 3 million defective Evenflow child safety seats. He has also led the fight to enact "lemon laws" in forty-six states.

Ditlow sees his mission and that of CAS as "socializing" the automobile. He's not out to ban the car, just improve it. He once told Lee Iacocca, a fellow Lehigh University alumnus, "when you stop making bad cars, we'll stop recalling them." Iacocca invited Ditlow into the inner sanctum of a Chrysler board meeting in March 1991, where Ditlow presented his case for safer cars and trucks.

If there is a key concept Ditlow would place in the forefront of safety policymaking it is "crashworthiness," and the belief that even in the smallest cars occupants can be protected by building-in—through better engineering—improved structural and other safety features. On the big car-small car question, and the growing number of SUVs, Ditlow maintains that all the extra weight of the bigger vehicle doesn't really offer its occupants proportionally greater protection than smaller cars. But SUVs do pose more risk to the occupants of smaller vehicles. He calls them "urban assault vehicles." Higher off the ground, SUVs pose a special risk to smaller cars, as they can "ride over" the smaller vehicle's side impact beams. But the big issue, for both Ditlow and Joan Claybrook and many of their safety colleagues, is the weight differential among vehicles out on the highways today. Combining the growing number of SUVs and light trucks with the loosened speed limits of recent years is a recipe for more violent accidents and continued loss of life. The goal, as Ditlow and Claybrook see it, is to even out the weight differential, and that means reducing the weight and size of bigger vehicles, not increasing the size of smaller ones.

Today, Ditlow believes his work, and that of his staff, is to help the auto industry become more competitive, not less. In fact, Ditlow will point out to anyone who will listen that safety and fuel economy regulations have helped the industry improve its technologies, and thereby, its competitive position. Among improvements CAS is still seeking are antilock brakes as standard equipment; higher crash standards to prevent serious injury; prohibiting secret warranties; requiring manufacturers to publicize widespread defects; increasing CAFE to 50 MPG (at least); and improving highway design.

CAS receives 30,000 to 50,000 complaints and queries from automobile consumers annually. Among the publications dispensed to its members and the public are the *Car Book*, an annual assessment of new models, and the *Lemon Book* which gives advice to owners of problem-plagued cars. Ditlow and his lawyers are not only in demand to help disgruntled consumers, and frequently appear as expert witnesses in automobile liability and personal injury cases, they are also important players in the front lines of federal policymaking, pushing the government to uphold its laws.

Described by the *New York Times* in 1997 as "the splinter the industry cannot remove from its thumb," Ditlow is shown grudging respect by his adversaries in Detroit on occasion, though sometimes he is treated with derision by a few or cast as a lone voice on the shrill fringe. Yet Clarence Ditlow is an engineer at heart; a thoughtful advocate who believes the world can be made a safer place through ingenuity, talent, and determination.

House-Senate conference. During that debate Evans found some inconsistency in the automakers's "free market" positions. The auto companies' "response to competition from Japan," he said, "was to cry out for import restrictions. Now they are saying let the market decide whether fuel efficiency standards are required."[18] Others saw the automakers rolling over public policy. "If all the statute is designed to do is ratify what GM and Ford want to do on their own, there isn't much purpose to the statute," charged C.F. Hitchcock, an attorney with Public Citizen. "The statute is designed to be market forcing."[19]

In early October 1986, NHTSA agreed to a second CAFE rollback, reducing the 1987 and 1988 requirements to 26 MPG and extending the deadline for 27.5 MPG to 1990. Thus, the original 1985 goal of EPCA—setting a 27.5 MPG CAFE standard for 1985—was now pushed back five years. "DOT's decision to roll back the 1987 and 1988 standards to 26 MPG makes a mockery of the law," said Lee Iacocca. "For a long-lead-time industry like ours, this kind of eleventh-hour decision is unfair to manufacturers who have based their product plans on federal standards established several years ago."[20]

Emboldened by their 1985 and 1986 victories at NHTSA, GM and Ford did not stop with these rollbacks. By August 1988, with their 1989 models poised on their assembly lines, officials of Ford and GM met with DOT secretary James Burnley seeking to relax the CAFE standard for those models. A month later, Ford vice chairman Harold Poling told an audience in Cleveland that fuel economy standards should be relaxed so that American automakers could better compete with foreign manufacturers.[21] GM's president Robert Stempel told the Detroit Economic Club that large-car and station wagon assembly plants in Texas and Georgia were vulnerable to closing unless the CAFE standard was relaxed again. GM might be forced to cut 60,000 jobs in 1989 and 110,000 jobs in 1990, and other plants in Michigan and Missouri might have to close as well. The higher CAFE standard, said Stempel, would "affect American employment not just in assembly plants but in plants that manufacture engines, seats, and components."[22] Congressman Bob Carr (D-East Lansing) was also helping to push for more auto industry relief. "If I were a Japanese auto manufacturer and I wanted to write a law in the United States that would help me and hinder American automakers, I couldn't write a better law than CAFE," said Carr.[23] GM's Stempel, in fact, stated in September 1988 that "the CAFE law should be repealed," calling, in the interim, for a rollback of the 1989 standards.[24] In early October 1988 he got his wish: DOT once again rolled back the 27.5 MPG standard to 26.5 MPG for 1989 models.[25]

What had gone almost completely unnoticed in the CAFE and auto emissions debates, however, was that these programs were helping to make America more competitive with the Japanese. The regulatory programs, in fact, were a key factor in forcing innovation within the US auto industry. Looking back on the programs, three analysts from the Massachusetts Institute of Technology's International Motor Vehicle Program—C. Kenneth Orski, Alan Altshuler, and Daniel Roos explained that although the American automakers "had doubted the 1985 CAFE standards could be achieved without size and performance sacrifices that the public would find unacceptable, foreign companies led the way in demonstrating that the combination of excellent performance and low fuel consumption was both technically feasible and attractive in the market." Further, had it not been for the government's intervention with CAFE and emission regulations, noted the MIT auto analysts, "the [American] automotive sector would be even worse off [via the Japanese competition]...." Inside Detroit, in fact, a mini-revolution was going on precisely because of the government regulations. "[P]ractically every recent move by US automakers to adopt advanced features—lightweight metals, high-strength plastics, electronic ignition management devices—can be traced to the influence of government regulations."[26]

## THE RISING HEAT

After the November 1988 election of George Bush, the anti-environment rhetoric and practice of the Reagan era establishment gradually began to move to more moderate middle ground. George Bush, during his 1988 campaign and the first year of his presidency, began responding to heightened public concerns about the environment. The fuel economy issue became part of this new politics, especially as concern over global warming began to emerge.

Prior to the election, in June 1988, during one of the hottest summers on record, Congress heard NASA scientist James Hansen declare that the greenhouse effect "has been detected, and it is changing our climate now." Hansen told his listeners he was "99-percent confident" that the continued rise in global temperature was not just a random event, but a real sign that global warming was underway. By early 1989, air pollution was still a major problem in many US cities. Los Angeles proposed one of the strictest air pollution control plans in the nation, calling for heavy use of alternative fuels in automobiles by the 1990s and even eliminating the gasoline engine by 2007. Then in March 1989, the *Exxon Valdez* oil tanker ran aground off Alaska, spilling millions of barrels of crude oil into pristine Prince William Sound. All of this served to heighten public concern over the environment and the nation's rising use of, and dependency on, fossil fuels. But thanks to the CAFE rollbacks of the 1980s, the fuel efficiency of America's cars and trucks had begun to decline. Meanwhile, a coalition of eighteen environmental groups had asked that CAFE be raised to 45 MPG, now suggesting global warming as an additional reason for pushing fuel economy.

Congress, too, had become noticeably more active on environmental issues, introducing a number of bills that incorporated automotive fuel economy provisions. Representative Claudine Schneider (R-RI) had already introduced the Global Warming Prevention Act in the House with 123 cosponsors. Schneider's bill, among other things, called for the equivalent of 45 MPG for cars and 35 MPG for light trucks by 2000, with a prohibition on any rollback of targets. Representative Barbara Boxer (D-CA) had also introduced a bill calling for CAFE standards to rise to 45 MPG by 2004. On the Senate side, Tim Wirth's National Energy Policy Act with thirty-three cosponsors and Al Gore's (D-TN) World Environment Policy Act also called for extending CAFE standards. Max Baucus (D-MT) had introduced the Global Environmental Protection Act whose transportation section called for 50-percent reduction in auto $CO_2$ emissions by the year 2000, at which point average automotive fuel economy would reach 55 MPG. Among all of these measures, however, it would be Richard Bryan's bill, S.1224, that would become the main focal point for legislative sparring. The Bryan bill, as it came to be called, proposed a 20 percent increase in fuel economy by 1995 and a 40 percent improvement by the year 2001.

Initially, George Bush's secretary of transportation, Samuel Skinner, was also supporting an "increase" in the CAFE standard—or more correctly, restoring it to where it should have been by 1985: at 27.5 MPG. By May 1989, other administration officials from the Department of Energy and EPA were also talking about improved automotive fuel economy, reducing America's energy dependence, and reducing greenhouse gas emissions.[27]

All of this activity caused the automakers to back off some of their Reagan era stridency. General Motors, for example, had previously urged that fuel economy requirements be abolished altogether. By May 1989, GM began a somewhat toned-downed approach. "Right now I'm saying let's not make them [CAFE standards] any more stringent," said James D. Johnston, then vice president of industry-government relations. Johnston admitted GM's new position was "an adaptation to current realities."[28] Ford Motor was also sounding conciliatory. "You can't just simply come forward and talk about all the things you can't do," explained Helen Petrauskas, Ford's vice president for environmental and safety engineering. "If you want to participate in the shaping of public policy, you have to step forward and contribute to the solution, or else you can't be a player. . . ."[29] Consumer and environmental groups insisted technology was available, offering proof that relatively painless gains could be made. Still, Ford and GM opposed higher CAFE standards in Senate testimony, arguing that such standards would limit consumer choice and reduce US competitiveness.

## SUPPLIER PUSH

Meanwhile, in something of a surprise move, auto suppliers began to speak out on fuel economy. The industries that sold Detroit raw materials and other components were becoming concerned about the automakers' hard line on CAFE. The suppliers felt the Big Three should take a proactive position on fuel economy and emissions before the federal government forced them to do it. [30] An August 1989 survey of US auto suppliers revealed they would have no problem meeting a 45 percent improvement in fuel economy: domestic cars could meet fuel economy goals of 33 MPG by 1995 and 41 MPG by 2000. This position came in stark contrast to the Big Three's opposition to meeting those kinds of numbers. "The survey results are surprising because of the attitude it reveals among the supplier industry," said Earl Landesman, with A.T. Kearney, Inc., the consulting firm conducting the survey. "They're very gung-ho to meet the challenge. The public has the impression that the auto industry is running out of steam on improving fuel efficiency because there hasn't been much progress in the past two years. But here's the supplier industry saying it's their responsibility, too, and they can do it."[31]

The suppliers believed that weight reduction throughout various vehicle components was one key way to achieve the needed fuel economies. Lighter metals for chassis components, casting and wheels, as well as some use of new plastic compounds, developed jointly with the carmakers, could all make a difference. "Everybody tends to look at the powertrain for the answer," explained Landesman, still citing his survey

## TOYOTA VS. FORD: 1988

In May 1989 Senate testimony, Clarence Ditlow of CAS offered one very clear example of how existing technology—in this case, multi-valve engines—could make a significant difference in automotive fuel economy without sacrificing size, speed, or quality. He compared a similar-sized Ford Tempo with a Toyota Camry, the major difference being the Camry's use of multi-valve technology.

"The 4-valve Camry is nearly 100 pounds heavier than the Tempo but gets almost 20 percent better fuel economy and does 0-60, a full 1.6 seconds faster than the Tempo," said Ditlow. "Toyota has found this technology so impressive that all its 1988 models were 3 or 4 valves per cylinder." Here are the numbers Ditlow presented in his table "Benefits of 4-Valve Per Cylinder Technology:"

| | 1988 Toyota Camry | 1988 Ford Tempo | Comparison Tempo-to-Camry |
|---|---|---|---|
| Curb weight | 2810 lbs | 2721 lbs | -4% |
| Engine size | 122 cu. in. | 140 cu. in. | +15% |
| Camshaft | DOHC | OHC | — |
| Valves/cylinder | 4 | 2 | — |
| Output power | 115 HP @ 5200 RPM | 100 HP @ 4400 RPM | -15% |
| Torque | 125 ft.lb @ 4400 RPM | 130 ft.lb @ 2600 RPM | +4% |
| Interior volume | 89 cu. ft. | 90 cu. ft. | 0 |
| Trunk volume | 12 cu. ft. | 13 cu. ft | 0 |
| Transmission type | 5-spd. manual | 5-spd. manual | — |
| Axle ratio | 3.74 | 3.75 | 0 |
| *Performance(seconds)* | | | |
| 0-30 MPH | 2.9 | 3.3 | +14% |
| 0-60 MPH | 9.2 | 10.8 | +17% |
| 0-k mile | 17.0 | 17.8 | +5% |
| 30-50 MPH (top gear) | 14.2 | 14.6 | +3% |
| 50-70 MPH (top gear) | 16.2 | 15.3 | -7% |
| *Fuel Economy (MPG)* | | | |
| EPA city | 28.8 | 23.1 | -20% |
| EPA highway | 41.7 | 36.3 | -12% |
| EPA combined | 33.3 | 27.6 | -17% |

Source: *Car and Driver* and "EPA 1988 Test Car List"

results, "but the majority think that weight reduction is the first key." They also pointed to additional efficiency gains through engine enhancements, the development and wider use of alcohol fuels, improved aerodynamics, and, only as last resort, vehicle downsizing. The suppliers emphasized they did not want to return to the day of poor performing "econo-boxes" that gave American cars a bad name.

But the bottom line for these suppliers was business, pure and simple. They were worried about their economic future if US automakers dug in their heels and were suddenly caught off guard by new law. If Congress were to require a 50 MPG standard, for example, the suppliers believed they and Detroit would lose business. The Japanese automakers, European plastic producers, and automotive electronic manufacturers would be the winners. US losers would include the Big Three, steel companies, and stamping and casting firms, among others.

Back in the US Senate, hearings were held in September 1989 on the Bryan bill, with the Big Three opposing any CAFE increase. Howard Metzenbaum (D-OH), for one, reminded the automakers of their 1974 prediction that new mileage standards would force them to produce only Pinto-sized subcompacts by 1985. "The automakers were obviously dead wrong," said Metzenbaum. Senator Bryan added, "Their testimony now is almost a carbon copy of their testimony in 1974, the thrust of which is: It can't be done." Environmentalists meanwhile, were pushing for tougher standards, pointing to available technology. "The technology that will be required to achieve a 45-miles-per-gallon fuel economy standard is already on the shelf and is just not being put on the cars by most of the manufacturers," said the Sierra Club's Dan Becker. "These are not exotic technologies."[32]

## NEVADA POLITICS

Senator Bryan, meanwhile, was being targeted by the auto industry for early retirement. In his first year in the US Senate, the fifty-two-year-old former Nevada governor had taken on fuel economy almost from the day he arrived. Not long thereafter, however, Bryan began hearing from angry constituents. In early 1990, a group of local citizens and businessmen calling itself Nevadans for Fair Fuel Economy Standards began writing to fellow Nevadans urging them to contact Bryan and other Nevada politicians about the senator's fuel economy bill. They opposed the measure and took the position that it would mean the demise of large cars in America. This campaign had all the appearances of a grassroots operation until it was disclosed that Nevadans for Fair Fuel Economy Standards was organized and funded by a Big Three consultant, the FMR Group of Washington, DC.[33]

At least two of the citizens whose names were used on the group's letterhead told a *Detroit Free Press* reporter they did not know the campaign was organized by the Big Three. One, George Balaban, owner of Desert Cab Co. of Los Vegas, said he probably would have participated even if he knew the Big Three were involved, but still resented not being told. "I don't think that's fair," he said. "I can guarantee you that the guy who talked to me did not tell me that the auto industry was involved."[34]

"I'm just astounded," said Tim Ransdell, the FMR organizer who went to Nevada to orchestrate the campaign. "I told them right off the bat I was working for the three automakers, Chrysler, Ford, and GM. That was always the first or second thing I said to them." Another businessman who lent his name to Nevadans for Fair Fuel

Economy Standards—Thomas Bordigioni, owner of a recreational vehicle company in Reno—said he was also not informed about the campaign's sponsors. "I'm not happy about that," he said. "I feel like I was misled." GM's William Noack, speaking for the Big Three, said FMR was instructed to disclose the automakers' role. Bryan was also notified when the campaign began, according to the automakers.[35]

Senator Bryan, although not bothered by anyone coming into his state to fight him on an issue, was not happy with how the Big Three conducted themselves. "The troubling aspect of the auto manufacturers efforts," he said, "is that they came into my state under false colors. They put out a misleading mailing; they failed to disclose their organizing and financing of this effort."[36]

On April 3, 1990, Bryan's bill (S. 1224) was approved by the Senate Commerce, Science, and Transportation Committee by a 14-4 margin.

### 1990 FLOOR VOTE

As the Bryan bill headed for the Senate floor, it still called for 40 MPG by the end of the 1990s. "That would be disastrous," said David Cole of the University of Michigan of the MPG goal. "That would hand the market to the Japanese." Ford Motor's David Hagen, general manager of the company's engine division, acknowledged that some improvement in CAFE was likely, but going to 40 MPG was "ridiculous" and would eliminate anything bigger than "compact and subcompacts."[37] Ford and General Motors opposed Bryan's bill outright, while Chrysler asked for more gradual changes. Still, Bryan's bill seemed to have a good chance.

Iraq's invasion of Kuwait in August 1990 helped the prospects for the bill. On September 14, 1990 it received a favorable 68-to-28 vote on a procedural question whether to consider the bill, which George Bush had threatened to veto. But the procedural vote signaled that Bryan had enough votes to both override a veto and cut off a filibuster—the two most likely threats. Bryan's seeming advantage, however, would soon erode. At a hastily called press conference after the September 14 vote, Secretary of Transportation Samuel K. Skinner stated, "The goal set in the Bryan legislation is completely unrealistic, irresponsible, and more important, unattainable from a technology viewpoint."[38] Yet in France, a Citroen AX-10 was capable of getting 76 MPG at highway speeds of 56 MPG and a Honda Civic then being sold in the US was capable of 55 MPG. The Bush administration—which was more aggressive on auto emissions—sided with the auto industry on fuel economy, and together, they stepped up the lobbying heat on a few targeted senators. By twisting arms in the Senate, Bush and the Big Three began to peel away senators from Bryan's side one by one.

By the time the Bryan bill was scheduled for floor action, Senator Donald Riegle (D-MI), working on behalf of his Detroit constituents, was signaling his intent to add amendments to reduce the bill's appeal and prevent it from coming to vote. The political geography of the auto industry beyond Michigan was also working its will.

New auto assembly plants had begun operating in Tennessee, Delaware, and California, which coupled with the new Japanese plants in Kentucky and Ohio, which affected some votes. Bryan soon lost his filibuster-proof margin. "What cost us the vote of [Senator Jim] Sasser was the Nissan and GM plants in Tennessee," recounted US PIRG lobbyist Bill Magavern. "In Ohio, [Senator Howard] Metzenbaum is a big supporter, but auto plants there cost [Senator John] Glenn's vote."[39] Bryan and his cosponsors saw the writing on the wall and soon withdrew their bill, essentially killing the measure for the 101st Congress.[40] Bryan was clearly not happy. "Every parent of a son or daughter in the Persian Gulf ought to ask his congressman, 'What's your plan to reduce our dependency on foreign oil?'" he said after pulling his bill. Bryan believed that addressing fuel economy in the nation's cars and trucks was the most direct way of getting at America's increasing dependence on foreign oil. He vowed to return with his bill the following year.

### BIG 3 HYPOCRISY

Even as the Big Three fought furiously to kill the Bryan bill in 1990, they used Madison Avenue to sell their cars on the basis of, above all things, their "fuel efficiency." Most of the claims, even for luxury cars, were blatantly deceptive and misleading.

In September 1990, for example, on the heels of Iraq's invasion of Kuwait, Chrysler and General Motors both made adjustments to already completed advertisements, adding new taglines to the ads that touted the featured car's fuel efficiency. One Cadillac ad, for example, used the line "The EPA estimated 26 MPG highway [rating] is the highest highway mileage of any V-8 powered luxury automobile." Peter R. Levin, Cadillac's director of marketing, was reportedly worried that potential Cadillac buyers would fear being branded as irresponsible for their choice of car. GM proceeded to tout the 1991 EPA highway MPG estimate for the Cadillacs in a series of TV and print ads featuring the De Ville, Fleetwood, Eldorado, and Seville models. Although the 26 MPG EPA estimate was used prominently in the adjusted ads, GM did not bother to disclose in the ads the Cadillacs' 16 MPG estimate for city driving. In fact, the combined rating for these Caddy models was only 20 MPG, well below the 1990 national average rating of 28 MPG. GM had also run Buick and Oldsmobile ads touting these models' fuel efficiency, even though in both of these cases, the models used could not match the national average 28 MPG.[41]

Consumer and environmental groups were furious. US PIRG in Washington issued a stinging review of GM and other ads featuring their cars' so-called fuel efficiencies. "At the very same time as General Motors' lobbyists were telling Congress that Americans did not want to purchase fuel-efficient cars, GM's marketers were trying to sell consumers on the efficiency of their luxury cars." The Middle East crisis and high oil prices had once again provided a grim reminder of America's vulnerability to oil supplies. "Did GM respond by easing its opposition to fuel-saving legislation, or by telling its engineers to design more efficient vehicles?" asked

PIRG. "No. Instead, GM marketers repackaged gas-guzzlers as socially responsible cars, and sought to soothe the conscience of buyers with the message that Cadillac's cars are as 'responsible to own and they are responsive to drive.'" Auto industry lobbyists, meanwhile, dug in their heels on Capitol Hill and refused to budge from their position that fuel-efficient cars would not sell.[42] The CAFE fight, however, was far from finished.

## BRYAN BILL II

In late January 1991, when the 102nd Congress convened, America and its allies were still in Kuwait, approaching the date for a planned ground assault on the Iraqi army. Introducing S.279 as Desert Storm assault loomed, Senator Bryan said his new CAFE bill would "begin the process of changing the conditions that make us so dependent on the unstable Middle East." Achieving the fuel economy standards in his bill, he said, would reduce America's energy consumption by 2.5 million barrels per day by the year 2005 and also reduce carbon dioxide emissions by 440 million tons annually.

US automakers, recognizing that public sentiment over the war had raised the prospects for fuel economy legislation, embarked on a multiple-front strategy to insure some control over the outcome. First and foremost, they claimed that meeting the Bryan standard was technologically impossible without drastically downsizing large cars. Second, on the House side, John Dingell and his ally, Phil Sharp (D-IN), chairman of the House Commerce Subcommittee on Energy and Power, were crafting a more modest fuel economy bill that could be used to counter Bryan's bill if it emerged from the Senate. Third, Senator Bennet Johnston (D-LA) was crafting an omnibus energy bill of his own that might also be used to water down or derail Bryan's attempt. Fourth, the auto industry would push amendments to any CAFE bill requiring that DOT have the sole authority to specify CAFE standards, not Congress.[43] And finally, if CAFE standards were to pass, the Big Three had already assured that each manufacturer would boost its CAFE by the same percentage, as distinct from the "specified MPG number approach" used in the 1970s.* Even at that, the percentage increase in the Bryan bill was too much for the automakers. "Over the next seven years," wrote General Motors in March 1991 comments to the Senate Energy Committee,

---

*This ploy was aimed primarily at penalizing the Japanese, who by this time had no trouble selling smaller cars and were in fact now competing in the luxury car market with more upscale Lexuses and Acuras. "No one will come right out in their statements and say we're bashing the Japanese on this, but that's definitely part of the strategy," explained one congressional source in May 1991. "Detroit, behind closed doors, will say if Congress is going to do something on CAFE, it had to be a percentage increase, because that helps us." Foreign automakers called this provision, already in the CAFE bills, "a big protectionist boondoggle." See Margaret E. Kriz, "Going the Extra Mile," *National Journal*, May 11, 1991.

"we see no technologies, not currently commercialized, that would improve fuel savings . . . anywhere near the percentage being proposed."[44]

US automakers and dealers were painting all kinds of scenarios if tough CAFE standards were enacted. GM vice president James D. Johnston claimed that mergers would occur* and that companies would take losses to lower their corporate fuel averages. "We think CAFE is flawed," he said, "and when you fix it, it's like fixing the income tax." GM and other automakers maintained that CAFE itself wasn't responsible for the fuel savings of the 1970s and 1980s. Higher gasoline prices were. Senator Bryan disagreed: "public policy" was the reason automotive fuel economy had moved from 13.2 to 27.5 miles per gallon. Over at the US Department of Energy (DOE), a May 25, 1990 internal memo to Carmen Difliglio, then DOE's director of energy demand policy, concluded, "The CAFE standards have worked; the industry responded to CAFE (and rising fuel prices) by delivering greater technology-based fuel economy without sacrificing consumer need or reducing transportation activity. Over two million barrels per day of fuel are being saved because of this increased fuel economy."[45]

But by this time, even Honda, which had itself become a more upscale car producer in America, had joined the chorus of naysayers. "It is our estimate that a 4 percent improvement in CAFE is all that is achievable by the refinement of existing technologies," said Thomas Elliot, executive vice president for operations at American Honda in February 1991. "Any increase greater than that will require us to downsize those models with the highest sales volume. . . . We do not believe consumers are ready to accept such a big change in vehicle size and performance, especially when accompanied by price increases which are inevitable."[46] Ford's Peter Pestillo, vice president for corporate relations, put it more bluntly, "Reducing size and weight is the only way to achieve significant additional improvements. That is the law of physics, not policy." Proponents of improved fuel economy disagreed. Improvements, they maintained, were found in technology—technology the automakers were choosing not to deploy.

## Big-Car Baloney

"A lot of the big car-little car arguments in terms of CAFE are baloney," said Steven E. Plotkin, then a senior associate with the congressional Office of Technology Assessment (OTA). Plotkin believed that some of the technologies used to boost accel-

---

*Walter Huizenga, then president of the American International Automobile Dealers Association, also talked of mergers. "I guarantee you're going to see a revamping of the industry that has not been seen since the end of the Second World War" if the Bryan bill passed, he warned. "Companies will acquire companies simply to acquire their CAFE standards or to acquire the production of a given model to shift their CAFE mix." In either case, he said, "nothing will be done to save fuel." Kriz, "Going the Extra. . . ," p. 1095.

eration could be used to save fuel. "The perfect example is the four-valve engine, which allows you to get more power out of an engine with the same displacement."

An April 1991 review of CAFE from 1974 through 1991 completed by the Center for Auto Safety found, in part, that CAFE improvements over that period came largely from technology, not small cars. CAS found, for example, that 86 percent or 11.8 MPG of the 13.8 MPG improvement during that period came from technologies; 13.1 percent or only 1.8 MPG from weight savings; and only 1.4 percent or 0.2 MPG came from a shift to smaller cars.[47]

The American Council for an Energy-Efficient Economy (ACEEE), a nonprofit organization focused on improving national energy efficiency, concurred. "It is technologically feasible to achieve a level of fuel economy by the year 2000 of about 44 miles per gallon, . . ." said the group in Senate testimony. "[And] to reach 40 MPG, it would cost $700 per car." The automakers countered that long planning lead times— five years in most cases—precluded the technological improvements ACEEE cited.

## COALITION FOR VEHICLE CHOICE

By early spring 1991, the Big Three had begun to unleash a multimillion dollar lobbying and "grassroots" organizing campaign built around the Coalition for Vehicle Choice (CVC)—the brainchild of the Washington public relations and lobbying firm of Bruce Harrison & Co. In addition, the Big Three's trade group, the MVMA, had also hired the Bruce Harrison group for $500,000. Before long, former NHTSA official Diane Steed was hired to head up the CVC at $12,000 a month. CVC soon added a number of groups to its cause, including major parts suppliers and their trade associations, and practically any organization that had the need of a motor vehicle, from the National Cattlemen's Association and the American Farm Bureau, to the Association of Chiefs of Police and the American Recreation Association.[48] Before long, the CVC would spend $8 million on the anti-Bryan CAFE effort, launch a nationwide media blitz, and enlist more than 200 groups into the CVC.

Separately, the Big Three also began using their executives in appealing to the media, politicians, and the public, which Micheline Maynard of *USA Today* described as "a furious two months of US auto industry image building and support seeking in Washington." The chief targets were the Bryan bill and the Japanese competition. In March 1991 the Big Three executives—GM's Robert Stempel, Ford's Harold Poling, and Chrysler's Lee Iacocca—met with George Bush seeking White House support on the continuing Japanese import problem. In May, the industry flew two planes full of congressmen to Detroit for a tour of Big Three operations. Then in early June 1991, as fuel economy and national energy policy were being debated in Congress, Stempel, Iacocca, and Poling made an unprecedented joint appearance on Ted Koppel's *Nightline*, which ran a special one-hour show on the automakers. Their TV appearance was used to puff up Detroit's image, boasting on the air that their operations and products had improved. "We're not whining," said Stempel.

"We're doing something about it.... When you look for fuel economy, US makers lead. When you look for safety, US makers lead."[49] In the aggregate, however—especially on fuel economy— US makers did not lead. The Japanese did.

Senator Bryan, meanwhile, was open to negotiating with the industry on his bill, but the automakers weren't willing to talk. "We'd be willing to consider what Detroit says they can do," offered Bryan in May 1991, "but there has been a real reluctance on their part to talk."[50] The automakers and the Coalition for Vehicle Choice (CVC) were trying to sink Bryan's bill, period. CVC's opening salvo against the new bill was that it would "limit consumer choice to mostly smaller and lighter models," as Diane Steed put it, repeating the industry's 1970s mantra.[51] Then came the safety scare.

## SCARE TACTICS

In 1991, NHTSA released some new auto safety studies. These studies "indicated that occupants of smaller, lighter cars were more likely to suffer serious or fatal injury ... than occupants of larger heavier cars, . . ." according to Jerry Curry, then NHTSA administrator. Curry testified in February 1991 before a Senate committee that NHTSA's studies "indicated that over 1,300 fatalities and 6,300 serious injuries occur annually as a result of the [automobile] downsizing." NHTSA estimated that the 1,000 pounds eliminated from the fleet's average curb weight between 1975 and 1982 reduced highway safety below levels that would have been achieved without the downsizing.[52]

CAFE proponents and auto safety advocates countered with a new round of data. In April 1991, CAS and MCR Technology of Goleta, CA—using DOT vehicle safety data—released "The Safe Road to Fuel Economy," which found that since 1974, the traffic fatality rate dropped 40 percent from what it had been in 1990. What had occurred over that time span, this study asserted, was an improvement in the crashworthiness of smaller cars *and* improved fuel economy—especially in models such as the VW Rabbit and the Honda Civic. Safety proponents maintained all along that both fuel economy and vehicle safety could be improved simultaneously, that the technologies were different. "Another CAFE boost would give manufacturers a second opportunity to implement advanced safety technologies like airbags, padded interiors, high-strength/low-weight materials [special side-door safety glass], and anti-lock brakes."

"In crashes," Clarence Ditlow would often explain, "what is important is whether the occupant survives the crash, not whether the car survives the crash." All cars, small and large, he asserted, could be made much safer through technological improvements to their structures and interiors—without sacrificing fuel economy. But what really infuriated the consumer groups, however, was the discovery that Transportation's Samuel Skinner and NHTSA administrator Curry were involved in staging big-car/small-car crashes, filming those crashes, and distributing the videos around the country to make the case against CAFE standards—and specifically, suggesting that improving such standards would endanger lives.

Photos of the DOT-run crashes appeared in full-page newspaper ads run by the CVC. A CVC video used in TV spots also included the DOT-made crashes. It would later be revealed that these video-taped crashes were repeated using the smallest car versus the largest car until the desired footage was attained, but with certain results regarding injury withheld.

## BEYOND THE BELTWAY

Meanwhile, the debate over fuel economy moved beyond the beltway and out into the country as each side began demonstrating on behalf of its views. The industry-sponsored CVC organized conferences and other public gatherings designed to get its views into local media. In Georgia, a CVC-sponsored conference provided one opportunity for local business people, labor, and farm groups to tell their stories to the media. "Mandated higher fuel economy standards would limit the sales of most family-sized cars, . . ." said Ford assembly plant manger Robert Anderson, parroting the Ford line nationally. "Our concern is this," said Herb Butler, a UAW representative from a GM plant in Doraville, Georgia, "if Congress passes an extreme CAFE bill [i.e., Bryan's bill], we will lose jobs."[53]

In Wilmington, Delaware, in June 1991, autoworkers and the Delaware Chamber of Commerce held a rally protesting the Bryan bill, raising questions about job loss at a local GM plant. Russell Peterson, the state's former governor, who also headed the National Audubon Society from 1979 to 1985, joined six environmental organizations a month later responding to the autoworkers. "I'm concerned the autoworkers will lose their jobs if they don't produce cars with better fuel efficiency because the Japanese and the Germans will," said Peterson. "They'll take that market away from us." Peterson also explained that the Bryan bill would help slow global warming and reduce US dependence on foreign oil, saving approximately 2.5 million barrels a day, or 16 percent of the country's oil consumption. "In one fell swoop," he said, "we would wipe out our reliance on Middle Eastern oil."[54]

Back in Washington, Public Citizen was distributing a fifty-one-page report entitled "Driving up the Heat," which concluded that worsening fuel economy in the nation's cars and trucks was contributing to global warming. The report ranked more than nine-hundred 1991 model cars, vans, and light trucks in terms of fuel efficiency, lifetime gasoline consumption, lifetime carbon dioxide production, and impact on global warming. It found that cars then on the road produced nearly 20 pounds of $CO_2$ pollution for every gallon of gas burned. While acknowledging that fuel efficiency for new cars reached 28.8 MPG in 1988, by 1990, that number had fallen to 28.1 MPG. For trucks it was worse, falling from a high of 21.7 MPG in 1987 to 20.8 MPG in 1990. Overall, of the 400 vehicles it examined, Public Citizen found 103 declined in fuel efficiency, 109 improved, and 188 remained the same.[55]

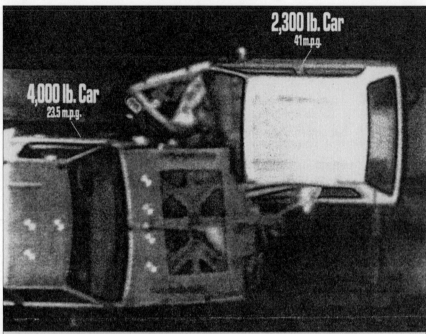

2,300 lb. Car
41 m.p.g.

4,000 lb. Car
23.5 m.p.g.

*Actual Department of Transportation crash test photo.*

# "THE LAWS OF PHYSICS CANNOT BE LEGISLATED AWAY."

–JERRY RALPH CURRY, National Highway Traffic Safety Administration
U.S. Department of Transportation, Media Roundtable, May 1, 1991.

EVERYONE KNOWS that larger cars are safer than smaller cars.* But we also know that larger cars get poorer gas mileage than smaller cars. The larger the car, the safer and the fewer miles per gallon.

Congress is now considering legislation that will call on the automotive industry to achieve dramatically higher fuel economy standards in the next few years. It will leave them little choice but to build smaller, lighter cars—at the expense of safety. Government safety experts say that today's fuel economy standards already result in nearly 2,000 deaths and 20,000 serious injuries each year.

Government should not mandate fuel economy standards that compromise safety and reduce your choice of vehicles.

Fuel economy is important, but safety is vital.

* Given equivalent safety technology and safety features on both small and large vehicles

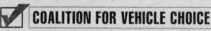 **COALITION FOR VEHICLE CHOICE**

*CVC REPRESENTS MORE THAN 200 AUTOMOTIVE AND OTHER BUSINESS, CONSUMER, FARM AND SAFETY ORGANIZATIONS.*

*This June 1991 CVC ad used a clip from a DOT big car/small car crash test—a test that was rigged, according to Public Citizen and Center for Auto Safety.*

## "A SORDID TALE"

The CVC began a multimillion dollar campaign against the Bryan bill in May 1991 and included a TV ad showing a crash test between a large and a small car. In the ad, the small car appears to be severely damaged as well as its crash dummy. In the background, the narrator's voice explains, "Everyone wants better gas mileage. But if proposed new laws force gas mileage too high, manufacturers will have little choice but to build mostly smaller cars. And when small cars like the one on the right collide with large cars, the results are clear. While smaller cars can save gas, US government safety experts say they could cost you something more precious. Fuel economy is important but safety is vital."

In late October 1991, Public Citizen and Center for Auto Safety held a press conference in which they released videotapes, internal documents, and memos obtained in a Freedom of Information lawsuit that showed DOT officials had misled Congress and the public about the safety of small cars. "The Department, on direct orders from Samuel Skinner, staged a series of car crash tests specifically designed to bolster assertions that small cars are unsafe," the two groups said, laying out evidence they compiled after hundreds of hours of piecing together what had happened inside the agency.

"Even we, the skeptics, were not prepared for what we found," said Joan Claybrook as she summarized their findings.

*It turns out that the idea for the large car/small car crash tests as a lobbying tool came from the secretary of transportation himself and was coordinated with the White House.*

*It turns out that the first crash tests the agency conducted at Secretary Skinner's request— side impact tests—clearly showed the small car performed better than the large car. These tests were submerged until now and have not seen the light of day.*

*It turns out that . . . Jerry Curry [NHTSA administrator] misled the press on May 1, [1991] when he released the frontal large car/small car crash tests in a private "roundtable" meeting and said they were part of the agency's ongoing research program.*

*It turns out that the agency interrupted its ongoing research program testing compact and mid-size cars with air bags to conduct concocted large car/small car tests instead.*

*It turns out that Administrator Curry selected the very largest car and the very smallest cars each representing a very small percentage of vehicles on the highway for testing to make sure he got what the Secretary wanted—graphic visuals making small cars look unsafe. . . .*

*It turns out that Administrator Curry personally ordered the tests to be conducted without air bags to make sure the instrumented dummies registered maximum injury. He did this even though all new cars will have air bags installed when the proposed fuel efficiency legislation is scheduled to take effect in 1996. . . .*

*It turns out that the full test reports were not released until six months after the tests were conducted and three months after the films were released.*

*It turns out according to the test data that even without air bags, the occupant/driver of the small cars would have survived the crash despite implications to the contrary by announcers for both the government and the CVC video tapes.*

*It turns out that the Department spent over $200,000 on this effort to influence public opinion and lobbying on the fuel efficiency legislation.*

> *This is indeed a sordid tale, particularly for a government agency whose credibility is based on its scientific analysis of the facts. . . .*
> *. . . We call on Congress to investigate this illegal lobbying campaign to help prevent others in the future. . . .*

## CAFE vs Alaska Lands

In the US Senate, meanwhile, the fuel economy debate had become part of a much larger struggle over national energy policy—or more precisely, the lack thereof. In the Senate Energy and Natural Resources Committee, Bennett Johnston (D-LA), committee chairman, was trying to move S. 341, the National Energy Security Act of 1991 (NESA). Johnston's bill, supported by the Bush administration, was generally more generous to energy production than it was energy conservation. However, it did include a CAFE section. But unlike Bryan's bill, which by March 1991 had been approved by the Commerce Committee in separate action, Johnston's CAFE provision did not include *specific* fuel economy standards. Johnston's bill allowed for an undefined percentage increase in CAFE and left the specifics to the discretion of the secretary of transportation—an approach generally liked by the auto industry but opposed by environmentalists. Counting votes on his energy bill—which also included a controversial provision allowing for oil development in the ecologically sensitive Arctic National Wildlife Refuge (ANWR), one of the most disputed pieces of real estate in the United States—Johnston began to see he did not have the support of senators who wanted tighter CAFE provisions. In late March 1991, he proceeded to meet with each of the US automakers to seek their help in crafting specific CAFE numbers for his bill. By mid-May, Johnston returned to his committee with a fortified CAFE amendment, this time with specific numbers: 30.2 MPG by 1996, 34 MPG by 2001 and 37 MPG by 2006.

Johnston believed that if his bill had enough "balance" in it—conservation provisions offsetting production provisions—he had a chance of getting a national energy bill passed. Environmentalists, however, would not give away ANWR for any reason, regardless of how strong a CAFE provision the bill might contain. They held that each policy—protecting wilderness and promoting conservation—was vital in its own right, and that in fact, tougher fuel economy standards would help make it unnecessary to exploit ANWR in the first place. For example, in a February 1991 report, "Looking for Oil in All the Wrong Places," Robert Watson of NRDC concluded, "America's largest unexploited oil and natural gas reserves lie not in environmentally sensitive coastal or Alaskan fields, but in our inefficient buildings, appliances and transportation system." Indeed, using various projections of fuel economy through the years 2000 and 2010, Watson found that potential savings in the automobile sector alone would exceed by a factor of five the total economic energy resources in both ANWR and the unleased offshore resource base.* An earlier study completed by Brooks Yeager, then with the Sierra Club, found that merely restoring the 27.5 MPG standard on new vehicles by 1993 would yield a greater contribution to national energy needs (4.6 billion BBLS) than would ANWR's expected production (3.2 billion BBLS).[56]

Nevertheless, in May 1991, Johnston's committee approved a bill to allow oil drilling in ANWR, but did not contain any provisions for boosting CAFE. During the committee's final consideration of the bill, the Bryan bill had been offered as an amendment, but lost 15 to 5. Then Johnston's CAFE compromise was offered, but it lost as well, 13 to 7. Johnston then delayed the vote of the final bill until the next day thinking he might still be able to effect a compromise. Nothing changed however. The vote on the final Johnston-Wallop bill without CAFE was 17-3. Senator Dale Bumpers, one of the three committee Democrats to vote against the bill, said it was "almost meaningless" without higher fuel efficiency standards.[57] A *New York Times* headline reporting on the committee's action said it all, "Panel Backs Arctic Drilling, But Not Fuel-Efficient Cars."[58]

Environmentalists promised an all-out fight when the measure came to the Senate floor. Dan Becker of the Sierra Club called the Johnston-Wallop bill "the environmental destruction act of 1991."[59] The ANWR proviso became the symbol of America as energy glutton, going for more and more oil at any price, while the Senate failed to include even a modest provision for improving automotive fuel economy.

Two months later, in July 1991, Honda and Mitsubishi reported advances in engine technology that produced greater fuel efficiency. Both automakers announced plans to incorporate "lean burn" engines in some of their 1992 models, engines they said would increase fuel economy by 10 percent to 20 percent. Mitsubishi said its version, which would be sold in Japan, would get more than 20 percent improvement during idling and about a 10 percent improvement at 60 MPH. Honda's version, to be sold in the US in its Civic models, was estimated to get about 48 miles to the gallon.[60]

Lean-burn engine technology had its problems, however. While good on fuel economy, there were problems with controlling emissions in cars that used these engines, especially nitrogen oxides, and particularly in larger engines. Detroit seized on this problem, saying the new engines would only work in smaller cars. "If Honda would introduce in the mid-size Accord an engine that showed an improvement of 6 miles per gallon, or about 20 percent, in EPA tests, that would really get my attention as an engineer," said David Cole of the University of Michigan's Automotive Transportation Program. Still, the Honda and Mitsubishi announcements stirred the pot on fuel economy at a crucial time. Thomas Hanna of the MVMA rushed to defend

---

* In thirty-year projections Watson found 31.5 billion BBLS oil equivalent in potential MPG savings vs. 6.1 billion BBLS in economically extractable oil and gas. See Watson, "Looking for Oil," figure 20, p. 32.

the Big Three, "The three domestic car companies spend enormous sums to increase fuel efficiency. It's not necessary to infer from this one instance that everyone else is a laggard."[61]

True, at the time, GM's Geo Metro, a small car built by Suzuki for GM, was the highest mileage car then being sold in the US, rated at 53 MPG city, and 58 MPG highway. Yet there were still questions about why the Big Three were not moving quicker on fuel economy technologies across all their models to protect future market share. "These engines are quite exciting," remarked Richard Ko, analyst with Barclays de Zoete Wedd in Tokyo, of the new Honda and Mitsubishi engines. "Ford and General Motors are working on the same technologies, I am sure, but the speed with which Japan is bringing these to market will open the gap even further."[62]

"As usual, the American industry has been fighting the regulations rather than making much progress in improving the technology to meet the regulations," added auto analyst Stephen Usher with Kleinwort Bensen International in Tokyo.[63]

## An Unholy Alliance

Back in the US Senate, as a likely floor vote on Johnston's bill approached in October 1991, each side was preparing amendments to make their arguments for supporting or opposing the measure. Johnston was still working to incorporate a stronger CAFE provision to woo liberals to his side. Environmentalists, however, determined not to have ANWR violated, were also making some interesting entreaties. One, oddly, was with the automakers. "We would be willing to enter into an unholy alliance with the auto industry to defeat the energy bill," explained Dan Becker of the Sierra Club. The plan was to have Bryan's CAFE bill waiting in the wings as a threatened amendment to the Johnston bill, which would then make the bill unpalatable to the auto industry. "It's the poison pill the auto industry can't swallow," said Becker.[64]

The deal went like this: If the auto industry would help prevent a cloture vote on the filibuster that was blocking the Johnston-Wallop energy bill—in effect killing the bill for that session of Congress—environmentalists would promise not to bring up Bryan's CAFE bill. By mid-October the deal was struck, with auto lobbyists acknowledging, however, they were not exactly bosom buddies with their new environmental allies. Still, environmentalists were soon helping to persuade Michigan senators Don Riegle and Carl Levin to join the filibuster. Only a year earlier, Riegle had led the filibuster that killed Bryan's first CAFE bill. For the automakers, however, it was clear why they were willing to strike a deal with environmentalists. In late October 1991, the American Automobile Association released a national poll which revealed that 85 percent of Americans favored tough new fuel economy standards, and that seven out of ten believed those standards could be met without major changes in automobile size or safety.[65] With those kinds of numbers, the Big Three would have danced with the devil if they had to.

## FORD RECEPTION

Just as Johnston's energy bill was about to be debated in the Senate, Ford Motor Co. hosted a reception on Capitol Hill for US senators. Attending the session was Ford's chairman Red Poling, and various Ford lobbyists, such as Robert Howard. Poling, Howard, and other Ford personnel at the event did their best to urge the lawmakers not to adopt any new CAFE measures[66] But some senators just went away shaking their heads. "They spend all their money lobbying saying why they can't do it," explained Patrick Leahy (D-VT) of the automakers' resistance to improved fuel economy, "and the Japanese go ahead and do it."[67]

On November 1, 1991—with the Gulf War over but national energy policy still in the balance—the Johnston-Wallop energy bill came to the Senate floor, but was quickly blocked by a filibuster. The Sierra Club, Friends of the Earth, NRDC, and others had been working intently, calling people around the country and lobbying key senators on the expected filibuster showdown. Every vote was key, either allowing the filibuster to continue, thereby dooming the Johnston bill, or imposing cloture, shutting off the filibuster, and releasing the bill for a Senate vote. Fortunately for environmentalists, the bill contained so many other unsavory provisions that a formidable array of interests were either ambivalent or unhappy about it. Among the offending provisions were partial deregulation of the electric utility industry; expedited approval of nuclear power plants and interstate pipelines; removing the government from the uranium enrichment business; and requiring owners of fleets of cars and light trucks to switch to alternative fuels.

When the cloture vote came, both sides thought it would be tight. In the end, the environmentalists and those senators insisting on more balance prevailed by a substantial margin. Johnston needed sixty votes to invoke cloture and stop the filibuster, but he got only fifty. He declared later the bill was dead for the session. Michael Stanton, lobbyist for the MVMA, when asked about the industry's deal with environmentalists, insisted the auto industry had simply refused to take a position on the filibuster vote. "We really and truly didn't do anything," he said.[68] But "anything" in this instance might have helped make the difference.

Environmentalists and their supporters in the Senate were ecstatic over saving ANWR. "We have drawn a line in the tundra," said Senator Joseph Lieberman (D-CT) on one of the leaders of the filibuster. Other key Democrats included Senators Bryan, Paul Wellstone, Tim Wirth, and Max Baucus—all of whom supported tougher fuel economy standards.[69] Some saw an important shift in the way the Senate was thinking about national energy policy. "This vote is an indication that the Senate is not willing to play energy politics the way it has in the past...," said Peter Berle, president of the National Audubon Society. "This is a great moment for environmentalists and all Americans."[70]

Bennett Johnston, meanwhile, tipped his hat to his green adversaries. "While I lose, and I hope, lose graciously," said Johnston, "I certainly have great admiration for those who fought the fight. The environmental groups, I must say, wrote the textbook on how to defeat a bill such as this, and my admiration is to them for the political skill which they exhibited." But Senator Malcolm Wallop was more scornful of the environmental effort and other public interest groups who lobbied against the measure. "The public they serve," he charged, "might as well be in Baghdad."[71]

Yet others wondered if the problem of America's rising energy vulnerability wasn't more correctly placed in Detroit.

## CLINTON-BUSH CAMPAIGN

In November 1991, Arkansas governor Bill Clinton, then beginning his bid for the Democratic presidential nomination, told the League of Conservation Voters in a taped interview that he would "support legislation that would impose higher fuel standards." Again in 1992, while he was campaigning, Clinton indicated he supported an increase in CAFE standards from the current 27.5 MPG level. "No single energy measure appears to present such a significant opportunity for [energy] savings, national security, balance of trade and the environment." Clinton indicated at that time, in fact "the 45 MPG standard should be a goal of automakers and incorporated into national legislation."[72]

By the time the campaign found its way to Michigan, George Bush was pounding on the Clinton position. A flurry of advertising about the issue had ensued in the state raising the issue of jobs. During the presidential debate in October 1992, Bush again hit the issue of "those fuel efficiency standards of 40 miles per gallon." Such standards, Bush said, would "break the auto industry and throw a lot of people out of work."

Yet at the time, when other jobs-environment clashes were also paramount in the campaign—including the Spotted Owl vs. logging jobs in the Pacific Northwest—voters weren't automatically concluding that tougher environmental provisions meant job loss. Even in Michigan, some of those on the front lines of economic development were more open to how tougher standards might mean improved economic conditions. "It's seen as a competitiveness issue," said Janice Karcher, program manager of the Genesee Economic Area Revitalization project. "More fuel efficiency means better cars and could mean more jobs." Some Michigan autoworkers as well, like Dave Yettaw, president of the UAW local 599 in Flint, supported Clinton's position. "Stricter mileage standards will produce a whole new industry for new methods, new equipment, new techniques, and new technologies," he said. "Too often, we think about the immediate problems and not the long term. . . . [T]hat's what got us in our predicament in the auto industry. I think Clinton is right on this. He says we can have higher mileage cars and more jobs."[73]

Bill Clinton, meanwhile, was beginning to soften. Promising he would raise the standard in an April 1992 Earth Day speech in Philadelphia, Clinton began to temper his position after meeting with Big Three executives. A National Research Council study also suggested that it might only be technically possible to raise CAFE to 37 MPG by 2006. Cornered on the question during the October 1992 presidential debate, Clinton responded, "I never said, and I defy you to find where I said, that we ought to have a goal of raising the fuel efficiency standards to forty miles per gallon. I think that should be a goal. I never said we should write it into law if there is evidence that the goal cannot be achieved." [74]

## VISIONARY SEES "HYPERCAR"

As the politicians debated the pros and cons of 30-to-40 MPG vehicles in Washington and on the campaign trail, out in Snowmass, Colorado, at a place called the Rocky Mountain Institute, a few people were thinking much bigger. Amory Lovins, a many talented physicist and college dropout who rose to prominence in the 1970s by popularizing a "soft energy path" of environmentally friendly energy alternatives—mostly wind, solar, and energy conservation—began promoting a 150-to-300-MPG automobile he would call the "hypercar." The Lovins car would be a new kind of automobile, one that would made differently and powered differently, but would be safe, carry four adults, and be capable of going coast to coast on one tank of gas. This new car, however, wasn't something Lovins was making up out of thin air, or conjuring for the future. Rather, in Lovins' view, this was a car possible in the near term.[75]

No new technologies were needed, Lovins would explain as he wrote and spoke about his new car. In fact, he would eagerly point out that General Motors had already created such a car—or at least one close to it. In 1991, fifty GM experts built a prototype car of ultralight construction, he would explain. This car was called the Ultralite. It was sporty-looking, with four seats and four airbags. It essentially took the interior space of a Chevrolet Corsica and made it fit into a Mazda Miata. "Although it has only a 111-horsepower engine, smaller than a Honda Civic's," Lovins wrote describing the GM car, "its light weight (1,400 lbs) and low air drag, both less than half of normal, give it a top speed of 135 MPH and 0-60 acceleration of 7.8 seconds— comparable to a BMW 750iL with a huge V-12 engine." But the GM car was "more than 4 times as efficient as the BMW, averaging 62 MPG. . . ."

At the core of Lovins' critique of the conventional car is wasted and misapplied energy. First, in Lovins' view, there is little that can be done with a steel car, and in fact, steel is one of the automobile's central inefficiencies. Put simply, most of the energy the internal combustion engine generates is used to move heavy steel around, not people. "Less than two percent of the fuel energy actually ends up hauling the driver," says Lovins. The internal combustion engine itself is grossly inefficient, with most of the fuel energy it consumes going out the tailpipe. More energy is dissipated as friction and drag costs, as Lovins describes them, pushing wind aside, heating up the tires, road, and brakes.

If the car is made light to begin with, and its design "slippery" or aerodynamically efficient, Lovins explains, energy losses and inefficiency are cut dramatically.

Although automakers had produced light-weight cars and prototypes using aluminum, magnesium, and light-weight plastics, Lovins would go beyond these, using "composites made by embedding glass, carbon, polyaramid, and other ultrastrong fibers in special moldable plastics." These materials would be safe and "bouncy," capable of measuring up to crash-test standards of steel cars. Some Indianapolis race cars, he noted, use carbon fiber construction.

Lovins' choice for an engine and drive power are also key to high efficiency; what he calls a "hybrid system"—that is, power supplied in part by a gasoline engine and in part by batteries. A tiny onboard internal combustion engine fueled by any liquid or gaseous fuel would be used to make electricity to run small motors placed directly at the wheels. A few batteries would also be onboard to temporarily store and reuse recovered braking energy—known as regenerative braking. "Adding hybrid-electric drive to an ordinary production car increases its efficiency by one-third to one-half. And making an ordinary car ultralight doubles its efficiency," Lovins would say. "But doing both together can boost a car's efficiency by about tenfold."

Through the early and mid-1990s, Amory Lovins' ideas and thinking on his "hypercar" caught the attention of those working on the automobile's problems, and before long he found himself talking with most of the major auto manufacturers, as well as lecturing around the country about the virtues of hypercars.

But Amory Lovins was not alone in calling for revolutionary changes in the way automobiles were powered and built. Public officials in Los Angeles—a city still choking on smog and auto exhausts—were agitating for alternatives to the internal combustion engine too. In Los Angeles, electric cars were about to get a big push from a few determined local politicians, and then statewide from the California Air Resources Board.

# 14

## *Not Exactly Electrifying*

Our goal is to build an electric car with a range of around 100 miles and with a top speed of, say, 50 [MPH]. . . . If we could achieve that in a lightweight two-seater . . . we believe many urban families would use it as a second or third car.

—*E.M. Estes, president,*
*General Motors, February 1977*[1]

In 1988, Los Angeles city councilman Marvin Braude took his second ride in a General Motors electric vehicle (EV)—this one called the G-van. It was much like the ride he had taken ten years earlier in another General Motors EV. "There had been absolutely no change," said Braude, "and it just filled me with indignation. Here was a company selling literally billions of dollars of automobiles in the nation's worst smog area. It seemed to me they had an obligation to their customers to spend some real money developing an electric vehicle."[2]

Councilman Braude then pushed a novel idea through city council called the LA Initiative—an international competition to find an automaker willing to mass produce EVs. Adding to the initiative was the fact that the South Coast Air Quality Management District (AQMD) had found that in order to meet air pollution standards by the year 2010, virtually all of the vehicles in Los Angeles would have to be electric. In September 1990, when the results of the "LA Initiative" competition were announced, eighteen proposals had been received, but not one from the Big Three. Clean Air Transport, a Swedish firm, was chosen to deliver 10,000 electric cars to Los Angeles by 1995. The LA Department of Water and Power, administering the program, and Southern California Edison, which would supply the power, together put up $7 million. The Swedish firm put up $10 million, and the project was underway.

The Big Three, however, challenged LA's move toward EVs. In fact, according to Jerry Enzenauer, head of the AQMD's EV program, pressure from the big automakers in 1990 caused AQMD to dramatically scale back its twenty-year projections—from nearly all cars going electric by 2010 to a much lower 17 percent goal. "The air quality management plan is a policy statement that invites response, and the response from the car companies was loud and long," explained Enzenauer of the lobbying that lead to the change. "Their argument was basically, 'Look, the technology is not there to get enough electric vehicles by the time you want them, so don't even think about it.' They applied pretty heavy and unrelenting pressure, not only at public hearings but behind the scenes. The fact is, they [automakers] never make a move until the regulators force them."[3]

## ELECTRIC HISTORY

The major automakers say they have been working on electric vehicles for more than thirty years. But what does that really mean? Prior to World War I, electric-powered automobiles comprised one-third of all vehicles on the road. In fact, between the late 1890s and 1940, there were more than forty companies, GM and Ford among them, engaged in the manufacture of electric vehicles. A number of the vehicles were produced for limited runs, and others only custom-made. But a few were fairly sophisticated for their day.* The internal combustion engine soon prevailed, however. Cheap gasoline, longer driving range between fill-ups, and Charles Kettering's electric starter, which eliminated the hand crank, gave the internal combustion engine the edge. Electric cars didn't begin to reenter the picture until the 1960s, when rising urban pollution and energy problems brought them forward as possible alternatives. These electric vehicles, however, were produced mostly as experimental vehicles, rolled out at the annual auto shows.

In 1966, GM unveiled its Electrovair II model at US auto shows. The Electrovair was basically a converted Corvair powered by silver-zinc batteries. Ford Motor developed sodium sulfur batteries for prototype electric vehicles in the mid-1960s. But Henry Ford II made clear his company's position on electric vehicles in an May 1968 *Look* magazine interview, "[W]e have tremendous investment in facilities for engines, transmissions, and axles, and I can't see throwing these away just because the electric car doesn't emit fumes."[4] As Congress began probing more deeply into what the major automakers were doing with alternative vehicles a few years later, GM officials were not encouraging. Dr. Paul F. Chenea of GM, testifying before the House Commerce Committee in December 1969 on alternatives to the internal combustion engine, said that electric cars were still experimental and might prove hazardous to public safety on urban expressways. Range, speed, and cold-weather usefulness were also problems, he explained, as was finding a battery that met all the requirements for a general purpose passenger car.[5] In the late 1970s, following the energy crisis, GM continued to say it had goals of marketing an electric vehicle, but only for selected markets and urban driving. "Our goal is to build an electric car with a range of around 100 miles and with a top speed of, say, 50 miles per hour, . . ." said GM's president,

---

* James MacKenzie notes in his *The Keys to the Car*, for example, "In 1919, inventor Harry E. Dey introduced a vehicle with a unique integrated motor differential axle that allowed the motor to act as a generator and return power to the batteries while travelling downhill." See Lloyd Darling, "Going Jaunting in an Electric," *Popular Science*, January 1920.

E.M. Estes, in February 1977. "If we could achieve that in a lightweight two-seater with ample room in the back for groceries and such we believe many urban families would use it as a second or third car. . . ."[6] At about the time of the Iranian hostage crisis when energy prices once again climbed, GM began work on the Electrovette—a converted Chevette that ran on zinc nickel oxide batteries with a DC motor. However, cost was still high. When oil prices dropped, so did GM's enthusiasm for the Electrovette, which never moved beyond the demo stage.[7]

According to Ford representatives, their company's interest in electric cars reaches back several decades. The company was especially keen on sodium sulfur batteries. By the 1980s, Ford's electric version of its Escort model, called the EXT-1, was equipped with such batteries. By the late 1980s, the company had worked up a proposal for DOE to fund the design of an EV powertrain that could be adjusted to fit a van or a sports car. Still, the Ford effort in EVs was tiny. In late 1989, for example, Ford's John Wallace, who then headed up the company's Dearborn, Michigan, electronics lab overseeing more than 100 Ph.D.s, "began scratching for funds [for an EV program] in odd nooks of the company, begging, as he put it, with his tin cup in hand. By Christmas, he had $8 million."[8]

None of the electric prototypes the Big Three pursued between the 1960s and late 1980s, however, ever made it to commercial development. That would take the prodding of government regulation, and once again, the leadership of California.

## THE CALIFORNIA PUSH

Southern California's dirty air, though somewhat improved by 1990, was still a health hazard for many citizens. Although the average citizen's exposure to smog in the region had been cut in half from 1970 levels, it was still a long way from meeting the federal standards for ozone attainment. California authorities were then estimating 1,600 premature deaths annually among persons suffering from chronic respiratory diseases. Evidence was also accumulating that Los Angeles youth were suffering diminished lung capacity from the region's bad air. In fact, an estimated $9 billion annually in health costs was cited for the state's Southland residents.[9] Real estate and housing developers worried about restrictions on growth as public officials looked for ways to curb pollution.

In September 1990, the entire state, not just Los Angeles, faced the foreseeable future in "nonattainment" for ozone and the distinct possibility of federal sanctions: losing federal highway money unless it cleaned up its air. That's when CARB moved to adopt its "low emissions vehicle regulations," also known as LEV regulations. The LEV regs established progressively more stringent auto emissions standards for the three key auto pollutants—VOCs, CO, and NOx—with the goal of moving California toward cleaner air by the year 2010. CARB laid out a plan for various classes of vehicles that would meet progressively tighter emission standards, including the following categories, operative between 1994-2003:

TLEVs, or *Transitional Low Emission Vehicles*. CARB established that 10 percent to 20 percent of new car production in 1994-1996 must cut hydrocarbon pollution in half compared to '93 models— 0.125 g/mi. These standards, however, could be met by improved gasoline-powered vehicles.

LEVs, or *Low Emission Vehicles*. CARB established that 25 percent to 75 percent of new car production in 1997-2003 must meet HC standard of 0.075 g/mi and NOx at 0.2 g/mi. These vehicles could also meet the standard using improved gasoline or alternative fuels.

ULEVs, or *Ultra-Low Emission Vehicles*. CARB established that 2 percent to 15 percent of new car production in 1997-2003 must cut hydrocarbon emissions by 84 percent and NOx and CO by 50 percent. These standards could be met by using natural gas, for example, or cleaner gasolines.

ZEVs, or *Zero Emission Vehicles*. These vehicles must have no tailpipe or evaporative emissions.

In this latter category, CARB established that the seven major automakers in California—GM, Ford, Chrysler, Toyota, Nissan, Honda, and Mazda—must have at least 2 percent of their sales as ZEVs by 1998. By the year 2001, that requirement would rise to 5 percent, and again in 2003 to 10 percent. This meant essentially that battery-powered electric vehicles—the only zero emission automotive technology on the horizon—would be required in California beginning in 1998. When CARB announced its plans, it pointed, in turn, to an announcement General Motors' chairman Roger Smith had made six months earlier about an electric vehicle GM was developing, and which Smith later promised GM would produce in quantity.

## GM's "Breakthrough"

In January 1990, GM's Roger Smith announced that GM had produced a prototype electric vehicle for personal use. Posing for photographs with the car—a two-seat sports car called the Impact—Smith told reporters about GM's plan for the new vehicle. Although not yet in production, he said, explaining that considerable work had to occur on batteries, a new electric car was certainly "producible." In fact, such cars could be on the market by the middle of the decade, Smith said. He and GM had high hopes the Impact would be the first EV to bridge the gap between limited production and mass-produced electric cars.

"We've taken a big step, a very big step here," Smith said, cautioning that the vehicle would cost twice as much to operate as a gasoline-powered car, and that a cost-competitive EV was years away. Still, "this is no golf cart," he told reporters. At the press conference a tape was shown of the Impact outracing a Mazda Miata and Nissan 300 zx from a standing start to 60 miles per hour.[10] "What this shows is that a major corporation recognizes that California is serious in demanding clean cars and clean fuel," said Tom Eichhorn, spokesman for the South Coast AQMD.[11]

"We need to determine just how much public enthusiasm there is out there—not just here in California, but all over the country," Smith said.[12] GM officials cautioned that nationwide demand would have to exist to justify production. Smith said he would be most comfortable with 100,000 cars a year, not 20,000.[13]

Powered with thirty-two traditional lead-acid automobile batteries, the Impact could travel 120 miles before it needed to be recharged—or so GM claimed at the time. Design and technical improvements from earlier advances on a solar-powered vehicle called the Sunraycer, developed by GM and outside partners, were used in the Impact. It featured a tear-drop, aerodynamic design to reduce wind resistance, special tires to further reduce drag, and two efficient electric motors to drive each front wheel. "It's a total system approach," said John S. Zwerner, a top GM engineer. "Every detail has been important."[14]

## BEHIND THE SCENES

The details, in fact, were very important, and few were really disclosed the day Roger Smith made his announcement. Some speculated at the time that GM's unveiling was all for show: to boost GM's image in tough economic times and calm environmental regulators to keep politicians from putting tougher controls on the existing ICE. As for the Impact itself, there was a lot more to this car than met the eye at its January showing. For one, no reporter was permitted to drive it. For another, there was much work to be done to make it production-ready and even come close to Roger Smith's pronouncement of 100,000 cars a year. The Impact, in fact, wasn't GM's car at all, it was largely the creation of a small company GM had hired to build the prototype.

The Impact—a name chosen by GM for "the impact" the new car would have on the world—was delivered to GM in November 1989 by AeroVironment, a California start-up founded by "Cal techie" Paul MacCready. MacCready had made a name for himself with a few nonconventional vehicles and work in aerodynamics. He built a light-weight, human-pedaled flying machine called the *Gossamer Albatross* that traveled across the English Channel in 1979. A sun-powered *Solar Challenger* in 1981 also brought notice. But the electric vehicle that AeroVironment delivered to GM—built by a group of young technicians—was an extraordinary accomplishment, enthusiastically tested that November:

> ... [T]he engineers took turns whipping around the parking lot with squeals of burning rubber. Every time it took off, the car pinned the delighted driver against his seat. A gas engine took a few long seconds to reach its peak power. This thing flew forward as fast as the current could reach the wheels, which was to say, *instantly*.
>
> As soon as its doors were affixed, the car was taken by flatbed truck to GM's desert proving grounds in Mesa, Arizona. It weighed in at a remarkably light 2,200 pounds, including 843 pounds of batteries. On the track, it jumped from 0-60 in 7.9 seconds—faster than such sporty gas cars as a Mazda Miata or Nissan 300 zx—and quickly

reached 75 miles per hour, the top speed allowed by its controller software. On a high-way test, it went 124 miles at 55 miles per hour; on an urban test range, one with lots of stopping and starting to simulate city traffic, it did nearly as well. That was extraordinary. A gas car had at least a 300-mile range on the open road. In the city, however, its range was sharply diminished as it idled at stops and used extra fuel to accelerate. Slowing, the . . . car recouped energy from its [regenerative] braking. Stopped, it consumed no energy at all.

The show car's windows remained fixed, its suspension and handling were terrible, and it lacked amenities and such safety features as air bags. Despite these and other drawbacks, it *worked*. . . .[15]

GM then assembled its own team to rework the AeroVironment car into a production-ready vehicle—a tortured tale in its own right.* Between 1989 and January 1996, when the first of fifty Impacts would roll out of a GM plant in Lansing, Michigan, there would be a series of financial setbacks, false starts, technical twists and turns, and serious corporate infighting over the fate of this car. Through it all, GM's Impact would become a political lightening rod, not only for GM and the Big Three, but also for California, the federal government, and twelve northeastern states—all of which were agitating for cleaner cars and new technology.

## EARTH DAY SURPRISE

On Earth Day 1990, however, Roger Smith took the Impact beyond the company's January 1990, caveat-filled unveiling. At the National Press Club in Washington, Smith announced GM would be the first auto company to *produce and sell* electric cars. But not all of the Big Three were then as upbeat as Roger Smith. Working on electric vehicles, explained Chrysler's Lee Iacocca in April 1990, was simply "putting new skin on a golf cart." For Iacocca and Chrysler it was simply a matter of dollars and cents: consumers just wouldn't buy them. "Will people pay a premium to say, 'My tailpipe's cleaner than your tailpipe?' No!," said Iacocca.[16] Yet, when GM later went looking for potential test drivers for the Impact, it received thousands of responses, a few with down payments enclosed.

With Roger Smith declaring that GM would produce and sell EVs, California had all it needed to go forward with its ZEV mandate. And it would be this mandate, with its 2-percent-of-sales 1998 deadline, which soon touched off a broader politics around the issue of cleaner cars in other states as well. The automakers, in any case, were not happy with the ZEV mandate in California. "The plan is asking the industry to take on responsibility that it is not in any shape to fulfill at this point,"

---

* For a blow-by-blow account of the GM trials and tribulations during the 1989-1996 building of the Impact, see Michael Shnayerson, *The Car That Could: The Inside Story of GM's Revolutionary Electric Vehicle*, New York: Random House, 1996.

complained Marcel Helberstadt of the MVMA in Detroit. GM's Joseph Calhoun, assistant director of the company's emission control program, explained that GM would try to meet the California standards, but wanted some special provisions added. GM wanted periodic reviews of the technological progress the industry was making toward reaching the ZEV goal *and* the option for California to adjust the ZEV timetable if warranted. CARB agreed.[17]

## Playing the Game

GM had long experience in the auto emission wars by this time, and its man in the trenches on these critical, billion-dollar matters was Sam Leonard. Leonard would support the California mandate in testimony, but he was also a man experienced in the ways of obtaining regulatory advantage—even when it appeared his company was agreeing to do something it really didn't want to do. Leonard was known as "Mr. Emissions" at GM. He practiced a form of shuttle diplomacy between Detroit and Sacramento on one leg, and Detroit and Washington on another. Leonard would appear before CARB, congressional committees, and make the rounds at EPA. He would recite the engineering of the possible—the engineering that GM preferred. "Inevitably, he testified that GM could do less than the regulators hoped," reports Michael Shnayerson, "then fed his numbers to auto lobbyists and lawyers who might abet his campaign of persuasion. The game as he put it, was not to win. . . . The game was to forestall, to buy the time GM needed to develop technology to meet the next regs and keep the factories operating in the meanwhile. . . ."[18] Leonard told Shnayerson the car companies "had fought new clean-air standards time and again, claimed they couldn't meet them—'emissions impossible'—only to meet them after all." However, Leonard also pointed out that the car companies really hadn't met the standards—at least not by the dates Congress had originally set. "The technology hadn't been there," according to Leonard. In fact, he boasted to Shnayerson that 1993 "was the first model year we ever built a model certified to [1975] standards."

When Leonard appeared before CARB to endorse the California ZEV requirement in September 1990 it was not a sign he had suddenly been born again on environmental regulation. Rather, he endorsed the mandate because he had no choice. "[W]ith his own company saying EVs could be done, he could hardly say they couldn't," reports Shnayerson. CARB had also agreed to the technical reviews of EV progress as a basis for potentially changing the deadline. "Based on two decades of experience, Leonard thought the chances of EV R & D conforming to CARB's schedule were absolutely nil. . . ."[19] Still, what happens in California often becomes national policy, though not right away. "Our program has historically set the pace for the country and created the technology that has made reducing emissions feasible," said CARB's Bill Sessa in September 1990. "This proposal lays the groundwork for a whole new generation of cars and technology." Yet, some environmentalists at the time thought an even stronger push was needed. "We absolutely agree that there is no way to meet clean air standards [in California] without introducing clean vehicles in significant numbers," said the NRDC's Lynne T. Edgerton. "Having said that, we think the plan for phasing in the low-emission vehicles and the zero-emission vehicles is too slow."[20] But in the 1990s, California wasn't the only region of the country agitating for quicker action on smog. New initiatives were also being pushed in the northeastern states.

## POLLUTED MEGALOPOLIS

The Boston-Washington urban megalopolis of the eastern seaboard—a near-continuous carpet of highways, urban areas, and metropolitan regions—is also one of the most polluted regions in the United States, especially in the summer. The problem is ground-level ozone and the pollutants that make ozone. That means, in large measure, cars and trucks and the fuels that move them, which together account for more than half of the ozone in the region. Since the EPA began its air pollution program in the 1970s, Boston, New York, northern New Jersey, Philadelphia/Wilmington, Baltimore, Washington, northern Virginia, even Richmond, and lesser constellations in and around these cities, were perennially exceeding federal pollution standards. The problem continued through the 1980s. Nearly sixty of the region's largest metropolitan areas could not meet the 1988 deadlines for reducing ozone and carbon monoxide.[21] But in those years, EPA took little action to pressure polluted northeast cities. The Reagan administration refused to invoke its considerable federal powers for "encouraging" the states to get tough, i.e., holding back federal dollars for highways, sewers, and other public works projects. Thus, states and metropolitan areas continued to miss federal clean air deadlines.[22]

When Congress enacted the 1970 Clean Air Act, it prohibited states, except California, from adopting stricter standards. However, under the 1977 amendments, Congress did give states the option of adopting California's auto emissions standards. Until the late 1980s, no state had considered that route. By then, however, something new began to take hold in the northeastern and mid-Atlantic states: a regional approach.

## THE NORTHEAST & THE OTC

In November 1987, impatient with EPA's inaction, six New England states plus New York and New Jersey moved jointly to require more stringent controls on gasoline production—specifically to require oil refiners to remove ozone-forming butane from gasoline sold in those states.[23] By June 1989, the northeast states began pushing EPA to impose tighter rules on evaporative emissions from gasoline stations, which also contributed to smog. EPA, however, refused to issue the rules, and later proposed a watered-down version. Massachusetts then challenged EPA, and after it threatened to sue, EPA began approving state gasoline rules.[24]

By late 1990, the region received new leverage from Congress under the 1990 Clean Air Act, which among other things, officially sanctioned regional action on air pollution by creating the Ozone Transport Commission (OTC). The OTC included twelve northeast and mid-Atlantic states, plus the District of Columbia. It was created because urban smog—especially ozone formed in the summer months—did not honor political boundaries and moved wherever prevailing winds would take it. In the Northeast, ozone from Maryland, for example, was wafting up into coastal Maine. Western Massachusetts would sometimes receive pollutants from New York and Pennsylvania. This became the basis for adopting a regional approach. At the core of the northeast states' activities and a prod to the OTC was another body called NESCAUM—the Northeast States for Coordinated Air Use Management— which had already worked on the region's gasoline standards.

Shortly after the victory on the gasoline rules, discussions began in the region about taking the California approach to auto emissions standards.[25] NESCAUM had already issued a 1989 report that concluded that adopting the California rules would be an important step in cleaning up the region's air. "Excessive levels of ozone and carbon monoxide (CO) . . . are a persistent public health problem in the northeast states," said NESCAUM. The region was regularly in violation of the Clean Air Act standards. "Violations of the national ambient air quality standard for ozone . . . occur over broad regions of the Northeast in the summertime," said the report. "These violations occur at urban, rural and remote sites, encompassing densely populated areas as well as more pristine recreational sites." In addition, NESCAUM explained that with the expected increase in NOx emissions, "ambient concentrations of nitrogen dioxide, nitrate particles, atmospheric acidity and acidic deposition may all be expected to worsen. . . ."

". . . [T]here has been no clear progress toward attainment of the national ambient air quality standard for ozone throughout the 8 states. . . ," said the report. "Peak hourly ozone levels have remained at 2 to 2 1/2 times the 0.12 PPM standard."[26] Adopting the California program—even as it was in 1989, prior to the LEV regulations— would mean reductions of 16 percent HC, 39 percent CO, and 27 percent NOx for the Northeast beyond the federal standards. Massachusetts, acting on its own, became the first state to propose adopting the California approach.

## MASSACHUSETTS LEADS

In July 1989, Massachusetts Representative David Cohen (D-Newton), introduced a bill to require his state to adopt California's existing auto emissions standards. Cohen's bill also proposed to adopt California's auto emissions inspection and recall programs. Under the bill, the new standards would take effect by 1993. "We expect it will reduce smog-causing chemicals as much as one third to one half," said Cohen. Without the measure, he said, the air quality in the state would be even worse than it was in the mid-1970s. "The reason is not that the tailpipe standards don't work," he said. "but [that] people in Massachusetts are driving more." Even though each car was then emitting less, the additional driving was wiping out the gains. In 1990, Cohen's bill was introduced again, where it passed the House by a vote of 144-2.[27] The Massachusetts Public Interest Research Group (MassPIRG) was leading a lobby effort to pass the bill. "Without stricter auto emissions controls," said MassPIRG's Jenny Carter, lobbying the state Senate in December 1990, "it will be nearly impossible for Massachusetts to clean up its air. . . ."[28] The automakers were then working up their own strategy for the Massachusetts Senate—a strategy they hoped would slow the move toward California car standards.

The AAMA wanted an amendment to stipulate that the new standards would not take effect until all of Massachusetts' neighboring states adopted them as well. Representative Joseph Baerlein, representing the automakers, said that implementing the standards in advance of the other states would put Massachusetts dealers at a competitive disadvantage. "All we are saying is let's move forward in concert with everybody else," said Baerlein. Senator John Olver (D-Amherst), sponsor of the bill in the Senate, thought the automakers and dealers "still have hopes that somehow they can derail an overall move toward more stringent controls." State environmental commissioner, Daniel Greenbaum, accused the industry of trying to gut the bill with the maneuver. He called the bill containing the California approach "the most effective tool we have available to us today to reduce air pollution in one move." Olver said without the measure, additional restrictions on other industrial activities would be required. "Boston is ranked 11th worse in the nation in terms of air quality and smog problems," said MassPIRG's Jenny Carter. "If every state had the attitude that, 'I won't do it until everyone else does,' progress could never be made. In the meantime, Massachusetts' air . . . will only get worse."[29]

In the final day of the state's legislative session, the Cohen-Olver bill was passed, making Massachusetts the first state to adopt by law California's stricter auto emissions standards. By this time, Congress had passed the Clean Air Act of 1990, with provision for the OTC. In California, CARB had proposed its new LEV-ZEV regulations.

In mid-July 1991, while smog alerts were being issued in some of the northeast states, the environmental commissioners representing the twelve states of the OTC met in Boston to consider adopting the California standards. "We're all part of an airshed," said Thomas C. Jorling, New York's commissioner of environmental conservation. "The more widespread the California car becomes, the better."[30] By October 1991, the northeast states, voting as a bloc, proposed to adopt the California mandate. But each state had to either propose regulations or adopt legislation in order to assume the California program. Debate then shifted back to the individual states.

## NEW JERSEY

New Jersey at the time was faced with an ozone air pollution problem second only to Los Angeles. For twenty years, the state had been unable to achieve the federal air quality goals established under the Clean Air Act of 1970. Northern New Jersey had failed to meet the federal standard for carbon monoxide. With the Northeast acting in unison, New Jersey saw a chance to use the "California Car" mandate to help clean up its air. The administration of Governor Jim Florio (D) began studying whether the state could adopt the plan by using regulatory initiatives or if new legislation would be necessary. Initially, state authorities thought that by 1998 or so, at least 2 percent of the autos would be required to be EVs to meet the standard, depending upon what elements of the California plan were included. Eventually, it was thought that 10 percent of the cars marketed in the state would have to be EVs.[31]

"The only way to bring emissions down," said New Jersey Department of Environmental Protection and Energy's (DEPE) David West in November 1991, noting that a cobbled collection of other measures proposed by the auto and oil industries fell short by the year 2000, "is to bring in new, cleaner cars, including electric vehicles. To us, the program makes a lot of sense. We have no other way to go." William Winters, with GM's marketing staff, took issue with how DEPE was calculating emissions reduction. "We strongly suspect those projections, particularly if you don't require the specific fuels mandated under the California program," he said. "Even if you do meet those goals," he added, "is it going to be worth the $800 more it cost [per] car?" State officials, meanwhile, calculated California's program would cost about $175 per car, not $800.[32]

GM was also pushing for more focus on older cars and produced a study showing that the oldest 30 percent of cars in New Jersey were driven only 21 percent of the miles but contributed 61 percent of CO and HC emissions and 45 percent of NOx. "Off-road engines"—motor boats, recreational vehicles, etc.—came into the picture as well, accounting for a growing part of the state's pollution problem. Better inspection and maintenance programs, I & Ms, were also being pushed by industry, as well as cleaner gasoline. Together these latter strategies were labeled "control strategies" and they were given the complete backing of Big Oil and the Big Three as the alternative to the California plan in New Jersey. Big Oil also supported a state-assisted "clunker" buy-back program, modeled after a Unocal program in California that was then receiving some notice for its success. John Taunton, for Exxon—which then still owned the huge Bayway refinery in northern New Jersey—said that control strategies designated for New Jersey under the federal Clean Air Act would bring roughly an 85 percent reduction in VOCs by the year 2010. "We need to see where these control strategies take us," said New Jersey Petroleum Council lobbyist Jim Benton in November 1991. "We think the benefits are going to be significant. We think enhanced I & M is going to catch what we call the high emitters." On the other hand, said Benton, "We're very concerned with the challenges the California program brings to industry."[33]

New Jersey environmentalists, however, felt industry was being disingenuous in its support of I & M programs. State officials, for their part, kept pointing to rising numbers of vehicles by the year 2000. Faster gains in clean air would be made, they said, if the California plan was adopted in the Northeast. There would be 62 percent decline in HC and a 34 percent drop in CO, as compared with a 23 percent HC and 10 percent CO decline under the federal plan. "I just don't think we're going to meet the (Clean Air Act) goals unless we go with the California car," said Edward Lloyd, director of the Rutgers Environmental Law Clinic. "We have no choice," added Linda Stansfield, chairwoman of the New Jersey Clean Air Council and member of the American Lung Association of New Jersey. Stansfield said industry had raised the same objections when lead was to be phased out of gasoline. As for the automakers, she said, "What they're really worried about is the Japanese are going to get there first. The Japanese have complied with environmental mandates without kicking and screaming, and that's why their cars are selling."[34] New Jersey held public hearings on the proposal and continued to weigh the matter through 1992. In neighboring New York, a similar process was underway.

## NEW YORK

"Nearly 13.5 million New Yorkers, over two-thirds of the state's population, are now in areas where they breathe unhealthful air," Thomas Jorling would tell audiences across the state in 1991. Jorling, an old hand in the clean air wars who had served as a consultant to Ed Muskie's subcommittee during the drafting of the 1970 Clean Air Act, had become one of the main proponents of the Northeast adopting the California approach. New York was then confronting the daunting task of having to bring about a 48 percent reduction in ozone-creating pollutants between 1993 and 2007. The state was the third worst place in the country for generating ozone pollution.

By October 1991, the New York Department of Environmental Conservation (DEC) began holding public hearings around the state and taking comments on its plan to adopt the California program. The oil and auto industries were in attendance at most of these hearings, opposing the initiative. Michael J. Schwarz, an emissions expert with Ford Motor Co. and representing the MVMA, spoke at a DEC hearing in Long Island City. He pointed to the experience of the mid-1970s, saying that auto technology was pushed too hard by clean-air advocates, and problems resulted. Cars ran roughly, stalled, or would not start, he said. "Let California expose its public to a giant experiment," Schwarz said. If it worked out there, he said, then New Yorkers could adopt it later.[35]

The auto and oil industries knew full well that New York was a key state in the larger Northeast battle; if New York did not adopt, it was likely that the other states would fold as well. "New York is not California," said David R. Hayward, a Mobil vice president, suggesting the California standards were inappropriate for the state. And when the topic of electric cars came up, the oil companies were especially emphatic. "Is the motoring public going to be willing to turn the clock back 70 years and drive without the comfort of heaters, air conditioners, and defrosters?" offered Texaco's William Cummings, explaining that all of these items would not be included in EVs because they would reduce driving range.[36]

In December 1991, the New York State Automobile Dealers Association hosted a debate between state regulators and the automakers on the matter. The automakers flew in a team from Detroit to a Holiday Inn near New York's La Guardia Airport where the meeting was being held. "You will all remember 1981," said GM's Al Weverstad, manager of emission compliance. Weverstad was referring to the year when federal regulations required yards of extra vacuum tubing creating balky engines that caused what manufacturers described as "driveability" problems.[37] "Every time you force the technology, you take that risk." If the new rules were adopted, he warned, prices would rise $1,000 per car, performance would drop, and consumers will simply stop buying.

However, by early 1992, New York's environmental board, with Thomas Jorling in the chair, voted unanimously to adopt the California standards. That same day, however, the state Senate passed a bill that would delay putting the rules into effect. The bill's supporters charged that the new rules could cost the state thousands of jobs in the petroleum and auto industries, including auto manufacturing and assembly jobs. Jorling reminded members of the legislature that not only did the state stand to lose federal highway money if it failed to take measures moving toward compliance, but that the other alternatives for tightening down on pollution—including restricting consumer products like lawn mowers and barbecue grills or limiting industrial expansion—could be even more unpopular and economically damaging.

Complicating matters in the New York Assembly, where the Senate bill was heading next, was the fact the bill's chief sponsor, Michael J. Bragman, chairman of the Transportation Committee, was also chairman of the Democratic Campaign Committee, holder of election-year purse strings for incumbent Democrats. Some worried that Mr. Bragman would promote the anti-California bill to his colleagues as a way to collect election-year contributions from oil and auto interests.[38] However, by the time the bill came up for consideration in June 1992, Jorling and Assemblyman Maurice Hinchey (D-Ulster), chairman of the Environmental Conservation Committee, had rallied supporters. New York City mayor David Dinkins also played a key role, lobbying several Democrats to back away from the delay. The auto companies, however, did not go away empty-handed: they obtained a state study on the economic consequences of the standards and continued to charge that the new approach could add several hundred dollars to the cost of a new car. Jorling, however, said the costs would be closer to $100 per car.[39]

Jorling also preached the gospel of new economic possibility. "With this incentive," he said, after the Environmental Board adopted the California option, "a real market is now available for entrepreneurs to produce these vehicles quickly." The new standards, he said, should help wean autos from petroleum and encourage a trend toward natural gas, electricity, and eventually, fuel cells.[40] But weaning automobiles away from petroleum and toward other new engine technologies was precisely why the California Car initiative was being blocked in other northeastern states.

## VIRGINIA

In February 1992, in a key Virginia Senate committee weighing whether to advance Governor Douglas Wilder's plan to adopt the California standards in northern Virginia, the most polluted part of his state, the Senate Transportation Committee voted 8-to-6 to kill the bill. Car dealers and oil companies combined in a lobby effort to help defeat it. The Mobil Corporation, with its corporate headquarters in Fairfax, Virginia, charged that the alternative and reformulated fuels part of the package would require oil companies in California to spend $6 billion on their facilities, raising gasoline prices an average of 17 cents a gallon. "Obviously," said Mobil's Susan Sonnenberg of the committee's vote to kill the Virginia bill, "we're pleased."[41]

Russel Hinz, lobbying for the measure on behalf of the Virginia chapter of the American Lung Association charged that the committee vote was "a classic example of big business scoring a victory against health and clean air." The defeated bill would not come up for a vote again until 1993. Elizabeth H. Haskell, Virginia secretary of natural resources, said the California emissions standards offered the best chance for improving air quality in the state without imposing broad new regulations on all businesses. "It isn't a problem that is going to go away," she said, noting that Virginia was now in danger of missing federal deadlines.[42]

## ATTACK THE WAIVER

As the northeast states were moving unevenly on the California program, the auto and oil industries tried another move to stop their activity. The industries sought to derail the northeast effort wholesale by knocking out the California option at the federal level. Under the Clean Air Act's allowance for California to have its own, tougher program, there is a mostly perfunctory requirement that a waiver from EPA be granted before the state can enforce its program. Every time California went through the procedure in the past, it got the waiver—until the northeast states began adopting the California program. That's when the auto industry, aided in part by Mobil and Texaco, began lobbying EPA and the White House to block the waiver. With California stopped, there would be no California program for northeast states to opt into. "As a result of the other states deciding to opt in," explained CARB director Jananne Sharpless at the time, "it's becoming more politically problematic for California to get its waivers."[43]

In the spring of 1992, EPA held its normal public hearing and comment period on the waiver and was moving toward a decision. However, in July, the comment period was re-opened, a move some say was brought about in part by pressure from Vice President Dan Quayle's Council on Competitiveness. EPA at the time denied pressure from the White House. That's about the same time that Mobil Corp. began running newspaper and magazine ads across the country with the headline, "California Dreaming?" Major oil companies disliked the alternative fuels-reformulated gasoline parts of the California program, fearing their spread to others states, in addition to the ZEV requirement. Mobil resorted to quoting CARB's chief of staff, James D. Boyd, saying, "problems can arise . . . when other states adopt our programs. Our regulations are designed to protect air quality under conditions that occur in California, and may not always be suitable for other areas." CARB, meanwhile, charged Mobil with quoting Boyd out of context and reiterated its position that California regulations may well be appropriate and suitable for other states.[44] In any case, EPA later granted the waiver, continuing the California program.

## GM CANS THE EV

At General Motors, meanwhile, a boardroom coup was underway in late 1992 that would soon spread to the company's EV program. GM's CEO, Robert Stempel—and Stempel's hand-picked president and personal friend, Lloyd Reuss—were under fire. GM was hemorrhaging badly, losing billions. In 1990 it lost $2 billion. In 1991 it lost another $4.5 billion. GM's market share had been sliding since the mid-1980s and wasn't improving with Stempel. Between 1980 and 1990 GM lost more than 10 percent of its market share: in 1979 it held 46 percent of the 14 million cars and light trucks sold in the US; by 1991, that share dropped to 35 percent of 13 million vehicles. In November 1991, Standard & Poor's put GM on a credit watch and downgraded its rating. By December 1991, GM announced it would close twenty-one US plants and trim its white- and blue-collar workforce by 74,000, reducing its capacity by one-fifth. In 1992, GM's board was still not happy with what it saw. Heads were going to role, and Stempel and Reuss were at the top of the list. When the shake-up finally came, it was big news: Stempel was removed as chair of the board's executive committee, Reuss was demoted. Board member John Smale of Proctor and Gamble took charge for the board, installing Jack Smith as president and William Hoglund as CFO.

Caught up in all of this was GM's EV program, a 400-person, $300 million operation that Stempel and Reuss had supported from day one. Up until this time, GM was proceeding apace under Roger Smith's 1990 announcement to produce the Impact in Lansing and introduce it commercially by the mid-1990s. "If you've been waiting for us," said GM's Ken Baker, head of the EV program, reiterating the goal in March 1991, "the waiting is over. We're committed to deliver a product by the mid-90s." By October 1992, however, after Stempel and Reuss had been demoted, and Jack Smith and Bill Hoglund elevated, the EV program was on the chopping block. At an awkward briefing on the EV program led by Ken Baker for GM's new management committee, Stempel, Reuss, Jack Smith, and Bill Hoglund were all in attendance.

> . . . When Baker finished, Stempel spoke first. Like Reuss, he felt the program was too important to be stopped. The company couldn't expect it to make a profit in three

## Al Gore & the ICE

As GM, California, and the northeast states were debating the need for tighter auto emissions standards and the possible use of EVs, the 1992 presidential race was underway featuring the Republican ticket of George Bush-Dan Quayle vs. the Democrat's slate of Bill Clinton-Al Gore. One issue that came up briefly during the campaign was the internal combustion engine.

In August 1992, President Bush, then stumping for reelection in that most automotive of places, Michigan, attacked the Clinton-Gore ticket as an environmental threat to the auto industry. Bush singled out Gore for what he had written about the automobile and the internal combustion engine in his book, *Earth in the Balance*.

"[He] says the automobile industry—and I quote . . .'poses a mortal threat to the security of every nation that is more deadly than that of any military enemy we're ever again likely to confront,'" said Bush. "That is Mr. Clinton's running mate talking about the auto industry that means so much to our country. . . . And one page later, he calls for the 'elimination of the internal combustion engine,'" Bush continued. "What kind of people are we dealing with here?"

Bush's attack on Gore reverberated loudly across the auto capital; raised the hackles of some autoworkers concerned about their future; and also brought then-Vice President Dan Quayle into the fray, calling Gore's writing "bizarre stuff." Gore had indeed written that it was time to start thinking about phasing out the internal combustion engine, replacing it with something new, something cleaner, and more efficient—something better. Gore had written:

> ". . . We now know that [the automobile's] cumulative impact on the global environment is posing a mortal threat to the security of every nation that is more deadly than that of any military enemy we are ever again likely to confront. Though it is technically possible to build high mileage cars and trucks, we are told that mandating a more rapid transition to more efficient vehicles will cause an unacceptable disruption in the current structure of the automobile industry. . . . I support new laws to mandate improvements in automobile fleet mileage, but much more is needed. . . . [I]t ought to be possible to establish a coordinated global program to accomplish the strategic goal of completely eliminating the internal combustion engine over, say, a twenty-five year period."

years, but what program with all-new technology could? Forcing every project to account for itself would just bring short-term gain and long-term disaster. New technology would be obsolete almost as soon as it appeared, but GM had to keep developing it. Stempel thought the cost of Impact should be spread not just into one follow-on [model], but over the first three or four cars, while the learning curve was steep. By the fourth car GM would have a mature design at far lower costs. "What do you think, Jack?" Stempel concluded.

"Bob," Smith said, "you can't afford it." Then he stood up. "Please excuse me," he said. "I've got to get to another meeting."

An embarrassed silence fell over the room as he left. . . .[45]

GM's EV team of 400 people was cut by two-thirds and the project reduced to 50 hand-built models to be used for two years of performance and consumer testing. But there was also something else on the table: the possibility of a "Team USA" EV consortium of GM, Chrysler, and Ford. This venture—which Ken Baker had described to GM's board in December 1992 following the Clinton-Gore election—was billed as a possible model for working with the federal government. After all, Baker reminded the board in his pitch, Vice President-elect Al Gore had talked about getting beyond the internal combustion engine. Perhaps Team USA could influence the new administration's transportation policies. Besides, explained Baker, GM couldn't afford to do it alone, and any money that might come from the federal government would obviously help.[46] A Team USA approach for EVs—at least the Big Three only version—never came to fruition. But the idea of getting together with the federal government would surface again, later.

## MULTIPLE FRONTS

Back in the Northeast, the AAMA was in court challenging New York's move to adopt the California Car program. In January 1993, AAMA lawyers narrowly convinced a federal district court judge to rule that the northeast states wanting to adopt the California program had to adopt it in its entirety or not at all. Some of the northeast states, like New York, wanted to avoid the reformulated fuels part of the California program—and the politically sensitive issue of higher gasoline prices that might erode public support. In court, however, New York's plan to use a modified California program was struck down. The state then appealed, and the litigation dragged on.

The automakers and the oil companies were also at work in northeast state legislatures twisting arms. With factories and assembly plants in many of those states, the auto manufacturers, says Sonia Hamel, director of air policy and planning in the Massachusetts Office of Environmental Affairs, were "lobbying hard and threatening to move jobs to other states, or Mexico, if the legislatures adopted LEV." The oil industry, fearful that adopting a California-like LEV in the Northeast would bring with it the low-sulfur gasoline requirement and new refining expenses, also lobbied hard. "This is going to impose high costs," they told the legislators, says Daniel Greenbaum, director of the Massachusetts Department of Environmental Protection from 1988 to 1994. "You can't have the [low emission] cars without the California gasoline, and it's very expensive."[47]

In Maine, the DEP issued rules to adopt a LEV program in February 1993 with a ZEV requirement, but first required a technology review and consumer acceptance study before the rules could go into effect. The state legislature then added some stipulations, requiring that before such a program could go into effect, three other New England states would have to adopt LEV programs and 60 percent of the vehicles in the entire OTC region would have to be involved as well. The Maryland legislature failed to adopt a California-styled LEV program in 1992, but adopted a Maine-like "neighboring-states-first" proviso in 1993. In Pennsylvania, state representative Richard Cessar (R-Pittsburgh) offered a June 1993 resolution in the state legislature specifically opposing the use of electric vehicles. Delaware did, too. By this time, it was clear the state-by-state approach was in trouble. Critical deadlines now loomed as well. By November 1993, each state had to submit its implementation plan to EPA, and for northeastern states, this was now clouded by uncertainty about what neighboring states would or would not do regarding the adoption of the California program. Then the idea of adopting the California program on a regionwide basis was proposed, which the OTC could do if petitioned by a member state. In August 1993, Maine, Maryland, and Massachusetts called on the OTC to officially petition EPA to approve the California Car option throughout the Northeast.

The auto industry, meanwhile, was pressing California to back off its 1998 ZEV requirement. In August 1993, Ford Motor Co. vice chairman Alan D. Gilmour flew to California to lobby Governor Pete Wilson to relax the CARB mandate. He later wrote to Wilson to explain that Ford would have to spend some $2 billion by 1998 to comply with the mandate and that the company would lose money in the process. But Ford's $2 billion figure included setting up a dealer network and projected losses for the first few years of operation when volumes would be low and costs high. "The [Ford] comptroller threw in everything he could find," explained Ford's EV director, John Wallace of the $2 billion figure.[48]

General Motors, however, was working on another approach—born of an idea that came to GM's "Mr. Emissions," Sam Leonard, in September 1993. Leonard was trying to come up with a way to outflank the northeast states and spare the Big Three the trouble of fighting state-by-state. What he came up with was a gasoline car strategy that would produce "nearly clean cars" by the year 2001 without adopting the California program—and certainly not the ZEV portion of that program. Under Leonard's plan, the new cars could be sold in forty-nine states, not just the Northeast, thereby providing a "gift" to the entire nation. Leonard's idea gradually made its way into the political lexicon of auto emissions deal-making as "FED-LEV," for Federal Low Emission Vehicle (Leonard's name, not EPA's). But there was a quid pro quo for the gift: dropping ZEVs.

The gist of the FED-LEV plan would be to drop any reference to EV mandates and put in its place low-emitting gasoline-powered cars that would clean the air just as well as the California standards—or so the automakers said. The Big Three were clearly alarmed by the prospect of a regionwide ZEV, which when combined with California, would mean producing such cars for about 40 percent of the auto market. FED-LEV was designed to prevent that from happening. The strategy for the automakers was to get the forty-nine-state plan out on the streets prior to the scheduled February 1994 OTC vote on the California option, then several months away. On October 19, 1993, at an AAMA board meeting, the Big Three's CEOs agreed to lobby both against the California mandate and to push the forty-nine-state plan in the Northeast and nationally.[49] A division of labor was also established among the companies. According to the *LA Times*, Ford would focus on derailing the California program, while "GM leads the Big Three's fight against the spread of California's rules to the 12 Northeast states. . . ."[50] Environmentalists, however, were not standing still. A coalition of more than seventy environmental and public health groups wrote to the OTC in January 1994, urging it to support the California Car option.

The auto industry used its traditional arguments to push its preferred solution and derail the OTC-LEV move. Auto officials would point out that its vehicles were 96 percent cleaner than they were in the 1960s, with more improvements to come. Some regulators, still beset by ozone alerts and with nowhere else to turn for reductions, believed there was still room for improvement. "If I had four percent dirt in my beverage," argued Sonia Hamel, alluding to the 96-percent-cleaner-cars line, "I wouldn't drink it. . . . We've got almost 3.6 million cars on the road, and they travel 12,000 miles a years, so even a small amount [of a pollutant], less than a gram per mile, multiplied by trillions [of vehicle miles] is a lot of stuff." Electric vehicles offered a very attractive option for taking tons of pollution out of the air.[51] Yet, for the auto industry, this hit at the very core of their business, and indeed the whole automotive economy. As Max Gates of the AAMA later put it, the "basic paradigm of the internal combustion engine" was being questioned with the EV push.[52] So, in the mold of Sam Leonard's maxim about buying time, the industry persisted with its FED-LEV idea at the OTC and EPA.

Environmentalists fought from the other perspective. Peter Iwanowicz of Environmental Advocates in New York called the automakers plan "too little, too late." In fact, OTC examined the FED-LEV proposal and found it falling short of needed reductions. The California LEV option was better and would "emit 30 percent less hydrocarbons and 15 percent less NOx than . . . the proposed AAMA standards."[53] Others in the Northeast felt that pushing EV technology was crucial as well, but FED-LEV allowed none of that. Still, the vote in the OTC was uncertain, as there had been new governors elected in two northeast states, and some states were sympathetic to the FED-LEV idea.

## The OTC Vote

On February 1, 1994, the OTC formally voted to petition EPA to allow the Northeast to adopt the California program. The vote to approve was 9-4. "Today's action represents a significant step toward providing healthier air to breathe in the region and opportunities for a stronger economic future," said Arthur Davis, Pennsylvania's environment secretary and chairman of the OTC.[54] US Senator George Mitchell (D-ME) hailed the OTC vote noting that the regional body "was established precisely for the purpose of helping prevent the creation of pollution from upwind states which ultimately ends up in Maine." Dean Marriott, Maine's environmental commissioner, agreed, "We're going to get a lot of benefit from this because . . . in the summer we get a lot of the air pollution transported to our state from outside places."[55] New Jersey, Delaware, New Hampshire, and Virginia cast opposing votes, with some of those states asking for more time to consider the proposal. Others in the dissenting camp were more emphatic. "We are not interested in having any vehicles mandated onto the residents of Northern Virginia," said Becky Norton Dunlop, Virginia's OTC representative. EPA, however, still had to rule on the OTC vote, leaving industry an opening.

A few days after the OTC vote, both GM's Jack Smith and Ford's Alex Trotman, in separate appearances at a Chicago auto conference, said they could not meet the "California Car" mandate by 1998, either in California or the Northeast. "We don't have the know-how to get there with a vehicle that consumers will pay for," said Trotman, announcing his company would fight to roll back the California mandate.[56] Publicly, GM was taking the same position, although privately, it was reconsidering its canned EV program. Jack Smith had asked Ken Baker to make a case to GM's president's council for restarting the EV program, which he did*, and which the GM board later approved. But in March 1994, the GM effort was kept secret and out of the public limelight for fear of encouraging California regulators to stand firm on the EV mandate. GM still wanted to overturn the mandate and figured it had a shot at doing just that when CARB began its biennial review of the process in May 1994. So internally, the EV program at GM was on orders to "run silent, run deep."[57]

Meanwhile, on February 10, 1994, the auto industry received another bit of bad news. The US Court of Appeals for the 2nd Circuit upheld the State of New York's right to adopt the California emissions program, including the EV mandate. In the decision, the court criticized the automakers' contention that electric vehicles would

---

* It was in this briefing by Baker, if not before, that the "business lightbulbs" began clicking on for GM executives. By this time, they began to see that EV technology was a prelude, potentially, to a much bigger business, and offered something of a competitive edge to the "next technologies"—not to mention a potentially rich components business. EVs, hybrids, fuel cells, whatever—all would need new kinds of components; components that GM as a major auto industry parts supplier already, would be able to sell, especially if it stayed on the EV learning curve. Hybrids were on the way, said Baker, and in ten years might equal or surpass the range of conventional gasoline engines. Longer term, there was the fuel cell. Recounts Michael Shnayerson of Baker's presentation, ". . . If the hydrogen for a fuel cell came from natural gas or methane, a small amount of carbon dioxide would be produced. One day, though, that hydrogen might be produced onboard by *solar* power, the sun electrolyzing water into hydrogen and oxygen, the fuel cell reforming the water even as it created electricity, the whole an elegant closed loop of forming and reforming energy with no toxic emissions at all. That would be the free lunch, the ultimate car. . . .

". . . If the mandate held, Baker observed, GM would have to do EV's anyway. Why not seize the technological lead by producing Impact, and then *keep* ahead, along a continuum of car development that stretched not five or even ten years into the future, but half a century?"

not be economically feasible before the turn of the century. The court called that logic something akin to nineteenth-century reasoning that "anything that ever could be invented had already been invented."[58]

By this time in the Northeast, there were a range of interests beyond environmentalists and state regulators supporting the adoption of the California Car option. Electric utilities and new EV manufacturers, conversion businesses, and others all became involved in the lobbying, urging EPA to approve the petition. US Senators Max Baucus (D-MT), Barbara Boxer (D-CA), Daniel Patrick Moynihan (D-NY), James Jeffords (R-VT), Patrick Leahy (D-VT), and John Kerry (D-MA) also became involved, writing EPA administrator Carol Browner to support the petition. The senators noted, for example, that the industry proposals to the OTC and EPA— one of which had promised a certain level of emissions reductions in advance of given deadlines, but were not universally triggered for all locations under 1990 Clean Air Act*—were inconsistent with the act, and in their view "would prolong the exposure of Americans to serious health and environmental problems associated with polluted air."[59]

The Big Three and Big Oil, meanwhile, had enlisted paid consultants to get their story out, stressing costs. One of the firms employed was Sierra Research of Sacramento, run by a former CARB executive named Tom Austin. Austin was known to favor cleaning up gas cars as the best route to cleaning the air. His numbers found that the cost for gas cars at one level would be about $323 on average to meet the California standards. However for ZEVs, the cost would be much higher, adding about $21,000 to the cost of a gas car. Austin, in fact, would tell a Detroit newspaper reporter, "CARB wants GM to build Impacts at forty thousand dollars apiece. Then you have suckers in the Midwest subsidize them by paying ten thousand dollars more for every conventional car." Soon, this argument was rolling from the lips of Chrysler officials appearing in TV ads. Reg Maudlin, Chrysler's environmental affairs manager, stated in one spot, "On that window sticker for your . . . Dodge Neon . . . will be a line item that'll say twenty-seven hundred dollars extra charge. . . . Thank you for your contribution to your neighbor's electric car." According to Michael Shnayerson, "Chrysler, from its chairman Bob Eaton on down, had become by far the most vocally bitter of the Big Three on the mandate."[60] Chrysler mobilized its northeast dealers "to scare consumers with the promise of a $2,700 premium on all

---

* For example, the auto industry offered, in modified form, to accelerate its meeting of tighter Tier 2 emissions standards required under the Clean Air Act ahead of schedule. Under the act, however, the EPA could not impose Tier 2 standards until 2004. The industry proposal offered to bring part of the new national vehicle fleet in 2001 up to a modified Tier 2 auto emissions standard, and all new vehicles up to the modified standard by 2004. The proposal would have created a new national car provision. The OTC, for its part, rejected this proposal because its slated emissions reductions were too small and would come too late to help the northeast states come into compliance.

gas cars if EVs were forced into the market."[61] Bob Eaton, in fact, would later announce that Chrysler would impose a surcharge of up to $2,000 on gasoline-powered automobiles in some states to cover the cost of EVs. "The surcharge will be imposed in California and other states with 2-percent ZEV requirements by 1999," said the announcement.

Part of the automakers' campaign was aimed at CARB's spring 1994 review of the "2-percent-ZEVs-by-1998" requirement. They were hopeful, after their lobbying of Pete Wilson and the CARB board, that they might be able to derail or put off the mandate. A series of fairly contentious meetings and public hearings were held in California, with each side presenting their best case. After months of debate, however, CARB held its ground. "We heard from no one who claimed the mandate had not accomplished its stated objective of stimulating technological development and innovation," said CARB chairwoman Jacqueline Schafer in announcing the board's decision. "While electric vehicle and battery technology may not have advanced much between the turn of the century and the 1980s, there is no doubt that tremendous advancements have occurred since we adopted the zero emission vehicle regulation in 1990. We heard over and over again that the mandate caused or contributed to these advancements. I don't think we want to take any actions that would slow down or stall this progress. . . . The mandate must remain in place."

## FED-LEV Becomes NLEV

Back in the Northeast, the Big Three tried appealing to EPA in September 1994 to prevent the region from adopting the California approach. EPA was required to approve the OTC action. The automakers urged Browner not to approve. "We think that forcing an electric car on the market at this point would be way too expensive for the consumer and not beneficial to the environment," said Richard Klimisch for the AAMA. Yet, the OTC petition did not require ZEVs, but they were available to individual states as an option. Still, EPA was inundated with comments after it proposed a rule to approve the OTC petition and consequently missed its November 10, 1994 deadline for issuing a final decision. EPA was also stalling a bit, hoping that something might be negotiated between the states and the auto industry.

The auto industry by this time had revised its FED-LEV proposal, renaming it "the forty-nine-state plan"—later to be called NLEV for "national" LEV. This proposal sweetened the pot and raised the political ante somewhat with even cleaner cars, but still fell short of the California car. What is often overlooked in the industry's supposed "gift" to the nation was that if adopted, the new and improved forty-nine-state plan would, in effect, foreclose those forty-nine states from adopting the California program. In addition to the ZEV requirement, the California program also called for very significant reductions in hydrocarbon pollutants from regular old cars—ozone-forming pollutants known to insiders as "nonmethane organic hydrocarbons," or NMOG for short. Sonia Hamel of Massachusetts points out that the automakers were very careful in what they said they would and would not do in their proposal. "They didn't say to us, if you drop the ZEV program, we'll do the rest of the California program. . . . They said if you drop the ZEV mandate, we'll do . . . [NLEV] for the whole country, and then you lose your rights to anything that's cleaner than [that]." Electric vehicles, says Hamel, were only a small part of the story. "In 2003, for example, they [ZEVs] would represent only ten percent of the mix," she says. "We were really focused on the other 90 percent. . . . California's got the right to have a cleaner car *average* [emphasis added], and we wanted to have that too."[62]

EPA, meanwhile, was under the gun to finally decide on the OTC-LEV proposal, which the OTC had voted for, 9-4, in February. On December 19, 1994—one day before Massachusetts and environmental groups had planned to sue EPA for not making the OTC decision—EPA approved the OTC petition allowing for California programs in the twelve northeast states and Washington, DC.

The AAMA said it would continue to fight all state mandates or targets for the sale of advanced technology vehicles, whether cars or trucks, electric or natural gas. Discussions on the forty-nine-state plan were still ongoing after the EPA ruling, with some states willing to negotiate with mediation by EPA. EPA, however, was leaning toward the industry plan. "We believe this broader agreement would be the most cost-effective way of bringing clean air to Americans," EPA's Carol Browner said in a statement.[63] In some northeast states, EPA's position was viewed as a cop-out, or at the least, undermining the work of those states trying to move EVs forward.

## 1994: REPUBLICAN REVOLUTION

By late 1994, a new political dynamic was at work in Washington and across the country. Republicans had taken the Congress. Newt Gingrich's "Contract with America" was being supported by the auto industry and others. Environmental laws were likely targets. In New York and Massachusetts, new Republican governors were elected. Pete Wilson was re-elected in California. All around it appeared the environmental balance had shifted decidedly in industry's favor. GM scrapped its planned announcement on its resurrected EV program slated for the January 1995 LA auto show.

In the northeastern states and Washington, DC, the auto industry started running a series of radio spots in early 1995 to whip up sentiment against the California Car, while plugging the forty-nine-state plan. "It's hard to believe," intoned a narrator on the spot used in Maryland, "but right now some state government officials are actually considering California's costly and highly controversial auto emissions plan for Maryland. The other plan, called the forty-nine-state approach, cuts pollution just as much or more and costs consumers a lot less." The ad, modeled in part after the successful "Harry and Louise" series used on the health care issue, was also designed to coincide with the National Governors Conference in February and a meeting of the OTC governors, now with its new Republican members. "This could be a precedent setting meeting to consider what the rights are of the newly constituted members," said AAMA's Andrew Card. In January 1995, New Hampshire governor Steve Meril(R) wrote Senator Gregg Judd(R-NH) to sponsor legislation that would allow New Hampshire to pull out of the OTC.[64]

In Massachusetts, Republican governor William Weld was holding firm on his state's position to adopt the California Car option. Weld defended this choice, in part, on states' rights grounds. And there was also the small matter of Massachusetts' bad air. At least 43 percent of the state's ozone-producing pollutants came from cars and trucks, as opposed to 11 percent from utilities and 8 percent from industry. As for the automakers' proposed forty-nine-state plan, Weld wrote to fellow Republican governor John Engler of Michigan in a February 10, 1995 letter, "we wholeheartedly support the forty-nine-state car, and we welcome its introduction into Massachusetts and the other forty-eight states." But he also added, "we do believe the potential of ZEV for pollution reduction and economic development in Massachusetts is clear."[65]

Chrysler's Bob Eaton, meanwhile, was telling shareholders in his February 1995 report to beware of the electric car mandates California, New York, and Massachusetts had set for 1998. "Developing and producing [the EVs], although costly, does not represent an insurmountable technical problem," he explained. "We already produce electric minivans [technically, conversions]. The problem is, there is virtually no consumer demand for them. So we'll have to price them at thousands of dollars below cost in order to generate buyer interest and force our other customers to subsidize them through higher prices on conventional vehicles. We hope the states will repeal their anti-consumer sales mandates."[66] The Big Three also redoubled their public relations effort to derail state-based EV initiatives.

### "A CLIMATE FOR REPEAL"

In California, the automakers mounted a PR and grassroots campaign to attack the mandate. A confidential March 24, 1995 document prepared by the AAMA made no bones about what the Big Three wanted to do in California. "The AAMA is conducting a search for a qualified contractor to manage a statewide grassroots and educational campaign . . . to create a climate in which the [California EV] mandate . . . can be repealed." Sure enough, before too long, and together with the oil industry, there was all manner of "grassroots" activity generating a furor about government regulation and electric vehicles. Enlisted in the anti-EV crusade, with either auto or oil money, were public relations firms such as Woodward and McDowell of Burlingame, CA; Sierra Research, Inc. of Sacramento; McNally Temple Associates of Sacramento; and others.[67]

The oil industry was already well along in its own anti-EV campaign, having targeted California utilities in 1993-94 when they proposed a $630 million upgrade of electric infrastructure to accommodate EVs. The utility proposal included a six-year package of R & D and incentives on the customer side of the line to help move along EV acceptance. A six-cents-a-month surcharge was being proposed for ratepayers to pay for the upgrade. The upgrade package was needed to comply with existing law, the California EV mandate. The oil companies, then spending millions on their refineries to produce reformulated gasolines and obviously threatened by any inroads on gasoline, saw the utility upgrade and ratepayer surcharge as a way to attack the EV mandate generally. The Western Petroleum Association (WSPA) began backing a front group called "Californians Against Utility Company Abuse" (CAUCA), which, in turn, was run by a California PR firm, Woodward and McDowell. The automakers, although not directly involved in this fight, went along for the ride.

GM, for example, was beginning its June 1994 public "PrEView" test run of fifty Impacts for two-year trials with volunteer consumers and was joined by the utilities in Los Angeles announcing the program. Test drivers would have their garages rewired to accommodate Impact chargers. The utilities would also help troubleshoot for the volunteer testers if they had any problems along the way. Still, there was a political chasm between the automakers and the utilities on the larger issue of mandate politics. On the one hand, GM was working with the utilities on their Impact program. With the other, they were spending money on lobbying to undo the EV mandate. Southern California Edison and other utilities were angry with the automakers' silence as Big Oil whipped up a grassroots frenzy and poured money into public attacks on the utility rate increase proposals needed to pay for the EV infrastructure improvements. The Big Three would say their hands were clean in those campaigns and "piously lamented the Oilies' tendency to trash EV technology. . . ." Richard Klimisch of the AAMA, however, would acknowledge that "the interests of the Big Three and Big Oil were parallel." In Sacramento, meanwhile, environmental advocates like John White stood little chance of beating back both the Big Three and Big Oil.[68]

The oil and auto campaigns continued through 1995. That summer, as CARB conducted workshops and public hearings on the EV mandate, a Big Oil-backed group of firemen began making the rounds on talk shows raising questions about EV safety—what might happen in a crash. Would the batteries, for example, release explosive hydrogen gas?[69] The oil companies also urged the firemen to testify before CARB.*

---

* One of the reasons the oil companies fought so furiously against the EV mandate was the fear of losing markets not only in the US, but also abroad. Mike Wirsch with the Sacramento Municipal Utility District put it this way: Big Oil saw that potential huge overseas gasoline markets—like China, India, and Malaysia, where an extensive system of filling stations, pipelines, etc., was not yet established—could conceivably "leap frog" gasoline altogether by going to electric vehicles. So, nipping the EV movement in bud here, the oil companies figured, would also slow its spread globally, buying time to establish more extensive gasoline systems throughout the world. See, Nick Budnick, "Electric Smoke Screen," *Sacramento News & Review*, July 6, 1995, pp. 19-20.

In concert with the Republican revolution, the Big Three began singing the anti-regulatory tune, tagging EV mandates as unfunded and unwarranted intrusions in the market by government. "There is a perception by the automakers, the public and some legislators that it is time to bring some sense to these regulations," offered GM's Sam Leonard, putting his own spin on the new political climate in March 1995.[70]

Jason Vines, a Chrysler spokesman in Washington, charged that EVs would come at a high cost with little environmental benefit. Such costs, he asserted, amounted to an unfunded mandate in California's case. "We see the electric vehicle as a poster child for these issues," he said, alluding to the excessive regulation and unfunded mandate charge. Chrysler and the other automakers were pressing CARB on the cost issue, pushing the board to move up the scheduled 1996 review of the mandate to 1995. "We want them to look at it from a different perspective," said Eric Ridenour, director of environment and energy planning. "Cost-benefit analysis, sound science, and risk assessment are the buzz words."[71]

## Presidential Politics

During 1995, the LEV-ZEV issue had also begun to permeate the Republican presidential nomination process. Pete Wilson, then making a bid for the nomination, came under pressure from the midwestern Republican governors he was courting for support. In a May 1995 letter, Governors John Engler of Michigan, Tommy Thompson of Wisconsin, George Voinovich of Ohio, and Jim Edgar of Illinois, wrote to Wilson, saying that California's ZEV requirements would be of little environmental benefit. Buying the auto industry's argument, they also said that electric vehicles would be so expensive that they have to be subsidized by conventional vehicles, which would cost jobs in their states. The four governors said they endorsed the auto industry "compromise plan" calling for tougher emissions standards on conventional cars. "We are willing to organize and participate with you in an event here in any one of the Great Lakes States, or anywhere else, . . ." they wrote Wilson of a possible campaign event, "to announce your support for national clean car." All four states had their Republican primaries scheduled for late February 1996.[72]

Wilson, for his part, stopped short of throwing over the California mandate in favor of the industry plan, but he did request an audit of the California electric car program, which some believe was the camel's nose under the tent. "The Wilson administration and its appointees have consistently supported the [CARB] until he decided to run for president," said Joe Caves, then lobbying in Sacramento for the Union for Concerned Scientists and other EV proponents. "There's never been any indication before that this decision was going to be made on anything other than its importance to the California air quality program. . . ."[73] But now, Wilson was allowing for other factors, opening the door to the automakers' arguments about cost and sales.

In Massachusetts, meanwhile, Governor William Weld, who had become Pete Wilson's campaign finance chairman, was also under the gun of his own state's EV mandate, patterned after California's. The automakers were pressing Massachusetts and the other northeast states to adopt the forty-nine-state plan—and abandon any mention of ZEVs. The bottom line for industry's moving ahead with the forty-nine-state car, the automakers said, was eliminating the ZEV requirements in New York and Massachusetts. Weld, however, had a different idea. In March 1995, he put forward a compromise: Massachusetts would delay by two years, to the year 2000, the demand for ZEVs—if Detroit started building its forty-nine-state gas car immediately. Weld also wanted assurances from automakers that if a breakthrough EV battery was developed, they would bring it to market within one year. Weld hinted that some generous allowances might be allowed in the way his state counted "electric vehicles" meaning that hybrids might be made; that averaging of sales over several years might be possible; and that EVs in some states upwind of Massachusetts might also be counted.[74]

Some charged that Weld was caving in. "It's really giving the auto industry and the oil industry two more years to spend millions of dollars to kill the zero emission mandate," said Michelle Robinson of the Union of Concerned Scientists. State representative David Cohen (D-Newton), author of the Massachusetts law, said the state had fought too long for electric and other low emission vehicles to back down now. Weld's proposal was debated and considered for the next several months.[75]

## ULTIMATUMS

The automakers, however, were rigid in their position, pressing their ultimatum to adopt the forty-nine-state plan only. Andrew Card and his AAMA delegation angrily refused the Weld compromise in Boston. AAMA was also pushing a deadline: the states had to decide whether to accept the forty-nine-state plan by July 31, 1995, as the automakers were then under the gun to make 1997 tooling decisions. Trudy Coxe, Massachusetts' environmental commissioner, was incensed by the automakers' ultimatum. "[It] merely revealed the carmakers' callousness," she said. "If they *could* make a cleaner gas car sooner than the law required, why didn't they do so for the general good, rather than playing it as a chip in the game to knock out EVs?" After Andrew Card and his team struck out in Massachusetts they then "brought their terms—unchanged—to Albany. At a local Omni hotel, they met with state officials, who tentatively agree to a six-year delay on ZEVs. Yet the carmakers, angry and arrogant, refused even this deal. The ZEV mandate had to go."[76]

The Big Three continued to threaten the OTC (and later, EPA): if the states didn't agree by the end of July to drop EVs from their plans, the Big Three would not build the forty-nine-state car. The automakers' NLEV plan eventually would be adopted by EPA, but would become mired in rulemaking and legal entanglements for years.[77] Essentially, the Big Three got what they wanted, and there was always their old friend, delay. But soon, Detroit shifted its attention back to California, where CARB was beginning a series of reviews, focusing mostly on battery technology and cost.

On one level, the Big Three were going through the motions of ZEV-compliance-if-they-had-to, ready to use conversions and fleet sales large enough to satisfy the 2- percent-by-1998 mandate. In April 1995, for example, Ford announced it was taking the conversion route* and that Troy Design and Manufacturing Company in Redford, Michigan would convert Ford Ranger pickups to EVs for 1998. The converted Rangers would have a range of about 35 miles with lead acid batteries. "The Ranger at least allows us to put all componentry into production," said John Wallace at the time. "That's consistent with Ford's strategy. It minimizes investment in the vehicles. Because there's no market."

But Ford was also playing pricing games with its Rangers. The EV Rangers, Ford said, would retail for $30,000, which was about $11,000 more than the gasoline-fueled Ranger. Some environmentalists had obtained internal Ford memos revealing an earlier target price for the EV pickups at $21,000—the selling price originally scheduled for the 1998 vehicles. But during the crucial summer of 1995, as CARB was weighing the mandate, "Ford wielded its ["revised"] $30,000 estimate like a club over the California commissioners. At that price, Ford lobbyists told them, no one would buy the truck." They pressed their case in private as well. "Though the lobbyists were careful not to be overt," explains Michael Shnayerson, "the commissioners got the message: Ford would sabotage its own EV program, if necessary, to *make* the mandate fail."[78]

By August 1995, GM's Dennis Minano said he expected California to heed industry's arguments that the current crop of electric vehicles would not meet consumer's needs. "In my optimistic view," he said, "I think the facts in terms of engineering, marketing and infrastructure will carry the day and they'll make an adjustment."[79] California Governor Pete Wilson dropped out of the presidential race in September and began facing pressure back home to undo the ZEV mandate. Wilson pushed CARB's new chairman, John Dunlap, to convene a special panel of experts to investigate progress in EV battery technology, which the Big Three then made the focus of their technical attack. In the Northeast, meanwhile, the AAMA began to use its advertising muscle in Massachusetts and New York, running ads in Boston and New York newspapers during October and November of 1995. The ads skewered electric vehicles and urged adoption of the automakers' "cleaner car" program—the forty-nine-state plan. Supporters of EVs retaliated with their own ad, bringing up the industry's 1982 position on an earlier technology—air bags—and how that requirement was supposed to "kill the industry."

---

* Ford had run into problems with its sodium sulfur batteries in its Ecostar vans. In mid-1994, after two fires occurred, it recalled its fleet of thirty-four vans, and by November 1994, thought US Electricar might be able to retrofit Ford "gliders" with EV equipment, but that deal fell through after Electricar ran into trouble.

## DEMISE OF THE MANDATE

Back in California, by late November 1995, CARB's chairman John Dunlap was sig-naling compromise on the ZEV mandate. CARB began holding discussions with the auto companies about putting some ZEVs on the road sooner than 1998, but doing away with the mandate.[80] By December 1995, it became clear what the auto indus-try wanted: a six-year suspension, coupled with voluntary offers to produce about 2,000 electric cars between 1998 and 2000. Oil companies, on the other hand, wanted the mandate repealed altogether. EV proponents were charging that CARB was being pushed politically by Pete Wilson and the oil industry, and indeed environmental-ists and the electric utilities were excluded from the discussions.[81] CARB's Dunlap insisted the review was technical. Still, even some engineers serving on the Wilson administration advisory committee were dismayed with the discussions and what appeared to be unfolding. The battery panel, meanwhile, predicted in fact that advanced batteries were very close—batteries that could give electrics range comparable to gaso-line-powered cars and would be available by 2000 or 2001. Said one of the advisors, "This mandate was shaping up as a brilliant success. This program actually worked, with just a little time disparity between 1998 and 2000. Why are they crumbling now?"[82]

Marla Cone of the *LA Times*, reporting on the likely collapse of the ZEV man-date, observed, "Such a decision would mark the first time the California air agency had backed down after three decades of setting groundbreaking, aggressive limits for auto pollution. . . . [S]econd guessing the auto industry is exactly what the air board had done since its creation 28 years ago. . . . Virtually every regulation was enacted despite glum forecasts by the auto companies, which wound up proving them-selves wrong and meeting deadlines without exorbitant price increases. . . . Every-one involved agrees that the air board's zero-emission standard has pushed electric car technology beyond what anyone imagined a decade ago. . . ."[83]

Still others had warned against tinkering with the mandate for economic rea-sons, pulling out the underpinning of a newly developing EV industry. "Many com-panies are making substantial investments in future technologies and products based on that mandate," wrote University of California professor and transportation ana-lyst Daniel Sperling in late 1994. "Any indication that the mandate might be changed or abandoned would freeze investment in hundreds of companies, especially small companies dependent on outside financing." Sperling, in fact, could not say enough about the importance of the mandate. "The ZEV mandate had probably spurred more progress in electric propulsion technology in a few years than took place over the course of twenty years under the combined auspices of the auto industry and DOE." Almost entirely because of the mandate, he said "every major automaker in the world has now invested in electric vehicle development." In addition, "hundreds of companies are sprouting up to develop and commercialize critical technologies of the future, such as flywheels, batteries, ultracapacitors, and fuel cells. . . ."[84] All of that now appeared to be increasingly at risk.

*In October 1995, the Big Three ran ads like this one in New York (and Massachusetts) to try to prevent the adoption of California's more stringent clean-car programs.*

*In November 1995, this AAMA ad appeared in the* Boston Globe *and the* Boston Herald, *urging Massachusetts to abandon its adoption of the California program.*

# "Airbags are going to kill the automobile industry."

*-Automakers, 1982*

If only automakers knew then what they know now. They fought hard against lifesaving airbags. Today, they couldn't sell their cars without them.

And now they're doing it again. This time, the issue is giving consumers the choice to purchase electric vehicles. Massachusetts requires that automakers offer affordable, clean electric vehicles starting in 1998. But they'd rather have everyone believe electric vehicles are still part of science fiction.

Fact is, electric vehicles are made right here in Massachusetts. And they're available now. The requirement simply assures that automakers supply them in Massachusetts.

Not only are these vehicles better for the environment and public health in a region with air quality problems, but they also give you, the consumer, a choice. With all the models and options automakers offer, choice is something they should support, not fight.

We'd like your opinion. Call 617-248-1883 for more information on electric vehicles and the environment.

*Consumer, public health, labor, environmental, and utility interests ran this ad to remind the public of the automakers' reluctance on other new technology.*

Standing on the sidelines, but anticipating the worse, were New York and Massachusetts. "This is snatching defeat from the jaws of victory," remarked Massachusetts state representative David Cohen.[85] Sure enough, on December 14, 1995, CARB essentially repealed the 1998 mandate, letting stand the 2003 requirement for 10 percent ZEVs. The seven major automakers did agree to voluntarily produce 3,750 EVs among themselves by the year 2000. And they also pledged to continue funding advanced battery research and disclose confidentially to CARB their EV plans and capital expenditures through the year 2003. Beginning in the year 2001, the automakers also agreed to produce gasoline-powered cars nationwide that would meet clean air standards originally slated to take effect in 2004—essentially the forty-nine-state car that the automakers had been trying to sell in the Northeast.

Environmentalists were not happy with the deal. Roland Hwang, of the Union of Concerned Scientists, pointed up the industry's hypocrisy as well as weaknesses in the deal's fine print. "All along, the automakers were telling CARB they wouldn't build the 49-state car, while at the same time they're telling the Northeast states they would." As for the agreement committing the automakers to the forty-nine-state car nationally, Hwang called it "meaningless," saying it was full of loopholes. "There's no real enforceability if they don't make a 49-state car—automakers are only required to live up to the spirit of the agreement. . . . They can get reductions from stationary sources or scrappage if they want to. We need to get automakers to take responsibility for vehicle technology."[86]

For the Big Three, however, the repeal of the California provision was perceived as a great victory. "Among carmakers, a lot of crowing went on that Christmas season," recounts Michael Shnayerson after spending a few years with GM while it ran hot and cold with its EV program. "CARB, they said, had finally come to its senses. Invention on schedule never worked—why, with EVs, it has *slowed* the pace of progress, gummed it up. Now that it was gone, the carmakers declared, EVs would come to market just as fast as invention and demand impelled them. That was what free markets were all about."[87]

But Shnayerson also added, "If the carmakers really believed that, they were deluding themselves. Impact, to be sure, had reached the show car stage without a mandate. And in March 1994, GM had gone the high road by reviving it, rather than cobble together a simple conversion. Whether GM would have plunged back into EVs so soon *without* a mandate, however, seemed highly dubious. Certainly without the mandate, no other carmakers, large or small, domestic or foreign, would have instigated serious EV programs at all. . . ." Further, says Shnayerson, there was real technical accomplishment and innovation because of the mandate. "In 1989, two patents in the United States were granted for EV-related technology," he says. "In 1995, 200 patents were granted." What the mandate had done, in his view, "was to leverage the only force that could induce an industry as powerful and entrenched as the auto industry to challenge itself, to take technological risks, to change."[88]

The fight for EVs and clean cars, however, was far from over. Although the repeal of California's 1998 mandate was clearly a blow to EV proponents and raised troubling legal questions about what would now happen to the northeast states who had modeled their programs on California's, the ZEV mandate in California was still in place for 2003 and beyond. Equally important, but overlooked in all the hoopla over EVs, were the very considerable California emissions standards for conventional gasoline engines that could be brought into play in adopting states, regardless of ZEVs.

## THE EV-1

General Motors, meanwhile, as if to make a point that it did not need a mandate to produce electric vehicles, announced on January 4, 1996, that it would begin producing and leasing its "EV-1" models later that year on a limited scale in four cities. "It's time to get electric vehicles out of the lab, into the showroom and onto the road," said GM's Jack Smith before a very large audience at the Greater Los Angeles Auto Show announcing the new car. Smith called the EV-1 "a car designed for people—to commute, to shop, to run around town." And he added, "it's a car for people who never want to go to the gas station again." GM's electrics would be "sold" at $34,000 apiece through a leasing arrangement in four cities—Los Angeles, San Diego, Phoenix, and Tucson. The new vehicles would have a driving range of between 60 and 80 miles before recharging, and would produce zero emissions.[89] "When auto historians look back, they will see this car as the first in the new generation of vehicles," Smith said. "And they will note that GM made it."[90]

The EV-1, Smith explained to his audience that day, was closely tied to how GM sees itself in the future, "especially in our commitment to environmental stewardship." Part of the company's new vision, Smith said, "is to recapture our leadership in the public's mind as an innovative technology company.... This EV-1 is the first product in a portfolio of high-technology products that we will be bringing to market in the years ahead...."[91]

# 15

## EV Conspiracy?

They built electric cars for regulators, not for the market.

—*Bill Curtiss, attorney*
*EarthJustice Legal Defense Fund*

In early 1996, not long after the rollback of California's EV mandate, the Sierra Club Legal Defense Fund (SCLDF)* in San Francisco, working with the law firm of Preston Gates Ellis & Rouvelas Meeds, petitioned the US Justice Department (DOJ) alleging a conspiracy to stifle the development of electric vehicles.

"Based on a review of the extensive public record and interviews of a number of individuals who have been involved in US electric car programs," stated SCLDF in its brief, "there is substantial evidence of a conspiracy among the Big Three automotive producers to hinder the introduction of electric vehicles."[1] SCLDF also charged that oil companies had conspired to block utility companies from establishing the electric infrastructure needed to accommodate electric vehicles.

SCLDF petitioned two state attorneys general in the matter as well, California and Massachusetts. In a letter to James Boyd, executive director of CARB, SCLDF attorney Bill Curtiss charged that the auto and oil industries conspired "to discredit EVs as viable products." Curtiss asserted that the two industries attempted to cripple EV development by colluding to build substandard electric vehicles, by steering the industry-government battery consortium toward unachievable new technologies, and by muzzling announcements on battery breakthroughs.[2]

The Justice Department, for its part, did take an interest in the case and began an investigation. At least one DOJ investigator traveled around the country digging into records. However, nothing finally materialized. Still, the record compiled by Curtiss and others, plus the accounts of those interviewed, show at the very least

---

* The Sierra Club Legal Defense Fund (SCLDF) formally changed its name to Earth-Justice Legal Defense Fund in 1997.

there was a concerted effort by the auto and oil industries during the 1992-1996 period to cast EV development in a most unfavorable light. The two industries spent millions of dollars in the process—money that arguably would have been better spent on the technology itself. They worked instead, to discredit, downplay, and in some cases withhold, key information about the latest developments in EV battery technology. The automakers purposely skewed and inflated their own corporate cost accounting for EVs to make the vehicles appear more expensive than they actually would be in mass production. They, and their oil industry allies, consistently made public statements with the intent of lowering both consumer and regulator expectations about EV performance, especially regarding EV driving range and marketability. They hired outside experts, used political campaign contributions, and spent heavily on national and regional advertising to insure that both EV technology and government initiatives to promote the technology were seen as respectively premature and unnecessary. In some cases, the auto companies slowed down or withdrew their own EV investment dollars, or terminated outside contracts with EV suppliers, actions that had the net effect of dampening and discouraging investment in the start-up electric vehicle industry. And finally, in a move reminiscent of the 1950s collusion among automakers in holding back the development of smog-control devices for cars, the Big Three allied themselves with no less a force than the federal government in a collaborative effort purportedly designed to advance the key EV technology: batteries.

## BATTERY GAMES

The development of electric cars had always been hindered by the limitations of battery power. Pound for pound, batteries are typically less "energy dense" than gasoline, which is part of the reason why gasoline-powered vehicles won out in the early part of the century. The traditional lead-acid battery held a limited charge and therefore limited vehicles to a short driving range. Experimental electric vehicles labored under a "golf cart" image for many years because of their low power and limited range. By the late 1980s, however, a number of other battery candidates had come to the fore—sodium-sulfur, lithium polymer, lithium-ion, zinc-air, zinc-bromine, and nickel-based batteries to name a few. Many of these showed promise, but each had a drawback or two. Lead-acid, it seemed, was always the one left standing, the most familiar and most reliable. Lead-acid "battery packs" of many batteries were required to propel a vehicle over any major distance and added weight to the mix. Then there was the matter of recharging system that wasn't on-board the vehicle, requiring a separate infrastructure, which would likely involve the electric utility industry.

Thus, the battery, with all its trappings and uncertainties, became the key technological element in EV development—and as some saw it, a convenient technological scapegoat. The auto industry typically pointed to the "battery problem" when questions were asked about how soon electric cars would arrive. "The technology isn't ready yet" would be the typical reply. However, critics believed the technology "wasn't ready" because the auto and oil industries didn't want it to be ready. By the time of the California ZEV mandate, however, there was every appearance that battery R&D was now well underway and was, in fact, a major priority of the auto industry with considerable investment and talent behind it, including the federal government's.

## THE CONSORTIUM

In October 1991, an entity called the US Advanced Battery Consortium (USABC) was created. USABC was a collaboration between the federal government and the Big Three automakers. Formally launched in October 1991 by President George Bush at a ceremony in the Rose Garden, USABC was slated to run for twelve years. The Big Three's EV directors at the time—Ken Baker of GM, John Wallace of Ford, and Jean Mallebay-Vacquer of Chrysler—were all in attendance as George Bush praised the new effort and drove one of Chrysler's battery-powered electric minivans down a White House driveway to demonstrate the new vehicles of the future. Also parked in the White House driveway that day were GM's Impact and Ford's Ecostar.[3] None of these early prototypes, however, were ready for commercial production. USABC had all the appearances of a major effort to forge the necessary technology to put electric vehicles on the road.

The origins of the new consortium dated to 1990, when a DOE official, Michael Davis, began prodding the Big Three to consider the potential of adding federal funds to their own research efforts. Davis, a Bush appointee heading up DOE's advanced battery work, saw that DOE was giving out $20 million in funds to an assortment of research enterprises all over the country. Davis thought if the money could be pooled with the automakers', everyone would be pulling in the same direction, working on the most promising technologies. As initially envisioned, each of the Big Three would kick in a share of money, as would the federal government. But the federal share would be bigger. When Davis went to sell the idea to GM, Ford, and Chrysler, he suggested that "each of the Big Three would get, in effect, six dollars of R&D for every one spent."[4] But the benefits for the automakers went beyond money and individual projects.

In September 1990, the Big Three's EV directors met at GM's Tech Center to discuss the possibility of the battery consortium and agreed to go ahead with the venture, establishing a rotating chair, public relations director, and treasurer. They met monthly thereafter.[5] The Big Three, essentially, ran the program. Although money came from DOE, and the Electric Power Research Institute as well, the Big Three held the voting power within USABC even though they only contributed 16.5 percent of the money. In effect, the Big Three could decide among themselves which battery developers got the grants.

When word of the battery venture surfaced in January 1991, it was fully cast in "we-they" competitive terms. "You have to realize that your real enemy is not the guy next door to you, but somebody coming from another country," said Chrysler's Francois Castaing. Indeed, the Japanese were still hitting the Big Three hard. GM, Ford, and Chrysler had lost market share, dropping from 74 percent in 1980 to 65 percent in 1990. Others put an environmental spin on the new arrangement. "The government wants clean air, the people want clean air, and all manufacturers want to get there," explained John Casesa, securities analyst with the Wall Street firm Wertheim, Shroder & Co. "Why should we compete with ourselves to develop a new technology?"[6] It all sounded good.

## CALLING THE SHOTS

By March 1991, Baker, Wallace, and Mallebay-Vacquer were meeting regularly on USABC business and soon began issuing requests for proposals to battery developers.[7] However, according to SCLDF, and witnesses cited in its brief, the Big Three used USABC to control the pace of research. First, "at the behest of the automobile companies," says SCLDF, the USABC refused to fund any lead-acid battery research on the premise that it was "known technology" and so could not offer "advanced" products. "Lead-acid funding was withheld," charges SCLDF, "even though it was recognized that such batteries were the only technology available to meet the 1998 mandate."[8] Indeed, when GM embarked with AeroVironment in 1988 to begin working on the vehicle that would become the Impact, GM's Ken Baker and Runkle agreed with AeroVironment's Alec Brooks that going with lead-acid batteries was the right approach, especially if the point of their project was to show that EVs were feasible. Lead-acid, they agreed, was the only practical, producible battery then around, and it was cheap and reliable.[9]

Second, USABC, through the automakers, essentially defined goals for itself that enabled an indefinite postponement of progress. Explains SCLDF in its brief, "The mid-term goal [of USABC] is the development of a battery that could be used in an automobile with a 150-mile driving range and price that is comparable to similar internal combustion vehicles. This midterm goal, which the Big Three have widely cited as essential to the development of a commercially successful ZEV, far exceeds the distance traveled by most commuters and ignores the feasibility of a niche car that would meet the needs of most urban commuters even with current technology."[10] USABC, in other words, set its sights on the far future with its mid- and long-term goals, ignoring what was already available as a stepping stone—and a learning curve—to improved batteries and a larger market later on. USABC, however, judged on its far-future goals, would typically be found falling short, with more work to be done. Yet, clearly, in the 1998 time horizon, lead-acid battery technology was sufficient to begin the process, to move shorter-range, niche cars, trucks, and vans into the market, meeting a 2-percent-ZEVs-by-1998 goal easily. This was not a huge goal in any case, amounting to a California total of about 25,000 vehicles, split among seven domestic and foreign auto manufacturers.

Finally, USABC also provided a place where the Big Three could meet, collaborate, and conduct research unencumbered by any antitrust threats. But says SCLDF, "According to one witness who participated in it (John Dabels, formerly of GM), the automakers formed USABC to hinder rather than enhance product development by controlling research and development efforts." Such actions, charges SCLDF, "specifically violates the Cooperative Research Act" under which USABC was created.[11]

## ELECTROSOURCE

Start-up battery makers were a vibrant part of the emerging EV industry in California and several other states during the 1990s. One of these was a company named Electrosource, a 1987 spin-off of Tracor, Inc., a military and missile system defense contractor. Technical advances relevant to battery technology went to Electrosource in the spin-off, and the new company continued its own research as well. By 1990, Electrosource signed a contract with GM's Delco division to develop and advance the lead-acid battery. In late May 1992, Electrosource announced a breakthrough in lead-acid battery technology, when it also revealed an agreement with GM to produce the battery. But after Electrosource had made all of the investments needed to begin production under the deal, GM-Delco allowed the contract to lapse, leaving Electrosource holding the bag. According to Electrosource VP for marketing, Sam Smith, the prototype technology worked as expected, but GM-Delco was critical of the proposed manufacturing plan and it backed out of the contract. GM-Delco also used a similar complaint with another battery maker, Valance, working on lithium-ion battery technology. In both cases, GM-Delco was not satisfied with the way these manufacturers planned to scale up production for practical-use battery packs.

Meanwhile, battery makers like Electrosource, who pegged their future on a deal with GM-Delco, were then saddled with investment costs without prospect of any revenue. Electrosource, in fact, had to shut down until the Electric Power Resources Institute (EPRI) rescued it with a $5 million grant on September 1993. Yet the Electrosource lead-acid battery—developed without USABC funding—was found by the Department of Defense to be capable of delivering the range, power, and economy needed to meet California's 2-percent-ZEVs-by-1998 requirement. EPRI's Jack Guy, overseeing the Electrosource project, agreed. "Electrosource is the best bet we have for 1998," he said.[12] In January 1995, when the Electrosource battery was tested at the Argonne National Laboratory it was found to have enough energy to theoretically give it a third more driving range than the lead-acid batteries used in GM's first Impacts. The Electrosource battery also had some internal design problems that might affect its use over time. Still, the SCLDF brief charges that GM's termination of the deal with Electrosource—which caused Electrosource to shut down—contributed to pushing back the 1998 date when ZEV introduction could have occurred.[13]

Nor was GM the only automaker acting oddly with the start-up battery makers. Chrysler, for example, also had a contract with Electrosource for the company's Horizon lead-acid battery. The Chrysler deal, however, prohibited Electrosource from making any public or private statements about the battery without Chrysler's approval. Yet Chrysler, for its part, wasn't reticent about its own battery statements. According to Electrosource vp Sam Smith, Chrysler consistently understated the battery's capabilities. Smith, in fact, believes the automakers had agreed among themselves on an acceptable mileage rating for lead-acid batteries—a rating, in fact, that shouldn't go beyond a certain distance. Arizona Public Service, an electric utility, had tested the Electrosource battery and determined it could go 100 miles per charge. Chrysler said it got 60 miles per charge. When Electrosource challenged Chrysler's statements, Chrysler defended its reduction of range as reasonable, based on battery management problems in an actual vehicle. But Chrysler's numbers were bogus, according to Electrosource, especially since they were based on tests that utilized older Chrysler technology and vehicles, using less efficient drivetrains, vehicle design, and energy management techniques. Sam Smith is also critical of USABC for not funding lead-acid battery development and believes there was collusion among the Big Three in late 1992 to stop ZEV programs.[14]

## SCALING BACK

The Big Three also threw cold water on battery development with their own programs. In January 1994, Ford Motor began scaling back its plans to build a new electric car, saying that batteries were the problem. "We've pushed development to the point that we question the sense of doing any more vehicle development until there is in fact more progress in batteries," said Dennis Wilkie, Ford director of electric vehicles. Ford said it was not canceling its program, only scaling back, spending less money in 1994 on EV body design and other physical attributes until battery technology caught up.[15] GM officials too, whenever they had the chance, would use the battery issue to point up the problematic California mandate. "[I]t is very, very unlikely that the kind of breakthrough needed for electric vehicles will happen during the time frames the regulators [in California and the Northeast] are now talking about," said GM's Jack Smith in a February 1994 speech in Chicago. The regulations, said Smith, should be tied to developing better batteries rather than being arbitrarily set. "I think it would be nice if all the key players, especially in California, could step back and talk about what we've learned and what's the best way to continue the progress, rather than force investment in current technology for the sake of meeting arbitrary deadlines."[16]

A month before this speech was made, however, at a secret testing of a GM Impact

EV outfitted with a nickel-metal hydride (NiMH) battery pack, the GM car had gone 201 miles around the company's test track in Arizona at a steady clip of 55 MPH on one charge. USABC, in fact, had initially refused to allow the NiMH battery's developer—Stan Ovshinsky who ran a small battery company named Ovonic—to give a battery pack to GM for testing. USABC had given financial support to Ovonic. The company's NiMH battery appeared promising, potentially doubling the driving range of an EV beyond the typical 70-to-100 mile range. At least two people on GM's Impact team had urged Ovshinsky to get USABC to approve the NiMH battery pack for use in one of GM's first test Impacts. But Ovshinsky reported back to his GM Impact contacts that USABC was giving him the runaround, and that tests were needed, then scale-up, etc. It would take months, and all the while political pressure was mounting on California's EV mandate. Having the Impact showcase his battery in a test was tempting to Ovshinsky. He decided to make the Impact team a battery pack anyway—in secret.[17] And it was that battery pack that wound up in the Impact on the Arizona test track in January 1994.

Some of GM's top brass were embarrassed by the good showing the NiMH-powered Impact made. But by March 1994, GM made a deal with Ovonic's parent company, Energy Conversion Devices (ECD), to commercialize Ovonic's NiMH battery.[18] This deal, however, prompted questions from Ford and Chrysler, believing they were in a research-only arrangement with USABC. Although unsaid, Ford and Chrysler were really worried about GM's grabbing the technology first, thinking they had made a deal like they had back in the old smog conspiracy days, i.e., "nobody goes first; we all go together." Ford and Chrysler also wondered whether USABC might be entitled a return of the $18 million awarded ECD for development of the NiMH battery. John Wallace, director of Ford's electric vehicle program, said, "We are just basically interested in what [the GM/Ovonic deal] is and what the access of the partners [of USABC,i.e., Ford and Chrysler] is going to be."[19]

Then there was the matter of CARB's request to USABC to submit its latest findings for CARB's May 1994 review of the EV mandate. USABC was less than forthcoming and held back data on both the Impact test using the Ovonic battery and another run in a Chrysler vehicle that also showed promise with the Ovonic battery. USABC reported instead that the Ovonic battery failed to meet midterm goals and could not be considered commercially viable, at least in the near future.[20]

That very month, in fact, on May 7, 1994, Jack Smith was throwing more cold water on electric vehicles in a California speech he gave at the Stanford University manufacturing conference. "The Impact was unveiled at the Los Angeles Auto Show in 1990 and had been in the headlines ever since. However, despite all the positive publicity, the vehicle is still far from being a viable alternative for most car buyers today." The key issues "in the consumer mind," said Smith, "are price and practicality, which includes the vehicle's range and utility." Then he turned to the battery. "The only batteries available for electric vehicles today are lead-acid and nickel cadmium, and both fall far short of the customer's needs. . . ."

Smith also talked about the Big Three effort with USABC as "the kind of creative partnership America needs to maintain a competitive technological and industrial base" and touted USABC's midterm goals targeting new batteries for the late 1990s. "Some of these batteries have achieved significantly higher energy than current batteries," he said, "but none of them are anywhere near USABC's cost targets." Smith did acknowledge GM's work with Ovonic and that its nickel-metal hydride battery had shown "great promise in the laboratory." However, he added, "we still don't know if and when it might be commercially viable in the marketplace."[21]

## GM Bridles Ovonic

GM, for its part, appears to have controlled Ovonic's enthusiasm about its new battery on at least three occasions. The first incident of alleged interference with Ovonic publicly revealing its battery progress came in a news story discussing a competitor's battery technology—Electrosource's new Horizon lead-acid battery. That news account reported unnamed "Ovonic executives" who urged their top technology official "not to testify" before CARB during the agency's electric car hearings "because he would have to reveal that [Ovonic] is farther along than GM wants to admit."[22]

In March 1994, representatives of GM and USABC tried to prevent Solectria's James Worden from racing his company's electric car in the Phoenix 500 EV race—a car outfitted with an Ovonic's NiMH battery pack. Bob Stempel (GM's former CEO but by then on the boards of both Ovonic and its parent ECD) had encouraged Ovonic to lend Worden the battery pack. However, USABC held the rights to the new battery, and they and GM did not want the battery tested that soon. USABC and GM representatives were about to pull Worden and his car from the race when happenstance intervened. Sheila Lynch, executive director of the Northeast Alternative Vehicle Consortium, a public private partnership in the Northeast that works to advance clean transportation fuels, happened to be standing nearby and overheard the GM and USABC officials talking about the proposed cancellation. Also nearby was Matthew Wald, a reporter with the *New York Times*. When Lynch heard about the move to prevent Worden from driving the EV with the new Ovonic battery, she threatened to give the story to the *New York Times*.[23] The threat apparently worked, as Worden went on to race his car with the NiMH battery and win the race, which is what Ovonic had hoped for—to give its NiMH battery visibility. GM executives were not amused.

A few months later, as CARB was about to conduct one of its biennial reviews of the EV mandate, a Solectria Geo Metro with an Ovonic NiMH battery found its way to CARB, where it was tested, running 174 miles on a single charge. This evidence helped convince the CARB to hold firm on the mandate in May 1994. But Stan Ovshinsky was not happy with USABC and the Big Three. "They tried to stop us from going to California," he charged. "They threatened us! I said to them, 'Look, the Communist party no longer runs the world. The consortium is set up to make sure American public has an electric car. It was not set up to fight the mandate. . . .'"[24]

Dan Sperling, a professor at the Institute for Transportation Studies at the University of California, told SCLDF he believed the Big Three used USABC to limit or suppress battery technology development. He also said he thought GM used its Delco subsidiary to suppress technology development and information about battery technology advances. He pointed to Valance Company, funded by GM through Delco, which was bound not to reveal any technology advances, like Ovonic.[25] Yet another conflict arose between GM and Ovonic over the public dissemination of battery progress, more specifically, over a proposed advertisement in a business magazine.

## THE *Fortune* AD FLAP

In June 1995, Ovonic decided it was time to tell the world a little bit more about its battery progress. The company drafted an advertisement that was set to run in *Fortune* magazine with the headline, "Ovonic Batteries Make Electric Cars Practical." The ad—picturing Bob Stempel and Stan Ovshinsky standing beside an Ovonic battery pack for a GM Impact—claimed that an advanced battery was now a reality. The ad explained that the Ovonic battery would be recyclable and not environmentally harmful, that it could be recharged quickly, and most importantly, that it would take its passengers 200 miles. As the text of the proposed ad put it, "[the Ovonic battery] would make electric vehicles cost-competitive with gasoline powered automobiles." Ovonic's ad was certainly one of the most upbeat messages about battery technology and electric vehicles to come into the public arena. The only problem was it never made it to print.

Back in Detroit, Ovshinsky killed the ad "after heated words from [Jon] Bereisa and [Jim] Ellis, among others." Bereisa and Ellis were principal players on GM's Impact platform at the time. Publicly, Ovshinsky stated he pulled the ad at the last minute, fearing it might provoke a controversy. But there were other reasons as well. Ovonic's batteries, according to GM, were not as far along in their range potential as Ovshinsky's ad claimed they were. And the battery pack shown with the Impact displayed in detail the system of ducts and hoses that the GM/Ovonic team designed to keep the Ovonic pack from overheating, a key element that would have been revealed to potential competitors, according to GM/Ovonic.[26] But there was something else, too.

The *Fortune* ad, it turns out, would have run a few days before the Big Three were slated to make their case to CARB about why the 1998 mandate should be relaxed, if not rolled back. The advertisement would have certainly put the Big Three in an awkward position. Ovshinsky and the automakers denied the CARB meeting had anything to do with cancelling the ad. At the Big Three-CARB meeting a few days later, Ford's John Wallace laid out the Big Three's EV-battery woes. "We've interviewed more than 10,000 people, and most of them have told us they need an EV that can deliver at least 100 miles of range, at a cost not much more than their conventional vehicle. The dilemma is that today's batteries cannot satisfy these consumer needs. As anybody who is familiar with today's battery technology will tell you. EVs are not ready for prime time."[27] In July 1995, the AAMA's Richard Klimisch reiterated that "battery technology needed to successfully launch EVs in the 1998 model year is not available."

CARB, however, had also commissioned another technical review of battery progress with a blue ribbon panel of outside experts. In fact, one of the reasons CARB convened this panel was to have an independent battery review because it believed USABC was not neutral. Whenever CARB heard from USABC, it was John Wallace and Big Three speaking, not an objective USABC. The federal government's role in USABC appeared muted in all of this. The automakers, meanwhile, moved to outflank the new CARB panel. GM had already given a private briefing to CARB, stressing its battery findings, reiterating its "no-way-by-'98" position. Then, on the day before the CARB panel delivered its report in October 1995, the AAMA held a public briefing on battery technology in which it concluded the technology wasn't ready. The CARB panel, however, found that the ZEV mandate had pushed battery technology along, that current battery technologies would be available by 1997-1998, and that more advanced battery technology would arrive by 2000-2001 in a best-case scenario.

With the release of the CARB panel's report, each side vied to put its own spin on the findings. AAMA found the report generally consistent with its own assessments—"that existing technology is inadequate." Environmentalists, on the other hand, said the report "proved the success of the 1998 ZEV rule," citing the report's key finding that "fundamental technology has advanced remarkably over the past five years and that the mandate has been the critical factor in driving the progress." The following day, a news release reported that a Solectria EV, equipped with an Ovonic NiMH battery could travel 105 miles at 45 MPH, or 85 miles in city driving.[28]

## MOBIL'S ATTACK

Part of the effort to put negative spin on the battery panel report came from Mobil Oil in a November 1995 *New York Times* op-ed advertisement. Mobil's ad said the battery panel found that batteries were not ready, suggested that cleaner gasoline was far less expensive than EVs, and that EV technology was less advanced than claimed. About ten days after the Mobil ad, the CARB battery panel wrote to Mobil's chairman objecting to the ad, "We, the members of the impartial advisory panel on battery technology quoted in the ad, strenuously object to Mobil's distortion of our findings." The panel members objected to Mobil's negative characterization of a report that was generally positive on battery development. "Widely published, distorting, and one-sided opinion pieces such as yours," continued the letter, "do a disservice to objective reporting and the informed discussion of electric vehicles; they even could hinder the collaborative efforts and investments needed to realize them."[29] That, however, was exactly the point of Big Oil and the Big Three's efforts—to paint the technology as not even close to viability to discourage investment.

Mobil, in fact, was one of the most consistently shrill voices in the engineered controversy surrounding electric vehicles, both nationally and in California. The oil giant's incessant drumbeat of ads in major newspaper and magazines contributed mightily to the negative air around electric vehicles and the ZEV mandate. Using headline themes for a series of ads entitled "Clearing the Air" or "The Hidden Price Tag," Mobil ran quarter-page ads filled with its arguments against the ZEV mandate, alternative fuels, or electric vehicles. In *Time* of December 1994, Mobil's "Clearing the Air #6," stated that everyone will be "forced" to pay for electric cars through higher electric rates for infrastructure, government tax subsidies, and increased prices on gasoline cars. "Clearing the Air #10," appearing in *USA Today* in mid-January 1995, enumerated the costs and problems of using any alternative fuel other than gasoline. A May 1995 *Newsweek* ad opposed the California mandate, "Forcing the market to make the transition to alternative fuels prematurely will harm the economy, consumers, and taxpayers." Oil sources, Mobil assured the readers of this ad, were quite abundant "and won't run out in your lifetime nor your grandchildren's." In "Hidden Price Tags #5," run in June 1995, Mobil used the caption, "Electric Vehicles: A Promise Too Far." A week later "Hidden Price Tags #7" opposed the California mandate.[30]

Bill West, who managed the ZEV policy group at Southern California Edison (SoCal Edison)—an electric utility that had an extensive commitment to electric vehicles—believes the oil and auto company "negative spin" on the CARB battery panel report was calculated to discourage positive financial coverage that might lead to further investment in battery technology. West also believes the national ad campaigns by Mobil, Chevron, and Arco were part of a calculated strategy to discourage investors and government officials from believing the EV industry was making technological progress.[31]

Through SoCal Edison, West worked with GM in its 1990 electric van program and later on GM's Impact for recharging. In fact, West worked for more than twenty years on air quality issues in the Los Angeles Basin, dealing with the oil industry, in particular, with companies such as Chevron, Mobil, and Arco. West's company, SoCal Edison, knew a great deal about the status of battery research and had completed a technical review of what was available at the time of the mandate. West, like others, believes the US Advanced Battery Consortium (USABC) was controlled by the auto companies, which accounts for the lack of funding for lead-acid batteries. SoCal Edison's research, on the other hand, indicated that existing battery technology was good enough for niche car or truck use, and that consumers were ready to accept and use EV technology.

Also alleged in the whole West Coast EV affair, but unproved, is economic pressure by the oil companies on the California electric utility industry for its part in supporting an EV infrastructure program, including consumer incentives, which would have enabled the installation of charging systems in homes throughout the state. According to Bill West, a senior Chevron official is reported to have told a senior PG & E official that Chevron would use another natural gas supplier and bypass PG & E's service if PG & E did not eliminate or substantially reduce its EV infrastructure proposal before the state PUC. George Minter, vp of Pacific Enterprises, a holding company for SoCal Gas, had also heard of the Chevron/PG & E threat. Separately, Minter also reported that ARCO made a similar threat to SoCal Gas.[32] These "economic reminders" apparently had some effect, as the electric utilities did alter or downsize their ZEV infrastructure proposals.

## Skewing the Costs

John Dabels, former director of market development for GM's EV program, says GM purposely distorted its cost accounting on the Impact to make electric cars appear much more expensive than they would be under more realistic market conditions. GM intentionally piled cost upon cost solely on the Impact. Yet traditionally, in other auto development programs, such costs would be shared with a broader base of products and other parts of the company. This was intentional, according to Dabels, to make the Impact appear very expensive and unprofitable—which the automakers needed to show CARB to discredit and undermine the mandate. All of the R & D costs for the Impact, as well as the Impact's plant production costs in Lansing, Michigan, were attributed solely to that one car, contrary to traditional auto accounting.

Others in the electric vehicle industry saw through this as well, calling the industry's high-cost game a myth. "When smaller EV manufacturers like Solectria, US Electricar, Solar Car Corporation, and Renaissance Cars can produce and sell well-equipped limited production EVs in the $15,000-45,000 range," charged the Electric Vehicle Industry Association in September 1994, "there is no justification for Detroit to charge $100,000-$135,000. These are artificial figures, based upon the immediate recovery of prototype development costs. Using the same accounting methods, *any* new car would cost $100,000 or more. Instead, Detroit spreads the cost over hundreds of thousands of cars to be produced."[33]

## Pricey Ford Rangers

Environmentalists and EV proponents believe they caught Ford Motor Company manipulating EV prices for political effect in 1994-95, obtaining internal Ford memos that reveled short-term discrepancies in pricing. Ford was scheduling its Ranger EV pickup trucks to help meet the EV mandate and other California fleet sales requirements. The Ford Rangers were "conversions"—trucks to be retrofitted with electric drives, not specifically designed EVs. In November 1994, Ford began telling its prospective fleet buyers—government agencies and utilities required and/or given incentives to buy certain kinds of vehicles to boost technology—that the company's 1998 Rangers would be sold for "under $20,000." In March 1995 the price target was still $21,000. But three months later, in June 1995, Ford announced its Rangers would cost $30,000 each.

The $30,000 price announcement for the EV Ranger came two weeks before a scheduled CARB workshop on the marketability of ZEVs. "Until battery technology advances considerably, selling EVs in volume to a more widespread consumer base is not feasible," said Ford's Mike McCabe, making the announcement. "Our market research shows that prospective EV drivers want at least 100 miles between charges and that they won't pay much more than they would for a regular car. The limits of today's battery technology mean we have to target fleets to have any chance of meeting the mandate requirements."[34]

Although Ford was going through the motions with its announcement, environmentalists and EV proponents believed Ford's price increase was calculated to dampen consumer interest and get the attention of CARB decisionmakers. The environmental groups pointed to Ford's internal memos. And in contrast to Ford's $30,000 price, one Burbank, California company, Battery Automated Transportation International (BAT), was already selling converted Ford Rangers at just under $26,000 each. Those prices could drop another $4,000, said a BAT spokesman, if the company could buy "gliders"—Ford Rangers without the EV drives—to retrofit.[35] A day after Ford's announcement, the California Manufacturers Association released a survey paid for by the auto industry that said Californians didn't want EVs when they saw the high cost.

## Consumer Interest

In the early 1990s, consumers seemed to like what they found when they had a chance to drive EV test cars—even cars "converted" to electric drive, as opposed to specially designed EVs like GM's Impact. In test drives of converted Geo Metros and Ford Fiestas at the Rose Bowl in June 1991, drivers came away surprised at the quality and performance. Sixty-one percent said their opinion of EVs improved after the drive.[36]

Surveys later conducted to specifically measure narrower market segments—i.e., among families with two cars, one of which was a compact or a subcompact—views about potential electric car use and purchase were even more encouraging, especially with regard to the vehicle range. "We found that many households might be satisfied with less than a hundred miles of range," explained Daniel Sperling, of the University of California at Davis, who had conducted a small survey of fifty-one households in San Jose, Sacramento, and Los Angeles. "Half of the households indicated that fifty miles or less was all they needed for one of their cars—in most cases the recently purchased subcompact or compact car—and that ninety miles would suit in almost all circumstances." When Sperling expanded his study

# Ford EV "Ranger" Pickup
## Which one is Ford going to sell?

The one they told fleet buyers at major meetings in November 1994 would cost **less than $20,000,** and the one they told fleet buyers in March 1995 was **targeted at about $21,000...**

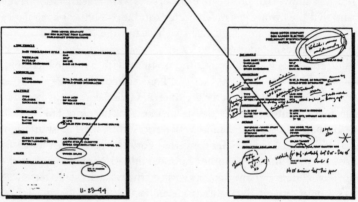

Or the one they told the press would cost **50% more -- $30,000** -- just two weeks before the CARB marketability workshop?

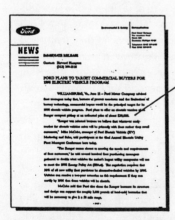

By the way, EV converters *already* sell the Ford Ranger converted to electricity for far less than $30,000...

*This analysis of Ford Motor's "price inflation" for its electric-powered Ranger pickup truck was made by the Planning and Conservation League of Sacramento, CA.*

to 600 households,* nearly half of the respondents were willing to buy EVs with ranges of 80 to 100 miles.[37]

By the time GM began offering consumers in twelve cities the chance to test drive a new EV in 1993-1994, the company began to see there could be a huge potential demand for electric cars. In cooperation with electric utilities, GM would slip notices of the free test drive into costumer's bills with an 800 telephone number. In Los Angeles, the first test city, there were 10,000 calls in two weeks. In New York there were 14,000 calls, and the lines were shut down a month ahead of time. The EV-1 was also getting rave reviews in *Motor Trend, Automobile,* and *Popular Mechanics.* By the time the actual tests began in late June 1994, GM had the help of the electric utilities in wiring up garages and working with testers on recharging. Although cooperating with the utilities on testing—presumably to comply with the mandate—the automakers were, with the other hand, lobbying and spreading money around to defeat it.

## THE SMOKING GUN

In fact, when the automakers discovered that consumer sentiment was more pro-EV in 1995, they and the oil companies redoubled their PR efforts and mounted an orchestrated "grassroots" campaign to turn public opinion around to help repeal the ZEV mandate. An internal March 24, 1995 memorandum from the AAMA detailed the industry's concern. "Recent surveys indicate a majority of Californians believe zero emission vehicles . . . are a 'workable and practical' means of reducing air pollution," said the AAMA memo. "This is a shift from survey and focus group results of 1993, and may indicate greater acceptance. . . ." With that, a concerted effort began to show just the opposite and hire contractors to do the job—or in the words of the AAMA "request for proposals" itself, "to manage a statewide grassroots and educational campaign . . . to create a climate in which the [ZEV] mandate . . . can be repealed." The memo instructed would-be contractors to submit their qualifications and budget by April 11, 1995. "Government affairs and public relations executives

---

* In this survey, according to Sperling, "We recruited 600 households from around California, including Fresno, giving each fifty dollars so that not all respondents would be EV enthusiasts. Again, only households with two or more vehicles were interviewed. First, we sent each household a questionnaire to obtain basic information on its demographics, environmental attitudes, and intentions regarding its next vehicle purchase. Then we asked respondents to complete a three-day trip diary for each vehicle they owned. In the last mailing we asked respondents to complete another questionnaire in which they were given various choices of vehicle including different sizes and driving ranges. They were told that the EV would cost about $4,000 more than a comparable gasoline car, but that $4,000 in tax credits and rebates would be available." For the 100-mile vehicle, respondents were told the cost would be $800 more than the 80-mile vehicle.

from AAMA and its three-member companies (Chrysler, Ford, and General Motors) will review the proposals and select three finalists."[38] A few weeks later, a pair of Sacramento organizers were hired to help move things along in California.

By June 1995, new public opinion polling began to appear, sponsored by the California Manufacturing Association, which found that Californians didn't want electric vehicles after all, especially when their high price was considered. But according to CALSTART, the NRDC, and the Coalition for Clean Air, "the poll asked only a series of misleading, negative questions using discredited information to achieve the result." The groups furnished the three-page questionnaire used by the Charlton Research Company of San Francisco to make their point.[39]

"This is deeply disturbing," said CALSTART president Michael Gage after he learned about the AAMA memo and the campaign being waged against the ZEV mandate. "What we have here is an organized, secret campaign of deceit to destroy a market the automakers know exists." Gage said the automakers were certainly free not to make ZEVs if they didn't want to, as the law allowed for others ZEV makers to supply the vehicles to meet the deadline. "But destroying a market is not only bizarre business practice, it crosses the line in acceptable business practice."[40]

John Dabels, formerly of GM's EV program, said GM's own studies and polling showed the likely success of electric vehicles, with strong support in Los Angeles, Boston, and Houston. Dabels found GM chairman Jack Smith to be a strong and consistent voice against California's EV mandate, even though other GM engineers, including chief engineer Jim Ellis, believed that the 2-percent-EVs-by-1998 requirement could be met.[41]

### "Sell a Lot More than We Think"

In fact, within GM, at the very highest levels, there were a few surprising perspectives on just how the company's electric car might fare in the marketplace. GM's chairman of the board in June 1994 was John Smale, the former Proctor and Gamble executive who had played a key role in engineering the GM board revolt of October 1992 when Bob Stempel was removed as CEO. Smale and Jack Smith then ran the company—Smale as chairman and Smith as CEO.

In advance of the June 1994 GM board meeting in New York, Smale asked to borrow one of GM's Impacts to test drive for a few days. He reported back, to the amazement of nervous engineers, that he and his wife very much liked the car. He put about 250 miles on it. He was especially impressed by its acceleration. On one outing he put 95 miles on the car without stopping, "with the charger still showing 5 percent."[42] Smale wrote a memo on his reaction to the car, offering suggestions on items small and large, from how the car ran to the need for a trunk release. People would react positively to the car's regenerative braking system, he wrote—the fact that it captured energy; an attribute he believed should be displayed on the instrument panel. On the larger question of just how far GM should go with its electric

# The "Smoking Gun"

Are the automakers performing honest assessments of technology and market, or simply joining together to destroy a market they admit exists, repeal the clean air rules of California, and crush a new industry?

### In their own words, the challenge is that there is a market:

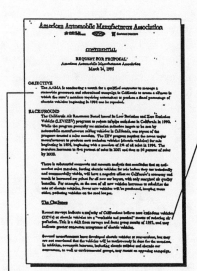

> *"Recent surveys indicate a majority of Californians believe zero emission vehicles (ZEVs) or electric vehicles are a "workable and practical" means of reducing air pollution. This is a shift from surveys and focus group results of 1993, and may indicate greater consumer acceptance of electric vehicles."*

### So their objective is to destroy that market so they can repeal the ZEV mandate:

> *"The AAMA is conducting a search for a qualified contractor to manage a statewide grassroots and educational campaign in California to create a climate in which the state's mandate requiring automakers to produce a fixed percentage of electric vehicles beginning in 1998 can be repealed."*

*Environmentalists were outraged when they discovered this confidential March 1995 auto industry memo seeking contractors to overturn the ZEV mandate in California. (Planning and Conservation League, Sacramento, CA)*

vehicle—knowing full well the company did not want regulatory authorities "to go off the deep end" with California-style mandates elsewhere—Smale still sided with taking the car to market.[43]

". . . I could be dead wrong," he wrote, "but it seems to me as you begin to get the Impact exposed to the marketplace in California and other cities around the country, we're going to generate a lot more excitement than you anticipate. . . . I don't think we would want to be in a position of stating the car is experimental and is not something which might find broad scale use in the future.

"I realize the risk of getting the car to the market might preclude California changing their regulations, but I also think we'll get a lot of credit if we do this well, for trying to do the right thing. . . . Again, it's pure speculation, but my instincts are that we could sell a lot more of these cars than we might think. Certainly it's a niche market and will remain so for a long time. But I think if we can get there first, the niche may be big enough to allow us to get profitable with an electric vehicle."[44] But "getting profitable" with EVs really wasn't in the strategic game plan at GM or any other automaker. The Big Three really weren't thinking much beyond the regulators. Sure, there was talk about the "big build" from time to time. Remember Roger Smith? In 1990, he said 100,000 Impacts would be built.

## No Real Plan

Joe Caves, a California lobbyist in Sacramento who was in the thick of the EV battle there, believes the automakers never really had an EV marketing plan. "They never envisioned a market" for EVs, he said, "They didn't see a second car possibility, a run-around car. To them, the market is what the market was."[45] What Caves means, of course, is that GM or any of the other Big Three, was not going to do any more than they had to do to satisfy regulators. GM executives, in fact, had talked about EVs as a second car as early as the mid-1970s. They just refused to build EVs and market them on a scale that would allow their cost to come down so that consumers would buy them. Sure, they would lease a few hundred to the technically curious and those who could afford a novelty car.

SCLDF's Bill Curtiss agrees. He believes the Big Three never had any intention of competing on electric vehicles. "They built electric vehicles for regulators not for the market," he says. Curtiss sees the automakers "predisposed to act collectively" whenever their core product is faced with fundamental change. With the EV mandate in front of them, the automakers joined together to insure that none of them separately would go out ahead of the others—although GM clearly had the technological lead. "How much has GM's EV-1 really changed since 1991?" Curtiss asks. "How much did they really improve it between 1991 and 1996?"

Curtiss is not a man consumed with conspiracy theories, despite his brief to the Justice Department. He is a lawyer, working the system. "It's about fear," he says, trying to explain the corporate response—"fear that EVs might surge ahead; fear that they might produce an electric Edsel; fear about heads on the line. It's about turf threatened and corporate lives at stake." More than anything else though, Bill Curtiss is a man disappointed with Detroit; disappointed with how the automakers failed to respond to technological challenge. "Cab-forward design," he says mockingly of Chrysler's oft-heard line used in television ads about its roomier sedans—"as if that puts them on the leading edge. Is that the best they can do?"[46]

## EVOLVING TECHNOLOGY

Despite the best efforts of the automakers to hold down the advancement of battery-powered EVs, key elements of electric vehicle technology generally are now advancing and will play a role in hybrid vehicle development. Battery-powered EVs are also finding niche markets today and will continue to have a piece of the alternative vehicle market. EV technology, says Sheila Lynch, "is an evolving thing." The first phase, she says, was the battery-powered EVs, "which have a limited market." Lynch, who has owned and driven a battery-powered EV as her personal car in the Boston area for three years, says that EV advocates were "overly exuberant" about the prospects for battery-powered EVs as a mass-market technology. But the core "electric drivetrain technology is advancing," says Lynch and will provide the means for successful mass-marketing of EV vehicles tomorrow. She predicts that hybrids "will become mass-market vehicles." Lynch credits California's ZEV mandate with "broadening the range of vehicles now in development."[47] Lynch acknowledges, however, that the automakers haven't done all that they could to bring EVs to market, and that they were up to their eyeballs in West Coast and Northeast lobbying to unravel and/or prevent EV mandates. "What they fear most," Lynch says, "is government interference." Still, it is only by such goading that the US automakers have moved at all. Now the Japanese and Germans are helping push the envelope on hybrids and fuel cells, but even these developments are owed to the California ZEV mandate and the efforts of consumer and environmental groups. And while SCLDF's efforts to raise conspiracy questions in the EV fight may have failed to move the Justice Department, and to some extent were eclipsed by changing technology, it is nevertheless clear that the need to hold large industrial actors to a high standard of performance and accountability will persist in the years ahead.

# 16

## *The Honda Effect*

More than any other automaker in this decade, Honda has risen to the challenge of producing cleaner, low-polluting vehicles.

*—John Dunlap, chairman,*
*California Air Resources Board*

As the Big Three and Big Oil did what they could in the 1990s to slow down or overturn the EV and clean car standards in California, one car company—Honda Motor Company of Japan—was increasingly in the limelight for complying with the toughest California clean car standards. In January 1995, for example, Honda announced that its Accord passenger car, the company's most popular US model and among the top five best-sellers nationally, had passed the 100,000 mile certification test for California's ultra-low emission vehicle (ULEV).

"Honda has exceeded our expectations by achieving ultra-low emissions before requirements apply," explained CARB's Tom Cackette. He called the Accord "the cleanest such pre-production automobile we have ever tested." Honda planned to put the Accords on sale in California in late 1997, more than two years ahead of the state's deadline. Honda's achievement also stunned the Big Three. One anonymous industry source allowed at the time, "It's a significant development because the US industry has maintained . . . that [meeting the standard] would put so much extra cost on the vehicle that it would be economically unfeasible."[1]

The Big Three had said in order to pass the ULEV standard, cars would have to burn an ultra-clean fuel, like natural gas, which would boost the cost of cars by $2,000 or more compared to gasoline models. Chrysler, for example, had also certified a natural gas minivan, but it cost $4,500 more than a normal minivan and travelled 160 miles between refuelings. Honda, however, had certified its Accord with no such caveats. Honda met the ULEV standard by adding $200 to $300 in new emissions hardware—essentially a beefed-up catalytic converter moved closer to the engine so it would heat up faster. Honda also became the first automaker to begin selling gasoline-powered cars under the LEV standard in October 1995, offering its 1996 model year Civics in California. But Honda didn't stop with California.

## "Your Air Bags"

In August 1997, Honda went public with its plans to sell its low emission Accords in other states, too. In provocative newspaper and magazine ads featuring a pair of human lungs—colored pink in a *Newsweek* version—Honda's ad carried the headline, "For a Change, We'd Like to Talk about Your Air Bags." In the ad, Honda said it would sell its 1998 Accord LEV in 50 states, and a limited number of Accord ULEVs. "This fall," explained the ad, "Honda will become the first automobile maker to bring advanced Low-Emission Vehicle technology to everyone in America. All fifty states. Voluntarily."[2]

Not only was Honda ahead of regulatory requirements in California and the rest of the country with this move, the company also provided a sharp counterpoint to the Big Three, who were then fighting a group of northeast states who wanted to adopt California's stricter standards, including its ZEV requirement. The Big Three favored a weaker plan—NLEV, for National Low Emission Vehicles, Honda's LEV and ULEV Accords went well beyond NLEV. Honda was showing that the old ICE could be cleaned up beyond what the automakers were advocating.

Honda's 1997 ad was also an important break with traditional automotive advertising, showing that at least one car company believed there was market value in trying to sell cars on their environmental performance, and that such interest could be tapped in consumers. In fact, Honda was spending more than $100 million on advertising built around its cleaner cars, one portion of which used Proctor & Gamble's "Mr. Clean" cartoon character to drive home the point.[3]

## The Car Company That Could

Honda, in fact, had a history of "environmental firsts" in the US, in part because of the company's philosophy. In the late 1960s, Honda sent a young engineer named Hiroyuki Yoshino—who later rose to top positions at the company—to the US to study the need for a cleaner-burning engine. Back in Tokyo, Honda began working on ways to cut the pollution of its engines, and by February 1971 had developed the "Compound Vortex Controlled Combustion engine," or CVCC engine, as it came to be known. It was an engine, Honda said, that could meet the 1970 US Clean Air Act emissions standards.

At the time, it was commonly thought that the best way to clean up auto exhaust was through the use of a catalytic converter. But Soichiro Honda, the company's founder, told his engineers, "At our company, let us try to clean up the exhaust gases inside the engine itself without relaying on catalytic converters."[4] And that's exactly what Honda did with the "Compound Vortex Controlled Combustion engine," or CVCC, the engine that met the 1970s Clean Air Act standards and upstaged the Big Three. The CVCC was an important engineering accomplishment because it brought existing technologies together in a new way to achieve a cleaner burn. What this engine did essentially was burn the fuel twice—or more accurately, pre-burn a portion of the fuel in a smaller

# For a change, we'd like to talk about *your* air bags.

Take a deep breath. Relax. Get comfortable. You are about to read some good news.

This fall, Honda will become the first automobile maker to bring advanced Low-Emission Vehicle (LEV) technology to everyone in America. All fifty states. Voluntarily.

It comes in the form of the all-new 1998 Accord. You see, the LX and EX 4-cylinder models will feature an engine which meets California's very strict Low-Emission Vehicle standard. But this autumn, you'll be able to buy one not only in California, but in Michigan. Georgia. Texas. Ohio. In other words, wherever you live.

The all-new Accord meets a 70-percent-lower emission standard for non-methane organic gases than is required by the most stringent federal standard.

And, because it uses our VTEC engine technology, there will be no sacrifice in performance. Or any cost penalty.

Plus, in California and certain northeastern states, we'll be the first to introduce our remarkable new Accord ULEV, which stands for Ultra-Low Emission Vehicle, the cleanest gasoline-powered production car sold in the United States.

Ever.

You might be wondering if one car can really make a difference in the air we breathe. Well, based on our sales figures from last year, you'll see more than 250,000 LEV and ULEV Accords on the road within the next year, which is more than 65 percent of all Accords sold in the United States.

But this news isn't really surprising. Since the Honda Civic with its CVCC engine made its historic debut in 1975, we've had a long history of developing innovative products that combine low-emission technology with high fuel efficiency.

After all, at Honda, we think about more than the products we make. We think about the people who use them, and the world in which they live.

Which, in the end, helps us all breathe a little easier.

## HONDA

---

*Honda, an automaker that has tried to integrate environmental values into its products and marketing, used a public health theme to tout its low-emission Honda Accords in August 1997.*

chamber followed by a second burn within the cylinder. It prolonged the burning of the gasoline air mixture, burning out more of the impurities.

Detroit scoffed at Honda's accomplishment initially, saying it was only possible because it was a small Honda Civic. Yet Honda engineers soon successfully tested the CVCC in a Chevy Vega. Not long thereafter, Detroit began banging on Honda's door for the new technology. In July 1973, Ford Motor signed an agreement with Honda for a CVCC license. In September 1973, Isuzu (then partnering with GM) and Chrysler signed contracts with Honda for the CVCC as well.[5] The basic idea of what Honda had done with the CVCC was embodied in the automobile literature on the stratified charge engine, which had been around since 1966—fully five years before even Honda began working on it. Still, this was a particularly stunning accomplishment for Honda, a company that had only been producing automobiles for about five years. Before that Honda was primarily a motorcycle manufacturer. The first car Honda sold in America—the N-600, a 42-miles-per-gallon commuter car—came in 1970. The Honda Civic hatchback and the Honda Accord quickly followed, with much success in subsequent years.

In the mid- and late 1970s, when fuel economy became a front-burner issue, Honda again came to the fore. By 1977, Honda's Civic CVCC was ranked first in fuel economy among all models by EPA, and it held that position through the early 1980s. Detroit claimed that meeting emissions and fuel economy standards simultaneously was impossible and would later push for weakening air pollution standards in trade for gains in fuel economy. Yet Honda had already shown it could do both simultaneously, at least in its smaller engine. Again, in 1985, when GM and Ford were pushing to rollback fuel economy standards, Honda was the first to bring a 50-mile-per-gallon automobile to the US market with its Honda Civic CRX-HF model.

Later, as global warming began to enter the debate, Honda offered a 1991 TV ad carrying the theme, "Think What You Can Save," using time-lapse photography showing a rain forest sprouting up around a Honda Civic VX (which was EPA rated at 58 MPG highway). Honda's ad was so beguiling, in fact, it was challenged by the Competitive Enterprise Institute and the US Business and Industrial Council, among others. The groups charged that Honda's ad implied that Civics preserved rain forests. Honda replied the ad only conveyed the car used less gasoline, which meant it would produce lower emissions, including the carbon dioxide that contributes to global warming.[6]

In the early 1990s, as Honda became more of an upscale car producer with its Acura line of luxury cars, it appeared to pull back on fuel economy, at least in the policy arena. By February 1991, Honda joined the Big Three in opposing a fuel economy bill by Senator Richard Bryan. "It is our estimate that a 4 percent improvement in CAFE is all that is achievable by the refinement of existing technologies," said Thomas Elliott, executive vice president for operations at American Honda. "Any increase greater than that will require us to downsize those models with the highest sales volume. . . . We do not believe consumers are ready to accept such a big change in vehicle size and performance, especially when accompanied by price increases which are inevitable."[7]

Still, in July 1991, Honda and Mitsubishi reported advances in engine technology that produced greater fuel efficiency. Both automakers announced plans to incorporate "lean-burn" engines in some of their 1992 models, engines they said would increase fuel economy by 10 percent to 20 percent. Mitsubishi said its version, which would be sold in Japan, would get more than a 20 percent improvement during idling and about a 10 percent improvement at 60 MPH. Honda's version, to be sold in the US in its Civic models, was estimated to get about 48 miles to the gallon.[8] Lean-burn engine technology had its problems, however. While good on fuel economy, there were problems with controlling emissions in cars that used these engines, especially nitrogen oxides, and particularly in larger engines. Detroit seized on this problem, saying the new engines would only work in smaller cars. "If Honda would introduce in the mid-size Accord an engine that showed an improvement of 6 miles per gallon, or about 20 percent, in EPA tests, that would really get my attention as an engineer," said David Cole of the University of Michigan's Automotive Transportation Program. Still, the Honda and Mitsubishi announcements stirred the pot on fuel economy at a crucial time. Thomas Hanna of the MVMA rushed to defend the Big Three, "The three domestic car companies spend enormous sums to increase fuel efficiency. It's not necessary to infer from this one instance that everyone else is a laggard."[9]

True, at the time, GM's Geo Metro, a small car built by Suzuki for GM, was the highest mileage car being sold in the US, rated at 53 city and 58 highway. Yet there were still questions about why the Big Three were not moving quicker on fuel economy technologies across all their models to protect future market share. "These engines are quite exciting," remarked Richard Ko, analyst with Barclays de Zoete Wedd in Tokyo, of the new Honda and Mitsubishi engines. "Ford and General Motors are working on the same technologies, I am sure, but the speed with which Japan is bringing these to market will open the gap even further."[10]

Yet, as tighter CAFE standards in the US market seemed increasingly less likely given the continued blockage in Congress, Honda quietly backed away from some of its most fuel-efficient models. In 1995, Honda pulled its 56 MPG Civic VX off the market—some say, the result of a gentlemen's agreement made with GM, which also backed away from its high-mileage Geo Metro around the same time. In the Northeast, Honda also disappointed environmentalists when it agreed to endorse the Big Three-favored NLEV alternative rather than giving states the option to adopt the stricter California car option. Honda's cars already went beyond NLEV, so environmentalists wondered what was going on. Still, in its R & D work, Honda continued to push forward with new engine technology, announcing in September 1997 that it was working on a hybrid vehicle featuring, among other things: a "pumped-up" three-cylinder, 1.0 liter direct-injection gasoline engine, an ultracapacitor capable of storing and delivering electric power faster than a battery, a continuously variable transmission, regenerative braking, and other features. The vehicle, said Honda, would be capable of achieving about 70 miles-per-gallon fuel economy.[11]

## HONDA STUMBLES

In June 1998, Honda made headlines in a major pollution case. The US Justice Department and EPA announced that the Honda agreed to pay $17.1 million in fines and restitution to settle allegations it intentionally hid likely pollution problems in its automobiles.

Honda, it seems, installed computerized diagnostics in 1.6 million of its cars, which would, in effect, allow these cars to spew more pollution into the environment unbeknownst to driver or government. This problem was not voluntarily reported by Honda, but was discovered inadvertently by California inspectors. Honda, for its part, decided to settle the case, paying fines to the federal government and California without admitting wrongdoing, calling the whole affair a difference in regulatory interpretation, just as GM had done in a similar 1995 case involving computer-related controls on Cadillacs. Still, Honda was at fault in the eyes of the law. Honda, in effect, had programmed pollution control computers to ignore spark plug failures. The computer software would not activate the dashboard display that says "check engine." A spark plug failure or other engine misfire meant that an uncombusted hydrocarbon cocktail was pushed through the exhaust system and into the air. Twice as much smog-causing hydrocarbon could result without driver or government ever the wiser. On top of that, catalytic converters might be damaged by the misfires, allowing even more exhaust to escape. California inspectors had discovered the problem when trying to certify Honda cars to meet federal standards. They found that an engine misfire was not diagnosed by the required On-Board Diagnostic System—a system that is governed by specific regulations. The inspectors found that the Honda system was designed not to pick up the misfires. The avoidance, in other words, was deliberate and designed-in.

"American Honda acknowledges that, regrettably, the company interpreted these regulations differently than the EPA and California officials," said Honda's managing counsel, Bill Willen. While not admitting wrongdoing in the case, Honda did agree to pay $10.1 million in federal fines, $2.5 million in California fines, extend warranties on emission control parts and service, and spend another $4.5 million in environmental research projects in California and nationally as restitution. "Today's action," said Willen, "reinforces American Honda's long standing commitment to the development of cleaner burning, low emission and nonpolluting vehicles." Well, maybe.

Honda's stumbling on computer diagnostics and software "miscalculations" was disappointing to many consumers and environmental leaders who had cheered Honda over the years as the one car company that would build cleaner, fuel-efficient cars. On balance though, even with this problem, Honda's otherwise strong commitment to clean-car engineering was a positive goad for American automakers.

At the Tokyo Auto Show in October 1997, Honda's leaders were showing off more green hardware and their leaders were making a green pitch. Honda President Nobuhiko Kawamoto said his company's clean car efforts were its "biggest responsibility," and that more had to be done in future years. "Emissions of toxic gases we can overcome with some costs, but the use of energy itself must be reduced also. We must have the reverse of the industrial revolution. This materialism embraces a structural problem in that it will exceed the earth's limits." Kawamoto even bordered on capitalist heresy when he suggested that profits might have to suffer to accommodate environmental change. "For a short time, profit may be lower. But we are looking at hundreds of years. We must have cleaner emissions for our next generation. If what we hear about global warming is true, we have no lead time and no remedy at all."[12]

Some American automakers attending the Tokyo show dismissed the Japanese hype as rhetoric and posturing for the then-upcoming global warming talks. But to that, American Honda spokesman Kurt Antonius replied, "You heard the same things when we unveiled the ULEV Accord . . . in Los Angeles two years ago, but now we're selling it. These are not just show cars. These things are going to happen."[13]

Honda also unveiled a cleaner internal combustion engine at the Tokyo show, one that it called a "zero emissions" vehicle but which still emitted some pollution. Using an advanced version of its 2.3 liter, four-cylinder Honda Accord ULEV engine, Honda added high-tech variable valve timing, new computer controls, and a new dual-function catalytic converter. These features allowed the so-called Honda Z-LEV to register very small levels of pollutants: yielding, for example, smog-producing hydrocarbons at 0.004 grams/mile, compared to California's 0.04 g/mi and 0.25 g/mi for the average car. But Honda's Z-LEV was not a California ZEV, even though the company was reaching for that label. CARB's Richard Varenchik called Honda's new engine "good technology," but it did not meet the state's ZEV mandate. "It certainly looks promising, but it's not a zero-emission vehicle."[14] In fact, Honda was pushing the boundary so much with its cleaner internal combustion engines that some environmentalists worried it could have the perverse effect of stretching out the ICE era, diverting resources from the alternative engine push.

Yet Honda was working hard on a range of hybrid and alternative engine vehicles. In December 1998, the company announced it would introduce for sale in late 1999 the first hybrid vehicle to be sold in the United States. Code named VV at the time, Honda said the two-seat, lightweight aluminum vehicle would meet California ultra-low emission standards and have a mileage rating of 70 MPG. The new hybrid, with both a small three-cylinder lean-burn internal combustion engine and a nickel-metal-hydride battery, would be capable of travelling 600 miles between fuel stops. The new car, which is "very sporty and very aerodynamic" according to a Honda spokesman, would weigh 1,740 pounds compared to a Honda Civic at 2,500 pounds. American Honda's executive vice president Tom Elliott said the car was an example of the advanced technologies being developed by Honda and its commitment to "bringing environmentally responsible vehicles to market ahead of the competition."[15] Honda's hybrid later earned EPA's highest mileage rating in advance of its expected 1999 launch—61 MPG city, 70 MPG highway. In the EPA rating, Honda's hybrid—called the Insight—surpassed several diesel powered models by more than 20 MPG. It also provided outstanding safety features, meeting all current US, European and Japanese standards as well as 2003 side impact and head-injury protection standards.[16]

Honda was also working on the fuel cell and projected a commercial launch of vehicles using that power source for 2003. But in April 1999, Honda upset California EV advocates and regulators when it announced it was going to pull its electric vehicle—EV Plus—off the market. Honda and other automakers, it appeared, were betting on the hybrids and/or fuel cells, even though hybrids technically would not qualify as zero emission vehicles to meet California's "10-percent-ZEVs-by-2003" requirement, which was still on the books.[17] Some believed the rules would be changed to accommodate the new generation of low emission hybrids, however.

In mid-1999, Honda began to prime the market for its forthcoming hybrid with some full-page newspaper and magazine ads that showed the new aerodynamic-looking automobile on a plain page by itself with the headline, "The new hybrid vehicle from Honda. What's next, perpetual motion?" In a short paragraph at the bottom of the ad, designed both to educate consumers and tout its new creation, Honda explained, "By combining an ultra-low emission engine with an electric motor, the Honda hybrid vehicle has brought the future of automotive transportation a little closer. Sooner than you might imagine. And before anyone else. You see, the Honda hybrid vehicle will be available late this year. At Honda, we're committed to developing environmentally responsible vehicles that reduce emissions and improve fuel economy. The future is, well, here."

Honda's existing ICEs, meanwhile, continued to be among the cleanest cars on US roads, becoming more so with each passing year. In October 1999, the company announced it would begin selling Honda Accords in California that would meet the state's SuLEV standards—Super Low-Emission Vehicle. Honda would meet this standard four years ahead of the required date and ahead of all the other automakers. At the same time in Washington, as EPA's Tier 2 proposal to tighten national auto emissions standards for the years 2004 and beyond was being debated and fought by the Alliance of Automobile Manufacturers and especially GM, Honda was supporting the proposal. In public testimony Honda explained, "the Tier 2 standards proposed by EPA are technically feasible. We believe that the technology to meet the proposed standard is well known and understood."

Greener performance in automobile engines was definitely coming of age as the new century dawned, a development traceable in part to an emergent Japanese approach that focused on the engine. And despite its stumbles here and there, for nearly thirty years Honda had been the key, and sometimes the lone, competitive voice for cleaner engineering. But times were changing, and even Honda might succumb to the powers of globalization. A series of megamergers began sweeping over the auto industry in the late 1990s and Honda made an inviting target for some of the bigger automakers—especially those needing a good small-car capability.

## HONDA'S INDEPENDENCE

Honda is not a member of the auto industry's newest power circle—the "Global Six"—comprised of Ford, GM, Toyota, Volkswagen, DaimlerChrysler, and Renault-

Nissan. Smart money says these companies are the entities likely to rule the auto world in the upcoming century. But Honda is more profitable per vehicle than any one of the Big Six and has a more innovative track record than most. Honda's R & D budget ($3.2 billion) is about one-third of GM's ($9 billion), but has arguably done more with it. "There's absolutely no proof that monstrous size conveys competitive advantage," says Maryann Keller, at ING Baring Furman Selz in New York.[18] Honda has a long independent history, a reputation for quality and persistence, and works very hard once it's committed and moving in a particular direction. Although a latecomer to the minivan business, for example, its Odyssey van is now taking market share from both Ford's Windstar and Chrysler's Voyager, even though the Odyssey is priced $1,500 to $2,000 higher. Honda went back to the drawing boards with the Odyssey after its initial launch went awry. Its technicians studiously observed how Americans use their vans and then went to work on a remake. By late 1999, Honda couldn't keep enough Odysseys in stock. Honda has also produced a hot little roadster, the S-2000, which has one of the most powerful engines on the road that meets LEV standards.[19] Honda does not shop around for engines as other automakers do; it makes its own. But there's something else too.

Honda's leaders have always placed a premium on what society thinks of its performance as a business. Company founder Soichiro Honda noted this a number of years ago when he said, "We are entering an age which requires a new sense of values, a fresh feeling for harmony between business and society, and a new way of management based on these." Those who have followed Soichiro Honda as leaders of the company have more or less adhered to and embellished his philosophy, reflected over the years in the company's environmental contributions, as well. "Honda's approach is to create products that balance our customers' desire for fun and performance with society's need for less pollution and lower fuel consumption," said Nobuhiko Kawamoto, who ran the company through 1998. "Over time, the technologies that achieve this balance will change—but our commitment never will."

By late 1999, Honda began selling its new hybrid vehicle, the Insight. Honda had beat Toyota's Prius to market in the US, notching another first in its string of environmental accomplishments. Toyota's Prius would not be far behind, however.

There was a bit of the 1970s in all of this, a time when the Japanese first came to the American market with small, fuel-efficient cars just as two energy crises hit, snapping up new American customers and market share. However, this time there was no energy crisis. But the market was changing in a fundamental way. Indeed, GM's Jack Smith saw this coming in 1997 as he viewed in amazement all the new green technology that both Toyota and Honda had showcased at the Tokyo Auto Show. He worried about GM's product line. GM would have to become a leader in high-mileage cars with extremely low emissions, he said. "It crystallized in my mind we needed to do a good job on that."[20] But why hadn't GM done a good job on emissions and mileage all along? Was Smith now saying that GM would have to play catch up? And could GM really become the leader? Certainly, with GM's one sixth of the global market share at stake, the company had a lot to lose. In any case, the ICE was edging out of the picture—however slowly. Environmental and energy values were permeating the marketplace in a new way. And it appeared, once again, that the Honda Motor Company had a big hand in making that happen.

In late December 1999, General Motors announced it would buy low emission V-6 engines and transmissions from Honda as part of a "worldwide partnership," whose immediate effect was that of helping GM meet California's future low emission standards. Honda's V-6 Ultra-Low Emission Vehicle engines were the leading candidates in the race to meet those standards, and GM apparently didn't have similar capability. This too seemed to repeat a pattern of the 1970s when GM and other automakers went to Japanese firms to strike deals or buy new technology. GM president Richard G. Wagoner said the new partnership reflected GM's strategy of using its global reach to bring new products to market quickly. "We have a tremendous respect for Honda's technical heritage," said Wagoner. "Together we can strengthen our abilities to develop future technologies." The deal would bring some GM diesel engines to Honda for sale in Europe, and would also give Honda access to other GM technology. But GM was really after about 100,000 Honda engines annually over the next five years. The deal was valued at $2.1 billion. Honda would also supposedly have access to GM's latest alternative fuel engines, which some believed Honda might be hard-pressed to develop on their own, financially. For GM, however, the deal was an admission that it hadn't been paying much attention to low emission engine work and now was simply buying its way back in. It was also one of the few times in GM's history when it would put another manufacturer's engine—the heart and soul of the business—into GM's North American cars.[21] And that brought a few hot complaints from some GM loyalists back in Detroit.

"The fact that GM would even consider outsourcing engines from Japan is a national disgrace and a slap in the face to every American and to every GM employee," offered Ray T. Bohacz, a technical writer sounding off to *Automotive News*. "GM has the greatest engineering resources in the world, but it refuses to let its engineers do what they do best—design engines. GM has spent millions of dollars trying to re-establish its brand identities. What brand identity will be left when there is a Honda powertrain under the hood of a GM car?"[22]

Environmentalists, however, worried that Honda might be sucked up entirely into the GM gulag, never to be heard from again. But Honda's president Hiroyuki Yoshino insisted there was no such merger in the works. "Honda is firmly committed to an independent path," he said. "This relationship will strengthen our ability to maintain this course."[23] For the good of the planet, let's hope Yoshino is right.

# Ozone Alert

The effects of ozone are not that serious. I hate to say that. But what we're talking about is a temporary loss in lung function of 20 to 30 percent. That's not really a health effect.
—*Richard Klimisch, AAMA*
*November 1996*

The current standards do not adequately protect human health.
—*Carol Browner, EPA administrator*
*November 1996*

When Carol Browner worked as a young Legal Aid attorney near Gainesville, Florida, she became frustrated with her inability to help her clients. The system was beating her at every turn; there just wasn't the same access for the poor as for others. The laws were inadequate and Browner soon discovered she was only helping around the edges at best. She then set out to work in the policy arena at the state level in Tallahassee, and from there to Washington where she became an activist and later, a legislative aid to US Senator Al Gore (D-TN). In 1991, she returned to Florida to head up the state's Department of Environmental Protection. After the Clinton-Gore election, Browner was summoned back to Washington in 1993 to head up EPA. She was thirty-seven years old.

In Florida, Browner had been raised in a family where hard work was exhibit A: her father, a high-school dropout who emigrated to the US from Ireland, had worked his way up—from truck driver to college professor. Browner's mother imbued Carol and her two sisters with the value of public service. Both parents became teachers at Miami-Dade Community College. Carol graduated from the University of Florida, receiving both her undergraduate and law degrees there. By the time she came to EPA, Browner had a five-year-old son, Zachary, who helped remind her of EPA's responsibilities. "Kids fundamentally get it," she told a reporter in 1993. "Why would you hurt your environment? Why would you hurt the place that you live in? Just in conversation with my kid, I find that he just doesn't understand why you wouldn't take care of what's around you." Browner's role as a mom helped her see EPA's responsibilities through a new lens. Nor did she forget about her earlier work in Florida with those less well off.

"It's a matter of looking at the people who are most at risk and designing your protection for them, as opposed to what we've tended to do, which is to focus on middle-class, middle-aged white males, whose lifestyle is very different from senior citizens, from children, from lower income minority communities."[1] Browner was just beginning her EPA tenure. She realized what a big opportunity she had been given—"more than anybody could ever hope for," she said not long after her confirmation—and she pledged to dig in and make a difference.

On the job, one of the first issues Browner confronted was a pollutant known as ground-level ozone, the chief ingredient in urban smog. EPA had struggled with the nation's ozone standard for more than twenty-five years, making little progress with each passing administration. But in 1994, after a previously filed legal action forced the Clinton administration to act, Browner began the arduous scientific and political process of revising the ozone standard and reviewing the medical science behind it. It would prove to be one of the major environmental battles of the 1990s—still being fought today.

## Ozone History

Under the Clean Air Act, EPA is required to periodically review its clean air standards—those for carbon monoxide, lead, nitrogen dioxide, sulfur dioxide, ozone, and particulate matter—and change them if scientific studies warrant. In revising and setting standards, known formally as National Ambient Air Quality Standards (NAAQS), the EPA administrator must establish them with an "adequate margin of safety" to protect public health. The ozone standard was originally set in 1971 for a group of pollutants called "photochemical oxidants" (later changed to just ozone), not to exceed an hourly average level of 80 parts per billion, or PPB* more than one hour per year. The ozone standard at the time was based, in part, on studies that showed increased asthma attacks in areas where ozone levels were high. By 1979, the standard was formally changed to adopt ozone as the indicator rather than photochemical oxidants, and the level was relaxed to 120 PPB ozone. EPA arrived at the revised standard after finding adverse health effects for sensitive individuals in the 150-to-250 PPB range, setting the standard at 120 PPB, providing what it then believed to be an adequate margin of safety. EPA also changed the violation threshold from a one-hour exceedance to a one-day exceedance. Compliance with the national standard for ozone—meaning whether a particular city or county had attained the standard—was determined over a three-year period. If an area had four separate days over three years in which the ozone concentrations exceeded 120 PPB—based on a

---

* In the early debate over the ozone standard, the units of measure were expressed as "parts per million." This was later changed and standardized to "parts per billion." For consistency sake and reader sanity, "parts per billion" will be used throughout this chapter and elsewhere, even though earlier agency literature and the scientific and political debates of 1970s and 1980s used "parts per million." In other words, 0.120 "parts per million" will now become 120 "parts per billion."

averaging method of all monitoring stations in that area—it would then be classified as a "nonattainment" area for ozone. EPA and the states were required by law to identify nonattainment areas, which was not a popular exercise in most places, since being in nonattainment for ozone (or other pollutants as well) could mean the imposition of additional requirements on a city, state, or locality—such as auto inspections, restrictions on certain kinds of traffic-generating activities or construction, and other measures to insure attainment or compliance. In extreme cases, if adequate plans weren't designed by state authorities, federal grants could be stopped, or as a last resort, EPA could take over the program.

In 1979, there were 317 counties and 31 metropolitan areas in nonattainment for the ozone NAAQS. The counties were given until the end of 1982 to meet the standard, while the 31 metropolitan areas were given extensions until the end of the year in 1987. By that date, however, there were 194 counties not meeting the ozone standard, while none of the 31 metropolitan areas had met the standard either.[2] As Congress began hearing about all the cities that would miss the deadline for ozone compliance, some of EPA's science advisors were calling for a tighter ozone standard.[3] As early as March 1986, EPA was finding new evidence that exposure to ozone levels below the 120 PPB standard was causing health effects, and in some cases, reducing lung capacity. Some EPA studies were recommending tightening the standard from 120 PPB to 80 PPB, noting the present standards "leave little or no margin of safety." By this time, however, EPA was in the middle of a major agency scandal involving then administrator Anne Gorsuch and superfund director, Rita Lavelle, which diverted both the agency's focus and that of Congress.* Nor was the auto industry keen on revisiting the ozone standard. GM's Richard Klimisch asserted in a congressional hearing that EPA's advisors had "made a mistake" in calling for a new look at the ozone standard. If exposure to 120 PPB ozone reduced lung function 10 percent, he said, that is "the same kind of effect you get from walking out into the cold," and "within the normal healthy range."[4] Ergo, no need to tighten. Then came 1988, one of the worst years on record for ozone pollution.

"This summer, especially in the East," explained EPA administrator Lee Thomas in late August 1988, "many cities have experienced severe ozone problems. While weather conditions have played a large role, it is indisputable that the pollutants leading to the formation of ozone must be reduced, in some cases, substantially, so everyone can breathe healthful air."[5] EPA would report that more than 110 million Americans lived in counties that exceeded the NAAQS for ozone in 1988.

"[T]here are days so bad you feel as if you're wearing a pair of those sunglasses with a yellow lenses that turn everything—air, ocean, even your own skin—a jaundiced hue,"

---

* In March 1983, Rita Lavelle was fired by Ronald Reagan after investigations into mismanagement and conflict of interest. Lavelle would later be convicted of perjury. Also in March, Anne Gorsuch was found in contempt of Congress and was forced to resign.

reported columnist Anne Taylor Flemming from her home in Los Angeles in March 1989. "On such a day I have stood on the bluffs overlooking the Santa Monica Bay, my favorite curve of any coast, and stared at the water through stinging eyes. . . . "[6] Los Angeles, of course, had been the worst of the lot for a long time, exceeding 100 on the Pollution Standards Index ("unhealthful") by more than 178 days in 1988, and 132 in 1989. But Los Angeles wasn't alone. By 1989, according to the American Lung Association (ALA), 60 percent of Americans were living in areas that failed to meet the federal standards for air quality, most of those in ozone nonattainment areas.

In May 1989, the NRDC released a study that charged that smog levels in many US cities were considerably worse than those reported by EPA. NRDC found that EPA was only using data from one monitoring station per area rather than including all the monitoring stations available. As a result, NRDC found considerably more days of high ozone than EPA did and wrote the Bush administration's EPA administrator, William Reilly, urging that EPA use data from all monitoring stations.[7]

Ozone exposure, even at below-standard levels, was now believed to be taking a quiet toll on public health. "We've got enough evidence now that we think there is a long-term effect attributable to smog," said John Holmes, research director for CARB in 1989. "We're convinced this does occur."

*Days Ozone Standard Exceeded, 1987*

| City | NRDC | EPA |
| --- | --- | --- |
| Houston | 54 | 20.8 |
| New York | 32 | 19.2 |
| Atlanta | 24 | 15.0 |
| Hartford | 23 | 11.6 |
| Baltimore | 23 | 11.1 |
| Wash., DC | 18 | 10.5 |
| St. Louis | 13 | 8.0 |
| Dallas | 11 | 5.2 |
| Baton Rouge | 11 | 5.1 |
| Boston | 9 | 4.3 |
| Cincinnati | 9 | 2.1 |
| Ashland, KY | 8 | 5.2 |
| Charlotte | 8 | 4.0 |
| Cleveland | 7 | 2.2 |
| Richmond | 5 | 3.0 |

The NRDC column shows the number of days between Memorial Day and the end of August 1987 when that city exceeded federal ozone standards, according to NRDC's research. The EPA column shows the number of days each city exceeded the standard according to EPA. California cities are excluded because some data were not available.[8]

Some auto industry scientists, however, were not convinced. Dr. Christopher Green of GM Research Labs told Congress that the health effects of smog were the subject of "considerable overstatement." Green asserted that most exposure to ozone and CO results merely in "adaptive physiological effects" that revert back to normal at the end of the exposure, rather than "adverse health effects," which do not revert and are irreversible.[9]

That's not what EPA scientists were finding. Bruce Jordon, chief of the ambient standards branch at EPA's Office of Air and Radiation in Durham, NC, noted new studies that suggested breathing ozone over a long period of time might lead to premature aging of lungs or inflammation that could signal permanent damage. Animal studies were also suggesting that ozone could reduce immunity to disease.[10]

At an April 1989 hearing of the Senate Environment and Public Works Committee, Dr. Robert Phalen of the University of California at Irvine said ozone could kill lung cells; interfere with the lung's self-cleaning mechanisms; decrease the lung's ability to kill viruses and bacteria; and impair the immune system. "The scientific evidence is very clear. Ozone is harmful to health, even at relatively low concentrations. It is an unusually toxic chemical."[11]

US Senator Joseph Lieberman (D-CT), hearing such testimony, had grown especially impatient with those who asserted that ozone's health effects were "transitory and self-limiting," as one former Reagan administration OMB official had written in the *Washington Post*. "Given its deadly nature," said Lieberman in June 1989, "I believe ozone pollution is a crisis, and I believe the American people are willing to make sacrifices to achieve cleaner, healthier air." Vast improvement in air quality could be made, said Lieberman, "by enacting stricter controls on automobiles, not on people." Lieberman proposed adopting tailpipe emissions standards as tough as California's, auto pollution control gear built to last 100,000 miles rather than 50,000 miles, and on-board controls such as gas-tank canisters to capture refueling emissions. "All of these changes would add only about $140 to the price of the average automobile," he said. "Compare that with the $220 price tag for power windows."[12] Despite a few pushing for change in Congress, however, nothing much happened, even though by this time it was clear that a tighter ozone standard was needed.

Ed Flattau, a nationally syndicated environmental writer for Gannett News, who had his own first-hand respiratory problems with Washington's summer smog, was among those agitating for a tougher standard. In August 1991 Flattau called for a standard that would be revised to 80 PPB or 90 PPB rather than the existing 120 PPB. "The federal standard is based on measurement of a single hour in a day, thereby omitting situations where measurements between 80 PPB and 120 PPB are recorded for six or seven hours straight." That summer, Washington exceeded the existing standard on five days. But using 80 PPB threshold instead, Flattau explained, the city would have had thirty-seven days exceeding the standard in the same period. EPA's reluctance to move to a tighter standard seemed foolish to Flattau, given the projections for auto growth. About 70 percent of Washington's ozone was then caused by motor vehicles—which were slated to double in number across the metropolitan area over the next 10 to 20 years. Tighter standards were needed sooner rather than later, Flattau argued, doubting that cleaner reformulated gasoline or the existing schedule of Clean Air Act changes set for 1995 would come soon enough.[13] And it wasn't just metropolitan areas anymore either. Smog and ozone alerts were moving to new ground, spreading outward, following the highways to suburbia. Metropolitan smog was now engulfing once rural counties beyond the urban fringe; counties that were now being developed and experiencing heavier traffic.

In October 1991, Washington, DC's four outlying suburban counties—Stafford County, Virginia, and Frederick, Charles, and Calvert Counties in Maryland—considered rural only a decade earlier, were now so polluted by commuter traffic that EPA added them to the official metropolitan smog zone. This was happening in other metropolitan areas as well. Smog was mobile, and it could be transported by prevailing winds over long distances.[14]

By this time, researchers conducting autopsies on Los Angeles youth killed in homicides or automobile accidents were finding that nearly 80 percent of their subjects had some abnormality in lung tissue; 27 percent had severe lung tissue damage unusual in subjects so young. Some of the abnormalities could have been caused by smoking or drug use, the researchers acknowledged, but smoking generally takes years to cause as much damage as found in these young victims.[15]

## EPA: No Revision

In the summer of 1992, as George Bush and Bill Clinton were reaching peak form in the presidential election campaign, EPA was finally about to move on its long overdue revision of the ozone standard—a process that should have been completed seven years earlier. The ALA, joined by NRDC, EDF, and five northeastern states, had sued the agency in October 1991, resulting in a court-ordered deadline. In responding, EPA met the deadline in August 1992, but chose not to revise the ozone standard, opting to continue using the existing standard. Robert D. Brenner, head of EPA's air policy office, acknowledged the agency did not review the growing body of scientific studies on ozone's health effects in making its decision. Brenner, whose office was also tied up drafting regulations required under the 1990 Clean Air Act, said EPA did not have time to compile all the studies and complete the review by August 1, 1992.[16]

"That's a pretty weak excuse," said Morton Lippman, a member of the EPA's Science Advisory Board and a leading ozone researcher at New York University. "New published data was available since 1988 and could have been reviewed in time. They recognized if they incorporated the new data, they would no longer be capable of defending the current standard." Nor was announcing a new standard months before the November elections part of the Bush administration's re-election plan. Had the standard been revised, dozens of additional cities and counties would be forced to crack down on pollution from automobiles and industrial sources. ALA and environmental groups charged the decision was based on politics rather than science.[17]

"The additional data that has come out [on ozone exposure] would certainly lean towards making things more stringent," added Bernard Goldstein, director of the Environmental Health Services Institute at Rutgers University. Researchers were finding that healthy people exposed to ozone in laboratories for several hours lost 40 percent of their lung power and also had more severe reactions when exposed to ozone in fresh air. Asthmatics exposed in similar testing had more severe reactions to certain allergens. In addition, some animal studies by this time were showing that chronic, long-term exposure to ozone was causing lung scarring similar to that caused by smoking.[18] And finally, an extensive review of the medical literature in 1993 concluded that the National Ambient Air Quality Standard for ozone—the 120 PPB standard—contained "no margin of safety against short-term adverse health effects and might also be inadequate to protect the public from effects resulting from chronic exposure. . . ."

Meanwhile, cities across the country continued to experience ozone levels below the existing standard, but in the range of concern to many scientists. In mid-July 1993 in Philadelphia, for example, the average ozone levels were placed at 81 PPB. Health studies at the time were showing reductions in lung capacity when ozone levels reached 80 PPB.[19]

## "SMOG & SOOT" REVIEW

EPA in 1993—now in Carol Browner's hands—had inherited the Bush administration's refusal to revise the ozone standard. And again, ALA and others had taken EPA to court in two separate actions: one for failing to revise the ozone standard on time, and another to revise the standard for particulate matter—tiny microscopic particles resulting from combustion and other processes, generically referred to as soot.

Fine particles, it turned out, were doing more damage than scientists had previously thought. EPA had established a standard of "PM 10," which meant, like ozone, that cities and counties had to keep emissions of particles below 10 microns in size in the ambient air. Research was sparse on the health effects of tiny particles, but a new body of literature was finding that the smaller they were, the more damage they did, penetrating deep into lungs, often carrying other microscopic toxins with them. "Particulate pollution" was linked to increased deaths and hospitalizations among people with lung and cardiac problems—especially among the elderly. One Harvard Medical School study estimated that particles kill more than 60,000 people annually in the United States. Many industrial processes were implicated—especially steel production, mining, and electric utilities burning coal. But cars and trucks were contributors, too, involved to a limited extent at PM 10 levels—contributing 6-to-7 percent of the problem, but would account for a larger share should the standard be tightened. Diesel engines, for example, then most commonly used in trucks and busses, had an especially high output of particles. Diesels, however, were also on the drawing boards for increasing use in cars, SUVs, and pickup trucks. This meant, potentially, millions of new vehicles would be affected in a regulatory context, and so, the "soot standard" became a matter of much greater import to the auto industry.

EPA had been ordered by the courts to meet a December 1996 deadline on the particle standard. On ozone, the agency was already moving on an agreed-upon review and voluntary deadline. By 1994, Browner had EPA reviewing both standards on the court-ordered schedule and instructed her agency to undertake a comprehensive review of the scientific studies on ozone and particulate. In the end, more than 271 studies were more carefully reviewed and evaluated—186 on ozone and 81 on small particles. EPA also assembled a special committee of outside scientists called the Clean Air Scientific Advisory Committee (CASAC) to review the studies and propose options and recommendations for agency action.

## SUMMER OF '94

During the summer of 1994, ozone levels all across the country were nearing or exceeding the existing 120 PPB standard. Along the mid-Atlantic coast and in the Northeast, a near solid block of nonattainment counties ran from Washington, DC to northeast Maine. During one stretch of days between June 14 and July 8, 1994, ozone levels were recorded in 130-PPB-to-170-PPB range throughout the region (see 1994 map). Even vacation spots like Kennebunkport, Maine and Acadia National Park on Mount Desert Island off Maine's southeast coast were reaching 100 PPB and above. In late July, readings at coastal locations in Maine and other northeastern states demonstrated how pre-formed ozone, and the pollutants that combine to make ozone, were being carried into the upper Northeast by the prevailing winds. But winds of another kind—those of political change—were about to bring a new kind of environmental politics to the nation.

After the midterm elections of November 1994, Republicans took control of Congress and many state houses as well. Newt Gingrich's "Contract with America"—the Republican pledge to fix the federal government—had a distinctly antiregulatory agenda, with environmental laws, regulations, and agencies among its chief targets.[20] Over at EPA, meanwhile, CASAC was still working through its review of the scientific studies on ozone and fine particle pollution. The ALA, by this time, had called on EPA to revise the ozone standard to 70 PPB, averaged over eight hours rather than the existing one-hour standard of 120 PPB. EPA's scientific advisory panel, however—the CASAC—did not settle on a firm recommendation. Instead, CASAC and EPA staff together suggested a revision in a range between 70 PPB with one allowable exceedance a year and 90 PPB with five allowable exceedances a year. These seemingly small numbers, however, had big implications. Setting the standard at 70 PPB with one allowable exceedance per year, as the ALA wanted, would mean that virtually every monitored area in the country would be out-of-

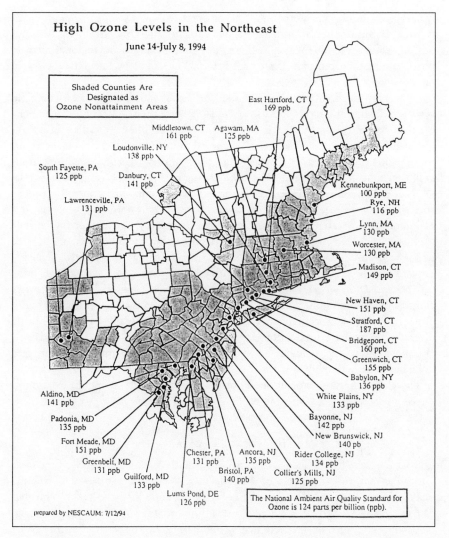

High Ozone Levels in the Northeast
June 14-July 8, 1994

Shaded Counties Are
Designated as
Ozone Nonattainment Areas

East Hartford, CT
169 ppb

Middletown. CT
161 ppb

Agawam, MA
125 ppb

Loudonville. NY
138 ppb

South Fayette, PA
125 ppb

Danbury, CT
141 ppb

Kennebunkport, ME
100 ppb

Lawrenceville, PA
131 ppb

Rye, NH
116 ppb

Lynn, MA
130 ppb

Worcester, MA
130 ppb

Madison, CT
149 ppb

New Haven, CT
151 ppb

Stratford, CT
187 ppb

Bridgeport, CT
160 ppb

Greenwich, CT
155 ppb

Babylon, NY
136 ppb

White Plains, NY
133 ppb

Bayonne, NJ
142 ppb

New Brunswick, NJ
140 pb

Aldino, MD
141 ppb

Padonia, MD
135 ppb

Fort Meade, MD
151 ppb

Greenbelt, MD
131 ppb

Guilford, MD
133 ppb

Chester, PA
131 ppb

Ancora, NJ
135 ppb

Bristol, PA
140 ppb

Rider College, NJ
134 ppb

Collier's Mills, NJ
125 ppb

Lums Pond, DE
126 ppb

The National Ambient Air Quality Standard for
Ozone is 124 parts per billion (ppb).

prepared by NESCAUM: 7/12/94

compliance. Alternatively, 90 PPB with five allowable exceedances per year, the majority of areas then designated as out-of-compliance would suddenly comply.

By November 1995 EPA was reporting under its existing standards that there had been progress in bringing some ozone-plagued metropolitan areas into compliance. Still, there were 90 million people living in 33 metropolitan areas with a continuing ozone problem. San Diego, for example, had improved slightly, moving down a notch from *severe* to *serious*. Sacramento, on the other hand, moved in the other direction, from *serious* to *severe*. Phoenix, AZ; Louisville, KY; Portland, ME; and

Mantowoc County, WI were among those areas with a *moderate* ozone problem. Atlanta, Baton Rouge, Boston, and Beaumont-Port Arthur were among the serious, while Chicago, New York-Northern New Jersey-Long Island region, Philadelphia-Wilmington-Trenton, Houston-Galveston, Milwaukee-Racine, and others were rated severe.[21]

These classifications were not just idle labels; they translated into very tangible actions that state and local officials had to take in order to show progress in attacking their respective problem—or else face the loss of millions of dollars in federal funding. *Marginal* regions had to set up special monitoring sites, and businesses in those regions emitting more than 100 tons per year of VOCs had to adopt certain pollution control technologies. A *moderate* rating meant the region must force polluters to cut emissions by a specified percentage; set up emissions controls at industrial sites; cut VOCs 15 percent in six years; adopt automobile inspection and maintenance programs (I & M programs); and require vapor recovery systems at gas stations. *Serious* areas had even tough requirements, including "enhanced" I & M for autos; use of clean fuels; and even possible "transportation controls," meaning measures such as car pool lanes, all with the goal of reducing average emissions by 3 percent a year. *Severe* zones were required to use reformulated gasolines; order controls on certain public activities and consumer products that contributed to the problem; initiate enforcement action on polluters; and generally stay on a schedule of graduated pollution reduction. In *extreme* areas—only Los Angeles to date— "advanced control technologies," such as electric vehicles were among the strategies to be implemented to cut smog.

These cleanup requirements soon got the attention of the Republicans around the country and soon became targets on Capitol Hill.

## REPUBLICAN ATTACK

During 1995, the Republicans began to chip away at certain provisions of the 1990 Clean Air Act. In November, for example, after a vigorous campaign by Republican governors such as Richard Allen of Virginia and Christine Todd Whitman of New Jersey, Congress extended the deadline for states to set up strict vehicle inspection programs designed to help bring many areas of the country into compliance, allowing states to institute their own programs rather than the centralized program established under the act. In December, another Clean Air Act program—one to require large corporate employers in heavily polluted metro areas to organize employee car pools—was scrapped altogether. Fortune 500 companies—oil and autos among them—were in the vanguard of those objecting to such programs. A 1995 Sun Oil study, for example, charged that auto repairs under the emissions inspection program cost as much as $450 per car and did not always reduce emissions. But the attack on the Clean Air Act and its enforcement went beyond removing or weakening these provisions, as legislation was drafted to make major portions of the act optional, while others advocated opening the law up for complete revision.[22]

EPA, in this atmosphere, began taking a decidedly more moderate profile—too moderate for some. "The act is simply not being enforced," charged David Hawkins of the NRDC, "the effect on air quality is negative, and public health is suffering." Carol Browner, caught in the middle, tried to assure environmentalists that no key standards were being relaxed. "We are not backtracking on the objectives of the statute. There are some in Congress who believe that the Clean Air Act would be repealed. By giving the states flexibility in enforcing the law, we hope to avoid a congressional fight over the act." Still, others worried about the tone EPA was setting, including, quite formidably, Senator Ed Muskie, the father of the Clean Air Act.[23]

"The promise of the clean air has been undermined by bureaucratic timidity at the EPA," charged Muskie in a February 1996 statement released through the Clean Air Trust, which he and former Republican senator Robert Stafford had founded to defend the act. "By showing weakness in the face of threats to amend the law, EPA encourages the adversaries of the air act." Muskie's criticism of EPA personally shook Browner. Yet publicly, she and EPA took the position that progress was being made. Fifty-five of the 98 areas that fell below the federal standard for ozone in 1990 now met that standard, said Browner. Smog in Los Angeles had been cut in half. "We could not have made that kind of progress if we were lax in our approach to the act," said Mary Nichols, assistant EPA administrator.[24]

Still, environmentalists found that only three states were on track to meet the Clean Air Act deadlines and that cities such as Baltimore and Houston had registered significant violations of the ozone standard every summer for the last decade. Texas, whose congressional delegation was one of the most vocal in attacking the act, exceeded the federal ozone standard 135 times in summer of 1995. "We'll never be able to get clean air in areas like that without stricter enforcement of the act," complained David Hawkins.[25] Meanwhile, drafts of EPA's plans for revising the smog and soot standards were beginning to receive attention on Capitol Hill. And although these revisions were on a court-ordered timeline, it appeared the Republican reformers, with some key help from conservative Democrats and industry, might have their way.

## INDUSTRY CAMPAIGN

By early spring 1996, well before EPA had offered a formal revision of either the ozone or the particulate standard, industry trade groups began sharpening their knives to attack whatever might emerge. Initially, a few industry groups had mobilized on the particulate standard, while others began working independently on the ozone proposal. Soon, both groups came together in one large coalition, and a well-financed national campaign to bash the regulations would soon follow.

As early as May 1996, several Fortune 500 companies and industry trade groups—

among them, AAMA, API, the National Mining Association (NMA), and the National Association of Manufacturers (NAM)—gathered in Washington to draw up their plan. Contributions for the venture were solicited from among the trade groups' member companies—up to $100,000 per company was expected from the larger firms. GM, Ford, Chrysler, Chevron, and Mobil were among the leading firms. They also set out to enlist small business in their cause, help fund grassroots groups, and lobby other federal agencies to put pressure on Browner, EPA, and the White House. In the end, more than 500 companies came together in what would be called the Air Quality Standards Coalition (AQSC), which operated from the headquarters of NAM.

Also a principal player in the industry coalition was C. Boyden Gray, former counsel to President Bush. A partner in the Washington law firm of Wilmer, Cutler, and Pickering, Gray had industry clients whose businesses would be affected by any tightening of the regulations.* Gray went out on the hustings, giving speeches to local business owners, warning that the forthcoming smog and soot regulations would bring costly restrictions. At one point in the debate, he suggested that the problem of dirty air might be solved by "getting poor people better air conditioning in the summertime."[26] Gray also helped coordinate lobbying activity in Washington and designed parallel grassroots organizations and strategies. Citizens for Sound Economy (CSE), a conservative think tank with Gray as president, released a report condemning EPA's proposed standards. CSE also ran a series of radio and TV spots attacking the EPA proposal. Another "grassroots" group was the Foundation for Clean Air Progress, a group backed by a some twenty trade groups and companies, but primarily funded by the oil industry. This group worked out of the offices of Burson-Marsteller, a high-powered, Washington, DC public relations firm.[27] The main tactic of the larger AQSC was to challenge and undermine the scientific basis of EPA's proposal. It typically cast the standards as "scientifically

---

* According to Margaret Kriz of the *National Journal*, "Gray said he became involved in the air quality standards debate primarily because he represented the Geneva Steel Co., a Provo (Utah) firm that's a founding member and leader of the industry coalition. Geneva Steel was the subject of a 1989 health study that linked pollution from the company's plant to increased respiratory problems in the region. That scientific analysis, which recorded a significant drop in the number of hospital visits for respiratory problems when the steel plant was closed, is being used by EPA to prove that tougher pollution controls are needed. Geneva Steel . . . is owned by Joseph A. Cannon, who was EPA's assistant administrator for air, noise, and radiation during the Reagan administration. In 1992, Cannon ran in the Republican primary for the Utah Senate seat vacated when Republican Jake Garn retired. Cannon spent $5 million of his own money, but lost to Sen. Robert F. Bennett. . . .[L]ast November [1996] . . . Cannon's brother, Christopher B. Cannon, beat three-term Utah Democrat Rep. Bill Orton. The brothers were partners in the purchase of Geneva Steel, although Christopher Cannon is no longer with the firm."

unjustifiable," charging that the revisions would "produce no significant improvement in public health."

On Capitol Hill, the auto industry's archangel and protector, John Dingell, was not happy with EPA's planned revisions. In late April 1996, Dingell orchestrated a letter from forty-two House Democrats to the White House seeking a meeting with the president on the proposal.[28] By June 1996, there hadn't been a formal response to the letter, at which point Dingell spoke directly with Clinton when he attended the White House on another matter. Although Clinton acknowledged the EPA proposal would receive careful review at the White House, he did not promise significant changes or to shelve the entire package, as Dingell had sought.[29]

By mid-October 1996, there were other attempts on Capitol Hill to outflank EPA. Senator Christopher Bond (R-MO), who chaired the Senate Appropriations subcommittee with jurisdiction over EPA was making noises about the particulate standards, and how it might be "premature" for the agency to propose new ones. Bond's staff was hearing from an array of industries, including the automakers, telling them that the existing standards were good enough. "All the major car companies say those standards are fine," said one of the senator's staff. "We're not jumping the gun. We're not telling EPA what to say. We want to see more research. That's why Senator Bond was adamant about getting $18.8 million for more health effects research."[30]

"We're always in favor of more health-effects research," responded the ALA's Paul Billings. "But research shouldn't be used as a delaying tactic."[31]

In early November 1996, meanwhile, the industry coalition working to block new air regulations was turning up the heat on its members to help one of its key allies—the National Governors Association (NGA). Notes from a November 5, 1996 meeting of the coalition in Washington indicated a discussion among coalition members "to pony up more cash for the NGA," meaning in this case, contributions from big business to the NGA's research arm, the Center for Best Practices. That center, coincidentally, raised nearly $1 million in 1996 from companies active in the clean air fight, including GM, Sun Oil, Mobil, and others. NGA denied there was any link between those funds and the NGA activity on the clean air fight. However, before the fight was over, at least fifteen governors wrote to the White House opposing the air quality rules.[32]

By November 1996, the EPA proposal was being reviewed by the White House Office of Management and Budget (OMB), which examines all federal proposals for their economic and budgetary impact. The AAMA took that opportunity to write OMB, warning that the implications of the proposed revisions, "are potentially enormous for state and local government, and for virtually the entire industrial sector of the economy."[33] By this time, too, a number of governors and big-city mayors had written letters to EPA, the White House, and/or their congressional delegations attacking EPA's draft proposal. Governor George Voinovich of Ohio said the proposed rules would "erode public support for environmental programs," while Mayor Dennis Archer of Detroit said they would "significantly injure Detroit's economic recovery." Governor Paul Patton, worried that more Kentucky cities would not measure up, asked President Clinton to "intervene in this crucial, ill-conceived proposal by the EPA to add costs where no benefit will be achieved." Environmentalists were furious with the governors' positions. "Why governors have taken it upon themselves to do this after hearing only the polluters' side of the story is pretty puzzling," said David Hawkins.[34] The answer, however, was found in the handiwork of the industry coalition.

The packaging of the soot and smog issue was now shifting to an antigrowth message. "In some ways, the opposition of local officials is the most important part of all of this," Gray would later say. "You do this and you stop growth. There's nothing worse if you're a governor or a mayor."[35] Meanwhile, the industry coalition and Boyden Gray were also targeting key political constituencies on Capitol Hill and around the country—among them, the Blue Dog Democrats, a conservative faction of the Democratic Party seen as sympathetic to industry arguments and as a way to roil Democratic party politics. All of this lobbying and political activity, however, was occurring in advance of any formal proposal being made by EPA.

## BROWNER ACTS

With one day to go before the court-ordered deadline, on November 27, 1996, Carol Browner officially proposed the new rules for ozone and small particles. The ozone standard was proposed at 80 PPB. The duration for measuring the ozone incident was changed to an average over 8 hours rather than the current 1 hour. "By averaging over 8 hours," EPA explained, "the standard helps protect people who spend up to 8 hours a day working or playing outdoors—a group that is particularly vulnerable to the effects of ozone."[36] The particle standard was tightened from PM 10 to PM 2.5.

"Today," said Browner, "EPA takes an important step for protecting public health and our environment from the harmful effect of air pollution."[37] Smog and soot, she explained, "are contributing to serious respiratory diseases, aggravated asthma attacks, and even premature death." The new standards, explained Browner, would prevent 20,000 premature deaths, 9,000 hospital admissions, 60,000 cases of bronchitis and 250,000 asthma cases—*every year*. The cost of implementing the new measures would be $8.5 billion, but the disease prevention and public health benefits were estimated at $100 billion annually. "What the extensive scientific review found," said Browner, "is that the current standard for both ozone and particles leaves too many people at risk." The new ozone standard, said Browner, would "provide protection for the 122 million Americans—46 percent of the population—including 33 million children, who are regularly exposed to harmful levels of ozone pollution."[38]

Industry, including the Big Three, wasted no time in voicing its dissent. "Given the tremendous progress America has made in cleaning the air, . . ." said Andrew Card of the AAMA in December 1996, "it is incomprehensible why the EPA is seeking to tighten the standards for ozone and particulate matter."[39] Owen Drey of

NAM, one of the industry trade groups in the vanguard of the opposition, predicted the rules would have "a chilling effect on economic growth."[40]

The huge, industry-backed AQSC began spending $1.5 million it had set aside for challenging and casting doubt on the science of small particles. AQSC's strategy was to call for more research. GM's George T. Wolff, who had chaired EPA's CASAC on the ozone and particulate proposal, said the committee could not agree on a safe level for fine particles because many felt the research was inadequate. "There's not much data out there yet," said Wolff.[41] Wolff had also voiced his opinion earlier on Browner's position. "I don't think the standards that have been chosen reflect the advice the CASAC has given the administrator," said Wolff in December 1996.[42] Browner admitted it was a policy matter. "The argument isn't really about science," she explained. "The argument is over whom do you protect, and against what effects. Now that the science has reached this point, this is where EPA is drawing the line."

## People "Can Adapt"

Still, it was industry's view that the health effects EPA cited were overblown or could be avoided. "It is clear to us that the ozone standard doesn't need to be changed— no ifs, ands, or buts," said Paul Bailey, director of health and environmental affairs for the API. "The effects that are typically seen are very short-term and very reversible and people exposed to ozone actually adapt to it. . . ."[43] Richard Klimisch, speaking for the automakers, went even further, "The effects of ozone are not that serious. I hate to say that. But what we're talking about is a temporary loss in lung function of 20 to 30 percent. That's not really a health effect."[44] One oil industry lobbyist suggested an avoidance strategy. "People can protect themselves," he explained. "They can avoid jogging. Asthmatic kids need not go out and ride their bikes."[45] The industry's reaction to the small particle standard was similarly insensitive. Excess deaths being reported from particle exposure, according to another auto industry official, were elderly people and others with severe diseases who would have died within days anyway.

Medical scientists and environmentalists were appalled by such statements. "Tens of thousands of hospital visits and premature deaths could be prevented each year by more stringent air quality standards for these two pollutants," said George Thurston of the Institute of Environmental Medicine at NYU School of Medicine. The current standards, he maintained, "are not sufficiently protective of public health."[46] EPA's review of the scientific studies had found a link between serious respiratory problems in American cities on days when ozone levels were high. A UCLA study had found that air pollution's damage to lung function resembled that of smoking tobacco. Other researchers found higher hospitalization rates and more missed days at work and school, especially among asthma sufferers, children, and the elderly.[47]

Industry, meanwhile, raised arguments intended to rouse public concern. "We even see the return of long lines for gasoline," said AAMA's Richard Klimisch, hinting

## BATTLE OF THE ADS

Radio, TV, and newspaper advertising during the fight over EPA's smog and soot regulations reached a fevered pitch in 1996 and 1997. Citizens for a Sound Economy (CSE), for example, ran a radio ad in early 1997 that focused on one of the opponents' favorite themes: government intrusion into everyday activity, from barbecuing to the use of snowblowers and lawnmowers. But the ad went beyond even those items, suggesting the regulations could prohibit fireworks on the 4th of July because they would emit pollutants. "Imagine that," intoned the narrator, "a new government regulation that takes away our freedom, to huh, celebrate our freedom." Another ad sponsored by the same group featured a father-and-son conversation, with the father also being a pediatrician. The narration for one version, used in the Chicago area, went as follows:

ANNOUNCER: The following paid for by Citizens for a Sound Economy

VOICE 1: Hey, Dad!

VOICE 2: Hi Son. How's the new job?

VOICE 1: I'm worried. It's the impact those EPA air quality regulations will have on my job. You're a doctor. What do you make of the health claims of the EPA?

VOICE 2: Son, they just don't have the science to back 'em up. Even EPA's own Science Advisory Committee admits that. And the EPA won't make public its data.

VOICE 1: Really?

VOICE 2: I'm a pediatrician. Kids with asthma? Most of it's caused by bad indoor air. You know, dust mites, stuff like that.

VOICE 1: Sounds like the bureaucrats in Washington are scheming to keep their jobs.

VOICE 2: Son, air quality has been getting better the way it is. I guess they gotta have something new to work on.

VOICE 1: Well, these new regulations would drive up the price of cars, force people into carpooling, maybe even end up banning things like barbecue grills and lawnmowers.

VOICE 2: Force us to change the way we live, huh?

VOICE 1: I read in the *Sun-Times* where it could cost Chicagoans $17 billion!

VOICE 2: Amazing, since it can't be justified for health reasons.

ANNOUNCER: Call Congress toll-free (888) 412-4064 and tell them you oppose their proposal for air quality regulations because the need just isn't there.

Sierra Club and ALA field reps in Illinois, hearing the $17 billion Chicago *Sun-Times* cost figure cited in this ad, urged radio stations to pull the spot, arguing it misled the public because the cost figure had only appeared as an *industry estimate* in a Chicago *Sun-Times* story.

Some of CSE-sponsored ads were aimed specifically at farmers. One radio and TV spot in North Dakota had a narrator offering these observations, "I suppose the EPA is going to tell us we can't plow on dry, windy days." This ad also explained that the farmer's "new worst enemy . . . seems to be the Environmental Protection Agency." Dust from fields and roads are sources of "particulate" pollution EPA does seek to reduce under some circumstances. However, the agency explained during the debate that most natural dust is of the coarse-grain variety, too large to be subject to EPA's fine particle regulations. The fine-particle variety EPA is most concerned about comes primarily from combustion sources, such as industry smokestacks, electric utilities, and diesel engines.

Other radio and TV ads sponsored by the Foundation for Clean Air Progress, another industry-funded group, targeted cities such as Baltimore, Boston, Nashville, and Richmond, Virginia, claiming the local air quality had dramatically improved since the 1960s. The ads run in Richmond happened also to be in the congressional district of Republican Thomas J. Bliley Jr., chairman of the House Commerce Committee with jurisdiction over the Clean Air Act.

ENVIROS COUNTERPUNCH. On the environmental side, the Washington-based Clean Air Trust began running a thirty-second TV ad that appeared in Washington and ten other media markets. Opening with a montage of smokestacks, then health-effects headlines superimposed across a backdrop of the US Capitol, the ad featured a young boy's hospitalization from a severe asthma attack. "The cost of dirty air, . . ." explained the announcer, "is children who literally can't breathe." The group's executive director, Frank O'Donnell, said the ad was in response to the industry's "multimillion-dollar misinformation campaign." The narration also stated, "We know asthma's worse when kids have to breathe dirty air. Yet now some in Congress are trying to block tougher standards for cleaning up our air. The special interests claim it'll cost too much." In April 1997, the Sierra Club also launched a series of radio ads supporting strong clean air standards. The spots ran in twelve cities, including Denver, St. Louis, and Tampa. Environmental organizations in Washington, working with the ALA, US PIRG and others, pooled their resources to run a series of cleverly crafted print ads designed by Rose Communications, run by Bob Rose, former aide to Ed Muskie. One of these ads attacked industry's "fairy tale" arguments and offered point-by-point rebuttals on each industry claim. Another run in *Roll Call*, the daily newspaper of Congress, charged that "The Polluter P.R. Just Doesn't Measure Up to Peer Reviewed Science," offering brief citations from a dozen health effects studies. Another, also run in *Roll Call*, asked: "When It Comes to Clean Air, Who Should You Trust? The Spin Doctors . . . or the Real Doctors?"

at short supplies that would follow requirements to make gasoline cleaner. EPA held its ground, however. "Some in industry are telling the same kinds of horror stories that we've heard in the past about environmental regulations," said Carol Browner in December 1996 as her agency prepared for public hearings. "They say life as we know it will grind to a halt. That's not going to happen."[48]

In January 1997, EPA held hearings in Chicago, Boston, Salt Lake City, and Durham, North Carolina. Some environmental organizations, such as the Sierra Club, made an extra effort to get people out to the hearings. In Durham, North Carolina, for example, the turnout of citizens on behalf of clean air even impressed the officials holding the hearing. "The EPA people were stunned," explained Deborah Shprentz of the NRDC, who also testified. "They can't remember the last time environmentalists outnumbered industry nearly 3 to 1."[49] "This was the first time in history that we really turned out the breathers of America and took the issue away from the polluters town by town," explained Carl Pope, the club's executive director and longtime activist on clean air issues.[50]

Back in Washington, however, industry was turning up the heat on its targeted list of politicians and bureaucrats. On Capitol Hill in February 1997, Representative Thomas Bliley (R-VA) blasted the Clinton administration for withholding documents he sought to obtain from OMB. In the agency review process, a draft OMB report on the EPA proposal apparently highlighted some differences between the two agencies, detailing disagreements on costs and science which Bliley and the opposition were anxious to see. These differences however, were not in the final report, leading Bliley and others to wonder whether EPA sought to muzzle OMB's concerns. "Just from our initial review," said Bliley, "it appears OMB had serious questions about EPA's cost-benefit review."[51] Carol Browner, however, did not.

## COST VS. HEALTH

In her appearances before various congressional committees, Browner would remind her listeners that the Clean Air Act required EPA to set health standards without regard to cost. Cost could be considered in how implementation was carried out, but not in setting the standard. That was the fundamental, cornerstone of the Clean Air Act of 1970; a principle stating that the protection of public health came first, monetary considerations second. Public health was not to be a simple cost-benefit calculation. "How do I put a dollar value on reductions in a child's lung function or the premature aging of lungs or increased susceptibility to respiratory infection?" Browner asked in prepared testimony for one Senate inquiry in March 1997. She argued that since the Clean Air Act's debut in 1970, the total public health benefits to society were many times the direct costs of the regulations. Still, industry persisted, aided by Boyden Gray, waving around numbers as high as $200 billion a year.[52]

". . . There are a lot of C. Boyden Gray types out there, trying to cloud the issue," said Daniel Rosenberg of the US PIRG in Washington. "They're trying to scare

This ad, sponsored by public health and environmental groups during the "smog &
soot" fight, refuted industry's "fairy tale" arguments against EPA's new standards.

# The Polluter P.R. Doesn't Measure Up to Peer-Reviewed Science

*Recent peer-reviewed studies confirm the need for EPA action:*

Air Pollution Causes
Premature Death
*Dockery et al. 1993*
*Pope et al. 1995*

Fine Particles
Specifically
Responsible for Daily
Mortality
*Schwartz et al. 1996*

Above Average
Ozone Levels
Increase Death Rate
*Kinney & Ozkaynak 1991*
*Hoeck et al. 1997*

Common Summer Air
Pollution Linked to
Hospital Respiratory
Admissions
*Thurston et al. 1994*

Asthma Emergencies
Increase with "Safe"
Ozone Levels
*Weisel et al. 1995*

Ozone Debilitates
Healthy and
Asthmatic Children at
Summer Camp
*Thurston et al.
1992, 1997*

Common
Summertime Ozone
Levels Cause
Respiratory
Inflammation in
Children
*Frischer et al. 1993*

Air Pollution's
Damage to Lung
Function Resembles
That From Smoking
*Tashkin et al. 1994*

Ozone Exacerbates
Allergies in People
with Asthma
*Molfino et al. 1991*

Long Term Exposure
to Ozone May Affect
Severity of Asthma
*Abbey 1991, 1993*

Air Pollution Causes
Increased School
Absences
*Ransom & Pope 1992*

People with Asthma
Suffer Under "Legal"
Particulate Pollution
*Forsberg et al. 1993*

Ozone Limits
Exercise
*Brunekreef et al. 1994*

The big polluters are spending millions of dollars trying to challenge the scientific support for EPA's new health standards. But polluter P.R. can't cover up the overwhelming conclusions of independent scientists.

EPA has examined more than 270 peer-reviewed scientific studies, and new studies are being published every month. The bottom line: Air pollution diminishes lives. Shortens lives. Steals from the young, the elderly, and the chronically ill. That's why EPA has proposed the new standards, and why the nation needs them.

**Help keep our kids on the playground and out of the hospital.
Support EPA's proposed clean air standards.**

A message from: Natural Resources Defense Council • American Lung Association • Environmental Defense Fund
• Environmental Information Center • Izaak Walton League of America • National Wildlife Federation
• Physicians for Social Responsibility • Sierra Club • U.S. Public Interest Research Group.
*Full citations for these studies are available on the American Lung Association web site at www.lungusa.org.*

*Another ad, also run by environmental and public health groups, took particular exception with industry's attempts to downplay scientific findings about air pollution's health effects.*

small business owners. But until they have the PTAs and the school nurses and the people whose kids carry inhalers clamoring for weaker clean air standards, they don't have grassroots support."[53] Others believed industry wasn't really sure of the numbers it was using anyway. "Industry hides behind the shrill cry of costs and benefits without knowing what they all are, . . ." charged Paul Billings of ALA during the height of the industry attack in March 1997. "They want breathers, instead of their own enterprises, to bear all the costs." Industry's track record on costs typically had run on the high side of the ledger. During the 1990 acid rain debate it argued acid rain controls for sulfur dioxide would cost $1,500 a ton. EPA placed its bet around $450 to $600 a ton. By 1997, the actual costs were less than $100 a ton.[54]

## "CRYING WOLF"

Representative Henry Waxman, meanwhile, was reminding his colleagues and the public about industry's "crying wolf" in the past: "[T]he last time EPA set a standard for smog [in 1979]. . . ." wrote Waxman in the *New York Times*, "the American Petroleum Institute predicted that 'extreme social and economic disruption' would follow and 'impossible' controls would be imposed across the country. General Motors advised Congress that the rule would cause 'widespread inflation and employee layoffs.'" Well, said Waxman, EPA adopted the rule and calamity didn't follow. A decade later, as Congress was writing the 1990 Clean Air Act, the auto industry said meeting tougher tailpipe requirements was impossible. "Mobil predicted that cleaner gasoline standards would result in major supply disruptions and dramatic price increases, . . ." said Waxman. But that wasn't what happened. "In fact, automakers have manufactured cleaner cars ahead of schedule, cleaner gasoline is being sold without price or supply problems. . . ."[55]

Waxman believed that industry was up to something else this time. "[I]ndustry's real goal isn't just to challenge EPA's proposed standards," he explained, "its ultimate aim is to weaken the Clean Air Act's fundamental structure. . . . They are now convinced that the moment is here to repeal the law's health-based standards and replace them with ones driven by economic projections."[56]

As the industry campaign reached full force in 1997, it had a "strike force" in Washington of some seventy-five veteran lobbyists, many who were former congressional staffers, working the phones or making the rounds on Capitol Hill. To their cause, they had enlisted 250 congressional supporters who signed letters opposing or questioning the standards. Citizens for Sound Economy had by this time recruited a team of scientists to help debunk EPA's science. Individual companies were doing their part, too. Exxon, for example, was enclosing notices in its credit card billings urging consumers to oppose the EPA regulations. Other companies helped pay for TV and radio ads. Estimates of total industry spending on the campaign went as high as $30 million, making it one of the biggest such campaigns in history.[57] "This has been far and away the best organized and most heavily financed campaign I have seen in 30 years," remarked Leon Billings.[58]

Carol Browner, meanwhile, was playing defense. On Capitol Hill, she appeared before more than a dozen various House and Senate committees defending the proposed regulations. She also did battle within the administration, with officials at DOT, DOE, Treasury, and Commerce—all of which were being pressed in turn by industry. Browner heard forceful complaints from OMB, the White House Science Office, and the President's Council of Economic Advisors. In fact, officials and OMB and Treasury had advised Clinton for months to turn against Browner. Donna Shalala, secretary of Health and Human Services, and Interior Secretary Bruce Babbitt supported Browner.[59] In public, Browner made speeches and engaged industry and public officials in debates. "The misinformation from the industry really forced us to respond," she later recalled. "It would have been irresponsible of me not to respond."[60]

Slowly but surely, EPA's defense of the proposed regulations was making a difference. Support came from some welcome corners. "These proposed standards seem to us to lean in the right direction within the realm of reasonableness," wrote the editors of the *Washington Post*. "They ought to be allowed to take effect."[61]

## WAVERING WHITE HOUSE

By late May 1997, however, as the decision moved closer to Bill Clinton's desk, it appeared Carol Browner was being hung out to dry. White House support for Browner was not apparent. Even Al Gore wasn't saying much. "The silence from Gore on this one is deafening," said US PIRG's Gene Karpinski, who was also then chairing the Green Group, a consortium of environmental and public interests groups fighting for tougher standards. In Congress, although the Democratic Leadership Council had endorsed the standards, party leaders like Representative Dick Gephardt (D-MO)—being pressed by unions to oppose the rule—weren't helping. "They want the blood on Browner's hands," remarked one environmentalist of the White House distance on the proposal.[62]

The business lobby was also making sure they paid particular attention to the issue in big industrial states that Al Gore might be thinking about for his expected year 2000 run for the White House. "We've clearly recognized that Al Gore is going to be running for president," said one industry lobbyist, "and we've targeted electoral states."[63] Democratic members from the congressional delegations of Illinois, Ohio, Pennsylvania, and Texas were sending letters down to 1600 Pennsylvania Avenue opposing the new rule. John Dingell was singing electoral politics, too, claiming the rule would undermine Democratic possibilities for recapturing the House, particularly by alienating constituencies in the industrial heartland and among labor. The White House was only hurting its friends, offered one of Dingell's aides.[64] Midwest mayors Richard Daley and Dennis Archer were also opposing the standards. Mayor Daley, in fact, had taken offense to the ALA's criticism of his opposition to the rules—"holding themselves up as almighty God," as he put it. ALA, for its part, was banking on the public. "People know what the air quality is like in their communities," said ALA's Paul Billings, "they know about kids with asthma."[65]

Browner, meanwhile, was holding her ground. "While I have not made a final decision," she said in late May 1997, "I can tell you that we have not found anything in the public comments, no new science, that causes us to question the science of what we are proposing." Inside the White House, some of the president's economic advisors had been sympathetic to the industry view that the rules would cost more than they were worth. Others there said that was not the issue. "It is not at all about the money," explained Kathleen McGinty, the top White House environmental aide. "These are health standards. . . . The requirement that needs to be met at the end of the day is you have to protect the public health with an adequate margin of safety. That is the policy decision. What constitutes that adequate margin of safety? Because there is always more protection you could give. There is always more that you can do."[66]

On Capitol Hill, for some Republicans, that was precisely the problem and might eventually mean zero tolerance. But here again, the bottom line was what the law required. EPA was required to be extra protective, to have a built-in margin of safety that considered the most vulnerable populations, such a children, asthmatics, and the elderly. "You are working under a precautionary statute" is how John Backhman, EPA's associate director for science policy put it. "To do otherwise could mean allowing deaths and serious health effects to occur without taking any preventive steps."[67]

## Waiting for Al Gore

By early June 1997, environmentalists were still waiting for Al Gore to weigh in on Browner's side. "Since this is the top priority issue for the national environmental community at this time," said Gene Karpinski pointedly in early June 1997, "any weakening of public health protection by the White House would certainly be a huge negative for Vice President Gore that would not be forgotten."[68] Gore, however, was in a particularly tough spot. If he supported the regulations, he risked losing the big-city mayors and governors—often, the political "infrastructure" of presidential victories. If he opposed the recommendations he would jeopardize his support among environmentalists, a special constituency that Gore had always placed at the heart of his politics. In other EPA efforts, Gore had been a more visible supporter of Carol Browner, his former senate aide, and had stood by her side earlier in other controversies—as, for example, when she sought to make toxic chemical reporting by manufacturers tougher and more available to the public. Environmentalists, meanwhile, had been hammering on the White House to get behind Browner—so much so, that Clinton personally lit into the Sierra Club's Carl Pope at one social gathering for the club's public criticisms. Pope took that as a signal the club's tactics were working.

Public opinion polls, however, appear to have played a key role. A May 1997 sur-

# Is Anyone Listening?

## 228 Members of Congress
## 74 Mayors
## 27 Governors

And hundreds more state and local officials—Democrats and Republicans alike—
are objecting to the Environmental Protection Agency's plan to expand the
standards regulating ozone and fine particles. In a wave of letters to the
Clinton Administration, they are expressing widespread concern that the EPA's plan
has no clear health benefits and is not scientifically defensible. It promises
billions of dollars in new costs to consumers and regulations that would
unfairly burden state and local governments. And it clearly shows
EPA is ignoring the nation's
unprecedented 25-year record of increasingly cleaner air.

This advertisement is one in a series. To find out what other people are saying about EPA's air quality plan, call (800) 257-1292

*This May 1997 ad, run by the industry-backed Air Quality Standards Coalition
(AQSC), was industry's attempt to pressure the White House to stop EPA's new smog
regulations.*

# Is anyone listening . . .

# . . . to the people?

Dear Mr. President and Mr. Vice President:

Big polluters are spending millions of dollars in a scare campaign to block your Administration's attempt to update clean air health standards for smog and soot. Don't be fooled by their claims.

After reviewing nearly 300 recent, peer-reviewed medical studies, the Environmental Protection Agency concluded the health standards need to be updated to protect children with asthma, senior citizens, and tens of millions of other Americans who breathe unhealthy air.

The people overwhelmingly support stricter new standards. And they want the truth about air pollution. How do we know? A well-regarded national pollster* has just asked them. He found:

> **83 percent favor stricter clean air health standards.**
>
> **92 percent say they have a right to know what levels of air pollution affect their health, regardless of the cost of cleanup.**

Please, listen to the people, not the polluters. Support EPA's update of clean air health standards.

| | |
|---|---|
| **American Lung Association** | **U.S. Public Interest Research Group** |
| **American Oceans Campaign** | **National Parks and Conservation Association** |
| **Defenders of Wildlife** | **National Wildlife Federation** |
| **Environmental Defense Fund** | **Natural Resources Defense Council** |
| **Environmental Information Center** | **Physicians for Social Responsibility** |
| **Friends of the Earth** | **Sierra Club** |
| **Izaak Walton League of America** | **Wilderness Society** |
| **League of Conservation Voters** | **Zero Population Growth** |

* Penn, Schoen & Berland Associates, Inc., national omnibus poll of 1,004 adults, conducted May 19-21, 1997.

For more information U.S. PIRG, 218 D Street, SE, Washington, DC 20003. Email uspirg@pirg.org

*Countering the industry ad a few days later, public health and environmental groups ran their own version, suggesting the Clinton administration listen "to the people" rather than the special interests.*

vey completed by Penn, Schoen & Berland Associates, a polling firm that had done work for the White House, found that 56 percent of respondents strongly favored stricter standards. Another 27 percent indicated they somewhat favored the proposal. Twelve percent opposed tougher rules.[69] Poll numbers like those might even keep Congress at bay. In addition, public health agencies in the states were supporting the rule change, as were some governors, including William Weld (R) of Massachusetts, George Pataki (R) of New York, Christine Todd Whitman (R) of New Jersey, and others in the Northeast. Governor Pataki, in fact, was quite outspoken on the need to strengthen the smog and soot regulations, so much so that the coalition of environmental and consumer groups supporting the new regulations publicly thanked Pataki with a full-page ads in some New York newspapers—with a pointed message to New York's other politicians. Still, back in Washington, environmentalists were uncertain about what the White House would finally do, as the pressure was still mounting from industry, mayors, and Democrats.

Days before the White House decision was expected, the United State Conference of Mayors, meeting in San Francisco in late June 1997, adopted a resolution by Detroit mayor Dennis Archer opposing the new EPA standards. "I don't think there's a mayor anywhere that doesn't want clean air," said Archer. "In this instance, I think we've gone too far too fast."[70] Back in Washington, however, a key development was about to unfold. Senator Alfonse D'Amato (R-NY), up for re-election in 1998 and goaded in part by environmentalists praising Governor Pataki, wrote President Clinton in support of the new regulations. "I want to make sure you are aware," said D'Amato in his letter to the president, "that I will take a leadership role in fighting any legislative effort to delay, weaken or block these important new public health safeguards." D'Amato's letter was seen as a very important lever among Republicans, especially since he was a key party fundraiser. "Pollution hurts us all," D'Amato wrote Clinton. "It is one of the major causes of diseases ranging from cancer to respiratory diseases including asthma. In New York state alone, more than 30,000 children suffer this painful and serious disease, including four of my own seven grandchildren. It is serious and we can do something about it."[71]

## BROWNER SUPPORTED, PRAISED

In the end, Bill Clinton and Al Gore stood behind Carol Browner. In late June 1997, the smog and soot rules she had pushed for were, with a few changes, supported by the White House. "I approved some very strong new regulations today that will be somewhat controversial," said President Clinton with Al Gore at his side in a speech at Vanderbilt University in Tennessee. He added, "but I think kids ought to be healthy," emphasizing EPA's findings that children were one of the groups at risk under the old standards. Clinton held out the promise of flexibility for state and local officials, some of whom were upset over the changes. "Read the implementa-

*During the final days of the Washington fight over the smog & soot rules, environmental and public health groups heaped praise on Governor George Pataki of New York in hopes of pressuring other NY politicians to follow his example.*

tion schedule," he urged, "Work with us. We will find a way to do this in a way that grows the American economy."[72] Carol Browner, meanwhile, was clearly pleased at the outcome. "The final product, I am delighted to say, is a major step forward for protecting the public health of the people of this country," said Browner at a Washington press briefing the same day. "These new standards will provide new health protections to 125 million Americans, including 35 million children."[73]

"This is a huge victory," said Paul Billings of the ALA. "We commend the president and Ms. Browner for standing strong and with great courage against the massive lobby designed to kill the standards."[74] Browner, in particular, was given high marks for her persistence and determination. "Her successful defense of the clean air rules," wrote *New York Times* reporter John Cushman, ". . . was a remarkable piece of bureaucratic bravura. . . ."[75] Bruce Bertelsen at MECA thought she had rejuvenated a moribund agency with her stand, and that "not since [Bill] Ruckelshaus in the early '70s" had he seen such a good fight on behalf of clean air.[76] "She did an incredible job under intense criticism from within the Administration," said S. William Becker, director of STAPPA-ALAPCO. "Her tenacity and persistence were the critical ingredients in the success of the clean air effort," added Gene Karpinski, president of US PIRG.[77]

"They really stood up to the worse that industry could throw at them," said Philip Clapp, head of the Environmental Information Center, who had criticized Gore earlier but was now commending the administration for its stand. The oil industry, however, had a different view. "The administration lacked the courage to do what is right," said Charles DiBona of the API. "Those who worked hard to bring reason to this debate, including some 250 members of Congress, 27 governors and more than a thousand mayors and other state, county and local officials, were simply ignored."[78] Two days later in Michigan, Andrew Card, president of the AAMA, said the air quality rules "are ill-conceived, economically disadvantageous to the country and will put a particular burden on the auto industry and the people of Michigan." In Washington, the AAMA began lobbying Congress to block the rules.[79]

Even with White House approval, the measure could still be derailed in Congress, which had a sixty-day window to overturn any new regulatory actions. John Dingell for one was not about to go quietly into the night. "I don't want to fight my president," said Dingell of doing battle with Bill Clinton, "but if the administration doesn't back off I am prepared to go to war."[80] Dingell said he was committed to reversing the decision, either by a congressional vote, imposing funding restrictions on EPA that would prevent implementation, or undoing the rules entirely by rewriting the Clean Air Act itself.[81] During July and August 1997, the industry coalition went to Congress in an attempt to overturn the measure, but its efforts went to no avail, at least for the moment. With public opinion holding firm in favor of clean air, and Republican and conservative Democrats reluctant to risk their political futures with a vote against public health, it appeared the action would hold. EPA's new regulations were issued in the summer of 1997. However, the new standards would not become legally binding in many locations for years.

## '97 SMOG SEASON

Meanwhile, the smog and bad air days continued. "Heat and Ozone at Danger Level," said the front-page headline of the *Washington Post* on July 15, 1997. At one monitoring station on Staten Island, NY, for example, smog exceeded the federal standard on six days between June 21 and July 28, the most recorded at that location in the 1990s. Maryland also notched its highest-ever reading in the 1990s on July 15, 1997.[82] In August, there was a run of bad air days, too. "Twenty million people between Philadelphia and Boston were breathing unhealthy air two days ago," reported Jason Grumet, director of NESCAUM in mid-August 1997, "and I don't think most people knew that." Indeed, ozone levels throughout much of the Northeast in 1997 weren't much better than they were three years earlier (see, for example 1994 and 1997 NESCAUM maps).

In Atlanta, Georgia, a city in the 1990s confronting an increasingly serious ozone problem, had ten bad air days through August, and in early September, monitors there were recording ozone at between 132 PPB and 138 PPB. There were a total eleven bad air days in Atlanta during 1997. Atlanta was already on EPA's ozone nonattainment list. "The Atlanta region's failure to meet official regulations on ozone has a profound impact on economics, health and the financial outlook of the area," said Thomas L. Weyandt, Jr., associate director of Research Atlanta.[83] Atlanta met a 1999 EPA deadline to come with a plan to move the region toward compliance, but it was questionable whether the plan would be implemented. More than fifty other metropolitan areas were also designated as ozone "nonattainment areas."

In 1998, a number of states began using the new eight-hour ozone standard to warn local residents of high ozone days. It soon became clear that with the tougher eight-hour ozone standard there would be a lot more "bad air" days, in some locations tripling the number of monitor exceedances and unhealthy days. US PIRG and the Clean Air Network, using available ozone exceedance data from state and local officials for twenty-six states, produced a report that found over 5,200 exceedances or monitor-recorded violations of the 80 PPB ozone standard in the April-to-September season. This compared to 231 exceedances in those same states under the old 120 PPB standard. There was also a noticeable rise in the number of "unhealthy days" posted. Among the top ten were California (79 days), North Carolina (68), Texas (62), Georgia (55), Pennsylvania (47), New Jersey (41), Maryland (40), New York (40), Indiana (39), and Ohio (38).[84] Back in Washington, meanwhile, there was a new development.

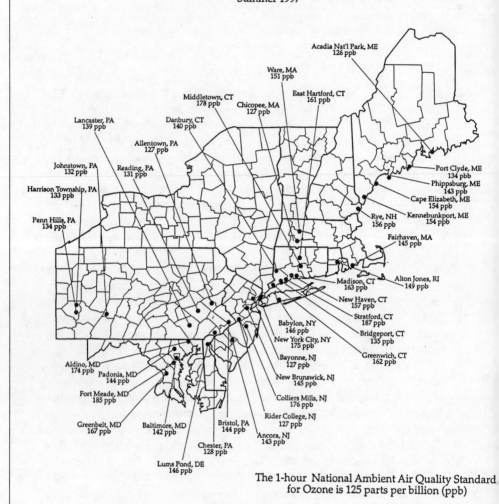

# High Ozone Levels in the Northeast
## Summer 1997

Acadia Nat'l Park, ME
126 ppb

Ware, MA
151 ppb

East Hartford, CT
161 ppb

Middletown, CT
178 ppb

Chicopee, MA
127 ppb

Danbury, CT
140 ppb

Lancaster, PA
139 ppb

Allentown, PA
127 ppb

Johnstown, PA
132 ppb

Reading, PA
131 ppb

Port Clyde, ME
134 pbb

Phippsburg, ME
143 ppb

Cape Elizabeth, ME
154 ppb

Harrison Township, PA
133 ppb

Kennebunkport, ME
154 ppb

Rye, NH
156 ppb

Penn Hills, PA
134 ppb

Fairhaven, MA
145 ppb

Alton Jones, RI
149 ppb

Madison, CT
163 ppb

New Haven, CT
157 ppb

Stratford, CT
187 ppb

Babylon, NY
146 ppb

Bridgeport, CT
135 ppb

New York City, NY
175 ppb

Aldino, MD
174 ppb

Bayonne, NJ
127 ppb

Greenwich, CT
162 ppb

Padonia, MD
144 ppb

New Brunswick, NJ
145 ppb

Fort Meade, MD
185 ppb

Colliers Mills, NJ
176 ppb

Greenbelt, MD
167 ppb

Baltimore, MD
142 ppb

Bristol, PA
144 ppb

Rider College, NJ
127 ppb

Chester, PA
128 ppb

Ancora, NJ
143 ppb

Lums Pond, DE
146 ppb

The 1-hour National Ambient Air Quality Standard
for Ozone is 125 parts per billion (ppb)

*prepared by NESCAUM 10/99*

*In the summer of 1997, unhealthy ozone levels were recorded throughout the Northeast, as these sample readings plotted by NESCAUM illustrate.*

## OZONE POLLUTED CITIES: 1997
### EPA-Designated Nonattainment Areas

Birmingham, Alabama
Phoenix, Arizona
Los Angeles, California
Sacramento metro, California
San Diego, California
San Joaquin Valley, California
Santa Barbara, California
Southeast Desert, California
Ventura County, California
Greater Connecticut, Connecticut
Washington, DC metro: DC-MD-VA
Sussex County, Delaware
Atlanta, Georgia
Chicago-Gary-Lake County, IL-IN
Evansville, Indiana
Louisville, IN-KY
Baton Rouge, Louisiana
Springfield (W. MA), Massachusetts
Boston-Lawrence-Worcester, MA-NH
Baltimore, Maryland
Kent & Queen Anne Counties, Maryland
Knox & Lincoln Counties, Maine
Lewiston-Auburn, Maine
Portland, Maine
Muskegon, Michigan
St. Louis, Missouri
Manchester, New Hampshire
Portsmouth-Dover-Rochester, NH

Atlantic City, New Jersey
Sunland Park, New Mexico
Reno, Nevada
Albany-Schenectady, New York
Buffalo-Niagara Falls, New York
Essex County (Whiteface), New York
Jefferson County, New York
New York metro area: NY-NJ-CT
Cincinnati-Hamilton, OH-KY
Youngstown-Warren, OH-PA
Altoona, Pennsylvania
Erie, Pennsylvania
Harrisburg-Lebanon, Pennsylvania
Johnstown, Pennsylvania
Scranton-Wilkes-Barre, Pennsylvania
Philadelphia-Wilmington: PA-DE-MD/NJ
Allentown-Bethlehem, PA-NJ
Providence (all of Rhode Island)
Beaumont-Port Arthur, Texas
Dallas-Fort Worth, Texas
El Paso, Texas
Houston-Galveston, Texas
Richmond, Virginia
Smyth County (White), Virginia
Door County, Wisconsin
Manitowoc County, Wisconsin
Milwaukee-Racine, Wisconsin

Source: EPA, "Condensed Non-Attainment Areas List," August 20, 1997

## STUNNING REVERSAL

The courts had always loomed in the background during the long fight over EPA's smog and soot rule change. And as EPA expected, the coalition of auto, oil, trucking, utility, and chemical interests that had fought the proposal in 1996-97, also filed a lawsuit challenging EPA's authority to implement those standards. That was just the way things were done in Washington; the other side always challenged. EPA was nonetheless confident in its procedures and its science. But in a stunning surprise, a three-judge panel of the US Court of Appeals reviewing the industry lawsuit voted 2-1 in May 1999 to block EPA's implementation of the new regulations. Not only did the court's panel send the regulations back to EPA for redrafting, it also charged that the Clinton administration had overstepped its constitutional authority in adopting them. In drawing this conclusion, the panel used an older bit of law known as the "nondelegation" doctrine. That doctrine holds that certain issues are too important for Congress to delegate to agencies like EPA. The ruling therefore not only had ramifications for EPA's new standard, but the entirety of government regulation. "If [the Appeals Court panel] is saying that EPA can't do it that way, then other agencies can't do it that way, either," said Robin Conrad, senior vice president of the US Chamber of Commerce's National Chamber Litigation Center.[85]

Environmentalists viewed the ruling as a dangerous setback, relying on stale legal authority that hadn't been used in years. Greg Whetstone, NRDC's legislative director and a former aide to Representative Henry Waxman, said the panel's reliance on the nondelegation doctrine "reeks of old 1930s case law. . . . If that rationale is to govern, not only these standards but decades of air standards are at risk." The dissenting judge on the panel, David S. Tatel, a Clinton appointee, said the ruling ignored decades of legal and judicial tradition in interpreting the federal Clean Air Act, including the "last half century of Supreme Court jurisprudence."

Frank O'Donnell of the Clean Air Trust saw public health as the loser. "For now, it means that millions of Americans could be exposed to unhealthful levels of air for longer periods of time. This could also unsettle the plans by states to meet the new standard—unfortunate because most states had become comfortable with the process."[86]

Back at EPA, Carol Browner and her legal team quickly saw that this could not only undo years of hard work, but also, if successful, could be used to challenge other standards as well. "I think it's a very extreme opinion," Browner said. "It reaches back 60 years to find a principle that it can rely on. It flies in the face of 25 years of Clean Air Act interpretation. We are going to pursue all of our legal avenues to see that it is set aside."[87]

But some in the industry coalition, meanwhile, were suggesting another possibility if this ruling were to stand: the chance that EPA's forthcoming Tier 2 standards—specific auto emissions and other standards for 2004 to be set by EPA as required under the 1990 Clean Air Act—could also be challenged. Said Ford Motor's Janet Mullins, vice president for Washington affairs, "[The court's action] changes the dynamics of the conversation, especially for those industries that might want to state unequivocally that Tier 2 shouldn't exist."

Carol Browner, however, wanted to be clear about where the agency was heading with ozone, and her intention was to call for tough car and truck emissions standards in the Tier 2 process. "When you look at vehicle miles traveled, when you look at the quality of air today, when you look at the prior ozone standard, which continues in effect today, it is warranted," she said.[88] The tighter NOx and VOC emissions standards Browner would propose under Tier 2, would be another way to get at the ozone problem. She hadn't been entirely outmaneuvered by industry and the courts. And there was also a likely US Supreme Court case to come, the last fight over EPA's long struggle to clean up the air. Still, Carol Browner was doing what she had set out to do in those early days back in Florida: putting into play the ingredients of power that would make a difference for millions of people.

# 18

## Political Cover

The "Supercar" project is the US auto industry's contribution to the global warming solution. . . .

—*Robert Eaton, chairman*
*Chrysler, July 1997*

They stood together in the Rose Garden at the White House on a warm September day in 1993: President Bill Clinton, Vice President Al Gore, and the top executives of the Big Three US automakers—Jack Smith of General Motors, Robert Eaton of Chrysler Corporation, and Harold Poling of Ford Motor Company.

"Today we're going to give America a new car-crazy chapter in her rich history," said President Clinton in opening the ceremony. Clinton and the Big Three were in the Rose Garden to announce a ten-year agreement between the government and the automakers to develop a new clean, super-efficient automobile by the year 2003. "We are going to try to . . . launch a technological adventure as ambitious as any our nation has ever attempted," said Clinton, comparing the endeavor to the ten-year Apollo project that put a man on the moon in the 1960s.[1]

"We're taking a clean sheet of paper and writing the goal without prejudging which technologies will be chosen," said Vice President Al Gore.[2] GM's Jack Smith said the sought-after fuel efficiency gains would amount to "nothing less than a major, even radical, breakthrough. We are proposing a whole new class of car."[3] The agreement set a goal of developing a "production prototype" automobile capable of getting 80 MPG without reductions in size or safety by 2003. However, at the ceremony, senior industry officials acknowledged that depending on the prototype, it could take several years, or perhaps even several decades after that, to put such a vehicle into mass production.[4]

### "WORLD CAR"

Still, on this day, it was the big picture that received the notice. "We intend to do nothing less than to define the world car of the next century, to propel the auto industry to the forefront of world automobile production and to make this industry the source of imagination for young people of the future," said Vice President Al Gore.[5] The vice president, in fact, was the administration's point man on the "Supercar" project, as it came to be known, negotiating with the industry for some months before the announcement could be made.

Six months earlier, the two sides had been meeting to discuss the possibility of such a venture. It was thought that the technological interests of Detroit might be linked to the regulatory strategies of Washington and that it might be possible to advance environmental and energy performance of the automobile, while securing the US automakers' competitive future through new automotive technologies.

Commerce department officials and the White House science office were then taking the lead in the discussions, and it was clear there was more than environmental protection at issue. The talks were part of a broader administration effort to help US industry become more competitive. "For a long time in America there has been a big debate about whether we ought to have any kind of national economic policy," said Ron Brown, then Secretary of Commerce. "I think it's time for that debate to end. This is no longer about philosophy or ideology or about partnership. It's about results, it's about doing what's best for the economic growth and economic future of our country."[6]

"There's clearly a lot of interest in Washington, I'm glad to say, in getting us all together in a much more cohesive way," said Alex Trotman, then president of Ford Motor Co's worldwide automotive operations. "I think we're seeing the dawning of a more enlightened America . . . an interface between the United States government and the auto businesses."[7]

But all of this sweetness and light between the automakers and the federal government had come about *after* the education of Bill Clinton.

## THE CLINTON-GORE THREAT

In April 1992, presidential candidate Bill Clinton made an Earth Day speech that sent shock waves through Detroit. Clinton supported increasing CAFE standards from 27.5 MPG to 40 MPG by the turn of the century—not a big deal for most environmentalists who had been pushing for even tougher standards in Congress, but a perceived economic threat to the automakers, then suffering through a recession. Clinton took the traditionally sensible position that improved fuel economy would help the environment and reduce the nation's dependence on foreign oil. The automakers, however, went on the attack. Clinton's CAFE proposal, charged the MVMA, would mean that between 150,000 and 300,000 jobs would be lost in the auto industry. The Bush-Quayle campaign began parroting the same numbers. But the automakers' numbers were wrong.

After a *Los Angeles Times* reporter investigated the details of the MVMA's very large numbers, it was revealed that the MVMA assumed the automakers would have to close down *all* of their assembly lines for *all* cars that didn't meet those standards, laying off all the workers on those lines. In truth, however, something far less draconian—like redesigning cars with most workers still involved—was the more likely reality.

By August 1992, with Clinton's election prospects rising, the automakers resorted to a more direct approach. Harold "Red" Poling, CEO at Ford Motor, spoke to Robert Stempel of GM and Lee Iacocca of Chrysler, suggesting they try to meet with Clinton to learn more about his views. Clinton agreed to a meeting on a campaign swing through Michigan, as he was scheduled to speak at the Detroit Economic Club. In his meeting with the automakers, Clinton showed signs of flexibility, describing a 40-MPG standard as a "goal" rather than a mandate. By the time Clinton reached the presidential debates, he was sending the Big Three even more good tidings, "I have never said we should write it into law if there is evidence the goal cannot be achieved."

Although the automakers were encouraged by Clinton's conciliatory tone in the latter days of the campaign, after the elections, with the Democrats holding Congress and Clinton and Gore heading for the White House, the Big Three worried that Clinton would play his party's strong hand. Still, political cross currents began working in the automakers' favor. Clinton wanted something else more than fuel economy: health care reform. And for that, the automakers could be a powerful ally. In Congress, meanwhile, the automakers still had John Dingell.

## LITTLE ROCK MEETING

In January 1993, not long before Clinton and Gore were to be sworn in, the Big Three automakers met again with the new president- and vice president-elect. This meeting, held in Little Rock, Arkansas, was also arranged by Ford's Red Poling. Poling had struck a favorable chord with Clinton during the campaign and would later be the only auto executive to be invited to Clinton's first economic summit as he prepared to take control of the government. The Little Rock session, however, focused on three main issues of concern to the automakers—trade, health care, and regulation. The buzz word cutting across all three, however, was "competitiveness," a political concept amenable to Bill Clinton. The automakers, facing growing medical costs with retiring workers, supported health care reform, and saw in Clinton's health care reforms cost cutting that would save them money in future years. In the trade arena—as subsequent events with the NAFTA and GATT trade agreements would show, as would the administration's tough negotiations with Japan on auto parts and American-made cars—Clinton and the automakers were also in accord.[8] Regulation and fuel economy, however, were somewhat more difficult.

Environmentalists were expecting the new administration to deliver on its CAFE promise, especially in order to meet the nation's obligations under the Rio Treaty— the 1992 international agreement to begin cutting global warming gases. But in Little

Rock, when the automakers said that tougher fuel economy standards would hurt their competitive position, Clinton backed off. Bob Rose, former aide to Ed Muskie and now head of Rose Communications, Inc. in Washington, believes that it was in Little Rock that the broad outlines of a deal on fuel economy began to take form.[9]

In Little Rock, the auto executives also brought up the fact that other countries were doing a much better job fostering economic cooperation between industry and government. "I lived in Europe for six and a half years," said Red Poling. "It was entirely different. They [government and industry] work closely together. So I was hopeful that we could get a change in our [domestic] relationship."[10] That also seemed to strike a responsive chord with Clinton. Congress and previous administrations had already traveled down the road of bringing government and industry closer together, so Clinton wouldn't be breaking totally new ground.

## THE NEW COOPERATION

In the mid-1980s, with the rise of the Japanese economic juggernaut, "competitiveness" became the new government-business mantra. Legislation followed in short order to help US corporations compete in world markets, simultaneously setting aside fears that new joint ventures would bring antitrust action. A new legal framework for business-government cooperation began to take shape with three new laws. In 1984, the National Cooperative Research and Development Act was passed, allowing companies to work together on pre-competitive technologies. In 1989, the National Competitiveness Technology Transfer Act was approved, allowing federal laboratories to establish cooperative research agreements with industry. And, in 1993, the National Cooperative Research and Production Act was approved, facilitating cooperative product programs. With this framework in place, it wasn't much of stretch for the Clinton administration to come up with its Partnership for a New Generation of Vehicles (PNGV), the formal name of the Supercar project.

The automakers, in fact, had been ruminating on possible cooperative ventures for several years and began taking steps among themselves in the late 1980s. In early June 1989, for example, Big Three executives Roger Smith of GM, Donald Peterson of Ford, and Gerald Greenwald of Chrysler, held a private meeting in Dearborn, Michigan. The Big Three were meeting on how to deal with some Bush administration clean air and energy conservation measures then on the Washington legislative agenda. Bush had refused to roll back CAFE standards, and the administration was also preparing its Clean Air legislation. The press was assured the joint discussions were strictly on "noncompetitive" matters.[11] Yet one of the items discussed by the auto executives at the Dearborn meeting was the possibility of a joint research initiative on energy and environmental concerns. The Big Three had already formed their first joint "precompetitive" research effort to explore automotive applications for plastic composite materials. Ford's Helen Petrauskas, vice president for environmental and safety engineering, told a Senate subcommittee in April 1989 that Ford could support a "pooling of industry and government research efforts" on energy and environmental technologies. She added, however, that "some modification in US law might be required to permit the automakers to work together."[12] That would come, soon enough.

## US CAR

In fact, in 1989, the Big Three became the "Big We," as GM's vice president Don Runkle later put it, when the early seeds were planted for the United States Council for Automotive Research, or USCAR, a first step toward more automaker cooperation in R & D and a bridge to the federal government.[13] GM, Ford, and Chrysler had already begun some smaller joint research ventures among themselves. But in 1992, they decided to formalize USCAR as an umbrella organization to focus on "pre-competitive" technologies. This would help industry and nation, they claimed, improving the competitive position of the United States. "It's an American type of thing that is bubbling up here," said David Cole, director of an automotive think tank at the University of Michigan. "We want to cut our competitors' throats more than we want to cut each other's throats, . . ." he explained in April 1993 on the occasion of USCAR's first joint patent for a lightweight material that could replace steel in car bodies.[14]

It was also a way of saving money. A joint research project exploring the best battery for electric cars, explained John P. McTague, Ford's vice president of technical affairs, could save "hundreds of millions" of dollars. According to McTague, it simply made sense to cooperate in areas such as emissions control that do not affect competition in the showroom. "In those areas," said McTague, it makes sense to do something once rather than three times. Doing something like safety three times does not make vehicles three times safer."[15] Yet, others worried that doing it once poorly would make all vehicles less safe.

USCAR became a working entity in the early 1990s. It soon had thirteen projects under its wings, ranging from an oil-auto panel on air quality to various ventures on advanced materials and USABC, the battery venture. But PNGV, in particular, would become especially important to the automakers, for political reasons as much as technological ones.

### GLOBAL WARMING

When Bill Clinton came to power in early 1993, he and his administration inherited George Bush's signing of the global warming treaty at the 1992 Earth Summit in Rio de Janeiro, Brazil. That treaty called for developed nations to voluntarily reduce their greenhouse gases to 1990 levels by the year 2000. Carbon dioxide ($CO_2$) was identified as the major culprit, although other gases were also involved.* Motor vehicles accounted for a 25 percent share of US CO-2 and a rising share of global CO-2. Clinton and Gore initially made the terms of the Rio Treaty a major goal of their administration, which is why they had campaigned to raise the CAFE standard to 40 MPG by the year 2000 and 45MPG by 2015. But now the administration was listening to the automakers. Voluntary initiatives and joint research ventures were the way to go, they said. Red Poling had assured Clinton earlier in Little Rock that the image of the automakers being "totally opposed to all actions in the safety and environmental area" was all wrong. The auto companies, he explained, were comprised of people who wanted to do the right thing. They would take reasonable steps to meet environmental and safety goals if only the government would abandon its mandate approach—what they pejoratively termed "command and control." However, when Clinton's team began to analyze how far the country would need to go to meet the Rio treaty, they realized that a 40-to-45 MPG fuel economy goal would not be enough to satisfy the treaty's goals. In fact, the White House Office of Science and Technology Policy (OSTP) calculated that in order to return the United States to 1990 levels of greenhouse gases—the US goal under the Rio Treaty—Americans would need vehicles that were three-to-four times as fuel efficient as those then on the road. Clinton's team was prepared to go to Congress to ask for 40 MPG, a 50 percent increase, but 80-to-90 MPG was out of the question. That's when the administration began to think more about the industry's suggestion for a cooperative venture. Jack Gibbons, formerly head of the Congressional Office of Technology Assessment (OTA) became Clinton's science advisor and head of OSTP. Hours after Clinton was inaugurated on January 20, 1993, Gibbons contacted John McTeague at Ford Motor about setting up a dialogue with the Big Three on building cars that would be both cleaner and more competitive. Was he interested?

"My first reaction to it was, yeah, that's fine, but we have to be very careful that we don't go chasing a will-of-the-wisp and use up all of our resources in such a way that we are not improving today's products," said McTague. "I said that any such cooperative activity should also involve the improvement of today's vehicles, and most particularly the improvement of manufacturing because the key to this is clearly cost. . . . So I mentioned these other two things, and he [Gibbons] said, 'Yeah.'"[16]

McTague contacted colleagues at GM and Chrysler, who later agreed to hear Gibbons' pitch. Gibbons explained the administration wanted to form a "clean car task force" as part of its forthcoming economic plan and a report entitled, "Technology for America's Economic Future." The idea for involving the automakers was to catalogue the technical capability of both government and industry, while identifying the obstacles to building a super efficient car. R & D projects would flow

---

* Nitrous oxide and methane are also greenhouse contributors, as are hydrofluorocarbons (HFCs), perfluorocarbons (PFCs), and sulfur hexafluoride (SF6).

from this initiative to solve some of the problems. The auto industry, for its part, would gain access to the ten national research labs operated by DOE, NASA, DOD, DOT, and others. But the auto industry was skeptical, especially as Gibbons reiterated the administration's environmental commitments, meaning in particular that tightening CAFE was still a possibility.

"When they proposed the program that they did," recounted Red Poling, "we were very apprehensive because there was tremendous pressure to increase the CAFE standard at the time. And we were concerned that they would jump on early indicators [of the auto industry's technological capabilities] and raise CAFE standards too quickly and inappropriately...."

In the end, the automakers agreed that being on the inside of the White House process was better than being on the outside looking in. If nothing else, it would give them a political edge. They would get an early heads up, for example, on any CAFE bill heading to Congress.[17]

## Shaping the Deal

On February 22, 1993, when the administration released its "Technology for America's Economic Growth," it included plans for "reestablishing technological leadership and competitiveness of the US automobile industry." A major new program would be proposed "to help the industry develop critical new technology that can all but eliminate the environmental hazards of automobile use and operate from domestically produced fuels and facilitate the development of a new generation of automobiles." The resulting "clean car" of the future would "be safe and perform as well, if not better than existing automobiles, cost no more to drive than today's automobiles, consume only domestic fuels such as natural gas and renewables, and produce little or no pollution." But this was only the broad outlines of the proposal. Important details had yet to be agreed upon.

In April 1993, the industry and the administration team began negotiating on the finer points of the arrangement. Fuel efficiency was first broached in terms of some undetermined increase—as "x-times" the fuel efficiency of current vehicles over a ten-year period. But even a vaguely worded notion of any fuel efficiency target upset the industry. "...All of a sudden it began to get negotiated as goals, and we began to talk about CAFE. And everybody says whoa," recalls Don Walkowitz, then director of USCAR. "...So that's when our industry government relations people said we better start telling [Representative John] Dingell what we're doing." Dingell gave the project his blessing, but warned the Big Three to be careful.[18]

In May 1993, the distance between the two sides on fuel economy became clear. The Clinton team, focusing on what was needed to meet the Rio Treaty obligations, wanted an increase of three-to-four times current levels in ten years—that meant something on the order of 82 to 110 MPG. The automakers were stunned. "Impossible!" the industry's negotiators charged. Yes, they acknowledged, it was technically possible to do that, but not in mass production. Maybe one-and-a-half times current levels was reachable in ten years, they said—about 40 MPG, a 50 percent increase. Beyond that, cost and performance would suffer, they insisted. Clinton's team, however, held to its position. By late April 1993, in an Earth Day speech, Clinton publicly committed his administration to meeting the Rio treaty: bringing greenhouse gases down to 1990 levels by the year 2000.

Industry, meanwhile, was still looking for assurances on CAFE. "Our concern was they would accelerate the ten-year time frame dramatically," said Red Poling. And although the president's campaign pledge to raise CAFE standards to 40 MPG was reportedly never on the table as a bargaining chip, Clinton's team did offer informal assurances to the automakers: if they agreed to a goal of tripling fuel efficiency within the venture, the administration would not support tripling or quadrupling of CAFE standards.

By June 1993, the emerging ten-year clean car initiative was still hung up on the prospect of tripling fuel economy in the program. The Clinton team wanted the Big Three to commit to tripling. The Big Three continued to say it could not be done while producing a car that met cost and performance requirements. By July, the Big Three CEOs had a private meeting with Al Gore. Red Poling said he felt the industry was being "set up" on the goal and was doomed to fail, bringing public criticism on industry. Gore held his ground. By mid-September 1993 a second meeting was held. This time, in the meeting of CEOs, Gore, and Gibbons, the Big Three agreed to tripling fuel economy, but only after a crucial wording change of "*up to* three times" was made. In that meeting, there was no outright quid pro quo from the government side. However, the Big Three understood what was going on, and so did the administration. "I think they felt an urgency to help demonstrate that we can get away from command and control regulation and move to more cooperative ventures," said Jack Gibbons. "We tried to get a commitment that they wouldn't increase the CAFE levels, but they wouldn't agree to that," said Red Poling. "It became a matter of trust. It was that simple."[19]

Yet consumer and environmental interests saw the outcome a bit differently. "You can't fault the concept of taking a long-term look at the future of the auto," explained Joan Claybrook, of Public Citizen. "But the perversion of it is that the auto industry has used the opportunity to lobby against higher standards.... What the industry wants is delay."[20]

## POLITICAL COVER

PNGV came three years after California had laid out its LEV-ZEV plan to help push electric vehicles. "Detroit will use this new partnership to argue against California's zero emission standard," predicted California state Senator Tom Hayden (D-Santa Monica) in November 1993. "'We're working with the president toward better internal combustion engine cars,' they will claim," said Hayden of the Big Three, "'so why build electric cars for those crazy Californians?'"[21]

In fact, in June 1993, when the automakers and the administration were only initially discussing PNGV as a possibility, the Big Three saw clearly there might be room for using the venture as a way to maneuver around or weaken the California ZEV mandate. As Michael Shnayerson observed, "To the CEO's, the offer was compelling not only on its own terms but as a possible alternative to the California mandate. If they anted up their share and agreed to work hand-in-glove with the government, the mandate might go away. A vaguely defined clean car with an even vaguer deadline and a billion-dollar budget would be a lot better than EVs in 1998."[22] PNGV included no reference to electric vehicles when first unveiled. And less than a month after the Rose Garden announcement, Chrysler's Robert Eaton sharply criticized the California ZEV requirement, saying, "There is absolutely no economic basis for electric vehicles in the world. Not even in Italy, where gas is four times the cost of gas in California." And Red Poling told the *Detroit News* about the same time that Ford opposed the California mandate, too.[23] At an October 1993 meeting of the AAMA—barely a month after the Big Three had thrown their support to the "clean car" initiative—the automakers were discussing how to enlist Vice President Al Gore in their fight against California's pending electric car rule. "Having thrown their support behind Mr. Gore's car-of-the-future program," wrote the *Wall Street Journal's* Oscar Suris, "the Big Three now want the support of Vice President Gore and California Gov. Pete Wilson."[24]

In a May 1994 speech at Stanford University, GM's Jack Smith was charging that mandates like California's were "not the way to go." He warned that "a premature introduction of EVs could turn off consumers." However, in the same speech, Smith sung the praises of the new PNGV venture with the White House as "one of the most promising and far-reaching examples of government, academia, and industry working together.[25]

"This partnership is aimed at a quantum leap in making the automobile and automotive manufacturing more compatible with the environment. It's the most ambitious and proactive joint project ever undertaken by government and the auto industry. . . ." What Smith also touched upon in his speech was the subject of risk, and why ventures such as PNGV and USABC were needed to deal with the challenges ahead. "The risks and costs of seeking a 80 MPG prototype vehicle, for example, are too great for any one company to go it alone and still be competitive in today's marketplace," he explained. "And, the nature of research requires the involvement of the best minds and laboratories in academia as well as the support of the federal government and its labs."[26]

The environmental community soon began to view PNGV as a diversion, providing the Clinton administration and the auto industry with shelter from the tougher issue of advancing fuel economy standards, a strategy widely believed to be one of the quickest ways for the US to reduce $CO_2$. In May 1994, Alden Meyer of the Union of Concerned Scientists in Washington warned that PNGV and other collaborative efforts between the automakers and the federal government "shouldn't be used as political cover to avoid near-term action on fuel efficiency and vehicle technology."[27]

But that appeared to be exactly what was happening. The Clinton administration's plan for addressing global warming—its Climate Change Action Plan, unveiled a month after PNGV—had already made clear that increased CAFE standards would not be part of the nation's effort to reduce greenhouse gases, at least for the time being. Instead, the administration's plan, based mostly on voluntary industry actions with a sprinkling of government incentives, called for a collection of some fifty measures and programs—from tree planting to more efficient office lighting. It soon became apparent the administration was basing its hopes on a lot of hypothetical reductions, including "breakthroughs" to come from the PNGV project. Neither the Rio goals, nor those set by the administration's Climate Action Plan, would be met.

The White House, meanwhile, continued its upbeat message about the PNGV venture. In mid-October 1994, Bill Clinton and Al Gore were distinctly positive about the project. "We have to do this," said Clinton, referring to PNGV. "We simply don't have an option. If you look at what's happening to greenhouse gas emissions, if you look at what's going to happen to automobile growth throughout the world, we have to do it."[28] But knowing full well its Climate Action Plan was weak on fuel economy, and that the results of the PNGV effort were still nine years away, the White House moved to shore up its political flanks among consumer and environmental groups who had been pressing the administration on Clinton's campaign promises to raise CAFE standards.

## CAR TALKS

In September 1994, a month before the PNGV anniversary event at the White House, President Clinton formed an advisory panel specifically on greenhouse gas emissions from motor vehicles. This panel was given the untenable name, "The Policy Dialogue Advisory Committee to Assist in the Development of Measures to Significantly Reduce Greenhouse Gas Emissions from Personal Motor Vehicles." Later sensibly dubbed "Car Talks" by its participants, this panel consisted of some thirty scientists, environmentalists, government officials, auto and oil executives trying to figure out how to cut motor vehicle CO-2.

In the yearlong talks that followed, there were a range of proposals discussed—from the radical to the mundane. In one early session, for example, a wide range of proposals were discussed, including, restricting the number of vehicles per family, requiring the elderly to give up their licenses, more taxes on gas-guzzling cars and trucks, higher age for beginning drivers, alternative driving days for commuters, and others.[29] The idea was to promote a freewheeling discussion of what might be possible by way of cutting the motor vehicle's share of greenhouse gases. That's how it began. But when specific proposals came to the table, it became clear that any agreement was a long way off.

Environmentalists and consumer groups tried to begin with President Clinton's 1992 campaign promise: fuel economy standards of 45 MPG for cars and 34 MPG for trucks. But that went nowhere. "The auto guys resisted talking about CAFE from day one," says the Sierra Club's Dan Becker, an invited participant. "It became obvious the auto industry would not agree with us on anything reasonable." He described the whole affair as "a very difficult, unpleasant effort."[30]

Automakers, for their part, tried to shift the emphasis to gasoline taxes. One group of automakers, consisting of GM, Ford, Chrysler, plus delegates from BMW and Honda, offered a proposal to curb driving by boosting gasoline taxes $1.50 over thirty years. But even over thirty years, the oil industry found that proposal too severe. Toward the end of the project, a proposed consensus report was prepared, but that died as well when the auto industry objected to the inclusion of direct measures to increase fuel economy. As the time approached for making a report to the president after a year of discussion, it was clear that a consensus position among the groups would be difficult at best.

On September 19, 1995, when the Car Talks panel held its last session, there was still no agreement. A draft report had been completed, which was put on the public record for comment, but it was not formally sent to the president. Among the elements considered in that report were land use changes that would reduce the public's dependence on cars, improved fixed-route and on-demand transit, support for the supercar-PNGV project, bike lanes, employee incentives for car pooling, accelerated retirement of low-MPG vehicles, support for alternative-fuel vehicles, and others. These measures, had they been agreed to, would reduce greenhouse gases by 93 million metric tons (MMT) by 2005, 171.5 MMT by 2015, and 383 MMT by 2025.[31]

As the Car Talks panel was finally dissolving, the API's William O'Keefe emphasized that the Clinton administration should "avoid any temptation to adopt mandatory requirements." Similarly, John Slaes, director of the Global Climate Coalition, representing industry trade groups and corporations, stated that "current voluntary programs should be given adequate time to work before any further actions are considered."[32] Frustrated at not having something more substantive to put on the record, a subgroup of the Car Talks panel—comprised of public officials, environmental representatives, and energy experts—began working on what they called a majority report. "There really is a center to our group," said Sonia Hamel, a member of the Car Talks panel and director of Air Policy Planning in the Massachusetts Governor's Office of Environmental Affairs, as she began the task of pulling the report together.[33]

As the majority report was being written, however, some of the industry representatives learned which members of the Car Talks panel were moving to the majority side. One of those was Missouri state representative Patrick Dougherty, a sixteen-year veteran of the Missouri House of Representatives. Dougherty was the chairman of the House Atomic Energy Committee and also served on the Energy and Environment committee, the Science and Technology Committee, and others. He had worked on state clean air bills, alternative-fuels legislation, energy efficiency measures, and other environmental bills throughout his career. He had been placed on the Car Talks panel because of this experience. But as word leaked out that Dougherty was going to sign the majority report, he was suddenly visited in his home state by representatives of the auto companies. These emissaries from Detroit told Dougherty that he might not fare well in his reelection bid if he chose to side with the majority on the Car Talks panel.[34]

By December 1995, the Car Talks majority report—with Dougherty included among the seventeen signing members—was sent to President Clinton. It recommended that fuel economy standards be raised annually beginning in 1998 and that other steps be taken to encourage the use of electric and low-emission vehicles, the development of alternative fuels, and a shift to other forms of transportation.[35] However, boosting fuel economy through the CAFE standard was the centerpiece of the majority report's recommendation.

"Looking ahead 10, 20, or 30 years, continued progress in fuel economy can significantly reduce greenhouse gas emissions," said the report. "Between now and 2015, improvements in fuel economy can produce greater greenhouse gas reduction than any other policy."[36] Fuel economy measures, this group found, could comprise 43 percent of total reduction by the year 2005 and 53 percent by 2015. The majority report further noted that the fuel economy improvements it was using as targets were modest—amounting to 1.5 MPG annual fleet average improvement over the 1998-2007 period, resulting in new cars reaching a 45 MPG standard and new light trucks, 34 MPG by the year 2007. That would mean raising fuel economy standards from the current 28.2 MPG for cars and 20.9 MPG for trucks—overall, a 60 percent improvement. By 2015, the annual rate of improvement—though still meeting the greenhouse target goals by that date—would drop to 1.0 MPG per year on average. Still, that would mean another 40 percent increase in fuel economy, raising levels by then to 58.7 MPG for new cars and 43.5 MPG for trucks.[37]

"We produced a very good report that makes clear that if the president is serious, he's got to raise CAFE standards. Nothing else will curb global warming as much," said Dan Becker.[38] But by late 1995, a distinct antiregulatory mood was sweeping over national policy. Representative Fred Upton (R-MI), at the behest of his auto company constituents, introduced a bill to revoke the president's authority to raise CAFE standards.

"TECHNO PORK"

Congressional Republicans, working under their Contract with America, soon discovered PNGV, and they were not favorably inclined to support it. The Cato Institute, a conservative think tank, called ventures like PNGV "techno-pork" and the label was used liberally on Capitol Hill. Since the Big Three earned $13.9 billion in profits between them in 1994, many thought the government's support was unnecessary. Robert Walker (R-PA), then chairman of the House Science Committee, vice chairman of the House Appropriations Committee, and friend of House Speaker Newt Gingrich, wanted to eliminate PNGV's funding. Some liberal and moderate Democrats—also unhappy with PNGV for diverting regulatory initiatives—were not sad to see the venture under the Republican spotlight. By early 1995, the Big Three and the White House joined together in a lobbying effort to forestall the Republican assault on PNGV. The White House, in fact, had requested a 40 percent increase in PNGV funding. The automakers were becoming increasingly comfortable with the political linkage they had forged with the White House and were not about to walk away.

"We believed, in the industry, that . . . [PNGV] was a net good for us both intrinsically and also because it was getting the government to understand our industry a lot better," said McTague. "From that perspective, we saw [PNGV] as advantageous to continue."[39] And both the automakers and the White House began the lobby effort to save the program.

Deftly, the Big Three took the techno pork label and began to put their own spin on it, showing Democrats and Republicans how the money was being spread around various congressional districts to suppliers and researchers. They also insisted that this wasn't really new government money, but rather, better management of existing programs. They went directly to the Republican power brokers to argue their case. The Big Three's McTague, Mueller, and Castaing met with Representative Robert Walker (R-PA), who also happened to be an auto enthusiast. They urged Walker to continue the program, asserting that the alliance with government was beneficial and should continue over the long term. "He said he would support us and he did," said McTague of the meeting with Walker.[40] PNGV didn't get the 40 percent increase the White House had requested, but Walker did save the program from extinction, giving it a 3 percent increase when other programs where being eliminated.

At the White House, Al Gore began to take a leadership role in moving PNGV along, convening technical symposia and hosting informal receptions at his private residence for the engineers and scientists involved. By mid-1996, PNGV published "Technical Accomplishments," listing sixty-one new technical advances from the twenty federal agencies taking part in the project and their industry partners. Yet, something closer to the truth came from Robert Chapman, former government relations VP for Allied Signal who came to PNGV in 1994, "They are in effect, picking through technologies that are there. . . . So, the result might be by the year 2002 a 65-mile per gallon car that is quite a bit lighter and has reduced emissions but not zero emissions and so on and so on. So they'll sift their way through [until they find] something they think would be favored by the public. And that's what's going on. It's very competitive."[41]

Yet others saw PNGV more clearly as a raid by Detroit on the federal laboratories. Any "competition" would come down to which one of the Big Three could make off with most valuable federal technology first.

## PNGV's POLLUTION

In June 1997, a group of five environmental and public health organizations—the Union of Concerned Scientists, ALA, NRDC, ACEEE, and the Environmental and Energy Study Institute—wrote to Vice President Al Gore about PNGV. Basically, this group had two concerns: PNGV's lack of attention to improving air quality and using the partnership as the government's sole approach to improving fuel economy.

"The weak emissions targets set out by the partnership offer little progress in reducing urban ozone and could permit next-generation vehicle designs to emit four to eight times more particulate than today's gasoline cars," wrote the group in their letter to Gore. In particular, the group viewed PNGV's plan to use diesel engines as the project's lead technology for building an 80-MPG prototype as a serious public health threat. PNGV also had another serious omission: it was only a passenger car project and did not address light trucks and SUVs, thereby neglecting what had become a 45 percent share of the new vehicle market.

On fuel economy, the group charged that PNGV by itself was insufficient to move the nation to improved vehicles, especially since the effort was being guided largely by industry's interests. "Not only is the R & D based strategy [of PNGV] incomplete, but the automobile industry is using PNGV to oppose action on fuel economy standards that are critical to delivering near-term gains and guiding the market towards more efficient vehicles. Although in principle we are highly supportive of R & D in the public interest, the concerns outlined above indicate our serious reservations about whether PNGV can deliver substantial returns on the federal investment," they said. "We therefore urge you to reevaluate PNGV's current direction and its role in federal energy and environmental policy."[42]

But nothing had riled up the environmentalists more than PNGV's move toward the diesel engine.

## THE DIESEL THREAT

In early 1996, Chrysler unveiled an electric-diesel hybrid automobile at the Detroit auto show. It came from research that both Ford and Chrysler had underway in the PNGV venture on diesel and hybrid engines.[43]

"We're excited about diesels because of their efficiency," explained Steve Barnhard of Chrysler's advanced technology group. "Diesels are the most efficient engines available today."[44] Indeed they were, a fact known since the energy crisis of the 1970s. Even then, diesels were 20 percent to 30 percent more fuel efficient than conventional ICEs. At one point in the 1970s, there were predictions that diesels would soon comprise 25 percent of the market. But diesels peaked at about 6 percent of sales in 1981 and went rapidly downhill thereafter. Diesels in the 1970s and early 1980s performed badly. GM, in particular, produced a trouble-plagued diesel—a gas-engine-converted Oldsmobile—that landed the company in court for several years. "GM set diesels back a long time," says Dan Ustian, vice president of engine business for Navistar, a major diesel engine manufacturer. By 1986, GM abandoned the diesel, at least in passenger cars. By 1998, less than 1 percent of all passenger vehicles in the US were diesel powered, and those were sold mainly by Volkswagen and Daimler-Benz. The Big Three sold diesels in about 5 percent of their pickups and SUVs. But as global warming concerns grew in the 1990s, and with the automakers falling behind in fuel economy, diesels began to get renewed consideration.

Combustion in a diesel engine occurs somewhat differently than in does in a conventional spark-plug-based ICE. Although the diesel is an ICE, combustion is initiated by heat and high compression, not a spark. But diesels have a reputation for being noisy, sluggish, and poor cold-weather starters. And they also emit problem pollutants, including NOx and particulate. Newer diesels, compared to older diesels, use very sophisticated fuel-injection systems, which result in vehicles that have better acceleration with reduced emissions, vibration, and noise. "Advanced diesels are much quieter, cleaner and responsive," says Charles McClure, president of Detroit Diesel, a major engine maker. But they still weren't as clean as the best conventional ICE.

On matters of fuel economy and overall energy efficiency, however, the diesel is a champ. Diesel fuel itself requires less energy to refine, the engines are about 25 percent more fuel efficient, and emit 20-to-30 percent fewer greenhouse gases than do equivalent ICEs. According to the experts, the diesel has a high thermal efficiency—meaning its power output relative to the potential energy in the fuel it burns is generally greater than that in conventional ICEs. But that is also part of its problem, too, as the higher temperatures increase NOx formation. Reducing the temperature lowers NOx but increases particulate. California, in fact, had for all practical purposes banned diesel engines in the early 1990s, as none of them could meet the state's emissions standards. By 1993, however, with low-sulfur diesel fuel, VW and Mercedes had models that passed state tests. Still, as of 1996, no diesel had qualified for California's LEV standards, although Daimler-Benz was working on some four-valve technology that might pass muster.[45]

By July 1997, PNGV began moving to select engine technologies that would lead to its 80-MPG family sedan for 2003. One of the engines then in the running was the "4SDI," a four-stroke, direct-injection diesel with a fuel efficiency 40 percent better that the standard ICE. At one of the PNGV technical symposia that month, Vice President Gore explained the challenge facing the PNGV team with the 4SDI diesels.

". . . [D]iesel engines are one of many internal combustion engine technologies being considered. This is because advanced diesels have the potential for fuel efficiency 40 percent better than current gasoline engines. Since there is a direct relationship between fuel burned and carbon dioxide emissions, this would mean a 40 percent reduction in carbon dioxide emissions as well." Some critics, however, felt this was generous arithmetic on Gore's part, saying the greenhouse reduction potential was actually closer to 30 percent. Still, Al Gore was the administration's man on global warming, which was driving the PNGV venture. But Gore made clear, however, that he saw the emissions problem. "Simply stated, while PNGV is primarily focused on a leap forward in fuel efficiency, we will not trade off clean air to achieve that goal, any more than we would trade off safety to do so." PNGV's engineers must meet several challenges at once, said Gore. If diesel engines are to be used in PNGV vehicles, "they must not only meet fuel efficiency challenges . . . they must [also] have significantly reduced emissions." PNGV's design criteria called for an 80 percent reduction in NOx emissions compared to current diesels, Gore noted, and a 50 percent reduction in particulate emissions. "This is well beyond regulatory requirements. Of course the PNGV vehicles also would be required to meet all regulatory requirements in effect at the time of production. If they can't do that, they are not appropriate candidates for PNGV."[46]

Yet, outside of PNGV, in the real world of production, the automakers could do whatever they pleased. And it appeared diesel engines were on the near-term drawing board for light trucks and SUVs in a big way. If PNGV happened to validate the trend by 2004, so much the better. Still, there were serious questions about the diesel's health effects. In California, a study examining the possible carcinogenic role of diesel fumes was underway and was slated to be released in early 1998. PNGV's diesels might not meet California standards by the time they were unveiled. That worried environmentalists who believed PNGV would be used to weaken new, tighter emissions standards slated to come out in California and at EPA—or as Jason Mark of UCS put it, using PNGV to include "diesel-friendly exemptions."

By mid-1997, however, US automakers began turning their attention to the upcoming international talks on a treaty to curb global warming, slated to take place later that year in Kyoto, Japan.

## OPPOSE TARGETS

A long history of scientific discussion, high-level panels, and previous international agreements, such as the Rio Treaty of 1992, had preceded what was scheduled to occur in Kyoto. The Rio Treaty, for example, had produced an agreement calling on nations to voluntarily reduce greenhouse gases to 1990 levels by the year 2000. None of the nations signing the Rio agreement, however, seemed close to reaching that goal in 1997.

The auto companies, like other businesses, opposed any tough measure to regulate greenhouse gas emissions. While a treaty per se might be acceptable, one that contained strict deadlines or targets would be dead on arrival. Environmentalists and climatologists, on the other hand, were emphatic about the need for tough targets. "Unless the United States accepts and implements binding emissions reduction targets and timetables," said Jonathan Lash, president of the Washington-based World Resources Institute, "no other country will do so, and Kyoto will be a failure."[47]

Historically, the auto-industrial lobby had taken the position that global warming was theory, not scientific fact, and that measures invoked to adjust emissions would simply be premature and damaging to the US economy. In July 1996, as US delegates were heading to Geneva for talks on global warming, executives from more than 100 US companies—including Jack Smith of GM, Bob Eaton of Chrysler, and Alex Trotman of Ford—signed a letter to President Clinton, expressing their views. "We are deeply concerned," they wrote, that the negotiations underway "may lead to premature agreements that will severely disadvantage the US economy and US competitiveness simply to meet an arbitrary deadline."[48] The letter raised other issues that typified industry's arguments in opposition to any treaty that placed tough restrictions on greenhouse gas emissions.

First, the letter maintained the problem was still uncertain. "While there is reason for concern about global climate change, the models that are relied upon to make climate change projections are evolving and there remains great uncertainty about the extent, timing, and effects. Each time the models have been improved, the estimates of the potential environmental impact have been significantly scaled back." Yet by this date there had already been evidence of Rhode Island-sized chunks of the Larsen ice shelf breaking off Antarctica and floating into the sea, and 2,500 of the world's leading climate scientists had agreed there was a serious problem.[49]

Next, the letter suggested that research was a better course than mandatory reductions of greenhouse gases (GHGs). ". . . [G]iven the long term nature of the issue, there is time to determine optimum strategies—that are economically sound, comprehensive, market-based and can be adjusted over time as new data and technologies become available. For example, a policy of accelerated research and development efforts leading to breakthrough technologies may achieve the same or better results with less cost and economic disruption than near-term strategies aimed at incremental reductions in greenhouse gas emissions."

Third, the letter warned that "the US should not accept other nation's agendas," focusing on the proposal to exempt developing nations from certain requirements, a theme that industry was especially concerned about and continued to focus on. "The US has the most to lose and will pay the highest cost for many of the proposals currently on the negotiating table." Yet it was the position of many leaders in the talks that the US and other developed nations must be leaders in the reductions, especially at first.

In conclusion, the US CEOs asked for more research on climate change cause and effect, and "a thorough study of all proposals with respect to their cost effectiveness and economic, social, and international competitiveness impacts." The US, said the executives, "should not agree to any of the three proposed protocols presently on the negotiating table." The letter to Clinton, displaying 119 CEO signatures was also run in full-page ads in the *Washington Post* and national publications. In Geneva, however, the delegates reached agreement that a new treaty with binding targets needed to be adopted. They agreed to meet in Kyoto, Japan in December 1997 to fashion the terms and finalize the new treaty.

Back home, the US auto industry continued to hone its opposition to the treaty. By mid-1997, Andrew Card, president of the AAMA was making sure his peers knew the stakes involved. "There is probably no more significant issue for the industry as whole that the global climate debate. Its ramifications will last for decades and its will affect production decisions, investment decisions, product decisions, and lifestyle—how vehicles are used and where they are available." The AAMA was also looking down the road, seeing Al Gore in the wings and the possibility of his being in the White House beyond 2000. Others in the industry thought they had already signed on with the Clinton administration to deal with the problem.

## PNGV & Global Warming

Chrysler's chairman Bob Eaton, for one, offered his view that the industry's new venture with the White House—PNGV—was the best way to prepare for global warming. Writing in a July 1997 *Washington Post* op-ed, Eaton characterized the Supercar project as "the US auto industry's contribution to the global warming solution." Eaton even proposed that the project "serve as a model for a much broader joint research effort involving all the major industries in the country and all the research resources of the federal government." Eaton was arguing in effect, for a worldwide PNGV, extended to *all* global warming-related industries. "This effort would dwarf the Manhattan Project and the space program in scope and cost," he wrote. "It would have to be a global program to be feasible, with everybody taking his fair share of the responsibility and cost."[50] Eaton's proposal would also be one way to string out the debate—and put off any real action—for endless years into the future.

"This is the sensible approach to global warming," Eaton continued, "not an international treaty based on inconclusive science that would have no chance of solving the problem (if we have one) but which would have disastrous economic consequences for all Americans. . . ." Environmentalists and many climate scientists, of course, took the opposite position, arguing that the disastrous economic consequences lay in not taking action now, imposing huge costs on generations to come. They advocated a "no regrets" policy.

The Big Three warned their colleagues at the annual University of Michigan auto industry seminar in August 1997, charging that the proposed global warming treaty could lead to higher energy costs, more expensive cars, and a transfer of jobs to less developed countries. "The stakes are absolutely enormous," said Ford's Alex Trotman. "We all ought to be scared stiff." Others hammered on the "faulty science" theme. "Our industry has worked too long and too hard to allow our efforts to be swept away by the tide of suspect science," said Chrysler's Thomas Gale, executive vice president of product development.[51] Chrysler's Ronald Boltz, vice president for product strategy, pointed to PNGV as the industry's preferred approach to developing cleaner vehicles—better than either federal regulation or global treaties. "We're simply as an industry suggesting that [PNGV] is a better course of action than having the United States enter into a treaty that sets some form of rigid timetable or target," said Boltz. PNGV would produce an 80 MPG four-door sedan, he said, in less than a decade. "The technology to do that hasn't been mandated," Boltz added, "it's gradually being discovered by that partnership. PNGV is a model of research proceeding before regulation."[52]

## ADVERTISING BLITZ

Back in Washington, the Big Three, already active in helping to form and help bankroll the Global Climate Coalition (GCC)*, put up more money in September 1997 to form the Global Climate Information Project (GCIP), which promptly announced it would spend $13 million on advertising to influence public opinion, Washington politicians, and the Kyoto negotiations. The money came primarily from the Big Three. Interestingly, the American International Auto Manufacturers Association (AIAM)—comprised largely of Japanese and German automakers—did not join GCIP, as its members were "uneasy" about how the campaign might boomerang on their "well earned green reputations," according to AIAM president Philip Hutchinson.[53]

At first, the industry ad campaign tried to confuse the public by saying global warming was based on bad science and was only theory, not fact. To advance its argument, the coalition used a small group of scientists time and time again who kept pounding home that message. At one point, the GCIP cited a purported Gallup poll in which the views of a large percent of the members of the Meteorological Society and the American Geophysical Society were incorrectly stated, suggesting that a large number of them did not believe in global warming.** Shortly thereafter 2,500 scientists went public, saying that global warming was fact and currently unfolding. The industry group re-engineered its own ad campaign, shifting to economics, now claiming that a greenhouse treaty would bring an economic disaster. In reply, 2,000 economists signed a statement disputing that charge. During the last quar-

---

* By 1993, the AAMA was itself spending about $100,000 on the global climate change issue and membership dues to the GCC. In 1994 and 1995 the GCC spent more than $1 million on the climate change issue and another $1 million in 1996.

** It turned out that there was no "Gallup poll" per se, but rather a study that Gallup had conducted for another group, some responses of which were then taken out of context, which led to a faulty attribution. Writing to the *Wall Street Journal*, whose editorial page had also misused responses from the study, Harry E. Cotugno, vice president at Gallup, offered the correction, noting however, that there was one important question and response that had not received much notice, "'In your opinion, is human-induced greenhouse warming now occurring?'" the study had asked. "Sixty-six percent of the scientists surveyed answered 'yes.'"

ter of 1997, the GCC orchestrated an intense campaign of TV, radio, and print ads opposing the treaty, playing on themes ranging from higher gasoline prices to the exclusion of developing countries. One TV ad, for example, showed a person with a pair of scissors cutting out various countries from a world map, with the tag line, "It's unfair!" Another showed gasoline prices being posted at the corner gas station at exorbitant levels.

By early December 1997, however, there was little evidence that the GCC ad campaign had affected public views. According to one *New York Times* poll of those who saw the ads opposing the treaty, two-thirds said they were not influenced.* But the ad campaign's real target was the public policy arena. "The goal of these sorts of campaigns is not ordinarily to change the attitudes of the public," said Kathleen Jamieson, dean of the Annenberg School for Communications at the University of Pennsylvania. "It is to persuade the legislative body that you are a player. You are involved, and you have ads on. And thus, in the next election campaign, you will have an effect by ultimately using advertising against them."[54] The US Senate, in fact, had already gotten the message.

Earlier in 1997, the Senate passed a resolution sponsored by Senators Robert Byrd (D-WV) and Chuck Hagel (R-NE) that called on developing countries like China to take on a bigger role in addressing the problem. Still, on the floor of the Senate as that resolution passed unanimously, Senator John Kerry (D-MA) was able to convince Senator Byrd that he did not mean developing countries would have to take on the same obligations as the developed world. Industry's GCC continued to oppose any treaty that contained targets or timetables. "My members support voluntary standards," said Gail McDonald, president of the GCC. Environmental leaders from seventeen organizations, meanwhile, sent their pleadings to Clinton, asking that he seek strong reductions in greenhouse gases to below 1990 levels no later than 2010.[55]

In late September 1997, the Department of Energy released a study showing that US greenhouse gas emissions could be cut to 1990 levels by the year 2010 without dire economic consequences, emphasizing new end-use technologies in four key sectors—transportation among them. Ford Motor's spokesman Al Chambers said Ford "is very much in favor of technology initiatives and pushing forward as quickly as possible on all of the different alternatives that exist." However, he added, "if you think this can be achieved why would you need to have legally binding targets? If this is all possible, it builds the case for doing this with voluntary measures."[56] Still, forty years of wrangling with the auto industry over urban air pollution and fuel

---

* In fact, in a November 1997 *Newsweek* poll, although most respondents indicated modest concern about global warming—that it wasn't a top concern—strong majorities indicated that measures could be taken to address the problem: 63 percent said the greenhouse effect could be reduced in ways that would not hurt the economy; 82 percent indicated they would pay an extra $50 for an energy-efficient appliance; 74 percent would buy a car with better fuel economy, and 51 percent would pay 12 cents more for gasoline.

economy suggested that the Big Three, in particular, needed something more than merely their verbal commitment to get the job done.

## WHITE HOUSE MEETING

As the Kyoto summit approached, US automakers went directly to the White House with their appeals. On the evening of Thursday, October 2, 1997, the Big Three CEOs—Alex Trotman of Ford, Jack Smith of GM, and Robert Eaton of Chrysler, plus Stephen Yokich of the UAW—met privately with President Clinton and several cabinet members. "We had a very good hearing . . . in the Oval Office with the president and his key people, . . ." recounted Alex Trotman. "We had quite an engaged discussion about ways that we might turn the 150 million vehicles that are now in the United States into much more energy efficient vehicles over the next decade or so."[57]

When Trotman first emerged from that meeting, however, he slammed the president's support for a treaty. "We believe the treaty would be bad for the United States in terms of jobs and the economic vitality of the country," said Trotman. The treaty, industry maintained, would increase gas prices 50 cents a gallon and boost electricity prices by 20 percent, raising the cost the making cars.[58] Not long thereafter, the Coalition for Vehicle Choice ran another ad in the *Washington Post* with that same message—that the treaty would be "bad for America." It included the names of 1,300 business, labor, and other local civic groups across the US that endorsed the statement. Still, in late October 1997, President Clinton offered the US proposal: reducing greenhouse gases to 1990 levels in the 2008-to-2012 time frame and calling for an aggressive program of incentives and tax breaks to encourage businesses to cut their emissions.

## JAPANESE UPSTAGE DETROIT

Meanwhile, at the 1997 Tokyo Auto Show, also in October, the Big Three received a wake-up call about the future of automotive technology. At center stage was Toyota's new car, the Prius. It was unlike any car on the road in America or anywhere else, and the Big Three didn't have one—at least not one as far along as the Prius which was about to go on sale in Tokyo. Known in the business as a "hybrid," the Prius was the first in a distinctly new wave of vehicle: a half gasoline-half electric-powered automobile that was far more fuel efficient and far less polluting than any vehicle of its time. Rated at 66 MPG for fuel economy, the Prius offered Toyota a competitive advantage in a warming world, producing half the carbon dioxide of a conventional car. The Prius also emitted 90 percent less of the vexing hydrocarbons and NOx that cause smog, a problem plaguing many of the world's major cities.

The Big Three, meanwhile, were caught somewhat flatfooted in Tokyo with their conventional vehicles, pushing a distinctly American lineup of big luxury cars, pickup trucks, and high-powered muscle cars. "At the Chrysler Corporation booth, where smiling women in hot pants lounged on fake brown boulders, the limelight was on the Viper sports cars," wrote Yuri Kageyama of the Associated Press from Tokyo. ". . . At $90,000, the Viper costs five times as much as the Prius and gets less than a fifth of the mileage at about 12 miles a gallon." Chrysler's Robert Bowen, president of Japanese sales, said that showing off the 450-horsepower Viper helped to build the company's reputation. "It creates a much stronger message that we are a hipper kind of car company," he said.[59] Chrysler wasn't alone. Ford had its Lincoln Continental and Town Car on display, GM had its Cadillac Seville and a V-8 Corvette, and there were also a few sport utility vehicles and big wagons, such as Ford's Tremor SUV and GMC's Yukon. The Japanese had a few of their own "sport utes" on display as well, and the Big Three had one or two small cars, such as GM's Opel and Ford's Ka headed for overseas markets. Still, the overwhelming impression was big American vehicles versus thrifty and environmentally improved Japanese versions. "America has remained true to its muscle-car heritage," said John Middlebrook, Chevrolet's general manager.[60]

Yet others saw the contrast between Detroit's muscle cars and pickups versus the Japanese seemingly clearer vision of a greening world and worried about the future. "I think the US automakers run the risk once again falling behind technologically," said Joseph Phillippi of Lehman Brothers, who viewed US automakers as preoccupied with high-profit pickups and SUVs.[61] Maryann Keller of Furman Selz Inc., agreed, "Green cars could be yet another issue that puts Japan in a leadership position."[62]

Ironically, Toyota's Prius—and the Japanese push into green car technology generally—was instigated at least in part by PNGV. The Japanese redoubled their R & D upon learning about PNGV. At Toyota, in particular, the effort focused on producing a highly efficient car. Toyota's chief engineer, Takeshi Uchiyamada, proposed the new car would be 30 percent more fuel efficient. However, another Toyota executive, Akihiro Ada, head of R & D, said 30 percent wasn't good enough. "He said our goal was too low and that we would have to increase fuel efficiency by two times." Uchiyamada went back to the drawing board, surveyed a stable of possible engines— electrics, hydrogen-based fuel cells, and others—but none could be mass-produced for a decade or more. In the end, the choice was a hybrid system. After four years of work—from 1993 to 1997—what Toyota produced was the Prius.[63] PNGV, by this time, was only at the halfway mark.

## THE OKUDA CHALLENGE

At the Tokyo Auto Show, the Big Three also appeared to play the wrong media message prior to the global warming conference. "Big Three executives spent most of the auto show's press preview pleading for more time and resources to find practical and more affordable solutions to global warming," reported Dave Phillips of the *Detroit News*, "while the Japanese auto executives gave every appearance of fully embracing the challenge to reduce dangerous emissions."[64]

Indeed, one of the most outspoken Japanese on this count was Toyota's Hiroshi Okuda. "We're determined to take the initiative in tackling environmental issues," he said. "We're coming to terms with the need to prevent global warming, to reduce pollution, and to conserve energy and other resources. The environment is our top priority."[65]

Okuda had become president of Toyota in August 1995 and immediately began pushing for a new business model—one founded in part on environmental performance. "A successful business model is good for about 40 years," says Okuda. After that, companies that persist with the same old model wither away. "Only companies that adopt new business models can continue to grow and prosper over the longer term." Toyota had jumped into its new business model embracing a range of new technologies, which include electric, hybrid, and fuel-cell engines, as well as improvements to existing internal combustion engines.

In addition to unveiling the Prius, Toyota engineered a bit of a media coup prior to the global warming talks. It became the exclusive advertiser in a special November 1997 issue of *Time* devoted to global environmental issues. The *Time* issue, entitled "Our Precious Planet," was also distributed to all the delegates at the Kyoto conference. In the *Time* issue, Toyota had twenty-one full pages of advertising, featuring its newly minted environmental philosophy, a range of Toyota's new green hardware, including the Prius, and a photo of its youngish, vigorous-looking new chairman, Hiroshi Okuda. Toyota used the *Time* issue as a platform to pitch its new philosophy. "We have the means—and therefore the responsibility—to explore a wide range of technologies," said Okuda in the *Time* spread. "We don't have a moment to lose. Customers are looking for cars they can feel good about owning. And they won't wait."

The Big Three initially dismissed the Japanese "green car" cavalcade, charging it to PR and posturing before the global warming talks. "This show is like this because of Kyoto," said Francois Castaing, Chrysler's VP for Powertrain Operations. "And if you read between the lines, none of the Japanese inventions here today are going to the US. I don't believe they are ahead of anybody else."[66] True, the Prius wasn't coming to the US—at least not right away. But the automotive technology that was bubbling up in Japan and elsewhere surely suggested that market conditions were about to change substantially. The Big Three said they could produce hybrid vehicles, too, but only if they made money on them, sniping at Toyota's loss-leader approach with the Prius. "We're really interested in what is economically sound, and what is honest development progress, before we put stuff out there and make a big song and dance about it," said Ford chairman Alex Trotman.[67]

Meanwhile, back home, PNGV was still the automakers' favorite refuge when confronted about progress on clean cars or fuel economy. In November 1997, after a coalition of environmental groups led by the Surface Transportation Policy Project (STPP) reported that improving automotive fuel economy could decrease global warming emissions by 200 million tons per year—or nearly half of that needed to reach 1990 levels—the auto industry responded by pointing to PNGV. The AAMA's

Mike Stanton said the STPP study "ignores all the work that is being done to increase fuel efficiency up to three times in today's midsize vehicle," reiterating the PNGV target of a clean 80 MPG car.[68] But PNGV's vehicle wouldn't be on the street until 2004, and only then as a prototype.

Environmentalists were also pressing the White House to take a tougher position at the Kyoto talks. In December 1997, more than 200 US environmental groups wrote to Clinton and Gore saying the White House had broken its promise on global warming, some citing Al Gore's book *Earth in the Balance* as a reminder of the vice president's earlier position. "Unless the US shows flexibility in Kyoto and takes a stronger position," said Phil Clapp of the National Environmental Trust, "its policy on climate change will become a character issue for Gore in the 2000 [presidential] race."[69] Heading into the talks, environmentalists favored a tougher European proposal, which called for 15 percent below 1990 levels by 2010. Industry, however, was well represented as the talks began. The GCC sent a delegation of 100 executives from oil, coal, and auto companies who stood at the ready in a suite of rooms across the hall from the US delegation.[70]

As proposals and counter proposals came and went, some received more serious consideration than others. Among the latter were pollution trading rights, underwhich companies and nations might swap pollution credits among themselves as a way of lowering overall $CO_2$ emissions. Looking ahead at how they might conduct business on the post-Kyoto chess board, some in the auto industry began figuring how they might use pollution trading rights. The following example was offered by *Automotive News*:

1. In 2002, Detroit-based carmaker "A" forecasts that rising sales of its sport utilities will soon produce more $CO_2$ emissions than allowed by international agreement.
2. Rather than cut its sales, "A" looks for a trading partner abroad. It turns to developing country "B," which want to build a coal-fired electric power station.
3. "A" pays to install an ultramodern pollution control system in the plant, thereby winning credits for lowering the plant's emissions. Those credits cover the additional sport utilities "A" plans to sell. The cost of plant's pollution control system is more than offset by the profits from the extra sport utility sales.[71]

Thus, as environmentalists had argued, trading would allow some companies to continue polluting and keep using older technology, as long as they bought emissions reductions elsewhere. Back at the negotiations, however, the whole process appeared like it might unravel as a wide North-South gulf opened up over which countries would participate and to what extent.

## "It Won't Work"

In the end, after a month of haranguing and posturing by all sides—and some last-minute heroics by Al Gore that helped hold the convention together—the delegates from 159 countries agreed to go forward with a treaty. Thirty-eight industrial nations agreed as a group to reduce their total greenhouse gases by an average of 5 percent below 1990 levels by the year 2012. The US, the largest greenhouse polluter, pledged to reduce its greenhouse gas emission by 7 percent below 1990 levels. Japan pledged a 6 percent reduction, and Europe an 8 percent reduction. DOE calculated that the US pledge would mean cutting 550 million metric tons of carbon by 2012—which meant achieving a 30 percent cut by that date. "This agreement represents unilateral economic disarmament" is how the American Petroleum Institute's William O'Keefe described what he saw.[72] "... It won't work," said Ford's Alex Trotman. "The protocol will impose significant costs on the United States and other developed economies without achieving genuine environmental benefit."[73] Chrysler's Bob Eaton added, "For months we have urged the administration not to bind the country to reduction of greenhouse gas emissions with arbitrary deadlines. Innovation and invention don't often come with dates certain. The administration chose to do that anyway."[74]

In any case, the treaty had a long road to travel before it became a legally binding document—a process that industry knew well it could use to delay and raise doubts. There were also a number of loose ends left to be worked out after Kyoto, including, importantly, enforcement, tradable pollution rights and credits, and whether major developing countries such as India and China would agree to make voluntary cuts in their greenhouse gases. Each of these could provide opportunities for the opponents.

"The administration can't submit (the Kyoto treaty) to the Senate. Not only would it not get 67 votes, ... it would be lucky to get 40 votes," predicted Chrysler's Washington lobbyist Robert Libertore. "Without Senate approval, do they try to do this through regulation? I hope they won't."[75] What the Big Three feared most was that the administration acting unilaterally to show the world community that it was willing to make reductions might come forward with a package of programs that included raising CAFE standards. To prevent that from happening, however, the industry had bills pending in Congress to keep the White House from taking such action. And there was also PNGV.

## PNGV POLITICS

PNGV, in fact, could be raised every time the Kyoto Protocol, CAFE, or new vehicle technologies were raised. "We're working with the White House on this" or "Congress has funded us to build a clean car" would be likely responses. PNGV might also turn out to be a refuge of sorts for some members of Congress worried about how their voting on environmental issues might be perceived. "It's my belief that Congress will recognize that it needs to have a response to climate change, regardless of [their] feelings with respect to Kyoto," said Michael Marvin, executive director of the Business Council for Sustainable Energy in Washington. PNGV funding levels, mused Marvin, could be among the chief beneficiaries.[76] Voting against Kyoto ratification—the priority for many in Congress—could be offset for some members by their support for PNGV and similar programs. They could vote against Kyoto, but could still say they supported research on climate change by funding PNGV, and thus could not be labeled antienvironment.

On the other hand, PNGV could become politically moot if technologically eclipsed by outside developments—in fact, as had already occurred with Toyota's Prius, another promised by Honda, and advances being made in the fuel cell. "While we were talking about hybrids," says Victor Wouk, a hybrid-vehicle consultant, "the Japanese were building one."[77] And PNGV diverted attention from the main event, too—SUVs. "While PNGV was going on," says Tom Gage, a former Chrysler official who charges that PNGV was set up to appease environmentalists, "light trucks captured 50 percent of the market, with their fuel economy in the 13-to-17-MPG range. We're back to the 1970s again."[78]

So what exactly has PNGV accomplished? When the Big Three PNGV directors were asked by *Scientific American* reporter Glenn Zorpette how PNGV helped their respective prototype new-car programs targeted for 2000 and beyond, none could identify a specific technology in their vehicles that had come from the collaboration. All insisted there was more to come. The benefits, it appeared, were mostly political. Ford's PNGV man, Victor Fazio said PNGV was instrumental in fostering "a significant amount of trust between Washington regulators and the industry." GM's PNGV man, Ron York explained, "we have learned to use collaborative work and competitive work in combination to get the job done." Indeed, no more worries about antitrust! Daimler-Chrysler's Steven Zimmer agreed, noting that "we have an ability to at least have a dialogue on the agendas" of the government agencies at the PNGV table, including EPA. This "inside track" and political access, in fact, is something Red Polling envisioned as a key advantage for joining PNGV back in 1993.

As of the year 2000, PNGV still had a few years left in its ten-year lifespan and conceivably could take a turn for the better to incorporate meaningful work on hybrids and/or fuel cells. But it might also be used to ratify the move toward diesel engine technology, prevent tighter auto emissions regulations from emerging, and thereby slow the clean-up of urban smog. And it would surely be used to fend off any tinkering with CAFE and could be used to slow action on the Kyoto treaty. Whatever lay ahead, PNGV had served a very useful purpose for the auto industry. It not only helped keep CAFE at bay for another decade, it also provided a cooperative R & D foil which at the very least slowed technological competition among the Big Three, diverted industry and government talent and dollars, and continued funneling limited financial resources—including public funds—into the 100-year-old internal combustion engine.

# 19

## The High Ride

There is no need for a customer to feel apologetic about buying an SUV.
—*Alex Trotman, chairman,*
*Ford Motor Co.*

These [SUVs] are nothing more than $35,000 pollution machines.
—*Dan Becker, Sierra Club*

On January 5, 1998, about a month after representatives of 156 nations had gathered in Kyoto, Japan, to discuss global warming, the Ford Motor Co. announced in Detroit it would clean up tailpipe emissions in its pickup trucks and SUVs. At Kyoto, SUVs, in particular, had come under a heavy round of pounding after an article by *New York Times* reporter Keith Bradsher had shown them to be fuel-hogging, carbon-belching behemoths, accounting for a rising share of urban pollution and greenhouse gases.[1] SUVs also epitomized for some the excesses of rampant American consumerism.

At the Tokyo Auto Show prior to the Kyoto talks, American automakers had been upstaged by the Japanese with a number of new green vehicles, and Ford decided that it was time to shine up its own image a bit with an environmental announcement. At the Detroit Auto Show, Ford said that by 1999 all of its light trucks—SUVs, pickups, and vans—would be as clean as cars. At a cost of a little more than $100 per vehicle, adding better catalysts, SUVs like the Ford Explorer and the Lincoln Navigator, and vans like the Windstar would no longer pollute at rates nearly twice that of cars.

"Now we call them CUVs—clean utility vehicles"—quipped Jacques A. Nasser, Ford's president.[2] Well, not entirely. There were still some emissions loopholes and public health concerns, especially if SUVs started using diesel engines. And there was also the small matter of global warming, and in particular, carbon dioxide. "These vehicles are horrible on carbon dioxide emissions," said the Sierra Club's Steven Pedery. They were horrible, in fact, because as a group, these SUVs and light trucks were gas guzzlers, most rated in the 12 MPG to 17 MPG range, well below most cars, then getting 27.5 MPG on average.

In 1998, America's 65 million SUVs, trucks, and vans already matched the greenhouse contribution of the nation's 125 million cars. EPA projected that light trucks would be the fastest growing source of US greenhouse gasses during 1998-2008. A Dodge Durango SUV emitted 57 percent more CO-2 than a Dodge Intrepid full-size passenger car. Light trucks and SUVs also emitted twice as much urban pollution as cars—175 percent more NOx than even the biggest passenger cars. Poor fuel economy only made both problems worse.

But Ford was in the limelight for the moment, collecting credit for cleaning up its vehicles and taking voluntary action. "This should neutralize the debate between cars and SUVs in the industry," said Jac Nasser, hoping for the best. But it wouldn't do that, especially since all light trucks—pickups, SUVs, and minivans—were getting a free ride of sorts, benefitting from the emissions and fuel economy loopholes inserted into the law more than two decades ago.

## The Twenty-Five-Year Loophole

In 1975, when Congress passed the Energy Policy and Conservation Act, the law establishing fuel economy standards, it excluded light trucks. At the time, there were about 20 million light trucks on the road, far fewer than today. Yet, even then there were clear signs that a new growth area was at hand. Between the late 1960s and mid-1970s, in fact, light truck sales had more than doubled, from 1.2 million per year in 1967 to 2.7 million per year in 1976. But with the Arab oil embargo of 1974, automotive fuel economy came front and center. Light trucks then were getting an average of about 12 miles to the gallon. Although Congress had specified levels of fuel economy to be achieved for passenger cars under the law, light trucks were another matter.

Allied with farmers and construction workers, the automakers argued in Congress that fuel economy standards for trucks would result in smaller and less powerful trucks, thereby hampering the work of homebuilders, farmers, and others. Congress punted and allowed DOT to establish separate standards for trucks. That task soon wound up in the lap of Joan Claybrook.

Claybrook, a young lawyer and public interest advocate who had schooled with consumer advocate Ralph Nader, had become Nader's chief Washington lobbyist by 1973. With the election of Jimmy Carter in 1976, Claybrook was nominated to head up the National Highway Traffic Safety Administration (NHTSA) at DOT. In 1977, when Claybrook arrived at NHTSA she faced a major battle with US automakers over fuel economy standards for light trucks.

The automakers expected they would have to give some ground and make some efficiency improvements in their trucks and vans. However, they were hoping for a NHTSA proposal of no more than about 6 percent a year. But in December 1977, Claybrook went well beyond that, pushing for a 30 percent increase—based on what her engineers found to be "technologically and economically feasible," as specified in the law by Congress. Claybrook was asking for an increase from 14.6 MPG in 1979 to 19.2 MPG in 1980 and 20.5 in 1981, for two-wheel drive vans and trucks. For four-wheel-drive vehicles, she was proposing 16.2 MPG in 1979 and 17.7 MPG in 1981. Part of the reason Claybrook was pushing improved fuel economy in light trucks was that more and more of them—along with vans—were being used for personal transportation. Claybrook was also proposing that the standard would apply to trucks, and in particular, heavier light trucks, increasing the weight of vehicles covered from 6,000 pounds to 8,500 pounds.[3] Fuel savings of about 1 billion gallons of gasoline per year were predicted by NHTSA under the Claybrook proposal—enough to build 100,000 new homes or heat the entire city of Detroit for ten winters. Over the life of the vehicle, Claybrook estimated that 12 billion gallons of fuel would be saved, and that by 1981, the improved fuel economy in the light truck category would mean consumers would save a net $553 to $652 annually, even after higher vehicle prices were considered.[4] The automakers, however, called Claybrook's proposal unreasonable, and they went to war, mounting a three-front campaign to derail the regulations.

First, they went to the White House and cabinet-level officials. Having obtained a leaked version of the standards before they were made public, a top GM executive arranged a meeting with Secretary of Transportation Brock Adams to complain about claybrook's proposal. Over in the White House, Henry Ford II contacted Kitty Schirmer, then a top-level energy analyst on the president's Domestic Council. Schirmer later told the *Detroit Free Press* that Ford enlisted congressmen to begin contacting other Cabinet officials about the matter. Longtime auto industry friend, John Dingell, chairman of the powerful House Commerce Subcommittee on Energy and Power, and then a key player on President Carter's National Energy Act, made his concerns known to both Adams and the White House. Carter wanted his energy bill to move and the fuel standards were becoming a problem. "Kitty Schirmer called me and asked about the timing of the standards," Claybrook recounted. "She said the timing was awkward. I thought about it overnight and called her the next day to say we were going ahead."[5]

The automakers used their auto dealer network and other interests to lobby congress and NHTSA. Even some rural postal carriers complained that tough fuel economy standards would put a drag on rural mail delivery. One farmer from Blackfoot, Idaho, even wrote Representative George Hansen (R-ID) to suggest that Claybrook was about to take his 10 mile-per-gallon pickup truck away. Letters of complaint poured into NHTSA at a steady clip. More than 200 separate sets of comments on the proposal were also received. "There's been a tremendous amount of lobbying on this issue by the automobile manufacturers," said Claybrook at the time. "They thought they had to use extra pressure to make me reasonable. That's unnecessary.... We put forward our methodology. Our proposal was based on it and it was based on their information." In fact, Chrysler had originally provided Claybrook's engineers with data that supported the standards. But once the standards came out, Chrysler called them impossible. "We were shocked to see the way [our] information has been used," said Chrysler vice president S.L. Terry.[6]

## ECONOMIC BLACKMAIL

Chrysler fought back, playing its final hand very deftly on one issue: jobs. Chrysler's John Riccardo announced if the standards went into effect, the company would have to lay off 3,000 workers in Detroit, a city in the throes of high unemployment. Chrysler had plans to convert its Jefferson Avenue auto plant into a factory for light trucks and vans. That plant conversion, said Chrysler, would be shelved if the standards went into effect. "It was sheer economic blackmail," reported *Environmental Action*'s editor Debbie Baldwin, who covered the NHTSA decision. Before long, though, Chrysler's threat was working. GM and Ford piled on, claiming jobs would be lost at their shops, too. The NAACP joined the opposition, saying there was a "relative certainty" that black autoworkers would be laid off. The UAW's Donald Fraser called Chrysler's Jefferson Avenue threat "propaganda," but the UAW was still concerned about potential layoffs. Jesse Jackson's People United to Save Humanity, PUSH, also opposed the standards.

"If the automakers are so interested in jobs," said Clarence Ditlow, of the Center for Auto Safety, "they should compete directly with the foreign manufacturers. There's no conflict between fuel economy and consumer needs. . . . You can have the trucks and the fuel efficiency too." But in politics, perception is what matters.

On March 15, 1978, Brock Adams announced to the press that Claybrook's proposal to increase van and light truck fuel economy by 30 percent had been cut to 10 percent. New technical data from the industry and a change in DOT's thinking about the economic impact of the rules were cited as reasons. "Sheer capitulation," charged Ditlow of NHTSA's final decision. "If this is a balancing of interest," he said, "the rocks are all on one side." Indeed they were, and in more ways than generous fuel economy rules.

## A PROTECTED MARKET

US automakers were, in fact, already benefiting from a special tariff on imported trucks. In 1964, President Lyndon Johnson placed 25 percent tax on all imported light trucks, a move that at the time was taken in retaliation for European restrictions on American agricultural products. Volkswagen was making inroads on the American market then, primarily with the Beetle, but also with its van, and Johnson took the action in part under the guise of protecting American jobs. In Congress, during the 1970s, there was more generosity.

After NHTSA failed to advance tough fuel economy for light trucks in 1977-78, Congress exempted light trucks from the gas-guzzler and luxury vehicle tax when it re-wrote tax rules in 1978. At the time, with energy issues still very much a concern, lawmakers thought that buyers of bigger, more luxurious vehicles that consumed more gasoline, adding to the nation's oil import problem, should then pay the price for their energy indulgence. The gas-guzzler tax established that manufacturers whose vehicles' fuel economy fell below 22.5 MPG would pay an escalating "gas-guzzler" tax, ranging from $500 to $3,850 per vehicle, depending on how far below the standard their gas mileage was. The only catch was that gas-guzzling trucks and vans—some with gas mileage far worse than luxury cars—were exempt.

The automakers also managed to secure special treatment for light trucks under the Clean Air Act Amendments of 1977. Emission standards for light trucks and vans were made less stringent than those for cars. In fact, for the 1981-84 model years—set by the '77 Act—the gulf in emissions standards between cars and trucks began to really open up. Light trucks by then were permitted to emit 2.3 times more NOx than cars; 4 times more hydrocarbons; and more than 5 times the CO. With all the good fortune bestowed on the automakers by Congress and the federal agencies, Detroit was well on its way to riding a new wave of protected "light truck" prosperity. By lobbying tough in Congress and playing hardball with NHTSA, the auto industry had secured the legal basis to produce vehicles that both consumed more fuel and produced more pollution.

## ADVERTISING SHIFT

During the 1970s debates in Congress and at NHTSA, automakers would typically cast their trucks and utility vehicles as the workhorses of America, vital to the economy. Trucks and vans, they would say, were essential to construction workers, farmers, and for moving commercial cargo. Yet in their advertising campaigns for these vehicles, they were already featuring them in noncommercial roles. The Center for Auto Safety, in fact, found in one review of 1960s-1970s pickup truck, van, and jeep ads, that the industry's advertising strategy had "clearly shifted" from selling light-truck type vehicles "as heavy load-carrying, commercial vehicles to substitutes for passenger automobiles."[7]

As early as 1968, and through the early 1970s, automaker ads were beginning to test the new messages. Some pitched pickups and vans for recreation, shopping, second cars, and more. One 1968 Chevrolet truck ad, for example, touted pickup trucks "for work, recreation or both." A few Jeep ads at the time also stressed recreational use. A Ford ad, featuring its club Wagon, Bronco, and Camper Special models, pushed a second car purchase, "Maybe your second car should be more than just a second car." By 1970, recreational uses were the focus of ads for Chevy pickup campers and Jeeps. American Motors, in fact, launched one campaign—"The 2-Car Car"—which stressed the Jeep's suitability as both a recreational vehicle and a family car. Jeeps were also shown in the woods, in front of country clubs, and parked along suburban streets. In the mid-1970s—though fuel economy was now a national concern—

jeeps, vans, and pickups appeared in ads head-to-head with cars. Chevy Blazer ads showed the vehicle loaded with groceries, touting them as "big at the supermarket." An AMC ad characterized its Jeep as "4-wheel drive for the family man" and compared it to a station wagon. Comfort, convenience, and styling in these so-called workhorse vehicles were also getting air time. Options mentioned in Ford van ads included woodtone effects, carpeting, chateau trim, and pivoting captain's chairs—clearly not "workhorse" features. A Dodge Ramcharger's options included cruise control, automatic transmission, air conditioning, and a console ice chest. Another Dodge ad showed a van at the beach, with the ad's text stating the vehicle was "ready to take on a weekend's worth of dirt bikes, surfboards, scuba gear, camping equipment. And friends." Vans were generally becoming something more than commercial and utility vehicles, as a craze swept across the country making them the equivalent of mobile lounges, with deep pile wall-to-wall shag carpeting. In 1976, Dodge featured recreational uses for its trucks in a series of ads, using the theme "the adult toys from Dodge." AMC ads of the late 1970s cast its Jeep CJs as "built this tough for the fun of it."

An October 1977 General Motors ad appearing in *Sports Illustrated* and titled, "Realizing Your Next Car Should Be a Truck," offered its view on how average people were then just stumbling into "this whole truck thing":

> There you were, strolling along just minding your business, when all of a sudden there it was, all big and red and tough and shiny, practically cooing to you from the showroom floor. Buy a truck?—*You?* Oh well, it can't hurt to look, can it? So in you go. What you discover, of course, is how civilized a GMC is. Glory be, this seating's comfortable. And look at all the goodies you can order: available power steering, automatic transmission, air conditioning, stereo, cruise control. Gosh, the instrument panel's as nice as you'd find in a car. . . .
>
> A test-drive? Oh, you couldn't . . . but then again, what's life without a little adventure, anyway? Besides, anything with such a good view of the road is bound to be ball to drive, right? Well, okay . . . but just around the block.
>
> Boy, sure is smooth up here. And all that cargo space—just imagine the stuff a guy could haul back there.
>
> *Buy* it? Oh, you couldn't . . . could you?
>
> Come to think of it, *sure* you could.[8]

In May 1977, Ford Motor's Robert Gillosky, the company's truck advertising manager, stated quite plainly that "the compact pickup primarily is a personal use vehicle with only a small percentage of buyers using it for business." Gillosky explained that about a third of the buyers—"an extraordinarily high percent"—attach a camper shell to the truck's body. "Our advertising," he assured *Advertising Age* at the time, "will recognize this and play strongly [to] the personal use market."[9]

In late 1977, *Business Week* editors, citing auto industry experts, confirmed that light trucks were hauling more passengers and less cargo. "Indeed, truck marketing executives report that only one-third of all light trucks now sold are used primarily as commercial vehicles—the reverse of the situation a decade ago. Most are now used for personal transportation. . . ." By this time, in fact, Ford Motor was reporting that half of the trade-ins for new pickups were cars, and passenger cars were also accounting for 60 percent of trade-ins for vans.

Still, in 1977-78 when Congress and NHTSA were handing out their favors and exemptions to the automakers for their "workhorse" vehicles, more than two-thirds of those vehicles were being used no differently than cars. Yet the special treatment of trucks, vans, and emerging SUVs—founded on the inflated premise that these were commercially vital vehicles—would continue for at least another twenty years. Detroit, meanwhile, would go about filling up its "light truck" category with many new creations.

## THE MINIVAN

In 1980, Lee Iacocca and Harold K. Sperlich at Chrysler began planning the Chrysler minivan, which would later be introduced with great success in 1983-84. The origins of the Chrysler minivan date back to Ford in the late 1960s when engineers began ruminating about a modernized, efficient station wagon—something between a commercial van and conventional station wagon—but a vehicle that women could use as well as men. Recalls Lee Iacocca,

> . . . Shortly after the first OPEC crisis, while Hal Sperlich and I were working on the [Ford] Fiesta, we designed a project we called the Mini-Max. We had in mind a small front-wheel-drive van that was compact on the outside and roomy on the inside. We built a prototype and fell in love with it.
>
> Then we spent $500,000 to research it. And in the process we learned three things. First, step-up height had to be low enough to appeal to women, who mostly wore skirts those days. Second, we had to make the car low enough to fit into a garage. Third, there had to be a "nose" with an ending up front to provide a couple of feet of crush space in case of an accident.
>
> If we took care of these things, the research shouted, we were looking at a market of eight hundred thousand a year. . . .[10]

Those numbers meant the Mini-Max would do better in its first year than even the popular Mustang—which had sold 400,000 in its first year. But the kicker for Iacocca was profit: the research showed that Ford could charge a high price for the Mini-Max—$8000 to $10,000 each, which was considerable in the mid-1970s. But despite the backing of Iacocca and Sperlich, Henry Ford canned the project; he didn't want to experiment. After Ford fired Iacocca for reasons more to do with personality than automobiles, Iacocca, Sperlich, and others from Ford went over to Chrysler. There they revived the Mini-Max project. In the fall of 1980, with Iacocca and Chrysler on the ropes financially, and on the federal dole, the decision was made to proceed with the minivan. In the fall of 1983, the Chrysler minivan was introduced to rave reviews and great success. *Fortune* called it one of the year's ten most innovative projects. By mid-1984, Chrysler's production of the new minivan was completely sold out.[11] The company sold 132,000 Voyagers and Caravans in 1984, and 236,000 in 1985. Chrysler's earnings soared to a record $2.4 billion in 1984, with more good earnings in 1985 and 1986. Shortly thereafter, Ford, GM, and Toyota brought out their minivans.

Although minivans were carlike in handling and were built upon automobile chassis, the automakers purposely designated them as light trucks so they could take advantage of the less stringent emission standards. The federal government was also enforcing the new 25 percent tariff on all imported trucks. After foreign makers, principally the Japanese, had taken 20.5 percent of the light truck market in 1981, tougher enforcement of the tariff helped push the foreign share down to 15.2 percent. But the Japanese were still able to produce small pickups at competitive prices even with the tariff, and by June 1983, Nissan for one, began producing compact trucks in Tennessee, avoiding the tariff. By 1985, foreign makers had raised their light truck share to 17 percent.[12]

Meanwhile, Ford and AMC's Jeep unit began selling more of their early sport utility vehicles. By 1984, Jeep introduced its Cherokee and Wagoneer models and Ford offered its Bronco II. Bronco sales tripled between 1984 and 1985. The light truck segment was beginning to look better and better as consumers bought more and more of the new vehicles, many outfitted with the latest options.

Back in Washington, Ford and GM were hammering on Congress and the federal agencies to roll back light truck fuel economy standards. In November 1983, Ford had petitioned NHTSA to push back the 1984 and 1985 light truck standards. Ford wanted the 20 MPG 1984 standard rolled back to 19 MPG and the 21 MPG standard pushed back to 20 MPG. For the 1983 model year, Ford's light trucks had eked out a 19.1 MPG level, surpassing the requirements by 0.1 MPG. But for 1984 and 1985, Ford was facing penalties if the standards weren't eased.[13] By August 1984, Ford was joined by GM lobbying Congress for a one-year reduction in the light truck standard. NHTSA, by this time, acting on Ford's request, had already reduced the 1985 standard from 21 MPG to 19.5 MPG. But Ford was still pushing NHTSA to reduce the 20 MPG 1984 standard to 19 MPG. GM agreed, supporting Ford's request. At a congressional hearing, Ford vice president Helen Petrauskas said the lower fuel economy standard for light trucks was needed because of an unexpected surge in consumer demand—mostly from business, she said—for trucks with big V-8 engines.[14]

Yet, despite Petrauskas' suggestion that commerce and business needs were once again behind this surging market, the Department of Commerce had found two years earlier, in 1982, that 73 percent of light trucks then on the road carried no freight whatsoever.[15] So what was going on here?

## Yuppie Cargoes

By the mid-1980s, it was clear that the commercial purpose of most light-duty trucks—especially pickup trucks—had shifted to new recreational and yuppie lifestyle cargo: snowmobiles, ski boats, motorcycles, and camping gear. "The yuppies and their toys are a key target market," explained Peter Guptill, vice president of North American Sales at American Motors in December 1985. "On weekends, they want to get away with their toys. A truck fits right into their lifestyle."[16]

Ford, for one, was giving appropriate upscale names to some of its SUV models, like the "Eddie Bauer Bronco." Ford's Bronco sales had tripled between late 1984 and late 1985. Minivans were doing well, too; some 450,000 were sold in 1985, with Chrysler doing especially well. Chrysler's Voyager and Caravan models lept from 132,000 units in 1984 to 236,000 in 1985. Car buyers were continuing to move toward bigger vehicles. Minivans at the time were attracting car buyers, not the traditional truck buyers, explained John Hammond, auto analyst with Data Resources.[17] Ford Motor, in fact, began pushing internally for more truck spending—meaning pickups, minivans, and SUVs. "[W]hat we've got to do is move our spending to trucks," explained Ford's top technical executive Louis Ross at an August 1986 meeting with the top brass, including CEO Don Peterson and president Red Poling. "We want to spend 70 percent more on truck programs in the next five years than we have in the last five. . . ." Ross pointed to the 25 percent import tax on two-door trucks "which holds back the Japanese." So, he concluded, "why the hell don't we, as a company, redirect our resources substantially to our trucks?"[18] And Ford did exactly that—and with pickup truck sales in particular, would soon become the undisputed king of the hill.

A year later, in August 1987, Chrysler acquired American Motors Corp (AMC) from Renault and soon began to reap a windfall known as the Jeep. At the time of the AMC acquisition, Chrysler itself was considering a truck-based sport utility vehicle. AMC, too, was then developing an upgraded Jeep, code-named Jeep ZJ. After the acquisition, Chrysler made some up-scale modifications to the AMC Jeep project, and in 1992 the new Jeep was unveiled. It was called the Jeep Grand Cherokee.[19] Meanwhile, over at Ford, the new Explorer had already been launched in 1990. These two vehicles, the Jeep Cherokee and the Ford Explorer, fully ushered in the modern SUV era.

Environmentalists were still raising the issue of fuel economy, with most of their effort targeted to CAFE in cars. But trucks also received attention. In 1990, Marc Ledbetter on behalf of the American Council for an Energy Efficient Economy, testified before a House subcommittee that average efficiencies of 35 MPG were feasible for light trucks by the year 2000.[20] Yet, few in Congress were listening. Detroit was on a roll.

## THE FORD EXPLORER EFFECT

By late 1992, it was becoming clearer and clearer that the US share of oil consumption and therefore, global warming emissions, was rising, not falling. And behind this rising greenhouse were a couple of trends in which the burgeoning light truck segment figured prominently.

First, American drivers were traveling more in the vehicles they bought—known as vehicle miles of travel, or VMT. In 1990, VMT was 2.2 trillion miles, double what it was in 1970. A growing share of national VMT was occurring in larger, less fuel-efficient vehicles, namely vans, pickups, and SUVs. Horsepower was climbing upward as well, also due in part to the light truck segment. And finally, by the early 1990s, pickups, vans, and SUVS comprised more than 40 percent of all vehicle sales.

The Ford Explorer, for example, one of the most popular vehicles in America by the time Senator Richard Bryan's CAFE bill was being buried in Congress, had a highway rating of 20 MPG. But even a luxury Lincoln Town Car would get 25 MPG. One SUV like the Explorer, in fact, could wipe out energy conservation gains being made in other sectors of the economy. Take, for example, efficiency in building lighting, then being pushed by EPA in a voluntary 1992 business program called Green Lights, aimed also at reducing greenhouse gases.

American Express joined the program and began installing new energy efficient lighting in its offices. At the company's fifty-one-story office building in Manhattan, American Express saved up to 40 percent on electricity bills while cutting carbon emissions. Together with offices in five other cities, American Express cut annual $CO_2$ emissions by 3,000 metric tons. Yet on the national ledger of carbon give and take, this impressive savings by American Express was wiped out by the $CO_2$ emitted by 700 Ford Explorers—less than one day's production of that model.[21]

Throughout the early 1990s, light truck and SUV sales continued to climb. New models proliferated. New four-door SUVs helped fuel the sales fire. GM's S-10 Blazer, as well as imports such as the Nissan Pathfinder and Toyota 4 Runner came on the market. The automakers couldn't keep up with demand. The pickup market was booming, too. By 1993, Chrysler designers were playing to the machismo fantasies of would-be tractor-trailer buffs, designing their Dodge Ram pickup with a huge ornamental grille to attract those buyers who wanted the "big-rig" effect and the look of tractor trailers. But the Ram also carried a driver-side air bag and a center console wide enough for a laptop computer. And it wasn't just male machismo that was powering the new light truck-SUV surge. Women were also attracted, especially to SUVs. According to Laurel Cutler, a female executive in the auto industry, "Women particularly love them [SUVs] because there is such a feeling of power sitting way up high and seeing the whole road and feeling in control. Nothing like it. I tell you it's a tremendous feeling to sit up high. It's marvelous. I mean you feel like the king of the road. Tall, tall, tall . . ."[22]

Sales of full-size pickups and upscale SUVs were also being powered by a certain public perception. "For a lot of buyers, those vehicle represented a better image than cars," explained Joe Pitcoff, a research manager at Ford Motor. "They became a surrogate for the luxury car." The SUV-light truck craze was clearly making Detroit happy. "I don't know how well we are doing at predicting how big this will get," said Fred Cook, director of marketing for GM's GMC truck division in August 1993, "but we are enjoying it."[23] By then, the margins were very good for light trucks and SUVS, pulling in $6,000 to $8,000 per Ford Explorer or Jeep Grand Cherokee, before deducting corporate overhead costs. As a group, trucks and SUVs had lower sales costs than cars, even in tough times. "When sales are a little slow, it takes, on average, a lot less in advertising and rebate money to move light truck models than cars," explained Jerry Paul, a New York auto analyst in August 1993.[24]

Trucks, vans, and SUVs made up 59 percent of Chrysler's vehicle sales in 1993, 47 percent of Ford's, and 38 percent of GM's. "Demand has outstripped supply pretty much across the board," said Allan Spitzer in early 1994, happily describing the Chevy pickups, Plymouth Voyagers, and Ford Explorers moving briskly off his lot in Elyria, Ohio. "I don't know where the top is." With the Big Three making several thousand dollars more profit per light truck vehicle than the average midsize passenger car, they were doing everything they could to increase production. GM began running a minivan plant in Flint, MI round the clock in May 1994 and also designated another that made C/K pickups in Pontiac, MI to add a third shift. Ford turned up the line speed at its Wayne, MI plant to crank out more Broncos and F-Series pickups. Chrysler's Ram pickup and Jeep Grand Cherokee production were maxed out; a new Dodge Ram plant was opened in Mexico in June 1994. Ford by then had begun producing its Windstar minivan in Ontario.[25]

Through the early 1990s, US automakers were still beneficiaries of the 25 percent import tariff on light trucks. In 1993 trade negotiations, for example, the auto industry warned the Bush administration that it would withhold its support from any trade agreement that reduced the tariff on imported trucks. The administration went along with the automakers position, despite Japanese protests. The tariff was later reduced to 2.5 percent for minivans and SUVs, but the 25 percent rate on pickup trucks remained.

## CLINTON & TRUCKS

By 1994, SUVs and light trucks accounted for 40 percent of all vehicles sold in the country, also accounting for a rising share of fuel. The truck CAFE standard was 20.6 MPG, but unlike the passenger car standard set by Congress, this standard could be adjusted by the Executive Branch. So when the Clinton administration made it known that the fuel economy standard for this class of vehicles was under consideration, Detroit became very concerned. Such a move "would have a very destructive effect on our business," said Robert Liberatore, Chrysler's vice president for Washington affairs. "CAFE doesn't work. It doesn't save energy," added William

Noack, GM's director of public affairs in Washington. "It's just a command-and-control rule that just bumps people around in the marketplace."[26] The automakers argued that if light truck fuel economy standards were raised, it would give the Japanese a bigger piece of the light truck market. The Japanese, as they had done with cars, were also making efficient truck engines. "It scares us," said Mike Stanton of the AAMA, about the prospect of a Japanese surge into a market the Big Three held firmly.[27]

In 1994, NHTSA had indicated that it was going to raise the standard for light truck fuel economy, with rules that wouldn't go in effect until model year 1998. Barry Felrice, NHTSA's associate administrator for safety performance standards told a congressional committee in July 1995 that "in light of the rapid growth in fuel consumption by light trucks" NHTSA began looking into what "could be done to improve light truck fuel economy." Felrice added that a 1992 National Academy of Science report had found a "technologically feasible" light truck fuel economy level of 26 to 28 miles a gallon by 2006. Environmentalists thought it should be even higher, noting that automakers had neglected technologies that would make fuel economy gains in light trucks fairly painless.[28] On Capitol Hill, meanwhile, Representative Tom Delay, Texas Republican and majority whip, stepped into the fray, charging that NHTSA's proposed fuel economy action would hurt domestic automakers and "would be devastating to the nation's economy."[29] He added a proviso in the House appropriations bill for DOT that prevented NHTSA from raising the standard for one year, an action repeated several times since.

When NHTSA finally did venture to raise the CAFE standard for light trucks under an earlier authorization, it was only by one-tenth MPG. Thus, light trucks in 1996 and 1997 would meet a 20.7 MPG standard. Yet, more than a decade earlier, in 1983, the average light truck fuel economy had already reached 20.7 MPG. It had fallen and stagnated ever since. In Congress, meanwhile, the Republican majority continued to prohibit NHTSA from raising the standard, giving automakers the green light to build more gas guzzlers.

## MORE TRUCKS THAN CARS

In 1995, for the first time in its ninety-three-year history, Ford sold more trucks than cars. The Ford F-Series full-size pickup outsold the Ford Taurus, the nation's no. 1 car, by 325,000 units. In that year, four of the nation's top ten vehicles were trucks. By 1996, Chrysler was selling nearly 280,000 Grand Cherokees and more than 148,000 regular Cherokees annually. The Jeep Grand Cherokee became Chrysler's third best-selling vehicle, right behind the Dodge Ram pickup and the Dodge Caravan.[30] By mid-1996, light trucks and SUVs were outselling cars in seventeen states. Profits were rolling in like never before.

Times were so good for SUVs and pickups that the Big Three were converting car plants to produce more of them. By mid-1995, GM had phased-out its Cadil-

lac Fleetwood, Buick Roadmaster, Chevy Impala, and Caprice models at its Arling-
ton, Texas plant, where it began building SUVs and pickups. In Newark, Delaware,
Chrysler converted one of its car factories to make new Dodge Durangos, a big SUV.
At the opening day ceremony for the plant in September 1997, Governor Thomas
Carper (D) noted that Chrysler's $623- million investment in the new plant worked
out to about $1,000 for every person in Delaware. Both of the state's senators were
also on hand—Joseph Biden (D) and William Roth (R). They had lunch with
Chrysler chairman Bob Eaton, during which Eaton raised, among other things, the
dangers of raising fuel economy standards. Governor Carper, asked about environmental issues surrounding light trucks, and possible CAFE fights ahead, offered his
assistance. "If they need our help," he said, "we'll give it to them."[31]

## REALLY BIG UTES

The automakers, meanwhile, began planning to manufacture even bigger sport utility vehicles and pickups—vehicles that tipped the scales at more than 5,000 lbs, carried big V-8 engines, and practically required a second mortgage to finance. By
building SUVs and pickups that were bigger, heavier, and more costly, the automakers became eligible for additional federal benefits. First, if the new vehicles cost more
than $36,000, they would be exempt from federal luxury taxes normally paid on
luxury passenger vehicles. Second, if they exceeded 6,000 lbs, they became exempt
from gas-guzzler tax, a provision that was supposed to discourage fuel waste. And
finally, if they were really big, moving into the over 8,500 lb category, they became
commercial vehicles, then exempt from even the light truck fuel economy standards.

King of the road in the big SUV category for many years was the Chevy Suburban, weighing in about 5,200 lbs in its lightest version and getting between 13-to-
17MPG. First introduced in 1977, some twenty years later, the Suburban had become
a bit larger than its predecessor, able to accommodate nine adults, growing to eighteen feet or more in length, and using a gigantic 7.4 litre V-8 engine. Other
GM/Chevrolet "big utes" would include the Chevy Tahoe and GMC Yukon models, also in the 4,500-to-5,000 lbs range, and built on a Suburban platform.

In the early 1990s, GM was doing quite nicely in the big SUV market, having
few competitors. Between 1990 and 1996, sales of Suburbans alone went up by 60
percent, reaching 137,000 per year in 1996. GM even found itself running short of
manufacturing capacity and couldn't keep up with demand. That's when Ford revealed
its big Expedition model (14 MPG city, 18 highway), designed to take market share
away from the Suburban. The Expedition was a little bit smaller, but still carried a
4.6 litre V-8 and seating capacity for nine people. Ford expected to sell 130,000 annually. A year later it was producing Expeditions at an annual rate of 240,000 and could
not meet demand. Ford pocketed $15,000 profit on each Expedition sold. But it
didn't end there. Ford's Mercury division began planning a luxury SUV that would
be called the Lincoln Navigator. By this time as well, foreign manufactures had also

introduced new luxury SUVs. Lexus introduced its first sport utility, the LX 450 in 1996, weighing in at 6,500 LBS with a 13/16 MPG city/highway fuel economy rating. Lexus introduced the model to keep its car buyers from defecting to Range Rovers, Jeep Grand Cherokees, and Suburbans. The SUV "arms race," as it would later be called by environmentalists, was well under way.

## BEYOND THE GARAGE

In June 1997, Ford revealed it was planning an even bigger SUV—one that hadn't been named yet. Chrysler was also working on a bigger version of its Dodge Durango SUV, making it a foot longer than its biggest Jeep Cherokee. GM was planning a redesign of its Suburban as well. But Ford's new mystery vehicle took the prize: it would be longer and heavier than any other SUV on the road. In fact, at its planned nineteen-foot length, the new Ford SUV would surpass the Suburban by about a foot and would not fit in many conventional passenger car garages. The new Ford SUV would also have an optional 6.8 liter V-10 engine, weighing-in at 8,500 pounds. At that weight, the new vehicle would also be exempt from the luxury tax and federal fuel economy standards. Toyota's Land Cruiser, when fully loaded with extras, also pushed it into the more lenient commercial category. The heaviest Chevy Suburbans would get there, too.[32]

Meanwhile, the Sierra Club, learning that Ford had not yet named their new extra large SUV, opened up a "Name-That-Gas-Guzzler" contest on their web page. "We want you to help Ford find a name for their new personal global warming machine," said the club in opening its contest. Among a few of the names the club offered to get its viewers in the mood were "The Ford Damage—At Ford, Pollution is Job #1," and "The Ford DumbVee—DumbVees Kill Our Planet."[33] The club would report the results of their contest when the model came to market.

## SUVs UNDER FIRE

By 1997, SUVs and light trucks had already begun to receive some unfavorable notice from federal agencies. The US Department of Transportation released a study in June 1997 that concluded that SUVs, pickup trucks, and minivans posed a growing danger to the occupants of smaller passenger cars. SUVs and light trucks themselves, long purchased for their perceived safety and security—a fact not disputed by DOT or other safety advocates—were now being seen as a public safety problem because of their size and towering design. DOT's study noted that because most light trucks and SUVs come with four-wheel drive and high road clearance in a collision they tend to override the strongest body sections of a passenger cars, often fortified to withstand crashes. In such collisions, the pickups and SUVs drive right into the passenger compartment at bumper level. When it was revealed in June 1997 that Ford Motor was planning a big sport utility model that would outsize the Chevro-

## T-REX & THE SIDEWINDER

Not to be outdone by bigger and bigger SUVs, pickup trucks, too, were ready to enter the big brute sales wars, appealing to certain kind of machismo.

At the November 1996 show of the Specialty Equipment Manufacturers Association in Las Vegas, Chrysler president Robert Lutz unveiled two "bulked-up" Dodge Ram pickups that gave new meaning to the term "urban assault vehicle." One of the trucks was named T-Rex and the other the Sidewinder. Both were Dodge concept trucks, not necessarily intended for mainstream buyers, of course. Yet the pitch given them by Bob Lutz made them sound like very real possibilities. First the T-Rex, a Ram pickup truck with an 8-liter, 500 horsepower, V-10 Magnum engine.

"We think T-Rex can outrun, out-tow, out-maneuver, out-haul and out-off-road anything in its class—and do it with a lot more driver comfort." T-Rex, Lutz explained, is the world's first full-time 6x6 (that's right, 2 more than 4x4) light truck "designed for personal use." T-Rex stands for Technology Research Experimental Vehicle, Lutz explained, adding that the dinosaur acronym was appropriate since its namesake was one of the meanest, nastiest beasts of its day. "This is what happens when you put a Dodge Ram on steroids," Lutz said. T-Rex was designed and built in little more than year, with minimal investment, Lutz explained.

Next came the Sidewinder.

"We like to think of it as a sidewinder missile for the street," Lutz said, introducing the Dodge Dakota concept truck that was part Dakota pickup and part Viper sports car. The Sidewinder came equipped with a Viper GTS-R 600 horsepower V-10 engine. To start the engine, the driver flips a switch labeled "arm" that activates the fuel pump and then hits a switch labeled "ignite" to start the engine. "The main influence is the all-American hot-rod," said Lutz, explaining that the Sidewinder was designed "by the hot rodders at Chrysler."

Asked if Chrysler would ever launch the T-Rex or the Sidewinder as production vehicles, Lutz said that Chrysler had no plans to do so at the time. "Fundamentally, it's feasible to do it," he added, not dismissing the possibility altogether. "We'll see how the economy goes and if the truck craze continues."

let Suburban, Adrian K. Lund of the Insurance Institute for Highway Safety, a group of insurers seeking to reduce the cost of accident claims, worried about the growing weight differential between big SUVs and passenger cars. "From a public health vantage point, clearly it's better not have such a weight mismatch."[34]

As the SUV-light truck wars heated up over issues of the environment and safety, Detroit responded with some of its heavy hitters. "When the government comes to take away the customer's sport utility because it supposedly is not environmentally friendly enough or supposedly poses a safety threat to people in small cars," offered Bob Eaton in a January 1998 speech before the National Automobile Dealers Association. "We may suddenly find we have the strongest possible ally," referring to SUV consumers. "Maybe Washington won't listen to us, but Washington will definitely listen to our customers."[35]

But perhaps not all customers would rise to the occasion as Eaton saw it. "Customers are viewing the role of sport-utilities negatively," said Bo Annvik, a vice president with Volvo North America in April 1998. "They don't want to sit in a vehicle that can harm others in a passenger car. They want to stand for something more rational when it comes to those safety issues."[36] On urban air pollution, too, light trucks and SUVs were getting more notice from California and EPA. Because of the growing truck and SUV share of vehicle miles traveled (VMT), EPA was finding it needed to tighten national standards for these vehicles.

In reviewing the needed air pollution control strategies for 2004 and beyond, EPA found that 60 million Americans would still live in areas that did not meet national air quality standards* unless more was done to clean up vehicle-based smog. Light trucks and SUVs—accounting for nearly half of all vehicle sales—were eating up the progress that had been made in smog control. Among the cities that would be particularly at risk by 2004 were New York, Chicago, Baltimore-Washington, Philadelphia, Pittsburgh, Houston, Dallas-Fort-Worth, Cincinnati, and Atlanta.

"We need to do something as soon as possible to reduce the emissions from light-duty trucks," said Margo Oge, director of EPA's Office of Mobile Sources, noting that light trucks were being used increasingly as substitutes for cars. If nothing is done to curb this source of emissions, she warned, light truck emissions would exceed emissions from cars by 60 to 80 percent in 2007.[37] California was also proposing to tighten its truck emission standard. "We did not expect trucks to be this popular," said Steven G. Albu, a year earlier as his agency began drafting rules for California's 7.5 million light trucks and SUVs. "It undermines our efforts to get to the federal clean air goals."[38]

## Abandoning Cars?

SUV and light truck sales in the US continued to soar through 1998. Some automakers were pointing to declining passenger car sales—Pontiac down 20 percent, Saturn off 15 percent, and Chevrolet Lumina down 30 percent—as evidence that consumers no longer cared about fuel economy in an era of cheap gas. Others took a somewhat different view. "A better explanation," offered Jamie Lincoln Kitman, a columnist for *Automobile* and *CAR* magazines, "is that as Detroit focuses ever more resources on SUVs and trucks, its cars have become less competitive." How else to explain the best-selling success of the Honda Civic or the Toyota Camry, wondered Kitman? Honda Accords and Toyota Camrys were built in America by American workers. What was

---

* When areas vulnerable to air pollution levels that can aggravate asthma and other chronic respiratory diseases are added, a larger population of 113 million Americans is at risk.

going on here? "American passenger cars too often have been starved of attention and needed development funds," explained Kitman"—time and monies that instead have been used to design new and larger SUVs, expand SUV-light truck production capacity, and hatch ever more grandiose SUV marketing schemes."[39]

Indeed, the automakers were building SUVs in every model category. No brand of automobile, it seemed, was without an SUV of its own. At first it was only the Bronco and the Jeep. But by late 1997, there were more than thirty different SUV models on the market. Some foreign makers, anticipating a market for smaller SUVs, were quick to fashion smaller SUVs, with Mercedes introducing its ML 320 model in the fall of 1997 and Toyota with its RAV-IV. Honda followed with its CR-V. The Big Three, meanwhile, kept turning out new models and redesigns of older SUVs, looking for every possible market niche. Dodge introduced its Durango SUV—bigger than the Ford Explorer and Chevy Blazer, but smaller than the Ford Expedition and the Chevy Tahoe. "The Durango," said one *Business Week* reviewer, "wears its blue color like a badge of honor. More than 70 percent of its components are carried over from the Dodge pickup truck, and Durango sports the same brawny front end as Dakota and its big brother, the Ram."[40] By November 1997, Chrysler announced it would spend $60 million to advertise the Durango in one campaign of six TV spots and six print ads.[41] After Ford introduced its luxury Lincoln Navigator SUV, Cadillac followed with its Cadillac Escalade, a gussied-up version of a GMC-Yukon Denali. Whatever they brought to the showroom in SUVs they sold.

"[D]uring much of the past 15 years, demand for sport utilities has consistently exceeded production, creating a situation in which the Big Three and importers alike could sell all they could make, without resorting to hefty discounts or rebates," observes *Barron's* Jay Palmer. "The popularity of sport utilities, moreover, meant that Detroit got fewer complaints if each one came loaded with expensive, highly profitable extras like eight cylinder engines, sun roofs, CD players, leather seats, and the like. All that adds up to big bucks."[42]

Profit was calling the tune, clear and simple. At Ford, for example, truck sales in 1997 accounted for $4 billion of the company's record $6.5 in profits. Ford's stock had more than doubled in a year, and light trucks were part of the reason. In Louisville, Kentucky, Ford took one of its largest manufacturing plants that was turning out low-margin heavy truck tractors and converted it to producing high-riding Super Duty pickups. Introduced in February 1998, the big pickups were immediately popular, selling at $24,000 each. By April 1998, Ford moved about a thousand workers from unprofitable car plants in Ohio and began operating the Super Duty line around the clock. Ford sold its heavy truck business in 1997 and discontinued a half dozen passenger car lines, including the Probe, Aspire, and Thunderbird. Wall Street analysts predicted the new Super Duty line would add $600 million in pretax profits to Ford's coffers.[43]

The Super Duty was also another of those heavyweights of 8,500 pounds or more that would be exempt from federal fuel economy standards. Ford was increasingly betting that gas would remain cheap, shifting more of its production to trucks and fewer cars. It was also betting that federal regulators would not tighten fuel economy standards for trucks. Could the company be inviting economic disaster for itself and its workers? "Ford has some serious vulnerabilities," observed the *New York Times'* Keith Bradsher. "Few of its car models other than the Mustang have produced much enthusiasm in the marketplace. That could prove to be a serious problem if gas prices rise or if sport utilities go out of favor."[44]

## TRUCK GAMES

Ford and GM were already confronting the problem of meeting existing CAFE standards for their smaller trucks and SUVs. GM, for one, began to alter its production runs to stay one step ahead of the law. In early 1998, GM began manipulating its SUV and light truck production schedule, extending and/or shortening certain model-year runs to avoid CAFE calculations. GM cut production of some of its biggest sport utility models in January 1998 because it feared it would be in violation of the fuel economy law. It also began simply calling '98 models '99s. As of January 31, 1998, after six months of production that began the previous year, GM stopped calling its 1998 Chevrolet Tahoes, GMC Yukons, and Suburbans '98s and began producing them as 1999 models.[45] By doing so, GM's 1998 light truck fleet average automatically improved, as the Tahoes, Yukons, and Suburbans were bigger gas-guzzlers. That was a nifty production trick. But there was still more.

In March 1998, moving in the other direction, GM notified dealers that it planned to extend the 1998 model year for its more thrifty minivans and small pickups, which would boost its overall light truck CAFE. On other models, the company found ways to completely exempt some models from any CAFE worry. It beefed up the suspension systems on its smallest Suburbans, qualifying them as medium trucks, thereby exempting them from CAFE calculations altogether. GM's Sam Leonard said the change was due to customer demand for more heated seats and other options the Suburbans offered.[46] As a result of GM's clever ledgermain, the company predicted its light truck 1998 average would be 21.2 MPG, beating the government standard set at 20.7 MPG. Of GM's latest moves, especially altering model-year runs to suit its CAFE needs, even *Automotive News* commented, "General Motors complied with the *letter* of CAFE law, but General Motors made a mockery of the *spirit* of the CAFE law."[47]

Ford and Chrysler were having problems meeting CAFE for their light trucks, too. Ford was predicting 20.1 MPG and Chrysler 20.0 MPG—both falling short of the 20.7 federal standard, and therefore, each facing potential fines of $5.50 per car for each one-tenth MPG off the standard, amounting to penalties in the tens of millions of dollars. However, the monetary penalties in themselves were a small sum to companies making profits in the billions, what the Big Three feared more was the public stigma of flouting the law and the possibility of opening themselves up to shareholder lawsuits for violating federal law.

GM's Jack Smith, commenting on his company's light truck difficulties, repeated the oft-heard automaker complaint about federal fuel economy regulation—that it "just introduces distortions to the marketplace, and that's disastrous for the auto companies."[48] Yet CAFE had been around for twenty years by this time, and surefooted companies would be planning for those requirements years ahead, as they do for any other model change, so that "distortions to the marketplace" could certainly be avoided, and last-minute shell games with production lines made unnecessary.

In fact, in a somewhat surprising April 1998 editorial, *Automotive News* called for CAFE reforms, tougher fines, and better enforcement, citing, in particular, GM's maneuvering around CAFE. "If we must have corporate average fuel economy standards, [NHTSA] should enforce them," said the *Automotive News* editors. "At present, enforcement is downright weird. If a vehicle manufacturer is in danger of missing the car or light truck mandate, it draws on credits it has built up in years in which it did meet the mark and avoids a fine. Or, it borrows from expected credits for future years and again escapes the penalty. That should not be permitted. Each year should stand on its own."

Singling out GM for what it called its "masterpiece of dipsy-do" turning '98 Suburbans into '99 Suburbans, the editors suggested that such loopholes should be eliminated and "maybe the fines for missing the CAFE target should be increased." The fine is currently $5.50 for each one-tenth of an MPG by which an automaker misses the standard, multiplied by number of vehicles produced. "That can be substantial— $55 million, for example, for a maker that builds 1 million trucks and misses the truck CAFE by 1 MPG. Maybe the fine should hurt even more." The editors also raised the matter of the difference between the car and truck CAFE standards—27.5 MPG for cars and 20.7 MPG for trucks. "That was OK long ago when trucks were purchased as commercial vehicles. Today, they're bought as personal vehicles, and they account for 47 percent of the new vehicle sales. Why should trucks get a break of 6.8 MPG? Enforcement of CAFE is fine. Fair and logical enforcement of CAFE is even better."[49]

The *Automotive News* editorial did not go unnoticed in the industry. Diane Steed, president of Coalition for Vehicle Choice commented, "Your editorial position fails to recognize that absent a technological breakthrough (which at this point is not even a gleam in some engineer's eye), the only way to achieve a 33 percent increase in light truck fuel economy is to make them smaller and lighter—and therefore less safe for occupants." Denny Minano of GM explained on his company's behalf that the loopholes the *Automotive News* editors singled out weren't loopholes at all but rather provisions of law intended by Congress to provide the automakers "flexibility."

## THE DUAL-FUEL CHARADE

Another bit of "flexibility" provided automakers by Congress—and one that allows them to skirt the law and sell more gas-guzzlers—is the allowance for dual-fuel or flexible-fuel vehicles. In 1988, Congress adopted a provision of law to foster the use of ethanol in cars and trucks. At the time, the action was taken to stimulate the use of ethanol—made from corn—and ostensibly help hard-pressed farmers. However, automakers who made flexible-fuel vehicles—those capable of running on either gasoline or ethanol, or blends thereof—would also get a handy windfall: they could count such vehicles as fuel-economy credits even if the vehicles sold never burned a drop of ethanol. And the credits were generous, too, amounting to the equivalent of a 60 mile-per-gallon vehicle for each dual-fuel vehicle produced. That meant roughly a two-car credit or more when computed over an entire fleet. So, when Chrysler and Ford ran into trouble meeting their light-truck CAFE standards in 1997, they decided to use the dual-fuel option big time. Ford, which had produced 5,000 such vehicles a year before, announced its plan to produce 250,000 dual-fuel vehicles over the next five years—Windstar minivans, Ranger pickups, and Ford Taurus sedans. Ford said the program was part of its corporate commitment to clean air. Chrysler followed a week later with a similar program. The move was really a no-brainer for the automakers, and would not put off consumers since there was really no visible change in the vehicle except for a stainless steel fuel system capable of handling gasoline or ethanol, and a sensor instructing the engine on which fuel was being used. The sticker price remained the same.* Yet it was unlikely that many of the dual-fuel vehicles sold would burn anything but gasoline, since at the time there were only about 40 ethanol service stations available nationally, all in the Midwest and Idaho.[50]

Philip M. Norvell, general sales manager for Ford-brand cars, said the expanded production of the dual-fuel vehicles "enhances our ability to comply with the law, and we will be in compliance." But what the arrangement really enhanced was Ford's ability to sell more giant SUVs and big pickups. Ford's Michael T. McCabe, an alternative-fuel vehicles manager, calculated that with the dual-fuel CAFE credits Ford could now effectively sell two of its giant Expedition SUVs for every dual-fuel vehicle it produced.

The Sierra Club's Dan Becker called Ford's move "a cynical ploy" to undermine the intent of CAFE, while allowing out-of-compliance automakers to continue selling gas-guzzling SUVs. The automakers, he charged, were producing cars "for which there is no fuel."[51] In any case, the dual-fuel vehicle loophole helped to bail out Ford and Chrysler, both then failing to meet the light truck CAFE standard of 20.7 MPG.**

Environmentalists, meanwhile, continued to pound away at SUVs as being big

---

* However, if the vehicle actually did use the ethanol fuel, a blend known as E85, the car would get fewer miles to the gallon since the energy value of E85 is less than that of gasoline, and so, its cost per mile would also be about 15 percent higher, according to Ford.

** It should be pointed out that the CAFE average is generously interpreted by NHTSA, which allows automakers essentially to average this average over a seven-year period, allowing each automaker to compute its CAFE for any one year *with the three years both before and after it.*

resource hogs. "SUVs are allowed to waste 33 percent more gasoline than passenger cars," charged Friends of the Earth. "Since 1990, the inefficiency of light trucks have led Americans to wasting an extra 70 billion gallons of gasoline." [52] SUV and light truck inefficiency also meant more $CO_2$ and more smog. But by 1998, both California and EPA began to focus on the big emission loopholes for light trucks.

## CARB CLAMPS DOWN

On the West Coast, CARB wanted light trucks to meet the same standards as passenger cars and had been encouraged by Ford Motor's January 1998 announcement that it planned to produce cleaner SUVs. CARB, in fact, had taken a Ford Expedition, given it a bigger catalytic converter, and with some other tinkering, enabled it to meet the proposed emission levels in testing. In early November 1998, CARB adopted new rules, effective in 2004, which would apply automobile standards to all vehicles up to 8,500 pounds. That would cover about 90 percent of SUVs, vans, and pickups.

"I'm shocked," said GM's Sam Leonard after CARB adopted the proposal in El Monte California. Leonard was miffed that CARB did not give more consideration to a plan the automakers had put forward. That plan would have reduced passenger-car emissions to levels even below those proposed by CARB. The automakers also agreed to apply that standard to smaller SUVs like the Chevy Blazer and Ford Explorer. But there was a catch. Full-size SUVs and pickups under the automakers' plan would still be allowed to emit twice as much NOx as cars, one of the main smog-forming culprits. Overall, the automakers' proposal still had 10 percent more pollution than CARB's and was rejected by the agency. It was also opposed by the Japanese and Asian automakers whose passenger cars dominate the California market and would have borne the brunt of deeper passenger-car reductions proposed by Detroit.[53]

The CARB action, said GM's Leonard, would probably mean that California drivers would be paying more for their vehicles "and probably . . . have a smaller selection." Toyota spokesman Matt Kevnik agreed that his company's lineup might also be limited. "We're really not sure how to get the rest of our lineup to look like our star performers," he said. "Today, we can't say how we're going to get there."[54]

Yet CARB engineers had a Ford Expedition on display outside of the meeting that they said met the new standards. And they had also retrofited a Ford Explorer that complied as well. All they did, according to CARB mechanics, was upgrade the catalytic converter using harder metal and add an air pump. "We feel if we could do this in our lab for a couple of hundred bucks," said CARB spokesman Jerry Martin, "what can the biggest car manufacturers in the world do with all the facilities they have? And we're giving them five to seven years to do it."[55]

But the bombshell in CARB's new regulations was the stance taken on diesel engines, which was essentially to ban them for use in light trucks. Back in Detroit,

GM's Denny Minano was reportedly apoplectic over the diesel prohibition. And in Washington—where EPA was also drafting new rules that might allow diesels, and the PNGV project was moving closer to an 80 MPG prototype supercar that could be diesel-based—the California action did not go down well either. But CARB had been confronted with a very credible and careful scientific study that found diesel fumes to be carcinogenic. Diesel exhaust, said UCLA toxicologist John Froines, who chaired the panel investigating the pollutant, "is without a doubt the most toxic set of constituents that you could ever find." Diesel exhaust consists of thousands of gases and particles, including more than 40 compounds such as benzene, dioxins, and formaldehyde, many of which are already classified carcinogenic. CARB really had no choice.

CARB did agree, however, to a couple of light truck concessions. First, it created a "medium-duty" category for vehicles 8,501 LBS to 14,000 LBS gross weight, that would have nearly as stringent standards. And second, a "work truck" allowance would permit up to 4 percent of each manufacturer's light trucks to meet a less stringent standard provided they could meet a freight-hauling test. Still, GM's Sam Leonard said it might not be technically possible to make full-size SUVs like the GMC Yukon, or pickups like the Chevrolet Silverado, meet passenger car standards.[56] But Leonard was thinking about other ways GM's vehicles might avoid the strictest standards. "A fully loaded Suburban," he noted, "could get shoved over 8,500 pounds."[57]

## HI HO SILVERADO!

GM, it turns out, was dong quite well with its pickup trucks and was betting heavily on them and SUVs as a way to improve both profitability and market share. After a labor strike slowed production of trucks in August 1998, GM went full bore on truck production at the end of the year to make up for lost time. The result: fourth quarter profits shot up sharply, more than doubling to $1.7 billion. Trucks, SUVs, and minivans accounted for 47 percent of GM's total vehicle sales in 1998, and the company wanted to push that share much higher in the future.[58]

GM's Silverado pickup truck, the company's best-selling vehicle, is now seen as a key part of GM's future. The Chevrolet Silverado, first introduced in the 1970s, was redesigned for 1999. The big Silverado has been very good to GM, accounting for some 13 percent of the company's North American sales in 1998, worth about $14 billion all by itself. The Silverado, in fact, was a bigger business than Time-Warner, McDonald's, or Microsoft, according to Kurt Ritter, Silverado brand manager. Nor is GM sparing any expense to sell its favorite pickup, deciding in 1998 to go all out in hyping its "new and improved" Silverado, launching a $135 million advertising campaign to spread the word, one of the largest-ever ad campaigns for a single vehicle.[59]

Silverado advertisements show cowboys and industrial workers in state-of-the-art TV spots marvelling over the new truck, which features, among other things, an extended cab. But the ad pitch is aimed at rugged use, building on GM's "Like a

Rock" theme used for other pickups. Still, 70 percent of full-size pickups bought in 1998 were purchased for personal use, not heavy work. No matter, a theme is a theme. It's what people think they're buying. In fact, GM's market research found that white-collar buyers like the blue-collar imagery. In 1999, GM planned to produce more than 975,000 Silverado and GMC Sierra pickups. Some analysts were projecting the company's aftertax pickup truck profits would grow by $1 billion that year.

## "KING KONG" OF SUVs

In February 1999, Ford unveiled its new giant SUV, which it named the Excursion. Getting between 10 to 18 MPG, depending on the engine type (a 7.3 litre, V-8 diesel was available in some models) the nearly nineteen-foot-long vehicle beat the Suburban by a more than half a foot. Priced at between $45,000 and $50,000, the Excursion could yield profits on each vehicle in the $12,000-to-$20,000 range. Environmentalists, led by the Sierra Club, felt the Excursion was an abomination. The contest the club was running to name the new vehicle concluded: the winning entry was "The Ford Valdez," adding the tagline, "Have you driven a tanker lately?" The club also gave Ford the Exxon Valdez Environmental Destruction Award. *USA Today* called the Excursion "an emblem of excess." Ford tried to put the best green spin it could on its huge vehicle, although that proved difficult for a couple of reasons. First, because it exceeded 8,500 pounds, the Excursion was allowed to emit more smog-producing hydrocarbons and NOx than cars and other light trucks. Second, because of its weight, it was exempt from fuel economy standards, and Ford would not have to count its poor mileage (10 to 15 MPG gasoline, or 16 to 18 MPG diesel) in its CAFE computation—nor would it lead to any CAFE penalties. Its mileage calculation for consumers was also not federally certified. With all of this, Ford still tried to call the Excursion "a low-emission vehicle," saying the giant SUV was "as clean as most new cars on the road today."[60]

"I wish Ford would be more precise about how polluting these vehicles are," said Roland Hwang of the Union of Concerned Scientists. "When Ford calls it a low-emission vehicle, that is not the same thing as a low-emission car," he said. "There is confusion out there that works to Ford's advantage." Setting the record straight, Hwang explained that the Excursion and other such vehicles "are about three times more polluting that the average new car in California."[61]

The Sierra Club's Dan Becker used the Excursion's debut to criticize Ford chairman, William Clay Ford, who had promised to move the automaker in a greener direction. "Ford needs to put its vehicles where its mouth is," said Becker.[62] Over its lifetime, the Excursion would emit three times more carbon into the atmosphere than the average car, said Becker. William Clay Ford, however, said his company's actions, green or otherwise, must also succeed as a business proposition. "A zero emission vehicle that sits unsold on a dealer's lot is not reducing pollution," he said.[63] The Ford Excursion, however, would not be left on the dealer's lot. Ford said it expected to sell 60,000 in the first year. Still, for some, there was a question about need and excess. "It's pretty clear that most ordinary Americans don't need this kind of vehicle," said Roland Hwang of the Union of Concerned Scientists. "This is a troubling direction Detroit is going in. It's almost like an arms race."[64]

Meanwhile, in Washington, EPA was following through on its plan to tighten emissions standards for trucks. As expected, the agency proposed in early 1999 that light trucks would have to meet the same emissions standards as cars—but not in the same time frame. The Clinton administration really had little choice, given the continuing smog problem and the fact that light trucks had both a CAFE *and* an emissions loophole, making their contribution that much worse for every mile they were used. Still, under the administration's proposal trucks would be given some leeway for NOx. Under the proposal, cars are required to meet a 0.07 GPM NOx standard by 2004. Trucks would be required to meet a 0.20 GPM NOx standard by 2004, and the 0.070 standard by 2009. And unlike California, EPA had made some exception for diesel engines, which did not please environmentalists.[65]

When EPA began its hearings on the proposal, the AAM supported the 0.07 standard, but said it should be pushed back to 2011 for large trucks and SUVs like the Suburban. Honda, not a member of the AAM, favored the same standards for cars and all light trucks. STAPPA-ALAPCO supported phasing-in the standards for all vehicles by 2007.[66] US PIRG's Rebecca Stanfield urged EPA to eliminate all of the SUV and large truck loopholes. PIRG also had in tow, outside on the sidewalk for the media, a giant fourteen-foot inflatable SUV it called the Exterminator with the words "Clean Cars Now" emblazoned on its side.[67] As the Tier 2 proposal headed for the White House in late 1999, it appeared something close to EPA's original proposal would be accepted.

## New SUV Markets

As the new century dawned, some industry analysts were predicting the SUV market in particular might be targeted for extinction, not because of pollution or fuel economy concerns, but rather, because baby boomers—then turning fifty at the rate of 10,000 per day—were looking to downsize. Smaller, more carlike vehicles might be on the way back, the analysts predicted. But the automakers were ready for anything—or at least some of them were. Subaru, Mercedes, and Toyota had begun building SUVs on car rather than truck chassis. Soon, all the other automakers were following suit. A new type of vehicle was being designed to cater to the boomers' new desire: a "hybrid" sport utility (not to be confused with hybrids so named because of their *engines*). The hybrid sport utilities are designed to be smaller, more agile, less trucklike. These vehicles, however, would also cut into the old passenger car market. But would the automakers take the opportunity of this vehicle redesign to also improve environmental and energy performance? William Clay Ford did say that Ford and Mazda would be making some smaller SUVs at a plant in Kansas.

"Hybrids are coming on like gangbusters," said Ford's CFO John Devine in late 1998, "But this isn't a static business. . . .[W]e have products coming out that will help us remain a leader. We are not going to go to sleep and let this important segment of the market get away from us."[68] Ford was then working with Mazda on a new hybrid ute based on Mazda's 626 platform, had plans to start building new hybrids by 2001, and was also considering a combination car, minivan, and SUV blend for another new vehicle. GM was looking at the possibility of a sport wagon. New designs were part of the perpetual new-model dictum laid down years ago by Alfred Sloan. "Keep them buying up," or in today's market at least, buying different.

Globally though, some still saw a robust market in SUVs and light trucks, especially in the developing world. "Our product line of trucks probably lends itself to faster expansion [in emerging markets] than fighting it out in the very competitive small-car business," said Chrysler's president Tom Stallkamp in May 1998. Stallkamp was referring mainly to his company's Jeep and pickup trucks, and the fact that the newly merged DaimlerChrysler would likely accelerate Chrysler's expansion plans outside of Europe and North America. There is less competition with trucks in new markets, Stallkamp explained, and Chrysler's Jeep brand is recognized around the world.[69]

The high ride, it appeared, would continue for some time to come, in America and everywhere else.

## 20

## *Slow Dance to Supercar*

... What we see is a slow phase-off of the internal combustion engine. . . .

*—Jack Smith*
*General Motors, 1997*

In twenty years, the internal combustion engine will still be on top.
*— Akihiro Wada, vice president, R & D*
*Toyota Motor, May 1997*[1]

In mid-1998, the US auto industry changed rather suddenly and dramatically when the Chrysler Corporation merged with Daimler-Benz, the largest industrial firm in Germany, maker of Mercedes-Benz, aerospace equipment, rail systems, and more. The politics and economics of the auto world would never be quite the same. A new world order was taking form, some said. Larger, global auto companies were the order of the day. But DaimlerChrysler—the new merged entity—raised other interesting questions about the future, especially how this new colossus might approach environmental problems.

Historically, neither Daimler nor Chrysler had been in the vanguard of the clean car movement. Chrysler, in particular, had been the most flatfooted of the Big Three in the environmental arena, and its executives the most vitriolic in their disdain for new green technologies, such as electric vehicles. With the possible exception of supporting federal fuel economy standards in the mid-1980s, there was little Chrysler could claim under the environmental banner. In its 1990s' comeback from a second economic stumble, Chrysler became the company that preferred to tout its 10-cylinder, 400-horsepower Viper muscle car, and whose in-your-face TV ads featured cherry-red Dodge Ram trucks smashing through glass walls. "We're breaking all the barriers," their ads said. Well, perhaps not all.

Daimler, for its part, had paid millions of dollars in US gas-guzzler fines for years rather than meet US fuel economy standards. Daimler's diesel technology was far from clean. Still, Daimler was viewed by some as the greener of the two. Daimler was more R & D oriented, a leader in safety design, and certainly knew the meaning of quality. Daimler had also formed a joint venture to produce the Swatch, a small European car. And Daimler had also begun work on the fuel cell—a potential power system for automobiles that many environmentalists called the holy grail.

"Fuel cells are electrochemical engines that generate electricity by harnessing the reaction of hydrogen and oxygen," explains Fuel Cells 2000, a nonprofit group in Washington, DC promoting the new technology. A fuel cell produces power through a controlled reaction of hydrogen and oxygen—actually by combining the two electrochemically to form water, and in that process, heat and electricity as well. Fuel cells produce little or no emissions.

Although something of a novelty in the automotive world, fuel cells are not new. The basic chemistry of a fuel cell's reaction has been known about for more than 150 years, when an amateur scientist in England discovered the reaction. In the US space program, they have been in use for more than thirty years. General Electric built fuel cells for on-board electric power in the Gemini spacecraft of the 1960s. The earliest use of a fuel cell to power a motor vehicle in the US is believed to be a 1950s tractor built by farm-equipment manufacturer Allis-Chalmers. In 1968, General Motors built a fuel-cell powered minivan, which was almost entirely occupied by the fuel-cell hardware needed to operate the vehicle. The bulky hardware and high cost made fuel cells unattractive for most of the automakers, although a few continued operate fuel-cell research programs.

In 1990, after California signaled to the world that automakers selling cars there would be required to have very low or zero emissions, the fuel cell began to receive more attention. Many of the automakers had research programs that included work on fuel cells, but no one company seemed to have embraced the fuel cell as the sine qua non. However, a small Canadian firm based in Vancouver named Ballard Power Systems had been working on fuel cells since 1979 and was quietly making progress. Ballard actually obtained some of its fuel-cell technology from NASA, after NASA auctioned off some development rights to Canada's defense department. In 1984 Ballard received an initial two-year grant from the Canadian government to develop military and commercial uses for fuel cells.[2] By 1990, Ballard began to focus on making fuel cells for small-scale power generation and low emission cars.

The following year, Ballard began supplying fuel-cell stacks to Daimler-Benz, which had a research program at the time, but no special commitment to fuel cells. In 1994, Daimler unveiled a research vehicle it dubbed NECAR-1 for "New Electric Car." It was a Mercedes minivan full of fuel-cell hardware. There was room for one driver. Still, Daimler proudly displayed its white van at auto shows and other fairs, with "No Emissions—Fuel-Cell Electric Car" emblazoned on its sides.

The Big Three, meanwhile—at least as of 1995—saw no immediate future for the fuel cell and said so, calling the research "blue sky" stuff that would take decades to come to market. But Daimler apparently thought otherwise and kept at its research. In 1996, Daimler unveiled NECAR-2, still a hydrogen-tank laden laboratory on wheels, but now six people were riding in the van. Daimler was reducing the bulk of the fuel-cell system. In fact, each time Daimler engineers rolled out their test vehicles, they were surprised by the progress they were making. "To our way of thinking, the fuel cell is the most promising alternative drive technology," said Mercedes-Benz chairman Helmut Werner at a Berlin news conference in May 1996. "It can offer a way out of the problem of storing energy in heavy batteries of limited capacity."[3]

In 1996, Daimler made an important calculation about the fuel cell's potential that became something of a turning point. In theory, an ICE-powered automobile is capable of transforming as much of 35 percent of its fuel's chemical energy into useful work. In practice, as Amory Lovins and others have shown, it's typically much less, usually 20 percent at best. Daimler-Benz, with one of its best diesel ICEs, had succeeded in getting 24 percent energy efficiency. Yet when they projected the energy-conversion values out to 2003 for both a diesel and a fuel cell they made a rather profound discovery: the diesel might be bumped up a few points to as much as 26 percent, but the fuel cell could go to 40 percent to 50 percent when fully developed—though some called that a stretch.[4] Still, that's when Daimler became much more serious about the fuel cell.

## "COMPETE AGAINST THE ICE"

In April 1997, Daimler stunned the auto world by announcing it would begin selling fuel-cell powered vehicles by 2005—and not just a few hundred either. "We are not aiming for a niche market," said Daimler's senior vice president Ferdinand Panik. "The objective is really to concentrate on mass production. We want to compete against the internal combustion engine, and the numbers will be high. We will start with a minimum of 100,000 units."[5]

The "100,000 cars" promise had been made before. Remember GM's Roger Smith in 1990? He also promised 100,000 cars—electric cars. In Germany though, there had been aggressive activity on global warming. In the posturing over the Kyoto treaty, for example, Chancellor Helmut Kohl of Germany pledged a 25 percent cut in $CO_2$ below 1987 levels by 2005. Although that goal might not be achieved, German utilities had begun switching from lignite to natural gas. Daimler, as a high-flying player in Germany's economy, had every reason to want to be a leader on the automotive side.

At the time of its announcement, Daimler also agreed to pump up its relationship with Ballard Power Systems, putting another $350 million into Ballard to launch a fuel-cell engine company and to take a 25 percent equity position in Ballard. Two joint ventures were created: one to license the technology to other companies, and another to sell fuel cells and fuel-cell engines. Both would be "open for business" with other automakers.

Still, Daimler's pledge of 100,000 cars by 2005 had a long, rough road ahead. Daimler's competitors, however, were not nearly as far along. Toyota had the Prius and was clearly the leader and first to reach the market with hybrid technology. GM had its EV-1, leasing several hundred by that time. GM and Chrysler were also working on the fuel cell, but were "several years" behind Daimler by one estimate. Ford was closer, saying it expected to have a prototype up and running by 2000. One key problem for all the researchers, however, was the fuel source to be used to power the hydrogen-making reaction in the fuel cell.

Initially, it was thought that a fuel-cell powered vehicle could use hydrogen directly. But that proved a major obstacle in terms of the bulky hydrogen tanks on the vehicle itself, not to mention developing a hydrogen infrastructure to refuel the vehicles. Soon, other fuels and strategies emerged as possible contenders. Hydrogen would be produced on board the vehicle from other fuels in a reformer to supply the fuel cell with hydrogen. Gasoline and methanol emerged as the leading reforming fuels, although in the long term it might be possible that the sun's power could be harnessed to produce the hydrogen, doing away with fossil fuels completely.

In October 1997, the US Secretary of Energy Frederico Pena announced that the DOE, with research assistance from Arthur D. Little and the federal governments weapons labs, had developed a gasoline-powered fuel cell that could lead to ultra clean cars that would achieve twice the fuel economy. "We have a terrific breakthrough here," said Pena, also citing the fact that with gasoline, the fuel infrastructure was already in place, and a separate network of refineries, pipelines, trucks, and service stations would not have to be developed.[6]

At the time of the DOE announcement, alternative vehicle advocates cautioned against thinking any one solution was the ultimate answer. Sheila Lynch, executive director of the Northeast Alternative Vehicle Consortium, an organization supporting electric and hybrid technology, noted that Toyota's Prius had just come to market in Japan, and that new battery-powered vehicles were then testing at 250 miles on a single charge. Acknowledging the fuel-cell progress, Lynch nevertheless cautioned, "it does not mean we should wait around for many years to see if this technology is commercially viable."[7]

Still, the progress being made on fuel cells seemed to signal a change in thinking about the likely mass-produced car of the future. "This blows the doors off any battery-powered electric vehicle," said Jeffery M. Bently, a vice president at Arthur D. Little, citing the ease of a five-minute fill-up at any gas station versus the long recharging times for battery-powered EVs. But battery-powered EVs would still get a piece of the action, despite ADL's hype. Secretary Pena suggested that developing countries looking to add millions of cars in the coming decades could "leapfrog us" with fuel-cell cars "like they did with cell phones."[8] But the worrisome part of the DOE-ADL announcement was its emphasis on gasoline to power the fuel cells—a strategy that Chrysler had also supported.

"[T]he government's proposal to cram gasoline into fuel cells makes them dirtier, more complex and expensive," said Jason Mark of the Union of Concerned Scientists in Berkeley. "Powering a twenty-first century technology with twentieth-century fuel seems anything but visionary. Limited federal finances would seem better aimed at breaking down barriers to new fuels that unleash the full potential of fuel cells rather than facilitating the longevity of petroleum dinosaurs."[9]

In December 1997, Ford Motor joined the fuel-cell sweepstakes. Ford decided to put $422 million into fuel cells through a joint venture with Daimler-Benz and Ballard. The partners said they expected to have fuel-cell vehicles on the road by 2004.[10] Ford's announcement "was more than sufficient in the testosterone-charged and PR-conscious auto industry, to set off a round of 'top this' announcements," observed *Barron's* Kathryn Welling. "Virtually every car maker not in need of Viagra unveiled a program to develop fuel-cell powered green machines—targeting [2004] or sooner—at the big January auto shows."[11]

By March 1998, GM was claiming that its fuel-cell program was "at least as big" as its hybrid or battery-car projects. GM's program has "significant dollars," said Byron McCormick, executive director of global alternative propulsion at GM. "We are totally serious," he said of the company's fuel-cell work. "The fuel cell is so compelling because of its enhanced efficiency and low pollution that we just have to go after this aggressively."[12] And it wasn't just the automakers who were involved. International Fuel Cells, a division of United Technologies Corporation that works on fuel cells for the space shuttle and the utility industry, announced it was launching a venture to commercial fuel cells for cars.[13]

However, in early May 1998, before the Daimler-Chrysler merger surfaced, Daimler seemed to be hedging a bit on its earlier 100,000-cars-by-2005 promise. "What we've really said is that we are going to decide *whether* to go into production at all in 1999," said a Daimler spokesman.[14]

By December 1998, Daimler was discounting a gasoline-powered fuel cell, leaning toward methanol. "The [gasoline] technology ... is still very immature," explained Chris Borroni-Bird, senior manager of technology strategy planning at Daimler-Chrysler. "It's not realistic to expect we can commercialize gasoline fuel-cell technology by 2004. Maybe 2010, but not 2004." But Barroni-Bird did say that DaimlerChrysler was capable of moving in any direction. "We believe we're now positioned to respond to wherever the market leads," he said, "whether it's a push toward hydrogen or methanol or continued work on improving gasoline. We have a leadership position in all of these aspects of the fuel cell."[15]

DaimlerChrysler announced at the Greater Los Angeles Auto Show in January 1999 that it planned to put a methanol-based fuel-cell system into a prototype Jeep Commander SUV, and that production was slated for 2004, five years away.[16] The company's announcement came a little more than a month after California became the first state to adopt rules requiring SUVs and trucks to meet the same pollution standards as cars. DaimlerChrysler seemed to be saying it could meet those standards in all its vehicles with fuel-cell technology. DaimlerChrysler's announcement was also encouraging on the methanol front, since this hydrogen-making route was preferred by environmentalists and regulators over gasoline. In addition, the sulfur content in gasoline can destroy a fuel cell.

## "Affordability" Race

In March 1999, at a Washington DC press conference, with EPA's Carol Browner participating, DaimlerChrysler unveiled its fourth version of a fuel-cell car, the

NECAR 4, a compact car that could go 280 miles before refueling and travel up to 90 MPH. "We have solved the most challenging technical problems," boasted Juergen Schrempp, one of DaimlerChrysler's cochairs. "So let me say today we declare the race to demonstrate the technical viability of fuel-cell vehicles over. Now we begin the race to make them affordable."

NECAR 4, however, was using liquid hydrogen to fuel the hydrogen-oxygen reaction, still a highly impractical fuel. But the technological achievement in the fuel-cell hardware itself was something to brag about. Ferdinand Panik, the company's fuel-cell project director called the NECAR 4 "a major breakthrough," being the first to pack a fuel-cell system into a smaller car with room for several passengers. In the NECAR 4, the fuel cells are positioned in stacks beneath the floorboard and the liquid hydrogen tank occupies part of the car's small trunk. "Five years ago," said Panik, "you needed a large van to contain all the fuel-cell hardware. Now that's simply no longer an issue." The downsizing of the technology, he explained, was comparable "to the impact the microchip had on the computer industry." Still, on an engine-by-engine basis, the fuel-cell system cost about $30,000 each vs. an internal combustion engine, at $3,000 apiece. And DaimlerChrysler's Panik was now talking about 40,000 fuel-cells vehicles by 2004 and 100,000 by 2006, which appeared to be a revision of the original 100,000-by-2004 statement made in April of 1997.[17] As NECAR 4 was being touted in Washington, the Big Three began meeting with methanol makers in Dearborn to begin working out a common standard for the composition of methanol that might be used to power fuel-cell cars.[18] Environmentalists, meanwhile, were cheering the progress and the test runs, pulling for the fuel cell. "We can't wait to see more fuel cells on the road," said Dan Becker. "We are looking forward to a healthy competition to see who makes the cleanest car."[19]

By April 1999 in California, DaimlerChrysler, Ford, and Ballard announced that by 2000-2001, they would begin putting a fleet of as many as fifty demonstration fuel-cell vehicles on the road in California. The venture was named "The California Fuel Cell Partnership—Driving for the Future," and on hand that day were two fuel-cell powered cars for reporters to drive—a Mercedes NECAR 4 and a Ford P-2000 sedan.

"I thought I would never see fuel cells advance this far in my lifetime," said former CARB executive director James Boyd, recalling that a decade ago he had driven one of the first fuel-cell prototypes in Frankfurt, Germany. "And here I stand seeing fuel-cell vehicles driving off at the steps of the Capitol. . . ." But the goal of the program, as Governor Gray Davis reminded the assembled officials and reporters, was clean air. "Our long-term goal is very simple," he said, "zero emissions in the air. . . . The real test is not whether [fuel-cell car] can drive, but whether it holds up under day-to-day traffic and whether its emissions are as low as predicted."[20]

Joining California and the automakers in this venture were Texaco, ARCO, and Shell to supply the low-sulfur "feeder fuels" for the fuel-cell engines and to help develop a system of new fueling stations. At the ceremony, ARCO's chief executive Mike Bowlin declared that the days of the internal combustion engine were numbered. The fuel cell, he said, is the technology "that will replace the internal combustion engine."[21] But in what form was the question. Would gasoline be involved or methanol? "I am not talking about a revolution here," Bowlin added. "I am talking about evolution. It may be a decade or two before fuel cells begin to make a significant dent in the gasoline fleet."[22]

The California press conference—as well as a May 1999 announcement that GM and Toyota were forming a joint venture to develop alternative vehicles—had come in advance of EPA's expected tightening of smog and gasoline standards. The automakers were trying to show the world and Washington they were committed to new technology to reduce emissions, and so, strict new measures weren't needed.[23]

Jason Mark of UCS had seen it all before—the automakers or the oil companies putting out "good news" of a technological breakthrough or some planned research initiative "to stave off strong government policies." In his view, neither industry will move quickly to change the economic ground rules for the internal combustion engine; their interests are too interwoven. He says a "technological cartel" has been forged between the internal combustion engine and petroleum over the last century.[24] Half of the top ten Fortune 500 companies, he points out, are either auto or oil companies. And auto-oil partnerships are especially worrisome—a sign that both the ICE and gasoline will be around a good bit longer. "New research partnerships between Ford and Mobil as well as GM and Amoco, have extended auto and oil's relationship beyond the lobbyists to the engineers," he says. These efforts and others, including the work on diesels and the move to gasoline-based fuel cells "will keep oil in the picture for some time to come."[25] Might the auto and oil industries therefore continue to work together to keep the ICE era going indefinitely?

It is true the two industries are now at odds over sulfur in gasoline—the automakers want it removed to make fuel cleaner so they can meet auto emission standards easier, and the oil industry has vowed to fight EPA's tighter low-sulfur gasoline standards. Although the Clinton administration's Tier 2 regulations proposed tighter gasoline standards as well as new auto emissions rules, Senator James M. Inhofe (R-OK), head of the Senate Public Works Subcommittee on Clean Air, had prepared a bill to prevent the new gasoline rule.[26] The sulfur fight to come, in fact, shows that the ICE system— whether fuel or hardware—is well entrenched and well connected, and will not yield easily, even if better technology is in the offing.

## EMBEDDED REALITIES

In 1990, when General Motors' EV-1 team began trying to build an electric car, they also came up against some of the ICE's entrenched power base and its "in-the-system" biases when they began to lay out their plans with the company's in-house and supposedly friendly chain of suppliers. They found instead "the princes," as Michael Shnayerson would describe the heads of GM subsidiaries or fiefdoms, which essentially controlled certain parts of the business. "The princes didn't merely have dibs," wrote Shnayerson. "They had letters of charter, signed by GM's top executives. Delco Remy *would* do all batteries and motors and alternators for GM cars. Delco Electronics *would* do all radios and electronic controllers."[27] This huge system of embedded capital—one devoted primarily to the ICE—will be slow to change with new technology, and as history well shows, politically empowered to derail or slow down whatever comes along to threaten it.

Fuel cell, battery-electric, and hybrid vehicles each bring a new overlay of supplier relationships and technology to the R & D dance and the auto assembly process. Marketing contracts and jobs are involved. With the newer technologies, there will be fewer parts, especially fewer engine parts—the guts of the ICE system. On the other hand, the electronic parts and components that come with hybrids and fuel cells are likely to multiply, or at least have a newness about them that will offer some offsetting investment and jobs benefit. Yet there can be no mistake that the vast network of ICE industrialism will still be a powerful factor in the changeover to whatever comes next in the automotive world.

In fact, even the Clean Air Act regulatory apparatus that governs auto emissions is based upon the ICE. Since the late 1960s, when the auto industry assured Congress that the internal combustion engine was indeed the only viable engine out there, an enormous body of law, regulation, and federal court opinions have essentially sanctioned the ICE. By agreeing, in effect, to regulate the ICE, the Clean Air Act fortified the internal combustion engine both in public policy and in industrial capital for decades to come. Although in the late 1960s there had been a robust debate on alternative engines, and the 1970 law itself included a provision for EPA to review progress in alternative engines, the Clean Air Act and its regulations, in effect, became partner to the internal combustion engine. The standards, testing procedures, and other apparatus of legal oversight essentially began to conform to the world of the ICE and how it performed, good and bad. This was not necessarily the fault of Congress, or those diligent and concerned members who had pushed the alternative engine debate. Given Detroit's insistence that no economically viable clean-engine alternative existed, Congress had little choice but to regulate the ICE. For the automakers, this was a good deal, despite their complaint to the contrary. They didn't have to risk large amounts of capital developing new engine technologies. It was then, and continues to be today, pretty much business as usual for the ICE system and its owners.

True, the Clean Air Act and its regulations were "technology forcing," but only for those pollution-control technologies that "fit the ICE"—crankcase fixes, exhaust gas recirculation, catalytic converters, and improved carburetion. Detroit could live with these—although in its own good time. Over the years, or course, emissions control became more sophisticated with sensors, software, and computer chips, but the object of all this technological affection was still the ICE. The auto industry, in effect, has only been pushed to innovate at the margin, not its technological core.

Granted, the air has become cleaner with catalysts and other supporting technologies—no question. Yet the gains have been incremental, hard fought, and year-to-year. And the struggle to maintain gains has been an annual contest of squeezing more and more performance out of the applied, add-on technologies, only to see such gains eroded in subsequent years by auto growth and VMT. Only in recent years—as in the case of California's ZEV requirement—has "technology forcing" pushed the automakers to go "out of the ICE box" for change. California's initiatives forced Detroit to go beyond the ICE world and seek the assistance and thinking of outside firms like AeroVironment and other "new tech" entrepreneurs, but only to a point. Daimler and Ford, too, have gone to Ballard to move the fuel cell along. Still, the ICE industrial base, its built-in marketing and regulatory biases, and its political network, will all weigh heavily against any fundamental shift to new technology. Or, as ARCO's man put in Sacramento at the fuel cell gathering—any new technology will be "evolutionary."

The supercar is coming, of course, but it might not be tomorrow.

# The Last Auto Fights?

... [T]he auto industry employs scores of lobbyists and spends more than $100 million a year to influence Washington decision makers....

—*Automotive News, December 1997*

"Americans love to drive, and we're driving more," said Bill Clinton in his weekly radio address in early May 1999. "But emissions from our cars, particularly from the larger, less efficient vehicles, threaten to erode many of the air quality gains America has achieved. As a result many of our cities and states are no longer on course to meet our vital air quality goals." Clinton's focus on clean air that day was tied to his administration's announcement of a proposed tightening the Clean Air Act's auto emissions standards as required under the 1990 amendments to that law. The administration was putting forward its Tier 2 proposal for cleaning up the ICE in the 2004-2007 period. Cars, trucks, and SUVs needed to reduce tailpipe emissions by another 80-to-95 percent to meet clean air goals. On the radio, Clinton said the benefits of the new program could outweigh costs by as much as four-to-one.

On Capitol Hill, Representative J.C. Watts (R-Okla), chairman of the House Republican Conference, said EPA should enforce existing laws before undertaking "new regulatory schemes of undetermined cost and scope." Others thought the agency should do both. The automakers, meanwhile, had argued for a longer phase-in of the new requirements—to 2011. The oil companies said the administration had not made "a compelling case" for why low-sulfur gasoline was needed.[1] It was politics as usual; it could have been 1970.

This time, however, EPA's Carol Browner had been meeting with the automakers in one-on-one meetings. She was playing, in part, to some of the industry's own green rhetoric. William Clay Ford had been in the news with his favorable environmental views. A few of the automakers began to see that tangling with the federal government in public again in a long battle over smog, children, and clean air would not look good for them. Environmental and consumer groups, meanwhile, kept up the drum beat for tougher standards. They pushed for four key provisions:

new cars meeting the proposed 90 percent reductions; closing the SUV and light truck loopholes; removing the special exemption for diesel cars; and making low-sulfur fuel available nationally.

This time, too, the automakers were supporting the low-sulfur fuel requirement as part of the Tier 2 package, which put them at odds with Big Oil. Still, inside the beltway it was business as usual for some of the automakers. In August 1999, GM submitted three volumes of public comments on the Tier 2 proposal, generally attacking the standards, calling them "arbitrary and capricious," asserting there was no need for Tier 2 emissions standards, and challenging EPA's ability to enforce them.[2] Ford had also been "one of the lead companies working to weaken the EPA's Tier 2 emission standards," according to US PIRG. In fact, Ford topped the list of 164 auto and oil-affiliated companies that reported more than $90 million in 1998 lobbying expenses. Ford alone spent $13 million.[3] As the lobbying ensued from both sides, EPA's proposal increasingly emerged as the centrist position, and it appeared that auto emissions standards would be tightened for the 2004-2007—with some allowances for the biggest SUVs. Yet, for the automakers, there was always Congress, the national elections, and the prospect of new occupants in the White House.

## THE AUTO LOBBY

Representing the auto industry—both through lobbying and public relations campaigns—is a big-time business. In Washington alone, the industry "employs scores of lobbyists and spends more than $100 million a year" to influence decision makers.[4] A build up of the automakers' Washington clout occurred not long after Bill Clinton was elected in 1993. The automakers doubled the AAMA's budget and "cabinet-level people" were brought in to do Detroit's bidding. Andrew Card, former Bush administration secretary of transportation, was hired at $500,000 a year to be AAMA's executive director. The AAMA at the time also hired Robert E. Moss, former Democratic National Committee official who worked at the US Treasury Department in the Carter years. Mell Bass and Ellen Shapiro were also hired around the same time. Bass was former tax counsel to Representative Sam Gibbons (D-FL) on the powerful House Ways and Means Committee. Shapiro was former senior policy analyst at EPA and would become AAMA's regulatory liaison manager. By mid-1994, Big Three lobbyists were crowing about their good relations with the Clinton team. "We have unprecedented access to all the Cabinet positions that relate to the auto industry—Treasury, Commerce, Labor, Transportation, and [the US Trade Representative's Office]," said Elliott S. Hall, then Ford vice president for Washington affairs.[5]

In 1998, however, after Chrysler merged with Daimler, the representation game in Washington became somewhat muddled, and the AAMA was at sea on how to represent its American trade group now that a third of it was a German-American conglomerate. The Big Three was now the Big Two. A new automotive group was mulled over, not only by Detroit's automakers, but also by some of the German and

Japanese auto companies. But in this process there was still some resentment left over from 1992 when the AAMA was called the Motor Vehicle Manufacturers Association (MVMA) and Honda, Volvo, and some other manufacturers were summarily kicked out, as the Big Three wanted a distinctly American trade group.* By September 1998, with the latest reconfiguration, the AAMA disbanded, and a new group, the Alliance of Automobile Manufactures (AAM) was created with a broader roster of members that now includes BMW, Daimler-Chrysler, Ford, General Motors, Mazda, Nissan, Toyota, Volkswagen, and Volvo, all of which have sales or manufacturing operations in the US. Honda, however, is not a member. Still, in the new group there were members and associate members, and either GM or Ford will retain the chair. At the head of AAM is the first woman to ever head a major automakers group, Josephine Cooper, a former assistant administrator at EPA. With Cooper at the helm, the automakers were sending a strong signal that environmental and safety matters would be at the top of their agenda.[6]

In addition to the new AAM, each automaker has its own Washington team as well, typically with eight to ten lobbyists and annual lobbying budgets in the $10 million-to-$15 million range. These offices are well staffed, with veteran lobbyists. Andrew Card, who was earning more than $600,000 annually when he left AAMA, is now with GM. Over at Ford, Janet Mullins heads up that company's national affairs team. Before coming to Ford, Mullins served with former Secretary of State James Baker and as an assistant for political affairs to President George Bush. Compared to environmental organizations, the automakers have little problem gaining access, and typically outgun the green lobby on Capitol Hill by a "more than 10 to one," according to the Sierra Club's Dan Becker. But Ford's Janet Mullins says the aim of both sides is the same. "Whether you are an environmentalist who has a $100 a month expense account or whether you're an industry lobbyist with a $1,000 a month expense account, your objective is the same, to get to know people a little bit."[7] And with $900 a month more, you can, presumably, get to know them better.

The Big Three have also financially supported, and in some cases, been instrumental in founding various think tanks, lobby coalitions, and so-called grassroots organizations, many of which bring a distinctly antienvironment message to legislative bodies and other public venues. They also prepare and churn out antienvironment studies and public relations material for the media, schools, and the general public. Ford and GM continue to support organizations that generally oppose environmental causes— groups such as the Heritage Foundation, whose quarterly journal has called the environmental movement "the greatest single threat to the American economy."[8] Ford, Toyota, Arco, Exxon, and AIAM are among the fun-

---

* Originally known as the Automobile Manufacturers Association (AMA), the organization changed its name to the Motor Vehicle Manufacturers Association (MVMA) in 1972 and later allowed foreign carmakers with US operations to join. In 1992, the trade groups' moniker became the American Automobile Manufacturers Association (AAMA), its headquarters shifted from Detroit to Washington with a suite of offices a block away from the White House, and Honda and other foreign automakers were asked to leave.

ders of the Cato Institute, a $13-million-a-year Washington DC think tank that has put out papers such as the 1995 report, "Health and Smog: No Cause for Alarm." GM, Ford, Texaco, and the American Petroleum Institute are among supporters of the Competitive Enterprise Institute (CEI), another Washington think tank, which has published work calling global warming a myth. CEI charged in May 1999 that EPA's proposed auto emission standards would "produce no reductions in smog," and have "no discernible effects on health." In August 1999, CEI began and anti-CAFE ad campaign whose message explained in part that fuel-efficient cars are less able to protect passengers in the event of an accident. Among the so-called grass-roots coalitions the automakers support are the Coalition for Vehicle Choice (CVC) and Citizens for a Sound Economy (CSE). CVC, which says its members include people "from all walks of life" and emphasizes "the freedom of Americans to choose the motor vehicles that meet their needs and their freedom to travel," is "dominated by auto and oil industry giants such as DaimlerChrysler, Ford Motor Co., General Motors, and the National Automobile Dealers Association," according to US PIRG. In the 1990s, the auto industry helped pay $500,000 to E. Bruce Harrison and Co. in Washington to set up CVC, which then began an $8 million PR campaign to defeat fuel economy legislation.[9] CVC's website and newsletters continue to urge the public to tell Congress to support the "CAFE freeze." CVC has also opposed tighter car and SUV emission controls, falsely asserting that tighter emissions standards would limit the availability of full-size truck models and truck performance. CVC includes other coalitions as members, such as the CSE, which is chaired by C. Boyden Gray, former White House counsel to George Bush and now partner at Wilmer, Cutler & Pickering. CSE lobbied against the EPA's smog and soot regulations in 1997, and has been an active opponent of the Kyoto Protocol. CSE's Gray, in fact, is credited with preparing a key amicus brief used by the court of appeals in making the 1999 decision to challenge EPA's smog and soot rule.

When the automakers have a public relations problem or need to gin up a grass-roots effort, they will simply hire the best in town, as they did in 1994 when they hired Daniel J. Edleman Public Relations, Inc. to run an image campaign, in this instance to show new members of Congress in particular, how important Detroit is to the national economy. Robert M. Teeter and Peter D. Hart also helped out on that effort. Extra lobbying power can also be acquired as needed. In recent years, GM has shelled out $120,000 to hire the Wexler Group and Chrysler has paid $280,000 to secure Timmons and Co. as its advisor in 1996. The Big Three, of course, are also upstanding members of the Business Roundtable, the US Chamber of Commerce, and the National Association of Manufacturers, organizations that have their own Washington clout. Also with a formidable Washington presence is the Association of International Automobile Manufacturers (AIAM) which represents the US subsidiaries of eighteen foreign automakers such as Honda, Nissan, Hyundai, Kia, and Volkswagen. The Japanese also have their own association in Washington, too—the Japanese Automobile Manufacturers Association (JAMA). All of this auto industry power is not solely trained on energy or environmental issues, of course, as the automakers have a long list of other needs in the trade, tax, and business-as-usual categories. But some of these issues have become more pressing for the Big Three.

In early 1999, as the new and improved AAM was being created, Ford, GM and DaimlerChrysler set up a separate group to focus on trade and international policy, called the Automotive Trade Council. This council, initially staffed by two former AAMA officials, focuses on issues such as "fast track" treaty negotiating power for the Executive Branch and rewriting "out-of-date" trade statutes. "We've been hired to be very visible public representatives of those three companies with senior levels of the US government and with other governments around the world on the views of these three companies," explained the council's new president, Stephen Collins. But there was something else, too, as *Automotive News* reporter Harry Stoffer observed, especially in the Asian theater. "In the long run, the council wants to persuade Asian governments and companies that industry consolidation and globalization of the market make economies of scale essential." Describing discussions at one meeting in the Asia Pacific region, for example, Stephen Collins explained, "every [nation] wanted to develop their own auto industry. Everybody wanted to be a huge exporter. No one wanted to have imports coming in. You could see this pattern developing, which was not healthy."[10]

There will also be plenty of other unhealthy auto-related social and environmental issues needing attention throughout the world, particularly in developing countries, ranging from global warming and the production of millions of cars and trucks with outdated pollution control equipment, to the mounting problem of auto-production and accessory wastes such as batteries, tires, paint, and toxic chemicals. Yet the major focus of the Big Six globally appears to be: securing a recognized "brand" of vehicle to sell in each of several global theaters, making production and joint-venture deals in places like China, and buying into one or more of the smaller foreign auto companies now in trouble. Back in the US, however, there were still some front-burner domestic issues that needed attention.

## CAFE SCARE

On fuel economy, the automakers were given a scare in mid-1999 as more and more members of Congress were beginning to see that CAFE standards needed to be raised. The automakers, as they had done for the past several years, were pushing a CAFE freeze amendment on an existing appropriations bill. In late May 1999, on the day that the House Appropriations Committee voted to pass the CAFE-freeze rider, a letter from thirty-one senators was sent to President Clinton urging him to raise the CAFE standards for SUVs and light trucks. "Because of the increasing number of light trucks, the average fuel economy of all new passenger vehicles is at its lowest point since 1980, while fuel consumption is at its highest," said the senators. "The freeze rider denies the purchasers of SUVs and other light trucks the benefits of existing fuel savings." US PIRG released a report showing that the SUV and light truck loophole in CAFE accounted for more than 1 million additional barrels of oil per day at the gas pump and 187 million tons annually in global-warming $CO_2$ emissions. Tightening the standard, environmentalists argued, would save SUV, light truck, and minivan owners money at the gas pump, would reduce global warming, and reduce the nation's oil consumption by more than 300 million barrels a year.

In the Senate, meanwhile, an attempt was made to require that CAFE standards be raised for SUVs and light trucks. All the old adversaries came out for the brief legislative fight. The Competitive Enterprise Institute, for example, began running ads during Rush Limbaugh's radio show pushing a "CAFE-means-small-cars-and-more-fatalities" message, claiming CAFE standards were responsible for an estimated 2,600 to 4,500 fatalities.[11] On the other side, US PIRG fired off several studies targeting SUVs and the political contributions of auto and other interests to members of Congress. During the last minute lobbying on the proposed bill, environmentalists were dismayed to learn that William Clay Ford had been in town to buttonhole key senators, pressing them to oppose the CAFE bill. When the measure came up for a vote in September, it was defeated on the floor by a 55-40 vote.

"We're thrilled," said Andrew Card, now vice president for governmental affairs at GM. "We applaud the rational thinking reflected in the Senate vote today." The Sierra Club's Dan Becker, however, found hope for the future in the support of 40 senators. "This strong vote is a warning that the days of gas-guzzler trucks are numbered."[12] Although the Senate version did not contain the same CAFE-freeze rider when the two bills came to conference, the House version prevailed and was sent to the White House for the president's signature. The bill was loaded with local highway and transit projects—pork for Democrat and Republican alike—making it difficult for Clinton to veto. Still, Al Gore urged the president to veto the bill. Environmentalists also lobbied Clinton for a veto. But in the end, the president signed the $50 billion bill, without fanfare in mid-October on a Saturday night.[13]

In the auto industry, however, there was a sign that at least some of the Washington insiders were getting the message. Ford lobbyist Janet Mullins, reacting to the growing strength of the environmental position in the US Senate, cautioned her colleagues in June 1999 that it was just matter of time before CAFE would receive more Congressional support, especially given the SUV issue and global warming pressures. She predicted CAFE would become more of an issue after the national elections in 2000, and that by then, "all bets would be off" even if a Republican were elected president.[14] In December 1999, Ford made another announcement that surprised environmentalists. The company withdrew from the Global Climate Coalition, the business group of oil, auto, utility and other interests challenging the Kyoto Treaty, and taking the position that there isn't enough evidence of global warming. In making the announcement, a Ford spokesman said the company was still opposed to the Kyoto Treaty, but believes that there is evidence of global warming and that businesses should work together to reduce carbon emissions.[15]

On yet another front—the year 2000 national elections—the clean car fight was also becoming part of the debate.

## THE GEORGE BUSH SURPRISE

In December 1999, just as the Clinton administration was about to finalize its Tier 2 regulations, Governor George W. Bush of Texas, then the Republican front-runner for his party's presidential nomination, made a surprise move. Bush proposed to the Texas Natural Resource Conservation Commission (TNRCC), then under the gun to come up with an ozone-reduction strategy in the state to meet national standards, that Texas consider adopting California's auto emissions standards. Gloria Bergquist, vice president of the Alliance of Automobile Manufactures (AAM) called the Bush's move "kind of a shocker" and unnecessary. Frank O'Donnell of the Clean Air Trust called it "presidential politics." Nonetheless, Bush's move elevated what the northeast states had been trying to do for the last several years in adopting California's stricter auto standards. The move also unnerved the automakers who thought they had that process bottled up. Al Weverstad, a GM emissions specialist who represented the AAM before the Texas NRCC considering the Bush proposal, warned the commissioners that the California rules would threaten the availability to Texans of a full range of vehicles, mentioning in particular, that favorite of Texas vehicles, the pickup truck.[16]

Bush, for his part, had been criticized nationally for the growing pollution problem in Texas, and his somewhat less-than-stellar record in helping to clean things up. With the presidential primary season heating up, environmentalists had run some ads in New Hampshire critical of Bush's clean air performance. Back in Texas, several cities, including Dallas, Houston, San Antonio, Beaumont, and Port Arthur, were having a persistent ozone problem owed in large part to automobiles, though in some cities like Houston, oil refining and petrochemical plants were also major culprits. Houston, in fact, had eclipsed Los Angeles as the city with the highest number of bad air days. Texas now had to show EPA that it had a plan to bring its ozone nonattainment area, into compliance by 2007. The TNRCC proposed a list of strategies for consideration ranging from driving restrictions and cleaner gasoline, to Bush's proposed California car option.[17] Bush's suggestion that his state consider the California plan had come on the heels of Governor George Pataki's announcement a month earlier that New York would adopt California's standards. Massachusetts was weighing the move as well. The states now weighing the California car option—with Texas now added to the mix—would comprise a sizeable share of the new car auto market, affecting economies of scale in production that might favor producing all new cars to the highest standard. The automakers, meanwhile, adopted the unusual tact of siding with EPA, urging Texas to wait for the Clinton administration's Tier 2 regulations that were about to be finalized. With EPA's rules, said GM's Denny Minano, it was "time for the states to move away from an independent, patchwork approach."[18]

Back in Washington, on December 21, 1999, Bill Clinton approved EPA's final package of Tier 2 regulations, which had everything environmentalists had hoped for, with the exception of a tough standard for diesel-powered vehicles, a decision that was postponed for later action.[19] But in the contest that now pitted EPA's program against California's, each side began to stake out their claims. EPA's Carol Browner argued that EPA's new regulations offered states more benefits that California's since it phased-in more vehicles, and larger SUVs, in a shorter period of time. "It makes our program deliver cleaner air faster," she said. Yet in Texas, the TNRCC still liked the California program. "We feel that long term, the California program appears to get more emission reductions," said Jeff Saitas, TNRCC's executive director. They also liked California's requirements for ZEVs and extremely low emissions vehicles, the exact features Massachusetts, New York, and NESCAUM had fought for in the Northeast for several years. Some state officials were also feeling that California's program might be a better bet politically as well, and a more certain path for them to follow if they wanted tighter standards, especially since EPA's new program might be challenged in Congress or in the courts.[20] In Texas, meanwhile, some believed the Bush move on the side of California program was a calculated strategy only designed for the presidential primary season, and would soon be crushed by a backlash of good old boys defending their pickup trucks and a general public outcry over the needed regulations.

In any case, it appeared "the last auto fights" of the twentieth century would not be the last word on the old ICE, as regulatory and public opinion battles over these and other auto pollution problems would continue through the presidential elections of 2000 and well into the twenty-first century.

# Miles to Go

It takes a lot of guts to obsolete your own technology, . . . [but] the worst thing would be to have the paradigm shift on you.
—*Robert Purcell, director, Advanced Technology Vehicle Program,*
*General Motors*[1]

The global automobile industry today is poised on the cusp of a new century of opportunity—a time for new vitality and new commitments. In the last few years, there have been some encouraging new words about the vehicles of the future, about cleaner cars and trucks, and some actual new automotive technology now on the road, with more promised to come. These developments all provide hope for cleaner air, a more frugal use of fossil energy, less carbon, and a safer, cleaner planet. Yet the major US corporations that dominated the automobile industry of the last century—some with corporate cultures little changed from the recent past—will now play a central role in shaping the technologies, business plans, and automotive context of the next century. How will this new era unfold?

Since the end of World War II, the American automobile industry has had numerous opportunities to capture the economic and environmental high ground of building better cars and trucks. Yet at least once a decade over the last fifty years, Detroit's best and brightest missed the mark. GM, Ford, and Chrysler repeatedly missed economic opportunity, missed becoming technological leaders, and missed the chance to cast their products and companies in an entirely different political light. Detroit failed to pick up the mantle of automotive leadership not because GM, Ford, or Chrysler lacked ability or technology, but rather, because they were too comfortable to change, were reluctant to take risks, refused to innovate, and lacked meaningful competition to make them perform any differently.

In fact, for a good twenty-five years, from the 1950s to the mid-1970s, there was very little outside influence on, or control over, the US auto industry. The Big Three, safe in the world of their US oligopoly, did whatever they wanted. There was little competition to worry about. Upstart carmakers like Preston Tucker or Henry J. Kaiser could not overcome the entrenched position of the Big Three.*

American Motors, which under the leadership of George Romney, flourished briefly in the small-car market in the 1950s and was more or less tolerated by the Big Three without much worry. During the "golden years," as auto historians call the 1950s and 1960s, GM, Ford, and Chrysler accounted for 94 percent of what was sold. The Big Three—led by GM—set the pace and made money by *not* taking risks. Models and more models proliferated and big cars ruled. Styling and horse-power reined supreme.** There was no need to innovate. "By the middle 1960s,"

---

* Tucker and Kaiser both introduced novel ideas and took engineering risks that would later prove their worth. Preston Tucker managed to produce fifty-one Tucker Torpedoes between 1947 and 1949 before his operation went under. Tucker's cars were rear-engine cars, and included classic styling and safety features. But Tucker became the focus of two US Securities and Exchange Commission investigations that dirtied his reputation and scared off his investors. Henry Kaiser, however, had considerably more means, having amassed a fortune during the war in aluminum and cement while mass-producing Navy ships. Kaiser and partner Joe Frazer formed the Kaiser-Frazer Corp. in 1945. The company produced 746,000 automobiles though 1954. Kaiser tried producing a front-wheel-drive car and an advanced precursor of the modern hatchback. Kaiser's most successful entry however, was the Kaiser-J, a small, no-frills car that peaked in 1950-51 at its launch with 65,000 sold.

** Perhaps no other element in Detroit's rise to power has been more important or has had more lasting effect than the annual model change—the idea that changing the appearance and style of a car every year would help to sell it. In the 1920s and 1930s when GM president Alfred E. Sloan first put the idea into play, it was a revolutionary notion, then resisted even by GM's management. Today, the annual model change is still a seductive and powerful marketing tool. It is the backbone of each year's new strategy, determining what is made and how it is sold. In the 1920s Henry Ford had established a more utilitarian standard by comparison—that only one kind of car and one color were all that was needed in a personal transportation vehicle. Sloan believed consumers would respond to style changes and other improvements in automobiles. He was right. Sloan's idea—initially "a car for every purse and purpose"—soon evolved into consumers "trading up" in the GM line, from Chevrolet to Buick to Cadillac. Historian Daniel Borstin described the Sloan plan as a "ladder of consumption" with social class distinctions. Regular cycles of major and minor styling change at GM were soon tied to one- and three-year manufacturing schedules. The annual model change became the way automobiles—and many other products as well—were sold and continue to be sold today. The problem with automotive styling, however, is that it became the dominant focus of how cars were built for such a long time. Styling usurped resources and talent for nearly thirty years in Detroit, resources and talent that might have been channeled into fuel economy, emissions control, and better automotive engineering. During the 1950s and 1960s, "the industry indulged in an orgy of non-functional styling that subordinated engineering to questionable aesthetic values," says auto historian James J. Flink. Also, as the industry moved from four- to six-cylinder engines in the 1930s; to small V-8s in everyday Fords and Chevrolets by the 1950s; to the overpowered Pontiac GTO and Dodge Charger muscle cars of the 1960s and 1970s; and finally, to today's big-engined SUVs—power, acceleration, and speed also took up a considerable share of Detroit's time and attention, especially within the key engine and powertrain divisions.

observes auto historian and former *Car and Driver* columnist Brock Yates, "GM had grown complacent and had become convinced that what looked like a perpetually growing market would be satisfied with relatively cheap annual styling changes instead of real automotive innovation. Emphasis at all the American automakers had shifted away from engineering towards marketing and finance."[2] But when the tide of economic change came rolling in, Detroit ignored the warnings and did little to change its ways.

## Ignoring the Cues

How many times did the Big Three receive a message that markets were changing? How many times did they hear—sometimes from their own people—that better, cleaner, and more fuel-efficient technologies were ready now and that pursuing them could mean better automotive engineering, better business, and more business? How many times did they refuse to act on what they knew?

In the 1950s, the first message was about smog, dirty engines, and automobile exhaust. The invasion of the VW Beetle in the late 1950s and early 1960s sent a message about basic transportation in a small, well-made package. Honda's CVCC engine in the early 1970s sent another message about "clean-engine" engineering. Congress and two energy crises during mid- and late-1970s sent still more warnings about the need for fuel economy, clean cars, and better automotive engineering. As Japan became the world's largest automaker in 1980 after Americans discovered that foreign imports were not only more fuel efficient, but well made, too, Detroit's problems seemed to worsen. In pursuing the fixes for pollution and fuel economy, the Big Three chose roundabout methods from add-on devices to deal with smog, to downsizing big- and mid-size cars to reduce vehicle weight to save fuel. Core engineering changes directed at the engine and driveline never really entered the picture—nor did strategic business makeovers to market such changes. GM would look to its inventory of old parts to fashion its fixes.* Designing totally new cars—or

---

* Consider GM's J-cars, the line of GM cars like the Chevy Cavalier that were launched in 1981 and billed by GM as an unconventional import fighters. But they were neither. J-cars were doomed from the start given the restraints under which GM engineers had to work. "While the basic structure of the J-car body would be entirely new, [J-car project director Bob] Brewbaker and his staff rifled through the General Motors parts inventory in an effort to find existing components," explains Brock Yates. This move saved GM millions of dollars that would otherwise be needed for tooling and manufacturing new parts. "Cannibalizing prior GM models was an economic expedient," observes Yates of GM's bid to save costs on the J-car. But in the end, the car was a failure, in part because of its borrowing heavier parts and engineering from the past. The engine GM had chosen for the "revolutionary" J-car "was scarcely different from ones that they had been using for over twenty years," says Yates—"a 1.8 liter, cast-iron four-cylinder engine with essentially the same pushrod-activated mechanism that Chevrolet had been using exclusively in its domestically designed engines since 1955." Yates, *The Decline and Fall of the American Automobile Industry*, pp. 28-29, 22.

"ground-up builds" as they are called—with new engineering and new platforms were rarely considered beyond hand-built show cars. Another part of the problem was execution. Quality suffered. Defects and recalls mounted. Corporate reputations were further damaged. Yet while Detroit was moving from fix to fix, there was a haunting past of dismissing or ignoring key technologies that might have been more transforming. Detroit, in fact, passed up important engineering opportunities that dated to the 1950s.

The modern era of front-wheel drive automobiles, for example, began in 1950s Europe. When oil supplies were threatened by hostilities at the Suez Canal in 1956, auto engineer Alec Issigonis went to the British Motor Corporation to design a low-MPG family car. The key breakthrough Issigonis came up with resulted in the Morris Mini, a small car that utilized a fuel-efficient transverse engine—i.e., a sideways-mounted engine placed over a front-wheel drive system. The Mini was small, but it seated four adults, offered good fuel economy and good road performance.[3]

Front-wheel drive with a transverse engine was a revolutionary development that offered a mother lode of automotive engineering potential. Not only was the front-wheel drive/transverse-engine arrangement more fuel efficient, it was also space-saving and reduced weight by eliminating the driveshaft, large rear axle, and older rear suspension. Front-wheel drive vehicles generally offer better stability in crosswinds because the center of gravity is farther forward and closer to the center of aerodynamic pressure. Front-wheel drive is also quieter, smoother, and offers better handling since it pulls the vehicle through curves. But this was not new technology. Front-wheel drive, in fact, had been introduced in limited numbers of commercial American cars as early as 1929, but for the most part was not considered by the Big Three until the 1970s energy crises. Although the Detroit automakers had heard from their own people about the virtues of front-wheel drive as early as the 1950s, and again in the early 1970s when they sent "scouts" to Europe to check out the competition, they resisted the change, even though the engineering and marketing advantages were there for those who would seize the initiative.

After Congress enacted fuel economy standards in the 1970s, the Big Three began to plan for some front-wheel drive models. Even then, Detroit's first response was downsizing, not front-wheel drive. Chrysler says it produced the first American built front-wheel drive car with a transverse engine in 1978.[4] GM's first major excursion with such cars came with its X-car lineup—Chevrolet Citation, Pontiac Phoenix, Oldsmobile Omega, and Buick Skylark. These cars did arrive on the production line in April 1979, just as America entered its second energy crisis. GM's X-cars did well, but not as well as they could have. GM couldn't keep up with demand, for one. Then quality problems plagued the X-cars, leading to their demise. In 1981, came GM's next import fighter, the J-cars, which had problems, too.[5] Chrysler produced its first full line of six-passenger front-wheel drive cars in 1981. But Detroit really didn't become competent with front-wheel drive until the mid-1980s—about the time Chrysler developed its front-wheel-drive minivans. But even then, the Big Three moved slowly in adapting their larger passenger cars to front-wheel drive.

Another key technology relevant to both emissions and fuel economy that Detroit neglected for years was fuel injection. First developed in Germany in the mid-1930s by the Robert Bosch Company for the German air force, fuel injection was eventually used by all the military forces in World War II. It was first used on a passenger car—a 300SL sports car—by Mercedes-Benz in 1954. Fuel injection is vastly superior to the use of a carburetor for delivering fuel to an internal combustion engine. The carburetor, which mixes air and fuel first, and then sends the mixture into the combustion chamber of the engine. A fuel injector, by comparison, is more elegant, and more efficient, spraying the fuel more precisely directly into each cylinder. It is the perfect technology for helping the ICE satisfy emission and fuel economy goals while not sacrificing performance. Fuel injection was used in Europe and by the Japanese in the late 1950s and 1960s. But not in Detroit. "Fuel injection is one of the vital advances Detroit rejected while the determined foreign competition utilized it to impress American car buyers," says Brock Yates.[6]

Finally, after the energy shocks of the mid- and late 1970s, Detroit began working on fuel injection. GM went halfway, according to Brock Yates, piecing together the Throttle-Body fuel injection system, "a bastardized standard carburetor modified to behave like an injector." One GM engineer told Yates, "The GM system had all the disadvantage of conventional carburetion with none of the advantages of fuel injection." Germany's Robert Bosch Co. by this time had developed a direct port fuel injection technique.* Not only were the Bosch injectors "better suited to modern emissions standards," said the GM engineer, "they provided a broader band of performance, higher fuel mileage, and were easier to maintain."[7]

Even into the late 1990s, Detroit was still diverting precious engine R & D into power, not fuel economy. More efficient technologies—engines with more valves and more sophisticated fuel injection systems and transmissions with extra gears—continued to appear and have been used in cars, vans, and SUVs since the mid-1980s. Yet these important advances were not being channeled or allocated into increasing fuel economy. "The trend has clearly been to apply these new technologies to increase average new vehicle weight, power and performance. . . ." said EPA. The agency found, in fact, that horsepower, vehicle weight, and 0-to-60 acceleration had all risen since 1986—horsepower up 58 percent, average vehicle weight up

---

* When Bosh engineers tried to sell their fuel injection systems in Detroit they were told that GM's Throttle Bodies then supplied by Rochester Products, a GM division, were cheaper and got the job done. "We had some young guys at General Motors who were pushing our stuff," recounts one Bosch representative, "but they didn't have much clout. If you're a new guy at GM, you better fit in or you're a dead duck. They knew they were out in left field talking about Bosch when GM had their own divisions . . . so they shut up." Yates, *The Decline and Fall*, p. 204.

20 percent, and 0-to-60 MPH acceleration up 19 percent. Fuel economy, meanwhile, fell by 7 percent in the same time frame. ". . . [H]ad the new 1999 light vehicle fleet had the same average weight and performance as in 1986," concluded EPA, "it could have achieved 5 MPG higher fuel economy."[8]

On smog, too, simple technologies for controlling at least a portion of auto exhausts were available for twenty years before the problem began receiving attention in Los Angeles. Positive crankcase ventilation, which the Big Three fought in the early 1960s, was a known principle in the 1930s. Fine-tuning engines and carburetors was also a familiar technique, dating to the 1920s. Pumping more air into exhaust systems to help burn up exhaust hydrocarbons before they left the tailpipe wasn't a stretch either. Catalytic converters may have been new to the auto industry, but the principles behind them date to 1890s France where early work was undertaken with catalysts to treat petroleum fumes. In the 1920s, researchers for the US Bureau of Mines and at Johns Hopkins University applied early catalytic converters to vehicles. Ford tried a vanadium pentoxide device in the late 1950s. Catalyst makers had workable devices ready to go in the mid-1960s. But catalytic converters weren't added to cars until 1975 and then only by the force of law. Still, one wonders how an industry that once tackled torpedo weapons with 5,000 parts in the early 1940s could be so slow on pollution control devices in the 1960s and the 1970s? Of course, there was always the matter of cost. But with costs, too, there was more than met the eye.

## Counting Beans

Cost control and financial considerations had become central objectives in Detroit following WWII, and when smog, safety, or fuel economy were raised, "high cost" was frequently rolled out in Washington or with the media as the major obstacle. Such improvements would cost too much and raise the price of cars and trucks, sending Detroit into a tailspin, went the refrain. But for an industry so concerned about cost, how well did Detroit do in managing its own house? When the automakers were telling Congress in the 1970s and 1980s about their economic concerns, how were the Big Three managing their own production costs?

In the early 1970s, Hal Sperlich, then with Ford Motor, toured a Japanese auto factory and was surprised to see that the Japanese had no repair bays along their assembly lines where defects and glitches would be fixed. Nor were there any inspectors in the plants. The Japanese didn't need either. They made it right the first time. A decade later, in the 1980s, when Sperlich moved to Chrysler, he was now preaching about "nonconformance costs"—all of the costs from glitches and mistakes that had to be paid for later with time, labor, and/or material fixes under warranty. "By Sperlich's estimates the cost of nonconformance for an American auto company was some 20 to 40 percent of revenues," wrote David Halberstam. "That, in turn . . . meant that if you did the car perfectly, if all the parts came in right and everything was done correctly the first time, not only would the cars be better and the company's reputation better, but you could reduce your costs by, say 25 percent, or finally about $2,500 a car, which was close to the Japanese price advantage."[9] That was in the 1980s.

Even in 1992, quality problems still plagued some Big Three assembly lines. GM trucks were barely reaching the same quality levels the Japanese had reached in 1986. GM's 1992 trucks, in fact, had the highest number of defects on average of any on the market. Some car lines weren't much better. For 1993 Cavaliers rolling off the Lordstown assembly line, there were 1.26 defects per car according to a GM survey—and that was after a "finesse line" was installed at Jack Smith's order to check cars for defects. "In every factory, inspectors were assigned to stations in the middle of each assembly line, at the end of the line, and even at the depots where cars were shipped to dealers," explained Paul Ingrassia and Joseph White. "In some plants, as many as twenty people would be arrayed along . . . a 'finesse line' to check finished cars for scratched paint, electrical glitches, and other goofs . . . ." In 1992, GM spent $3 billion on warranty repairs, or about $829 a vehicle in the US.[10] That kind of money can buy an awful lot of automotive engineering—and perhaps even a few energy and environmental improvements.

Robert Templin, who was the chief engineer at Cadillac from 1973 to 1984, found cost containment priorities skewed in questionable directions. "I was always impressed with the fact that I was being pushed to reduce engineering costs by ten dollars a car, when the sales incentives and warranty costs totaled something like a couple of thousand dollars a car, and that we must have the pressure on the wrong thing."[11]

In other cases, the cost accounting used was unreliable or even nonexistent. Chrysler's former vice chairman and president Bob Lutz recounts what it was like at Chrysler just before the late 1980s. "Prior to this time, not only did Chrysler have frequent variable cost overruns on product programs," he says, "we also had very little idea of how much those costs would be until after the car was built." Lutz said it was like navigating with a rearview mirror. "Every year, just after the launch of the new models, we'd have an October surprise as the actual bills for parts and components came in." So at the beginning of each year, Chrysler would have "to book hundreds of millions of dollars in contingency fees 'just in case'—money that obviously could have been put to much better uses, including, perhaps, in improving the product itself."[12] Chrysler was also missing a whole "domino effect" in the cost of new-model auto parts—which presumably should have been well understood by the 1980s. "What we never took into account," says Lutz, "is that there were lots of other parts connected to and/or affected by the [new model] part in question, and we were paying virtually no attention whatsoever to the costs of those parts (even though they would all have to be changed or updated as well). . . ."[13]

All of this was going on while a quality revolution was supposedly underway in the American auto industry. "Quality Is Job One"—remember? The truth of the matter is that the lessons of the quality revolution were not deeply or totally learned in Detroit, nor were they well integrated into all aspects of business practice. Quality improved, but not everywhere. Costs came down, but not always the costs that mattered most. And while the slogans and management mantras touted "total quality," there was nothing "total" about the quality revolution in the US auto industry. Energy and environmental values were left out, they were rarely if ever considered as core values—in design, engineering, or marketing. In the 1970s, 1980s, and 1990s, there were numerous occasions in the design, building, rebuilding and launching of new and improved models—or existing and new vehicle platforms, as they're called—during which environmental engineering could have been incorporated into the automaking process with little pain and only marginally increased costs. GM could have done more with the Saturn in the early 1980s and had plenty of other opportunities with other models before that. Ford, when it rolled the dice with the Taurus in the early 1980s, spending $3 billion to build that vehicle, could have then integrated environmental and fuel economy factors into that package. Chrysler could have done more with its LH cars on the environmental fuel-efficiency side.

Incorporating improved fuel economy and environmental performance into new vehicles, of course, can't take place in a marketing vacuum. A key to the success of such improvements, like any new vehicle attribute, is a corollary marketing and advertising program that emphasizes these features and makes them enticing and important, leading the market. Yet Detroit did none of this. Rather, the Big Three spent billions of profits in the 1980s buying up nonautomotive assets and empire building. The problem in the US auto industry has never really been about cost or talent; it's been about turf. The auto industry had the money—it was just spent poorly, wasted in the tens of millions.

## VULNERABILITY

Today, some American activists and politicians look at Detroit and worry that the mistakes and missed opportunities of the past may be repeated in the future. "There's a competitive threat coming, significantly, but not exclusively driven by environmental realities that Michigan leaders, both inside and outside the auto industry, are loathe to acknowledge," says Lana Pollack, a former Michigan state senator who now heads up the Michigan Environmental Council. "Foreign manufacturers and domestic startups pioneering the new technologies could take a huge market share before the slower-moving traditional auto industry has had the opportunity to adapt and recover." Pollack is now working with labor and other interests in Michigan to persuade the automakers to heed the warning signs. "We lost market share that we never fully regained," she says, referring to the 1970s. "Now we face a similar threat. . . . Not being first out of the box could have a tremendous, more or less permanent depressive effect on the domestic auto industry. This isn't a matter of environment over economics. Either they move together, or we're going to inflict tremendous damage on ourselves."[14]

Others look at the rising tide of SUVs and light trucks, rising oil imports, declining fuel economy and a volatile world—particularly in the perennially troubled Middle

East—and believe it's just a matter of time before America has another big energy crisis. This time, though, it will be a lot uglier than it was in the 1970s. Detroit is riding high on the SUV and light truck good times. Profits are soaring. Car plants have been converted into truck and SUV plants.[15] New SUV plants have been springing up too. But what other investments have the Big Three been making? One sudden energy shock could create a very nasty surprise that would ripple through all parts of the American economy quickly and without mercy. Are we ready for this? What might an alternative economic vision look like if cars and trucks that were not as vulnerable were designed? What might an alternative business plan look like that incorporated energy and environmental values into vehicle design, engineering, and marketing? What if rational vehicle design, strategic business planning, and advertising were to incorporate these values as central goals?

Energy and environmental values in the automobile business have at best been on the periphery. They have never been part of the core business philosophy, a central element of the engineering ethic, or a key element in strategic business planning. What if—as now appears to be the case with safety features after years of resistance—energy and environmental improvement of the product was sought out and built-in to sell it? Why haven't energy and environmental improvements been regarded as "value added?" For the last thirty years or so the automakers have said consumers aren't looking for those features.

## A Better Message

The automakers, however, have been hiding behind a convenient marketplace maxim that pretends that consumers determine what Detroit builds. And indeed, all manner of demographic, focus-group, and marketing surveys bolster "consumer preferences." But demand is more complicated than just what comes out of the mouths of consumers. And in fact, consumer demand is powerfully influenced, if not shaped, by the endless—and in some late-night TV markets—mind-numbing barrage of automobile, truck, and SUV advertising.

True, there are clearly consumer interests and inclinations that emerge in the marketplace or in focus groups—and these are often seized upon, amplified, and writ large on contemporary culture by an awesome army of marketeers and Madison Avenue mavens. Between 1980-2000, US automakers spent *$80 billion* urging people to buy their cars and trucks—more money than what was spent on any other consumer product.[16] It is not uncommon to find the cost of an advertising campaign for *one model line* of a major automaker to exceed the annual profits of many average-size businesses. GM decided in 1998 to go all out in hyping its "new and improved" Silverado pickup truck, launching a $135 million advertising campaign to spread the word, one of the largest-ever ad campaigns for a single vehicle.[17] SUVs are also getting a lot of advertising air time: Chrysler spent $136.4 million in 1998 on its Jeep Grand Cherokee. What if that same kind of money were used by GM and Chrysler to take the lead in fuel economy or to promote the virtues of new hybrids?

The automakers, of course, are not only advertising products when they tout their cars, trucks, and SUVs, they are also conveying and shaping values and attitudes. And sometimes the messages sent are truly outrageous, as they were in the case of GM's 1994 antitransit ads that appeared in US subway stations and subway cars.

Other ads convey values ranging from machismo to conquest to escape, and more. Some SUV ads portray the world "out there" like a war zone, carrying a message which says, in effect, "you need our gigantic vehicle to be safe." One TV spot for GM's Cadillac SUV, the Escalade, uses a female voice to explain that the female driver feels "safe and secure" in her new luxury SUV, and can "overcome the barriers" as the video shows the vehicle deftly moving through some foreboding-looking urban territory. Other ads appear to have nothing to do with vehicles, until the very end, after a snowboarder goes flying across a mountain face with a hard-driving rock score blaring behind the scene—"I have to get away—yeah!"

Ford Motor is running TV and print ads that make it appear more like an outdoor equipment manufacturer or travel agent than an auto company. "All the gear you need," says Ford in one full-page, outdoorsy print ad featuring its Explorer, Expedition, and Excursion SUVs. One tag line beneath the blue Ford oval shown with an environmentally friendly icon is the phrase, "No Boundaries. Ford Outfitters." Then superimposed over a river meandering through a forest is more text, "The best lineup of SUVs on the planet is here at your local Ford dealer. Go where reservations aren't necessary and nothing is off limits. . . ."[18] Other TV spots using the same theme feature kayakers in rough water, men and women climbing cliffs or jumping into pristine lakes, and hikers scaling a snow-covered, Himalayan-type mountain. In many of the shots, no vehicles are pictured. In this series, one TV spot featuring mountain-climbing scenes, TV actor John Corbett of *Northern Exposure* fame sets the scene, "Out here, the stories unfold like a map, stories written across the sky with the tip of an eagle's wing or . . . between the lines of a sheer rock face." More outdoor scenes appear, then Corbett returns, "You'll need an outfitter for the journey, an outfitter for your dreams. Introducing Ford Outfitters, offering the most far-reaching sport utilities on Earth, created to take you where the stories begin and never end." As part of the campaign, Ford dealers are being given tents, kayaks, and other outdoor gear to set up in their showrooms. Joseph C. Collins, Jr., Ford's brand manager for SUVs explained, "SUVs are about image, they're about taking people where they want to go, not necessarily where they really go." In 1998, Ford and its dealers spent $63.7 million of advertising for the Expedition, $61.8 million for the Explorer, and $13.7 million for ads featuring the two SUVs together. Overall in 1998, Ford spent $1.2 billion on advertising, and those numbers would be exceeded in 1999 and 2000.[19] True, some Ford ads tout "football fields-full" of recycled car parts or display how many Eiffel Towers could be built with the saved material. All to the good. But really, let's get to the engine here—the core part of the smog and global warming problem. Ford could help the environment more by using its advertising muscle to help explain how

## GM's TRANSIT HIT

In 1994, GM's Oldsmobile division began running a series of print advertisements that were placed on trains and in the subway stations of Washington, Philadelphia, New York, Boston, and Chicago. These ads carried a clear antitransit message. Some ads showed an Oldsmobile accompanied by a headline that read "Next Time, Catch The Express." In Washington, Lawrence G. Reuter, general manager of Metro, noticed the ad while riding the subway and was infuriated. "It's unconscionable that a major car manufacturer would come out with an ad trying to view us as a competitor," he said.

"The ad sends an antitransit message, not a pro-Aurora message," observed Metro's Patricia A. Lambe. She also

noted that in the Washington area, at least, on major highways like the Capital Beltway there was nothing "express" about auto travel. Metro's Lawrence Rueter and Jack R. Gilstrap, vice president of the American Public Transit Association, wrote to GM officials and told them their ads targeted one of the few industries trying to reduce the environmental damage caused by the auto industry's products. "If the millions of daily transit users took your advice literally," wrote Gilstrap to GM's chairman, Jack Smith, "both cars and trucks would risk being stuck in commuter traffic from dawn to dusk." GM ended the ad campaign in December 1994, with Oldsmobile's PR director Gus Buenz promising, "we won't stumble again."

hybrids and fuel cells work, and why these new technologies are "good buys" for consumer, nation, and planet. Madison Avenue is certainly capable of bringing good ideas to the table for casting and selling these themes. The entire auto industry needs to be a lot more sophisticated and creative with its marketing and advertising dollars than simply using the outdoors and green-sounding rhetoric to surround and hype existing cars and SUVs that pollute the environment.

Auto executives, too, often in the public eye, need to be mindful of their leadership opportunities. On the *Charlie Rose Show* one night in March 1999, for example, Richard Wagoner, an up-and-coming GM executive then in New York for the auto show and other business, came on Rose's show to talk about GM. Rose served up to Wagoner a softball question he could have hit out of the park about what big issues or strategies GM might be considering for the future. In reply, the one innovation Wagoner came up with was the company's "North Star" system, the telecommunications locational technology. Nothing was said about the fuel cell, EVs, or hybrids. Perhaps Wagoner's answer showed GM's real priorities—electronics, satellites, and telecommunications—as GM is still a major owner of Hughes Electronics.

Automotive and highway electronics, in fact, may well become the twenty-first century equivalent of the annual model change—the sales gimmick that keeps customers coming back, diverting money and talent into nonfunctional engineering, and doing more for marketing than safety, efficiency or a clean environment. True, electronics now play a key role in emissions control and can also contribute to improved safety and fuel economy. Yet if the gimmick side of this technology dominates vehicle development, coupled with illusions about traffic-management-by-computer, the vehicles and roads of the twenty-first century may not be than much better off than they are today. Much of this, of course, will depend on what investments the auto industry makes, and most importantly, how competitive it will be in the twenty-first century.

## THE COMPETITION

In May 1999, General Motors and Toyota announced they were forming a five-year joint venture to build alternative vehicles. It was an awesome combination: the No.1 US industrial corporation and the No. 1 Japanese automaker were joining forces to make green cars. "With environmental concerns so critical on a global scale, no single auto manufacturer can realistically expect to find all the technological answers on its own, let alone in a timely manner," said GM's vice president Harry Pearce, announcing the deal. "Fierce marketplace competitors like GM and Toyota must explore innovative ways to solve our common challenges."[20] But were Toyota and GM really the "fierce competitors" Pearce said they were? And would their new venture really advance the ball all that much on alternative vehicles?

Economic competition is supposed to be the all-powerful force that will bring innovation, technological advancement, and product improvement. Yet competition among the Big Three in the US has been in short supply. When competition for better vehicles did arrive in the US, it came from the foreign manufacturers—from the Swedes and Germans on safety, and from the Japanese on quality, fuel economy, and emissions control. But even the foreign automakers slowed down once they realized the Big Three weren't moving. Or they were compromised through contracts, joint ventures, or they were simply acquired.* Today, the foreign compe-

---

* For nearly thirty years now, the Big Three have been making deals with Japanese and other automakers, beginning in 1971 when GM, Ford, and Chrysler each began equity plays for stakes in, respectively, Isuzu, Mazda, and Mitsubishi. By 1972, Chrysler was importing Mitsubishi subcompacts and selling them as Dodge Colts; GM was marketing Isuzu-built Chevy LUV "pup pickups"; and Ford was marketing Mazda-built Courier pickups. In 1973, Ford, Chrysler, and GM signed agreements with Honda to use the CVCC engine. In the 1980s, as the Japanese began building US manufacturing plants, other joint ventures were made. In 1985, Chrysler and Mitsubishi built a joint assembly plant in Bloomington, IL. By 1986, Ford Mustangs were being mostly built by Mazda in Japan and shipped to Flat Rock, MI, where they received Ford engines. The following year, Mazda opened a car plant with Ford in Flat Rock

tition appears to be even less of a factor, especially given the latest round of mergers, acquisitions, and joint ventures.

The most recent venture between GM and Toyota on alternative vehicles is not surprising. In 1983, when Japanese imports were taking market share from the Big Three, GM and Toyota created a joint manufacturing venture in California called NUMMI—New United Motor Manufacturing, Inc.—which soon began cranking out identical cars under the Chevrolet Nova and Toyota Corolla nameplates. But Toyota did surprise GM with its Prius. After GM chairman Jack Smith saw the Prius at the October 1997 Tokyo Auto Show, he realized GM might be a little behind in the alternative vehicle race. But now, by hooking up with Toyota, GM had at least hedged its bets. The deal with Toyota might give GM a leg up in the hybrid car race should these new vehicles really catch on. GM was also mindful of global-scale risks involved, having learned a few things from the past. Harry Pearce touted the venture as putting GM back in the race.

"We believe we can lead the way in terms of setting [alternative vehicle] standards," said Pearce. "We see a lot of advantage to size." To be sure, there would be what economists call economies of scale and ways to spread costs out with two big companies footing the bill. But there was something else, too, as the *Wall Street Journal*'s Jeffrey Bell put it, "Through sheer combined size, GM and Toyota hope to dictate the parameters that their competitors will have to follow in building and selling cleaner, more fuel-efficient vehicles."[21] Indeed, together, GM and Toyota held about one-quarter of the global auto market at the time of their announcement. Not only might alternative-vehicle standards be determined by these two global powerhouses, but how quickly or slowly such new technology might penetrate the market. In the US, GM has a long tradition of using its dominant market share to move the market its way. For years, GM's 50 percent-plus market share in the US determined the automotive fashion of the day. How quickly would this new GM-Toyota venture move? GM, it should be noted, held the lead in EV technology too, but chose not to move ahead of its competitors. It held back, and joined in the Advanced Battery Consortium with Ford, Chrysler, and the federal government. On fuel economy too, it chose to join and help create PNGV. In fact, now that GM and Toyota were teaming up, how did that affect PNGV? GM's Harry Pearce suggested that Toyota, and perhaps other foreign automakers, should be admitted to this part federally funded program.[22] But wasn't PNGV created to help make the US more competitive with the foreign automakers?

---

to produce Ford Probes, Mazda 626s, and Mazda MX-6s. Other ventures were formed in the 1990s. Ford and Volkswagen agreed in 1992 to build vehicles in Portugal for the European market. In 1996, GM and Isuzu began producing pickups and minivans in Louisiana. In 1998, GM and Chrysler negotiated with Mitsubishi to buy direct-injection engine technology. Suzuki announced in 1998 it would produce compact cars for GM Opel in Europe. In 1998 and 1999, Ford and GM were making deals and taking equity in Korean automakers.

## THE BIG SIX

At the dawn of the twenty-first century, a new round of auto-industry mergers and joint ventures is occurring that will hold very fundamental ramifications for the environmental and energy future. Consider, for example, what has occurred in the last few years. In May 1998, Daimler and Chrysler merged. In March 1999, Renault paid $5.4 billion for a major stake in Nissan. In April 1999, Ford, which already owns Mazda, Jaguar, and Aston Martin, acquired Volvo for $6.5 billion. In May 1999, GM and Toyota announced their joint venture. Daimler-Benz and Ford have entered a multimillion dollar fuel-cell venture. In November 1999, Mitsubishi was rumored to be a takeover target and Honda was having discussions with GM about building new GM engines. In December 1999, DaimlerChrysler made no secret about the fact that it would like to buy Honda. GM announced that same month it would pay $1.4 billion for Subaru parent Fuji Heavy Industries, and it also appeared GM would acquire Daewoo, an ailing Korean auto company. Toyota and Ford meanwhile, had expanded their ties with Yamaha for engine work. The industry, said one insider, is becoming "one big inbred family."[23] The conventional wisdom was pointing to a Big Six that would soon rule the auto world—Ford, GM, Toyota, Volkswagen, DaimlerChrysler, and Renault-Nissan. Today, these six account for nearly 65 percent of global vehicle sales. Adding in GM's latest acquisitions, plus Honda, and that share rises to nearly 75 percent.

"[I]f you want to keep an industry out of a rut," counseled former Michigan governor and American Motors chairman George Romney as he gave testimony before Senator Estes Kefauver's 1958 Antitrust and Monopoly Subcommittee, "have enough companies in it so that some of those companies have got the sheer necessity of invention. When you get down to a few— and they are all prospering—millionaires and billionaires don't pioneer."

The global auto industry of the twenty-first century, it appears, will operate in highly managed markets with, at best, muted competition among models, brands, and geographic territories. Technological change and product improvement under these circumstances will not be revolutionary, to say the least. Some new technologies will come, of course, but they will likely not displace conventional technologies like the internal combustion engine very rapidly—say for another twenty-five years or more. With less competition and managed markets, it will be left to outside forces to keep the pressure on—and that means activists, political leaders, investors, consumers, and regulators.

## COUNTERVAILING POWER

If there is a lesson in the long and tortured clean-car fight, it is one of countervailing power, and why a government presence and outside pressure are important, indeed essential in moving the auto industry forward. In the US, the Big Three have been quick in recent years to use the "command and control" pejorative to demean government regulation, offering in its place "voluntary initiatives" and "government-industry collaboration." Yet the record in this industry, as troubled as it is still, suggests things would be much worse without the deadlines and regulations that have so far been put into law. The outside mandates have helped save the American auto industry from complete economic disaster, pushing it to innovate. "Much as I hate to admit it," said Chrysler's Charlie Heinen, director of vehicle emissions in the late 1970s, "the EPA accelerated the pace at which we studied combustion. The knowledge we've gained is important, whether applied to emission control or fuel economy." Henry Ford II also admitted the law was the spur. "We wouldn't have the kinds of safety built into automobiles that we have unless there had been a federal law. We wouldn't have had the fuel economy unless there had been a federal law, and there would not have been the emission control unless there had been a Federal law."[24] Outsiders—ranging from the National Academy of Sciences to journalists who have taken up residence inside one or more of the automakers for periods of time—have said the same thing: laws and regulations have, on balance, been a good thing for Detroit. "[P]ractically every recent move by US automakers to adopt advanced features—lightweight metals, high-strength plastics, electronic ignition management devices—can be traced to the influence of government regulations," concluded Massachusetts Institute of Technology analysts C. Kenneth Orski, Alan Altshuler, and Daniel Roos. [25]

Clearly, though, this is an industry that will need to be pushed and challenged on many fronts. From heads of state who see the public health costs and diseconomies in their own countries caused by runaway auto culture, to moms and dads in suburban America who want cleaner air for their kids and communities. But more than just casual activism is needed. Organized pressure must continue. The Clean Air Act, CAFE, and global warming initiatives all need to be pushed and supported by a broad base of citizen and grassroots groups, as well as national consumer, environmental, and labor organizations. These coalitions, in fact, should be broadened, adding local health groups, PTAs, meteorologists—the broader the better. Even within the automobile industry, alliances should be sought. Local car dealers, for example, should be considered in a new light, as they will play an enormous role in educating their customers about new car choices and which cars are the cleanest and most fuel efficient. Consumer education will obviously be important as new hybrid, electric, and fuel-cell vehicles begin to arrive in showrooms. The early days of introduction for these vehicles will be critical in terms of consumer acceptance, so the educational role at the local level will be very important. Among publications that have already begun to inform the public about these new choices is the *Green Guide to Cars and Trucks*, published annually by the American Council for an Energy Efficient Economy in Washington, and *The Car Book*, published by the Center for Auto Safety. Informed consumers can help make Detroit pay attention. Investors can also get the automakers' attention, too—especially large institutional investors. Public employee pension funds, universities and colleges, unions, religious organizations, and foundations all hold huge blocks of stock in many of the automakers. Organizing this shareholder "voting bloc" and uniting it with the holdings of smaller brokerages, concerned individual investors, and other social investors could prove to be an effective voice for raising clean-car and auto-industry issues. There are existing organizations working this route now, such as the Interfaith Center for Corporate Responsibility in New York and the Coalition for Environmentally Responsible Economies in Boston. Yet, these efforts are small in comparison to the investor clout found throughout the global economy today. Indeed, making sound environmental and public health investments should be a part of the fiduciary responsibility of company and shareholder alike.

State, local, and regional air pollution officials—ranging from NESCAUM, the Northeast State for Coordinated Air Use Management; OTC, the Ozone Transport Commission; and STAPPA-ALAPCO, the State and Territorial Air Program Administrators and the Association of Local Air Pollution Control Officials—add the voice of practitioners and important local organizations to the fight. These bodies also represent the home territory of millions of people and have often been the critical element in bringing forward the scientific and technical information that has made the difference in national legislation and regional initiatives.* They have also, importantly, broadened the political base in these fights and will continue to do so. The United Auto Workers has, of necessity, sided with its employers in many of the auto emission and fuel economy fights, although it appears that at least on a few occasions it was misled by management. Energy and environmental improvements and new engine technologies can obviously create jobs, and the UAW should be in the vanguard of those calling for leadership in the green car race, new capital investment, and company R & D. The competition, as the UAW well knows, can and will take jobs away.

At the national policy level, leadership and determined activism from consumers, environmental, and public health organizations will be more important than ever as the twenty-first century begins. Leadership in the White House and in the Congress will be decisive in determining the scope and outcome of several pending environmental and energy issues now facing nation and planet, making the present round of national elections absolutely key. These elections will also set the tone for policymaking in the early part of the century. But in addition to the normal channels of

* In addition to the organizations mentioned, there are also other important commissions, regional bodies, and organizations currently engaged in short and longer term research and data gathering that will prove important in the years ahead, much of it related to the ozone problem, but also air pollution generally. These are, for example, the Ozone Transport Assessment Group; the Grand Canyon Visibility Transport Commission; the Southern Appalachian Mountains Initiative; the Lake Michigan Ozone Study and Ozone Control Program; the North American Research Strategy for Tropospheric Ozone; the Southern Oxidants Study; and various North American and international study commissions and monitoring agencies.

policy struggle and public relations battles, there may also be some unexpected venues in which auto industry accountability emerges as a paramount concern.

## THE TOBACCO PARALLEL

There is, for example, the possibility that the US auto industry may soon find itself the target of a class-action lawsuit brought by cities, state attorneys general, insurance companies, tolltakers, asthma sufferers, or any number of private groups and/or public bodies seeking damages or the recovery of health costs attributable to auto exhausts. Far-fetched? Maybe so. Yet, at a time in our nation's history when tobacco and gun manufacturers are the targets of lengthy legal battles to recoup financial compensation for the public health damage their products have inflicted, should automobile manufacturers—with a fifty-year resume of resistance and technological negligence—be treated any differently?

The American Lung Association estimates that *annual* health costs from motor vehicle pollution could be as high as $93 billion. And scientists have found that air pollution's damage to lung function resembles the damage done by cigarette smoking. Some nonsmokers living in LA have experienced as much damage to their breathing capacity as pack-a-day cigarette smokers. Other health studies on ground-level ozone pollution have found that at smog-alert levels, ozone contributes to premature death, increased hospital admissions for asthmatics, causes respiratory inflammation in children, exacerbates allergies for those with asthma, and can have negative effects on healthy people, particularly those who work outside, and those who exercise. Pollutants from car engines and cigarette smoke stand equally ready to attack the human immune system. A few years ago, a group of Harvard University researchers studying respiratory disease and death found that 30,000 people die every year in the United States from respiratory illness attributable to the automobile's airborne toxins. These toxins, the researchers found, were also responsible for another 120,000 premature deaths each year.

Today we know that at least 30 percent of nitrogen oxides, a chief ingredient in smog, is caused by motor vehicles. We know, too, that nitrogen oxide levels in the US are rising and that ground-level ozone concentrations are no longer declining. We know that ozone is a health hazard, and that exposure to ozone can make people more suspectable to respiratory infection and aggravate pre-existing diseases such as asthma. We know that hospital admissions for respiratory ailments rise when ozone levels are high. We know that the incidence of new asthma is rising. We know that 85 percent of the airborne benzene, a carcinogen, comes from gasoline, and that 1.3 million tons of benzene are emitted each year into the air by gasoline-powered vehicles. More seriously, it appears that much of this has been known for a good many years, and that at least some of it might have been prevented with speedier action on motor vehicle pollution control, cleaner fuels, and/or alternative engine development.

So is a tobacco industry-styled lawsuit aimed at the auto industry plausible or appropriate? One attorney who has represented the tobacco industry in recent litigation seems to believe there are some parallels. Mark Pickrell is a Nashville, Tennessee attorney became involved in a free speech case defending a citizen's right to publish material regarding Ford Motor Company's SUV emissions and the possibility of automaker collusion on that matter. "As I look at [this case]," he said, "I keep saying, 'It's like tobacco.' The similarities that I've seen are unbelievable."[26] Pickrell should know; he was an associate with a New York law firm in 1996 defending a large cigarette maker against lawsuits filed by the states of Mississippi and New Jersey.

Admittedly, trying to ferret out exactly the auto or fuel share of certain diseases and disease costs may be difficult. But such tabulations are not impossible. Each urban area can compute quantities and share of pollutants by type. Exposures and cause-and-effect are more tricky, to be sure. The tobacco litigants had difficult variables, too. But the evidence compiled, plus the united front of state attorneys general presented in mounting the case, apparently was sufficient to move that industry toward societal compensation. If a similar suit were to be initiated in the case of the auto industry, it would not only serve to recoup monetary compensation for health costs and losses if that were the goal, but would also bring a measure of accountability to the corporate decision-making process that sanctioned a continuation of health-damaging technology when safer prospects existed. Tort law is one of society's key instruments of business accountability, and in this case there are grounds for allowing that process to work its will. Indeed, even as this book goes to press, there is a fresh round of charge and countercharge about what automotive technology is being put forward by Detroit's automakers versus that which is allegedly being held back. And while this particular case may not have a direct bearing on evidence in a tobacco-styled case, it nevertheless suggests possibilities for what might be uncovered through the discovery process.

## BlueOvalNews.com

Robert Lane is a thirty-three-year-old publisher of an internet newsletter and web site called BlueOvalNews.com, a site that has been critical of the Ford Motor Company. Lane, who has also run other web sites critical of Ford in the past, lives several blocks from Ford's Dearborn headquarters. In the summer of 1999, and over an eighteen-month period, Lane received some boxes full of documents. The boxes, mailed anonymously, contained internal Ford papers and memos, some of which pertained to Ford's plans for dealing with its SUVs, EPA air pollution standards, and fuel economy. Lane put this information on his web site, BlueOvalNews.com, and, within days, Ford went to court seeking and obtaining a restraining order. Lane, however, was allowed to use the information gleaned from the documents as any journalist would. Ford is appealing that part of the initial ruling and is also trying to permanently shut down BlueOvalNews.com. Lane subsequently hired an attorney and the matter is still tied up in appeals.[27] However, the documents Lane received were briefly posted on the web site and some of the materials surfaced in the press. The documents disclosed that Ford was in the process of developing technologies to improve fuel economy by as much as 15 percent and also had improved technologies—including some cleaner diesel technology—that could meet tougher proposed federal emissions standards. However, only a month earlier, in August 1999, Ford's Jacques Nasser stated that the company would seek to make every new model it produces be 5 percent more fuel efficient—not 15 percent.[28] At the time, Ford officials were lobbying Congress to extend the freeze on CAFE and had also argued their company would have to create new technologies and new work loads for their engineers in order to meet emissions standards. Nor did these latest Ford documents seem consistent with the company's publicly stated promises about its new environmental commitment, run in full-page newspaper ads only months before. "We're not promising you the world, just a cleaner one," said the headline, in the *Wall Street Journal* and other newspapers in mid-May 1999. Ford further explained in its ad:

> Last year, we introduced low emissions sport utility vehicles and a low emissions Ford Windstar minivan, advancing a strategy coined "Cleaner, Safer, Sooner." Meaning whenever technologically possible as well as affordable to our customers, we would make our products even safer and more environmentally friendly. Now, we're taking the next step. In the year 2000, our Ford F-Series pickups will have their smog-forming emissions lowered by an average 25 percent—without sacrificing performance or increasing cost to our customers. We've taken this initiative years in advance of any federal mandates—because there just isn't a reason to wait.[29]

Yet, the documents BlueOvalNews.com had received suggested that Ford was holding back on the technologies it had in-house, meting them out only as it saw fit. Competitively, however, the Ford documents were particularly important in the booming truck and SUV market, since in effect, they were saying that Ford could still produce big vehicles that would meet emissions standards and make fuel economy gains without sacrificing horsepower and pulling power. So why were they withholding the knowledge? "It's quite clear the company has the technology to build greener vehicles," said Jason Mark, who had seen the documents.[30]

Meanwhile, Lane and his attorney have filed a counterclaim in response to Ford's original complaint. Lane, who is also the owner of two Ford F-150 pickups and a Ford Mustang that were built between 1984 and 1997, alleges that during that time, Ford, GM, and Chrysler had a gentlemen's agreement to limit the introduction of technology that would improve fuel economy and cut emissions. Lane alleges personal economic injury and says in his suit that he has been forced to pay higher fuel costs than he would otherwise have paid if Ford had installed the improvements the documents indicate it was capable of making. Under certain circumstances, private parties can file antitrust claims against corporations. Ford, which has hired the Washington, DC law firm of Hogan & Harston, well-known in antitrust, does not believe Lane has the legal standing to file such a claim and has asked the court to throw it out. The case is scheduled to be heard in US District Court in Detroit in early 2000.[31]

Back in Washington, some environmental, consumer, and public health organizations were considering using these latest revelations as a basis to petition the US Department of Justice to begin an investigation of Ford's activities and those of the Alliance of Automobile Manufacturers. Separately, Ralph Nader had already written the Justice Department requesting that it look into the possibility the automakers conspired to delay the installation of pollution control equipment in SUVs. To date though, DOJ has taken no public action on the Ford or related auto industry matters.[32]

## LOVE AFFAIR ENDING

On another front, all of the major automakers will be hearing more about how their cars, trucks, and SUVs affect people and communities. William Clay Ford is right when he says the honeymoon with the automobile is over. In fact, in some places, the love affair may soon be over as well, especially as gridlock grows. A combination of rising vehicle numbers, more miles of travel for those vehicles, and seemingly endless road construction and repair projects are pushing many metro areas to the brink. In the Washington area, for example, a major point of congestion on the Capital Beltway, known as the Springfield mixing bowl—an interchange with Interstate 95—is undergoing an *eight-year* reconstruction and repair job that will last through the year 2007. Road rage incidents are up in Washington and other cities. A study by the AAA Foundation for Traffic Safety reported that road rage incidents have increased 60 percent between 1991 and 1996, resulting in 218 deaths.[33] People are enraged in part because they expect uninhibited movement at all times— a value emphasized throughout forty years of auto advertising. Politicians are now courting suburban voters who have had it with traffic and sprawl, with some even advocating land use controls—once the kiss of death for any politician. Al Gore is crafting a message around "livability" issues and seems to have struck a chord. Voters across America have approved nearly 200 initiatives aimed at controlling or limiting sprawl and preserving open space. The American Institute of Architects found that 68 percent of state and local executives and policymakers say they believe concern over "livable communities" is growing. AIA, in fact, has briefed both political parties, convinced the trend goes beyond traditional partisan politics. The automobile and Detroit—though not entirely to blame for sprawl and poor land use planning—are implicated, nonetheless. Heading into the new millennia, the auto industry will be tested like never before on environmental and energy matters. As the economic and social expense of living with, operating, and owning motor vehicles rises in the future, the automakers will need every ounce of good will they can muster to stay even with consumers and most social institutions. At the very least, they should begin pulling in the same direction on the significant issues: smog, global warming, safety, and traffic congestion. This year—not ten years from now—the automakers could push Congress to enact CAFE levels that reflect their technological capabilities. Increasing the average fuel economy of new cars and light trucks by 75 percent is technically and economically feasible, according to the Energy Foundation, and "would reduce US carbon emissions in 2010 by 108 million metric tons—more than one-fifth of the reduction needed to meet [the US] Kyoto target."[34] Although hybrids are here and the fuel cell may be coming, there is no reason why existing ICEs shouldn't be as clean and as thrifty as soon as possible. Waiting another five or ten years is irresponsible. The automakers should also make other public commitments to demonstrate their involvement in reducing global carbon, either by showing annual improvement in carbon reductions per vehicle somehow—perhaps even making a showing of this on the new and used car price stickers—and by reporting annually to shareholders on such progress and taking other positive actions in advertising and public forums to demonstrate their commitments. Ford's December 1999 departure from the Global Climate Coalition, the industry-backed trade group fighting global warming initiatives, is an encouraging step.

The Big Three and other automakers might also begin spending money in novel ways in the private sector to demonstrate real social commitment to repairing the urban fabric. Perhaps they could up spin-off development corporations dedicated to urban redevelopment, novel community-based transportation projects, or tackling a few especially troubled metropolitan transportation corridors. Enhancing economic value along abandoned rail lines by resurrecting some form of rail or trolley service, and coupling such undertakings with community development projects, old and new, could prove attractive business opportunities. Examples of such projects already exist. More are needed.

## HERE COMES CHINA

In March 1997, on a trip to China with Al Gore, GM finalized a $1.3 billion fifty-fifty joint venture with Shanghai Automotive Industry Corp. that will eventually produce 100,000 Buick Century and Buick Regal automobiles every year in China.[35] In June 1999, Ford announced that its Chinese partner, First Automobile Group of China, would begin producing new cars by the end of the year—a line of luxury sedans named the Big Red Flag that would be based on Ford's Lincoln Town Car. Toyota, Volkswagen, and Honda are also producing new cars in China. After China agreed to enter the World Trade Organization and struck a trade deal with the US in November 1999, it opened the doors to American and other automakers a little wider, dropping tariffs on automobiles by the year 2006 from current 80-percent-and-above levels to 25 percent, allowing foreign financing of car purchases, and giving foreign automakers full distribution and trading rights.[36] With that agreement, the global automobile race sped up, making environmental and energy issues more urgent as well. Millions and millions more cars and trucks will soon begin rolling off assembly lines. How many will have state-of-the-art pollution control equipment? How many will burn the cleanest fuels possible? Congestion and smog will certainly become worse in many developing countries not prepared to cope with a major surge of auto growth. And a mountain of auto production waste and used auto equipment—batteries, tires, paint, toxic chemicals—will soon begin accumulating as well. Indeed, there is a long road to travel in the twenty-first century, and auto-related problems will be among the thorniest and most intractable.

### "Great Industrial Responsibility"

In 1941, GM's famous leader Alfred Sloan, Jr., offered his observations about big corporations and their role in society. In *Adventures of a White Collar Man*, Sloan wrote, "Some see a danger in bigness. They fear the concentration of economic power that it brings. . . . That is in a degree true." But Sloan saw that with corporate growth, "management must expand its horizons of responsibility. It must recognize that it can no longer confine its activities to the mere production of goods and services. It must consider the impact of its operation on the economy as a whole in relation to the social and economic welfare of the entire community. . . . Those charged with great industrial responsibility must become industrial statesmen. . . ."

Today, with colossal global firms running the planet, business leaders have great industrial and social responsibility. The auto-industrial system, in particular—with the increasing demands cars and trucks will be placing on the earth, living space, and atmosphere—has an enormous responsibility. To become true statespeople of the twenty-first century, the men and women of today's automobile industry must rise above their past performance and truly provide transportation that will, as William Clay Ford has put it, undo the excesses of the prior industrial revolution and provide personal mobility with no social trade-offs.

# *Notes*

## INTRODUCTION

1. Motor Vehicle Manufacturers Association of the United States, Inc. *Motor Trucks of America,* University of Michigan Press: Ann Arbor, 1979, p. 171.

2. *Automobile Quarterly Magazine, General Motors: The First 75 Years of Transportation Products.* Produced under the auspices of General Motors in observance of its Seventy-Fifth Anniversary, Detroit, MI, 1983, p. 109.

3. Frank Coffey and Joseph Layden, *America on Wheels, The First Hundred Years: 1896-1996,* General Publishing Group: Los Angeles, 1996, pp. 124-126, and, Motor Vehicle Manufacturers Association, *Automobiles of America,* Wayne State University Press: Detroit, 1974, pp. 107-114.

4. Motor Vehicle Manufacturers Association of the United States, Inc. *Motor Trucks of America,* p. 174.

5. Coffey and Layden, *America on Wheels,* pp. 124-126.

6. Coffey and Layden, *America on Wheels,* pp. 124-126.

7. Doron P. Levin, *Behind the Wheel at Chrysler: The Iacocca Legacy,* New York: Harcourt Brace & Co., 1995, p. 15.

8. Ernie Suggs, "Month of Ooozing Ozone Enough to Make You Sick," *The Atlanta Journal-Constitution,* August 15, 1999, p. C-1.

9. Charles Seabrook, "Warning! Smog Season Choking the Life Out of Atlanta," *The Atlanta Journal-Constitution,* June 20, 1999, p. A-1.

10. Greg Jaffe, "Is Traffic-Clogged Atlanta the New Los Angeles?" *The Wall Street Journal,* June 18, 1998, p. B-1.

11. American Lung Association, *Health Effects of Outdoor Air Pollution,* 1996, pp. 14-15.

12. Rebecca Burns, "Is Traffic Killing Atlanta?" *Atlanta,* January 1998, p. 62.

13. Suggs, "Month of Ooozing Ozone Enough to Make You Sick," p. C-1.

14. Lucy Soto, "Take It From a Kid Who Knows: Bad Air Hurts," *The Atlanta Journal-Constitution,* October 6, 1999, p. B-1.

15. Arthur Allen, "Breath of Life," *The Washington Post Magazine,* October 31, 1999, p. 10.

16. Susan A. Korrick, Bruce Hill, and others, "Effects of Ozone and Other Pollutants on the Pulmonary Function of Adult Hikers," *Environmental Health Perspectives,* vol 106. no. 2, February 1998, pp. 93-99.

17. Marcia Myers, "Polluted Air Hits Asthmatics Hard," *The Baltimore Sun,* September 29, 1999, p. 1-A.

18. Gita M. Smith, "Smog Is Gone; Debate Lingers," *The Atlanta Journal-Constitution,* September 30, 1999, p. D-1.

19. David Firestone, "In Atlanta, Suburban Comforts Thwart Plans to Limit Sprawl," *The New York Times,* November 21, 1999, p. 1.

20. Randall Edwards, "Season's First Smog Alert Hits 3 Ohio Cities," *The Columbus Dispatch,* May 16, 1998, p. 4-C; "Summer Ground-Level Ozone in Region May Exceed Last Year's, Forecast Says," *Business Wire,* May 21, 1998; Tom Johnson, "Sixth Unhealthy Day, Yet First Ozone Alert," *The Star-Ledger,* May 30, 1998, p. 2; Greg Jaffe, "Is Traffic-Clogged Atlanta the New Los Angeles?" *The Wall Street Journal,* June 18, 1998, p. B-1; Marilyn Chase, "Pollution from Ozone Is a Lot More Harmful to Us Than It Looks," *The Wall Street Journal,* June 22, 1998, p. B-1; Jacques Kelly, "Code Red Alert Issued for a Second Day," *The Baltimore Sun,* June 26, 1998, p. 2-B; Daniel B. Wood, "Searing Heat Leaves US Cloaked in Smog," *The Christian Science Monitor,* July 24, 1998, p. 1; Michael Mansur, "Stalled Weather System Prompts Ozone Alert," *The Kansas City Star,* August 18, 1998, p. B-1; Ernie Suggs, "Fun in the . . . Ozone—A Health Issue 'Seen as a Traffic Issue,'" *The Atlanta Constitution,* July 22, 1998, p. D-1; Tom Held, "DNR Issues Ozone Alert for Milwaukee-Area Counties," *The Milwaukee Journal Sentinel,* July 13, 1998, p. 3; "Ozone Alert Ends, Thanks to Clouds, Lower Temperatures," *The Plain Dealer,* June 27, 1998, p. 3-B; "Hot Time in the Old Town Means an Ozone Alert," *The Plain Dealer,* July 14, 1998, p. 3-B; Darryl Campagna, et. al., "Oh, No, We're in the Ozone Smog," *Chicago Tribune,* June 25, 1998, p. 1; George McLaren, "Hot Weather Prompts City To Announce Ozone Alert," *The Indianapolis Star,* June 8, 1999, p. A-1; Associated Press, "State Wants to Reduce Ozone Levels in Central Arkansas," August 3, 1999; Fern Shen, "For Asthmatics, A Cruel Summer," *The Washington Post,* August 14, 1999, p. B-1; Associated Press, "Wichita Air Quality Teetering on Clean-Air Violation," August 23, 1999; Matthew L. Wald, "'A Bad Year but not a Hideous Year' for Smog," *The New York Times,* September 10, 1999, p. A-13; Marcia Myers, "Polluted Air Hits Asthmatics Hard," *The Baltimore Sun,* September 29, 1999, p. 1-A; Pennsylvania Department of Environmental Protection, "Pennsylvania See One of Worst Summers for Air Pollution," Update, October 1, 1999, p. 13; "State's Summer Tally for Bad Air Days: 33," *The Hartford Courant,* October 4, 1999, p. B-5; Ann S. Kim, "Summer Smog Sends Nearly 700 People to Hospital in New Hampshire," Associated Press, October 6, 1999; and "The Smoggiest City of Them All," CNN.com, October 28, 1999.

21. CNN.com, "Report: America's Vacation Spots Have Dirty Air," August 5, 1999.

22. Angela Doland, "'Day Without Cars' in French Cities," Associated Press, September 22, 1999.

CHAPTER I

1. Remarks of William Clay Ford, Jr., Chairman of the Finance Committee and the Environmental and Public Policy Committee, Ford Motor Company, before the Society of Auto-

motive Engineers, Greenbriar Conference in White Sulfur Springs, West Virginia, October 10, 1997, p. 1.

2. Oscar Suris, "Job One: William Clay Ford Jr. Stands Ready to Steer the No. 2 Auto Maker," *The Wall Street Journal*, September 23, 1996, p. A-1; Micheline Maynard, "Ford Succession Buzz Generates Denials, But...," *USA Today*, December 2, 1997, p. 4-B; and Ron Stodghill, II and Joseph R. Szczesny, "The Ford in Ford's Future," *Time*, December 8, 1997, p. 74.

3. Remarks of William Clay Ford, Jr., p. 2.

4. David Versical, "Don't Ignore Global Warming, Ford Warns," *Automotive News*, October 20, 1997, p. 14.

5. Remarks of William Clay Ford, Jr., pp. 2-3.

6. Remarks of William Clay Ford, Jr., p. 3.

7. Remarks of William Clay Ford, Jr., p. 4.

8. Remarks of William Clay Ford, Jr., p. 6.

9. David Versical, "Don't Ignore Global Warming, Ford Warns," p. 14.

10. Earle Eldridge and Traci Watson, "Carmakers Lobby against Global Warming Treaty," *USA Today*, October 3, 1997, p. B-1.

11. Remarks of William Clay Ford, Jr., p. 8.

12. David Versical, "Don't Ignore Global Warming, Ford Warns," p. 14.

13. Oscar Suris, "Job One: William Clay Ford Jr. Stands Ready to Steer the No. 2 Auto Maker," *The Wall Street Journal*, September 23, 1996, p. A-1.

14. Ron Stodghill, II and Joseph R. Szczesny, "The Ford In Ford's Future," p. 74.

15. Micheline Maynard, "Ford Succession Buzz Generates Denials, But...," *USA Today*, p. 4-B.

16. Remarks of William Clay Ford, Jr., p. 9.

17. "Big Screen in the Big Apple," *Automotive News*, May 17, 1999, p. 4.

18. Darren Gersh, Interview with William Clay Ford, Jr., *The Nightly Business Report*, July 22, 1999.

CHAPTER 2

*Sidebar*

1. "They Have a Responsibility"
John C. Esposito, *Vanishing Air*, the Ralph Nader Study Group Report on Air Pollution, Grossman: New York, 1970, p. 37; and, statement of Kenneth Hahn, County Board of Supervisors, Los Angeles County, Hearings Before a Special Subcommittee on Air and Water Pollution of the Committee on Public Works, US Senate, 88th Congress, 2nd Session, "Field Hearings Held on Progress and Programs Relating to the Abatement of Air Pollution," Los Angeles, California, January 27, 1964 (and five other cities), pp. 24-26.

1. Kenneth Hahn, "Health Warning: Record of Correspondence between Kenneth Hahn, Los Angeles County Supervisor and the Presidents of General Motors, Ford, and Chrysler on Controlling Air Pollution," Los Angeles, California, May 1972.

2. E. Ainsworth, "Fight to Banish Smog, Bring Sun Back to City Pressed," *Los Angeles Times*, October 13, 1946, cited in James E. Krier and Edmund Ursin, *Pollution and Policy: A Case Essay on California and Federal Experience with Motor Vehicle Air Pollution, 1940-1975*, Berkeley, University of California Press, 1977, p. 53.

3. Air Pollution Foundation, *Final Report* (Los Angeles, CA, 1961) pp. 40-41, cited in James E. Krier and Edmund Ursin, *Pollution and Policy*, Berkeley: University of California Press, 1977, p. 6, 75-76.

4. Technically, *smog* is a misnomer. Derived from a synthesis of smoke and fog and used to describe the type of pollution in the past for places like London, it is not chemically accurate for the hydrocarbon and photochemical variety of air pollution found today in most cities. Yet, in popular usage the term has become synonymous with today's urban pollution.

5. Ashleigh Brilliant, *The Great Car Craze: How Southern California Collided with the Automobile in the 1920s*, Santa Barbara: Woodbridge Press, 1989, p. 17.

6. Letter of John M. Campbell, administrative director, engineering staff, General Motors, to Kenneth Hahn, Los Angeles County Supervisor, March 26, 1953.

7. Krier and Ursin, *Pollution and Policy*; Robert E. Bedingfield, "A Student of Air Pollution by Automobiles," *The New York Times*, February 1, 1970, section 3, p. 3; "Auto Engineers Arrive in LA to Study Smog," *Daily Press*, January 27, 1954; and "Automotive Industry Aid Pledged in Fumes Study," *Los Angeles Times*, February 3, 1954.

8. James E. Krier and Edmund Ursin, *Pollution and Policy*.

9. Letter from J. Campbell, administrative director, engineering, General Motors Corp., to K. Hahn, March 26, 1953, in *Smog: A Factual Record*, p. 6; and Letter from D. Chabeck, news dept., Ford Motor Co., to K. Hahn, March 3, 1953, in *Smog: A Factual Record*, p. 4.

10. Air Pollution Foundation, *1954 President's Report*, p. 8; L. Hitchcock, "Diagnosis and Prescription," in Proceedings of Second Southern California Conference on Elimination of Air Pollution, November 14, 1956, pp. 76-78; Air Pollution Foundation, *1956 President's Report*, p. 12; "Smog Fighters Claim Car Fumes Last Unlicked Pollution Trouble Source," *Daily Press*, February 13, 1958.

11. Hearings before the Subcommittee on Public Health and Welfare of the Interstate and Foreign Commerce Committee, US House of Representatives, *Air Pollution Control Progress*, February 23-24, 1960, pp. 7-10.

12. Holcomb B. Noble, "W. Lain Guthrie, 84, Jet Pilot Who Refused to Dump Fuel," *The New York Times*, April 4, 1997.

13. Mitchell Gordon, *Sick Cities: Psychology and Pathology of American Urban Life*, Baltimore: Penguin Books, 1963, pp. 100-102.

14. Krier and Ursin, *Pollution and Policy*, p. 110, citing: R. Dyck, "Evolution of Federal Air Pollution Control Policy" (Ph.D. diss., University of Pittsburgh, 1971), pp. 33-35, 40-42; and R. Ripley, "Congress and Clean Air: The Issue of Enforcement, 1963," in *Congress and Urban Problems*, ed. F. Cleveland et. al., Washington, DC: The Brookings Institution, 1969, pp. 232, 234.

15. Gordon, *Sick Cities* p. 101.

16. Gordon, *Sick Cities*, p. 102.

17. Krier and Ursin, *Pollution and Policy*, pp. 172-173.

18. Krier and Ursin, *Pollution and Policy*, p. 174.

19. Subcommittee on Public Health and Welfare, Committee on Interstate and Foreign Commerce, US House of Representatives, *Clean Air Act Amendments*, June 1965, p. 288.

20. Subcommittee on Public Health and Welfare, *Clean Air Act Amendments*, p. 112.

21. Irving S. Bengelsdorf, Ph.D., ". . . That Breathing by the People Shall Not Perish from the Smog," *The Los Angeles Times*, August 15, 1969.

22. "Air Pollution Control," *CQ Weekly Report*, March 3, 1967, p. 300.

23. "Air Pollution Control," *CQ Weekly Report*, p. 299.

24. "Environmental Currents," *Environmental Science and Technology*, February 1968.

25. Virginia A. Ball, "GM Study Notes Cuts in LA Auto Smog," *Automotive News*, August 18, 1969, p. 35.


CHAPTER 3

*Sidebar*

1. "Ripping Out the Tracks"
Steve Nadis and James J. MacKenzie, *Car Trouble*, Boston: Beacon Press, 1993, pp. 4-5; Jonathan Kwitny, "The Great Transportation Conspiracy," *Harper's*, February 1981, p. 15.; and Morton Mintz, "GM Still Faces Monopoly Suit," *The Washington Post*, May 24, 1974.


1. The suit was filed January 10, 1969, in Los Angeles, with the US District Court for the Central District of California—*US v. Automobile Manufacturers Assn., Inc; General Motors Corp.; Ford Motor Co.; Chrysler Corp.; and American Motors Corp.* Named as coconspirators but not as defendants were Checker Motor Corp.; Diamond T Motor Car Co.; International Harvester Co.; Studebaker Corp.; White Motor Corp.; Kaiser Jeep Corp.; and Mack Trucks Inc.

2. S. Griswold, "Reflections and Projections on Controlling the Motor Vehicle," paper presented at annual meeting of the Air Pollution Control Association, Houston, Texas, June 25, 1964.

3. Frank V. Fowlkes, "GM Gets Little Mileage from Compact, Low-Powered Lobby," *National Journal*, November 14, 1970, p. 2502.

4. US Department of Justice, press statement, September 11, 1969, 5 pp., with statement of Dr. Lee A. DuBridge, science advisor to the president, September 11, 1969, 1 pp.

5. Ralph Nader, letter to Hon. Richard W. McLaren, assistant attorney general, antitrust division, Department of Justice, Washington, DC, September 15, 1969, and Steven V. Roberts, "Auto Smog Pact on Coast Opposed," *The New York Times*, September 28, 1969.

6. See, for example, US House of Representatives, "Congressmen Urge Open Trial in Smog Control Antitrust Case," *Congressional Record*, September 3, 1969, pp. H7441-H7450.

7. Ray Zeman, "Release of Secret Smog Testimony to be Sought," *Los Angeles Times*, September 25, 1969.

8. "Brown Resolution Calls for Stronger Action in Smog Conspiracy Case," Hon. George E. Brown, Jr., *Congressional Record*, extensions of remarks, October 6, 1969, pp. E-8195-96.

9. Hon. Phil Burton, "Smog Control Antitrust Case," *Congressional Record*, May 18, 1971, pp. H4063-4074, including the internal memorandum of the US Justice Department, Antitrust Division, citing grand jury evidence, exhibits, and transcript references, as cited below hereafter.

10. ibid.

11. Morton Mintz, "Justice Dept. Had '68 Memo on Auto Plot," *The Washington Post*, May 19, 1971, p. A-2; John Lanan, "Probe Is Asked of Auto Makers Pollution 'Plot,'" *The Washington Star*, May 19, 1971, p. A-9; Morton Mintz (*LA Times-Washington Post* service), "Auto Makers Faced Criminal Suit on Smog," *The Detroit News*, May 19, 1971, p. 4-C; and, "Chrysler Defends Role in Reducing Auto Pollution," *The Washington Post*, May 21, 1971, p. A-3.

12. Memorandum of the US Justice Department, Antitrust Division citing grand jury transcripts, volume XXXXV, pp 46, 51-53.

13. Memorandum of the US Justice Department, Antitrust Division, citing grand jury exhibit 583.

14. Memorandum of the US Justice Department, Antitrust Division, citing grand jury transcripts, volume XXXXV, pp 46, 51-53.

15. Memorandum of the US Justice Department, Antitrust Division, citing grand jury exhibit 339 and grand jury transcripts, volume XX, p. 78.

16. Memorandum of the US Justice Department, Antitrust Division, citing grand jury exhibit 542.

17. Memorandum of the US Justice Department, Antitrust Division, citing grand jury exhibit 542.

18. Memorandum of the US Justice Department, Antitrust Division, citing grand jury exhibit 345, December 3, 1962, and grand jury transcripts, volume XX, pp. 105-106.

19. Memorandum of the US Justice Department, Antitrust Division, citing grand jury transcripts, vol. XX, pp. 49-50 and 75-77.

20. Memorandum of the US Justice Department, Antitrust Division, citing grand jury transcripts, volume XXIX, p. 72 and volume XXXVI, pp. 15-16.

21. John C. Esposito, *Vanishing Air*, New York: Grossman, 1970, p. 50.

22. Automobile Manufacturers Association, "Memorandum on the US Department of Justice Investigation," (also known as the green book).

23. Memorandum of the US Justice Department, Antitrust Division, citing grand jury exhibit 555.

24. John F. Gordon, president, General Motors, letter to Kenneth Hahn, Los Angeles County supervisor, October 18, 1960.

25. Memorandum of the US Justice Department, Antitrust Division, citing grand jury exhibit 365.

26. Representative John E. Fogarty, US House of Representative, *Congressional Record*, May 17, 1961, pp. 7689-7690.

27. Memorandum of the US Justice Department, Antitrust Division, citing grand jury exhibit 504 and grand jury transcripts, volume XXXXV, pp 71-76.

28. Memorandum of the US Justice Department, Antitrust Division, citing rough draft of paper presented at ECS-APCA Meeting, by James M. Chandler, Chairman, VCP-AMA, entitled, "Current Status and Future Work on Vehicle Emissions Control Devices," grand jury exhibit 381.

29. Memorandum of the US Justice Department, Antitrust Division, citing grand jury exhibit 504 and grand jury transcripts: volume XXI, pp. 32-33; volume XXII, pp. 49-50; volume XXIX, pp. 107-110, 130-133; and grand jury exhibits 360 and 442.

30. Memorandum of the US Justice Department, Antitrust Division, citing grand jury exhibit 504 and grand jury transcripts, volume XXXVII, p. 7 and grand jury exhibit 509; see also, transcript volume XXX, pp. 27-32, and grand jury exhibit 373.

31. John C. Esposito, *Vanishing Air*, p. 50.

32. Memorandum of the US Justice Department, Antitrust Division, citing grand jury exhibit 507.

33. Memorandum of the US Justice Department, Antitrust Division, citing grand jury transcripts, volume XXVI, pp 149-152 and exhibit 507.

34. Memorandum of the US Justice Department, Antitrust Division, citing grand jury exhibit 478.

35. Memorandum of the US Justice Department, Antitrust Division, citing grand jury transcripts, volume XXXXI, p. 25.

36. Memorandum of the US Justice Department, Antitrust Division, citing grand jury transcripts, volume LVII, p. 73.

37. S. Griswold, "Reflections and Projections on Controlling the Motor Vehicle," and Esposito, *Vanishing Air*, p. 49.

38. Memorandum of the US Justice Department, Antitrust Division, citing grand jury transcripts, volume XLV, pp. 29-30 and exhibit 182.

39. Memorandum of the US Justice Department, Antitrust Division, citing grand jury exhibit 418.

40. Memorandum of the US Justice Department, Antitrust Division, citing grand jury exhibit 195, dated April 22, 1960.

41. Memorandum of the US Justice Department, Antitrust Division, citing grand jury exhibit 196.

42. Conversation with Dr. W. Stanley Briggs, Bridgeton, NJ, October 2, 1998.

43. Memorandum of the US Justice Department, Antitrust Division, citing grand jury transcripts, volume XXII, pp. 14-15 and exhibit 402.

44. Memorandum of the US Justice Department, Antitrust Division, citing grand jury exhibit 407.

45. Memorandum of the US Justice Department, Antitrust Division, citing grand jury exhibit 599.

46. Memorandum of the US Justice Department, Antitrust Division, citing grand jury transcripts, volume XXXVIII, pp. 16-17.

47. Esposito, *Vanishing Air*, p. 48.

48. ibid, p. 51.

49. Richard Corrigan, "Administration Looks to Industry to Control Automotive Air Pollution," *National Journal*, pp. 17-19.

50. Charles M. Heinen, "We've Done the Job—What Next?" paper delivered before the Society of Automotive Engineers, April 9, 1969, p. 1.

51. US Department of Health, Education, and Welfare, *Progress in the Prevention and Control of Air Pollution*, Senate document No. 92, 90th Congress, 2nd Session, June 28, 1968, p. 19.

52. Society of Automotive Engineers, April 9, 1969.

## CHAPTER 4

*Sidebar*

1. "The Great Dirty Cloud"
"Handwriting in the Sky," editorial, *The New York Times*, July 30, 1970; "A Cloud No Bigger than the Eastern Seaboard," editorial, *The Washington Post*, July 1970; "Tokyo Curbs the Car, Beats the Smog," *The Washington Post*, August 3, 1970.

2. "Leon G. Billings"
Leon G. Billings, Leon G. Billings, Inc., Washington DC; Bernard Asbell, *The Senate Nobody Knows*, pp. 74-75; and author conversations with former House staff members, Leon Billings' colleagues, and Washington lobbyists.

1. US Senate, Joint Hearings before the Committee on Commerce and the Subcommittee on Air and Water Pollution of the Committee on Public Works, *Electric Vehicles and Other Alternatives to the Internal Combustion Engine*, on S.451 and S.453, Washington, DC, March 16, 1967, p. 238.

2. US Department of Commerce, *The Automobile and Air Pollution: A Program for Progress*, vol. II, December 1967.

3. Robert Fairbanks, "Senate Passage of Combustion Engine Ban Elates Petris," *The Los Angeles Times*, July 26, 1969, p. 1.

4. ibid.

5. ibid.

6. Virginia A. Ball, "Measure Draws Attack in Automotive Circles," *Automotive News*, August 4, 1969, p. 34.

7. Fairbanks, "Senate Passage of Combustion Engine Ban Elates Petris," *The Los Angeles Times*, July 26, 1969, p. 1.

8. Joe Kugelmass, "California Warned of Danger in Gas Engine Ban," *Automotive News*, August 4, 1969, p. 1.

9. "California's Senate Approves Bill to Ban Smog-Causing Engines," *The Wall Street Journal*, July 28, 1969, p. 21.

10. ibid.

11. Ball, "Measure Draws Attack In Automotive Circles," p. 34.

12. ibid.

13. Fairbanks, "Senate Passage of Combustion Engine Ban Elates Petris," p. 1.

14. Kugelmass, "California House Kills Auto Ban," *Automotive News*, August 11, 1969, p. 6.

15. ibid.

16. Senator Nicholas Petris, telegram, reprinted in letters to the editor, "Petris Files Complaint on California Story," *Automotive News*, August 25, 1969.

17. Kugelmass, "California House Kills Auto Ban," p. 6.

18. ibid.

19. Senator Nicholas Petris, telegram, "Petris Files Complaint on California Story," August 25, 1969.

20. Kugelmass, "California House Kills Auto Ban," p. 6.

21. Senator Nicholas Petris, telegram, "Petris Files Complaint On California Story," August 25, 1969.

22. "Air Quality Act Amendments," *1969 CQ Almanac*, *Congressional Quarterly*, Washington, DC, p. 523.

23. ibid.

24. Judith Robinson, "Many New Cars Fail Federal Pollution Tests; Agencies Seek Added Controls," *National Journal*, April 11, 1970. p. 755.

25. Charles B. Camp, "Detroit Pushes Search for Answer to Problem of Pollution by Autos," *The Wall Street Journal*, March 31, 1970, p. 1.

26. "Air Quality Act Amendments-Related Hearings," *1969 CQ Almanac*, *Congressional Quarterly*, p. 524.

27. Robinson, "Many New Cars Fail Federal Pollution Tests," p. 755.

28. President Richard M. Nixon, Message on the Environment to the Congress of the

United States, February 10, 1970, appendix C, President's Council on Environmental Quality, *Environmental Quality*, August 1970, p.261. "An alternative to the internal combustion engine may be necessary if it cannot meet the increasingly stiff [air pollution control] standards," wrote the Council on Environmental Quality (CEQ) in its first annual environmental quality report, August 1970. CEQ noted that President Nixon had specifically asked for an R & D program to conducted under the direction of CEQ and an incentive program to private developers, through government purchase of privately produced unconventional vehicles for testing and evaluation. (CEQ report, pp 79-80.)

29. Charles B. Camp, "Detroit Pushes Search for Answer to Problem of Pollution by Autos," p. 1.

30. Denis Hayes, letter to Jack Doyle, August 9, 1998, 2pp.

31. ibid.

32. E.W. Kenworthy, "A Clean-Air Bill Passed by House," *The New York Times*, June 11, 1970, p. 1, and "House Votes to Expand Clean Air Law, 374-1; Measure Goes to Senate," *The Wall Street Journal*, June 11, 1970.

33. Hon. Gaylord Nelson, "Amendment of Clean Air Act—Amendment No. 815," and "Pollution Crisis And Business As Usual," *Congressional Record*, Senate, August 3, 1970, pp. 26932-26936

34. ibid.

35. Frank V. Fowlkes, "GM Gets Little Mileage from Compact, Low-Powered Lobby," *National Journal*, November 14, 1970, pp. 2508-2509.

36. Henry Ford II, letter to Robert Dunlop, CEO Sun Oil, January 27, 1970, Dunlop Papers, Acc. 1317, box 47, EMHL., cited in, Arthur M. Johnson, *The Challenge of Change: The Sun Oil Company, 1945-1977*, Ohio State University Press: Columbus, 1983, p. 283.

37. Author conversations with individuals formerly employed at Corning and other catalyst scientists wishing to remain anonymous, 1997 and 1998.

38. "Bill to Ban Polluting Cars by 1975 Gains in Senate," *The New York Times*, August 21, 1970, p.1.

39. ibid.

40. Barone, Ujifusa, and Matthews, *The Almanac of American Politics 1976*, New York: E.P. Dutton, Inc., 1975, pp. 343-344.

41. Richard E. Cohen, *Washington at Work: Back Rooms and Clean Air*, Boston: Allyn & Bacon, 2nd edition, 1995, p. 14.

42. Krier and Ursin, *Pollution and Policy*, pp. 173-174.

43. Barone, Ujifusa, and Matthews, *The Almanac of American Politics 1976*, p. 343.

44. Bernard Asbell, *The Senate Nobody Knows*, Baltimore: Johns Hopkins University Press, 1978, p. 240; Barone, et. al., *The Almanac of American Politics 1976*, New York: E.P. Dutton & Co., 1975, p. 343; and Cohen, *Washington at Work: Back Rooms and Clean Air*, p. 14.

45. Theo Lippman, Jr., and Donald C. Hansen, *Muskie*, New York: W.W. Norton & Co., 1971, p. 143.

46. Fowlkes, "GM Gets Little Mileage from Compact, Low-Powered Lobby," p. 2509.

47. L. A. Iacocca, executive vice president, Ford Motor Company, "A Statement on Pending Changes to the Clean Air Act," Dearborn, Michigan, September 9, 1970, p. 1.

48. Letter from Edward N. Cole, president, General Motors, to US Senator Edmund S.

Muskie, September 17, 1970, reprinted in Senate Committee on Public Works, Legislative History of the Clean Air Act Amendments of 1970, 93rd Congress, 2nd Session, 1974, committee print, Washington, DC, p. 358.

49. Fowlkes, "GM Gets Little Mileage from Compact, Low-Powered Lobby," p. 2511.

50. ibid.

51. "GM Offers New Antipollution Standards; Calls Government's '75 Goal 'Unattainable,'" *The Wall Street Journal*, November 18, 1970, p. 8.

52. Krier and Ursin, *Pollution and Policy*, p. 204.

53. Remarks of Senator Edmund Muskie, *Congressional Record*, September 21, 1970, p. 16091.

54. Cohen, *Washington at Work*, p. 14.

55. Senator Edmund Muskie, "The Clean Air Act: A Commitment to Public Health," *Environmental Forum*, January 1990, p. 14.

56. "Cole, Riccardo Deride Lack of Scientific Approach," *Automotive News*, March 8, 1971.

57. "Clean Air Standards Termed 'Unrealistic,'" *Automotive News*, March 8, 1971, p. 52.

58. National Archives Nixon Project, National Archives at College Park, College Park, MD, "Conversation Among President Richard M. Nixon, Lide Anthony Iacocca, Henry Ford II, and John D. Ehrlichman," The Oval Office, The White House, Washington, DC, April, 27, 1971 (transcript, pp. 1-30).

59. Helen Kahn, "AMA Challenges Standards for Ambient Air Quality," *Automotive News*, March 22, 1971.

60. "Clean Air: The View from General Motors," *National Journal*, July 28, 1973, p. 1089.

## CHAPTER 5

*Sidebars*

1. "Someone Is Lying"

Transcript of proceedings, US Environmental Protection Agency, "Motor Vehicle Pollution Control Suspension Request," Testimony of Chrysler Corporation, Engelhard Industries, etc., Washington, DC, March 15, 1973, pp. 1070-1416; Donald A. Colbun, "Chrysler Grilled on Hot Seat," *Automotive Industries*, May 1, 1973, p. 11; Before the administrator, US Environmental Protection Agency, Washington, DC, In Re: Applications for Suspension of 1975 Motor Vehicle Exhaust Emission Standards, American Motors Corporation, Chrysler Corporation, Ford Motor Company, General Motors Corporation, and International Harvester Company, Applicants, *Decision of the Administrator on Remand from the United States Court of Appeals for the District of Columbia Circuit*, April 11, 1973, pp. 40-43. See also, letter of Ralph Nader to William Ruckelshaus, administrator, US Environmental Protection Agency, March 15, 1973.

2. "John Z. DeLorean"

"DeLorean DMC-12," *Automotive Industries*, September 12, 1978; William H. Jones, "Views in GM Book Confirmed," *The Washington Post*, November 15, 1979, p. B-1; Patrick J. Wright, *On a Clear Day You Can See General Motors* (New York: Avon), 1979; Ralph Nader & William Taylor, *The Big Boys: Power & Position in American Business* (New York: Pantheon), 1986; Hobart Rowan, "Stunning Account of How GM Works," *The Washington Post*, November 18, 1979, p. G-1; and Clarence Ditlow, "Making It at GM," *Environmental Action*, February 1980, p. 2829.

1. Michael Shnayerson, *The Car That Could—The Inside Story of GM's Revolutionary Electric Vehicle*, New York: Random House, 1996, p. 50.

2. Elsie Carper, "Clean Air Hearings Focus on San Clemente Meeting," *The Washington Post*, January 27, 1972, p. A-3, and James Miller, "Air Pollution," *Nixon and the Environment: The Politics of Devastation*, James Rathlesburger (ed), League of Conservation Voters Report, (Village Voice: New York), 1972, pp. 23-24. This meeting was reportedly organized by Representative Victor Veysey, a first-term California Republican, who said "the White House had nothing to do with the conference." Veysey said he obtained the use of the facility through the University of California at Riverside. The university, also a cosponsor, was permitted to use the San Clemente facility for nonpolitical meetings. On Capitol Hill, Representative Paul Rogers, then holding hearings on the Clean Air Act, focused some attention on the meeting, concerned that the "sanction of the White House" was given to a meeting attended by representatives of the auto and oil industries.

3. US Senate, Public Works Subcommittee on Air and Water Pollution, *Oversight Hearings on Implementation of Clean Air Act Amendments of 1970*, March 27 & 28, 1972, and, "Clean Air," *CQ Weekly Report*, April 8, 1972, pp. 802-803.

4. ibid, US Senate.

5. John Quarles, *Cleaning Up America*, Boston: Houghton Mifflin Co., 1976, pp. 179-180.

6. ibid.

7. Victor Cohn, "Clean-Car Device Makers Oppose Delay on '75 Rules," *The Washington Post*, April 13, 1972, p. A-3.

8. Quarles, *Cleaning Up America*, pp. 179-180.

9. William Ruckelshaus, administrator, US Environmental Protection Agency, Testimony before the Senate Public Works Subcommittee on Air and Water Pollution, *Oversight Hearings on the Clean Air Act Amendments of 1970*, May 22, 1972.

10. Quarles, *Cleaning Up America*, pp. 179-188.

11. See, Applications for Suspension of 1975 Motor Vehicle Emission Standards, Decision of the Administrator on Remand from the United States Court of Appeals, District of Columbia Circuit, April 11, 1973, hearing transcript, at 29-30, cited in Clarence Ditlow, "Federal Regulation of Motor Vehicle Emissions under the Clean Air Act Amendments of 1970, *Ecological Law Journal*, 1975, pp. 495-504; and, "EPA—Auto Emission Standards," *Congressional Quarterly*, March 17, 1973, p. 600.

12. "Honda and Clean Air," *Congressional Quarterly*, (*CQ Weekly*), March 24, 1973, p. 639.

13. "Auto Pollution Control Deadline Postponed," *1973 CQ Almanac*, pp. 653-654.

14. Chrysler Corporation, "Let's Have Clean Air—But Let's Not Throw Money Away," booklet, 1973.

15. Richard Corrigan, "Clean Air Goals in Doubt as Deadlines Near for Traffic Controls, Car Emissions," *National Journal*, March 10, 1973, p. 349.

16. Hearings before the Subcommittee on Air and Water Pollution of the Committee on Public Works, US Senate, *Decision of the Administrator of the Environmental Protection Agency Regarding Suspension of the 1975 Auto Emissions Standards*, Part 1, April 16, 1973, p. 2.

17. Editorial, "A Matter of Emphasis," *The Wall Street Journal*, April 13, 1973.

18. Hearings before the Subcommittee on Air and Water Pollution of the Committee on Public Works, US Senate, *Decision of the Administrator of the Environmental Protection Agency Regarding Suspension of the 1975 Auto Emissions Standards*, pp. 86-87.

19. "Auto Pollution Control Deadline Postponed," *1973 CQ Almanac*, p. 654.

20. ibid, p. 655.

21. ibid.

22. John F. Burby, environment report, "Challenges to Health Statistics Push Senate to Review Clean Air Act Implications," *National Journal*, July 28, 1973, p. 1088.

23. Tom Kleene, "Ford's Crusade to Ease EPA Rules Hits the Road," *Akron Beacon Journal*, June 13, 1973, p. E-9.

24. ibid.

25. Neil Robblee, Oregon Student Public Interest Research Group, Portland, Oregon, letter to Clarence Ditlow, Public Interest Research Group, Washington, DC, July 6, 1973.

26. John F. Burby, "Challenges to Health Statistics Push Senate to Review Clean Air Act Implications," p. 1088.

## CHAPTER 6

*Sidebars*

1. "False and Misleading"
Barbara B. Wooley, "Energy Actions—Senate Recommits Energy Bill, 57-37...." *National Journal*, February 2, 1974, p. 187; and "EPA Debunks Chevrolet," *Environmental Action*, February 16, 1974, p. 14; and George C. Wilson, "Exploitation Seen in Fuel Crisis Ads," *The Washington Post*, December 1973.

2. "Hal Sperlich's Epiphany"
David Halberstam, *The Reckoning*, New York: William Morrow & Co., 1986, pp. 512-513.

3. "Beyond Tree Huggers"
Bernard Asbell, *The Senate Nobody Knows*, p. 200, and author interviews with sources wishing to remain confidential.

1. Maryann Keller, *Rude Awakening: The Rise, Fall and Struggle for Recovery of General Motors*, Harper Perennial: New York, 1989, p. 52.

2. John J. Riccardo, president, Chrysler Corporation, Detroit, MI, Letter to Hon. Jennings Randolph, US Senate, Washington, DC, October 9, 1973, p. 1.

3. Richard Witkin, "Agency Bars Stay on Auto Pollution," *The New York Times*, November 7, 1973, p. 19.

4. Tim O'Brien, "Big Three Ask Clean-Auto Rule Freeze," *The Washington Post*, November 6, 1973, p. A-3.

5. Richard Witkin, "Agency Bars Stay on Auto Pollution," p. 19, and Tim O'Brien, "Big Three Ask Clean-Auto Rule Freeze," p. A-3.

6. *1975 CQ Almanac*, p. 247.

7. Quarles, *Cleaning Up America*, p. 193.

8. Keller, *Rude Awakening*, p. 52.

9. ibid.

10. Richard Egan, "Energy-Environment Fights Shape up over Autos, Oil and Coal," *The National Observer*, February 8, 1975, p. 3.

11. Karen J. Elliott, "Is There a Joker in the Gas Mileage Deal?" *The Wall Street Journal*, February 28, 1975, p. 10.

12. John Emshwiller and Albert Karr, "Auto Men Use Slump in Seeking Slowdown on Safety, Pollution," *The Wall Street Journal*, January 9, 1975, p. 1.

13. ibid.

14. ibid.

15. ibid.

16. ibid.

17. Arthur J. Magida, "EPA Study May Bring Reprieve for Catalytic Converter," *National Journal*, April 12, 1975, p. 553.

18. ibid.

19. ibid.

20. Asbell, *The Senate Nobody Knows*, pp. 36-37.

21. ibid., p. 37.

22. ibid, p. 38.

23. ibid, pp. 315-319.

24. Telephone conversation with Leon Billings, September 12, 1997.

25. *The Wall Street Journal*, May 15, 1975.

26. "Congress Faces Hard Choices on Clean Air Act, Auto Emissions," *1975 CQ Almanac*, p. 250

27. Asbell, *The Senate Nobody Knows*, p. 102.

28. ibid, p. 131.

29. Halberstam, *The Reckoning*, p. 462.

30. Timothy Jacobs, *Lemons: The World's Worst Cars*, Greenwich, CT: Bompton Books Corporation, 1987, pp. 125-128.

31. Stephen B. Shepard and J. Patrick Wright, "The Auto Industry," *The Atlantic*, December 1974, pp. 18-27.

32. ibid.

33. Halberstam, *The Reckoning*, pp., 513, 519.

34. ibid, pp. 22-23.

35. ibid, pp. 23-24.

36. ibid, p. 24.

37. Asbell, *The Senate Nobody Knows*, p. 125.

38. ibid, pp. 133-34

39. Brian T. Ketcham, P.E., vice president and staff engineer, Citizens for Clean Air, Inc., New York, NY, letter to Hon. George E. Brown, Jr., US House of Representatives, Washington, DC, September 25, 1975, p. 2.

40. US Environmental Protection Agency, Washington, DC, fact sheet, "Future Emissions Standards," FS-46, MSAPC, September 1975.

41. Asbell, *The Senate Nobody Knows*, p. 320.

42. Senator Edmund Muskie, "Automobile Emissions Standards," *Congressional Record*, September 1975.

43. ibid.

44. Dick Kirschten, "It's Washington Taking on Detroit in the Auto Pollution Game," *National Journal*, January 1, 1977, pp. 14-15.

## CHAPTER 7

1. Kirschten, "It's Washington Taking on Detroit in the Auto Pollution Game," p. 14.

2. Krier and Ursin, *Pollution and Policy*, pp. 181-182.

3. Kirschten, "It's Washington Taking on Detroit in The Auto Pollution Game," p. 14.

4. ibid.

5. Tom Quinn, chairman, California Air Resources Board, Sacramento, CA, letter to The Honorable Jimmy Carter, February 15, 1977.

6. ibid.

7. "Debating a Clean-Air Timetable," *Business Week*, February 28, 1977, p. 80.

8. ibid.

9. "Muskie Hearings Open," *Motor Vehicle Industry Report*, February 14, 1977, p. 1.

10. "Energy and the Environment: Having it Both Ways," *National Journal*, April 30, 1977, p. 663.

11. Margot Hornblower, "Delay Is Sought in Enforcing Auto Emission Rules," *The Washington Post*, April 19, 1977, p. A-1.

12. "One-Year Delay in Auto-Emission Rules Is Urged, as Expected, by Administration," *The Wall Street Journal*, April 19, 1977, p. 17.

13. Hornblower, "Delay Is Sought in Enforcing Auto Emission Rules," p. A-1.

14. "Energy and the Environment: Having It Both Ways," p. 663.

15. Documentary film, *H.R. 6161: An Act of Congress*, produced by Jerry Colbert, December 1976 through January 1978, and first shown on national public television in April 1979 (the fifty-eight-minute film is available for rental or purchase through the Learning Corporation of America, 1350 Avenue of the Americas, New York, NY,). See also, *Viewer's Guide*, "H.R. 6161: An Act Of Congress," written by Albert R. Hunt of *The Wall Street Journal*, edited by Jerry Colbert.

16. ibid.

17. Hon. Gary Hart, "Dear Colleague" letter to members of the US Senate, April 29, 1977.

18. US House of Representatives, *Clean Air Act Amendments of 1977*, Report by the Committee on Interstate and Foreign Commerce, (to Accompany H.R. 616), May 12, 1977, 95th Congress, 1st session, report no. 95-294, p. 240. See also, EPA report, "Automobile Emission Control—the Development Status, Trends, and Outlook as of December 1976," April 1977, pp. 3-18 to 3-23.

19. ibid, p. 244. See also, EPA report, "Cost/Technology Analysis," April 11, 1977 (revision copy), pp. 1-8.

20. "On Driving and Breathing," *The Washington Post*, May 19,1977, p. A-16.

21. Tomio Kubo, president, Mitsubishi Motors Corp., Tokyo, Japan, letter to Senator Edmund S. Muskie, Washington, DC, April 27, 1977.

22. ibid.

23. US Senate, Committee on Environment and Public Works, committee print, *A Legislative History of the Clean Air Act Amendments of 1977*, prepared by the Environmental Policy Division of the Congressional Research Service, Library of Congress, for the Committee on Public Works and the Environment, August 1978, volume 3, serial no. 95-16, pp. 744-745.

24. "GM Chairman on Issue of 'Clean Cars,'" *The Washington Star*, June 14, 1977, p. A-1.

25. "GM Unveils Plan to Phase in New Device for Cleaner Air on All Its Autos by 1982," *The Wall Street Journal*, May 24, 1977, p. 5

26. US Senate, *A Legislative History of the Clean Air Act Amendments of 1977*, p. 749.

27. ibid.

28. "On Driving and Breathing," *The Washington Post*, May 19, 1977, p. A-16.

29. "Major Clean Air Amendments Enacted," House floor action, *1977 CQ Almanac*, p. 638.

30. Philip Shabecoff, "House Vote Delays and also Weakens Curb on Auto Fumes," *The New York Times*, May 27, 1977.

31. US House of Representatives, *Clean Air Act Amendments of 1977* (report to accompany H.R. 616), pp. 252-265.

32. "Auto Workers, Manufacturers and Dealers United . . . To Dilute Auto Standards in House Clean Air Bill," *1977 CQ Almanac*, p. 637.

33. Shabecoff, "House Vote Delays and also Weakens Curb on Auto Fumes," p. A-1.

34. Ron Sarro, "Detroit Wins Big on Pollution," *The Washington Star*, May 27, 1977, p. A-2.

35. Mary Russell, "House Votes to Weaken Clean Air Act Revisions," *The Washington Post*, May 27, 1977, p. A-5.

36. Shabecoff, "House Vote Delays and also Weakens Curb on Auto Fumes," p. A-1.

37. Spencer Rich, "President Opposes Auto Cleanup Delay," *The Washington Post*, June 9, 1977, p. A-2.

38. Spencer Rich, "Carter: Victories on Air," *The Washington Post*, June 10, 1977, p. A-1.

39. Lee Dembart and Lawrence Fellows, "All Three States Are Doing What They Can for Clean Air," *The New York Times*, June 19, 1977, section 3, p. 6.

40. US Senate, *A Legislative History of The Clean Air Act Amendments of 1977*, p. 707.

41. Manufacturers of Emission Controls Association, "Demonstration Tour of Automobile Pollution Controls," 1977, Appendix, Pollution Charts & Graphs by city, Washington DC, March 10, 1978.

42. US House of Representatives, *Clean Air Act Amendments of 1977*, (report to accompany H.R. 6161), p. 253. See also, EPA report, "Air Quality and Health Effects of Alternate Exhaust Emission Standards for Light Duty Vehicles," March 21, 1977.

43. George Will, "Another Setback in the Quest for Clean Air," *The Washington Post*, June 26, 1977.

44. Thomas Love and John Holusha, "Automakers at Fault on Emissions—Hart," *The Washington Star*, July 15, 1977, p. A-2.

45. ibid.

46. ibid.

47. "Carter Urges Action on Emission Guides for '78 Model Autos," *The Wall Street Journal*, July 27, 1977, p. 2.

48. "Major Clean Air Amendments Enacted," conference action, *1977 CQ Almanac*, pp. 643-645.

49. ibid, p. 645.

50. ibid.

51. United Press International, "Hill Agreement Averts Auto Industry Crisis," *The Washington Star*, August 3, 1977, p. A-1.

52. Dick Kirschten, "The Clean Air Conference—Something For Everybody," *National Journal*, August 13, 1977, p. 1262.

53. "Major Clean Air Amendments Enacted," p. 645.

54. ibid.

55. ibid.

56. Arlen J. Large, "Conferees Agree to Delay Curbs on Car Emissions," *The Wall Street Journal*, August 4, 1977, p. 3.

57. "Major Clean Air Amendments Enacted," final action, *1977 CQ Almanac*, p. 646.

## CHAPTER 8

1. Thomas Love, "Recall of 1 Car in 5 May Cost Buyers $120 Million," *Washington Star*, May 11, 1978, p. B-5.

2. Letter of New Jersey resident, Charles E. Archbald, II, of Mantoloking, NJ, to Ralph Nader, January 17, 1974.

3. William D. Ruckelshaus, administrator, US Environmental Protection Agency, Washington, DC, letter to automobile manufacturers, July 12, 1972.

4. Warren Brown and Pierre Thomas, "Emissions Case Costs GM Fine, Cadillac Recall," *The Washington Post*, December 1, 1995, p. A-1.

5. Phil Frame, "Procedural Quirks Blamed for Cadillac's EPA Fines," *Automotive News*, December 18, 1995, p. 8.

6. Warren Brown and Pierre Thomas, "Emissions Case Costs GM Fine, Cadillac Recall," p. A-1.

7. Frame, "Procedural Quirks Blamed for Cadillac's EPA Fines," p. 8.

8. Brown and Thomas, "Emissions Case Costs GM Fine, Cadillac Recall," p. A-1.

9. ibid.

10. Phil Frame, "Fiend or Friend? GM Boils after Skewering by Feds," *Automotive News*, December 4, 1995, pp. 4, 45.

11. ibid.

12. Frame, "Procedural Quirks Blamed for Cadillac's EPA Fines," p. 8.

13. Judith Robinson, "Many New Cars Fail Federal Pollution Tests; Agencies Seek Added Controls," *National Journal*, April 11, 1970, pp. 754-756.

14. ibid.

15. Robert Harris, director, Bureau of Abatement and Control, and Paul Spaite, director, Bureau of Engineering and Physical Sciences, National Air Pollution Control Administration, confidential report to Commissioner John T. Middleton, October, 13, 1969.

16. Senator Edmund S. Muskie, letter to Hon. Elmer B. Staats, comptroller general of the US General Accounting Office, Washington, DC, May 25, 1972.

17. US General Accounting Office, *Examination into the Adequacy of the Environmental Protection Agency's Motor Vehicle Certification Activities*, June 12, 1972.

18. ibid.

19. Unless otherwise noted below, this section is based on Russell Mokhiber's "Ford and Emissions Testing," chapter 13 in, *Corporate Crime and Violence*, Sierra Club Books: San Francisco, 1988, pp. 207-211.

20. Text of Henry Ford II's speech at International Conference on Transportation and Environment, May 31, 1972.

21. "Court Fines Ford $7 Million in Suit in Pollution Test," *The New York Times*, February 14, 1973, p. 1.

22. Robert W. Irwin, "Chrysler Working on Recall," *Automotive News*, March 7, 1974

23. "Chrysler to Recall '73 Models to Fix Pollution Device," *The Wall Street Journal*, March 7, 1974, p. A-2.

24. "Ford Models Fail Auto Pollution Tests," *National Journal*, February 12, 1977, p. 260, and "EPA Orders Ford Motor Co. to Stop Making Granada and Monarch Models," *The Washington Post*, February 1977.

25. ibid, "EPA Orders Ford Motor Co. To Stop Making Granada And Monarch Models."

26. "Ford Motor Company Ordered to Recall 21,000 Cars for Nitrogen Oxides Emissions," *Environment Reporter*, June 10, 1977, p. 222.

27. Joseph M. Callahan, "Tightening the Emissions Screws," *Automotive Industries*, September 15, 1977, pp. 24-25.

28. ibid.

29. ibid.

30. United Press International, "EPA Demands Chrysler Recall," *The Washington Star*, December 11, 1976, p. A-11

31. *Chrysler Corporation, Petitioner v. United States Environmental Protection Agency and Douglas M. Costle, Administrator, Respondents*, no. 78-2273, US Court of Appeals, District of Columbia Circuit, 203 US App. DC 283; F.2d 865.

32. "Chrysler Loses Ruling in Test of EPA Order," *The Wall Street Journal*, February 13, 1978, p. A-5.

33. *Chrysler Corporation, Petitioner v. United States Environmental Protection Agency and Douglas M. Costle, Administrator, Respondents*, F.2d 865.

34. "Supreme Court Refuses to Review Air Act Case on Auto Maintenance," *Environment Reporter*, December 5, 1980, p. 1179.

35. Associated Press, "US Investigation of GM Seeks Pollution Violations," *The Washington Post*, May 5, 1978, p. F-5.

36. "EPA Probe of GM's Emission Tests Sent to Justice Agency," *The Wall Street Journal*, March 17, 1978, p. 7.

37. Leonard M. Apcar, "GM Sues EPA to Bar Spot-Checks of Cars to Predict Adherence To Pollution Rules," *The Wall Street Journal*, May 1, 1978, p. 4.

38. Associated Press, "US Investigation of GM Seeks Pollution Violations," p. F-5.

39. Thomas Love, "Recall of 1 Car in 5 May Cost Buyers $120 Million," *Washington Star*, May 11, 1978, p. B-5.

40. Thomas Love, "AMC Is Ordered to Recall 310,000 1976 Cars, Jeeps," *The Washington Star*, May 10, 1978, p. A-17

41. "US to Recall All '76 AMCs for Faulty Emission Control," *The Washington Post*, May 10, 1978, p. A-6.

42. Love, "AMC Is Ordered to Recall 310,000 1976 Cars, Jeeps," p. A-17

43. ibid.

44. Thomas C. Austin, deputy executive director, Air Resources Board, California, letter to Eric O. Stork, deputy assistant administrator for Mobile Source Air Pollution Control, US Environmental Protection Agency, February 10, 1978.

45. ibid.

46. T.M. Fisher, General Motors, director, Automotive Emission Control, environmental activities staff, General Motors Technical Center, Warren, MI, (letter to selected local air pollution control officials), February 14, 1983.

47. ibid.

48. Andy Pasztor, "GM's 700,000 Recall Is Reinstated by Appeals Panel Ruling on Pollution," *The Wall Street Journal*, October 29, 1984.

49. Helen Kahn, "GM Recall Case Needs Second Look," *Automotive News*, December 1983.

50. Warren Brown, "Court Expands Authority of EPA to Recall Autos," *The Washington Post*, September 8, 1984.

51. Andy Pasztor, "Court Rules Auto Makers Must Repair Free Pollution-Control Systems on Older Cars," *The Wall Street Journal*, September 10, 1984.

52. "High Court Won't Hear Appeal on Recall of 1975 Cadillacs," Dow Jones News Service-*Wall Street Journal*, April 29, 1985.

53. Marc Ross, Rob Goodwin, and Rick Watkins, physics department, University of Michigan; Michael Q. Wang, Argonne National Laboratory, and Tom Wenzel, Lawrence Berkeley Laboratory, *Real World Emissions from Model Year 1993, 2000 and 2010 Passenger Cars*, November 1995.

54. Marc Ross, "Why Cars Aren't as Clean as We Think," *Technology Review*, February/March 1994, p. 72.

CHAPTER 9

*Sidebars*

1. "Our Japanese Strategy"
Maryann Keller, *Rude Awakening*, pp. 84-88.
2. "They Keep Coming at You"
Author interview with Mike Walsh, Washington, DC, September 25, 1997.
3. "Albuquerque Blues"
"16 Areas Will Never Meet CO Standard if Auto Limit Is Relaxed, Coalition Says," *Environment Reporter*, December 11, 1981, pp. 974-975; "Senate Panel Delays Auto Standard Vote to Consider New Controversial Analysis," *Environment Reporter*, December 18, 1981, pp. 1004-1005; "Predictions of Benefits Speculative, Report on Carbon Monoxide Standard Says," *Environment Reporter*, January 29, 1982, pp. 1263-1263; and conversation with David Hawkins, NRDC, Washington, DC, September 17, 1997.

1. Lee Iacocca with William Novak, *Iacocca: An Autobiography*, Bantam: New York, 1984, p. 239.

2. ibid, p. 227.

3. ibid, p. 230.

4. ibid, pp. 232-233.

5. ibid, pp. 235-236.

6. ibid, pp. 234-235.

7. ibid, pp. 238-239.

8. Interview with Leon Billings, Washington, DC, April 8, 1997.

9. Flink, *The Automobile Age*, pp. 339-340.

10. Mark Rechtin, "Import Restraints Proved to Be Political, Not Practical," *Automotive News*, June 26, 1996, p. 144.

11. Flink, *The Automobile Age*, p. 342.

12. *The US Automobile Industry, 1980*, Report to the President from the Secretary of Transportation, January 1981.

13. Melissa Merson, "Environmental Regulation of the Automobile," *Environment Reporter*, Bureau of National Affairs, Inc., monograph no. 31, December 17, 1982, pp. 48-49.

14. ibid.

15. William C. Chapman, director of technical liaison, government relations, General Motors, Washington DC, letter to Jim J. Tozzi, assistant director for Regulatory and Information Policy, US Office of Management and Budget, Washington, DC, January 28, 1981.

16. Melissa Merson, "Environmental Regulation of the Automobile," pp. 48-49.

17. Jonathan Lash (with Katherine Gillman and David Sheridan), *Season of Spoils: The Story of the Reagan Administration's Attack on the Environment*, New York: Pantheon Books, 1984, pp 22-23.

18. Remarks of Boyden Gray, *Transcription of Hall of Flags Reg. Reform Briefing*, April 10, 1980, p. 20; reprinted in, "Role of OMB in Regulation," Hearing Before the Subcommittee on Oversight and Investigations, House Energy and Commerce Committee, No. 97-70, June 18, 1981, p. 90

19. "GM Proposed Air Act Amendments Give Far Greater Compliance Flexibility," *Environment Reporter*, April 3, 1981, p. 2170.

20. Philip Shabecoff, "General Motors Urges Revamping of Clean Air Act," *The New York Times*, April 1, 1981.

21. "Administration Proposes Rule Changes It Estimates Would Save $800 Million," *Environment Reporter*, April 10, 1981, p. 2188.

22. The White House, *Actions to Help the US Auto Industry*, April 6, 1981, attachment A: Regulatory Relief for the Auto Industry, Notice of Intent Transmitted to Federal Register on April 6, 1981, by Acting EPA Administrator Walter C. Barber, Jr., pp. A4-A27.

23. "Administration Proposes Rule Changes It Estimates Would Save $800 Million," p. 2188.

24. Testimony of George Eads, General Motors, "Role of OMB in Regulation," Hearing before the Subcommittee on Oversight and Investigations, House Energy and Commerce Committee, No. 97-70, June 18, 1981, p. 15.

25. Jonathan Lash (with Katherine Gillman and David Sheridan), *Season of Spoils*, p. 27.

26. 1981 *CQ Almanac*, p. 511.

27. "Pollution Control Manufacturers Oppose Relaxing Air Act Requirements," *Environment Reporter*, May 22, 1981, pp. 131-132.

28. Melissa Merson, "Environmental Regulation of the Automobile," p. 51.

29. 1981 *CQ Almanac*, p. 511.

30. Bill Keller, "Auto Firms Find Slow Going for Changes in Clean Air Law," *Congressional Quarterly Weekly Report*, December 12, 1981, p. 2444.

31. ibid.

32. The Harris Survey, 1981, no. 47, June 1981.

33. Kathy Koch, "Senate Committee Begins Clean Air Revision," *Congressional Quarterly Weekly Report*, November 7, 1981, p. 2191.

34. Roger Smith, chairman, General Motors, speech before the Engineering Society of Detroit, September 1981, reprinted in part as "GM On Clean Air" in *The New York Times*, October 4, 1981.

35. ibid.

36. Bill Keller, "Auto Firms Find Slow Going for Changes in Clean Air Law," p. 2444.

37. Andy Pasztor, "Attempts to Soften Basic Clean-Air Laws May Bring Major Struggle, Some Changes," *The Wall Street Journal*, May 8, 1981, p. 52.

38. Koch, "Senate Committee Begins Clean Air Revision," p. 2191.

39. Governor John D. Rockefeller IV, chairman, Committee on Energy and Environment, National Governors' Association, Washington, DC, letter to Hon. Robert T. Stafford, chairman, Committee on Environment and Public Works, United States Senate, December 10, 1981.

40. General Motors, "Clean Air Amendments: General Motors Urges Prompt Enactment of Provisions Contained in the Luken-Madigan Bill, HR 5252," March 10, 1982, GM/WCC.

41. "Congress Begins Rewrite of Clean Air Act," *CQ Almanac*, pp. 508-509.

42. General Motors, "Clean Air Amendments," March 10, 1982.

43. "Congress Begins Rewrite of Clean Air Act," pp. 508-509.

44. General Motors, "Clean Air Amendments," March 10, 1982.

45. ibid.

46. Frank O'Donnell, "Tailpipe Johnny," *The Nation*, April 21, 1982, p. 10.

47. General Motors, "Clean Air Amendments," March 10, 1982.

48. "Congress Begins Rewrite of Clean Air Act," pp. 508-509.

49. "Extension Urged of Ban on 'Smog Conspiracy,'" *Automotive News*, November 14, 1977, p. 13; "Adams Presses for Renewal of Automotive Consent Decree," *Automotive News*, June 26, 1978, p. 7; Jake Kelderman, "US Seeks to Extend Smog-Conspiracy Rule," *Automotive News*, November 6, 1978, p. 1.

50. The events leading up to the legal actions began with GM agreeing to sell Chrysler some prototype emissions and safety technology—an action, at least for the emissions equipment, which appeared to contravene the stipulations of the decree. The Justice Department, however, announced it would not challenge the GM-Chrysler arrangement. Within days, Ford Motor Co. then petitioned the US District Court renewal of the decree citing the GM-Chrysler deal. The court then agreed with Ford, overturning the decree's extension. This ruling, however, was appealed, but the appeal was not decided until April 1981 when the Court of Appeals reversed the District Court, thus upholding the decree for ten more years.

51. Merrill Brown, "Consent Decree Ended after Reagan Request," *The Washington Post*, September 4, 1981, p. D-11; Merrill Brown, "Antitrust Chief Amenable to Joint Auto Ventures," *The Washington Post*, September 5, 1981, p. C-7; "Administration Eyes Vacating 'Smog Conspiracy' Decree," *Automotive News*, September 14, 1981, p. 6; "DOJ Drops Consent Decree Provisions Allowing Automakers to Share Emission Control Research," *Air/Water Pollution Report*, September 14, 1981, p. 335; "At a Glance," *National Journal*, September 12, 1981, p. 1650; and Center for Auto Safety, "History of Smog Conspiracy Consent Decree," August 15, 1982.

52. Helen Kahn, "Suit Tries to Revive 'Conspiracy' Ban," *Automotive News*, October 19, 1981, p. 3; UPI, "Auto Safety Unit Suing over Emissions Decree," *The New York Times*, October 20, 1981, p. C-4; Alan Parachini, "Smog Device Competition Sought," *Los Angeles Times*, October 21, 1981, section IV, p. 1; "Court Stalls Easing of Curb on Research Among Auto Firms," *The Wall Street Journal*, November 25, 1981, p. 19; Helen Kahn, "Easing of Smog Decree Is Up in the Air Again," *Automotive News*, November 30, 1981, p. 2; "Judge Requires Notice For Consent Decree," *Legal Times*, December 7, 1981, p. 6; David Ranh, "Consent Decree Changes Made Tougher," *The National Law Journal*, December 21, 1981, p. 5; Comments of Clarence Ditlow III, director, Center for Auto Safety, Washington, DC, Re: *United States v. Motor Vehicle Manufactures Association*: Proposed Modified Final Judgment and Competitive

Impact Statement (47 Fed. Reg. 7529), submitted to Bernard N. Hollander, chief, Judgment Enforcement Section, Antitrust Division, Department of Justice, Washington, D.C., April 20, 1982, 23 pp; and, letter and comments of James D. Boyd, executive director, California Air Resources Board, Sacramento, Re: *US v. Motor Vehicle Manufacturers Association, et al.* submitted to Bernard N. Hollander, chief, Judgment Enforcement Section, Antitrust Division, Department of Justice, Washington, DC, April 20, 1982, 12 pp.

53. "Smog Conspiracy Ruling Extended for 10 Years," *Automotive News*, April 16, 1979, p. 7; Leonard M. Apcar, "Data-Sharing Bar on Auto Makers to Be Restudied," *The Wall Street Journal*, June 8, 1979, p. 4; Helen Kahn, "'Smog Conspiracy' Decree to Die," *Automotive News*, July 23, 1979, p. 1; Stephen Duthie, "Auto Firms Win Right to Share Technology," *Detroit News*, July 19, 1979, p. 1-A; letter of Joyce K. Kinnard, staff attorney and Clarence Ditlow III, executive director, Center for Auto Safety, Washington, DC, to: William F. Baxter, assistant attorney general, Antitrust Division, Department of Justice, Washington, DC, September 3, 1981; and press release, "Justice Department Secretly Drops Consent Decree;" and, Center for Auto Safety, "History of Smog Conspiracy Consent Decree," August 15, 1982.

54. Letter of Kingsley Macomber, general counsel, California Air Resources Board, Sacramento, CA, to Mr. John H. Shenefield, assistant attorney general, Antitrust Division, US Department of Justice, August 21, 1978.

55. Letter of James D. Boyd, executive officer, California Air Resources Board, Sacramento, CA, to Mr. Bernard M. Hollander, chief, Judgement Enforcement Section, Antitrust Division, US Department of Justice, Re: *United States v. Motor Vehicle Manufacturers Association, et al.*, April 20, 1982, p. 6.

56. Letter of Representative Henry Waxman to US Justice Department, May 19, 1978.

57 Author conversation with Clarence Ditlow, Washington, DC, June 12, 1997.

## CHAPTER 10

1. Robert A. Lutz, *Guts: The Seven Laws of Business that Made Chrysler the World's Hottest Car Company*, New York: John Wiley & Sons, Inc, 1998, p. 16-17.

2. Keller, *Rude Awakening*, pp. 169-170.

3. Peter Behr, "Auto Maker Seeks Breakthrough," *The Washington Post*, June 9, 1985, p. H-1.

4. Keller, *Rude Awakening*, p. 175.

5. Paul Ingrassia and Joseph P. White, *Comeback: The Fall & Rise of the American Automobile Industry*, New York: Simon & Schuster, 1994, pp-91-92, p. 78.

6. ibid, pp. 111-112.

7. Alex Taylor III, "US Cars Come Back," *Fortune*, November 16, 1992, p. 55.

8. Doron P. Levin, *Behind the Wheel at Chrysler: The Iacocca Legacy*, New York: Harcourt Brace & Co., 1995, pp. 91-92.

9. Taylor, "US Cars Come Back," p. 62

10. ibid.

11. Keller, *Rude Awakening*, pp. 186-187.

12. Ingrassia and White, *Comeback*, pp. 225, 230.

13. ibid, p. 218.

14. Taylor, "US Cars Come Back," p. 68.

15. Ingrassia and White, *Comeback*, pp. 93, 98.

16. ibid, p. 80.

17. Taylor, "US Cars Come Back," p. 62.

18. ibid.

19. Lutz, *Guts: The Seven Laws of Business*, p. 16-17.

20. Peter Passell, "Capitalism Victorious (Thanks, Everyone)," *The New York Times*, Money & Business, May 10, 1998, section 3, p. 1.

21. John Holusha, "GM Earns $1.3 Billion in Quarter," *The New York Times*, February 8, 1984, p. D-1.

22. Mark Rechtin, "Import Restraints Proved to Be Political, Not Practical," *Automotive News*, June 26, 1996, p. 144.

23 *Los Angeles Times*, February 21, 1985 and March 2, 1985; William J. Hampton, "Can Detroit Cope This Time?" *Business Week*, April 22, 1985; and Flink, *The Automobile Age*, p. 343.

24. Taylor, "US Cars Come Back," p. 57.

25. ibid.

26. ibid, p. 58.

27. Micheline Maynard, *Collision Course: Inside the Battle for General Motors*, New York: Carol Publishing Group, 1995, p. 10.

28. Motor Vehicle Manufacturers Association, *Position on 1983 Clean Air Act Amendments*, June 10, 1983, 6 pp.

29. General Motors, *Modifying the Clean Air Act: The GM Position*, spring 1983.

30. T. M. Fisher, director, automotive emission control, GM Corporation, GM Technical Center, Warren, MI, letter to local air pollution official, February 14, 1983.

31. Democratic National Committee, Campaign '88, "Bush's Top 100 Environmental Hits," September 1988, p. 2, and Hawley Truax, "Does This Man Deserve Your Vote? George Bush Is Courting the Environmental Vote," *Environmental Action*, September 1988.

32. Robert E. Taylor and Andy Pasztor, "Reagan Administration's Deregulation Offensive 'Stopped in Its Tracks' on Environmental Issues," *The Wall Street Journal*, January 8, 1985.

33. Taylor and Pasztor, "Reagan Administration's Deregulation Offensive 'Stopped in Its Tracks' On Environmental Issues," January 8, 1985

34. Bruce Stokes, "Auto Glut," *National Journal*, September 23, 1989, p. 2321.

## CHAPTER 11

1. Robert E. Taylor, "Despite Nearly 2 Decades of Federal Efforts, Many in the US Still Breathe Unhealthy Air," *The Wall Street Journal*, April 6, 1987, p. 56.

2. ibid.

3. Thomas J. Knudson, "Western Cities Move Aggressively to Clear up Smoggy Skies," *The New York Times*, November 24, 1987, p. A-16.

4. ibid.

5. ibid.

6. ibid.

7. ibid.

8. Michael Weisskopf, "Under EPA, A Regulatory Breakdown," *The Washington Post*, June 4, 1989, p. A-1.

9. ibid.

10. ibid.

11. Robert E. Taylor, "Despite Nearly 2 Decades of Federal Efforts, Many in the US Still Breathe Unhealthy Air," p. 56.

12. Janet Braunstein, "Vehicle Industry Fighting Proposed Clean Air Act," Associated Press, November 18, 1987.

13. ibid.

14. Cohen, *Washington At Work*, pp. 124-125.

15. ibid.

16. Alexandra Allen, "The Auto's Assault on the Atmosphere," *Multinational Monitor*, January-February 1990, pp. 25-26.

17. Cohen, *Washington At Work*, pp. 51-55.

18. ibid.

## CHAPTER 12

1. Gregg Easterbrook, *A Moment on the Earth*, New York: Viking-Penguin, 1995, p. 196.

2. Philip Shabecoff, "President Urges Steps to Tighten Law on Clean Air," *The New York Times*, June 13, 1989, p. A-1; Barbara Rosewicz, "Bush Proposes Revision of Clean-Air Law that Would Cut Acid Rain by 2000," *The Wall Street Journal*, June 13, 1989, p. A-3.

3. Rosewicz, "EPA Supports Alternate Fuels Use in Autos," *The Wall Street Journal*, June 2, 1989, p. A-3.

4. Philip Shabecoff, "California Acts to Promote Switch from Gasoline to Methanol Fuel," *The New York Times*, May 23, 1987, p. 1.

5. Rosewicz, "Bush Proposes Revision of Clean-Air Law," p. A-3.

6. Jeff Alson, "The Methanol Debate: Clearing the Air," in Wilfrid L. Kohl (ed), *Methanol as an Alterative Fuel Choice: An Assessment*, 1990, p. 406.

7. Representative Henry Waxman, chairman, House Health and Environment Subcommittee, "Clean Air Bill Doesn't Go far Enough," *The Wall Street Journal*, 1989.

8. Philip Shabecoff, "Draft of Anti-Pollution Bill Falls Short, Critics Say," *The New York Times*, July 12, 1989, p. B-5.

9. Larry Margasak, Associated Press, "Subcommittee Agrees to Tighten Car Pollution Standards," October 2, 1989.

10. ibid.

11. "Clean-Air Bill Moves in Both Chambers," *1989 CQ Almanac*, p. 667.

12. Matthew L. Wald, "ARCO Offers New Gasoline to Cut up to 15% of Old Cars' Pollution," *The New York Times*, August 16, 1989, p. 1.

13. ibid.

14. Easterbrook, *A Moment on the Earth*, p. 197.

15. Patrick Lee, "Arco to Introduce Low-Emissions Gas to Replace Leaded Regular on Sept. 1," *The Los Angeles Times*, August 16, 1989, part IV, p. 3.

16. Easterbrook, *A Moment on the Earth*, p. 196.

17. Lee, "Arco to Introduce Low-Emissions Gas to Replace Leaded Regular on Sept. 1," Part IV, p. 3.

18. Wald, "ARCO Offers New Gasoline to Cut up to 15% of Old Cars' Pollution," p. 1.

19. Easterbrook, *A Moment on the Earth*, p. 196.

20. Cohen, *Washington at Work*, p. 158.

21. Margaret E. Kriz, "Politics at the Pump," *National Journal*, p. 1331.

22. Michael Weisskopf, "Key Provision of Bush Clean-Air Bill under Siege," *The Washington Post*, October 10, 1989, p. A-4.

23. Michael Weisskopf, "House Panel Votes to Weaken Clean-Air Bill," *The Washington Post*, October 12, 1989, p. 1-A.

24. Steven Thomma, "Legislators Scrap Provision to Require 'Clean Fuel' Cars," *Detroit Free Press*, October 12, 1989, p. 1-A.

25. "Clean-Air Bill Moves In Both Chambers," *1989 CQ Almanac*, p. 671.

26. George Hager, "Closed-Door Talks on Clean Air Anger Environmental Groups," *Congressional Quarterly*, February 10, 1990, p. 386.

27. Richard E. Ayres, "Clean Air: What's the Deal?" letter to the editor, *The Washington Post*, March 17, 1990, p. A-28.

28. George Hager, "Senate-White House Deal Breaks Clean-Air Logjam," *CQ Weekly Report*, March 3, 1990, p. 654.

29. George Hager, "Clean-Air Deal Survives First Senate Assaults," *CQ Weekly*, March 10, 1990, p. 739.

30. Phil Kuntz, "The 'Super Tuesday' of Clean Air . . . Nothing but a Quirky Footnote," *CQ Weekly Report*, March 24, 1990, pp. 902-903.

31. ibid.

32. Cohen, *Washington at Work*, p. 163.

33. Gary C. Bryner, *Blue Skies, Green Politics: The Clean Air Act of 1990 and Its Implementation*, Washington, DC: CQ Press, 1995, pp. 124-125, and Kriz, "Politics At The Pump," p. 1329.

34. Cohen, *Washington at Work*, p. 163.

35. Kriz, "Politics At The Pump," p. 1331.

36. ibid, p. 1329.

37. ibid, p. 1330.

38. ibid.

39. Representative Henry Waxman, Gregory S. Wetstone, and Philip S. Barnett, "Cars, Fuels, and Clean Air: A Review of Title II of the Clean Air Act Amendments of 1990," *Environmental Law*, 21: 1947 (1991).

40. Kriz, "Politics at the Pump," p. 1332.

41. ibid.

42. Cohen, *Washington at Work*, p. 171.

43. "In Speedier Process, House Yields Clean Air Bill Close to Senate's," *Inside EPA*, June 1, 1990, p. 11

44. "Interest Groups to 'Pick And Choose' Among Senate/House CAA Bills," *Inside EPA*, June 1. 1990, pp. 12-13.

45. Allan R. Gold, "New York Wants Cleanest Air Act," *The New York Times*, September 23, 1990, p. 35.

46. Allan R. Gold, "New York Sets Stricter Rules on Emissions," *The New York Times*, September 28, 1990, p. B-1.

47. 1990 *CQ Almanac*, p. 247.

48. Keith Schneider, "Congressional Negotiators Agree on New Curbs on Car Emissions," *The New York Times*, October 11, 1990, p. A-22.

49. 1990 *CQ Almanac*, p. 246.

50. Roberta J. Nichols, "The Transition to New Sources of Energy Using Sustainable Energy Strategies," paper presented at "Car Talks" workshop, Washington, DC, undated.

51. 1990 *CQ Almanac*, pp. 246-247.

52. Alyson Pytte, "Clean Air Conferees to Tackle But Differences Loom," *CQ Weekly*, October 6, 1990, p. 3210.

53. Cohen, *Washington at Work*, pp. 183-84.

54. Francesca Lyman, "The Gassing of America: A High-Octane Campaign Against Toxic Fuel Additives," *The Washington Post*, April 13, 1990.

55. J.M. Colucci, General Motors Research Laboratories, Warren, MI, and J.J. Wise, Mobil Research and Development Corporation, Princeton, NJ, "Auto/Oil Air Quality Improvement Research Program," December 18, 1990, p. 2.

56. Daniel Sperling, *Future Drive*, Washington, DC: Island Press, 1995, p. 26.

57. Nadis and MacKenzie, *Car Trouble*, p. 63

## CHAPTER 13

*Sidebars*

1. "Toyota vs. Ford: 1988"
Statement of Clarence M. Ditlow III, director, Center for Auto Safety, before the Consumer Subcommittee of the Senate Committee on Commerce, Science and Transportation, Washington, DC, May 2, 1989, p. 10.

2. "A Sordid Tale"
Statement of Joan Claybrook, president, Public Citizen, on Department of Transportation Manipulation of Safety Crash Test Data, National Press Club, Washington DC, October 28, 1991; press release, Public Citizen, Washington, DC, "Department of Transportation Manipulated Crash Test Data, Violated Lobbying Law to Discredit Fuel Economy Bill," October 28, 1991; Center for Auto Safety, Washington, DC, "Statement of Clarence Ditlow on DOT CAFE Cover-Up," October 28, 1991.

3. "Clarence M. Ditlow"
Author conversations with Clarence Ditlow, 1996-1999; Kirk Victor, "Fueling the Debate over Auto Safety," *National Journal*, August 18, 1990, p. 2025; "Chrysler Given Safety Lecture," *The New York Times*, March 8, 1991, p. D-3; Matthew L. Wald, "Detroit May Not Like Him, but He's the Crash Dummy's Friend," *The New York Times*, October 16, 1997; Robert D. Hershey Jr., "Center for Auto Safety's Point Man," *The New York Times*, p. 48; John E. Peterson, "20 Years Later, Auto Safety Center Keeps Fight Alive, *Detroit News*, p. 1-E.

1. National Highway Traffic Safety Administration, "Passenger Automobile and Light Truck Average Fuel Economy Standards; Model Year 1985 and Beyond," *Federal Register*, vol. 48, no. 16, January 25, 1981, pp. 8056-8062.

2. Christopher Conte, "Ford, GM Ask US to Ease Standards for Auto Fuel Use," *The Wall Street Journal*, March 6, 1985, p. 26.

3. ibid.

4. Warren Brown, "EPA Relaxes Fuel Standards for Ford, GM," *The Washington Post*, June 27, 1985, p. E-1.

5. Clarence Ditlow, director, Center for Auto Safety, statement before the US Department of Transportation, Washington, DC, August 8, 1985, p. 9.

6. James Baron, "Should Car Mileage Limits Be Kept?" *The New York Times*, June 17, 1985, p. A-16.

7. John D. Withrow, executive vice president, product development, Chrysler Corporation, Statement before the National Highway Transportation Safety Administration, Department of Transportation, Public Meeting on Passenger Automobile Average Fuel Economy Standards—Model Year 1986, Washington DC, August 8, 1985, p. 4.

8. Maria Recio and William J. Hampton, "The EPA Gives a Little on Gas Mileage," *Business Week*, July 15, 1985, p. 38.

9. Helen Kahn, "Battle over '86 CAFE Heats up," *Automotive News*, August 12, 1985, p. 2.

10. Linda G. Kincaid, "Corporate Average Fuel Economy Standards," Kennedy School of Government Case Program, Harvard College, C16-86-670, 1986, p. 8.

11. Hobart Rowen, "Cop-Out on Fuel Efficiency," *The Washington Post*, July 25, 1985, p. A-25; and Helen Kahn, "Battle over '86 CAFE Heats up," *Automotive News*, p. 2.

12. James Mateja, "Fine Has Iacocca Calling Foul on Foes," *Chicago Tribune*, September 20, 1985, p. C-3.

13. Warren Brown, "Fuel Economy Standards Lowered," *The Washington Post*, October 2, 1985, p. C-4.

14. Warren Brown, "Inside: National Highway Traffic Safety Administration Auto Fuel Economy Rule May Keep Backing up," *The Washington Post*, October 4, 1985, p. A-21.

15. Warren Brown, "Ford Threatens US over Fuel Economy Rules," *The Washington Post*, November 2, 1985, p. A-1.

16. Associated Press, "Ford Threatens to Build Big Car Engines Abroad," *Chicago Tribune*, August 27, 1985, p. C-7, and Richard Johnson, "Big Fords May Become 'Imports' to Meet CAFE," *Automotive News*, September 2, 1985.

17. Brown, "Ford Threatens US over Fuel Economy Rules," p. A-1.

18. Jacob M. Schlesinger, "Auto Companies' Lobbying Drive Aims to Poke Widest Loophole Yet in US Fuel Economy Law," *The Wall Street Journal*, October 1, 1986, p. 68.

19. ibid.

20. Warren Brown, "Fuel Standards Eased on '87, '88 Model Cars," *The Washington Post*, October 3, 1986, p. F-1.

21. Associated Press, "Ecologists Warn against Lowering of Fuel Standards," *Detroit Free Press*, September 14, 1988.

22. Marjorie Sorge, "Stempel: Mileage Rules Risk Jobs," *The Detroit News*, September 15, 1988, and "Geoff Sundstrom and Dutch Mandel, "Stempel: 4 GM Plants Periled if CAFE Rises," *Automotive News*, September 19, 1988.

23. Associated Press, "GM, Ford Oppose New Fuel Standard," *The Detroit Free Press*, September 18, 1988.

24. Robert C. Stempel, "Ease Up on Mileage Requirements," *USA Today*, September 21, 1988, p. 6-A.

25. John Holusha, "Government Agrees to Relaxation of Auto Mileage Standard for '89," *The New York Times*, October 4, 1988, p. 1.

26. C. Kenneth Orski, Alan Altshuler, and Daniel Ross, "The Future of the Automobile," *Transatlantic Perspectives*, March 1980, pp. 4-8

27. "DOT Decision on 1990 CAFE Level Expected this Week, Senators Told," Bureau of National Affairs newsletter, May 3, 1989.

28. Paul Ingrassia and Joseph B. White, "Debate over Pollution and Global Warming Has Detroit Sweating," *The Wall Street Journal*, May 4, 1989, p. 1-A.

29. ibid.

30. Lindsay Chappell, "Suppliers Say US Car Fleet Can Get 41 MPG in 10 Years," *Automotive News*, August 21, 1989, p. 10.

31. ibid.

32. Alyson Pytte, "Japanese Drive a Hard Bargain on Emissions Standards," *CQ Weekly*, January 20, 1990, p. 165.

33. David Everett, "Citizens Campaign on Mileage Funded by Big 3," *Detroit Free Press*, March 10, 1990, p. 9-A.

34. ibid.

35. ibid.

36. ibid.

37. Paul A. Eisenstein, "New Focus on Fuel Efficiency?" *The Christian Science Monitor*, August 14, 1990, p. 9.

38. John H. Cushman, Jr., "Mileage Bill Gets a Lift in Senate," *The New York Times*, September 15, 1990, pp. 31, 35.

39. Kriz, "Going the Extra Mile," *National Journal*, May 11, 1991, p. 1096.

40. "Fuel Efficiency Effort Defeated in Senate," *1990 Congressional Quarterly Almanac*, p. 279.

41. US Public Interest Research Group, *More Waste: Keep Filling—Deceptive Gas Mileage Advertising By the Automobile Industry*, April 1991, p. 2.

42. ibid.

43. Kriz, "Going the Extra Mile," p. 1096.

44. United States Senate, Committee on Energy and Natural Resources, *The National Energy Security Act of 1991* (Appendices to parts 1, 2, 3 and 4), 102nd Congress, 1st Session, February 28 and March 20, 1991, S. Hrg. 102-5, pt. 14, p. 631.

45. Kriz, "Going the Extra Mile," pp. 1095, 1097.

46. United States Senate, Hearings Before the Subcommittee on the Consumer of the Committee on Commerce, Science and Transportation, *The Motor Vehicle Fuel Efficiency Act of 1991*, 102 Congress, 1st Session, February 21, 1991, p. 80.

47. Center for Auto Safety, *The Safe Road to Fuel Economy*, April 1991, p. 1.

48. Jill Abramson, "Car Firms Kick Lobbying Effort into High Gear in Bitter Fight over Fuel-Economy Legislation," *The Wall Street Journal*, September 20, 1991, p. A-14.

49. Micheline Maynard, "Automakers Push for Voice on New Rules," *USA Today*, June 12, 1991, p. 1-B.

50. Kriz, "Going the Extra Mile," p. 1097.

51. *PR Newswire*, April 4, 1991.

52. United States Senate, Hearings before the Subcommittee on the Consumer of the Committee on Commerce, Science, and Transportation, *The Motor Vehicle Fuel Efficiency Act of 1991*, 102nd Congress, 1st Session, February 21, 1991, p. 52.

53. *PR Newswire*, April 4, 1991.

54. Maureen Milford, "Gas Mileage Bill Crucial, Groups Say," *The News Journal* (Wilmington, DE), July 10, 1991, p. B-8.

55. John E. Peterson, "Group Cites Global Warming in Fuel-Economy Rule Plea," *Detroit News*, April 2, 1991.

56. Brooks Yeager, *Wasted Energy: A Report on the Reagan Administration's Energy Program*, Sierra Club, Washington DC, 1989, p. 18.

57. Holly Idelson, "Senate Panel Moves Energy Bill without Mileage Standards," May 25, 1991, *Congressional Quarterly Weekly Report*, pp. 1369-70.

58. Richard L. Berke, "Panel Backs Arctic Drilling, but Not Fuel-Efficient Cars," *The New York Times*, May 24, 1991, p. D-1.

59. ibid.

60. Jacob M. Schlesinger, "Japan Car Firms Unveil Engines Lifting Mileage," *The Wall Street Journal*, July 30, 1991, p. B-1.

61. David Sanger, "Fuel Efficiency: New Japan Coup?" *The New York Times*, July 31, 1991, p. D-1.

62. ibid.

63. Schlesinger, "Japan Car Firms Unveil Engines Lifting Mileage," p. B-1.

64. Bryan Gruley, "Environmentalists Poised to Kill CAFE Bill," Gannett News Service, October 14, 1991.

65. Max Gates, "Senate to Tackle Energy Bill, CAFE Standards," *Automotive News*, October 28, 1991.

66. Holly Idelson, "Energy Policy Filibuster in Senate Fuel for Efficiency Standards Debate," *Congressional Quarterly Weekly Report*, November 2, 1991, pp. 3192-3193.

67. ibid.

68. Barbara Rosewicz, "Opponents of Drilling in Arctic Refuge Derail Efforts to Enact Energy Policy," *The Wall Street Journal*, November 4, 1991, p. A-4.

69. Thomas W. Lippman, "Senate Votes to Abandon Energy Bill," *The Washington Post*, November 2, 1991, p. 1.

70. ibid.

71. ibid.

72. League of Conservation Voters, "1992 Presidential Profiles," and, Energy America, "Energy and the Environment," presidential candidate questionnaire, 1992.

73. Keith Schneider, "Bush Stance on Mileage Seems to Lag," *The New York Times*, October 21, 1992.

74. ibid, and, Sierra Club handout, "Bill Clinton Quotes on CAFE Standards," 1992.

75. Amory Lovins and L. Hunter Lovins have written and lectured extensively about the "Hypercar" idea. Their first work on this subject appeared in the summer 1991 and spring 1992 editions of the *Rocky Mountain Institute Newsletter* and the thirty-two-page paper, "Supercars: The Coming Light-Vehicle Revolution," (Publication T93-10), also available from the Rocky Mountain Institute. Subsequent to 1991-92, Amory and Hunter continued writing and speaking about the Hypercar, most notably, for example, in a January 1995 feature article in the *Atlantic Monthly*, "Reinventing the Wheels."

## CHAPTER 14

1. General Motors, news release, February 17, 1977.

2. Dick Russell, "LA's Positive Charge," *The Amicus Journal*, spring 1991, pp. 18-23.

3. ibid.

4. A. Rothenberg, "Informal Visit with Henry Ford," *Look*, May 28, 1968, pp. 92-96.

5. "Air Quality Act Amendments—Related Hearings," *1969 CQ Almanac*, p. 524.

6. General Motors, news release, February 17, 1977.

7. Shnayerson, *The Car That Could*, p. 7.

8. Shnayerson, *The Car That Could*, p. 85.

9. James M. Strock, California secretary for environmental protection, "Rules of the Road on the Drive to Clean Air," before the Institute of Business Law, Los Angeles, CA, November 14, 1995.

10. Richard W. Stevenson, "GM Displays the Impact, an Advanced Electric Car," *The New York Times*, January 4, 1990, p. D-1.

11. ibid.

12. Rick Wartzman, "GM Unveils Electric Car with Lots of Zip but also a Battery of Unsolved Problems," *The Wall Street Journal*, January 4, 1990, p. B-3.

13. Stevenson, "GM Displays the Impact, An Advanced Electric Car," p. D-1.

14. ibid.

15. Shnayerson, *The Car That Could*, p. 25.

16. Russell, "LA's Positive Charge," p. 21.

17. Richard W. Stevenson, "California to Get Tougher Air Rules," *The New York Times*, September 27, 1990, p. A-1.

18. Shnayerson, *The Car That Could*, p. 49.

19. ibid.

20. Stevenson, "California to Get Tougher Air Rules," p. A-1.

21. Philip Shabecoff, "EPA Seeks Delay in Using Sanctions of Pollution Law," *The New York Times*, November 18, 1987, p. A-1.

22. ibid.

23. Matthew L. Wald, "Northeast Opens Drive to Cut Back Ozone Pollution," *The New York Times*, November 21, 1987, p. A-1.

24. Matthew L. Wald, "How the Northeast Asserted Itself on Smog," *The New York Times*, June 11, 1989, p. E-5.

25. ibid.

26. Northeast States for Coordinated Air Use Management (NESCAUM), *An Evaluation of Adopting the California Mobile Source Control Program in the Eight Northeast States*, executive summary, April 1989, p. 2.

27. Renee Loth, "Strict Rules Gain on Auto Emissions," *The Boston Globe*, March 28, 1990, p. 56.

28. Scot Lehigh, "Two Environmental Bills Await Senate Action," *The Boston Globe*, December 4, 1990, p. 32.

29. Scot Lehigh, "Last Chance for 2 Key Bills," *The Boston Globe*, December 17, 1990, p. 21.

30. Matthew L. Wald, "12 States Consider Smog Curb," *The New York Times*, July 15, 1991, p. D-1.

31. Tom Johnson, "Auto Industry, Jersey Tussle on Smog Policy, *The Star-Ledger* (Newark, NJ), November 25, 1991.

32. ibid.

33. ibid.

34. ibid.

35. Matthew L. Wald, "Stricter Rules on Car Emissions Draw Opposition," *The New York Times*, October 1, 1991, p. B-3.

36. ibid.

37. Matthew L. Wald, "Pollution Limits Debated for Cars," *The New York Times*, December 21, 1991, p. Y- 17.

38. Kevin Sack, "Delay Sought for Limits on Pollution," *The New York Times*, March 24, 1992, p. B-6.

39. Sam Howe Verhovek, "Assembly Leaders Reject Delay Enforcing Auto Emissions Rules," *The New York Times*, June 12, 1992, p. B-5.

40. Amal Kumar Naj, "New York Adopts California's Rule on Auto Emissions," *The Wall Street Journal*, March 24, 1992, p. A-18.

41. John F. Harris and John Ward Anderson, "VA Senate Panel Kills Wilder Bill on Car Emissions," *The Washington Post*, February 11, 1992, p. B-1.

42. ibid.

43. Matthew L. Wald, "California's Pied Piper of Clean Air," *The New York Times*, September 13, 1992, Section 3, p. 1-F.

44. ibid.

45. Shnayerson, *The Car That Could*, p. 118.

46. Shnayerson, *The Car That Could*, p. 127.

47. Esther Scott, "Low Emission Vehicles; The Pursuit of a Regional Program," based on research by Sylvia Sensiper, for Arnold Howitt, executive director of the Taubman Center for State and Local Government, for use at the John F. Kennedy School of Government, Harvard University, 1997, p. 11.

48. David Woodruff, "Assault on Batteries," *Business Week*, November 29, 1993, p. 39.

49. Shnayerson, *The Car That Could*, p. 168.

50. "Big 3 Try to Put Breaks on Push for Electric Cars," *The Los Angeles Times*, October 23, 1993.

51. Scott, "Low Emission Vehicles," p. 15.

52. ibid.

53. Scott, "Low Emission Vehicles," p. 17.

54. David Everett, "Northeast Acts to Toughen Smog Curbs," *The Philadelphia Inquirer*, February 2, 1994, p. A-1.

55. Staff and wire reports, "Regional Panel Pushing for Stricter Auto Standards," *Bangor Daily News* February 2, 1994.

56. Oscar Suris, "Detroit Steps up Push for Delay on Electric Cars," *The Wall Street Journal*, February 7, 1994, p. A-4

57. Shnayerson, *The Car That Could*, p. 191.

58. Oscar Suris and Margaret A. Jacobs, "Court Decides New York May Adopts Clean-Air Rules Fought by Car Makers," *The Wall Street Journal*, February 11, 1994, p. A-14, and Peter Stone, "Automakers' Electric Shock," *National Journal*, May 21, 1994, p. 1178.

59. Bryner, *Blue Skies, Green Politics*, p. 223.

60. Shnayerson, *The Car That Could*, p. 222.

61. ibid.

62. Scott, "Low Emission Vehicles," p. 16.

63. Oscar Suris, "EPA Backs Auto-Emission Plan Sought by Northeast Despite Industry Protests," *The Wall Street Journal*, December 20, 1994, p. B-8.

64. Margaret A. Kriz, "Harry, Louise on the Road," *National Journal*, February 25, 1995, pp. 490-491.

65. ibid.

66. Robert J. Eaton, chairman and CEO, Chrysler Corporation, "To Our Shareholders," *1994 Report to Shareholders*, February 3, 1995, p. 3.

67. Nick Budnick, "Electric Smoke Screen," *Sacramento News & Review*, July 6, 1995, pp. 19-20.

68. Shnayerson, *The Car That Could*, p. 217.

69. ibid, p. 248.

70. Donald W. Nauss, "Big Three Escalate Attack on Electric Car," *The Los Angeles Times*, March 24, 1995, p. 1.

71. ibid.

72. Matthew L. Wald, "Road Gets Bumpy for Electric Car, and Presidential Politics Is Blamed," *The New York Times*, June 24, 1995, p. 48.

73. ibid.

74. "Gov. Weld Offers Detroit Delay in Electric-Car Plan," *The Wall Street Journal*, March 8, 1995, p. A-5; Scott Allen, "Weld Offers to Stall Rule on Electric Cars," *The Boston Globe*, March 7, 1995, p. 21; and, Matthew L. Wald, "Plan Could Again Delay the Electric Car," *The New York Times*, July 4, 1995.

75. Scott Allen, "Weld Offers to Stall Rule on Electric Cars," *The Boston Globe*, March 7, 1995, p. 21.

76. Shnayerson, *The Car That Could*, p. 246.

77. Scott, "Low Emission Vehicles," 26pp.

78. Shnayerson, *The Car That Could*, p. 247.

79. Reuters, "GM Views California and the Electric Car," *The New York Times*, August 12, 1995, p. 43.

80. Matthew L. Wald, "Deal Is Likely on Cars Run by Electricity," *The New York Times*, November 19, 1995, p. 25.

81. Author conversations with Cecile Martin, deputy executive director, California Electric Transportation Coalition, Sacramento, CA, May 1999.

82. Marla Cone, "Air Panel Bending under Pressure," *The Los Angeles Times*, December 20, 1995, p. A-3

83. ibid.

84. Daniel Sperling, *Future Drive*, Washington: Island Press, 1995, pp. 140-141.

85. Marla Cone, "Air Panel Bending under Pressure," p. A-3

86. Mark Rectin, "CARB, Makers Agree on ZEVs, 49-State Car," *Automotive News*, Feb. 12, 1996, p. 8.

87. Shnayerson, *The Car That Could*, p. 254.

88. ibid.

89. Warren Brown, "Little Juice Coupes," *The Washington Post*, January 5, 1996, p. 1.

90. General Motors Corporation, news release, Los Angeles, CA, January 4, 1996, p. 2.

91. Brown, "Little Juice Coupes," p. 1.

## CHAPTER 15

1. Sierra Club Legal Defense Fund and Preston Gates Ellis & Rouvelas Meeds, "Evidence of a Conspiracy to Hinder Introduction of Electric Vehicles," Presented to the Antitrust Divi-

sion of the United States Department of Justice, January 17, 1996, with exhibits and attachments, p. 1, hereafter SCLDF brief.

2. Mark Rechtin, "Sierra Club Charges Anti-Zev Conspiracy," *Automotive News*, April 1, 1996, p. 1.

3. Shnayerson, *The Car That Could*, p. 89.

4. ibid, p. 82-83.

5. ibid, p. 89.

6. Gregory A. Patterson, "US Auto Firms Say Joint Effort Is Way to Gain Electric-Car Edge," *The Wall Street Journal*, January 21, 1991.

7. Shnayerson, *The Car That Could*, p. 89.

8. SCLDF brief, Overview memo, p. 3.

9. Shnayerson, *The Car That Could*, p. 19.

10. SCLDF brief, Overview memo, p. 3.

11. ibid.

12. Donald W. Nauss, "Battery Technology Fuels the Electric Vehicle Debate," *The Los Angeles Times*, May 11, 1994, p. 1.

13. SCLDF brief, p. 4 and exhibit 22.

14. SCLDF brief, "Witness Summaries," p. 7.

15. Reuters, "Ford Delays Electric Cars," *The New York Times*, January 13, 1994, p. D-20.

16. James Bennet, "GM Asks for More Time on Electric Cars," *The New York Times*, February 5, 1994, p. 39.

17. Shnayerson, *The Car That Could*, p. 178.

18. Joseph B. White, "GM, Energy Conversion Joining Forces to Develop New Electric Car Battery," *The Wall Street Journal*, March 10, 1994, p. B-5.

19. Oscar Suris, "GM's Link to ECD, Developer of Battery for Electric Car, Dents Big Three Effort," *The Wall Street Journal*, March 17, 1994

20. Shnayerson, *The Car That Could*, p. 181.

21. John F. Smith, Jr., CEO & president, General Motors, "Trends in Automotive Technology and Manufacturing," Stanford University, Stanford, CA, May 7, 1994.

22. SCLDF brief, "Chronology of Key Events," p. 19.

23. Telephone conversations with Sheila Lynch, April 9, 1998 and March 11, 1999.

24. Shnayerson, *The Car That Could*, p. 203.

25. SCLDF brief, "Witness Summaries," p. 8.

26. Shnayerson, *The Car That Could*, p. 243.

27. Nick Budnick, "Electric Smoke Screen," *Sacramento News & Review*, July 6, 1995, pp. 19-20.

28. SCLDF brief, "Chronology of Key Events," pp. 38-39 and exhibits 56 and 57.

29. ibid, exhibit 63.

30. ibid, see "Chronology of Key Events," pp. 21-40 and identified exhibits.

31. ibid, "Witness Summaries," pp 9-11.

32. ibid, overview memo, p. 7 and "Witness Summaries," pp 9-11.

33. Electric Vehicle Industry Association, Memorandum to Subcommittee on Mobile Source Emissions and Air Quality in the Northeast States, Response to the Disinformation Campaign against Electric and Hybrid Vehicles, September 24, 1994, p. 3.

34. Ford Motor Co., "Ford Plans to Target Commercial Buyers for 1998 Electric Vehicle Program," press release, June 12, 1995, p. 2.

35. Michael Parrish, "Ford to Build Electric Ranger for California," *The Los Angeles Times*, June 13, 1995, p. D-2.

36. Sperling, *Future Drive*, p. 60.

37. ibid, p. 61.

38. See, for example, cover letter sent out by Laura Q. Armstrong, director of communications, AAMA, Washington, DC, March 28, 1995, with accompanying confidential "Request for Proposal," American Automobile Manufacturers Association, March 24, 1995.

39. CALSTART, NRDC, and the Coalition for Clean Air, press release, "Automakers' Own Documents Show There's a Market for Electric Cars," with attachments, June 27, 1995.

40. ibid, p. 1.

41. SCLDF brief.

42. Shnayerson, *The Car That Could*, pp. 213-214.

43. ibid.

44. ibid.

45. Author interview with Joe Caves, Sacramento, CA, November 4, 1998.

46. Author interview with Bill Curtiss, San Francisco, CA, November 6, 1998.

47. Author conversations with Sheila Lynch, executive director, Northeast Alternative Vehicle Consortium, Boston, MA, April 1999.

## CHAPTER 16

1. Frank Swoboda, "Honda Announces Gas Engine Meets Anti-Pollution Goals," *The Washington Post*, January 7, 1995, p. 1.

2. Honda Motor Co., "For a Change, We'd Like to Talk About *Your* Air Bags," full-page advertisement, *The Wall Street Journal*, 25 July 1997, p. A-7.

3. Sally Goll Beatty, "Mr. Clean to Add Muscle to Honda's Claims," *The Wall Street Journal*, September 26, 1997, p. B-20.

4. Tetsuo Sakiya, *Honda Motor: The Men, The Management, The Machines*, Tokyo and New York: Kodansha International, 1982, p. 181.

5. ibid, p. 230.

6. "Groups Are Critical of Honda Commercial," *The New York Times*, October 18, 1991, p. D-15.

7. United States Senate, Hearings before the Subcommittee on the Consumer of the Committee on Commerce, Science and Transportation, *The Motor Vehicle Fuel Efficiency Act of 1991*, 102 Congress, 1st Session, February 21, 1991, p. 80.

8. Jacob M. Schlesinger, "Japan Car Firms Unveil Engines Lifting Mileage," *The Wall Street Journal*, July 30, 1991, p. B-1.

9. David Sanger, "Fuel Efficiency: New Japan Coup?" *The New York Times*, July 31, 1991, p. D-1.

10. ibid.

11. James B. Treece, "Honda Says Hybrid Produces High MPG," *Automotive News*, September 29, 1997.

12. James B. Treece, "Green Theme Dominates Tokyo," *Automotive News*, October 27, 1997, p.1.

13. ibid.

14. "Honda Unveils Cleaner Engine," *ACBNews.com* (and Reuters), October 20 & 24, 1997.

15. Donald W. Nauss, "Honda Will Sell Gas-Electric Vehicle in US," *The Los Angeles Times*, December 22, 1998.

16. PR Newswire, "Honda Insight Hybrid Earns EPA's Highest Mileage Rating Ever; Does Even Better In Highway Competition," October 1, 1999.

17. Deena Beasley, "Electric Car Glow Fades, But California Mandate Looms," Reuters, Los Angeles, April 30, 1999.

18. Emily Thornton, Kathleen Kerwin, and Keith Naughton, "Honda: Can the Company Go It Alone?" *Business Week*, July 5, 1999, p. 42.

19. ibid.

20. Keith Bradsher, "US Auto Makers Showing Interest in Fuel Efficiency," *The New York Times*, January 5, 1998.

21. Frank Swoboda and Warren Brown, "GM, Honda Team up to Lower Emissions," *The Washington Post*, December 21, 1999, p. E-1.

22. Ray T. Bohacz, "GM Should Build its Own Engines," letter to the editor, *Automotive News*, December 20, 1999, p. 12.

23. Frank Swoboda and Warren Brown, "GM, Honda Team up to Lower Emissions," *The Washington Post*, December 21, 1999, p. E-1.

## CHAPTER 17

*Sidebars*

1. "Battle of the Ads"
Margaret A. Kriz, "From the K Street Corridor," *National Journal*, December 7, 1996, p. 2647, Allan Freedman, "Advertisements Take an Emotional Tack," *CQ*, March 1, 1997, p. 531; Matthew Reed Baker, "From the K Street Corridor," *National Journal*, February 22, 1997, p. 376; "Dust Mites to Blame, Not Pollution, Claims Industry Ad," *The Planet*, newsletter of the Sierra Club, March 1997, p. 3; Joby Warrick, "A Dust-Up over Air Pollution Standards," *The Washington Post*, June 17, 1997, p. A-1.


1. William E. Gibson, Chicago Tribune News Service, "Carol Browner at Work with Mother Nature," *Portland Oregonian*, September 16, 1993, p. E-1.

2. US General Accounting Office, *Air Pollution: Ozone Attainment Requires Long-Term Solutions to Solve Complex Problems*, GAO/RCED-88-40, January 1988, p. 3.

3. Guy Darst, "Air Pollution Still Rampant in America's Large Cities," Associated Press, Washington Bureau, May 3, 1987.

4. ibid.

5. US Environmental Protection Agency, Office of Public Affairs, Washington, DC, "Congressional Moratorium Ends on Clean Air Sanctions," *Environmental News*, August 29, 1988, p. 2.

6. Anne Taylor Flemming, "Getting Serious About Smog at Last," *The New York Times*, March 29, 1989, p. C-8.

7. Rose Gutfeld, "Smog Levels in Many Cities Are Worse than the EPA Says, According to Group," *The Wall Street Journal*, May 23, 1989.

8. ibid.

9. Alexandra Allen, "The Auto's Assault on the Atmosphere," *Multinational Monitor*, January/February, 1990, p. 23.

10. D'Vera Cohn, "Future Hazy for Control of Ozone; Smog Can Impair Long-Term Health," *The Washington Post*, July 17, 1988, p. A-1.

11. Senator Joseph I. Lieberman, "Dirty Air Isn't Free, Either," letter to the editor, *The Washington Post*, June 18, 1989, p. C-6.

12. ibid.

13. Edward Flattau, "Regional Ozone Level Will Get Worse," *The News Journal*, August 17, 1991, p. A-6.

14. US Environmental Protection Agency, "National Air Quality and Emissions Trends Report, 1991," Washington, DC, 450-R-92-001, October 1992, pp. 1-2.

15. American Lung Association, *Why We Need Cleaner Cars*, Washington, DC, 1994.

16. Michael Weisskopf, "EPA Won't Tighten Urban Ozone Standard," *The Washington Post*, August 4, 1992, p. A-1.

17. "EPA Refuses to Tighten Main Standard for Smog," *The Wall Street Journal*, August 4, 1992, p. A-16.

18. Weisskopf, "EPA Won't Tighten Urban Ozone Standard," p. A-1.

19. Mark Jaffe, "Heat Wave Helps to Keep Smog Level Down," *The Philadelphia Inquirer*, July 14, 1993, p. A-8.

20. Margaret Kriz, "Clean Air Act's a Target," *National Journal*, January 14, 1995, p. 116.

21. H. Josef Hebert, "Thirty-Three Regions Don't Meet Smog Standards," Associated Press, November 6, 1995.

22. Gary Lee, "Compromising on Clean Air Act," *The Washington Post*, February 21, 1996, p. A-1.

23. ibid.

24. ibid.

25. ibid.

26. David Corn, "A Bad Air Day," *The Nation*, March 24, 1997.

27. Kriz, "From the K Street Corridor," p. 2647.

28. Harry Stoffer, "Rep. Dingell Promises 'War' if Clinton Toughens Air Rules," *Automotive News*, July 1997.

29. ibid.

30. Susan C. Hegger, "EPA Ruling on Air Particles Puts Bond in Midst of Dispute," *St. Louis Post-Dispatch*, October 16, 1996.

31. ibid.

32. Jim Drinkard, "Clean-Air Decision Follows Yearlong Lobbying Campaign," Associated Press, June 25, 1997.

33. Brad Knickerbocker, "Dust-up Ahead as Air Particle Rules Go Under Microscope," *The Christian Science Monitor*, November 19, 1996, p. 1.

34. John J. Fialka, "Group Gears up to Block EPA Proposals on National Air-Quality Standards," *The Wall Street Journal*, November 29, 1996, p. B-3.

35. Jim Drinkard, "Clean-Air Decision Follows Yearlong Lobbying Campaign," June 25, 1997.

36. US Environmental Protection Agency, Office of Air and Radiation, Washington, DC, "Proposed Revisions to the Ozone And Particulate Matter Air Quality Standards," EPA-456/F-97-003, March 1997, p. 2.

37. Kevin Galvin, "EPA Proposes Strict New Air Quality Standards," Associated Press, November 27, 1996.

38. Rae Tyson, "Too Many People At Risk, EPA Says," *USA Today*, November 29, 1996, p. 9-A.

39. Phil Frame, "Automakers Call EPA Rules Tough Enough," *Automotive News*, December 23, 1996, p. 26.

40. Galvin, "EPA Proposes Strict New Air Quality Standards," November 27, 1996.

41. Mary Beth Regan, "The Dust-up Over Dust," *Business Week*, December 2, 1996, p. 119.

42. John Merline, "Clean Air Rules under Attack," *Investor's Business Daily*, December 11, 1996, p. A-1.

43. Marla Cone, "EPA Proposes Tougher Limits on Soot, Smog," *Los Angeles Times*, November 28, 1996, p. A-1.

44. Joby Warrick, "Opponents Await Proposal to Limit Air Particulate," *The Washington Post*, November 27, 1996, p. A-1.

45. Margaret Kriz, "Heavy Breathing," *National Journal*, January 4, 1997, p. 9.

46. David Corn, "A Bad Air Day," *The Nation*, March 24, 1997, p. 7.

47. "Health Effects of Outdoor Air Pollution," *American Journal Of Respiratory And Critical Care Medicine*, volume 153, 1996, pp. 1-50.

48. Kriz, "Heavy Breathing," p. 9.

49. John Byrne Barry, "Clean Air Now!" *The Planet*, March 1997, p. 2.

50. Jenny Coyle, "Air Victory Good News for Those Who Breathe," *The Planet*, January 1998, p. 12.

51. Allan Freedman, "Advertisements Take an Emotional Tack," *Congressional Quarterly*, March 1, 1997, p. 531

52. Corn, "A Bad Air Day," p. 7.

53. Kriz, "Heavy Breathing," p. 9.

54. Corn, "A Bad Air Day," p. 7.

55. Representative Henry A. Waxman, "False Alarms on Clean Air," *The Washington Post*, March 5, 1997, p. A-21.

56. ibid.

57. Warrick, "A Dust-Up Over Air Pollution Standards," p. A-1.

58. ibid.

59. H. Josef Hebert, "Agencies Questioned Plan to Combat Air Pollution," Associated Press, *The Philadelphia Inquirer*, March 15, 1997, p. D-7, and David Corn, "Clearing the Air," *The Nation*, July 21, 1997, p. 5.

60. John H. Cushman, Jr., "On Clean Air, Environmental Chief Fought Doggedly, and Won," *The New York Times*, July 5, 1997.

61. "The Cleaner-Air Fight," *The Washington Post*, February 21, 1997, p. A-20.

62. "Washington Wire," *The Wall Street Journal*, May 30, 1997, p. A-1.

63. Margaret Kriz, "Business Lobby Divides Democrats," *National Journal*, May 17, 1997.

64. ibid.

65. ibid.

66. John H. Cushman, Jr., "Top EPA Official Not Backing Down on Air Standards," *The New York Times*, June 1, 1997, p. A-1.

67. Allan Friedman, "Latest Fight on Clean Air Rules Centers on Scientific Data," *Congressional Quarterly*, March 1, 1997, p. 532.

68. Cushman, "Top EPA Official Not Backing Down on Air Standards," p. A-1.

69. ibid.

70. Reuters, "Mayors Vote to Fight Plan on Air Quality," *The New York Times*, June 25, 1997, p. A-12.

71. John H. Cushman, Jr., "D'Amato Vows to Fight For EPA's Tightened Air Standards," *The New York Times*, June 25, 1997, p. A-13.

72. John H. Cushman, Jr., "Clinton Sharply Tightens Air Pollution Regulations Despite Concern over Costs," *The New York Times*, June 26, 1997, p. A-1, and Associated Press, "Clinton Gives Go-Ahead to Toughen Clean-Air Standards," June 26, 1997.

73. Cushman, "Clinton Sharply Tightens Air Pollution Regulations Despite Concern over Costs," p. A-1.

74. Associated Press, "Clinton Gives Go-Ahead to Toughen Clean-Air Standards," June 26, 1997.

75. Cushman, "On Clean Air, Environmental Chief Fought Doggedly, and Won," July 5, 1997.

76. Author conversation with Bruce Bertelsen, executive director, MECA, February 1996.

77. Cushman, "On Clean Air, Environmental Chief Fought Doggedly, and Won," July 5, 1997.

78. Cushman, "Clinton Sharply Tightens Air Pollution Regulations Despite Concern over Costs," p. A-1.

79. Keith Bradsher, "Auto Makers Seek to Halt Tough Rules on Clean Air," *The New York Times*, June 29, 1997, p. 16.

80. Harry Stoffer, "Rep. Dingell Promises 'War' If Clinton Toughens Air Rules," July 1997.

81. Cushman, "On Clean Air, Environmental Chief Fought Doggedly, and Won," July 5, 1997.

82. John H. Cushman, Jr., "Northeast States Pressuring EPA to Move on Smog," *The New York Times*, August 8, 1997, p. A-1.

83. Rebecca Burns, "Is Traffic Killing Atlanta?" *Atlanta*, January 1998, p. 62.

84. Angie Farleigh, Jayne Mardock, Gina Porreco, Felice Stadler, and Rebecca Stanfield, "Smog Threat '98: 1998 Summer Ozone Pollution Report," US PIRG Education Fund and the Clean Air Network, Washington, DC, October 8, 1998.

85. Joby Warrick and Bill McAllister, "New Air Pollution Limits Blocked," *The Washington Post*, May 15, 1991, p. A-1.

86. ibid.

87. Harry Stoffer, "EPA Pushes Forward with Tailpipe Rules," *Automotive News*, May 24, 1999, p. 4.

88. ibid.

# CHAPTER 18

1. Inquirer wire services, "US and the Big Three Will Attempt to Create an 82.5 MPG Auto," *The Philadelphia Inquirer*, September 30, 1993, p. A-1.

2. Bob Davis, "White House and Auto Firms to Unveil Joint Plan to Triple Fuel Efficiency," *The Wall Street Journal*, September 29, 1993, p. A-5.

3. Inquirer wire services, "US and the Big Three Will Attempt to Create an 82.5 MPG Auto," p. A-1.

4. ibid.

5. ibid.

6. Peter Behr and Warren Brown, "US, Big 3 May Join in 'Clean Car' Search," *The Washington Post*, April 16, 1993, p. A-1.

7. ibid.

8. Peter H. Stone, "Detroit's Smooth Ride," *National Journal*, May 21, 1994, p. 1177.

9. Conversation with Bob Rose, Rose Communications, Inc., Washington, DC, November 6, 1997.

10. John Buntin, "From Confrontation to Cooperation: How Detroit and Washington Became Partners," Case Program, Kennedy School of Government, Harvard College, with funding provided by the US Department of Commerce, April 1997 p. 5.

11. Melinda Grenier Guiles, "Bush Initiatives Are Discussed by Auto Makers," *The Wall Street Journal*, June 22, 1989, p. A-3.

12. ibid.

13. Gregory A. Patterson, "US Auto Firms Say Joint Effort Is Way to Gain Electric-Car Edge," *The Wall Street Journal*, January 21, 1991.

14. Oscar Suris, "Big Three Win Joint Patent, Marking a First," *The Wall Street Journal*, April 13, 1993, p. B-1.

15. Christopher Jensen, "Big 3 Work Together on Research," *Plain Dealer*, February 28, 1993, p. 1-E.

16. Buntin, "From Confrontation to Cooperation," pp. 8-9.

17. ibid, pp. 8-9.

18. ibid, pp. 10-11.

19. ibid, pp. 13-14.

20. Stone, "Detroit's Smooth Ride," p. 1176.

21. Tom Hayden, "Conspirators Are Targeting Electric Cars," op-ed, *Los Angeles Times*, November 2, 1993.

22. Shnayerson, *The Car That Could*, pp. 149-150.

23. Oscar Suris, "Big Three Discuss a Joint Crusade Against California's Electric-Car Rule," *The Wall Street Journal*, October 25, 1993, p. A-4.

24. ibid.

25. John F. Smith, Jr., CEO and president, General Motors Corporation, "Trends in Automotive Technology and Manufacturing," keynote address at the Stanford University Manufacturing Conference, Stanford, California, May 7, 1994.

26. ibid.

27. Stone, "Detroit's Smooth Ride," p. 1177.

28. Associated Press, "Gore, Clinton Mark Year of Partnership with Automakers on Future Cars," October 18, 1994.

29. Jayne O'Donnell, "Car Rationing? Just An Idea," *USA Today*, September 30, 1994, p.1.

30. B.J. Bergman, " 'Car Talks'—Motown Walks," *Sierra*, March-April, 1996, pp 36-37.

31. Phil Frame, "Car Talk Panel Agrees to Disagree—And Folds," *Automotive News*, September 1995.

32. John H. Cushman, Jr., "White House Considers Toughening Its Anti-Emissions Program," *The New York Times*, September 24, 1995, p. 31.

33. Jayne O'Donnell, "Auto Future Hits a Roadblock," *AutoWeek*, October 2, 1995, p. 4.

34. Reviewer note: This account relayed to the author in conversations with at least three members of the Car Talks panel.

35. Policy Dialogue Advisory Committee, "Majority Report to the President—To Recommend Options for Reducing Greenhouse Gas Emissions from Personal Motor Vehicles," October 1995. This report was signed by the following: Daniel Becker, director, Global Warming and Energy Program, Sierra Club; Scott Bernstein, president, Center For Neighborhood Technology; Joan Claybrook, president, Public Citizen; John DeCicco, senior associate, American Council for an Energy Efficient Economy; Clarence Ditlow, executive director, Center for Auto Safety; Hank Dittmar, executive director, Surface Transportation Policy Project; George Dixon, director, Greater Cleveland Regional Transit Authority; Patrick Dougherty, Representative, Missouri House of Representatives; David Freeman, former president, New York Power Authority; Sonia W. Hamel, director, Air Policy and Planning, Massachusetts Executive Office of Environmental Affairs; Daniel Lashof, senior scientist, Natural Resources Defense Council; Valerie Lemmie, city manager, Petersburg, Virginia; James M. Lents, executive director, South Coast Air Quality Management District, California; Lee R. Lynd, director of Process Development, Independence Biofuel, Inc. and associate professor of Engineering, Dartmouth College; Francis J. Murray, National Association of State Energy Officials, former commissioner, New York State Energy Office; Wayne Shackelford, director, Georgia Department of Transportation; and, Ann Shen Smith, vice president, Environment and Safety, Southern California Gas Company.

36. "Majority Report to the President," p. 15.

37. ibid, p. 19.

38. Bergman, " 'Car Talks'—Motown Walks," pp 36-37.

39. John Buntin, "Rallying Behind PNGV (Epilogue)," Case Program, Kennedy School of Government, Harvard University, with funding provided by the US Department of Commerce, April 1997, p. 1.

40. ibid.

41. ibid, p. 4.

42. Letter to Vice President Albert Gore, Jr., The White House, Washington, DC, from Jason Mark, Union of Concerned Scientists; John DeCicco, American Council for an Energy Efficient Economy; Fran Du Melle, American Lung Association; Richard Kassel, Natural Resources Defense Council; and Carol Werner, Environmental and Energy Study Institute, June 19, 1997.

43. Eric C. Evarts, "Will Diesels Make a Comeback on US Roads?" *The Christian Science Monitor*, June 18, 1996.

44. ibid.

45. ibid.

46. Remarks of Vice President Al Gore, Sixth Technical Symposium, Partnership for a New Generation of Vehicles, July 23, 1997, p. 2.

47. Jennifer Scarlott, "Forecast: Climate Watchers Offer Opinion on the Conference," *The Amicus Journal*, winter 1998, p. 20.

48. Letter to President Bill Clinton with 119 CEO signatories, July 6, 1996.

49. Ross Gelbspan, *The Heat Is On: The High Stakes Battle over Earth's Threatened Climate*, New York: Addison-Wesley Publishing Co., 1997.

50. Robert J. Eaton, "Global Warming: Industry's Response," *The Washington Post*, July 17, 1997, p. A-19.

51. Katherine Yung, "Auto Industry Knocks Clinton Global Warming Plan," *The Detroit News*, August 6, 1997, p. S-12.

52. John Flesher, "Companies Oppose New Regulations But Study Low-Polluting Vehicles," Associated Press, August 7, 1997.

53. Harry Stoffer, "Auto Lobby: $100 Million Voice," *Automotive News*, December 29, 1997, p. 31.

54. John H. Cushman, Jr., "Intense Lobbying against Global Warming Treaty," *The New York Times*, December 7, 1997, p. 28.

55. David Phinney, "Green Groups Push President," *ABCNews.com*, October 10, 1997.

56. Martha Hamilton, "Technology Can Cut Pollution without High Cost, Study Says," *The Washington Post*, September 26, 1997, p. A-1.

57. "At Risk: Profits and Jobs," *Fortune*, December 8, 1997, p. 120.

58. Earle Eldridge and Traci Watson, "Carmakers Lobby against Global Warming Treaty," *USA Today*, October 3, 1997, p. B-1.

59. Yuri Kageyama, Associated Press, "Brains vs. Brawn: High-Tech Japanese Show Up Muscle-Bound Americans in Tokyo," *Chicago Tribune*, November 30, 1997, p. 7

60. Bloomberg News, "Big Three Say Japanese Engine Breakthroughs Not Yet Available in Market," *The Plain Dealer*, October 26, 1997, p. 8-G.

61. Kageyama, "Brains vs. Brawn: High-Tech Japanese Show Up Muscle-Bound Americans in Tokyo," p. 7

62. Emily Thornton, Keith Naughton, and David Woodruff, "Toyota's Green Machine," *Business Week*, December 15, 1997, pp. 108-110.

63. ibid.

64. Dave Phillips, "Japan Carmakers Go Green at Tokyo Show," *The Detroit News*, October 26, 1997, p. C-1.

65. ibid.

66. James B. Treece, "Green Theme Dominates Tokyo," *Automotive News*, October 27, 1997, pp. 1, 53.

67. John Hughes, Associated Press, "American Automakers Want New Technology to Mean Profits," November 12, 1997.

68. Regina M. Roberts, "Study: Increase MPG to Curb Global Warming," *The Atlanta Journal/Constitution*, November 1997.

69. Jeffrey H. Birnbaum, "A Cloud on Gore's Horizon," *Fortune*, December 7, 1998, p. 122.

70. John J. Fialka, "A Curious Assortment of Adversaries Assemble in Kyoto for Talks on Global Warming Treaty," *The Wall Street Journal*, December 5, 1997, p. A-20

71. "Dirty Dancing," *Automotive News*, December 8, 1997, p. 49.

72. Jeffrey Bartholet and Karen Breslau, "Wake-Up Call," *Newsweek*, December 22, 1997, p. 67.

73. "What They're Saying," *Automotive News*, December 15, 1997, p. 48.

74. "Big US Industries Launch Attack on Warming Treaty," *The Wall Street Journal*, December 12, 1997, p. A-3.

75. "What They're Saying," p. 48.

76. Laura M. Litvan, "Paying Up for Global Warming," *Investors Business Daily*, February 23, 1998, p. 1.

77. Glenn Zorpette, "Waiting for Supercar," *Scientific American*, April 1999.

78. ibid.

CHAPTER 19

*Sidebar*

1. "T-Rex & The Sidewinder"
Ralph Kisiel, "Chrysler Unleashes the Beasts: Bulked-Up Ram, Retro Pickup," *Automotive News*, November 11, 1996, p. 44.

1. Right before the Kyoto global warming conference was to convene in Japan, *New York Times* reporter Keith Bradsher published a long story on how trucks and SUVs were bigger environmental polluters than cars, how they received special treatment for emissions and fuel economy under the law, and how they were contributing more to global warming. The article detailed the pollution, poor mileage, and greenhouse gas emissions of SUVs and light trucks, comparing popular SUV and pickup models with passenger cars. Bradsher used data from EPA and other sources. The piece created quite a stir, both in Kyoto and back home. See, Keith Bradsher, "License to Pollute—A Special Report: Trucks, Darlings of Drivers, Are Favored by the Law, Too," *The New York Times*, November 30, 1997, p. 1.

2. Keith Naughton, "Confessions of a Sport-Ute Owner," *Business Week*, January 19, 1998, p. 34.

3. "Fuel Economy Rules for Some Trucks, Vans Are Proposed by US," *The Wall Street Journal*, December 13, 1977.

4. ibid.

5. Deborah Baldwin, "Wheeling and Dealing in Washington," *Environmental Action*, March 25, 1978, p. 7.

6. ibid.

7. Center for Auto Safety, *Advertising Trends of Nonpassenger Automobiles*, January 30, 1978.

8. "Realizing Your Next Car Should Be a Truck," GMC ad, *Sports Illustrated*, October 17, 1977, p. 29, cited in Center for Auto Safety, *Advertising Trends*, p. 11.

9. "Ford Sets Ad Splash for Compact Pickup Courier," *Advertising Age*, May 16, 1977, p. 86, cited in Center for Auto Safety, *Advertising Trends*, p. 13.

10. Iacocca, *Iacocca*, p. 297.

11. ibid, and Halberstam, *The Reckoning*, pp. 561-566.

12. "Trucks Captivating American Market," *The New York Times*, November 18, 1985, p. D-1.

13. "Ford Asks US to Ease Fuel-Economy Rules for Light Trucks," *The Wall Street Journal*, November 29, 1983, p. 12.

14. Warren Brown, "Ford, GM Ask 1-Year Delay on Truck Fuel Ratings," *The Washington Post*, August 1, 1984.

15. US Department of Commerce, *Truck Inventory and Use Survey*, Bureau of the Census: Census of Transportation, 1982.

16. Jack A. Semonds, "Pickup Trucks Running Hot for Detroit," *US News & World Report*, December 16, 1985, p. 63.

17. ibid.

18. Taylor, "US Cars Come Back," p. 68.

19. Ralph Kisiel, "Grand Cherokee? AMC's Idea," *Automotive News*, August 4, 1997, p. 27.

20. Marc Ledbetter, Testimony on Light-Vehicle Fuel Economy before the House Subcommittee on Energy and Power, American Council for an Energy Efficient Economy, Washington, DC, September 15, 1990.

21. William K. Stevens, "With Energy Tug of War, US Is Missing Its Goals," *The New York Times*, November 28, 1995, p. 1.

22. Coffey and Layden, *America on Wheels*, p. 289.

23. Doron P. Levin, "The Cars That Are Hot Are Not," *The New York Times*, August 24, 1993, p. D-1.

24. ibid.

25. James B. Treece and Kathleen Kerwin, "Detroit: Highballing It into Trucks," *Business Week*, March 7, 1994, p. 46.

26. Neal Templin, "Detroit Girds for Fight over Fuel Economy," *The Wall Street Journal*, October 18, 1994, p. B-1.

27. James Bennet, "Truck's Popularity Undermining Gains in US Fuel Savings," *The New York Times*, September 5, 1995, p. 1.

28. ibid.

29. ibid.

30. Kisiel, "Grand Cherokee? AMC's Idea," p. 27.

31. Keith Bradsher, "License To Pollute—A Special Report," p. 1.

32. Keith Bradsher, "Start Expanding That Garage for Detroit's Next Generation," *The New York Times*, June 17, 1997, p. A-1.

33. The Sierra Club web page, www.sierraclub.org/global-warming/ford.htm, visited December 8, 1997.

34. Bradsher, "Start Expanding That Garage for Detroit's Next Generation," p. A-1.

35. Harry Stoffer, "Eaton Tabs Customer As SUV Defender," *Automotive News*, February 2, 1998, p. 8.

36. "What Industry Leaders Say About the New Breed of Sport Wagons," *Automotive News*, April 27, 1998, p. 40.

37. Keith Bradsher, "Emissions Rules May Tighten for Autos and Light Trucks," *The New York Times*, April 24, 1998, p. A-10.

38. Bradsher, "License To Pollute—A Special Report," p. 1.

39. Jamie Lincoln Kitman, "SUVs Won't Always Be Riding High," *Los Angeles Times*, May 27, 1998, p. B-7.

40. Bill Vlasic, "These Sport Utes Are Standouts," *Business Week*, November 3, 1997, p. 179.

41. Jean Halliday, "$60 Million Ad Drive Plugs Durango," *Automotive News*, September 29, 1997, p. 41.

42. Jay Palmer, "Have We Gone Too Far?" *Barron's*, December 28, 1998, p. 24.

43. Keith Bradsher, "The Road Ford's Taken," *The New York Times*, April 16, 1998, p. D-1.

44. ibid.

45. Keith Bradsher, "Auto Makers Seeking to Avoid Fines over Mileage Rules," *The New York Times*, April 3, 1998, p. A-22.

46. ibid.

47. "Enforce CAFE, But First Close CAFE Loopholes," *Automotive News*, April 13, 1998, p. 12.

48. Bradsher, "Auto Makers Seeking to Avoid Fines over Mileage Rules," p. A-22.

49. "Enforce CAFE, But First Close CAFE Loopholes," p. 12.

50. Keith Bradsher, "Ford to Raise Output Sharply of Vehicles That Use Ethanol," *The New York Times*, June 4, 1997, p. A-1.

51. ibid.

52. "The RoadHog Info Trough," at: http://WWW.suv.org/environ.htm#N_5_.

53. Keith Bradsher, "Light Trucks Face Tougher Air Standards," *The New York Times*, November 3, 1998.

54. Larry Gerber, Associated Press, "Stricter Emissions for Light Trucks," *The Sacramento Bee*, November 6, 1998, p. A-1.

55. ibid.

56. Bradsher, "Light Trucks Face Tougher Air Standards."

57. Joseph B. White, "New Clean-Air Rules for Light Trucks Set Battle Stage," *The Wall Street Journal*, November 9, 1998, p. B-4.

58. Kathleen Kerwin, with Joan Muller in Detroit, "Reviving GM," *Business Week*, February 1, 1999, p. 116.

59. Keith Bradsher, "Advertising," *The New York Times*, October 8, 1998, p. C-5.

60. Mary Connelly, "Too Big? Polluting? Ford Execs Rally Round Excursion," *Automotive News*, March 8, 1999, p. 6.

61. ibid.

62. Nichole Christian, "Ford's New Monster," *Time*, March 8, 1999, p. 50.

63. ibid.

64. Eric Fisher, "Ford's New Sport Utility Vehicle Irks Safety, Environmental Groups," Knight-Ridder Tribune Business News, *The Washington Times*, February 26, 1999.

65. Martha M. Hamilton and Warren Brown, "EPA Wants Light Trucks to Meet Car Standards," *The Washington Post*, February 18, 1999, p. E-1.

66. Harry Stoffer, "EPA Hearing Shows Divisions on Tier 2 Emissions Proposal," *Automotive News*, June 14, 1999, p. 49.

67. US Public Interest Research Group, "Doctors Testify for Cut in Auto Pollution," *US PIRG*, vol. 15, no. 1, p. 1, and US PIRG Education Fund, "The Dirty Truth About SUVs," July 1999.

68. Palmer, "Have We Gone Too Far?" p. 26.

69. Ralph Kisiel, "Chrysler Counting on Trucks to Speed Up Global Expansion," *Automotive News*, May 18, 1998, p. 52.

## CHAPTER 20

1. Donald W. Nauss and others, "Ways to Go," *The Los Angeles Times*, May 4, 1997, p. D-1.

2. Tamsin Carlisle, "Fuel-Cell Car Promises Less Pollution," *The Wall Street Journal*, July 5, 1996, p. B-10.

3. Scott Miller, Reuters, "Fuel-Cell Car Unveiled," May 15, 1996.

4. Stuart F. Brown, "The Automakers' Big Time Bet on Fuel Cells," *Fortune*, March 30, 1998, p. 122(F).

5. Brandon Mitchener and Tamsin Carlisle, "Daimler, Ballard Team to Develop Fuel-Cell Engine," *The Wall Street Journal*, April 15, 1997, p. B-8.

6. Matthew L. Wald, "In a Step Toward a Better Electric Car, Company Uses Fuel Cell to Get Energy from Gasoline," *The New York Times*, October 21, 1997.

7. ibid.

8. ibid.

9. Jason Mark, Union of Concerned Scientists, Berkeley, CA, "Clean Car's Wrong Turn," letter-to-the-editor, *The New York Times*, October 26, 1997, p. 14.

10. Valerie Reitman, "Ford Is Investing in Daimler-Ballard Fuel-Cell Venture," *The Wall Street Journal*, December 16, 1997, p. B-4.

11. Kathryn M. Welling, "Cell Out?" *Barron's*, May 11, 1998, p. 6.

12. Stuart F. Brown, "The Automakers' Big Time Bet on Fuel Cells," *Fortune*, March 30, 1998, p. 122(F).

13. ibid.

14. Welling, "Cell Out?" p. 6.

15. Brian S. Akre, "Methanol Focus for Fuel Cell Car," Associated Press, December 29, 1998.

16. Bloomberg News Service, "DaimlerChrysler Says Fuel Cells Are 5 Years Away," *Automotive News*, January 11, 1999.

17. Jeffrey Ball, "Auto Makers Race to Sell Cars Powered by Fuel Cells," *The Wall Street Journal*, March 15, 1999.

18. ibid.

19. Warren Brown, "Automakers Plan Fuel-Cell Cars," *The Washington Post*, March 17, 1999, p. A-14

20. Dow Jones News Service, "Calif. Gov. Davis Confirms Planned Fuel Cell Vehicle Tests," April 20, 1999.

21. Mark Glover, "California Officials, Automakers Hail Zero-Emission Car Engine," *The Sacramento Bee*, April 21, 1999.

22. Dow Jones News Service, "Calif. Gov. Davis Confirms Planned Fuel Cell Vehicle Tests," April 20, 1999.

23. Donald W. Nauss, "The Cutting Edge: Auto Makers to Test Fuel-Cell Vehicles in State," *Los Angeles Times*, April 19, 1999, p. C-1.

24. Jason Mark, "Who's in the Driver's Seat?" *dollars and sense*, July/August 1998, pp. 16-20.

25. ibid.

26. Keith Bradsher, "Tighter Rules Likely on Autos and Gas," *The New York Times*, April 14, 1999, p. A-20.

27. Shnayerson, *The Car That Could*, p. 39.

## Chapter 21

1. Lawrence McQuillan, "Clinton Emissions Plan Draws Praise, Criticism," Reuters, May 1, 1999, and Associated Press, "Clinton Proposes Clean Air Standards," May 1, 1999.

2. General Motors, Public Comments on EPA's Proposed Tier 2 Emissions Standards, August 1999, pp. 19, 39, 44, and 64.

3. US PIRG, "Dirty Dollars, Dirty Air—The Auto and Oil Industries' Continuing Campaign against Air Pollution Control," September 1999, 27 pp.

4. Harry Stoffer, "Auto Lobby:$100 Million Voice," *Automotive News*, December 29, 1997, p. 1.

5. Peter H. Stone, "Detroit's Smooth Ride," *National Journal*, May 21, 1994, pp. 1176-1181.

6. Anna Wilde Mathews, "The Big Two Shift Gears on the Best Way to Reach Washington," *The Wall Street Journal*, November 27, 1998.

7. Stoffer, "Auto Lobby:$100 Million Voice," p. 1.

8. John K. Andrews, et al., "The Vision Thing: Conservatives Take Aim at the '90s," *Policy Review*, Spring 1990, p. 4.

9. ibid.

10. Harry Stoffer, "Trade Council Mission Is Clear, Style Evolving," *Automotive News*, March 22, 1999, p. 6.

11. Richard Morin and Claudia Deane, "The Ideas Industry," *The Washington Post*, September 14, 1999, p. A-27.

12. Dina ElBoghdady, "Senate Kills SUV Fuel Bill," *The Detroit News*, September 16, 1999.

13. "Clinton Signs Highway Bill," *The Washington Post*, October 11, 1999, p. A-6.

14. Harry Stoffer, "31 Senators Back Higher CAFE," *Automotive News*, June 7, 1999, p. 8.

15. Warren Brown and Martha M. Hamilton, "Ford Shifts on Global Warming," *The Washington Post*, December 7, 1999, p. E-2.

16. Bill Dawson, "Bush Wants 'Bold' Plan on Smog," *Houston Chronicle*, December 16, 1999, p. 37, and Harry Stoffer, "Bush Backs Calif. Air Rules," *Automotive News*, December 20, 1999, p. 1.

17. Bill Dawson, "Smog Hit List Includes Far-Reaching Measures, *Houston Chronicle*, December 14, 1999, p. 1, and Connie Mabin, "Commission Adopts Pollution Rules, Seeks Comment," Associated Press, December 16, 1999.

18. Anna Wilde Mathews and Jeffrey Ball, "Auto Makers Are Left in Design Limbo as States Weigh EPA's Emissions Rules," *The Wall Street Journal*, December 22, 1999, p. B-12.

19. Warren Brown and Martha M. Hamilton, "EPA to Require Cleaner Fuels," *The Washington Post*, December 21, 1999, p. A-1, and Keith Bradsher, "Clinton Allays Criticism on New Pollution Rules," *The New York Times*, December 22, 1999, p. A-20.

20. Mathews and Ball, "Auto Makers Are Left in Design Limbo as States Weigh EPA's Emissions Rules," p. B-12.

## CHAPTER 22

1. Donald W. Nauss, "Gas Engine Is Not About to Go," *The Los Angeles Times*, January 11, 1998, p. D-1.

2. Yates, *The Decline and Fall of the American Automobile Industry*, p. 29.

3. Ray Hutton, "The Car in Europe," *Motor Trend*, Special Edition, "100 Years of the Automobile," 1985, p. 135.

4. Chrysler Corporation, advertisement, "60 Years of Chrysler Automotive Leadership," *Motor Trend*, special issue, "100 Years of the Automobile," 1985, p. 189.

5. Keller, *Rude Awakening*, p. 57

6. Yates, *The Decline and Fall of the American Automobile Industry*, p. 202.

7. ibid, p. 203.

8. Robert M. Heavenrich and Karl H. Hellman, "Light-Duty Automotive Technology and Fuel Economy Trends Through 1999," Advanced Technology Support Division, Office of Mobile Sources, US Environmental Protection Agency, EPA420-R-99-018, September 1999, p. iv.

9. Halberstam, *The Reckoning*, p. 716.

10. Ingrassia and White, *Comeback*, p. 427-428.

11. Keller, *Rude Awakening*, p. 28.

12. Robert A. Lutz, *Guts: The Seven Laws of Business That Made Chrysler the World's Hottest Car Company*, New York: John Wiley & Sons, Inc., 1998, pp. 35-36.

13. Lutz, *Guts: The Seven Laws of Business*, pp. 35-36.

14. The Joyce Foundation, "Countdown to Change," *Work in Progress*, September 1999, pp. 6-11.

15. See, for example, Joe Miller, "GM Slims Car Plan in Favor of Trucks," *Automotive News*, June 14, 1999, p. 1.

16. Stephanie Pollack, "Cars Are Evil . . ." (internal memo), Conservation Law Foundation, 1990, cited in *Car Trouble*, World Resources Institute, p. 169.

17. Keith Bradsher, "Advertising," *The New York Times*, October 8, 1998, p. C-5.

18. See, for example, Ford advertisement, "All The Gear You Need, . . ." *The Washington Post*, October 24, 1999, p. D-18.

19. Keith Bradsher, Advertising, "Ford Is Starting A Big Campaign, . . ." *The New York Times*, August 23, 1999, p. C-12.

20. Warren Brown, "GM, Toyota Team Up To Make Electric Cars," *The Washington Post*, April 20, 1999, p. E-4.

21. Jeffrey Ball, "To Define Future Car, GM, Toyota Say Bigger Is Better," *The Wall Street Journal*, April 20, 1999, p. B-4.

22. Ball, "To Define Future Car, GM, Toyota Say Bigger Is Better," p. B-4.

23. Aaron Robinson, "GM Goes Shopping For Engine Deals," *Automotive News*, November 1, 1999, p. 1.

24. "Meet the Press," October 1977.

25. C. Kenneth Orski, Alan Altshuler, and Daniel Ross, "The Future of the Automobile," *Transatlantic Perspectives*, March 1980, pp. 4-8

26. Keith Bradsher, "From Defending Big Tobacco to Fighting Ford Motor for a Lone Client," *The New York Times*, September 12, 1999, p. 18.

27. See, for example, BlueOvalNews.com; Warren Brown, "Web Site's Publication of Ford Secrets Halted," *The Washington Post*, August 27, 1999, p. E-10; Fara Warner, "Ford Motor Is Ordered to Help Restore the Web Site of Operator It is Suing," *The Wall Street Journal*, August 31, 1999, p. B-7; and Keith Bradsher, "From Defending Big Tobacco to Fighting Ford Motor for a Lone Client," *The New York Times*, September 12, 1999, p. 18.

28. Warner and Bell, "Ford Documents Reveal New Fuel-Economy Plan."

29. Ford Motor Co., advertisement, *The Wall Street Journal*, May 18, 1999.

30. Fara Warner and Jefferey Bell, "Ford Documents Reveal New Fuel-Economy Plan," *The Wall Street Journal*, September 3, 1999.

31. Michael Woodyard, "Ford Hires Help in BlueOval War," *Automotive News*, November 29, 1999, p. 10.

32. Warner and Bell, "Ford Documents Reveal New Fuel-Economy Plan."

33. See, for example, "'Oh My God, I Can't Believe I Shot Her,'" *The Washington Post*, November 16, 1999, P. 1-A.

34. The Energy Foundation, annual report, 1998, p. 16.

35. Kathy Chen and Hilary Stout, "Boeing, GM Obtain China Agreements," *The Wall Street Journal*, March 25, 1997, A-3, and John F. Harris, (*Washington Post*), "With Gore on Hand, China Signs Boeing and GM Deals," *The Philadelphia Inquirer*, March 25, 1997, p. A-1.

36. John Burgess, US, China Agree on Trade," *The Washington Post*, November 16, 1999, p. A-1.

# A Time Line of Technology, Commerce, and Politics

## The Automobile—From ICE to Fuel Cell

| | |
|---|---|
| 1864 | Nikolaus Otto invents internal combustion engine in Cologne, Germany. |
| 1886 | Karl Benz patents world's first practical motorcar. |
| 1896 | Henry Ford, tests a motorized "quadricycle"; Frank and Charles Duryea sell the first motor vehicles in US through Duryea Motor Wagon Co. |
| 1897 | Early and clean electric vehicles, easy to operate, gained popularity among women, lawyers, and physicians according to *Automotive Industries*. |
| 1898 | French report "catalytic reaction" to clean fumes from petroleum motors. |
| 1900 | First auto show in New York City—40 manufacturers show 300 cars; steam & electric vehicles outsell gasoline-powered vehicles. |
| 1901 | Spindletop "oil gusher" near Beaumont, Texas ushers in era of cheap oil, helps shift advantage to gasoline-powered vehicles. |
| 1903 | Ford Motor Company founded. |
| 1908 | General Motors holding company absorbs Buick, Oakland, and Oldsmobile (Chevrolet added in 1918); Ford's first Model-T produced in October. |
| 1910 | 468,500 US total vehicles registered: annual production, 180,000. |
| 1913 | Mass production begins, cuts making of Model-T from 12.5 hours to 93 minutes. A shaft-drive EV, made by Borland Electric, travels from Chicago to Milwaukee on a single charge. |
| 1920 | 9.2 million US vehicles registered: annual production, 2.2 million. EVs then regarded as "city cars." |
| 1922 | Early research on automobile exhaust begins to appear (*Franklin Institute Journal*) Catalysts being used in mines to control gasoline engine CO; Johns Hopkins researchers also experimenting with catalysts treating car exhaust. |

1923    Model-Ts being produced at 1.8 million per year.

GM initiates annual model change idea; later called "ladder of consumption" for buying up in the GM system—from Chevrolet to Buick to Cadillac.

1924    Walter P. Chrysler produces first car bearing his name.

1926    Daimler-Benz formed in Germany.

1927    A four-speed manual transmission is introduced.

1929    Growth of automobiles in Los Angeles is five times the rate of population growth.

Nationally, record 4.5 million cars produced, accounting for 20 percent of the nation's steel, 80 percent of rubber.

1936    W.S. James of Studebaker Co. reveals simple method of recirculating gases from crankcase to engine manifold for recombusting with piece of copper tubing—later called "positive crankcase ventilation" or PCV.

Research by the Society of Automotive Engineers indicates presence of hydrocarbons in automotive exhausts.

US Commerce Dept: 54 percent of US families own cars.

1937    Ford offers 60 and 85 horsepower engines; in Germany, first Volkswagen, or "People's Car" produced.

1938    Internal GM memo notes management's reluctance "to undertake the engineering and development of [exhaust control] devices, even though they appear to be based on sound principles."

Packard offers "Econo-drive," an overdrive transmission.

1940s   Detroit converts to military production for WWII; turns out munitions, aircraft, tanks, electronics, etc.

1943    Los Angeles has episodes of low-lying haze that cause coughing, wheezing, and much public complaint; "daylight dimout" occurs in September; public commissions form.

1947    California Air Pollution Control Act empowers local bodies to regulate pollution sources; Chevrolet initiates first automobile advertising on television.

1948    Honda Motor Company forms in Japan.

1950    Dr. Arie J. Haagen-Smit of Cal Tech advances theory of "smog" (ozone pollution), caused by a photochemical reaction of pollutants—primarily from oil refineries and automobiles.

49 million total US vehicles registered: annual production, 8 million.

1953    AMA forms the Vehicle Combustion Products Committee in December to begin "cooperative program" of industry research to address auto pollution and explore smog control devices.

1955    Air Pollution Control Act adopted by Congress; first federal attempt, only provides for research studies and financial and technical support to states.

AMA adopts legal agreement to assure new pollution control devices are jointly agreed to and cross-licensed so no one company reaps competitive advantage.

1956    European oil supplies threatened at the Suez Canal spurs significant small car breakthrough, the Mini, utilizing fuel-efficient transverse engine (mounted sideways) over front-wheel-drive.

US Highway Act calls for the construction of 41,000 miles of interstate highways; by this date, at least 190 US communities are collecting air pollution data.

1957    Representative Paul Schenck (R-OH) introduces bill to prohibit sale of vehicles discharging hydrocarbons in levels found dangerous by the Surgeon General; bill dies, becomes study.

Ford Motor tests early catalytic converter, vanadium pentoxide device.

1958    Toyota and Datsun (Nissan) go on sale in US for first time.

1959    AMA announces in November that a device to reduce crankcase emissions, PCV valve, will be offered on 1961 California cars; PCV essentially same principle as in 1938.

VW Beetle takes nearly 12 percent of US import market; Big Three compacts soon introduced—Chevrolet Corvair, Ford Falcon, and Plymouth Valiant.

1960    Dwight Eisenhower signs the Schenck Act, clean air law that, among other things, directs US Surgeon General to study auto pollution and public health.

California's Motor Vehicle Pollution Control Act creates Motor Vehicle Pollution Control Board to certify pollution control technology and require its installation.

GM begins voluntarily installing PCV device on its new 1961 California cars.

80 percent of US families own cars.

1961    Kennedy administration says 90 percent of population lives in localities with air pollution problems.

1962    Automakers begin installing PCV devices on 1963 model year cars, nationally.

Engelhard Industries begins testing catalytic converters on automobiles. GM builds a smog chamber for analyzing smog and uses mobile lab for sampling.

1963    Congress passes Clean Air Act of 1963; authorizes federal government to establish air quality standards; use of the standards, however, is optional for states.

1964    California certifies four exhaust devices by non-automakers triggering requirement for exhaust controls by 1966; automakers opt for engine controls (spark, timing), not catalytic converters.

1965    LA County requests US attorney general to investigate automakers lack of progress on pollution control and take action to prevent "further collusive obstruction;" DOJ internal activity already begun.

Federal Motor Vehicle Air Pollution Control Act passed; confusion remains about state vs. federal standards; Ralph Nader's *Unsafe At Any Speed* attacks auto safety.

1965    Muskie committee reports 84 million motor vehicles cause about half the nation's air pollution.

US annual auto production at 11.1 million vehicles.

1966    Ford and GM show prototype EVs. Neither are produced.

Congress passes National Traffic and Motor Vehicle Safety Act, brings safety belts by 1968; US Department of Transportation created.

1967 Clean Air Act of 1967 adopted, requiring states to adopt and implement standards consistent with federal criteria; California alone can adopt stricter standards; CARB created.

1968 California Pure Air Act prescribes increasingly tough auto emissions standards for 1970-1974 model years.

1969 US Justice Department files suit against US automakers in January under antitrust statute, alleges sixteen-year conspiracy (1953-1969) to prevent pollution control.

Detroit automakers gather at White House conference on environment, learn of Nixon's intention to propose tough auto emissions standards to be met in ten years, by 1980.

1970 US EPA created; first Earth Day celebration in April; Henry Ford II says his company will produce virtually emission-free ICE by 1975, other automakers say by 1980.

Senator Gaylord Nelson (D-WI) introduces bill in August to ban the sale of ICE by 1975; Senator Ed Muskie (D-ME) offers bill for 90 percent reduction of auto emissions by 1975.

Ford's Lee Iacocca, calls Muskie's proposed Clean Air bill "a threat to the entire American economy and to every person in America."

Clean Air Act of 1970 establishes NAAQS, 90 percent reduction in auto emissions by 1975, begins phase-out of leaded gasoline, and requires goal-attainment plans by states.

1971 Honda announces in February that its CVCC engine can meet the projected 1975 US auto emissions standards without a catalytic converter.

1972 EPA's William Ruckelshaus first refuses, but after litigation and re-hearing, grants automakers a one-year delay of auto emissions deadline from 1975 to 1976.

1973 First "energy shock"—OPEC stops oil exports to US in October, gas lines follow; average fuel economy of Big Three car fleet then at 13 MPG.

1974 Congress passes the Energy Supply and Environmental Coordination Act that delays auto emissions standards to 1977, with allowances for EPA to extend further.

President Nixon orders states to observe 55-MPH speed limit; 37 percent of US oil then imported.

Auto sales (US and imports) fall to 8.6 million units; Chrysler begins first "rebate" program in following year to help stimulate sales; Toyota surpasses VW in sales.

1974 Total US vehicles registered: 129.9 million.

1975 President Ford proposes to delay auto emissions standards to 1982 in exchange for Big Three pledge to improve fuel economy by 40 percent.

First two-way catalytic converters—treating CO and HC emissions—are used on automobiles; unleaded gasoline made available for first time.

1976    Government issues first fuel economy standards in October for improving gas mileage in cars—18 MPG to be achieved in 1978 models; Detroit begins downsizing programs.

1977    Congress amends Clean Air Act, extends auto emission deadlines to 1979 and pushes back original emission standards to 1981, also adds variety of waivers.

1978    EPA Deputy Administrator cites automakers' 12 million vehicle recalls for emission system failures as "dismal showing."

US annual auto production at 12.8 million vehicles.

1979    Second oil crisis, US gasoline prices double.

Chrysler and UAW lobby Congress and Carter administration for $1.5 billion federal bailout for Chrysler in the form of federal loan guarantees.

GM's Pete Estes says GM will produce EVs by mid-1980s, possibly as commuter car or delivery truck.

1980    GM, Ford, Chrysler, and American Motors suffer combined loss of $4.2 billion for the year; total vehicle sales fall below 9 million units.

1981    NHTSA proposes new CAFE standards in January, calls for 40 MPG by 1990 and 48 MPG by 1995. Reagan administration withdraws notice three months later.

Oil prices climb; Big Three seek congressional rollback of emissions standards.

Three-way catalytic converters begin to be used to treat auto exhausts.

Japanese automakers agree to begin "voluntary" export restraints, shortages of Japanese models occur thereafter in US.

Chrysler reports 1980 losses of $1.7 billion—the largest in American business history. Ford and GM also report heavy losses as Americans purchase fuel-efficient foreign cars.

1982    Japanese take 22.6 percent of US auto market—up from 9.3 percent in 1976.

1983    GM, CAFE slips to 24 MPG, below 27 MPG standard; GM misses standard again in following year, coming in at 24.8 MPG.

1984    Chrysler minivan heralds new multimillion vehicle segment in what soon becomes booming light-truck market.

GM and Toyota begin joint-venture in California to produce Toyota Corollas also sold as Chevy Novas & Prisms.

Detroit has record profits—Chrysler, Ford, GM, and AMC all post hefty gains.

1985    GM and Ford petition NHTSA in March to rollback 1986 CAFE standard. Chrysler opposes rollback, runs Lee Iacocca ads supporting CAFE. NHTSA capitulates, rolls back to 26 MPG.

As voluntary export restraints are eased on Japanese, they increase American sales by 25 percent to 2.3 million vehicles. Honda introduces Acura luxury model.

Chevrolet's S-10 Blazer introduced—first "compact" SUV; Ford Taurus introduced in fall.

1986   Oil price collapse; auto sales reach all-time high—more than 16 million vehicles, the peak year until 1999.

1987   Clean Air Act stalls in Congress on acid rain issue.

Chrysler buys American Motors, maker of Jeep; also buys Lamborghini.

1988   NASA's Jim Hansen tells Congress "greenhouse effect is here" and that he is 99 percent certain that global warming trend is caused by a buildup of carbon dioxide and other gases.

EPA's Lee Thomas in August, "indisputable" that ground-level ozone must be reduced, in some cases, "substantially"; 110 million Americans in areas exceeding NAAQS for ozone.

1989   Honda Accord is best-selling car in US in 1989, 1990, and 1991.

1990   Iraq invades Kuwait in early August; US auto sales plummet; Senator Bryan's pending CAFE bill receives favorable reception in Senate vote, may be veto-proof.

California adopts LEV-ZEV regulations in September, including a "2%-ZEVs-by-1998" deadline.

Congress adopts Clean Air Act Amendments: stricter tailpipe standards, cleaner-burning fuels, limits on fuel volatility, and clean-fuel fleets in nonattainment areas.

1991   Sen Bryan re-introduces CAFE bill in January; GM's Robert Stempel later tells press that atmospheric benefits of tighter fuel economy standards are "marginal,"

GM announces in March that Impact EV will be built in Lansing, MI and will be introduced commercially; delivery of EVs by mid-90s.

In October, Big Three establish US Advanced Battery Consortium, a joint industry research venture on EV batteries at the "pre-competition" level.

NRDC, EDF, ALA, and five northeastern states sue EPA over ozone standard, resulting in a court-ordered deadline by August 1992.

Auto sales drop 11 percent from mediocre 1990; GM, Ford, and Chrysler all deep in red; end of Persian Gulf War fails to ignite sales; GM to close 25 factories, slash 75,000 jobs.

1992   Oxygenated gasoline introduced in 36 cities in nonattainment for carbon monoxide (CO); EPA does not revise ozone standard.

Rio Treaty agreement on global warming calls on nations to voluntarily reduce greenhouse gases to 1990 levels by the year 2000.

1993   White House/Big Three "Partnership for a New Generation of Vehicles" launched in September; ten-year program to deliver 80-MPG prototype vehicle by 2003.

ALA and others sue EPA for failing to set smog & soot standards (ozone and particulate).

1994   EPA's Carol Browner instructs EPA to begin court-ordered review of "smog & soot" scientific studies to determine whether standards should be revised.

GM secretly restarts Impact EV program in March.

US drivers travel 2.35 *trillion* miles in their vehicles during the year.

1995 Honda Accord passenger car passes California ULEV emissions test more than two years ahead of deadline.

Congress repeals 55-MPH speed limit. US importing half its oil by this date.

Ford, for first time in its ninety-three-year history, sells more trucks than cars.

1996 GM's Jack Smith announces plans to sell EVs to the public—goes to market in December as leased vehicles in selected markets—CA, AZ, NM.

Sierra Club Legal Defense Fund, with law firm of Preston Gates Ellis, petitions US Justice Department alleging a conspiracy to stifle the development of electric vehicles.

In May, auto, oil, and other industries form Air Quality Standards Coalition to fight EPA's expected "smog & soot" reforms; companies contribute $100,000 or more each to join.

EPA's Browner proposes eighty-hour ozone standard at 80 PPB and small particle standard of PM 2.5.

1997 Daimler-Benz announces it will sell 100,000 fuel-cell-powered cars in 2005; launches $330 million joint venture with Ballard Power Systems; Ford later joins putting up $422 million.

Industry effort to stop smog & soot revisions includes seventy-five-lobbyist "strike force" and spending of $30 million; in June, President Clinton approves EPA's smog and soot rules.

In September, Big Three spend millions to bankroll Global Climate Information Project's $13 million advertising campaign to influence public opinion and Kyoto negotiation politics.

1997 Toyota unveils world's first hybrid vehicle in October, a half-gas, half-electric-powered car, called the Prius, rated at 66 MPG, with very low emissions; sold in Tokyo at first.

1998 In May, Chrysler and German automaker Daimler-Benz announce $40 billion merger to form DaimlerChrysler, the world's fifth largest automaker.

Big Six automakers—Ford, GM, Toyota, DaimlerChrysler, Renault-Nissan, and Volkswagen—account for nearly 65 percent of 1998 global auto sales.

1999 Ford announces $6.5 billion acquisition of Volvo; Renault makes $5.4 billion deal to become Nissan's largest owner.

GM and Toyota announce in May they will begin five-year joint venture to build alternative vehicles; Nissan unveils a gas/electric hybrid vehicle, the Tino.

A three-judge panel of US Court of Appeals votes 2-1 in May to block the implementation of EPA's new smog & soot regulations.

Honda becomes first automaker to begin selling a hybrid vehicles in US market when its gas-electric subcompact car, the Insight (70 MPG highway) goes on sale in December.

GM makes deal to buy Honda low emission engines for GM cars.

2000  Toyota's hybrid car, the Prius, goes on sale in the US and Europe; hybrid minivan to follow in US by summer.

2001  GM says it will produce an electric/gas-turbine hybrid capable of achieving 80 MPG by this deadline.

2003  California requires that 10 percent of all new vehicles sold in state by major automakers be ZEVs.

2004  PNGV's production-ready 80 MPG vehicle is to debut; Tier 2 auto emissions standards to begin as well; and Big Three fuel-cell vehicles slated to arrive.

2009  All new trucks and SUVs are to meet Tier 2 emission standards by this date.

2012  The US—the world's largest greenhouse polluter—to reduce its greenhouse emissions to a level 7 percent below 1990 levels if bound by Kyoto Treaty.

2019  Last of 8-to-10 million SUVs and trucks on US roads and highways certified under old Tier 2 emission standards will have reached ten years of vehicle life.

Sources: Motor Vehicle Manufacturers of the United States, Inc., *Automobile of America*, Detroit: Wayne State University Press, fourth edition, revised 1974; "100 Years of the Automobile," special edition, *Motor Trend*, 1985; "100 Years," special anniversary issue, *Automotive Industries*, July 1995; Scott Oldham and Michael Lamm, "Automobiles: Happy 100th!" *Popular Mechanics*, May 1996, pp. 47-59; Al Hass, "A History of Automobile Production in America," *The Philadelphia Inquirer*, June 2, 1996, p. E-1; Crain Communications, Inc., *Automotive News*, special editions, "The 100-Year Almanac," vol. 1, April 24, 1996; and "100 Events That Made the Industry," *Automotive News*, vol. 2, June 26, 1996; "Auto Industry Gets More Compact, 1954," Centennial Journal: 100 Years in Business, *The Wall Street Journal*; American Automobile Centennial Commission, brochures, timelines, charts and other material, 1996; and other source material already cited throughout this book.

# Big Three Auto & Truck Recalls for Emission System Problems & Defects, 1973–1998

## NOT MAKING THE GRADE

| Date | Company | Problem & Sample Models | Type Recall | Vehicles |
|------|---------|-------------------------|-------------|----------|
| Jul/Aug 73 | GM | improper vehicle weight; need to readjust emission system in selected '73 Suburbans & others | EPA influenced | 2,885 |
| 21 Jun 74 | Chrysler | probable failure of EGR system actuator (CCEGR valve) in selected '73 cars/trucks | EPA influenced | 769,281 |
| Oct 1974 | Ford | probable failure of EGR system actuator PVS valve in selected '73 & '74 models | EPA influenced | 226,058 |
| 6 Mar 76 | Chrysler | defect in sensing device for exhaust gas recirculation (EGR); selected '73 models, Dodge, etc. | EPA ordered | 825,000 |
| Sep 1976 | Ford | excessive HC emissions in selected Mustangs, Mavericks, & Mercury Comets | EPA influenced | 34,500 |
| 20 Oct 76 | GM | failure of cold temperature vacuum valve in '74 Pontiacs w/V-8s causing excessive NOx emissions | EPA ordered | 330,000 |

| Date | Company | Problem & Sample Models | Type Recall | Vehicles |
|------|---------|------------------------|-------------|----------|
| 8 Dec 76 | Chrysler | idle mixture misadjustment on selected 1975 Chryslers, Dodges, & Plymouths; excessive CO emissions | EPA ordered | 208,000 |
| 8 Feb 77 | Ford | excessive CO in selected '77 Monarchs and Granadas caused by overly rich carburetion | EPA ordered | 54,000 |
| 11 Feb 77 | Ford | excessive HC emissions suspected in '73 & '74 V-8 models due to failure of EGR carburetor spacer plate | company recall | 4,400,000 |
| 22 Mar 77 | GM | excessive CO emissions in selected '75 Cadillacs; defective carburetor design | EPA ordered | 135,000 |
| 27 Jan 78 | Ford | defective EGR backpressure transducer resulting in excessive NOx in selected Torinos, Rancheros, Cougars, & others | EPA ordered | 640,000 |
| 19 Apr 78 | Chrysler | excessive CO emissions in selected '78 Plymouth Fury, Dodge Monaco, Chrysler Cordoba & others | EPA ordered | 67,400 |
| 20 Apr 78 | Chrysler | 2x allowable CO levels in certain Dodge, Plymouth, & Chrysler models;carburetor problem on V-8s | EPA ordered; sales halt threatened | 77,000 |
| 9 May 78 | AMC | defective EGR backpressure transducer causing excessive NOx in selected Jeeps & federal vehicles (Post Office) | EPA ordered | 330,300 |
| June 1978 | GM | incorrect hose routing resulting in excessive emissions in selected Chevy and GMC trucks | company recall | 2,800 |
| August 78 | Ford | defective canister purge valve causing excessive HC emissions in all '78 LDV models & some CA trucks over 6000 LBS. | company recall | 1,417,000 |

| Date | Company | Problem & Sample Models | Type Recall | Vehicles |
|---|---|---|---|---|
| 22 Sep 78 | Chrysler | defective valve in air injection ystem resulting in excessive CO & HC in '76-'77 Dodge Colts & Plymouth Arrows | company recall | 198,500 |
| 31 Oct 78 | Ford | defective valve in air injection system in selected '78 Fairmounts & Zephyrs | company recall | 190,000 |
| Nov 1979 | GM | defective EGR backpressure transducer resulting in excessive NOx in selected '75-'78 Pontiacs | EPA ordered | 430,000 |
| Nov 1979 | GM | excessive CO emissions; failed SEA audit; Chevrolet Chevettes manufactured at Lakewood and Wilmington | EPA ordered (2 actions) 78,500 | 41,700 |
| 14 Dec 79 | Ford | accelerator pump weepage resulting in excessive evaporative emissions in '80 CA Pinto/Bobcat, Mustang/Capri, others | company recall | 6,100 |
| 1 Apr 80 | GM | defective EGR backpressure transducer & EGR clogging resulting in excessive NOx in selected '76 Buicks, Pontiacs, others | EPA ordered | 150,000 |
| 16 Apr 80 | Ford | excessive NOx; selected Broncos failed an EPA Selective Enforcement Audit | EPA ordered | 6,000 |
| 20 Jun 80 | GM | defective EGR backpressure transducer & EGR clogging NOx resulting in excessivein selected '76 & '77 Cadillac Sevilles | EPA ordered | 99,900 |
| 20 Jun 80 | GM | clogging of EGR passages resulting in excessive NOx emissions in selected '77 Oldsmobile Omega, Delta, & Cutlass models | EPA ordered | 65,100 |
| 25 Jun 80 | GM | excessive NOx in '76 Oldsmobiles & '77 Cadillacs; clogging of EGR with faulty joint | EPA ordered | 169,000 |

| Date | Company | Problem & Sample Models | Type Recall | Vehicles |
|---|---|---|---|---|
| 2 Sep 80 | GM | defective carburetor design in selected '75 Cadillac Eldorados, Devilles, others | EPA influenced | 95,000 |
| 8 Sep 80 | GM | defective EGR valves & burnt EGR hoses causing excessive NOx in selected Buick Centurys, Regals, & LaSabres | EPA ordered | 171,900 |
| 9 Dec 80 | GM | excessive NOx emissions in selected Buick, Pontiac, & Oldsmobile models | EPA ordered | 573,400 |
| 26 Jan 81 | GM | breakage of air pipes transmitting vacuum to distributor diaphragms in selected '80 Celicas, pickups, others | company recall | 318,800 |
| 9 Mar 81 7 Apr 81 22 Apr 81 | GM | excessive NOx emissions in selected '78 Pontiac, Chevrolet, & Oldsmobile models | EPA influenced | 121,000 |
| 9 Apr 81 10 Apr 81 25 Apr 81 | GM | EGR valve plugging; excessive NOx emissions in selected '77 Buicks, Oldsmobiles, & Pontiacs | EPA influenced | 424,700 |
| 25 Nov 81 | Ford | excessive CO emissions; failed audit, selected '82 Thunderbirds | EPA influenced | 4,200 |
| 10 May 82 | GM | excessive NOx due to EGR clogging and EGR backpressure transducer failure in selected '78 Cadillac Sevilles | EPA ordered | 52,000 |
| 21 Oct 82 | GM | excessive NOx due to EGR valve plugging in selected '78 Buick, Oldsmobile, Pontiac, and Chevrolet models | EPA ordered | 608,000 |
| 21 Dec 82 | GM | excessive NOx in selected Pontiac Sunbirds, Chevrolet Monzas, and Oldsmobile Starfires w/151 CID four-cylinders | EPA ordered | 131,000 |

| Date | Company | Problem & Sample Models | Type Recall | Vehicles |
|------|---------|------------------------|-------------|----------|
| 26 Jan 83 | GM | excessive NOx in '80 Buick Regals & Centurys, Pontiac LeMans, Grand Prix, Bonnevilles, Firebirds, others | EPA ordered | 174,000 |
| 28 Jan 83 | Chrysler | excessive HC & CO in '79 Mitsubishi Dodge Colts, Challengers & Plymouth Champs, Arrows & Sapporos | EPA influenced | 74,600 |
| 23 Mar 83 | GM | excessive NOx in '78 Chev. Malibu & Monzas, Pontiac Grand Ams & Sunbirds, Buick Regals, Olds Starfires, others | EPA ordered | 527,000 |
| 7 Apr 83 | GM | EGR valve plugging; selected '79 Buicks, Chevrolets, Oldsmobiles & Pontiacs | EPA ordered | 567,000 |
| 7 Apr 83 | GM | EGR valve plugging in selected '78 & '79 Malibu, Monte Carlos, El Caminos, GMC Caballeros & others | EPA ordered | 294,000 |
| 31 May 83 | GM | EGR passage clogging in selected '79 Cadillac Sevilles & Eldorados | EPA influenced | 64,400 |
| 12 Jul 83 | Ford | high altitude compensator miscalibration in selected '82 Escorts, Lynxes, Granadas, T-Birds & others | company recall | 20,400 |
| 18 Jul 83 | GM | catalyst plugging in selected '81 & '82 Chevrolets, GMCs & Pontiacs | company recall | 808,300 |
| 21 Sep 83 | Ford | failed CARB in-use HC & NOx testing for selected '80 Granadas, T-Birds, Cougars, Versailles & others | company recall | 17,200 |
| 20 Oct 83 | GM | excessive CO emissions in selected Chevrolet Chevettes | EPA ordered | 112,000 |
| 6 Mar 84 | GM | excessive CO in 1980 Oldsmobiles with 5.0L & 5.7L 8-cylinder engines | EPA ordered | 186,000 |

| Date | Company | Problem & Sample Models | Type Recall | Vehicles |
|---|---|---|---|---|
| 23 Apr 84 | AMC | excessive HC and CO emissions in selected '79 Concords, Spirits & Pacers. | EPA influenced | 62,400 |
| 24 Apr 84 | Ford | CARB new vehicle compliance testing showed HC & CO exceedances in some 1984 CA Ford Mustangs and Capris. | company recall | 3,700 |
| 7 May 84 | Chrysler | excessive HC and CO emissions in selected '80 Chrysler, Dodge, & Plymouth models. | EPA influenced | 235,000 |
| 13 Jun 84 | GM | EGR valve plugging in selected '80 Buick, Pontiac, Chevrolet, & Oldsmobile models. | EPA ordered | 550,000 |
| 1 Aug 84 | Chrysler | EGR valve diaphragm separates from housing, rendering inoperative in selected '84 Dodge & Plymouth models | company recall | 31,800 |
| 21 Sep 84 | Ford | CARB in-use vehicle enforcement testing showed HC exceedances in selected '81 CA Fairmonts, Mustangs, & others. | company recall | 18,800 |
| 5 Oct 84 | GM | plugging of dual-bed catalyst due to pellet fragmentation in selected '81 & '82 Pontiacs, Buicks, & Oldsmobiles | company recall | 750,000 |
| 17 Oct 84 | Ford | Ford end-of-line testing showed HC and CO exceedances in selected '84 CA Rangers & Bronco II LDTs | company recall | 8,300 |
| 18 Jan 85 | GM | plugging of dual-bed catalyst due to pellet fragmentation; selected '81 & '82 Buicks, Cadillacs, & others. | company recall | 225,000 |
| 25 Feb 85 | GM | plugging of dual-bed catalyst due to pellet fragmentation; selected '82 & '83 Cadillac models | company recall | 290,000 |

| Date | Company | Problem & Sample Models | Type Recall | Vehicles |
|---|---|---|---|---|
| 2 Apr 85 | Ford | excessive HC & CO in selected '81 Ford & Mercury models | EPA influenced | 180,000 |
| 29 Apr 85 | GM | EGR valve tearing & EGR deposit accumulation; selected '81 Buicks, Cadillacs, Oldsmobiles, & Pontiacs | company recall | 20,800 |
| 15 May 85 | Ford | excessive HC & CO in selected Cougars, Mustangs, T-birds & others; leaking choke pull down motor | EPA influenced | 119,000 |
| 30 Aug 85 | GM | excessive HC & CO due to corrosion of air tube assembly & damaged solenoid valve in selected '81 Chevy Chevettes & Pontiacs | EPA influenced | 454,000 |
| 4 Sep 85 | GM | excessive evaporative emissions —triple federal standard—in selected '81 Buicks & Pontiacs | EPA ordered | 82,600 |
| 22 Nov 85 | Chrysler | excessive HC & CO in selected '81 Omnis, Horizons, Reliants | EPA influenced | 340,000 |
| 2 Dec 85 | GM | plugging of dual-bed catalyst in selected '83 Buicks & Oldsmobiles | company recall | 186,000 |
| 7 May 86 | GM | excessive HC and CO due to corrosion of air tube assembly in selected '82 Chevettes & Pontiac T-1000s | EPA influenced | 133,000 |
| 19 May 86 | GM | CARB in-use Vehicle Enforcement Testing showed NOx exceedances in selected '82 Buicks, Chevrolets, Cadillacs, & others | company recall | 30,200 |
| 11 Sep 86 | Chrysler | excessive NOx emissions in selected '81 Dodge Omnis & Plymouth Horizons | EPA ordered | 93,000 |
| 6 Nov 86 | Chrysler | CARB in-use Vehicle Enforcement Testing showed NOx exceedance in selected '82 Horizons, Reliants, Omnis, & LeBarons. | company recall | 18,600 |

| Date | Company | Problem & Sample Models | Type Recall | Vehicles |
|------|---------|-------------------------|-------------|----------|
| 8 Dec 86 | Ford | excessive CO from calibration change in selected '86 Escorts, EXPs, & Lynxs | EPA influenced | 58,000 |
| 17 Dec 86 | Ford | excessive CO in selected '81 & '82 Ford LTDs, LTD wagons, Mercury Marquis & Marquis wagons | EPA influenced | 314,000 |
| 23 Dec 86 | Ford | excessive CO (Fed) and excessive CO HC (CA) in selected '82 Escorts, Lynxs, EXPs, & LN7s | EPA/CARB influenced | 226,000 |
| 24 Feb 87 | Chrysler | excessive HC in selected '82 Dodge Omnis & Plymouth Horizons | EPA influenced | 51,000 |
| 26 May 87 | Ford | electronic engine control module mal-function affects idle speed control in selected '87 Ford & Mercury models | company recall | 22,300 |
| 31 Jul 87 | GM | defective evaporative canister purge thermal vacuum switch in selected '82 Chevrolet, Pontiac, & GMC models | EPA influenced | 473,000 |
| 6 Oct 87 | Chrysler | excessive HC and NOx in selected '82 LeBarons, Dodge Aries, & Omnis, Plymouth Horizons, Reliants, & others | EPA influenced | 126,000 |
| 6 Oct 87 | Ford | excessive HC in '82 Ford Escorts and Mercury Lynx w/1.6 L engine & manual transmission | EPA influenced | 85,000 |
| 19 Nov 87 | GM | defective evaporative canister purge thermal vacuum switch in selected '83 Chevrolet, Pontiac, & GMC models | EPA influenced | 599,000 |
| 15 Mar 88 | Ford | excessive HC & CO emissions in selected Ford Escort, Escort Wagon, EXP & Mercury Lynx, Lynx Wagon & LN-7 models | EPA influenced | 185,000 |

| Date | Company | Problem & Sample Models | Type Recall | Vehicles |
|------|---------|-------------------------|-------------|----------|
| 12 Apr 88 | Chrysler | CARB in-use Vehicle Enforcement Testing showed HC & NOx exceedances in selected '83 Chrysler, Plymouth, & Dodge models | company recall | 23,200 |
| 19 Apr 88 | Ford | excessive HC & CO emissions in selected Ford Ranger, & Bronco II models. | EPA influenced | 106,000 |
| 28 Feb 89 | Ford | excessive HC & CO emissions in selected '83 Ford Mustang, LTD, Thunderbird & Mercury Capri, Cougar, & Marquis models | EPA influenced | 264,200 |
| 13 Mar 89 | Ford | excessive HC & CO emissions in selected '84-'85 Ford Escort, EXP, Escort Wagon, & Mercury Lynx & Lynx Wagon models | EPA influenced | 513,000 |
| 28 Mar 89 | GM | defective Evap TVS in selected '84 Buick and Oldsmobile models—Delta 88, & others | EPA influenced | 672,600 |
| 18 Apr 89 | Ford | CARB in-use Vehicle Enforcement Testing showed HC & NOx exceedances in selected '85-'86 Ford & Mercury models | company recall | 47,000 |
| 10 May 89 | Chrysler | excessive evaporative emissions due to deviation in carburetor bowl vent valve setting in '84-'87 vans, wagons, & trucks | EPA influenced | 568,000 |
| 10 May 89 | Chrysler | excessive CO emissions in '84 Chrysler E-Class, New Yorker, LeBaron, Laser, Dodge Datona, & others. | EPA influenced | 127,200 |
| 24 Jul 89- 7 May 90 | Ford | excessive HC & CO due to low pressure throttle body fuel injector leakage in selected '85-'87 Ford & Mercury models | EPA influenced | 1,281,800 |

| Date | Company | Problem & Sample Models | Type Recall | Vehicles |
|------|---------|-------------------------|-------------|----------|
| 23 Aug 89 | Ford | excessive HC emissions in selected '85 Ford Mustangs, & Mercury Capris & '85-'86 Ford LTDs, Mercury Marquis, & others | EPA influenced | 453,000 |
| 18 Sep 89 | Ford | excessive HC & CO emissions in selected '85-'86 Ford Escort, EXP, & Lynx models | EPA influenced | 493,200 |
| 24 Oct 89 | Chrysler | HC & NOx exceedance in CARB in-use Vehicle Enforcement Testing in selected '86 CA Jeep Wagoneer, Cherokee, & Comanche models | company recall | 15,000 |
| 25 Oct 89 | GM | camshaft misoriented to crankshaft by one geartooth (retarded or advanced) in certain '89-'90 Chevy & GMC vans, pickups & SUVs. | company recall | 7,700 |
| 8 Dec 89 | Ford | CARB in-use Vehicle Enforcement Testing showed HC exceedances in selected '86 Ford Mustang, LTD, T-Bird, & others | company recall | 32,000 |
| 11 Dec 89 | Chrysler | EPA proposes $666,000 penalty for denying owners warranty complaints coverage for work performed on emission-control parts | EPA investigation | 66 |
| 18 Dec 89 | Ford | CARB in-use Vehicle Enforcement showed HC exceedances in selected '86 Ford models | company recall | 64,000 |
| 16 Jan 90 | Chrysler | catalytic converter insulation blanket in some '86 Jeeps, Comanches, & Wagoneers causes catalyst overheating, breakdown | EPA influenced | 55,000 |
| 26 Jan 90 | Chrysler | catalytic converter insulation blanket in some '86 & '87 Alliances & Encores causes catalyst overheating, breakdown | company recall | 8,700 |

| Date | Company | Problem & Sample Models | Type Recall | Vehicles |
|---|---|---|---|---|
| 9 Feb 90 | Chrysler | catalytic converter insulation blanket in some '85 & '86 Alliances & Encores causes catalyst overheating, breakdown | EPA influenced | 52,000 |
| 28 Feb 90 | Ford | excessive HC & NOx in CARB In-Use Vehicle Compliance Testing in selected '86 CA Ford Escort & Mercury Lynx models | company recall | 16,000 |
| 18 Apr 90 | Chrysler | excessive HC and CO emissions in selected '83 Plymouth Horizons, Dodge Chargers, Dodge Omnis, Chrysler LeBarons, & others | EPA influenced | 72,000 |
| 7 May 90 | Chrysler | failure of choke delay valve causes excessive HC & CO emissions in '85 Plymouth Horizons, Dodge Omnis, & others | EPA influenced | 383,700 |
| 14 May 90 | GM | incorrect emission control module (ECM) in selected Chevrolet Van & Sportvan, GMC VanDura, & Rally models | company recall | 360 |
| 21 May 90 | Chrysler | catalytic converter insulation blanket in some '87 Jeeps, Comanches, & Wagoneers causes catalyst overheating, breakdown | EPA influenced | 11,100 |
| 1 Jun 90 | GM | excessive CO in selected '85 Buick, Oldsmobile, & Pontiac models | EPA influenced | 410,000 |
| 24 Sep 90 | Chrysler | excessive CO; fuel injectors shift rich due to lengthening of closing time in selected '87 Plymouths, Dodges, & others | EPA influenced | 106,000 |
| 24 Sep 90 | Ford | excessive nonmethane HC in CARB In-Use Vehicle Compliance Testing in selected '87-'89 CA F-150, F-250, & Bronco models | company recall | 12,600 |

| Date | Company | Problem & Sample Models | Type Recall | Vehicles |
|---|---|---|---|---|
| 2 Oct 90 | Ford | excessive HC and CO in selected Ford LTD, LTD Wagon, Thunderbird, & Mustang & Mercury Cougar, Marquis, & Capri models | EPA influenced | 228,500 |
| 15 Oct 90 | Chrysler | excessive NOx & defective exhaust manifold found in CARB compliance tests in selected Jeep Commanches, Cherokees, & Wagoneers | company recall | 19,100 |
| 29 Oct 90 | Ford | excessive CO in Ford Thunderbirds & Mercury Cougars with 3.8L engine | EPA influenced | 127,700 |
| 23 Jan 91 | Ford | excessive HC and evaporative emissions in selected '84 Ford F-150 & F-250 pickups & E-250 vans w/5.0L engine & dual fuel tank | EPA influenced | 61,059 |
| 19 Feb 91 | Chrysler | excessive evaporative emissions in selected '87 Dodge Dakota models | EPA influenced | 66,069 |
| 27 Mar 91 | GM | IDI coil cracks at high voltage terminals; external arcing, misfires, rough idle in selected '87-90 Buicks, Chevrolets, others | company recall | 376,363 |
| 13 May 91 | Ford | excessive HC emissions in selected '84-85 Ford Mustang, T-Bird, LTD, Crown Victoria,Lincoln-Mercury Cougar, Mark VII, & others | EPA influenced | 640,837 |
| 28 Aug 91 | Ford | excessive CO emissions in assembly line testing for selected '90 Ford Probes | company recall | 24,700 |
| 10 Sep 91 | Chrysler | excessive HC and CO emissions in selected '87 Plymouth Voyager, Dodge Caravan, & Ram Van models | EPA influenced | 96,300 |
| 25 Nov 91 | Ford | defective throttle sensor in selected '90-'91 Ford Tempo, Mercury Topaz, & Ford Aerostar models | company recall | 528,100 |

| Date | Company | Problem & Sample Models | Type Recall | Vehicles |
|------|---------|------------------------|-------------|----------|
| 2 Dec 91 | Ford | excessive HC emissions in selected '85-'86 Ford E-Series, F-Series, & Bronco trucks with 4.9L engines in high altitude areas | EPA influenced | 20,800 |
| 21 Jan 92 | Ford | excessive NOx emissions in CARB in-use testing in '88-'89 CA Ford Tempo & Mercury Topaz models with 2.3 L engine | company recall | 60,400 |
| 21 Feb 92 | Chrysler | excessive HC & CO in selected '86 Dodge Chargers & Omnis, Horizons, & others | EPA influenced | 141,000 |
| 31 Mar 92 | Ford | excessive HC & NOx in CARB in-use tests of '88 CA Ford Taurus, Mercury Sable, & Lincoln Continental with 3.8L engine | company recall | 17,900 |
| 8 Apr 92 | Ford | particulate exceedance in SEA testing of '91 Ford 7.8L heavy-duty diesel engines | EPA influenced | 80 |
| 8 May 92 | Ford | excessive CO in '87 Ford Taurus & Taurus Wagon; Mercury Sable, & Sable Wagon with 3.0L engine | EPA influenced | 306,000 |
| 8 May 92 | Ford | excessive HC found in CARB in-use testing for '88 Ford Rangers with 2.3L engine | company recall | 20,400 |
| 11 Jun 92 | Ford | excessive HC & CO due to mat-mount catalyst failure in selected '86-'89 Ford Mustang, Lincoln, T-Bird, Mercury Cougar, & Capri | EPA influenced | 821,900 |
| 16 Jun 92 | GM | excessive CO emissions in selected '87 Buick Regals & Grand Nationals with 3.8L turbocharged engine | EPA influenced | 25,000 |
| 18 Jun 92 | Ford | excessive CO due to TPS sensor wearing out prematurely in selected '90-'91 Ford Probes | company recall | 1,600 |

| Date | Company | Problem & Sample Models | Type Recall | Vehicles |
|------|---------|-------------------------|-------------|----------|
| 7 Jul 92 | Chrysler | excessive HC, CO, & NOx found in CARB tests in selected '87 CA Jeep Wrangler, J-10 truck, AMC Eagle sedan & wagon models | company recall | 5,246 |
| 13 Jul 92 | Ford | CO & NOx exceedance; NOx problem due to leaking diaphragm in PCV valve; in '86 Ford Escort & Mercury Lynx models | EPA influenced | 132,000 |
| 22 Jul 92 | Chrysler | excessive NOx found in CARB in-use testing of selected '88 CA Jeep Commanche, Cherokee, & Wagoneer models | company recall | 27,551 |
| 10 Aug 92 | Chrysler | carburetor defects result in high replacement rate per CARB regs in '90 CA Jeep Wranglers with 4.2L engine | company recall | 4,623 |
| 18 Aug 92 | Ford | excessive evaporative emissions due to PCV system problem in selected '88-'90 Ford Taurus, Mercury Sable, & Lincoln models | EPA influenced | 412,250 |
| 21 Aug 92 | NUMMI (GM/ Toyota) | CO exceedance in selected '88 Novas & Toyota Corollas. | EPA influenced | 3,363 |
| 18 Dec 92 | Isuzu/GM | excessive CO in selected '86 Spectrum & Isuzu I-Mark models | EPA influenced | 61,287 |
| 23 Dec 92 | Chrysler | excessive NOx in selected '87 Dodge Omni, Charger, Plymouth Horizon, & Turismo models | EPA influenced | 275,844 |
| 1 Mar 93 | Isuzu/GM | excessive CO in selected '88 Chevrolet Spectrum & Isuzu I-Mark models | EPA ordered | 82,681 |
| 26 Feb 93 | GM | PCV fresh-air inlet hose disconnects from air cleaner allowing blowby emissions to escape in '92 | company recall | 1,849 |

| Date | Company | Chevrolet Caprice models Problem & Sample Models | Type Recall | Vehicles |
|---|---|---|---|---|
| 13 Aug 93 | Ford | excessive NOx during CARB in-use testing in selected '89-'90 CA Escorts | company recall | 42,800 |
| 30 Aug 93 | GM | evaporative system hoses deteriorate in selected '88-'89 Corvettes. | company recall | 49,209 |
| 2 Nov 93 | Diamond Star | excessive CO due to oxygen sensor problems (Chrysler/Mitsubishi) in selected '90 Mitsubishi Eclipse, Eagle Talon, & Plymouth Laser models | EPA influenced | 41,097 |
| 15 Nov 93 | Chrysler | excessive HC, CO, & NOx due to silicon contamination of oxygen sensor in selected '87-'90 Jeeps, '88-'91 Eagles, Dodges, & others | EPA influenced | 726,873 |
| 22 Dec 93 | Chrysler | excessive HC; leaking fuel injectors in '88 Chrysler New Yorker & Dodge Dynasty models | EPA influenced | 112,700 |
| 23 Dec 93 | Ford | excessive CO in selected '88-'90 Ford Escort, Escort wagon, & EXP models | PA influenced | 636,137 |
| 14 Feb 94 | Ford | excessive NOx in 1988 Ford Rangers with 2.0L engine | EPA influenced | 27,612 |
| 7 Mar 94 | Chrysler | excessive CO & NOx in '86 LeBarons, New Yorkers, Dodge Omnis, Lancers, Plymouth Caravelles, & others | EPA influenced | 166,206 |
| 14 Mar 94 | Chrysler | excessive NOx during California in-use testing in selected '90 Dodge Ram Pickup, Ramcharger, & others | company recall | 13,715 |
| 17 Mar 94 | GM | excessive HC & CO in selected '91 Saturns | EPA influenced | 28,850 |
| 6 May 94 | Ford | excessive NOx due to incorrect computer calibration in '93 heavy trucks with 4.9L engine | company recall | 800 |

| Date | Company | Problem & Sample Models | Type Recall | Vehicles |
|---|---|---|---|---|
| 27 May 94 | GM/ Isuzu | excessive CO in selected '90 Geo Storms due to computer programming in electronic control module | EPA influenced | 54,231 |
| 8 Jul 94 | Ford | excessive CO in selected '88-'90 Taurus Sable models in high-altitude areas | EPA influenced | 20,500 |
| 26 Aug 94 | Chrysler | excessive CO in selected '88 Plymouth, Dodge, & Chrysler models | EPA influenced | 5,264 |
| 14 Oct 94 | Ford | excessive CO emissions in selected '86-'89 Fords & Mercurys | EPA influenced | 91,765 |
| 14 Oct 94 | Ford | overheating & eventual breakup of catalyst in selected '88-'93 F-series trucks due to EEC calibration error | company recall | 52,130 |
| 28 Nov 94 | Chrysler | excessive CO & HC found by CARB in testing due to defective PCV solenoid & decel valve in '90 Jeep Wranglers | company recall | 4,764 |
| 5 Dec 94 | Suzuki (GM) | excessive CO in selected GEO Metro, Metro LSi, Chevrolet Sprint, Pontiac Firefly, & Suzuki Swift models | EPA influenced | 3,827 |
| 14 Dec 94 | GM | Powertrain Control Module (PCM) software error causes deceleration stall in selected '95 Pontiacs & Oldsmobiles | company recall | 29,783 |
| 8 Feb 95 | GM | excessive HC found in CARB '91 CA Chevrolet & GMC C/K & G trucks & M vans all with 4.3L engine. | company recall | 20,078 |
| 24 Feb 95 | Ford | CO levels in selected 1990 Taurus, Probe, & Sable models exceeding standard, new catalytic converters to be installed | EPA influenced | 250,000 |
| 14 Apr 95 | Ford | recall of selected '86 Ford Esorts, EXPs & Mercury Lynxs repaired improperly & discovered during an EPA audit | EPA influenced | 41,217 |

| Date | Company | Problem & Sample Models | Type Recall | Vehicles |
|------|---------|-------------------------|-------------|----------|
| 25 May 95 | Chrysler | catlytic converter failure in selected '89-'90 Jeep Cherokee, Comanche, & Wrangler models with 2.5L engine. | company recall | 35,953 |
| 31 May 95 | Chrysler | CO levels in selected 1985-1990 Jeeps & Eagles exceed standard, PCV system fails to operate as designed, will replace with improved PCV system & other repairs | EPA influenced | 180,000 |
| 30 Jun 95 | Ford | excessive NOx in '95 2.5L Ford Contours & Mercury Mystiques corrected by installing a new powertrian control module with a different calibration | company recall | 11,000 |
| 2 Jan 96 | Chrysler | excessive HC, CO, or NOx in selected '89-'90 Jeep Wrangler, CJ-&, & others due to various PCV system failures | EPA influenced | 51,625 |
| 8 May 96 | Chrysler | catalytic converter failure in selected '91-'95 Jeep Cherokees, Comanches, & Wranglers due to thermal expansion of can | company recall | 124,150 |
| 1 Aug 96 | GM | replace catalytic converter catalyst beads in selected '92 Chevrolet & GMC trucks & vans with 4.3L, 5.0L, & 5.7L engines | company recall | 65,400 |
| 3 Sep 96 | GM | failed CO when climate control system used in selected '91-'95 Cadillacs, company in violation of Section 203 Clean Air Act | EPA ordered | 586,967 |
| 19 Mar 97 | Ford | vapor control valve in '96 flex-fuel Taurus with 3.0L engine may experience improper open/close oscillation | company recall | 5,164 |

| Date | Company | Problem & Sample Models | Type Recall | Vehicles |
|------|---------|------------------------|-------------|----------|
| June 1997 | GM | excessive emissions & non-conformance with CA emission rules by '91-'93 Cadillac Sevilles & others, GM to pay $1.3 million fine & replace emissions calibration software that regulates air-fuel mixture | CARB influenced | 44,000 |
| 9 Jul 97 | Ford | premature failure of catalyst substrate support system in selected '95-'96 Contour & Mystique models with 2.5L engine | company recall | 105,000 |
| Sept 1997 | Chrylser | catalytic converters in some '90-91 Jeep Grand Wagoneer models not lasting full useful life of the vehicle | company recall | 10,740 |
| May 1998 | Chrysler | powertrian control module in selected '96 Sebring, Cirrus, Dodge Stratus, & Plymouth Breeze models may inadequately control CO emissions during I/M testing | company recall | 100,000 |
| 12 Aug 98 | GM | exceedance of NOx emission standard in '94 Olds Ciera & Buick Century with 3.1L engine (CA & NY) | company recall | 33,906 |
| 17 Sep 98 | GM | exhaust gas recirculation valve failures in selected '98 Chevrolet Camaros & Pontiac Firebirds due to corrosion | company recall | 27,000 |
| 14 Oct 98 | Chrysler/ Mitsubishi | NOx emissions problem may result in some '95 Mitsubishi, Dodge, & Chrylser models due to aspirator system failure | EPA influenced | 48,878 |
| 16 Nov 98 | Ford | managed fuel air strategy in selected '97 Econoline Vans causes vehicles to run lean of air/fuel balance in certain conditions | company recall | 44,444 |
| 28 Dec 98 | GM | exceedance of CO emission standard in selected '93 Chevrolet, Oldmobile, Pontiac, & Buick models with 3.1L enigne | EPA influenced | 391,885 |

Sources: EPA, *Emission Recall Report* (issued annually, 1976-1998) and *Emission Investigations Report* (issued on an incident basis, 1976-1998); EPA news & press Advisories; EPA printout, "Recall Quick Reference—Model Years '78-86," February 19, 1986; and newswire, newspaper, and other sources, including, for example: EPA, Office of Public Affairs, "EPA Orders General Motors to Recall 170,000 Cars for Pollution Defects," *Environmental News*, March 1980; "EPA Orders Recall of 169,000 GM Cars over Exhaust Device," *The Wall Street Journal*, June 25, 1980, p. 2; Robert E. Taylor, "EPA Finds Fewer Cars Are Meeting Emissions Limits," *The Wall Street Journal*, May 28, 1985; EPA, Office of Public Affairs, "EPA Orders GM Recall," *Environmental News*, October 25, 1982; EPA, Office of Public Affairs, "EPA Orders Recall of GM Cars," EPA, *Environmental News*, June 21, 1984; EPA, Office of Public Affairs, "GM Volunteers to Fix Emissions Problem on 750,000 Cars," *Environmental News*, October 15, 1984; "Chrysler Will Recall 350,000 Cars that Fail US Pollution Limits," *The Wall Street Journal*, November 26, 1985; EPA, Office of Public Affairs, "EPA Orders Recall of 1981 GM Cars," September 4, 1985; EPA, Office of Public Affairs, "EPA Orders Recall of 1981 Chrysler Cars," *Environmental News*, September 11, 1986; EPA, Office of Public Affairs, "Chryslers, Dodges and Plymouths Recalled for Exhaust-Emission Fix," October 6, 1987; EPA, Office of Public Affairs, "Ford Recalls Cars for Emission Repair," *Environmental News*, February 28, 1989; EPA, Office of Public Affairs, "Chrysler Recalls Vans, Cars and Trucks for Emission Repairs," *Environmental News*, May 10, 1989; EPA, Office of Communications and Public Affairs, update of activities, from Lew Crampton, associate administrator, "Chrysler Denied Vehicle Owners Emission Warranty Coverage, EPA Charges," December 11, 1989; EPA, Office of Communication, Education, And Public Affairs, "EPA Announces Recall of AMC Jeeps with Faulty Catalytic Converters," *Environmental News*, January 16, 1990; EPA, Communications and Public Affairs, "Ford Recalls Pickups and Vans for Emission Repairs," *Environmental News*, January 23, 1991; EPA, Communications and Public Affairs, "Ford, Lincoln-Mercury Recalled for Emission Repair," *Environmental News*, May 13, 1991; EPA, Communications and Public Affairs," Plymouth, Dodge Vans Exceed Federal Emission Limits," *Environmental News*, September 10, 1991; EPA, Communications and Public Affairs, "Chrysler Cars Exceed Federal Emission Standards," *Environmental News*, February 21, 1992; EPA, Communications, Education, and Public Affairs, "Ford Recalls Cars for Emission Repair," *Environmental News*, June 11, 1992; EPA, Communications, Education, and Public Affairs, "Ford Cars Exceed Emission Standards," *Environmental News*, August 18, 1992; EPA, Communications, Education, and Public Affairs, Press Advisory, "Chrysler Recalls 276,000 Plymouth, Dodge Models," December 23, 1992; EPA, Communications, Education, and Public Affairs, "Chrysler to Repair Emissions Problem on over Half Million Vehicles," *Environmental News*, November 15, 1993; EPA, Office of Communication, Education, and Public Affairs, "High-Altitude Chrysler Jeeps Exceed Emission Standard," *Environmental News*, February 18, 1994; EPA, Office of Communication, Education, and Public Affairs, "GM Saturns Recalled for Emission Repair," *Environmental News*, March 21, 1994; EPA, Office of Communication, Education, and Public Affairs, "Ford Recalls High-Altitude Taurus And Sable Autos," *Environmental News*, July 8, 1994; See also, for example: letter to F. James McDonald, president, General Motors Corporation, from John W. Hernandez, Jr., acting administrator, US EPA, March 22, 1983; letter to Dr. Betsy Ancker-Johnson, vice president, General Motors Corporation, from Kathleen M. Bennett, assistant administrator for Air, Noise and Radiation, EPA, April 7, 1983; and letter to W.R. Kittle, director, Vehicle Safety and Emissions, Chrysler Corporation, from J. Craig Potter, assistant administrator for Air and Radiation, EPA, September 10, 1986.

EPA ordered: recall after EPA order
EPA influenced: voluntary recall after EPA investigation
Company recall: voluntary recall by company

Note: not a complete list, especially for California vehicles.

# Index

## About the Author

Jack Doyle is the founder and director of *Corporate Sources* and its principal investigator. Formerly a senior policy analyst with Friends of the Earth and the Environmental Policy Institute in Washington, Doyle has more than twenty years experience with national energy and environmental policy. He has served as a consultant to the President's Council on Environmental Quality and the former Congressional Office of Technology Assessment. He has appeared as an expert witness before US congressional committees, worked with citizen groups on strip mining and agricultural issues, and assisted social investors with shareholder filings at the SEC. Doyle has written books on agricultural biotechnology, the US oil industry, and rural electric utilities. His articles have appeared in the *New York Times*, the *Washington Post*, the *San Francisco Chronicle*, the National Academy of Sciences' *Issues in Science and Technology*, and other publications. Doyle holds degrees from Millersville University (PA) and Pennsylviania State University.

## Corporate Sources

*Corporate Sources* is a nonprofit research center dedicated to public education on business and environmental issues. Based in Washington, DC, *Corporate Sources* conducts independent, investigative analysis focusing on controversial business practice and specific case histories. *Corporate Sources'* reports, case studies, and business profiles are prepared for educators, investors, consumer and environmental organizations, journalists, and public officials. With fair and accurate reporting, *Corporate Sources* seeks to assist citizen action, inform public policymaking, and encourage business leadership. *Corporate Sources* is a sponsored project of the Tides Center of San Francisco, a 501(C)(3) organization that serves as *Corporate Sources'* fiscal agent. Tax-deductible contributions can be made to The Tides Center/Corporate Sources, Presidio Bldg. 1014, PO Box 29907, San Francisco, CA 94129-0907. The author's share of the royalties from the sale of this book are dedicated to *Corporate Sources*.